C++ Software Development for Technology Students

David Conger

Prentice Hall
Upper Saddle River, New Jersey   Columbus, Ohio

Library of Congress Cataloging-in-Publication Data

Conger, David.
C++ software development for technology students / David Conger.
p. c.m.
ISBN 0-13-370180-8
1. C++ (Computer program language) 2. Computer software-
-Development. I. Title.
QA76.73.C153C658 2000
005.13'3--dc21 99-426696
CIP

Cover Art: Benjamin Shearn/FPG International
Publisher: Charles E. Stewart, Jr.
Associate Editor: Kate Linsner
Production Editor: Alexandrina Benedicto Wolf
Production Coordination: Custom Editorial Productions, Inc.
Cover Design Coordinator: Karrie Converse-Jones
Cover Designer: Dan Eckel
Production Manager: Matt Ottenweller
Marketing Manager: Ben Leonard

This book was set in Times by Custom Editorial Productions, Inc., and was printed and bound by The Banta Company. The cover was printed by Phoenix Color Corp.

Printed in the United States of America

10 9 8 7 6 5 4 3 2

ISBN: 0-13-370180-8

Prentice-Hall International (UK) Limited, *London*
Prentice-Hall of Australia Pty. Limited, *Sydney*
Prentice-Hall of Canada, Inc., *Toronto*
Prentice-Hall Hispanoamericana, S. A., *Mexico*
Prentice-Hall of India Private Limited, *New Delhi*
Prentice-Hall of Japan, Inc., *Tokyo*
Simon & Schuster Asia Pte. Ltd., *Singapore*
Editora Prentice-Hall do Brasil, Ltda., *Rio de Janeiro*

Preface

Professional computer programming in C++ involves highly specialized skills; more than a proficiency with the C++ programming language, software developers need software design skills. The professional software designer must be able to look at a problem and see what it is and what it is not. Although that may sound strange, deciding what is not part of a programming solution is just as important as deciding what is. Sometimes those in management say they want their business entirely computerized. That is not always realistic or cost effective. Some parts of a business are just better done by hand.

Once we can define the problem that we need to solve, we must be able to break it down into smaller problems. If those portions are not small enough to enable us to code a solution, we break it down more. Good design means that we must be able to decompose all aspects of a problem into their most fundamental pieces. This is called *top-down design*, which is emphasized in this book.

C++ is an object oriented language. The task of programming has been mostly procedure oriented, not object oriented. Thinking in terms of objects and building programs with them is an increasingly vital ability for professional programmers to acquire. After the first few chapters, objects and object oriented design are used throughout.

Many of the examples and most of the exercises in this book focus on designing and developing a text editor. If you follow these examples and do the exercises, you will have a working text editor when you finish the book. This is not a formidable task. Using top-down and object oriented design skills, you will be able to break down the task of creating a text editor into very manageable pieces. Ultimately, every programming task can be handled this way.

Why Use This Book

If you are seeking to develop practical design and development skills using C++, this book is for you. It doesn't matter whether you are a student learning programming for the first time, a self-taught guru seeking C++ skills, or someone with a degree in computer science. The combination of C++ and design techniques will make reading this book worthwhile.

Because this book teaches top-down and object oriented design skills in addition to language proficiency, it is more suited than many other texts for those pursuing professional programming careers.

Also, you will be developing a complete system. Unlike other books, which present only small example programs, this book demonstrates the process of developing a completely working software system. Creating such a system is more than just writing code. It also involves the ability to organize that code into a form that is extensible, flexible, and maintainable.

To help you get the maximum value from the examples, they all follow a common format: Objective, Experiment, Results, and Analysis. First, an experiment with a definite objective or set of objectives is undertaken. This usually takes the form of writing some code to see what happens. We then look at the output of the experiment for the results. Finally, the experiment and results are analyzed to see what can be deduced about the C++ language, as well as designing and developing software in C++.

What You Need to Use This Book

To be able to do the exercises and reproduce the examples, you will need both hardware and software.

Hardware

You can use any computer that has a C++ compiler. The code examples in this book are platform independent.

Software

Any ANSI-compatible C++ compiler should run this code properly. Most of the codes presented in this book are written to the ANSI C++ standard. However, the version of the text editor presented in the final chapters must be compiled with a compiler that runs under MS DOS. The Tools and Examples CD that comes with this book contains a version of the text editor that can be compiled on computers using Microsoft Windows 95 or Windows 98. For more information, look in the Examples directory on the CD. You'll find a directory called TEdit. The TEdit directory contains the file Readme.1st. The Readme.1st file presents information on compiling the text editor as a Windows console application.

If your compiler doesn't supply one, you will also need to acquire a text editor to write your source code. In addition, a good debugger will help save you many hours finding errors.

A special student edition of the Metrowerks CodeWarrior compiler, CodeWarrior Lite, is also provided on the CD. It contains versions of CodeWarrior for Microsoft Windows-compatible computers. You will find instructions for installing and using CodeWarrior in the Appendix. *Note:* CodeWarrior Lite does not currently work with Windows 98. It supports Windows 95 and Windows NT/2000. The final version of the text editor can be compiled under Windows 98 if using MS VC++ or CodeWarrior Professional.

Acknowledgments

Reviewers who helped in the editorial process of this project assisted with many constructive ideas and criticisms. Thanks is expressed to Blayne E. Mayfield, Oklahoma State University; Michael A. Miller, DeVry Institute of Technology; and Daud Syed, ITT Technical Institute.

Contents

This book is dedicated to my children, even though they no longer believe I hunted dinosaurs as a kid.

1 A Brief History of C++

Objectives

After reading this chapter, you should be able to:

- Explain the evolution of computer languages from binary to object oriented languages.
- Name and explain the advantages of C++.
- Name and explain the disadvantages of C++.

Preview

Like most computer languages, C++ has evolved. It is the result of much thought and deliberation. Many talented people have had a hand in its creation. Knowing a bit about the history of the C++ language helps us understand its purposes. It also explains why C++ has developed into the form that we know today.

Beginning with Binary

The only thing computers understand are **binary numbers.** Binary numbers are numbers in base 2.

When computers filled entire floors of buildings, almost all data was put into them using switches. People flipped switches to input an instruction. They would then flip another switch to tell the computer they were going to input the next instruction. Each instruction would be entered into the computer in this manner. Eventually, even people who really enjoyed flipping switches decided that there had to be a better way.

Improving Things with Assembler

As time passed, some very perceptive people realized that we could write computer programs in a form more readable to humans. The computer could translate the programs into binary numbers. The first of these languages was called **Assembler,** or **Assembly Language.**

Assembly Language had instructions that were abbreviations of actual words. For instance, MOV instructed the computer to move a value from one spot in memory to another. ADD meant add, INC meant increment, and so on.

Assembly Language was easier than binary for people to read and write. It also enabled programmers to write portions of programs that could be reused. These chunks of program code were called **subroutines.** A program could jump to a subroutine, execute it, and come back to where it left off. Well-written subroutines could be used in many programs.

Function Oriented Languages

The next step in computer language design was to create languages that were even more readable than Assembler. Also, programs were becoming larger and more complex. Writing them from scratch each time was costly. Languages needed greater structure to make it easier to organize programs. They also needed to expand upon the utility of subroutines so that more and larger chunks of programs could be reused.

The result of these trends was what we now call *function oriented languages*. Computer programming languages began to use words such as PRINT and INPUT for their instructions. Subroutines were expanded into **functions** and **procedures** with formal parameter lists and return values. A parameter list is a way of getting information into a function. A return value is a way of getting information out of a function.

Hundreds, if not thousands, of programming languages were invented over the years to meet a variety of needs. Most of them are no longer used. Today we primarily use variations on a group of about two dozen computer languages. In fact, these days most programs are written in either Assembler, Basic, Pascal, Cobol, Fortran, C, or C++. There are other languages around (some of them are great to use; others are a nightmare), but these few are the dominant ones.

C

The C programming language was invented by Brian Kernigan, Dennis Ritchie, and some of their colleagues at Bell Labs in the 1970s. Many of computing's great milestones came from this group at Bell Labs.

The inventors of C designed it to be as flexible and as powerful as Assembler but more readable. The designers of C achieved that goal, and C became the favorite of many programmers.

The Advent of Objects

As time progressed and programs continued to become more complex, programmers began to see the limitations of function oriented languages. One of the biggest drawbacks is that function oriented languages do not make it easy to structure programs the way the data is structured. Function oriented languages tend to be structured around actions that are performed on data. They are seldom structured around the data itself.

Also, function oriented languages don't force programmers to encapsulate or hide data. If the access to data is not strictly controlled, data can easily become corrupted. It is common for someone working on a large project with hundreds or even thousands of programmers to write a piece of a program that will alter data when it shouldn't.

Because function oriented languages often result in data that is less structured and exposed to all parts of a program, they often contain errors that are difficult to find.

Eventually, the idea of **software objects** was born. A software object is something that encapsulates data. It also defines the operations that can be performed on the data. Through the use of polymorphism (a concept we'll discuss in detail later), objects can define those operations in a consistent way. Because objects support inheritance (also discussed later), we can use them as the building blocks of other objects.

C++

The C++ programming language is an expression of C in object oriented forms. That is, C was extended by Bjarne Stroustrup at Bell Labs into an object oriented language. Eventually, a committee from the American National Standards Institute (ANSI) took over the job of deciding what C++ is and how it is structured. Today, C++ is the most popular computer language for the development of new software.

Advantages of C++

The following are the primary advantages of C++.

- Most programmers find that the conversion from C syntax to C++ syntax is fairly easy. That is not to say that all who learn C++ write object oriented programs. However, people who know C can typically learn its syntax easily.
- C++ gives programmers much greater potential for code reuse than function oriented languages such as C.
- C++ provides for greater data encapsulation. In other words, it is easier to control the access to data. This helps ensure that the data is correct.

Disadvantages of C++

C++ does have some disadvantages as well, including the following.

- Programming in object oriented languages such as C++ takes a different mind-set than programming in function oriented languages such as C.
- If they are not used correctly, features such as inheritance and polymorphism can make it difficult to follow what a C++ program is doing. If used properly, however, they can make a program *much* easier to follow.
- Features such as operator overloading allow programmers to write nonstandard uses for operators. For instance, you wouldn't expect a + sign in a program to print output to a printer. You'd expect that it would add something onto something else. With operator overloading, a programmer can make a + sign do anything he or she wants. Usually we rely on the programmer's common sense to overload operators in an intuitive way.

Summary

Computer programming has evolved over the years. It started with binary and progressed to object oriented languages such as C++. Object oriented languages offer many advantages over function oriented languages. For example, they provide greater control of data and enable us to create parts of programs that are consistent, intuitive to use, and reusable.

Review Questions

1. What "language" do computers understand?
2. How was Assembly Language an improvement?
3. What is a subroutine?
4. What are the advantages of using subroutines in a program?
5. What is a function? What is a procedure?
6. How are functions and procedures different from Assembly Language subroutines?
7. What is a software object?
8. What are the advantages of designing and developing software with objects?
9. What are some of the advantages of C++?
10. What are some of the disadvantages of C++?

Chapter Glossary

Assembler, Assembly Language An early programming language that used words, or abbreviations of words, as program instructions.

Binary Number A number in base 2.

Function A procedure that returns a value. It therefore has a declared return type.

Procedure A named subroutine with a declared parameter list. Each parameter in the parameter list must have a declared type.

Software Object A module of code that encapsulates data and the operations that can be performed on it. Software objects also support inheritance and polymorphism.

Subroutine A reusable portion of a program that a program can jump to, execute, and return from.

2 Essential C++ Program Development

Objectives

After reading this chapter, you should be able to:

- Explain the process of writing, compiling, and linking a computer program.
- Type the programs in this chapter into a text editor or integrated development environment (IDE).
- Compile, link, and run the programs in this chapter.
- Use the `cin` stream and the extraction operator for input.
- Use the `cout` stream and the insertion operator for output.
- Name and explain the most essential parts of a C++ program.

Preview

In this chapter, we'll look at the most fundamental aspects of developing computer programs. We'll also see how to perform simple input and output using C++ streams.

This chapter is intended to be an overview. Therefore, it presents many essential software development concepts but explains only their basics. All of the ideas and techniques presented in this chapter will be covered in detail in later chapters.

What Is a Computer Program?

Look in your pocket or purse. What do you find there? Keys? Credit cards? A comb? Each of these is a tool for getting along or getting around in our world. A computer is no different. *A computer is nothing more or less than a tool.*

Computers are smart tools. Most tools, such as hammers and saws, can only do one thing or one small group of things. A computer has a very simple type of "brain" called a **microprocessor.** This allows computers to be many different kinds of tools. For instance, a computer can be used for word processing. The same computer can be used for accounting. It can also possibly be used to play music. In each case, the computer is a different type of tool.

Of course, a computer has no actual brain and it can't really think. However, the microprocessor of any computer can execute instructions. When we group these instructions together and store them in a file, we call the file a **program** or **software.**

Computer programs tell the microprocessor how to act. It is the program that the computer is currently executing that tells the computer what type of tool to be.

Programmers write computer programs for specific reasons. We use them to solve problems that we face in business and industry, and we market those solutions as products.

A Solution to a Problem

A computer program is a solution to a problem. It is the answer to some sort of question. Do you remember those word problems you always hated in your math classes when you were growing up? A computer program is a solution to a word problem.

Whenever a program gets written, somewhere, someone said something like, "Is there an easier way to do this task?" The resulting program is the answer to that question. Because a program is a solution to a problem, we as software developers must have good problem-solving skills. We also need organized ways to design and create our particular solution to the problem at hand.

We can solve problems in six basic steps.[1] These are

1. *Identify the problem.* You can't solve a problem if you don't know what the problem is. My experience is that if I can't write down what the essence of the problem is in one paragraph or less, then I probably can't solve the problem because I don't know what it is.
2. *Understand the problem.* The solution to a problem usually depends on who will use the solution. As an example, let's say that someone asks us to write a word processing program. If that person intends to use the word processor for only one- or two-page letters, we'll write a rather simple program. However, if the person wants to use the program to publish books and manuals, we'll write a much more complex program. Understanding the problem also involves familiarity with a set of tools that can be used to solve it. Programmers must know what computers are currently capable of doing. They must also know at least one programming language. The more languages programmers know, the better they are able to solve problems.
3. *Identify alternative ways to solve the problem.* As programmers, we tend to try to make problems we encounter fit solutions that we know. It's something we all do occasionally. It's good to recognize that tendency in ourselves. We need to be able to look at other technologies, computer languages, and even nontechnical solutions to the problems our employers give us. There are always many ways to solve a problem. Which solution is best depends entirely on the needs of the people who will use the software.
4. *Select the best way to solve the problem from the list of alternative solutions.* Evaluate the strengths and weaknesses of all of the solutions you come up with in terms of the users' needs. You must also consider cost, time, and quality.
5. *List instructions that enable you to solve the problems using the selected solution.* This list of instructions eventually becomes a computer program.
6. *Evaluate the solution.* This means that we must test our solution to see how well it solved the problem. Sometimes our solution is just what the users need. Other times we don't do so well at solving their problems. We need to know when we succeed and when we fail and find out why in both cases.

A Product

Usually, the program you write will be marketed as a product. It may be used to produce a product that our employer markets. Either way, we must consider our users to be our customers. Part of our job is keeping those customers happy. To do that, we need to communicate with them. The best programmers are good communicators.

When we begin program development, we should first identify everything that the user wants the program to do. This can involve interviews with users and user surveys. We must communicate well if we want to make the product fit the users' needs.

As we develop the product, we must communicate with other programmers, our managers, and our users. The program itself must communicate its functions to our customers.

Good communication skills are essential to developing a high-quality product.

A Set of Instructions

From an internal point of view, a *computer program* is a set of instructions. As we write the program, we are writing a set of instructions that tells the computer how to

[1]These steps are from Maureen Sprankle, *Problem Solving and Programming Concepts,* 4th ed. (Upper Saddle River, NJ: Prentice Hall, 1992), pp. 3–4. I highly recommend this book to all beginning programmers.

be a particular type of tool. Since computers can't understand human languages such as English or Japanese, we must learn to communicate with them in a language they do understand, such as C++.

Designing and Developing Programs

Good programs are designed before they are developed. They are also designed as they are developed.

Before we start writing a program, we should always design it. Trying to write a program with no design to follow is very much like building a house with no house plans. We're never quite sure what we'll end up with.

When we build a house, we first determine what our needs are. Do we want a roomy house with plenty of bedrooms for a large family? Or do we want a compact house for a retired couple? What's more important, energy efficiency or luxury? We answer all of these questions by picking a floor plan. We give the floor plan to an architect, who comes up with a design. The design then goes to a contractor, who builds the house.

Writing computer programs follows a similar process. We determine the users' needs and then design a solution or product to meet those needs. That design can be given to a team of programmers. They write a program according to the design.

In computing, the person who writes the program is often the person who designs it. Therefore, we typically need to be good at both design and development.

Developing Programs

Once we have a design, we can develop a program. To develop programs in C++, we must know the C++ language. We also need to know how to create a C++ program. So that's where we'll start.

We create C++ programs by

1. Writing the source code.
2. Compiling the source code into object code.
3. Linking the object code into an executable program.

Figure 2.1 illustrates the process of creating a computer program. We must compile source code into object code. We then link it into executable code. We'll look at each of these steps in the following sections.

Source Code

We store program instructions in files on a disk, CD-ROM, tape, or other storage device. Computers store files in two different formats, text and binary.

Text files contain characters from the ASCII (American Standard Code for Information Interchange) character set.[2] The ASCII character set contains the letters of the alphabet in uppercase and lowercase. In addition, it contains the numbers 0 through 9 and some punctuation marks. (It also contains additional characters, but that is not important at this time.) We'll look at the ASCII character set in greater detail in Chapter 4.

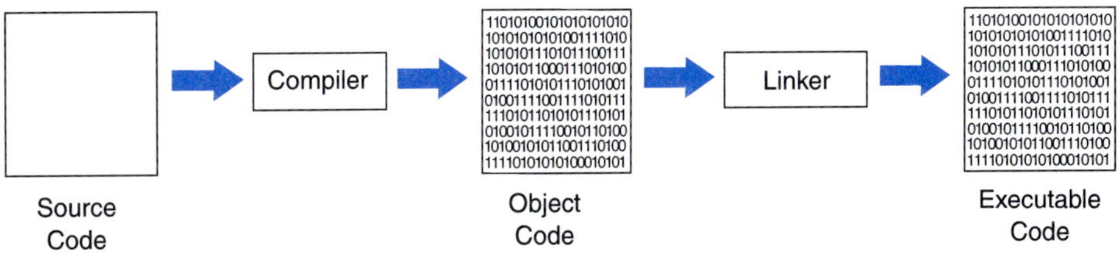

FIGURE 2.1 Creating a Computer Program

[2]IBM mainframe computers are the only exception to this. They use a different character set. We'll be using only the ASCII character set in this book.

Binary files contain binary numbers. All binary numbers are composed of 1s and 0s. When we write C++ programs, we store them in text files. The instructions in a C++ program are called **source code.** Programmers often build C++ programs from many text files of source code.

Because source code is stored in text files, we can use any text editor to create a C++ program. Many word processors will also enable you to store files as plain text, so we can use them as well. However, programmers generally find that word processors are not well suited to their needs.

There are many reasons for this. Word processing programs tend to insert tabs in ways that are inconvenient for programmers. Typically, they store documents in a binary format rather than as text files. If you use a word processor to develop programs, you must often take extra steps to export your program as a text file. Each line of a text file is terminated by a newline character. When you export your program as a text file, you may find that the word processor added or removed newline characters in unexpected places.

Actually, each line is terminated by a combination of a carriage return character and a line feed character. In C, these are represented by a single character called a *newline character*. In C++, we call this an *endline character*. C++ understands both the endline and newline characters. In this book, we'll primarily use the endline character.

Most software developers find that they get better usage out of a text editor that is written specifically for their needs. Many excellent program editors are available on the market today.

Compiling Source Code

Computers can't read source code. They only understand binary. We write programs called **compilers** and **interpreters** that translate programs from C++ (or any other computer language) into binary.

There is a definite difference between a compiler and an interpreter. A compiler, as the name suggests, compiles the entire program into binary at one time. An interpreter translates one line of code into binary instructions and then executes them. It then translates another line of source code. Interpreted programs execute much more slowly than compiled programs. C++ is a compiled language.

Each C++ compiler is used a bit differently. The Appendix provides a brief overview of how to compile a program using Metrowerks CodeWarrior, which is included on the CD that comes with this book.

When we compile programs, the compiler reads the statements in our source files. It converts them into binary commands that the computer understands and stores the result in a binary file.

However, compilers do not produce executable programs. Compilers change programs into **object code.** Object code is an intermediate form between source code and an executable program. The next step is to link the program into an executable file with a **linker.**

Linking

When a linker links a program into **executable code,** it links the object code linked together with libraries. A library is a collection of precompiled C++ objects and functions that perform a task or a group of tasks.

Someone wrote the library as source code. The programmer compiled it into object code and distributed the object code. You link your object code to the object code in the libraries.

In the case of a C++ program, there is a set of standard libraries that programs use for tasks such as input and output. Other libraries that we create, or are created by commercial library publishers, can also be linked into our C++ programs. This enables us to purchase libraries for special tasks such as creating user interfaces or doing database operations. Since we buy the libraries, we don't have to write those portions of the program ourselves. Linking to libraries can save programmers many hours of work.

When the linker finishes, we have converted our source code into an executable form.

Hello, World—Our First C++ Program

The first program that people write in a new programming language is traditionally a Hello, World program. So let's be traditional.

Hands On 2.1

Objective

Write a program that prints the string "Hello, World" on the screen.

Experiment

Type the following program into your text editor or integrated development environment (IDE). Compile it and run it.

```
//------------------------------Simple.cpp--------------------------------
/*
File name:  Simple.cpp
Comments:   This file contains a simple sample program.
*/

//------------------------------Include Files------------------------------

#include <iostream.h>

//----------------------------End Include Files----------------------------


int main()
{
   cout << "Hello, World << endl";
   return (0);
}

//----------------------------End Simple.cpp-------------------------------
```

Results

```
Hello, World
```

Analysis

If you compiled this program using a Windows-based compiler such as Borland C++ or MS Visual C++, you may have had problems. The first, and easiest to solve, is that there is no `WinMain()` function. When you create a project for any of the programs in this book, create it either as an EasyWin program, a console application, or a DOS program. See your compiler documentation for details.

If you did create this as an EasyWin program or a console application, it's likely that your compiler generated a warning stating that you have no definition file. Most Windows-hosted C++ compilers will use a default definition file if none is provided. That will be perfectly acceptable for all of the programs in this book. Therefore, that particular warning is safe to ignore for these programs. Normally, that would not be the case.

The first five lines of the Hello, World program are taken up with a file banner. This is a *minimal* example of how professional programmers document their programs. At the beginning of every program file that you create, there should be a file banner describing what is in the file. This helps people who are maintaining your code. It will even help you. You might be surprised at how rapidly you'll forget what any one piece of a large program you write is doing. File banners are just one aspect of proper program documentation that will help you remember.

A file banner is contained in one or more comments. A comment in a C++ program is indicated with either the symbols // (two slashes) or /* (a slash and an asterisk) followed by */ (an asterisk and a slash). The // symbol tells the compiler that the rest of the text on the line is a comment. The compiler will ignore all comments. They are just there for people to read, not for the compiler. Comments that begin with // can be only one line long.

On the other hand, comments that begin with /* may span as many lines of text as you like. When the compiler sees the /* symbol, it will treat all text in the file as comments until it sees a */ symbol. Be aware that forgetting the */ symbol at the end of a comment can cause many problems at compile time. The Troubleshooting Guide at the end of this chapter illustrates what can happen with unterminated comments.

Example 2.1 demonstrates the two types of comments in C++.

EXAMPLE 2.1 Comments in C++

```
// This is a one line comment.
/* This comment
can span multiple lines of text. */
```

Next in the program is an `#include` directive. This is a symbol recognized by the preprocessor, which the compiler automatically invokes when you compile a program. Using the `#include` directive essentially tells the compiler to read the text file that is specified in the angle brackets <> into the current file. In this case, it is the file iostream.h that comes with the standard libraries. You need to include iostream.h if your program is going to do input or output.

The new C++ standard is to omit the .h extension. So instead of `#include <iostream.h>`, you would `#include <iostream>`. Not all current C++ compilers support the new standard. Therefore, I use the old style throughout this book. If your compiler tells you that it can't find the file iostream.h when you compile, try changing `#include <iostream.h>` to `#include <iostream>`.

Every C++ program must have a `main()` function. The `main()` function is the **program entry point.** It is the spot in the source code where the program starts execution.

`main()` is a function and follows the format for functions. That is, it has a return type, which is `int`. It has a function name, `main`, and a parameter list, which in this case is empty. All of the commands within `main()` must be contained inside the curly brackets, { and }. When we discuss functions in more detail in Chapter 12, we'll see that they all use this format.

After the computer executes the last statement before the closing curly bracket, it terminates the program because that symbol marks the end of `main()`. The program terminates at the end of `main()`.

The last statement in the `main()` function is `return (0)`. We will discuss the purpose of this in Chapter 12. For now, just be aware that the last statement in `main()` should always be `return (0)`.

The only thing that the Hello, World program actually does is send the words "Hello, World" out to the screen. C++ performs input and output with data streams. If you want to envision a data stream, picture a stream of water flowing by. For our purposes, you can imagine data flowing in and out of the computer in the same manner.

The string of characters "Hello, World" is enclosed in quotes. That is always the case with **literal strings** in C++. A literal string is a sequence of characters that you actually type right into the source code, just like "Hello, World". Even though literal strings are not program instructions, they are part of the program. They are data.

C++ programs get output to the display by sending it to a stream called `cout` (pronounced *see-out*). This is a standard stream. We will talk about input and output with streams in detail in Chapter 20. For the purposes of this overview, all we need to be aware of is that `cout` is the data stream that flows to the screen. There is also a stream called `cin` (pronounced *see-in*) that flows into the program from the keyboard.

The direction of the stream is indicated by the C++ operator that is used on the stream. In this case, it is the insertion operator, which looks like this: <<. This operator inserts data into a stream. It points from the source of the data to its destination.

In this case, the source of the data is the literal string "Hello, World" and the destination is the stream `cout`. Once data is inserted in the stream, it flows out to the display.

Notice that the string "Hello, World" is followed by the symbol << and the word `endl`. The word `endl` stands for end of line. It causes a blank line to be printed after the program prints "Hello, World" on the screen. So the combined effect of the statement

```
cout << "Hello, World << endl";
```

is to tell the computer to send the literal string "Hello, World" to the stream `cout`. After that, the end-of-line character, also called the *endline character,* is inserted into that same stream. Another way to write that is with two separate output statements, like this:

```
cout<<"Hello, World";
cout<<endl;
```

Both of these methods of output accomplish the same thing. Which one you use is up to you.

Adding the Ability to Get Input with `cin`

The Hello, World program demonstrated the basics of writing a C++ program. One thing that it doesn't show, however, is how to get input from the keyboard. For our next Hands On, we'll modify Hello, World so that it reads data from the keyboard using the `cin` stream.

Hands On 2.2

Objective

Write a program that

Prints the string "Hello, World" to the screen.
Reads an integer from the keyboard.
Prints the integer to the screen.

Experiment

Modify the Hello, World program so that it is the same as the following program. The changes that you need to make are printed in bold type. They will not be in bold letters in your program.

```
//-------------------------------Simple2.cpp--------------------------------
/*
File name:   Simple2.cpp
Comments:    This file contains a modification of the Hello, World program.
*/

//------------------------------Include Files-------------------------------

#include <iostream.h>

//---------------------------End Include Files------------------------------


int main()
```

```
{
    cout<<"Hello, World<<endl";
    cout<<"Please type in a number and press Enter: ";
    int theNumber;
    cin>>theNumber;
    cout<<endl<<"The number you entered was "<<theNumber;
    return (0);
}
//----------------------------End Simple2.cpp--------------------------------
```

Results

```
Hello, World
Please type in a number and press Enter: 5
The number you entered was 5
```

Analysis

This program prints the literal string "Hello, World" and then prompts the user to enter a number. In the Results section of this Hands On, I typed the number 5. It is shown in bold print to emphasize that it is user input, not something that the program is supposed to print. The number the user enters will not actually be in bold on the computer's screen.

After the user types in a number, the program prints it back to the screen. As you can see, all output in this program is done to the `cout` stream by using the insertion operator.

When we want input from the `cin` stream (or any other stream for that matter) we use the extraction operator, which looks like this: >>. Like the insertion operator, the extraction operator indicates direction of the flow of data. The data flows from the `cin` stream into a variable called `theNumber`. For the purposes of this overview, it's necessary to know only that a variable is a place in memory where data can be stored. We will talk more about variables in the next chapter.

Hands On 2.2 demonstrated how we can get numeric input from the `cin` stream. As you might expect, we can also send numeric output to the `cout` stream. Hands On 2.3 demonstrates this.

Hands On 2.3

Objective

Write a program that sends character and numeric output to the screen.

Experiment

Type the following program into your text editor or integrated development environment (IDE). Compile it and run it.

```
//------------------------------IntOut.cpp----------------------------------
/*
File name:  IntOut.cpp
Comments:   This file contains a program that sends characters and numeric
            output to the display.
*/

//----------------------------Include Files-------------------------------
```

```
#include <iostream.h>

//----------------------------End Include Files-----------------------------

int main()
{
   cout << "How much wood would a woodchuck chuck ";
   cout << "if a woodchuck could chuck wood?";
   cout << endl << 42 << " logs." ;
   return (0);
}
//----------------------------End IntOut.cpp-----------------------------
```

Results

```
How much wood would a woodchuck chuck if a woodchuck could chuck wood?
42 logs.
```

Analysis

Hands On 2.3 demonstrates some C++ output techniques. First, it sends the literal string ”How much wood would a woodchuck chuck” to the `cout` stream. The next statement in `main()` sends the string ”if a woodchuck could chuck wood?” to `cout`. Notice in the Results section that these two strings print on one line. That is because the program did not send an endline character between the two strings. Your program can print as many strings on a single line as you want it to (or rather, as many as the display will allow).

After the program prints the two strings, it executes the statement

```
cout << endl << 42 << " logs." ;
```

This statement again demonstrates the fact that C++ can send multiple items sequentially to a stream. The items can be different types. In this example, it sends an endline character to `cout`. This forces subsequent printing to begin on the next line of the display.

The program then inserts the literal number 42 into the `cout` stream. Note that **literal numbers** do not need quote marks around them like literal strings do. Literal numbers are numbers that are typed right into a program's source code.

Lastly, this statement sends the literal string ”logs” to the `cout` stream.

As you can see, when we insert multiple items into a stream, the program inserts them in the order that they occur from left to right. That is how (in this example) they are printed on the screen.

Using Pseudocode

Developers currently can choose from many design methodologies. Most of them, at some point, have you write all or part of your program in **pseudocode.** When we write statements in pseudocode, we write generic, high-level statements of program actions. Example 2.2 shows the `main()` function from Hands On 2.2. One possible version of the pseudocode for this program is given in Example 2.3.

EXAMPLE 2.2 The `main()` Function from Hands On 2.2

```
int main()
{
   cout<<"Hello, World<<endl";
   cout<<"Please type in a number and press Enter: ";
   int theNumber;
```

```
    cin>>theNumber;
    cout<<endl<<"The number you entered was "<<theNumber;
    return (0);
}
```

EXAMPLE 2.3 Pseudocode Version of the Program in Example 2.2

```
Print "Hello, World" to the screen.
On the next line, print "Please type in a number and press Enter: "
Read an integer from the keyboard.
On the next line, print "The number you entered was ".
Print the integer to the screen.
```

The term *language-independent* refers to computer languages such as Pascal or C++, not human languages like English or Russian.

Pseudocode provides us with a language-independent description of what a program should do. For the remainder of this book, most of the Objective sections of the Hands On examples will contain a pseudocode description of what the program does.

Troubleshooting Guide

After reading this section, you should be able to:

- Recognize and fix problems caused by unterminated comments.
- Recognize and fix problems caused by missing semicolons.
- Recognize and fix problems caused by extra semicolons.
- Recognize and fix problems caused by unpaired curly brackets.

Unterminated Comments

One common mistake that even experienced programmers make is to forget to terminate comments. You'll remember that C++ uses two types of comments. One, marked by two slashes (//), ends at the end of the current line. The other can span multiple lines. It begins with /* and ends with */.

You can generally tell when you forget the */ mark when you compile your program. Most compilers will give you an error that says something like "Unexpected end of file". Some are even more helpful by saying something along the lines of "Unexpected end of file in comment beginning on line 2".

Many modern integrated development environments (IDEs) and programmer's editors use color and style coding to indicate language features. For instance, keywords such as `int` and `return` might be in bold. Comments might be in a particular color, say green or red. If you suddenly find that all the text in your program is in the color that indicates comments, you know that you've left off a */ somewhere.

Missing Semicolons

Forgetting a semicolon at the end of a C++ statement is one of the easiest mistakes to make. Even experienced programmers do it. However, it's also one of the easiest mistakes to detect. Often, your C++ compiler will tell you exactly what the problem is. It will print a message along the lines of "Semicolon missing before <statement>", where <statement> is the C++ statement that occurs right after the one missing the semicolon.

Unfortunately, some compilers are not so explicit. You may get error statements telling you that the compiler encountered something unexpected. For instance, it may say "Unexpected variable declaration" or "Unexpected function declaration". When this occurs, it will typically point you at the statement right after the one missing the semicolon. So if your compiler tells you it ran into something unexpected, look in the lines above for one or more missing semicolons.

Extra Semicolons

Another easy error to make is adding extra semicolons. Unfortunately, it can be *extremely* hard to detect. In some cases, adding an extra semicolon on the end of a statement makes no difference at all. Example 2.4 shows the Hello, World program that we saw earlier in this chapter. Notice that there is an extra semicolon after the closing curly bracket at the end of `main()`. Most C++ compilers will not complain about this, even though the extra semicolon is unnecessary.

EXAMPLE 2.4 Hello, World with an Extra Semicolon

```
#include <iostream.h>

int main()
{
   cout << "Hello, World << endl";
   return (0);
};
```

In this case, it's OK to leave the extra semicolon. It's not needed, but it causes no problems.

Example 2.5, however, shows a misplaced semicolon that definitely does cause problems. It occurs right after the last parenthesis of `main()`.

EXAMPLE 2.5 An Extra Semicolon After `main()`

```
#include <iostream.h>

int main();
{
   cout << "Hello, World << endl";
   return (0);
}
```

This little semicolon can cause you a world of problems. Your compiler may give you a very helpful warning, such as "Declaration terminated incorrectly" and indicate exactly where the extra semicolon is. Unfortunately, it may not be able to figure out what's wrong at all. It could point you at a statement several lines from where the extra semicolon occurs. The problem is that the compiler may actually think that you are trying to do something valid. Functions generally have prototypes. A prototype looks exactly like the first line of the function, except that it ends with a semicolon.

The point here is that the compiler may think you're trying to make a valid statement by putting a semicolon at the end of the first line of a function. It will continue compiling statements and encounter the function body. However, it will detect that it has not yet seen the proper declaration of a function, just its prototype. So it will basically ask you, "Why are you putting a function body here?"

Another reason extra semicolons may be hard to detect is that they can terminate statements correctly even if they're in the wrong place. For example, you can add an extra semicolon onto the end of the first line of an `if` or `while` statement. When you compile, you will get no errors at all. However, your program will not function correctly. It may not be immediately obvious why. We'll demonstrate techniques for tracking down problems like this in the Troubleshooting sections of the chapters that introduce these statements.

Unpaired Curly Brackets

Another source of "Unexpected <statement>" errors is unpaired curly brackets. This is a mistake that I remember making often when I was first beginning to program. The reason that I made this mistake so much was because I laid out my curly brackets in the style shown in Example 2.6.

EXAMPLE 2.6 Unaligned Curly Brackets

```
#include <iostream.h>

int main() {
   cout << "Hello, World << endl";
   return (0);
}
```

The compiler doesn't care if you do this. It's not wrong and not bad in any way. In fact, it's a common style that many experienced C++ programmers use. For experienced programmers, it's not a problem because they don't make this mistake very much. However my own experience as both a novice programmer and a teacher has led me to conclude that novice programmers will save themselves some time and frustration if they don't use this style.

For novice programmers, an easy way to solve this problem is to always put closing curly brackets under opening curly brackets. Example 2.7 illustrates what I mean.

EXAMPLE 2.7 Aligned Curly Brackets

```
#include <iostream.h>

int main()
{
   cout << "Hello, World << endl";
   return (0);
}
```

Notice that the opening and closing curly brackets for the block of code are aligned in the same column. If you print this program out, you can lay a ruler on the printout on the column where the opening curly bracket occurs and draw a line straight down to the closing curly bracket. If the closing curly bracket is missing, it becomes obvious immediately.

We'll see as we go along the great value of this simple technique. As your programs become more complex, you'll create code blocks nested inside of code blocks. Each block will have its own set of curly brackets that must be paired. If they're aligned in the same column, unpaired curly brackets will be easier to find.

Summary

Computer programs are groups of commands stored in text files. Computers don't read text files, so the commands must be translated into binary. Compilers and interpreters perform the necessary translations.

An interpreter translates one line of source code into binary and then executes it. The next line of source code is then translated and executed. This continues until the end of the program.

A compiler translates an entire program into binary at once. The program can then be executed repeatedly without having to translate the code again. Compiled programs execute faster than interpreted programs.

A C++ program must have a `main()` function. The `main()` function is the program entry point. The program terminates when it finishes executing all of the statements in `main()`.

C++ programs send output to the `cout` stream. They get input from the `cin` stream. Programs write output to the `cout` stream with the insertion operator. They read input from the the `cin` stream.

Review Questions

1. What does an interpreter do? What do you think the advantages or disadvantages might be in using an interpreter?
2. What does a compiler do? What do you think the advantages or disadvantages might be in using a compiler?
3. To what form does a compiler compile programs? Why?
4. What is a linker? Why are programs linked?
5. What is the purpose of the `main()` function in a C++ program?
6. What is `cout`? What is `cin`?

7. What does the << operator do?
8. What does the >> operator do?
9. What is a literal string?
10. What does `endl` stand for?

Exercises

1. Write, compile, link, and execute a program that gets three numbers from the user. Print them out in the opposite order than the user entered them.
2. Explain the difference between source code and object code.
3. Explain the difference between object code and executable code.
4. Explain why using code libraries might be helpful. Describe how a library is incorporated into a C++ program.
5. Look on the Tools and Examples CD in the directory \Chapt2. You will find a program called Ex_2_5.cpp. Load the program into your IDE or text editor. Compile and link it. Explain what errors you got and describe how you fixed them.
6. Look on the Tools and Examples CD in the directory \Chapt2. You will find a program called Ex_2_6.cpp. Load the program into your IDE or text editor. Compile and link it. Explain what errors you got and describe how you fixed them.
7. Look on the Tools and Examples CD in the directory \Chapt2. You will find a program called Ex_2_7.cpp. Load the program into your IDE or text editor. Compile and link it. Explain what errors you got and describe how you fixed them.
8. Look on the Tools and Examples CD in the directory \Chapt2. You will find a program called Ex_2_8.cpp. Load the program into your IDE or text editor. Compile and link it. Explain what errors you got and describe how you fixed them.
9. Look on the Tools and Examples CD in the directory \Chapt2. You will find a program called Ex_2_9.cpp. Load the program into your IDE or text editor. Compile and link it. Explain what errors you got and describe how you fixed them.
10. Look on the Tools and Examples CD in the directory \Chapt2. You will find a program called Ex_2_10.cpp. Load the program into your IDE or text editor. Compile and link it. Explain what errors you got and describe how you fixed them.

Chapter Glossary

Binary File A file that contains information stored in binary format.

Compiler A program that translates source code into object code. It translates entire files, or entire groups of files, each time it compiles.

Executable Code A binary file that a computer can execute. An executable program.

Interpreter A program that translates source code into executable code. It translates a program line by line.

Linker A program that combines object code programs and libraries into an executable program.

Literal Numbers Numbers that are typed into the source code of a program. They are not program instructions. They are pieces of data that are embedded in the source code.

Literal Strings Strings that are typed into the source code of a program. They are not program instructions. They are pieces of data that are embedded in the source code.

Microprocessor A microchip that can carry out a set of instructions. This is the "brain" of the computer.

Object Code An intermediate binary form between source code and an executable program.

Program A collection of instructions that a microprocessor can execute. The collection of instructions carry out a particular task or group of tasks.

Program Entry Point The point in the code where the program begins execution.

Pseudocode Generic statements that describe program actions.

Source Code Instructions in a C++ program that are stored in text files.

Software See **Program.**

Text File A file that contains data stored as text characters.

3 Atomic Data Types: Integer and Floating Point Variables

Objectives

After reading this chapter, you should be able to:

- Explain what atomic data types are and how they are used.
- Name and utilize all of the integer and floating point data types.
- Explain the differences between the various integer data types.
- Explain the differences between the floating point data types.
- Explain overflow and underflow.
- Demonstrate overflow and underflow in a program.

Preview

Computer programs aren't much good if they don't process data. This chapter presents some fundamental **data types** that we can use in our programs. Specifically, it explains some of the C++ atomic data types. It also discusses two potential problems with all data types, overflow and underflow.

What Are Atomic Data Types?

Before we ask what an atomic data type is, it is reasonable to define the term *data type*. Every piece of data in a computer has a type. If we enter the amount of a bank deposit into an ATM, we're entering data. That data is a numeric type. If you type a customer's name into a database program, you are entering a string of characters. The data you enter is of type character.

The ancient Greeks defined an atom as the smallest possible particle of matter. Of course, we now have discovered subatomic particles (and sub-subatomic particles, and so on). However, the word *atomic,* in its original sense, suggests something that is as small as it can get. It indicates something that can't be divided into smaller pieces.

When we describe a piece of data as atomic, we mean that it is in the smallest possible unit of data. It can't be broken down any further. In C++, the **atomic data types** are the data types that are built into the language. You use those as building blocks for other data types.

C++ comes with several numeric data types. It also has character data types. These can be used to build strings. When we begin to talk about objects, we'll see how all of these can be used to build larger data types that reflect real-world programming situations.

TABLE 3.1 **Examples of Integers and Non-integers**

Integers	Non-integers
5	5.0
–23	0.888
56,345	75.75

`int`, `short`, and `long`

The most commonly used data type in C++ programming is an `int`, which stands for integer. An **integer** is a number that has no fractional part. Table 3.1 shows some numbers that are integers and some that are not.

Notice in Table 3.1 that the number 5 is an integer. It is a whole number and has no fractional part. The number 5.0 is not an integer. It has a fractional part, even though the fractional part is zero. Any number that contains a decimal point in it is not an integer.

C++ programs store data that changes in **variables.** When we declare a variable in a program, we set aside a spot in memory that we have given a name and a type. In more technical terms, we allocate memory at a particular address. To create an integer variable in a program, we declare its name and type. Hands On 3.1 demonstrates how to declare and use variables.

Hands On 3.1

Objective

Write a program that declares and uses integer variables.

Experiment

Type the following program into your text editor or IDE. Compile it and run it.

```
int main()
{
    int i;
    int j,k=5;

    i=j+k; // This is wrong!
    j=7;
    i=j+k; // Now this is ok.
    cout<<"i="<<i<<" j="<<j<<" k="<<k;
    return 0;
}
```

Results

```
i=12 j=7 k=5
```

Analysis

This short example demonstrates several important points about variables. First, notice how the program declares integers. It declares the variable `i` on a line by itself. By stating the variable's name and type, the program allocates memory for one integer and names it `i`.

Programs can declare integers on a line by themselves, as `i` is. They can also declare them in groups, as the Hands On program does with `j` and `k`. When our program declares more than one variable on a line of a program, we need to separate the variable names with commas.

In addition to declaring the variable k, the program also initializes it. Using the assignment operator, which is an equal sign, the program gives k the value 5. A program can initialize any variable it declares.

The question then arises, what values do i and j have when the program declares them? The answer is, I don't know. No one does. There isn't any way to know in advance. Their values are undefined. Programmers must always remember this important characteristic of the C++ language. We must assume that any variables we declare in our programs contain random values if we do not explicitly initialize them.

Because the program does not initialize the variable j, the line that reads

TRAP: Whenever you declare a variable and don't initialize it, you must assume that it contains a random value.

```
i=j+k; // This is wrong!
```

gives unpredictable results. There is actually nothing wrong with adding the value in j to the value in k and storing the results in i. However, we have no way of knowing what j contains. Therefore, we have no way of predicting what value will be stored in the variable i. This statement is wrong only because it will yield unpredictable results.

TIP: The majority of C++ compilers initialize all uninitialized data to zero. However, some don't. You must not depend on that happening. Many program errors occur because the programmer uses variables that are not yet initialized. Therefore, always initialize variables before you use them.

The Hands On program then assigns the value 7 to the variable j. That means j now contains a known value. Our program can try the addition again and it's OK. It will yield a predictable result.

The line that reads

```
cout<<"i="<<i<<" j="<<j<<" k="<<k;
```

outputs the string "i= " to the screen. It then sends the value in the variable i. Next, it sends the string "j= " to the screen, followed by the value in j. Lastly, it sends the string "k= " to the screen, followed by the value in k.

When our programs declare variables, they set aside memory for the variables. You may wonder about the size of an integer. The number of bytes that the C++ compiler allocates for an integer determines the largest value that an integer can hold. So how many bytes does the compiler allocate? The answer is, it depends. The ANSI definition of C++ leaves the size of an integer implementation-dependent. It is 16 bits on some operating systems, and 32 bits on others.

Even if we may not know the size of an integer, C++ provides us with qualifiers to modify its size. Integers can be declared as `short` or `long`. Example 3.1 shows some ways that the `short` and `long` C++ keywords can be used.

EXAMPLE 3.1 `short` and `long` Variable Declarations

```
short int aShort;
long int aLong;
short anotherShort;
long anotherLong;
```

Short integers can be declared using the keywords `short int`, or just `short`. In the same way, long integers can be declared using the keywords `long int`, or just `long`. The compiler knows that something declared as `short` or `long` is a `short int` or a `long int`, respectively.

The ANSI definition of a `short` is that it can be no longer than an `int`. That means that it can be the same size as an `int`. The definition of a `long` is that it can be no shorter than an `int`. Again, it can be the same size as an `int`.

Although it's confusing to possibly have `short`s, `int`s, and `long`s all the same size, there is a very good reason for this. By leaving the definition somewhat vague, the ANSI committee enables compiler writers to decide how many bytes to allocate for each data type. They can create compilers with numeric types that best fit the particular computer that the compiler will run on. Companies writing compilers for computers on jet aircraft don't have to force their integer data to be the same size as integer data on a microcomputer. That kind of flexibility helps compiler manufacturers create efficient compilers. Because they can choose the best size for their data, the compilers can produce fast programs for whatever type of computer they run on. It also helps to increase the portability of programs.

Usually, compiler manufacturers write their compilers so that a variable of type `short int` has half the width of an `int`. Since it has half the number of bytes in it, using `shorts` can mean that your program uses less memory.

Long integers generally are implemented as twice the number of bytes as an `int`. Because it has more memory space, larger numbers can be stored in a `long`.

On a DOS-based PC, the `int` data type is typically 16 bits, or 2 bytes, long. That means that an `int` can store 65,536 integers. About half of that range is given over to negative numbers, so the highest value these `ints` can store is 32,767. The lowest value is –32,768.

Some operating systems for PCs (Windows 95, Windows NT, and Linux) support a 32-bit (4-byte) integer data type. We can compile the same program on the same computer using two different operating systems and get a different-sized integer.

Most operating systems these days support at least 32-bit integer data types. Some support 64-bit `ints`. The point is that we should never depend on a data type being a particular size. It should not matter to us how many bytes a compiler allocates for an integer (or any other data type).

Hands On 3.2 illustrates the differences between `short`, `int`, and `long`.

Hands On 3.2

Objective

Write a program that:

Declares and initializes two short variables.
Declares an integer variable.
Outputs the values in the short variables to the screen.
Multiplies the short variables and stores the results in the integer variable.
Outputs the result to the screen.
Declares and initializes another integer variable. Outputs the value in the new integer variable to the screen.
Declares a long variable and outputs its value to the screen.
Multiplies the two integer variables and stores the result in the long.
Outputs the result to the screen.

Experiment

Type the following program into your IDE or text editor. Compile, link, and run it.

```
#include <iostream.h>

int main()
{
   short aShortVariable=127, anotherShortVariable=120;
   int anIntegerVariable;

   cout<<"The value of the first short variable is: ";
   cout << aShortVariable << endl;
   cout<<"The value of the second short variable is: ";
   cout << anotherShortVariable << endl;

   anIntegerVariable = aShortVariable * anotherShortVariable;

   cout << "When you multiply " <<  aShortVariable;
   cout << " times " << anotherShortVariable;
   cout << " you get " << anIntegerVariable;
```

```
    cout << endl;

    int anotherIntegerVariable = anIntegerVariable + aShortVariable;
    long aLongVariable;

    cout<<"The value of the first integer variable is: ";
    cout << anIntegerVariable << endl;
    cout<<"The value of the second integer variable is: ";
    cout << anotherIntegerVariable << endl;

    aLongVariable = anIntegerVariable * anotherIntegerVariable;

    cout << "When you multiply " <<  anIntegerVariable;
    cout << " times " << anotherIntegerVariable;
    cout << " you get " << aLongVariable;
    cout << endl;

    return (0);
}
```

Results

```
The value of the first short variable is: 127
The value of the second short variable is: 120
When you multiply 127 times 120 you get 15240
The value of the first integer variable is: 15240
The value of the second integer variable is: 15367
When you multiply 15240 times 15367 you get 234193080
```

Analysis

This program begins by declaring two variables of type `short` and initializing them. As shown in Hands On 3.1, your program can declare more than one variable at a time if the variable names are separated by commas. It also declares a variable of type `int`.

This example program initializes the two `short` variables to 127 and 120, respectively. On some operating systems, most notably MS DOS, the `short` data type is 1 byte (8 bits) in length. Therefore, the maximum value it can hold is 127. If the `short` data type on your system contains more than 8 bits, it can hold larger values.

The program outputs the values in the short variables to the screen. It then multiplies the two values and stores the answer in the integer variable.

The first thing to notice in this example is that the variables that values are being stored into are always on the left side of the equal sign. When we do math, we can write equations like this:

$$\pi r^2 = c$$

with the multiplication on the left and the destination of the assignment on the right. However, that is not allowed in C++ statements. The destination of the assignment must always be on the left side of the equal sign, as shown in Example 3.2.

EXAMPLE 3.2 An Assignment Statement

```
anIntegerVariable = aShortVariable * anotherShortVariable;
```

This example program also demonstrates that C++ supports the multiplication operator. In math classes, we typically use an × for multiplication. However, in C++ we use the asterisk (*). After the program in Hands On 3.2 multiplies the two `short` variables together and stores the result in the integer variable, it prints the result to the screen.

Next, the program declares another integer variable and initializes it to a value by adding the variables anIntegerVariable and aShortVariable. It also declares a variable of type long.

It prints the values in the two integer variables and multiplies them. The program stores the result in the long. Finally, it prints the value in the long variable to the screen.

unsigned short, unsigned int, and unsigned long

The three integer types that we have presented so far, short, int, and long, are all signed data types. A **signed data type** can have a positive or a negative sign on its value. In other words, it can store numbers greater than zero or numbers less than zero.

The integer family of data types also includes unsigned data types. The **unsigned data types** can only hold positive numbers; no negative numbers are allowed. Because the data range is not split between positive and negative numbers, unsigned integers can store twice as many positive numbers as signed integers.

C++ provides us with three types of unsigned integers, unsigned short, unsigned int, and unsigned long. Unsigned integers are declared in a way that is similar to signed integers. Example 3.3 illustrates their use.

EXAMPLE 3.3 Variable Declarations of Unsigned Integer Types

```
unsigned short v int = 0;
unsigned short w = 127;
unsigned int x=5;
unsigned y=11;
unsigned long int z=22;
unsigned long a=54567;
unsigned b=-27;  // This is NOT allowed!
```

Notice that in Example 3.3, we were able to leave the word int out of the declarations of unsigned variables. C++ allows this.

Programs use unsigned data in exactly the same way they use signed data. They just can't store negative numbers in unsigned variables.

An unsigned int is the same size as an int. Variables of type unsigned short are no longer than an unsigned. It typically contains half the number of bytes as an unsigned. An unsigned long can be no shorter than an unsigned. It usually contains twice the number of bits as an unsigned.

float, double, and long double

We call numbers that contain a decimal point **floating point numbers.** Table 3.2 gives some examples of floating point numbers.

As you might expect by now, programs declare floating point numbers in essentially the same way as integers. Example 3.4 demonstrates the declaration of floating point numbers.

TABLE 3.2 Examples of Floating Point and Non-floating Point Numbers

Non-floating Point	Floating Point
5	5.0
–23	0.888
56,345	75.75

EXAMPLE 3.4 Declaration of Floating Point Variables

```
float f=7.2;
double aDouble;
long double d=.000005
```

The basic type in the floating point group is `float`. C++ compilers usually implement a `double` as twice the number of bits as a `float`. However, the ANSI C++ standard defines a `double` as no shorter than a `float`.

C++ also provides a `long double`. This is usually implemented as twice the width of a `double`. However, it is required to be no shorter than a `double`.

C++ compilers often implement a `float` as the same size as an `int`, but that doesn't have to be the case. In fact, many compilers for the PC and Macintosh promote variables of type `float` to type `double`. When a compiler promotes a data type, it substitutes a larger data type for the one you have stated. The types `float` and `short` are the ones that compilers most often promote to a larger type. They will do this without telling you and without changing your source code. So you generally don't need to worry about whether your compiler is promoting the data types in your programs.

Overflow and Underflow

Let's say we're working on a computer that uses a 16- bit (2-byte) integer. That gives us a data range of –65,538 to 65,537. Example 3.5 shows an integer variable declared on this 16-bit system. Notice that the program initialized the variable to the maximum value it can hold. The next line adds 5 to that variable. The question is, what happens next?

EXAMPLE 3.5 Overflow

```
#include <iostream.h>

int main()
{
   int anInteger=65537;

   anInteger=anInteger+5;
   cout << anInteger;
   return (0);
}
```

TRAP: When you try to store data in a variable and the data is too large for the type, the variable overflows. The result of an overflow is undefined.

The answer is, no one knows by just looking at this code. When data in a variable exceeds the maximum value that the data type can hold, it **overflows.** The ANSI C++ standard does not define what happens when overflow occurs. Typically, the numbers wrap around. That is, the variable in Example 3.5 might contain 4. It might not. Only your compiler writer knows for sure.

Underflow is just the opposite. Take a look at Example 3.6. Notice that the program tries to store a value that is too negative for the integer data type (we're still assuming we're working with 16-bit integers).

EXAMPLE 3.6 Underflow

```
#include <iostream.h>

int main()
{
   int anInteger=-65538;
   anInteger=anInteger-3;
   return (0);
}
```

What happens when a data type underflows is also undefined by the ANSI C++ standard. The moral is that you must be mindful of the data types that you use. Be sure to use types that are large enough for the data you want to store.

Students often ask, "How do you find overflow and underflow errors?" Unfortunately, it's difficult to look at output from a program and say, "Ah, that looks like an underflow error." If you have a good familiarity with the data that your program should be outputting, you might guess that overflow or underflow occurred. Often, overflow and underflow errors are caught by testers, not by programmers.

Overflow and underflow can also occur on floating point and unsigned integer data types.

Troubleshooting Guide

After reading this section, you should be able to:

- Understand problems with mixed-type operations.
- Understand and avoid precision errors.
- Prevent overflow and underflow by using a larger data type.
- Prevent overflow and underflow by data validation.

Mixed-Type Operations

The C++ programming language allows us to do mixed-type operations. Hands On 3.3 shows some mixed-type operations.

Hands On 3.3

Objective

Write a program that uses mixed-type mathematical operations.

Experiment

Type the following program into your IDE or text editor. Compile, link, and run it.

```
#include <iostream.h>

int main()
{
    short aShort = 100;
    int anInt;

    // Shorts can be stored in ints.
    anInt = aShort;
    cout << anInt;
    cout << endl;

    // This can be dangerous!
    anInt = 10000;
    aShort = anInt;
    cout << aShort;
    cout << endl;

    // Ints can be stored in floating-point types.
    float aFloat;
    aFloat = anInt;
    cout << aFloat;
```

```
    // Be sure this is what you want.
    aFloat = 100.123;
    anInt = aFloat;
    cout << anInt;
    cout << endl;

    return (0);
}
```

Results

```
100
10000.0
10000100
```

Analysis

The results that you get when you run this program may be different than what is shown in the Results section. You may also get warnings or errors from your compiler when you attempt to compile the program.

The program first declares two variables, one of type `short` and the other of type `int`. It initializes the variable `aShort` to 100. Compilers usually implement short integer variables so that they contain at least 1 byte. Your compiler may allocate more than 1 byte. Because a `short` is never less than 1 byte long, the value 100 will fit nicely into a `short` on almost any computer.

An `int` variable typically contains twice the number of bytes than a `short` does. If your compiler promotes `short` variables to type `int`, it will be the same size. Either way, anything you can store in a `short` can fit into an `int`. Therefore, the statement

```
anInt = aShort;
```

should be just fine on every computer.

The same is not true, however, of the statement

```
aShort = anInt;
```

This can potentially cause unexpected results. If your compiler promotes `short` variables to `int` variables, there will be no problem. Any value that you can store into an `int` can go into a `short`. If your compiler implements a `short` as half the number of bytes as an `int`, however, you can lose data by trying to assign the value of an `int` variable into a `short`. The `short` will only be able to hold half as much data as an `int`.

TRAP: Storing the value of a variable into a smaller data type can lose data.

TIP: Whenever you assign a value to a variable, avoid using smaller data types than the variables on the right side of the assignment operator (the equal sign).

Because the results of storing values from `int` variables into `short` variables are compiler-dependent, you should generally avoid doing it.

Integer data types generally fit into floating point types without a problem. Just be sure that the type of the variable on the left side of the equal sign is large enough to hold the value. The statement

```
aFloat = anInt;
```

is OK on *most* systems. There are systems where this assignment can cause problems, however. The trouble stems from how the compiler is implemented. Most compilers are fine with this statement because they convert the integer value to the same value with a zero after the decimal. In the Results section of Hands On 3.3, the value in the variable `anInt` was 10000. When we assigned that value into the variable `aFloat`, the program converted it to 10000.0.

Not all systems will do this. The computer allocates some of the bits in a floating point variable for the significant digits of the value that it stores. The rest are for the exponent. When you assign a value in an integer variable to a floating point variable, the compiler may interpret the pattern of the bits as a value and an exponent. The results will be very different than what is shown here.

The same is true when we assign floating point values into integer variables. When our program executed the statement

```
anInt = aFloat;
```

the compiler interpreted the bit pattern as that of an integer. The resulting value was very different from what we may have wanted.

TRAP: The results you get when you assign a floating point value into an integer variable varies from compiler to compiler.

When we assign floating point values into integer variables, some compilers will simply truncate everything to the right of the decimal point. They will store the value on the left of the decimal point into the integer variable. However, this behavior is entirely dependent on what compiler you use.

Precision Errors

Because each data type contains a set number of bits, it is possible to get errors in your floating point numbers if you don't use a large enough data type. The drawback to using a larger data type is that it is slower because there are more bits to manipulate. So you have to decide which is more important, speed or accuracy.

The errors you can get with floating point numbers are particularly tricky to deal with. Numbers can lose small fractional parts. A number such as 634721000000.0000005 is very likely to lose the fractional part if a large enough data type is not used. However, 0.000000005 is just fine.

The reason has to do with the way floating point numbers are stored in memory. Some of the bits for a floating point number are used to store the significant digits of the number. The rest of the bits are used to store an exponent.

If, for example, a program stores the number 12,300 in a floating point variable, it may actually store 123 and 2. When this value is used, it is treated as 123×10^2. The value 10^2 is the same thing as 10×10, or 100. As you can see, 123×100 is 12,300.

If we try to store a number such as 634721000000.0000005 into a `float`, it may not fit. The compiler allocates a limited number of bytes for the data type `float` to store the **significant digits.** Usually, a `float` can only accurately contain six or seven significant digits.

In the number 634721000000.0000005, the most significant digits are 634721. The .0000005 will get lost. In order to store the entire number, including the .0000005, the compiler must allocate enough bytes to store every digit in the number as a significant digit. A `float` will probably not be large enough for that.

If the number were 634721000000.0, however, there would be no problem. The significant digits are now 634721. There are only six of them, so it would probably fit into a `float`. A C++ program can store the number 634721000000.0 as 634721 and 6. To a C++ program, this means 634721×10^6, which is 634721000000.0.

Preventing Overflow and Underflow

There are two basic methods of preventing overflow and underflow. You can use a larger data type than you think you will actually need, or you can perform validation on the data before you store it into an integer or floating point variable.

Using a Larger Data Type If you are using variables of type `float` in your program and you think they might overflow or underflow, you can declare your `float` variables as `double` instead. Similarly, if you are using `int` variables, you can declare them as `long` instead.

Although this technique may prevent overflow and underflow, it is not without cost. Using larger data types is generally slower. Typically, though, the performance penalty is not severe.

Data Validation Another way to prevent overflow and underflow is to check data each time an operation is performed on it and ensure that it stays with acceptable limits. While this is always good to do, it requires extra code and more CPU time. However, this procedure is usually necessary to ensure that your program produces accurate results.

To perform data validation, your program must read all user input as strings (which we will discuss later). The program can check the data to ensure it contains digits and can also verify that the number the digits form is within the acceptable range for the data type you want to use. It must then convert the digits in the string into a number.

Summary

C++ provides atomic data types. Programs use the atomic data types as the fundamental data types. The atomic data types are also called the *built-in types* because they are built into the C++ language.

The ANSI C++ standard specifies two groups of numeric types: the integer group and the floating point group. Integers include the types `short`, `int`, `long`, `unsigned short`, `unsigned int`, and `unsigned long`. The floating point group includes `float`, `double`, and `long double`.

Integers are numbers that have no fractional or decimal part. Floating point numbers have a fractional part to the number. In C++, floating point numbers contain a decimal point.

The data type `short` can be no longer than the type `int`. The ANSI standard defines data type `long` as no shorter than an `int`.

According to the ANSI standard, an `unsigned short` must not be longer than an `unsigned int`. An `unsigned long` can be no shorter than an `unsigned int`.

The C++ language specification does not allow a `double` to be smaller than a `float`. A `long double` can be no shorter than a `double`.

If a C++ program stores a value into a variable that is larger than the data type can hold, the variable overflows. The C++ standard does not define the result of overflow.

If a value put into a variable is smaller than the data type of the variable can hold, the variable is said to underflow. The result of underflow is undefined.

Review Questions

1. What is an atomic data type? What is a built-in data type?
2. How many bits are in an `int`?
3. How many bits are in a `short`?
4. How many bits are in a `long double`?
5. What is a data type?
6. Identify which of the following are integers: (a) 6.0, (b) –21, (c) 764543, (d) –111.1.
7. What is the difference between an `unsigned int` and an `int`?
8. Why can data by lost from floating point numbers?
9. What value does a variable contain when it is declared?
10. Why do variables need to be declared?

Exercises

1. Write a C++ program that declares a different variable for each atomic data type that was discussed in this chapter. Initialize each variable to a value. Print the value in each variable to the screen.
2. Write a program that declares a variable of type `int` and prints out the value in that variable. Do not initialize the variable. Run the program at least five times. Explain what happened when you ran the program. Also explain why.
3. Write a program that declares a variable of type `double`. Set the variable to the value 430000.054. Print the value in the variable. Was it able to handle that number accurately? If the number was accurately printed, add a zero to each side of the decimal point so that you get 43000000000.0000000054. Compile and run the program again. If the number prints correctly, add five more zeros to each side of the decimal point and try again. Keep doing this until some of the information is lost. Explain what is happening when the program loses this information.

4. Write a program that initializes an `unsigned int` to –1. Explain what happened and why.
5. Write a program that declares an integer variable called `anInteger`. It should also declare a long integer called `aLongInt`. Assign the value 2000000000 into the variable `aLongInt` with the statement

```
aLongInt=2000000000;
```

Next, add the statement

```
anInteger=aLongInt;
```

Compile your program and run it. Explain the results.

Chapter Giossary

Atomic Data Type The built-in data types. The data types that are part of the C++ programming language.

Data Type Specifies the kind of information that can be stored in a variable. For instance, integers are stored in variables if type `int`. Floating point values are stored in `float` variables.

Floating Point Number A numeric value with a fractional part.

Integer A numeric value that has no fractional part.

Overflow Occurs when data in a variable exceeds the maximum value that the data type can hold.

Signed Data Type A data type that can store both positive and negative values.

Significant Digits The digits in a number with the highest, or most significant, numerical value.

Underflow Occurs when data in a variable is less than the minimum value that the data type can hold.

Unsigned Data Type A data type that can only store positive values.

Variable A place in memory that is assigned a name and a type. It stores a value that can vary as the program executes.

4 Atomic Data Types in C++: Characters

Objectives

After reading this chapter, you should be able to:

- Explain and use the `char` data type.
- Explain and use the `signed char` and `unsigned char` data types.

Preview

This chapter presents two more atomic data types: `signed char` and `unsigned char`.

char

Someday computers will be able to talk to us and understand our speech. Until then, the primary means of communication with computers is the written word. As a result, all computers must be able to recognize alphanumeric characters. **Alphanumeric characters** are the alphabet, both uppercase and lowercase, as well as the numbers 0 through 9.

All computers use a specific set of built-in codes to represent alphanumeric characters. Most computers use a set of characters called the **ASCII character set.** ASCII stands for American Standard Code for Information Interchange. With the exception of mainframe computers made by IBM, all computers recognize this set. IBM mainframes use a different character set. In this book, we will only discuss the ASCII character set.

In addition to the alphanumeric characters, the ASCII set also includes some punctuation marks and some other commonly used characters.

C++ programs declare character variables by using the `char` keyword. Example 4.1 demonstrates how programs declare and initialize character variables.

EXAMPLE 4.1 Declaring and Initializing Character Variables

```
char Variable Declarations
char aCharacter;
char anotherCharacter='C';
```

Example 4.1 declares the variable `aCharacter` and leaves it uninitialized. Therefore, we must assume it contains garbage until we put something in it. The second variable, `anotherCharacter`, is initialized to contain the character 'C'. Notice that in C++, all literal characters have single quote marks (') around them.

You may wonder, since characters in C++ are surrounded by the single quote marks, if C++ can store a single quote mark character in a character variable. The answer is yes, but you must precede it with a backslash, like this: '\''. The same is true for the backslash

TABLE 4.1 C++ Escape Sequence Characters

Escape Sequence	Represents
\a	Bell (beep)
\b	Backspace
\f	Formfeed
\n	Newline (same as endl)
\r	Return
\t	Horizontal tab
\\	Backslash
\'	Single quotation mark
\"	Double quotation mark
\00	Octal representation
\xhh	Hexadecimal representation

character, double quote marks, and some other special characters. Collectively, we call these characters **escape sequences.** Table 4.1 shows a list of the C++ escape sequence characters, all of which need to be preceded by a backslash.

A character variable may contain only one character at a time. Characters are stored as numbers. The numeric value in a character variable is the character's ASCII value. Table 4.2 contains the ASCII set of characters. Each character in the ASCII set is in the column on the left of the table. The other columns contain the value that is stored in memory for that character. In other words, when we store an 'A' in memory, what we really store is the number 65. Table 4.2 shows the numeric values as both decimal and hexadecimal (base 16) numbers.

TABLE 4.2 The ASCII Set of Characters

Character	Decimal Value	Hexadecimal Value	Represents
NUL	0	0x00	Null character
SOH	1	0x01	^A
STX	2	0x02	^B
ETX	3	0x03	^C
EOT	4	0x04	^D
ENQ	5	0x05	^E
ACK	6	0x06	^F
BEL	7	0x07	^G, Rings bell or beeps speaker
BS	8	0x08	^H, Backspace
HT	9	0x09	^I, Tab
LF	10	0x0A	^J, Line feed
VT	11	0x0B	^K, Vertical tab
FF	12	0x0C	^L, Form feed
CR	13	0x0D	^M, Carriage return
SO	14	0x0E	^N
SI	15	0x0F	^O
DLE	16	0x10	^P
DC1	17	0x11	^Q
DC2	18	0x12	^R
DC3	19	0x13	^S
DC4	20	0x14	^T
NAK	21	0x15	^U
SYN	22	0x16	^V
ETB	23	0x17	^W
CAN	24	0x18	^X
EM	25	0x19	^Y
SUB	26	0x1A	^Z
ESC	27	0x1B	Escape
FS	28	0x1C	^/

TABLE 4.2 Continued

Character	Decimal Value	Hexadecimal Value	Represents
GS	29	0x1D	^]
RS	30	0x1E	^=
US	31	0x1F	^-
SP	32	0x20	Spacebar
!	33	0x21	!
”	34	0x22	”
#	35	0x23	#
$	36	0x24	$
%	37	0x25	%
&	38	0x26	&
’	39	0x27	’
(	40	0x28	(
)	41	0x29	)
*	42	0x2A	*
+	43	0x2B	+
,	44	0x2C	,
-	45	0x2D	-
.	46	0x2E	.
/	47	0x2F	/
0	48	0x30	0
1	49	0x31	1
2	50	0x32	2
3	51	0x33	3
4	52	0x34	4
5	53	0x35	5
6	54	0x36	6
7	55	0x37	7
8	56	0x38	8
9	57	0x39	9
:	58	0x3A	:
;	59	0x3B	;
<	60	0x3C	<
=	61	0x3D	=
>	62	0x3E	>
?	63	0x3F	?
@	64	0x40	@
A	65	0x41	A
B	66	0x42	B
C	67	0x43	C
D	68	0x44	D
E	69	0x45	E
F	70	0x46	F
G	71	0x47	G
H	72	0x48	H
I	73	0x49	I
J	74	0x4A	J
K	75	0x4B	K
L	76	0x4C	L
M	77	0x4D	M
N	78	0x4E	N
O	79	0x4F	O
P	80	0x50	P
Q	81	0x51	Q
R	82	0x52	R
S	83	0x53	S
T	84	0x54	T

(continued on the next page)

TABLE 4.2 Continued

Character	Decimal Value	Hexadecimal Value	Represents
U	85	0x55	U
V	86	0x56	V
W	87	0x57	W
X	88	0x58	X
Y	89	0x59	Y
Z	90	0x5A	Z
[	91	0x5B	[
\	92	0x5C	\
]	93	0x5D	]
^	94	0x5E	^
_	95	0x5F	_
`	96	0x60	`
a	97	0x61	a
b	98	0x62	b
c	99	0x63	c
d	100	0x64	d
e	101	0x65	e
f	102	0x66	f
g	103	0x67	g
h	104	0x68	h
i	105	0x69	i
j	106	0x6A	j
k	107	0x6B	k
l	108	0x6C	l
m	109	0x6D	m
n	110	0x6E	n
o	111	0x6F	o
p	112	0x70	p
q	113	0x71	q
r	114	0x72	r
s	115	0x73	s
t	116	0x74	t
u	117	0x75	u
v	118	0x76	v
w	119	0x77	w
x	120	0x78	x
y	121	0x79	y
z	122	0x7A	z
{	123	0x7B	}
|	124	0x7C	|
}	125	0x7D	}
~	126	0x7E	~
DEL	127	0x7F	Delete

Since programs store characters in character variables as numbers, it is possible to store a numeric quantity in a character variable. Most modern C++ compilers will complain about that, though. They don't like mixing numeric and character data types, but they will allow it. Hands On 4.1 shows how this ability to treat characters as numbers can be useful.

Hands On 4.1

Objective

Write a program that converts characters to numbers and numbers to characters.

Experiment

Type the following program into your text editor or IDE:

```
#include <iostream.h>

int main()
{
    char aCharacter=' ';
    int anInteger=0;
    cout<<"Please input a number between 0-9 :";
    cin>>anInteger;
    aCharacter=(int)'0'+anInteger;
    cout<<"I have converted your number to the character ";
    cout<<aCharacter;
    cout<<endl<<"The ASCII value of that character is ";
    anInteger=(int)aCharacter;
    cout<<anInteger;
    return 0;
}
```

Result

```
Please input a number between 0-9 :1
I have converted your number to the character 1
The ASCII value of that character is 49
```

Analysis

This program demonstrates the equivalence of numbers and characters. First, the program declares two variables, one of type `char` and another of type `int`. The character variable is initialized to the value of space. The ASCII set includes a space in it. It is character number 32. A space character is generated every time you press the spacebar on your keyboard. The program initializes the second variable, `anInteger`, to zero.

The program then asks the user to type in a number between 0 and 9 inclusive. The characters '0' through '9' are also in the ASCII set. They are not the same as the numbers 0 through 9. The numbers 0 through 9 are integers that have the values of 0 through 9. The characters '0' through '9' are of data type `char` and have the ASCII values of 48 through 57.

This program converts the numbers 0 through 9 to the characters '0' through '9'. It uses the fact that the ASCII values in memory are really numbers. The ASCII value of the character '0' is 48. If the user types the value 0 into `anInteger`, then 48 + 0 gives 48. If the user types in a number 1, then 48 + 1 is 49, which is the ASCII value of the character '1'. This works for all the numbers in the range of 0–9. We add them to the ASCII value of '0' to get the ASCII value of the number that the user entered on the keyboard.

There are several important points to recognize about the conversion from integers to characters. First, notice the line that reads

```
aCharacter=(int)'0'+anInteger;
```

The word `int` is in parentheses. This tells the C++ compiler that we are treating the character '0' as if it were an integer. It is called a **type cast.** For this one statement only, we are asking the compiler to treat '0' as an `int` instead of a `char`. The integer value that '0' evaluates to is its ASCII value.

The program then tells the user that the conversion has been done. It also converts the character that the user entered to its ASCII value with the statement

```
anInteger=(int)aCharacter;
```

Here again, a type cast is used. For this statement only, the compiler will treat the `char` variable `aCharacter` as an `int`.

After it converts the character that the user typed to its ASCII value, the program prints the value on the screen.

`signed char` and `unsigned char`

We have seen that characters can be treated as numbers. We know that they are stored as numbers (their ASCII values) in memory. By default, characters are neither signed nor unsigned. Remember that a signed number is one that can take on either positive or negative values. An unsigned number can only store positive values. It is left to the implementor of the compiler to decide whether characters are signed or unsigned quantities.

In the past (particularly in C programming), the `char` data type was often used to represent a byte because a `char` is usually implemented as a byte. In that case, the programmer must be able to explicitly state whether the byte is signed or unsigned. C++ allows this. Example 4.2 demonstrates the declaration of signed and unsigned character variables.

EXAMPLE 4.2 Declaring `signed char` and `unsigned char` Variables

```
unsigned char anUnsignedChar = 'b';
anUnsignedChar = -5; // Not allowed.
signed char aSignedChar = -1; // This is ok.
```

The drawback to defining a byte in this manner is that it is often not portable. Many C++ compilers promote all `char` variables to `int`.

Troubleshooting Guide

After reading this section, you should be able to:

- Recognize and avoid nonportable character assignments.
- Find and fix accidental escape sequences in strings.

Nonportable Character Assignments

Many systems allocate 1 byte (8 bits) for character variables. A 1-byte character variable can contain any value between 0 and 255. However, if you look at the ASCII chart in Table 4.2, you'll see that the characters range in value from 0 to 127. What about the values from 128 to 255?

Some computers use the values from 128 to 255 for an **extended character set.** The extended character set is not standardized. You can use it in your programs, but it will not work the same way on every computer. For instance, the statement

```
char aCharVariable = (char)248;
```

is a valid C++ statement on most computers. It declares a variable called `aCharVariable` and stores the character whose value is 248 in it. If your program executes this statement on a PC, it will store a different character than if it executes the same statement on a Macintosh. The result will be different on nearly every different type of computer. Therefore, we say that this statement is nonportable.

It is best to avoid using the extended character set. Both C++ and many graphical user interfaces (such as Windows or the Macintosh operating system) provide tools to display the same characters that you find in extended character sets. These tools are generally more portable than extended character sets.

C++ provides a wide character data type that allows you to use a greater range of characters. (This is an advanced topic that is beyond the scope of this book.)

Accidental Escape Sequences

If you are using MS DOS or some version of MS Windows (Windows 3.x, Windows 9x, or Windows NT), it is possible to get accidental escape sequences in your programs. Example 4.3 shows a program fragment that demonstrates this.

EXAMPLE 4.3 Accidental Escape Sequences

```
cout << "The file you're looking for is located at ";
cout << "C:\adirectory\thisspot\bytes.txt";
```

This string contains three escape sequences: \a, \t, and \b. Whenever any of the characters in Table 4.1 occurs in a string, the C++ compiler will treat it as an escape sequence. Does this mean that we can't put strings containing directory and file names in MS DOS or MS Windows programs?

The answer is no. Any time we want the backslash character to occur in a string as a backslash and not as the beginning of an escape sequence, we must put '\\' in the string. This tells the compiler to treat it as a backslash character. Example 4.4 shows nearly the same string as Example 4.3. However, all of the backslash characters in Example 4.4 are doubled. The compiler will not treat them as escape sequences.

EXAMPLE 4.4 The Escape Sequences Removed

```
cout << "The file you're looking for is located at ";
cout << "C:\\adirectory\\thisspot\\bytes.txt";
```

Almost every programmer occasionally puts accidental escape sequences in their programs. When we program on other operating systems, such as Unix, we are less prone to this mistake. Unix does not use the backslash character in path names. However, we must watch out for it any time we want to use a backslash in a string.

Summary

Character variables are declared as type `char`. A character variable can contain, at most, one character. All computers except IBM mainframes use the ASCII set of characters.

There are some character values in C++ that are preceded by a backslash. These are called *escape sequences*.

The ANSI C++ standard does not specify whether the character data types are signed or unsigned by default. The implementor of the compiler can decide which way `char` variables should be. If you absolutely need a character to be signed or unsigned, you can force it to whichever you want.

Review Questions

1. What is the ASCII set?
2. What are alphanumeric characters?
3. How is a character variable declared in a C++ program?
4. What is a literal character? Give an example.
5. What is an escape sequence? How are escape sequences used?
6. In what way is a character really a number?
7. How can a character variable be treated (temporarily) as an integer in a program?
8. By default, are characters signed or unsigned?
9. How is a signed character variable declared in a program?
10. How is an unsigned character variable declared in a program?

Exercises

1. Write a program that accepts a character as input from the user and prints its ASCII value.
2. Write a program that tries to store the value –1 in an unsigned character variable. Explain the results of this experiment.
3. To find out whether your compiler uses signed or unsigned characters by default, declare a char variable in a C++ program. Assign the char variable the value of –1. Explain the results.

4. Write a program that accepts a number as input from the user. We will assume that the user will type in a number between 0 and 127 inclusive. Treat the number as an ASCII value and print the character that corresponds to that ASCII value.
5. Write a program that accepts a number as input from the user. We will assume that the user will type in a number between 128 and 255 inclusive. Treat the number as a character value and print the character that corresponds to it. Explain why this did or did not work on your computer system.
6. Find the errors in the following program.

```
#include <iostream.h>

int main()
{
   char aChar = Q;
   char aString = "This is a string";

   cout << "The letter " << aChar;
   cout << " is a very nice letter.
   cout << "Don't you think?" << endl;
   cout << endl << aString;
   return (0);
```

Chapter Glossary

Alphanumeric Characters Characters that are either numbers or letters.

ASCII Character Set American Standard Code for Information Interchange. A set of characters recognized by all computers except IBM mainframes.

Escape Sequence A special character that is preceded by a backslash (\) character. See Table 4.1.

Extended Character Set Nonstandard characters whose values fall between 128 and 255 inclusive.

Type Cast Temporarily casting one data type into another.

5 The Essentials of C++ Operators

Objectives

After reading this chapter, you should be able to:

- Use the addition (+), subtraction (–), multiplication (*), and division (/) operators in C++ programs.
- Explain what operator precedence is and how it can affect equations in programs.

Preview

This chapter introduces C++ operators. Part of the richness of the C++ language is its powerful set of operators. Some of the most commonly used operators in C++ are the arithmetic operators: addition, subtraction, multiplication, and division.

+, –, *, and /

We've already used operators in our sample programs. In most cases, their use is pretty straightforward. Hands On 5.1 demonstrates the use of the operators plus (+), minus (–), times (*), and divide (/).

Hands On 5.1

Objective

Write a program that demonstrates the use of the +, –, *, and / operators for integers.

Experiment

Type the following program into your text editor or IDE. Compile and run it.

```
#include <iostream.h>

main()
{
   int i=20;
   int j;

   // Print the value of i and j.
   cout<< "i=" << i << endl;
```

```
    cout << "j=" << j << endl;

    // Integer addition.
    j = i+5;
    cout << "j="<< j << endl;

    // Integer subtraction.
    i = j-10;
    cout << "i="<< i << endl;

    // Integer multiplication.
    i = i * j * 2;
    cout << "i=" << i << endl;

    // Integer division.
    j = i/10;
    cout<<"j="<<j<<endl;

    return (0);
}
```

Results

```
i=20
j=4217080
j=25
i=15
i=750
j=75
```

Analysis

When you compile this program, you will very likely get a warning about it. The compiler should tell you that you are trying to use the variable `j` before it has been initialized. However, the program should still compile and run.

The first thing the program does is to print the values of the variables `i` and `j`. We can see that `j` does in fact contain a random value. It will likely be different every time you run the program. Some compilers automatically initialize uninitialized data to zero. Don't get in the habit of depending on this, however, because many don't.

Next, the program does an integer addition and prints the result to the screen. It shows that the variable `j` now equals 25.

The program performs a subtraction and assigns the result to the variable `i`. It then prints the value in `i`.

Next is a multiplication. The line

```
i=i*j*2;
```

tells the computer to take the value in `i`, multiply it by the value in `j`, then multiply it by 2. The result in this case is 25 * 15 * 2, or 750. The program prints 750 to the screen.

It may seem funny to have the variable `i` on the right side of the statement

```
i=i*j*2;
```

This instruction tells the program that we want it to get the current value in the variable `i` (which is 25) and multiply it by the value in `j`, then multiply it by 2. We then want the result stored back in the variable `i`. So the new value of `i` becomes 750.

The example program performs an integer division. The value in `i` is divided by 10 and stored back in `j`. The result is 75, which the program prints to the screen.

The four basic C++ mathematical operators can be used with other data types. Hands On 5.2 shows the use of +, –, *, and / with unsigned integers.

Hands On 5.2

Objective

Write a program that demonstrates the use of the +, –, *, and / operators for unsigned integers.

Experiment

Type the following program into your IDE or text editor. Compile, link, and run it.

```
#include <iostream.h>

main()
{
   unsigned i=20;
   unsigned long j;
   unsigned short k=50;

   cout << "i=" << i << endl;
   cout << "j=" << j << endl;
   cout << "k=" << k << endl;

   // This will cause underflow!
   j = i-k;
   cout << "j=" << j;
   cout << endl;

   j = i+k;
   cout << "j=" << j << endl;

   // This can cause overflow!
   k=i * j * k;
   cout << "k=" << k << endl;

   j = j/5;
   cout << "j=" << j << endl;

   return (0);
}
```

Results

```
i=20
j=4217672
k=50
j=4294967266
j=70
k=4464
j=14
```

Analysis

When you compile this program, your compiler may give you a warning indicating that you are trying to use the variable j before it is initialized.

This sample program begins by declaring three variables: an unsigned integer, an unsigned short integer, and an unsigned long integer. It initializes the variables i and k. However, it does not initialize j to a known value. Therefore, we must assume that it contains garbage.

The program prints the values in i, j, and k. When it does, we see that j does, in fact, contain a random value.

The first mathematical operator that the program uses is a subtraction. Because the value in k is larger than the value in i, the subtraction will evaluate to a negative number. However, C++ doesn't allow us to store negative numbers in unsigned data types. Therefore, we are generating an underflow error through this subtraction. When the program prints the value of j, we can see clearly that it underflowed.

Next, the program does an addition. It assigns the result to the variable j. This assignment gives j a known value.

After performing the addition and printing the value of j on the screen, the program does a multiplication. It multiplies the value in i times the value in j, then multiplies that by the value in k. It assigns the result into k. Note that this may cause an overflow error. The Results section shows that it was OK in this instance. However, if your compiler defines `unsigned short` variables as 1 byte in length, this equation will cause an overflow error.

The program finishes by performing a division and printing the resulting value.

Hands On 5.3 demonstrates the use of +, –, *, and / on floating point data types.

Hands On 5.3

Objective

Write a program that demonstrates the use of the +, –, *, and / operators for floating point numbers.

Experiment

```
#include <iostream.h>

main()
{
    float i=1000.1001;
    double j=123.234567;
    long double k;

    k = i+j;
    cout << "k=" << k << endl;

    k = i-j+500.951;
    cout << "k=" << k << endl;

    j = j*i;
    cout << "j=" << j << endl;

    i = k/j;
```

```
    cout << "i=" << i << endl;

    return (0);
}
```

Results

```
k=1123.33
k=1377.82
j=123247
i=0.0111793
```

Analysis

This short program first declares three floating point variables, then uses them in an addition operation. It prints the result to the screen. It also performs a subtraction and prints the resulting value.

When the program prints the result of the addition and subtraction, it sets the number of digits to the right of the decimal point to two. It also rounds the answer. This is the default behavior for the compiler that I used for this example. Your compiler's default may be different. C++ provides ways to control this.

The program performs a multiplication and outputs the result. Notice that it rounded the value it printed to the next whole number. It did not print anything to the right of the decimal point. The compiler I used to create this example has a default column width. If a floating point number exceeds the column width, it tries to shorten the output by rounding to the nearest whole number. Your compiler's behavior may be different. We'll see later how to control this as well.

Finally, the program does a division. In order to print the significant digits of the result, it prints seven digits to the right of the decimal point.

Precedence

Not all operators are created equal in C++. Some operators have higher priority or **precedence** than others. Suppose, for example, that we want to type the equation in Example 5.1 into a program.

EXAMPLE 5.1 A Question of Precedence

$$\mathrm{i} = \frac{j+k}{3}$$

A natural reaction would be to type the statement

```
i=j+k/3;
```

into the program. However, that will not give us what we want. The reason is that the division operator has higher precedence than the addition operator. Therefore, the program does the division first. Next, it performs the addition. What we want is the addition done first, then the division. We can solve this problem using the parentheses operator, which has higher precedence than division. We would need to rewrite the preceding equation to the following:

```
i=(j+k)/3;
```

Because the parentheses operator has very high precedence, everything inside the parentheses is evaluated first. Afterward, the program does the division.

Hands On 5.4 demonstrates precedence.

Hands On 5.4

Objective

Write a program that demonstrates operator precedence.

Experiment

Type the following program into your IDE or text editor. Compile, link, and run it.

```
#include <iostream.h>

int main()
{
    int i,j=60,k=30;

    i=j+k/3;
    cout << "The answer to i=j+k/3 is " << i << endl;

    i=(j+k)/3;
    cout << "The answer to i=(j+k)/3 is " << i << endl;

    return (0);
}
```

Results

```
The answer to i=j+k/3 is 70
The answer to i=(j+k)/3 is 30
```

Analysis

The first equation uses normal C++ precedence. That is, the program performs the division first, then does the addition. The second equation contains parentheses that force the addition to be done first.

As we can see from Hands On 5.4, operators with higher precedence are performed first. Table 5.1 gives some more examples of equations whose precedence has been altered with parentheses. The left column contains several equations without parentheses. The center column shows how those equations will be evaluated. The right column gives an example of one way the precedence of the first equation can be altered with parentheses.

Table 5.2 shows a precedence chart. This chart lists all of the operators in C++ by order of precedence. Operators shown near the top of the chart have higher precedence than operators listed lower down.

At this point you may be asking, "What if I have an equation with two operators of equal precedence? Which one is done first?" You can find the answer for yourself by looking at the Associativity column in Table 5.2. The associativity of an operator tells us which operator to evaluate first if there are two operators of equal precedence.

TABLE 5.1 Altering Precedence

Equation	Evaluation Order	Forced Precedence
a=b+c*d	a=b+(c*d)	a=(b+c)*d
a=b/c*d+e	a=((b/c)*d)+e	a=b/(c*(d+e))
a=b–c/d*e	a=b–((c/d)*e)	a=(b–(c/d))*e

TABLE 5.2 Precedence Chart

Level	Operator	Associativity	Operation
1	()	L–R	Call function or force precedence
	[ ]	L–R	Array subscript
	->	L–R	Indirection membership (pointer)
	::	L–R	Scope resolution
	.	L–R	Direct membership
2	+	R–L	Unary plus (positive sign)
	-	R–L	Unary minus (negative sign)
	~	R–L	Negate bits (one's complement)
	!	R–L	Logical negation (logical not)
	++	R–L	Increment (pre- and post-)
	--	R–L	Decrement (pre- and post-)
	&	R–L	Address of (pointer)
	*	R–L	Dereference (pointer)
	new	R–L	Dynamically allocate memory
	delete	R–L	Dynamically deallocate memory
	sizeof	R–L	Size (in bytes)
3	*.	L–R	C++ dereference
	->	L–R	C++ dereference
4	*	L–R	Multiplication
	/	L–R	Division
	%	L–R	Modulus
5	+	L–R	Addition
	-	L–R	Subtraction
6	>>	L–R	Right shift or extraction
	<<	L–R	Left shift or insertion
7	>	L–R	Greater than
	!	R–L	Logical negation (logical not)
	>=	L–R	Greater than or equal to
	<	L–R	Less than
	<=	L–R	Less than or equal to
8	==	L–R	Equal to
	!=	L–R	Not equal to
9	&	L–R	Bitwise AND
10	|	L–R	Bitwise OR
11	&&	L–R	Logical AND
12	||	L–R	Logical OR
13	?:	R–L	Conditional
14	=	R–L	Assignment
	+=	R–L	Assign sum
	-=	R–L	Assign difference
	*=	R–L	Assign product
	/=	R–L	Assign quotient
	%=	R–L	Assign (modulus) remainder
	&=	R–L	Assign bitwise AND
	|=	R–L	Assign bitwise OR
	>>=	R–L	Assign right shift
	<<=	R–L	Assign left shift

Note: L–R indicates left-to-right associativity. R–L indicates right-to-left associativity.

Notice, for instance, that the multiplication (*) and division (/) operators are on the same level in the precedence chart. The rightmost column says that they have left-to-right associativity. That means in an equation like

```
a=b*c/d;
```

the multiplication will be done first, then the division. Even though they are of equal precedence, the multiplication is done first because it's the leftmost of the two operators.

Troubleshooting Guide

After reading this section, you should be able to:

- Find precedence problems.
- Fix precedence problems.

Finding Precedence Problems

Tracking down precedence problems in a program is primarily a matter of knowing and validating your output data. You should thoroughly test the output of every program, and every part of every program, before you release it.

Certain precedence mistakes tend to be made more often than others. For instance, you may write an equation in a program like this:

```
y=x/a+1;
```

when you really mean this:

```
y=x/(a+1);
```

The first equation will divide the value in x by the value in a. Next, the statement adds 1 to the result. It stores the result in the variable y. The second equation first adds 1 to the value in the variable a, then divides x by the result of the addition. It stores the final value in the variable y.

Similar precedence mistakes are common with multiplication.

Also, precedence mistakes often appear using the operators *= and \=. These are discussed in more detail in Chapter 6. However, it is important to note that they can be a common source of precedence errors.

Fixing Precedence Problems

Whenever you're unsure of the precedence of an equation, use parentheses to force it to what you want it to be. It's OK to overuse parentheses a bit. That's better than spending large amounts of time tracking down a precedence bug in your program. Using parentheses to force precedence doesn't cause your program to run slower. There is no performance penalty for this technique.

Summary

C++ supports arithmetic operations. This chapter presented the addition, subtraction, multiplication, and division operators.

Generally speaking, it's best not to mix types in an operation. That is, integers should be added to integers, floating point values to floating point values, and so on. If a program performs an operation (+, –, *, or /) on an integer type and a floating point type, it results in a floating point value.

Operator precedence controls the order in which operations are performed. Operators with higher precedence will be done before operators with lower precedence. Operators with equal precedence are evaluated in the order specified in the precedence chart in Table 5.2.

Programs can force precedence by using parentheses. Parentheses have very high precedence, so operations inside them are executed first.

Review Questions

1. What is the order of evaluation for the following equation? It doesn't matter whether you know what the operators do. Only the order in which they are evaluated is important.

```
a = b*c+d-e/f%d;
```

2. What data type is the answer to the following equation?

```
10/200.0;
```

3. What is stored in the variable `i`?

```
int i,j=5;
double d=7.6;
i=j+d;
```

4. What is stored in the variable `d`?

```
int i=5;
double d,e=7.6;
d=e+i;
```

5. What is precedence?
6. Why do operators have to have precedence?
7. What would be the result of the following equation if the addition and subtraction operators had higher precedence than the multiplication and division operators?

```
int i,j=5,k=9,m=1,n=21;
i=j+k*m-n;
```

8. Why would you not want addition and subtraction to have higher precedence than multiplication and division? Use Question 7 as an example.
9. In what order are operators of equal precedence evaluated?
10. How can the precedence of an equation be forced into a particular order?

Exercises

1. Write a program that gets four integers from the user, adds them, and prints the sum on the screen.
2. Write a program that implements the following equation:

```
a=(b-c)/(d*e);
```

Declare the five integer variables `a`, `b`, `c`, `d`, and `e` in your program. When the program runs, it should prompt the user for the values of `b`, `c`, `d`, and `e`. After it executes the equation, it should print the value of `a`.

3. Some of the equations from Table 5.1 are repeated below. Assume that `b` equals 7, `c` equals –3, `d` equals 29, and `e` equals 114. Write a program that assigns values to the variables and calculates an answer for `a` for each equation.

```
a=b+c*d      a=(b+c)*d
a=b/c*d+e    a=b/(c*(d+e))
a=b-c/d*e    a=(b-(c/d))*e
```

4. Write a program that gets an integer value and a floating point value from the user. The program should multiply them and store the result in an integer variable. It should then print the contents of the integer variable. Explain your result.
5. Write a program that gets an integer value and a floating point value from the user. The program should multiply them and store the result in a floating point variable. It should then print the contents of the floating point variable. Explain the result.
6. Write a program that:
   a. Declares two unsigned integer variables.
   b. Assigns the values 10000 and 1000 into the unsigned integers.
   c. Multiplies them and stores the answer into an unsigned short integer.

   Explain the result you get when you run this program.
7. Write a program that gets an integer from the user, multiplies the integer by itself (e.g., squares the number), and outputs the answer to the screen. The number that the user types in may be less than zero.

8. Write a program that gets a number from the user and divides it by 10. It should then output the answer to the screen. The number that the user types in may not be less than zero.
9. Write a program that gets a number from the user and multiplies it by 10. It should then output the answer to the screen. Explain what happens when the number that the user types in becomes very large.
10. Write a program that gets a number from the user and divides it by 100000.5. It should then output the answer to the screen. Explain what potential problems could occur when the number becomes too small.

Chapter Glossary

Precedence The order in which operators are evaluated. Operators with higher precedence are evaluated first.

6 Other Operators in C++

Objectives

After reading this chapter, you should be able to:

- Explain and use the preincrement and postincrement operators.
- Explain and use the predecrement and postdecrement operators.
- Explain and use the modulus operator.
- Explain and use the `sizeof` operator.
- Explain and use the `+=`, `-=`, `*=`, and `/=` operators.

Preview

In this chapter, we'll continue looking at C++ operators. In particular, we'll cover the use of the four increment and decrement operators, the modulus operator, and the `sizeof` operator. This chapter also presents the use of the `+=`, `-=`, `*=`, and `/=` operators.

Preincrement, Postincrement, Predecrement, and Postdecrement

A common operation in C++ is to increment or decrement the value of a variable by 1. Because these are such common operations, the C++ language provides us with operators for incrementing and decrementing.

Actually, there are two operators for incrementing and two for decrementing. When we want to increase the value in a numeric variable by 1, we can use preincrement or postincrement.

The preincrement operator is shown in Example 6.1. The `++` sign occurs before the variable. Look at the example. What do you think will be stored in the variable `b`?

EXAMPLE 6.1 Preincrementing a Variable

```
int main()
{
   int a=10;
   int b;

   b=++a;
   cout << "a=" << a << endl;
   cout << "b=" << b;
   return 0;
}
```

The program in Example 6.1 stores the value 11 in the variable b. A preincrement tells the compiler that you want to increment the variable before it you use it for anything else. Therefore, the program incremented the value in the variable a, then assigned it to b. When you run this program, it will print 11 for both a and b.

Example 6.2 shows nearly the same program as Example 6.1. In this case, however, the program uses a postincrement. What do you think the values of a and b will be?

EXAMPLE 6.2 Postincrementing a Variable

```
int main()
{
    int a=10;
    int b;

    b=a++;
    cout << "a=" << a << endl;
    cout << "b=" << b;
    return 0;
}
```

TIP: Remember that preincrement tells the compiler that a variable should be incremented before it is used for anything else. Postincrement tells the compiler that the variable should be used in an equation first, then incremented.

The answer may surprise you. This program will print the number 10 for the variable b and 11 for a. A postincrement tells the compiler to use the value in a variable, then increment it. Therefore, the program first assigned the value in the variable a into b, then it incremented the value in a. At the end of the program, the variable a has the value of 11; however, b contains 10.

Predecrement and postdecrement work in a way that is similar to preincrement and postincrement. Hands On 6.1 shows a program that demonstrates the difference between predecrement and postdecrement.

Hands On 6.1

Objective

Write a program that demonstrates the difference between predecrement and postdecrement.

Experiment

Type the following program into your IDE or text editor. Compile, link, and run it.

```
#include <iostream.h>

int main()
{
    int a=10;
    int b;

    b=a--;
    cout << "a=" << a << endl;
    cout << "b=" << b << endl;

    b=--a;
    cout << "a=" << a << endl;
    cout << "b=" << b;

    return (0);
}
```

Results

```
a=9
b=10
a=8
b=8
```

Analysis

The program in this Hands On first uses a postdecrement to decrement the value in the variable a by 1. The postdecrement made the program use the value in the variable a for the assignment first, then decrement it.

After outputting the values in a and b, the program uses a predecrement to decrease the value in a by 1 again. We can see from the Results section that it decremented the value in the variable a before it performed the assignment.

Modulus

An operator that gets used more than you might think is the modulus operator. The C++ language uses the percent sign (%) for the modulus operator.

The modulus operator gives the remainder of an integer division. Example 6.3 shows an integer division in a program. The answer should be 2.5. However, because we're using integers, C++ throws away, or truncates, the fractional part. So the program prints the number 2 to the screen.

The fractional part that is truncated is called the *remainder*. The real answer to 5/2 is that 2 goes two times into 5 with a remainder of 1. In other words, 2 * 2 + 1 = 5.

EXAMPLE 6.3 An Integer Division

```
#include <stdio.h>

int main()
{
   cout << "What is 5/2?"<<endl;
   cout << "The answer is ";
   int theAnswer=5/2;
   cout << theAnswer;
   cout << endl;
   return (0);
}
```

If we ever want to know the remainder of an integer division, we use the modulus operator. Example 6.4 demonstrates the result of using the modulus operator. Notice that it is almost the same program as shown in Example 6.3. The primary difference is that the division sign has been removed, and the modulus operator is used instead. If you type this program into your computer, compile it, and run it, you'll see that it prints the number 1.

EXAMPLE 6.4 Using the Modulus Operator

```
#include <stdio.h>

int main()
{
   cout << "What is 5%2?"<<endl;
   cout << "The answer is ";
   int theAnswer=5%2;
   cout << theAnswer;
   cout << endl;
   return (0);
}
```

sizeof

The `sizeof` operator evaluates to the number of bytes a piece of data requires when it is stored in memory. Hands On 6.2 demonstrates the use of the `sizeof` operator.

Hands On 6.2

Objective

Write a program that demonstrates the use of the `sizeof` operator with various data types.

Experiment

Type the following program into your text editor or IDE. Compile, link, and run it.

```
#include <iostream.h>

int main()
{
     cout << "On this computer, ";
     cout << "using this operating system,"<<endl;
     cout << "an integer is ";
     cout << sizeof(int) ;
     cout << " bytes."<<endl;

     cout << endl<<"A long is ";
     cout << sizeof(long);
     cout << " bytes."<<endl;

     cout << endl<<"A short is ";
     cout << sizeof(short);
     cout << " bytes"<<endl;
     return (0);
}
```

Results

```
On this computer, using this operating system,
an integer is 2 bytes.

A long is 4 bytes.

A short is 2 bytes
```

Analysis

This program displays the number of bytes that are needed in memory to store an `int`, a `long`, and a `short`. Any type name can be used with the `sizeof` operator, even types that you create yourself. The `sizeof` operator always evaluates to the size of a type in bytes.

When you run this program on your computer, you are likely to get a different answer for the size of the atomic data types than I did on mine. Unless you're using the same kind of computer, with the same operating system and compiler that I used, you can't guarantee that you'll get the answers that I got.

+=, −=, *=, /=

C++ provides some additional arithmetic operators that can be used as a kind of shorthand. For instance, the statement

```
anInteger += 5;
```

adds 5 to the value in the variable `anInteger`. It stores the result in `anInteger`. This notation is much more efficient than a statement such as

```
anInteger=anInteger+5;
```

There are similar statements for subtraction, multiplication, and division. They each take a value in a variable, perform an operation on it, and store it back in the variable.

Troubleshooting Guide

After reading this section, you should be able to:

- Find common problems with the increment and decrement operators.
- Be aware of possible mistakes that can be made with the `sizeof` operator.
- Find and fix precedence problems with the +=, −=, `*=`, and /= operators.

Confusion with the Increment and Decrement Operators

The most common problems that arise when using preincrement, postincrement, predecrement, and postdecrement occur when we try to get too fancy. C++ is a very flexible language; however, all programmers sometimes make the mistake of being just a bit too clever and creative with our use of C++. The result can be very surprising.

For instance, what do you think the following equation would evaluate to?

```
int i,j=5;
i=++j + j++ + --j - 1;
```

If you can predict what this will yield, you're borderline psychic. It is not always evaluated the way you anticipate. Experience with a variety of compilers has taught me that they all evaluate multiple increments and decrements on a single line of code differently. It's best to refrain from such tricky code and find a simpler way to express equations.

Surprises from `sizeof`

The `sizeof` operator is used to find the size of a data type. It can also be used to find the size of other things, but I recommend against such uses. The code in Hands On 6.3 illustrates some of the other uses of `sizeof` and demonstrates why there might be some confusion.

Hands On 6.3

Objective

Write a program that demonstrates the uses of the `sizeof` operator.

Experiment

Type the following program into your text editor or IDE. Compile, link, and run it.

```
#include <iostream.h>
int main()
{
   int anInteger;
```

```
    long aLong;
    double aDouble;
    int anIntegerArray[10];
    int *anIntegerPointer;

    cout << sizeof(anInteger) << endl;
    cout << sizeof(aLong) << endl;
    cout << sizeof(aDouble) << endl;
    cout << sizeof(anIntegerArray) << endl;
    anIntegerPointer = anIntegerArray;
    cout << sizeof(anIntegerPointer) << endl;
    return (0);
}
```

Results

```
2
4
8
20
4
```

Analysis

Notice that this example does not use the `sizeof` operator to find the size of data types. It uses `sizeof` to find the size of variables. Specifically, we're finding the size of an integer, a long integer, a double, an array of integers, and a pointer to an array of integers. We'll discuss arrays and pointers in later chapters.

Taking the size of the integer, long, double, and array gives the number of bytes that most people expect. The problem comes in with pointers. Notice that even though the pointer is pointing at the array, the `sizeof` operator didn't give the size of the array. It gave the size of the pointer.

There is a fundamental equivalence in C++ between pointers and arrays. In many cases, they can be used interchangeably. This is one instance in which they can't. Therefore, it can a source of great confusion—especially to maintenance programmers.

In general, the safest way to use `sizeof` is with types. That way, you clearly state to the maintenance programmer that you know what you're finding the size of. There can be no confusion between finding the size of pointers and finding the size of arrays.

Precedence with *= and /=

And now it's time for a pop quiz. The statement

```
thisInteger*=thatInteger-4;
```

is equivalent to which of the following?

a. `thisInteger=(thisInteger*thatInteger)-4;`
b. `thisInteger=thisInteger*(thatInteger-4);`
c. `(thisInteger=thisInteger)*thatInteger-4;`
d. `thisInteger=((thisInteger*thatInteger)-4);`

OK, time's up. A quick glance through the list of answers will eliminate some possibilities right away. Answer (c) is illegal. It won't compile. C++ equations are divided into two parts—everything to the right of the equal sign and everything to the left of it. The stuff on the right of the equal sign must evaluate to a value. Whatever is on the left must evaluate to a location in memory to store the answer. The formal name for these two parts of equations are **Lvalue** and **Rvalue,** for left value and right value. In answer (c), the parentheses span both sides of the equal sign. The compiler will not be able to separate that into an Lvalue and an Rvalue.

So now we know that (c) is wrong.

Answers (a) and (d) say exactly the same thing. The addition of the extra parentheses in (d) don't affect the results at all.

By the process of elimination, we find that the answer is (b). At first glance, you'd think it would be (a) and/or (d). It looks as if the multiplication should be done first because it has higher precedence. However, a glance back at the precedence chart in Chapter 5 (Table 5.2) will clear things up. The `*=` operator has much lower precedence than the subtraction operator. Therefore, C++ performs the subtraction first, not the multiplication. All of the operators in the group `+=`, `-=`, `*=`, `/=` operate in the same way. Everything on the right side of the equation is done first because these four operators have very low precedence.

Summary

To increment a variable means to increase its value by 1. To decrement it is to decrease its value by 1. C++ provides two increment and two decrement operators. They are preincrement, postincrement, predecrement, and postdecrement.

Preincrement increments the value in a variable before the program uses it for anything else. Predecrement decrements the value in a variable before the program uses it for anything else. Postincrement uses the value in a variable, then increments it. Postdecrement uses the value in a variable, then decrements it.

It is best to do only one increment or one decrement per line in a C++ program.

The modulus operator evaluates to the remainder of an integer division.

The `sizeof` operator evaluates to the size of a data type. The answer is in bytes.

The += operator tells the C++ compiler to add the value on the right of the += to the value in the variable on the left. It stores the answer in the variable on the left of the += sign.

The `-=` operator works in the same fashion as the += operator. The only difference is that it performs a subtraction instead of an addition.

Likewise, the `*=` and `/=` operators perform their operations similarly. The `*=` operator multiplies the Lvalue and the Rvalue and stores it in the Lvalue. The `/=` operator does the same with a division.

Review Questions

1. What does the preincrement operator do?
2. What does the postincrement operator do?
3. What does the predecrement operator do?
4. What does the postdecrement operator do?
5. What does the modulus operator do?
6. What does the `sizeof` operator do?
7. What is the `sizeof` operator used for generally?
8. Why is incrementing or decrementing a variable more than once per line generally not desirable?
9. What do the +=, `-=`, `*=`, and `/=` operators do?
10. What potential confusion might occur with the precedence of the *= and /= operators?

Exercises

1. Type the following program into your text editor. Save it and run it. Explain the results you expected and the results you got. Explain how the answers were obtained.

Also explain why you think code like this might be easy/hard for a maintenance programmer to understand.

```
#include <iostream.h>

int main()
{
   int i,j=5;

   i=j++ + ++j - --j;
   cout << "i=" << i;
   cout << endl;
   cout << "j=" << j;
   return (0);
}
```

2. Write a program that uses the % operator to find even and odd numbers. The user should be able to type in any number. Your program will output a 0 if the number is even. If not, it will output a 1. *Hint:* The remainder of any even number that is divided by 2 is 0. The remainder of any odd number that is divided by 2 is 1.
3. Type the program in Hands On 6.2 into your text editor or IDE. Compile and run it. Print out your results and submit it with this assignment. Explain why the output of the program might be different if you run the program on a different computer with a different operating system.
4. Write a program that uses the *= operator to square any number that the user types in, then output the result to the screen.
5. Write a program that uses the += and /= operators in the same equation. Explain why you think this usage might be confusing for maintenance programmers.
6. Write a program that uses the * and *= operators in the same equation. Tell whether you think a maintenance programmer would have trouble understanding this equation. Explain why.
7. Write a program that divides an integer that the user types in by 3. It should output the result of the division, as well as the remainder of the division.

Chapter Glossary

Lvalue Anything that can go on the left side of an assignment (=) operator. An Lvalue must be a location in memory where data can be stored.

Rvalue Any value or variable that can go on the right side of an assignment (=) operator.

7 Logical Operators

Objectives

After reading this chapter, you should be able to:

- Explain what logical operators are.
- Demonstrate the use of logical operators.
- Explain what truth and falsehood are in C++.

Preview

Programs can make rudimentary decisions based on information that they process as they run. The logical operators that this chapter presents are fundamental to that capability.

Logical Operators

Computer languages provide programs with the ability to make choices as programs run. Applications make decisions utilizing **logical operators.** A logical operator is an operator whose result evaluates to either true or false. But what is "truth" to a computer?

What Is Truth?

The C++ language defines truth with absolute certainty. Anything that is not 0 is true. Everything that evaluates to 0 is false. The logical operators usually evaluate to either 0 or 1, false or true. However, don't make the common mistake of assuming that 1 is the only value that is true. Table 7.1 demonstrates a few values that evaluate to true in C++, and some that evaluate to false.

Table 7.1 illustrates the idea that all nonzero numbers evaluate to true in C++. The type of the value does not matter. For instance, a character can evaluate to true or false. If the ASCII value of the particular character is nonzero, the character evaluates to true. There is only one character that has an ASCII value of 0. That is the null character '\0'.

The null character terminates every string in C++.

TABLE 7.1 Some Truths and Falsehoods in C++

Evaluates to True	Evaluates to False
5	0
–74	'\0'
'Q'	NULL
22.3	0.0

Arithmetic Values and Truth

Arithmetic expressions can also evaluate to true or false. The statement

```
anInteger+anotherInteger
```

can be used as a logical value. If the addition of these two variables results in a nonzero value, then the expression evaluates to true. If it results in a value of 0, it evaluates to false. We'll see how this can be used in the exercises for this chapter.

It is generally not a good idea to use arithmetic expressions as logical values. People testing and maintaining your code often find it difficult to understand what you mean when you write that kind of condition. Also, it is not uncommon for such tricky code to have unintended side effects. I'm not saying that you should never use arithmetic expressions as logical values. There are times when it's appropriate. Just be careful and try to make your code as clear as possible.

>, >=, ==, !=, <=, and <

Table 7.2 lists all of the logical operators in C++.

The next few Hands On examples illustrate how programs can use these operators.

TABLE 7.2 Logical Operators

Operator	Meaning
>	Greater than
>=	Greater than or equal to
==	Equal to
!=	Not equal to
!	Not
<=	Less than or equal to
<	Less than
&&	Logical AND
||	Logical OR

Hands On 7.1

Objective

Write a program that:

Gets a number from the user.
Outputs a 1 if the user enters a number greater than 0.
Outputs a 0 if the user enters a number that is less than or equal to 0.
Gets another number from the user.
Outputs a 1 if the user enters a number greater than or equal to 100.
Outputs a 0 if the user enters a number that is less than 100.

Experiment

Type the following program into your text editor or IDE. Compile, link, and run it.

```
#include <iostream.h>

int main()
{
    int aNumber;
    int theResult;
```

```
    cout << "Please type in a number greater than 0. ";
    cin >> aNumber;
    cout << "You will see a 1 on the next line ";
    cout << "if the number you typed is greater than 0."<<endl;
    theResult=(aNumber>0);
    cout << theResult;
    cout << endl<<"Please enter a number greater than or ";
    cout << "equal to 100. ";
    cin >> aNumber;
    cout << "You will see a 1 on the next line ";
    cout << "if the number you typed is greater than or ";
    cout << "equal to 100."<<endl;
    theResult=(aNumber>=100);
    cout << theResult;
    return (0);
}
```

Results

First Run

```
Please type in a number greater than 0. 5
You will see a 1 on the next line if the number you typed is greater than 0.
1
Please enter a number greater than or equal to 100. 200
You will see a 1 on the next line if the number you typed is greater than or equal to 100.
1
```

Second Run

```
Please type in a number greater than 0. -5
You will see a 1 on the next line if the number you typed is greater than 0.
0
Please enter a number greater than or equal to 100. 50
You will see a 1 on the next line if the number you typed is greater than or equal to 100.
0
```

Analysis

As you can see in the Results section, I ran this program twice. The program asks the user to enter a number greater than 0. In the first run, I typed in 5, which is shown in bold letters. The second time I ran the program, I entered –5. When the program reaches that point, it stores the result of the comparison

```
aNumber>0
```

in the variable `theResult`. The result of the comparison is a numeric value. It evaluates to 1 if the user types in a number greater than 0. If the user types in a number less than 0, as I did in the second run, the comparison evaluates to 0.

The program then asks the user for a number greater than or equal to 100. If the user enters a number greater than or equal to 100, the comparison

```
aNumber>=100
```

evaluates to 1. If the user enters a number that is less than 100, the comparison evaluates to 0.

The next Hands On example demonstrates the use of the == and != operators.

Hands On 7.2

Objective

Write a program that:

Gets a number from the user.
Outputs a 1 if the number was 10 or outputs a 0 if the number was not 10.
Outputs a 1 if the number was not 10 or outputs a 0 if the number was 10.

Experiment

Type the following program into your text editor or IDE. Compile, link, and run it.

```
#include <iostream.h>
int main()
{
   int aNumber;
   int theResult;
   cout << "Please enter the number 10. ";
   cin >> aNumber;
   cout << endl<<"You will see a 1 on the next line if you ";
   cout << "typed the number 10."<<endl;
   theResult=(aNumber == 10);
   cout << theResult;
   cout << endl<<"You will see a 1 on the next line if the ";
   cout << "number you typed wasn't 10."<<endl;
   theResult=(aNumber != 10);
   cout << theResult;
   return (0);
}
```

Results

```
Please enter the number 10. 10
You will see a 1 on the next line if you typed the number 10.
1
You will see a 1 on the next line if the number you typed wasn't 10.
0
```

Analysis

This short example illustrates the use of the == and != operators. If the user enters the number 10, the comparison

`aNumber==10`

yields a result of true. Since the logical operators use 1 for true, the program stores the value 1 in the variable `theResult`.

The comparison

`aNumber!=10`

evaluates to true if the user types anything other than 10. If the user enters 10, the comparison evaluates to false. A false result causes the program to store a 0 in `theResult`.

The logical NOT operator is used to turn true values to false and false values to true. The reason for doing this may not be immediately apparent, but it will become clearer when we discuss looping and branching. Hands On 7.3 demonstrates the use of the NOT operator.

Hands On 7.3

Objective

Write a program that:

Assigns a nonzero number to a variable.
Uses the logical NOT operator on the value in the variable.
Outputs the result.
Assigns 0 to a variable.
Uses the logical NOT operator on the value in the variable.
Outputs the result.
Uses the logical NOT operator with the greater than operator.
Outputs the result.

Experiment

Type the following program into your text editor or IDE. Compile, link, and run it.

```
#include <iostream.h>

int main()
{
   int aNumber;
   cout << "In this example, we'll use the NOT operator."<<endl;
   cout << "It is the exclamation point !"<<endl;
   cout << "If we assign a nonzero number to a variable, ";
   cout << "and use the !,"<<endl<<"this is what we get."<<endl;
   cout << "aNumber=5;"<<endl;
   cout << "!aNumber is equal to ";
   aNumber=5;
   cout << !aNumber;
   cout << endl<<"If we assign aNumber=0, what will we get from ";
   cout << "the statement !aNumber ?"<<endl;
   aNumber = 0;
   cout << !aNumber;
   cout << endl<<"Now here's an example of using ! with another ";
   cout << "logical operator."<<endl;
   cout << "What do you think the result of these statements ";
   cout << "will be?"<<endl;
   cout << "aNumber = 10;"<<endl;
   cout << "!(aNumber > 10)"<<endl;
   cout << "The answer is ";
   cout << !(aNumber > 10);
   return (0);
}
```

Results

```
In this example, we'll use the NOT operator.
It is the exclamation point !
If we assign a nonzero number to a variable, and use the !,
this is what we get.
aNumber=5;
!aNumber is equal to 0
If we assign aNumber=0, what will we get from the statement !aNumber ?
1
Now here's an example of using ! with another logical operator.
```

```
What do you think the result of these statements will be?
aNumber = 10;
!(aNumber > 10)
The answer is 1
```

Analysis

Whenever we use the NOT operator on a variable containing a nonzero number, we get 0. If we use the NOT 0, then we get 1.

Here's a pop quiz. The statements in Example 7.1 use the NOT operator. What value will be printed to the screen?

EXAMPLE 7.1 Using the ! Operator

```
int aValue=7;
aValue=!(!aValue);
cout << aValue;
```

I added parentheses to help clarify the meaning. However, they aren't required by C++.

In Example 7.1, the variable `aValue` is assigned the value of 7. The `!` operator is used to NOT the value in `aValue`. Another `!` operator is used to NOT it again. The result is stored back into `aValue`. What will be printed?

The answer is 1. The statement

```
int aValue=7;
```

declares the variable `aValue` and stores the value 7 in it. The condition `(!aValue)` evaluates to true if the value in of `aValue` is false. It evaluates to false if the value in of `aValue` is true. Since `aValue` contains the nonzero value of 7, it evaluates to true. NOT true evaluates to false. Remember that the C++ logical operators use the values 0 and 1 for false and true. Therefore, the condition `(!aValue)` in Example 7.1 evaluates to false. The condition `!(!aValue)` evaluates to true if `(!aValue)` is false. It evaluates to false if `(!aValue)` is true. In this example `(!aValue)` evaluates to false, so `!(!aValue)` is true. The C++ logical operators use 1 for true. So the value that Example 7.1 prints is 1.

If we NOT any nonzero value, we get 0. If we NOT 0, we get 1.

Hands On 7.4 will demonstrate the use of the < and <= operators.

Hands On 7.4

Objective

Write a program that:

- Gets a number from the user.
- Outputs a 1 if the number the user entered is less than 100, or outputs a 0 if not.
- Outputs a 1 if the number is less than or equal to 100, or outputs a 0 if not.

Experiment

Type the following program into your text editor or IDE. Compile, link, and run it.

```
#include <iostream.h>

int main()
{
   cout << "Please enter a number that is less than   ";
```

```
    cout << "or equal to 100. ";
    int aNumber;
    cin >> aNumber;
    int theResult;
    cout <<endl<< "If the number you entered is less than 100,";
    cout << " a 1"<<endl<<"will be printed on the next line."<<endl;
    theResult=(aNumber<100);
    cout << theResult;
    cout << endl<<"If the number you entered is less than or ";
    cout << "equal to 100,"<<endl<<"a 1 will be printed on the ";
    cout << "next line."<<endl;
    theResult = (aNumber<=100);
    cout << theResult;
    return (0);

}
```

Results

```
Please enter a number that is less than or equal to 100. 100
If the number you entered is less than 100, a 1
will be printed on the next line.
0
If the number you entered is less than or equal to 100,
a 1 will be printed on the next line.
1
```

TIP: The less than or equal to (<=) and greater than or equal to (>=) operators must be typed in the order you see here. The symbols =< and => won't work.

Analysis

In this Hands On example, the program highlights the difference between the less than operator (<) and the less than or equal to operator (<=).

Logical AND

The logical AND operator enables programmers to concatenate more than one logical condition. It's a way of saying, "This logical expression is only true if this condition AND that condition are true."

The logical AND operator is two ampersands, like this: &&. Example 7.2 shows the use of the logical AND operator.

EXAMPLE 7.2 Using the Logical AND Operator

```
#include <iostream.h>
int main()
{
    int anInteger=5, anotherInteger=10;
    cout << ((anInteger==5) && (anotherInteger<=10));
    return (0);
}
```

In this very contrived example, the condition will always evaluate to true. However, it demonstrates the use of the logical AND operator. The condition

```
((anInteger==5) && (anotherInteger<=10))
```

evaluates to true if the variable `anInteger` is equal to 5 and the variable `anotherInteger` is less than or equal to 10. Both conditions must be true for the entire expression

TABLE 7.3 A Truth Table for Logical AND

Exp1	Exp2	Result
0	0	0
0	1	0
1	0	0
1	1	1

to be true. If either one is false, the entire expression is false. Of course, if both conditions evaluate to false, then the entire expression is false.

Table 7.3 contains a truth table for the logical AND operator. A truth table shows the conditions that are required for the logical AND operator to evaluate to true. In this table, the label *Exp1* stands for the logical condition on the left of the && operator in an expression. *Exp2* stands for the logical condition on the right of the && operator. Since 0 evaluates to false in C++ and 1 evaluates to true, false and true values in the table are indicated by 0s and 1s, respectively.

The first line of Table 7.3 tells us that the entire expression evaluates to false if the conditions on the left and right of an && operator both evaluate to false. The next line says that if the condition on the left of the && operator is false, but the one on the right is true, the result is still false. The third line of Table 7.3 says that if the condition on the left of the && operator is true but the one on the right is false, the complete expression is again false. In fact, the only time the result is true is when both conditions evaluate to true.

Logical OR

Logical OR works very much like logical AND. It allows programmers to combine two conditions into one expression. The difference is that both of the conditions in an expression with a logical AND must be true for the expression to be true. A logical OR requires that only one condition be true for the expression to evaluate to true.

The logical OR operator is two vertical lines together, like this: ||. On many computer keyboards, the | character is on the same key as the \ character. Therefore, you would press Shift+\ to get a | character.

Hands On 7.5 demonstrates the use of && and ||. It also illustrates how some of the other operators are used.

Hands On 7.5

Objective

Write a program that:

Gets a number from the user.
Outputs a 1 if the number is greater than or equal to 0 and less than or equal to 100, or outputs a 0 if not.
Outputs a 1 if the number is less than 0 or greater than 100, or outputs a 0 if not.

Experiment

Type the following program into your text editor or IDE. Compile, link, and run it.

```
#include <iostream.h>

int main()
{
   cout << "Please type in a number that is in the "<<endl;
```

```
    cout << "range of 0 - 100. ";
    int userResponse;
    cin >> userResponse;
    int theResult=((userResponse >= 0) && (userResponse<=100));
    cout << endl<<"If the number you typed was greater than or"<<endl;
    cout << "equal to 0, and less than or equal to 100,"<<endl;
    cout << "a 1 will be printed on the next line."<<endl;
    cout << theResult;
    cout << endl<<"If the number you typed is less than 0, or"<<endl;
    cout << "greater than 100, a 1 will be printed on"<<endl;
    cout << "the next line."<<endl;
    theResult = ((userResponse < 0) || (userResponse > 100));
    cout << theResult;
    return (0);
}
```

Results

First Run

```
Please type in a number that is in the
range of 0 - 100. 50

If the number you typed was greater than or
equal to 0, and less than or equal to 100,
a 1 will be printed on the next line.
1
If the number you typed is less than 0, or
greater than 100, a 1 will be printed on
the next line.
0
```

Second Run

```
Please type in a number that is in the
range of 0 - 100. -10

If the number you typed was greater than or
equal to 0, and less than or equal to 100,
a 1 will be printed on the next line.
0
If the number you typed is less than 0, or
greater than 100, a 1 will be printed on
the next line.
1
```

Third Run

```
Please type in a number that is in the
range of 0 - 100. 200

If the number you typed was greater than or
equal to 0, and less than or equal to 100,
a 1 will be printed on the next line.
0
If the number you typed is less than 0, or
greater than 100, a 1 will be printed on
the next line.
1
```

Analysis

The program in Hands On 7.5 asks the user to type in a number between 0 and 100. If the number the user enters is greater than or equal to 0 and less than or equal to 100, the condition

```
((userResponse >= 0) && (userResponse<=100))
```

will evaluate to true. The program then uses the condition

```
((userResponse < 0) || (userResponse > 100))
```

to test to see if the number that the user typed in is less than 0 or greater than 100. Three runs were done on this program to demonstrate the different answers that the logical expressions will give.

The input for the first run was 50 (shown in bold in the Results section). The first condition evaluated to true, so a 1 was printed. The second condition evaluated to false (0) since 50 is not less than 0 and it is not greater than 100.

During the second run, I entered the number –10 from the keyboard. Since –10 is less than 0, the first condition of the expression

```
((userResponse >= 0) && (userResponse<=100))
```

evaluates to false. The program doesn't even need to check the condition on the right side of the && sign (and it usually doesn't) because only one side of a logical AND expression has to be false for the entire expression to be false.

Because –10 is less than 0, the first condition in the logical expression

```
((userResponse < 0) || (userResponse > 100))
```

evaluates to true. In this case also, the second condition doesn't need to be checked, and it probably won't be. If the left side of a logical OR is true, the right side doesn't need to be checked. It takes only one true condition in a logical OR expression to make the entire expression true.

The third run demonstrates the same ideas. The input was 200, which makes the expression

```
((userResponse < 0) || (userResponse>100))
```

false. The condition on the right side of the && is false, so the entire expression is false.

The expression

```
((userResponse >= 0) && (userResponse<=100))
```

evaluates to true. Because 200 is greater than 100, the condition on the right of the || sign is true. One true condition in a logical OR expression makes the entire expression true.

Troubleshooting Guide

After reading this section, you should be able to:

- Prevent common problems with the use of the assignment and equal to operators.
- Avoid confusion resulting from complex logical expressions.

== and =

The = and == operators look very much alike. It is extremely easy to accidentally use = for ==. In fact, that is one of the most common errors in C++ programs. What makes it worse is that the compiler won't always catch the error. It will compile and run, but your program won't work correctly.

If we think about the definitions of true and false in C++, we'll understand why the compiler can't catch this type of error. Recall that in C++, 0 is false and nonzero is true. That means that an assignment operation can be used as a logical condition. For instance, let's suppose we have an integer variable in our program called `anInteger`. The statement

```
anInteger=5;
```

evaluates to a value. The value to which it evaluates is the value of the assignment. This statement assigns a 5 to `anInteger`. So the value of the assignment operation is 5. The number 5 is not 0, so the statement is true.

TRAP: It is easy to accidentally use the = operator instead of the == operator. They both can be used as logical conditions.

Although there are some instances in which you will want to use the assignment operator (=) as a logical condition, that is rare. If you see a single = in a logical condition, be extremely suspicious. It is probably incorrect.

To avoid this error, some programmers put the number in the condition first. That is, they will use the condition

```
5==anInteger
```

instead of

```
anInteger==5
```

Although this looks funny to some, many programmers find it helpful. If you accidentally leave off one of the = signs, your condition is

```
5=anInteger
```

and the compiler will give an error. This is because you can't assign a value in a variable to a literal number such as 5.

Problems with Complex Conditions

Because we can combine logical expressions, it is easy to make them overly complex. Conditions are hard for people to read. They are also prone to errors. Example 7.3 illustrates this.

EXAMPLE 7.3 An Overly Complex Condition

```
#include <iostream.h>
int main()
{
   int result;
   int intOne=20, intTwo=30, intThree=40, intFive=50;

   result = intOne > intTwo && intThree <= intTwo ||
            intOne <= intTwo && intThree >= intTwo ||
            intFour == intFive;
   cout << result;
   return (0);
}
```

Note that the condition spans more than one line. That's fine with the compiler. It doesn't see the white space (characters like the newline, tabs, and spaces) except in strings.

Although the compiler can evaluate this condition, many programmers will struggle with it. A C++ compiler would evaluate this expression in the order of its precedence. Example 7.4 shows the same condition in a slightly more readable style.

EXAMPLE 7.4 A More Readable Condition

```
#include <iostream.h>
int main()
{
   int result;
   int intOne=20, intTwo=30;
```

```
        intThree=40, intFive=50;

        result = ((intOne > intTwo) && (intThree <= intTwo)) ||
                 ((intOne <= intTwo) && (intThree >= intTwo)) ||
                 (intFour == intFive);
        cout << result;
        return (0);
}
```

This version of the condition uses parentheses to specify a particular order of evaluation. It makes the expression more readable. The expression is true if the variable `intOne` is greater than `intTwo` and `intThree` is less than `intTwo`. The condition will also evaluate to true if `intOne` is less than or equal to `intTwo` and `intThree` is greater than or equal to `intTwo`. In addition, it will evaluate to true if `intFour` is equal to `intFive`.

Another way to simplify this condition is to break it up into multiple conditions. Example 7.5 illustrates this.

EXAMPLE 7.5 A More Readable Condition

```
#include <iostream.h>
int main()
{
        int finalResult, result1,result2,result3;
        int intOne=20, intTwo=30, intThree=40, intFive=50;

        result1 = (intOne > intTwo) && (intThree <= intTwo);
        result2 = (intOne <= intTwo) && (intThree >= intTwo);
        result3 = (intFour == intFive);
        finalResult = (result1) || (result2) || (result3);
        cout << result;
        return (0);
}
```

This example breaks the complex condition down into its component conditions. It is much easier to read. If you are writing a condition that you think the maintenance programmer might misinterpret, you can try this technique to help clarify it.

Summary

In C++, truth and falsehood are clearly defined. Expressions that evaluate to a nonzero number are true. Expressions that evaluate to zero are false.

Logical operators allow values to be compared. C++ programs use this ability to make decisions.

Review Questions

1. What are logical operators?
2. What are logical operators used for?
3. What is truth in C++?
4. What is falsehood in C++?
5. What do the following logical operators mean/do? (Write them out in words.)
    a. >
    b. >=
    c. <
    d. <=
6. What do the following logical operators mean/do? (Write them out in words.)
    a. ==
    b. !=
    c. !

7. Which of the following is true?
   a. 0.0
   b. –0.888
   c. 'b'
   d. 7
   e. 1
8. What is a truth table? What information does it convey?
9. Which of the following is false?
   a. 0.0
   b. 0
   c. '\0'
   d. !7
10. Which of the following is true if x is 10?
   a. `(x>=0) && (x<10)`
   b. `(!(x>10)) || (x<=100)`
   c. `!(x>=0) && (x<10)`
   d. `!(!(x>10)) || !(x<=100)`

Exercises

1. Explain the conditions under which the following expression will evaluate to true.

   ```
   ((x>5) && (x<=y))
   ```

2. Explain the conditions under which the following expression will evaluate to false.

   ```
   ((x-y) || (x!=1000))
   ```

3. Explain why the expression in Exercise 2 might be hard for a maintenance programmer to understand.
4. Write a program that gets a number from the user. If the number is greater than 1000 and less than or equal to 10000, your program should print a 1. If not, it should print a 0.
5. Write a program that gets a number from the user. If the number is equal to 1000 or equal to 10000, your program should print a 1. If not, it should print a 0.
6. Write a program that gets a number from the user. If the number is not greater than 1000 or not equal to 10000, your program should print a 1. If not, it should print a 0.
7. Write a program that gets a number from the user. If the number is not less than or equal to 1000 or not less than or equal to 10000, your program should print a 1. If not, it should print a 0.
8. Write a program that gets a number from the user. If the number is greater than 1000 and less than or equal to 10000 and not equal to 5000, your program should print a 1. If not, it should print a 0.
9. Write a program that gets a number from the user. If the number is even, your program should print a 1. If not, it should print a 0. *Hint:* Use the `%` operator.
10. Write a program that gets a number from the user. If the number is greater than 1000 and odd, your program should print a 1. If not, it should print a 0.

Chapter Glossary

Logical Operator An operator whose result evaluates to either true or false.

8 Control Flow: Branching

Objectives

After reading this chapter, you should be able to:

- Explain what flow control statements are.
- Use the `if-else` statement in programs.
- Use the `switch` statement in programs.
- Use the conditional operator in programs.

Preview

In the last chapter, we saw how logical and arithmetic operators can be used to evaluate logical conditions. In this chapter, we'll begin to use logical operators to enable programs to make decisions. By making decisions based on logical conditions, programs can conditionally execute portions of program code.

What Are Flow Control Statements?

Computers are able to make simple decisions and do tasks repeatedly. They do this by evaluating logical conditions, which we looked at in the last chapter. Whenever the flow of execution is altered by a logical statement, we say that the **control flow** of the program has changed.

There are two types of commands that enable computers to make decisions. One type, which we'll discuss in this chapter, is called **branching statements.** The other, which is presented in the next chapter, is called *looping statements*.

All control flow statements evaluate a logical condition as the program runs. They take action based on the value of the condition.

Branching

Most commands in a program execute sequentially one after another. If the program encounters a branching statement, it makes a decision based on a logical condition. If the condition is true, it does one thing. If it is false, it does something else.

C++ offers three branching statements, the `if-else` statement, the `switch` statement, and the conditional operator.

`if-else`

Branching statements using `if-else` in a C++ program are very much like a person walking along and coming to a fork in the road. The traveler has to decide whether to go left or right. If she chooses the left fork, she will not see what's down the road to the right. The result of the decision will be different because of the choice she made.

In the same way, an `if-else` statement changes the flow control of a program by providing it with two paths. The program makes a decision based on the condition of the `if-else` statement. If the condition evaluates to true, the program's flow control branches down one path. If the condition evaluates to false, it branches to the other path. Figure 8.1 illustrates the control flow for an `if-else` statement. Figure 8.2 shows its general form.

Hands On 8.1 shows a sample `if-else` statement. When a program encounters any `if-else` statement, it evaluates the condition. Both the `if` and the `else` portions of the `if-else` statement have blocks of code associated with them. The code blocks contain C++ statements. If the condition evaluates to true, the program executes the code block for the `if` portion of the `if-else` statement. If the condition is false, it executes the code block for the `else` portion.

FIGURE 8.1 The Control Flow of an `if-else` Statement

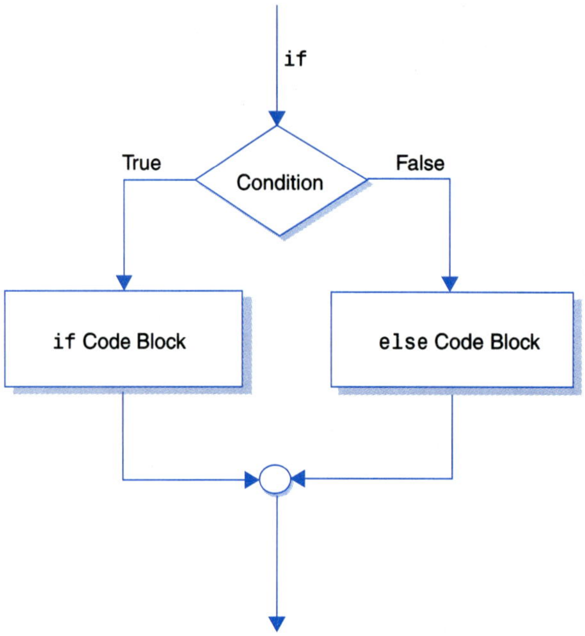

FIGURE 8.2 The General Form of `if-else` Statements

```
if (condition)
     statement; }Single-statement if body
else
     statement; }Single-statement else body



if (condition)
{
     statement; }
     statement; } Multiple-statement if body
}
else
{
     statement; }
     statement; } Multiple-statement else body
}
```

Hands On 8.1

Objective

Write a program that:

> Gets a number from the user.
> If the number is greater than 5,
>> The program prints a message that tells the user he or she typed in a number greater than 5.
>
> Else
>> The program prints a message that tells the user he or she typed in a number less than or equal to 5.

Experiment

Type the following program into your IDE or text editor. Compile, link, and run it.

```
#include <iostream.h>

int main()
{
   int inputValue;

   cout << "Please enter an integer: ";
   cin >> inputValue;
   if (inputValue>5)
   {
      // This is executed if the condition is true.
      cout << "Hold the phones, ";
      cout << "the input value is greater than 5."<<endl;
   }
   else
   {
      // This is executed if the condition is false.
      cout << "Don't worry, the input value is less than ";
      cout << "or equal to 5."<<endl;
   }
   return (0);
}
```

Results

```
First Run
Please enter an integer: 3
Don't worry, the input value is less than or equal to 5.

Second Run
Please enter an integer: 10
Hold the phones, the input value is greater than 5.
```

Analysis

In the `if-else` statement in this program, the `if` portion of the statement is executed if the variable `inputValue` is greater than 5. If the value of `inputValue` is less than or equal to 5, the program executes the `else` portion of the `if-else` statement.

The `if` portion of an `if-else` statement can contain more than one statement in its code block. If it does, the statements in the code block need to be between the opening and closing curly braces, { and }. If the code block contains only one C++ statement, you can omit the curly braces. Example 8.1 demonstrates an `if-else` statement with only one C++ statement in the `if` portion.

EXAMPLE 8.1 An `if` Without Curly Braces

```
if (inputValue>5)
   cout << "inputValue is greater than 5."<<endl;
else
{
   // This is executed if the condition is false.
   cout << "Don't worry, inputValue is less than ";
   cout << "or equal to 5."<<endl;
}
```

The `else` portion of the statement is not affected by the fact that the `if` portion does not use curly braces. The reverse is also true. If one has curly braces, it doesn't mean that the other must have them. Example 8.2 shows an `else` without curly braces.

EXAMPLE 8.2 An `else` Without Curly Braces

```
if (x>5)
{
   // This is executed if the condition is true.
   cout << "Hold the phones, ";
   cout << "x is greater than 5."<<endl;
}
else
   cout << "x is not greater than 5"<<endl;
```

The `else` portion of an `if-else` statement is optional. If you leave the `else` portion off of the statement and the condition is false, the program simply continues execution with the next statement after the `if`.

EXAMPLE 8.3 An `if` Without an `else`

```
if ((anInteger>=0) && (anInteger<=100)
{
   anotherInteger=100-anInteger;
   anInteger=100;
}
```

An `if-else` statement may contain any valid C++ statement, even other `if-else` statements. Example 8.4 shows an `if-else` statement inside of an `if-else` statement.

EXAMPLE 8.4 Nested `if` Statements

```
if (x>0)
{
   if (y>0)
   {
      cout << (x+y);
      y++;
   }
   else
      cout << x;
   x++;
}
```

The outside `if` statement contains two C++ statements in its code block. The first is an `if-else` statement, and the second is a postincrement statement. The entire inner `if-else` statement is seen as just one statement by the outer `if` statement. We indent all of the statements in a code block to the same level.

One final note about the `if-else` statement. I mentioned earlier that we indent each time we enter a new block of code. Common programming practice does, by convention, allow an exception to that rule. Example 8.5 shows an `if-else` statement with an `if-else` statement in its `else` section. That, in turn, has an `if-else` in its `else`, and so on. In a very real sense, these `if-else` statements are chained one onto the end of the other.

EXAMPLE 8.5 A Long `if-else` Statement

```
if (x>0)
{
   x++;
}
else
{
   if (x<640)
   {
      x--;
   }
   else
   {
      if (y>0)
      {
         y++;
      }
      else
      {
         if (y<480)
         {
            y--;
         }
         else
         {
            x=0;
            y=0;
         }
      }
   }
}
```

You can see from this example why indentation can be both good and bad. By looking at the indentation, we can see which block of code each statement belongs in. However, as we indent, our code drifts to the right. In this case, it moved over quite a bit. That can cramp the code and make it less readable.

Although the style in Example 8.5 is perfectly acceptable to both the compiler and most people reading your code, the majority of C++ programmers don't use it. Example 8.6 demonstrates the more common format for chained `if-else` statements.

EXAMPLE 8.6 Chained `if-else` Statements

```
if (x>0)
{
   x++;
}
else if (x<640)
{
   x--;
}
else if (y>0)
{
   y++;
}
else if (y<480)
```

```
{
    y--;
}
else
{
    x=0;;
    y=0;
}
```

TRAP: The common C++ style of indentation shown in Example 8.6 is only for `if-else` statements. This is the exception to the rule. Programmers will usually find your code less readable if you apply this exception to other C++ statements.

The code in Examples 8.5 and 8.6 say the same thing. The compiler doesn't detect any difference. However, the style shown in Example 8.6 does leave more room for statements in each block of code. Which style you use is entirely up to you.

switch

The C++ language provides a branching statement called the `switch` statement. A `switch` is used when there are many known values that a variable may take on. Figure 8.3 shows the control flow of a `switch` statement. Figure 8.4 gives its general form.

Hands On 8.2 illustrates how programs can use a `switch` statement.

FIGURE 8.3 The Control Flow of a switch Statement

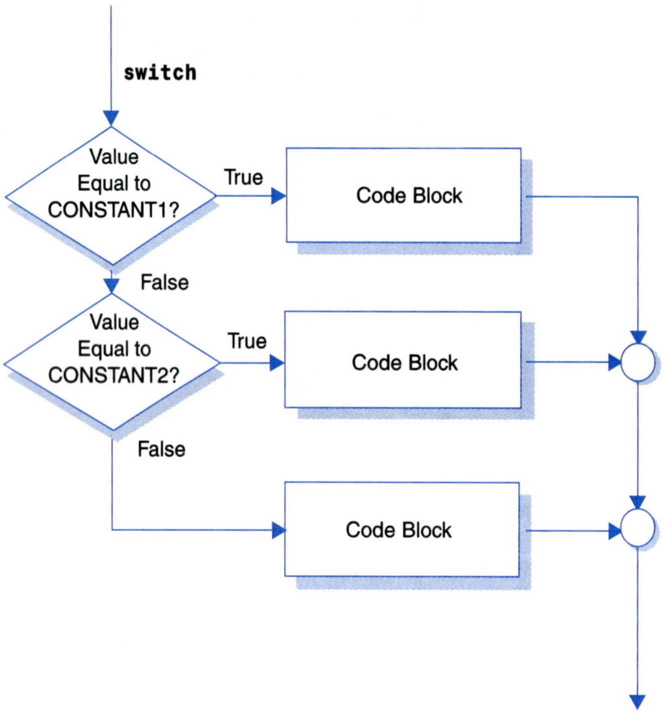

FIGURE 8.4 The General Form of a switch Statement

```
switch (value)
{
      case CONSTANT1:
         statement;
         statement;
      break;

      case CONSTANT2:
         statement;
      break;

      default:
         statement;
         statement;
         statement;
      break;
}
```

Hands On 8.2

Objective

Write a program that:

Gets an integer from the user.
If the integer is 0,
    The program increments the integer.
If the integer is 1,
    The program decrements the integer and increments another integer.
If the integer is –100
    The program increments the integer and decrements another integer.
In all other cases,
    The program sets both integers to 0.
The program outputs the result.

Experiment

Type the following program into your IDE or text editor. Compile, link, and run it.

```
#include <iostream.h>


int main()
{
   int anInteger;
   int anotherInteger = 1000;


   cout << "Please type in an integer: ";
   cin >> anInteger;

   switch (anInteger)
   {
      case 0:
         anInteger++;
      break;

      case 1:
         anInteger--;
         anotherInteger++;
      break;

      case -100:
         anInteger++;
         anotherInteger--;
      break;

      default:
         anInteger=0;
         anotherInteger=0;
      break;
   }

   cout << endl << anInteger << endl;
   cout << anotherInteger;
   return (0);
}
```

Results

```
First Run
Please type in an integer: 0

1
1000

Second Run
Please type in an integer: 1

0
1001

Third Run
Please type in an integer: -100

-99
999

Fourth Run
Please type in an integer: 50

0
0
```

Analysis

The `switch` statement in Hands On 8.2 says the same thing as the code in Example 8.7. That is, if the variable `anInteger` equals 0, then increment `anInteger`. If it equals 1, decrement `anInteger` and increment the variable `anotherInteger`. If `anInteger` equals –100, increment it and decrement `anotherInteger`. If `anInteger` equals none of those values, the program selects the `default` case.

EXAMPLE 8.7 The Same Code as Hands On 8.2 Using `if-else` Statements

```
if (anInteger == 0)
{
   anInteger++;
}
else if (anInteger == 1)
{
   anInteger--;
   anotherInteger++;
}
else if (anInteger == -100)
{
   anInteger++;
   anotherInteger--;
}
else
{
   anInteger=0;
   anotherInteger=0;
}
```

I ran this program four times to demonstrate each case and the default.

TIP: Always put a `break` after each case.

The `default` portion of a `switch` statement is optional, just like the `else` part of an `if-else`. If the `switch` statement does not contain a `default` case and the variable being switched on is not equal to any of the values in the `case` statements, program execution jumps to the next statement after the `switch`.

A `switch` statement can contain only one `default`. It can have as many `case` statements as you need. However, don't overuse cases. If you put in more than about a dozen, other programmers will have a tough time reading it.

You may be wondering what the `break` statements do after each `case` and the `default`. The `break` statement marks the end of the case. It causes program execution to jump to the end of the `switch` statement. What happens if the `break` is left off? Let's find out in the next Hands On example.

Hands On 8.3

Objective

Write a program that:

Gets an integer from the user.
If the user types in the number 0,
    Output the string "Zero" to the screen.
If the user types in the number 1,
    Output the string "One" to the screen.
If the user types in the number 2,
    Output the string "Two" to the screen.
If the user types in the number 3,
    Output the string "Three" to the screen.
If the user types in the number 4,
    Output the string "Four" to the screen.
If the user types in the number 5,
    Output the string "Five" to the screen.
    Output the string "Six" to the screen.
    Output the string "Seven" to the screen.
If the user types in the number 6,
    Output the string "Six" to the screen.
    Output the string "Seven" to the screen.
If the user types in the number 7,
    Output the string "Seven" to the screen.
If the user types in the number 8,
    Output the string "Eight" to the screen.
If the user types in the number 9,
    Output the string "Nine" to the screen.
    Output the string "Ten" to the screen.
If the user types in the number 10,
    Output the string "Ten" to the screen.
If the user types in anything else,
    Output the string "That wasn't a number between 0-10." to the screen.

Experiment

Type the following program into your text editor or IDE. Compile, link, and run it.

```
#include <iostream.h>
int main()
{
```

```
    cout << "This program contains a switch statement"<<endl;
    cout << "Please enter a number between 0-10 ";
    cout << "inclusive:";
    int userInput;
    cin >> userInput;
    switch (userInput)
    {
       case 0:
          cout << "Zero";
          break;
       case 1:
          cout << "One";
       break;

       case 2:
          cout << "Two";
       break;

       case 3:
          cout << "Three";
       break;

       case 4:
          cout << "Four";
       break;

       case 5:
          cout << "Five";

       case 6:
          cout << "Six";

       case 7:
          cout << "Seven";
       break;

       case 8:
          cout << "Eight";
       break;

       case 9:
          cout << "Nine";

       case 10:
          cout << "Ten";
       break;

       default:
          cout << "That wasn't a number between 0-10.";
       break;
    }
    cout << endl;
    return (0);
 }
```

Result

```
First Run
This program contains a switch statement
```

```
Please enter a number between 0-10 inclusive: 2
Two

Second Run
This program contains a switch statement
Please enter a number between 0-10 inclusive: 5
FiveSixSeven

Third Run
This program contains a switch statement
Please enter a number between 0-10 inclusive: 9
NineTen

Fourth Run
This program contains a switch statement
Please enter a number between 0-10 inclusive: -100
That wasn't a number between 0-10.
```

Analysis

In this program, I left the `break` statement off of the cases 5, 6, and 9.

In the first run, I typed in the number 2. The `switch` statement evaluated the variable `userInput`. Because the value of `userInput` was equal to the value for case 2, it jumped to case 2. When execution jumps to a case, the computer will execute all statements between the case value and the `break` statement. In this instance, there is only one statement that the program can execute before the `break`. The statement tells the program to write the string "Two" to the screen.

On the second run, I entered the number 5. The computer found that the value of `userInput` was equal to case 5, so it jumped there. The program printed the string "Five" to the screen. So far, so good. However, the next thing the program encounters is the label for case 6. C++ programs ignore this type of statement, except when it's being used as the destination of a branching jump. Since the program already jumped to case 5, it won't jump again unless it's told to. The label for case 6 is the destination of a jump, not the beginning of a jump. Therefore, the program ignores the label. It continues execution until it encounters a `break` statement or until it reaches the end of the `switch`. So it prints the string "Six". There is no `break` statement after case 6, so case 7 is executed. The program prints the string "Seven" to the screen. Finally the program comes to a `break` at the end of case 7. That causes execution to jump to the end of the `switch` statement.

The same type of situation occurred on the third run. When the program prompted me for input, I typed 9. Again, the `break` was left off the case. Both cases 9 and 10 were executed.

The fourth run simply demonstrates the use of the `default` statement.

TIP: Always put your cases in order in a `switch` statement. Both you and other programmers will find your code more readable if you do.

The cases in a `switch` statement don't have to occur in any particular order. I presented them in ascending numerical order for readability.

The Conditional Operator

C++ provides a nice shorthand for simple `if-else` conditions. The conditional operator, which uses both the question mark and the colon, is a concise way of performing an `if-else`.

Figure 8.5 shows the general form of the conditional operator. If the condition evaluates to true, the whole conditional operator statement evaluates to the true result. The true result is the value on the left of the colon. If the condition is false, the conditional operator statement evaluates to the false result. The false result is the value on the right of the colon.

Example 8.8 demonstrates a conditional operator.

FIGURE 8.5 The General Form of the Conditional Operator

```
value = (condition) ? true-result : false-result;
```

EXAMPLE 8.8 The Conditional Operator

```
finalValue = (currentValue < 1000) ? currentValue:1000;
```

The condition in this statement is enclosed in parentheses. If that condition evaluates to true, the whole conditional operator statement evaluates to the value in the variable `currentValue`. If it is false, the conditional operator statement evaluates to 1000.

Troubleshooting Guide

After reading this section, you should be able to:

- Recognize and fix common problems with `if` statements.
- Prevent possible problems with `switch` statements.
- Avoid problems with the conditional operator.

Common Problems with `if-else`

C++ compilers don't detect the indentation that we put into our programs. The indentation makes our programs easier for us to read. Normally, we indent to the right any time we begin a new block of code. The statements inside an `if-else` statement are in a new block of code, so we usually indent them.

Failing to indent can lead to unclear or misleading code. Example 8.9 demonstrates this.

TIP: Always indent code to the right when you enter a new block of code. Indent to the left when you exit a block of code. This improves readability.

EXAMPLE 8.9 Unindented Code

```
if (x>0)
if (y>0)
cout << x+y;
else
cout << x;
```

Just looking at this example, it's difficult to tell which `if` goes with the `else`.

Even if our code is indented properly, it's easy to make a mistake. Take a look at Example 8.10.

EXAMPLE 8.10 An Indention Mistake

```
if (x>0)
   if (y>0)
      cout << x+y;
else
   x++;
```

The question here is which `if` the `else` goes with. The indentation indicates that it goes with the outer `if`. However, the rule is that the `else` always goes with the closest `if`. So the `else` in Example 8.10 goes with the inner `if`. That may not be what the programmer intends. If it isn't, it can be changed by adding curly braces, as in Example 8.11.

EXAMPLE 8.11 Clearer Indentation

```
if (x>0)
{
   if (y>0)
```

```
        cout << x+y;
}
else
{
    x++;
}
```

TIP: In general, it's a good idea to put the curly braces on an `if-else` statement even if there is only one statement in the if or else code blocks.

By placing the inner `if` inside curly braces, we've forced the compiler to see that the inner `if` and the `else` are in two different blocks of code. The compiler can't connect the `else` to the inner `if`.

Back in Example 8.4, it may not have been clear that the `x++` was not in the code block of the `else` statement. We can clarify that by adding curly braces.

EXAMPLE 8.12 A Clarification of Example 8.4

```
if (x>0)
{
    if (y>0)
    {
        cout << x+y;
        y++;
    }
    else
    {
        cout << x;
    }
    x++;
}
```

Now, even inexperienced C++ programmers who might be maintaining your code should be able to tell that `x++` is not part of the `else` statement's code block.

Another common problem with `if-else` statements is misplaced semicolons. In Example 8.13, there is a semicolon after the condition on the `if` statement. This code will actually compile and execute with no warnings or errors.

EXAMPLE 8.13 A Misplaced Semicolon

```
if (x<y);
{
    x+=5;
}
```

The semicolon after the end of the `if` condition in Example 8.13 terminates the `if` statement. The compiler does not see the code block in the curly brackets as being connected to the `if` statement. It is just a block of code standing by itself. That is legal in C++. Therefore, the compiler gives no errors or warnings.

When the program executes this `if` statement, it will do nothing if `x` is less than `y` because there are no statements in the body of the `if` statement. It will unconditionally execute the block of code after the `if` statement. Because it is unconditionally executed, the block of code is executed every time.

Avoiding Problems with `switch`

The `default` statement can appear anywhere within the code block of the `switch`, which leads to a very interesting problem. I've been putting the `default` statements last in all of the `switch` statements presented so far. This is a common convention used by most C++ programmers. However, the C++ language doesn't force you to do that.

Because the `default` usually occurs last in a `switch`, programmers often leave the `break` statement off the end of the `default`. If the `default` is last, the missing `break` statement doesn't matter. After the `default` is executed, the program encounters the end of the `switch` statement.

However, if you do leave the `break` statement off the end of the `default` case, some maintenance programmer will invariably come along and stick another case after the `default` without noticing that there is no `break` between them. The other programmer thinks, "Oh well, it doesn't matter because the statements in a `switch` can occur in any order." This is a potentially nasty problem, because it's easy to overlook.

You may think, "Who would be stupid enough to stick another case after the `default` without checking for a `break`?" Well I would, and so would you. In fact, I can honestly say that I have made this very dumb mistake, and wasted a lot of time figuring it out. Many programmers have. For some reason, you can look at a `switch` statement over and over and not see that a `break` has been left off of the `default`. It's odd, but it's true.

Avoid the potential for problems. Always put a `break` after the `default` in a `switch` statement. Always put your defaults last. Never stick another `case` after the `default`.

Complex Conditional Operators

It is possible to combine conditional operators into complex operations. Example 8.14 illustrates this.

EXAMPLE 8.14 Nested Conditional Operators

```
maxValue =
(value1 > value2) ? (value1>value3) ? value1:value3 :
                    (value2>value3) ? value2:value3;
```

This complex use of the conditional operator is perfectly valid in C++. Since the conditional operator evaluates to a value, you can use it anywhere you would use any value. That means you can use it in another conditional operator.

Example 8.14 finds the maximum of three numbers and assigns that value to the variable `maxValue`. The first condition asks if `value1` is greater than `value2`. If it is, then it evaluates everything in the true result section of the conditional operator statement. The true result section contains another conditional operator statement. This statement

```
(value1>value3) ? value1:value3
```

will be evaluated if the condition

```
(value1 > value2)
```

evaluates to true. This statement has its own condition. If `value1` is greater than `value3`, it is the maximum of the three variables. Therefore, the conditional operator statement that is in the true section of the outer conditional operator evaluates to the contents of its own true section, which is `value1`. If the inner condition is false, the inner conditional operator evaluates to `value3` because it is the maximum of the three variables.

If the outer condition

```
(value1 > value2)
```

evaluates to false, another conditional operator in the false section of the outer conditional operator is evaluated. This nested conditional operator statement, which is this:

```
(value2>value3) ? value2:value3
```

tests to see if `value2` or `value3` contains the larger value. It evaluates to whichever is largest.

Confused? Most people are when confronted by multiple nested conditional operators. Experienced programmers try to live by the KISS rule. KISS stands for Keep It Simple, Stupid. If there is a simpler way to do something, it's generally best to use it. Therefore, it's a good idea to avoid multiple nested conditional operator statements.

Summary

C++ programs can conditionally execute blocks of code. When combined with the C++ branching statements `if-else` and `switch`, logical conditions enable a C++ program to decide whether or not to execute a block of code based on run-time information.

The `if-else` statements provide an alternative between two possibilities. That is, they evaluate a condition at run time. If the condition is true, the program executes the block of code associated with the `if` portion of the statement. If the condition is false, the program executes the block of code associated with the `else` portion of the statement. The `else` block is optional.

A `switch` statement enables a program to choose one of many alternatives. Each alternative block of code is contained in a case. End each `case` with a `break` statement. The `default` is optional.

Review Questions

1. What is the purpose of branching statements?
2. What is wrong with the following `if-else` statement?

```
if (x>100)
   x++;
   y++;
else
   x=0;
```

3. What happens when the condition on an `if` statement evaluates to false and there is no `else`?
4. Why do we indent to the right when we enter a block of code? Would the compiler care if we didn't? Why or why not?
5. Why is it usually a good idea to put curly braces around the code blocks of an `if` and an `else`, even if there is only one statement in the block?
6. How many cases can be in a `switch` statement?
7. What happens if we leave off the `break` from a case in a `switch` statement?
8. What happens if we leave the `default` out of a `switch` statement?
9. In what order do the cases go in a `switch` statement?
10. According to the rules of C++, where does the `default` of a `switch` have to go?

Exercises

1. Write a program that prints the word "Yes" on the screen if the user types in a number greater than or equal to 100. If the number is less than 100, your program should print the word "No."
2. Write a program that will print the word "Yes" if the user enters a number that is in the range of 0–100 inclusive. If the number the user enters is greater than 100 or less than zero, your program should print the word "No" to the screen.
3. Write a program that gets two numbers from a user and prints the larger, or maximum, of the two.
4. Write a program that gets a number from the user and uses a `switch` statement to convert it to a character. The numbers will be 0–9 inclusive. Your program should have two variables, one of type `int` and the other of type `char`. If the user enters a 0 into the `int`, your program should assign the character '0' into the `char`. If the user enters a 1, the `char` variable should be assigned a '1', and so on. After the number is converted to a character, print the character to the screen.
5. Write a program that will prompt the user to type in a character. It must print the word "Yes" if the user types in a 'y' or a 'Y'. It must print the word "No" if the user types in an 'n' or an 'N'. All other input should be ignored. Use a `switch` statement. *Hint:* This is an example of when it might be reasonable to leave the `break` statement off of the end of a `case`.
6. Write a program that determines whether a number that the user types in is even or odd. If it is even, your program should print the word "Even" on the screen. If it is odd, your program should print the word "Odd" on the screen.
7. Write a program that prompts the user for the radius of a circle. Use the radius to calculate the area of a circle. If you have a variable in your program named `radius`, the

area is found by multiplying `3.14159*radius*radius`. If the user types in a radius that is less than or equal to zero, your program should print an error message and exit.

8. Write a program that calculates a customer discount. The user must enter the amount of a purchase. (You'll probably want to use a float, double, or long double variable for this.) If the purchase is greater than $100, the user gets a 2 percent discount. If it is greater than $500, the user gets a 5 percent discount. If it is greater than $1000, the user gets a 10 percent discount. Print the user's total with the discount subtracted. Make sure that the user types in a number greater than zero.
9. Write a program that prompts the user for the number of hours a worker has worked during the week and calculates that person's gross pay. Assume that the worker gets paid $10 per hour. Ask the user if he or she has worked overtime. If so, the pay rate is time-and-a-half ($15 per hour). Calculate the tax the worker owes and subtract it from the gross pay. Assume that workers are taxed 10 percent if their pay is $300 or less. Tax the workers at 15 percent if their pay is greater than $300 and less than or equal to $1000. Anything higher than $1000 is taxed at 25 percent. Output the worker's gross pay and net pay.
10. Modify the program in Exercise 9 so that it presents a menu for the user. The menu should allow the user to select from standard pay rates, as the following example shows. The program should calculate the user's gross and net pay based on the number of hours worked and the pay rate. Be sure to adjust the overtime pay according to the user's pay rate.

    Standard Pay Rates

    a. $10.00 per hour
    b. $15.00 per hour
    c. $17.50 per hour
    d. $20.00 per hour

    Select the pay rate: _______

Chapter Glossary

Branching Statements C++ statements that cause execution to branch to another location. Statements in the code block of the branching statement will be conditionally executed depending on whether or not its associated condition evaluates to true.

Control Flow The flow of execution from one C++ statement to the next.

9 Control Flow: Looping

Objectives

After reading this chapter, you should be able to:

- Explain what looping statements are.
- Use `while` loops in programs.
- Use `do-while` loops in programs.
- Use `for` loops in programs.

Preview

In addition to making decisions at run time, a C++ program can use statements that repeatedly execute code blocks. This chapter will present the three basic loops used in C++: `while`, `do-while`, and `for`.

Looping: You Can Say That Again

A loop is a block of code that a program executes repeatedly. All loops have a condition either at the beginning or end. Loops that evaluate the condition first are called **pre-test loops.** Looping statements that evaluate the condition at the end of the loop are called **post-test loops.**

We build a loop's condition using the logical operators we saw in previous chapters. If the condition evaluates to true, the program repeats the code block attached to the loop. If the condition evaluates to false, the loop terminates.

The `while` Loop

The first looping statement we'll look at is the `while` loop. It is a pre-test loop. Like all pre-test loops, it may execute zero or more times. If the condition at the beginning of the loop never evaluates to true, the code block for the loop never executes. Figure 9.1 shows the control flow of a `while` loop. Figure 9.2 illustrates its general form.

Hands On 9.1 illustrates the use of a `while` loop.

FIGURE 9.1 The Control Flow of a `while` Loop

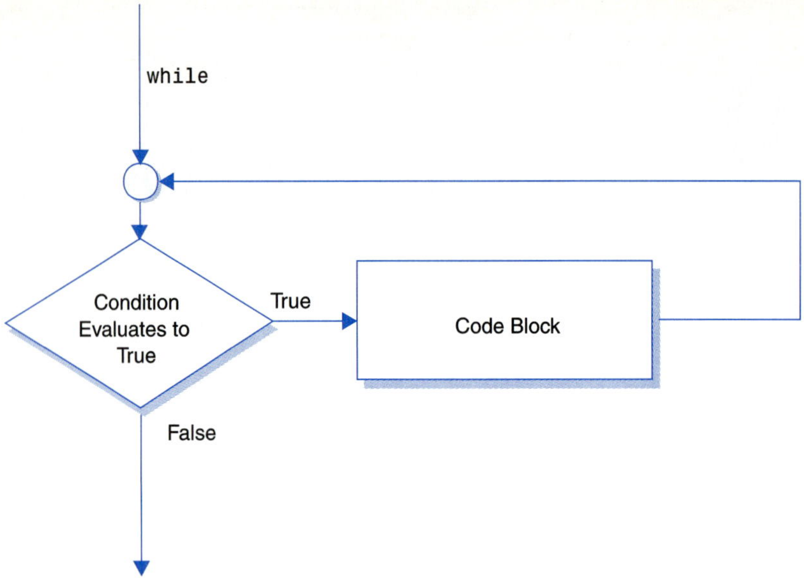

FIGURE 9.2 The General Form of a `while` Loop

```
while (condition)
      statement;     } Single-statement body


while (condition)
{
      statement;     )
      statement;     } Multiple-statement body
      statement;     )
}
```

Hands On 9.1

Objective

Write a program that:

Prompts the user for input.
Gets a number from the user.
Declares and initializes an integer counter variable.
While the counter variable is less than the number the user typed in,

Output the value of the counter to the screen.
Increment the counter.

Experiment

Type the following program into your text editor or IDE. Compile, link, and run it.

```
#include <iostream.h>

int main()
{
   int userInput;
   cout << "Please enter a number greater than 0:" ;
```

```
    cin >> userInput;
    int i=0;
    while (i < userInput)
       cout << "i=" << i++ << end/ ;
    return (0);
}
```

Results

```
First Run
Please enter a number greater than 0:10
i=0
i=1
i=2
i=3
i=4
i=5
i=6
i=7
i=8
i=9

Second Run
Please enter a number greater than 0:-9
```

Analysis

I ran this program twice to demonstrate the pre-test nature of the `while` loop. In the first run, the program asked for user input. I entered the number 10. After the program got my input, it initialized the integer variable `i` to 0. The computer thenencountered the `while` loop. Because the `while` loop is a pre-test loop, it first evaluated the condition. The variable `i` contained 0, which is less than 10, so the condition evaluated to true. Therefore, the program executed the loop's code block.

The code block attached to the `while` loop in Hands On 9.1 contains only one statement. Therefore, the curly braces are not required around the statements in the code block. If there had been more than one statement in the code block, the curly braces would have been required. I left them off in this example to demonstrate that they can be left off.

The line

```
cout << "i=" << i++ << '\n' ;
```

does several things in one statement. First, it sent the string "`i=`" to the stream `cout`, which of course is attached to the display. Next, the program sent the value of the variable `i` to the display via the `cout` stream. Notice here that the program uses the value in `i` first, then increments it. That's because we used a postincrement statement. After the program increments the variable `i`, it prints the endline character on the display.

The `do-while` Loop

The `do-while` loop is a post-test loop. That means that instead of the test being done at the beginning of the loop, it's done at the end. A `do-while` loop always executes at least once. Figure 9.3 presents the control flow of a `do-while` loop. Figure 9.4 shows its general form.

Hands On 9.2 demonstrates the use of a `do-while` loop.

FIGURE 9.3 Control Flow of a **do-while** Loop

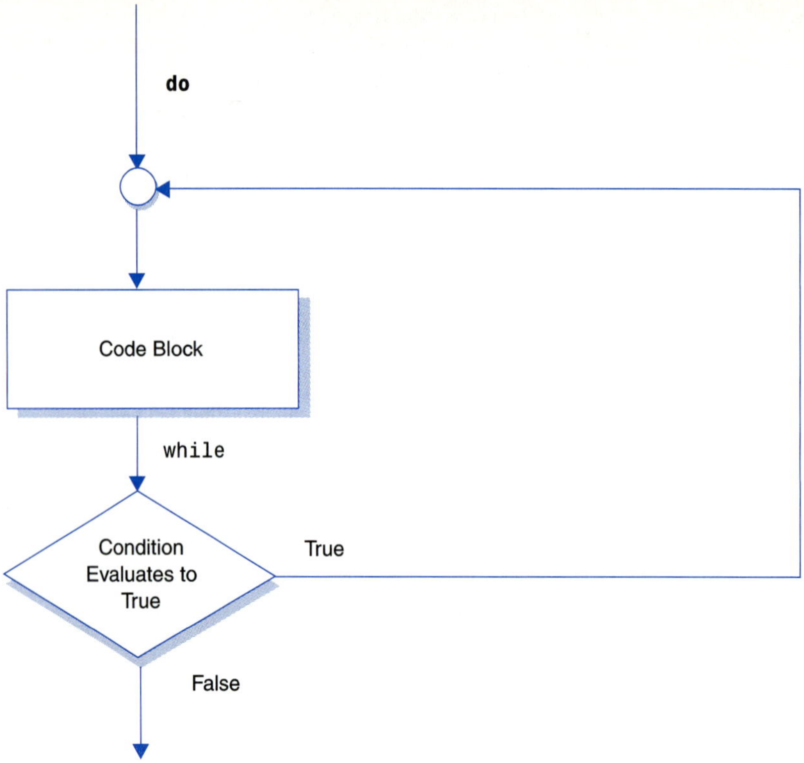

FIGURE 9.4 The General Form of a **do-while** Loop

```
do
{
      statement;
      statement;
      statement;
} while (condition);
```

Hands On 9.2

Objective

Write a program that:

Prompts the user for input.
Gets a number from the user.
Declares an integer counter variable.
Does the following repeatedly:

Prints the current value of the counter.
Increments the counter.

Until the counter is greater than or equal to the number the user typed in.

Experiment

Type the following program into your text editor or IDE. Compile, link, and run it.

```
#include <iostream.h>
int main()
{
    cout << "Please enter a number greater than 0 :";
    int maxLoopCount;
    cin >> maxLoopCount;
```

```
    int i=0;
    do
    {
       cout << endl;The current value of i is ";
       cout << i++;
    } while (i<maxLoopCount);
    return (0);
}
```

Results

```
First Run
Please enter a number greater than 0 :10
The current value of i is 0
The current value of i is 1
The current value of i is 2
The current value of i is 3
The current value of i is 4
The current value of i is 5
The current value of i is 6
The current value of i is 7
The current value of i is 8
The current value of i is 9

Second Run
Please enter a number greater than 0 :-10
The current value of i is 0
```

Analysis

Whenever this program runs, it prompts the user to enter a value. It stores the value that the user enters into the variable `maxLoopCount`. Next, it initializes the variable `i` to zero. When it enters the `do-while` loop, it prints out the current value of `i`. After the program sends the value in `i` to the `cout` stream, it increments `i`. The program encounters the end of the loop, so it performs the loop's test. The test compares the value in `i` to the value in `maxLoopCount`. If `i` is less than `maxLoopCount`, the loop continues. If that is not the case, the loop terminates.

TIP: Be careful when using post-test loops. Always make sure that it is OK for thc loop to execute at least once, because that's what it will do.

I ran this program twice to demonstrate the properties of the `do-while` loop. In the first run, I entered the number 10. As you can see, it made the loop execute ten times. The values 0 through 9 were printed to the screen.

In the second run, I entered the value –10 into `maxLoopCount`. Note here that the loop did execute once. The program printed the value of `i`, which was zero, to the screen. However, because `i` was found to be greater than `maxLoopCount` at the end of the loop, the loop terminated.

`for` Loops

The `for` loop is the most flexible and powerful looping statement in C++. Consequently, it tends to be the most complex to use. Figure 9.5 shows the control flow of the `for` loop. Its general form is shown in Figure 9.6.

The `for` loop, of course, begins with the word `for`. This is followed by the control portion of the loop, which is in parentheses. The control portion of the loop has three sections.

The initialization section comes first in the control portion of the loop. It is the first thing to be executed in the `for` statement. Typically, programmers use this section to initialize a loop counter variable. The initialization section of the loop is optional. You can leave it blank.

The second section of the control portion of a `for` loop contains the condition. Notice that the loop condition occurs before the loop's code block. That makes the `for` loop a

FIGURE 9.5 **Control Flow of a `for` Loop**

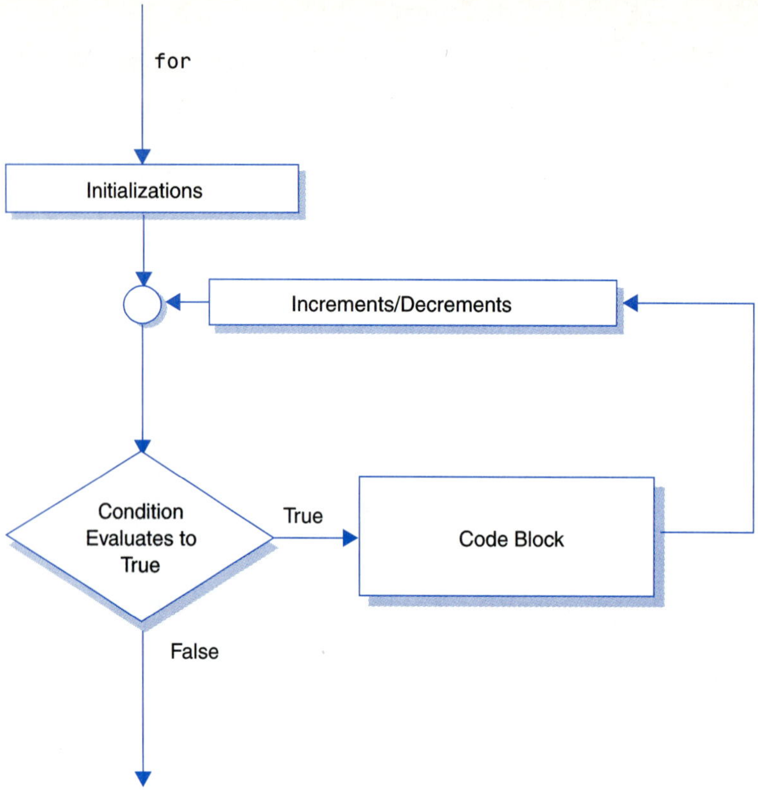

FIGURE 9.6 **The General Form of a `for` Loop**

```
for (initializations;condition;increments/decrements)
      statement;     }Single-statement body


for (initializations;condition;increments/decrements)
{
      statement;   ┐
      statement;   ├ Multiple-statement body
      statement;   ┘
}
```

pre-test loop. It will execute zero or more times. After the program executes the initialization section, it checks the condition. If the condition evaluates to true, the program performs the statements in the code block.

The third section in the control portion of a `for` loop is the increment/decrement section. It is only executed when the loop's code block is executed. If the loop condition is not true, neither the `for` loop's code block nor the increment/decrement section is executed.

Hands On 9.3 demonstrates a typical `for` loop.

Hands On 9.3

Objective

Write a program that:

Declares an integer counter variable and initializes it to 0.
For each value between the range of 0 to 99 inclusive,
  Output the value of the counter.
  If the counter variable is divisible by 5,
    Output an endline.

Experiment

Type this program into your word processor or text editor. Compile, link, and run it.

```
#include <iostream.h>

int main()
{
   int i;
   for (i=0;i<100;i++)
   {
      cout << "i=" << i << ' ';
      if (i%5 == 0)
      {
         cout << endl;
      }
   }
   return (0);
}
```

Results

```
i=0
i=1 i=2 i=3 i=4 i=5
i=6 i=7 i=8 i=9 i=10
i=11 i=12 i=13 i=14 i=15
i=16 i=17 i=18 i=19 i=20
i=21 i=22 i=23 i=24 i=25
i=26 i=27 i=28 i=29 i=30
i=31 i=32 i=33 i=34 i=35
i=36 i=37 i=38 i=39 i=40
i=41 i=42 i=43 i=44 i=45
i=46 i=47 i=48 i=49 i=50
i=51 i=52 i=53 i=54 i=55
i=56 i=57 i=58 i=59 i=60
i=61 i=62 i=63 i=64 i=65
i=66 i=67 i=68 i=69 i=70
i=71 i=72 i=73 i=74 i=75
i=76 i=77 i=78 i=79 i=80
i=81 i=82 i=83 i=84 i=85
i=86 i=87 i=88 i=89 i=90
i=91 i=92 i=93 i=94 i=95
i=96 i=97 i=98 i=99
```

Analysis

Hands On 9.3 demonstrates how programs typically use `for` loops. It declares a counter variable of type `int`. The program uses the variable to control how many times the loop **iterates,** or repeats, itself.

The `for` loop initializes the counter variable `i` to zero in the initialization section of the control portion of the `for` loop. It also checks the condition section. In this program, the condition states that the loop should continue for as long as `i` is less than 100. If that condition evaluates to true, the program performs the statements in the `for` loop's code block. The loop's code block is also called the *body* of the loop.

The `for` loop's code block contains two statements. The first sends some output to the screen. The second is an `if` statement. As you can see, the program doesn't print a newline character at the end of the first statement in the `for` loop. The second statement sends an endline character to the output, but only if the condition `(i%5==0)` evaluates to true. This condition is true only when `i/5` leaves a remainder of 0. In other words, we are sending an endline to the screen when `i` is divisible by 5. The output is shown in the Results section above.

After the program executes everything in the `for` loop's code block, it evaluates the `i++` statement. The program begins the loop again by checking its condition. If the condition evaluates to true, the loop continues. If not, neither the code block nor the increment is executed.

One of the features that was added to C++ that C doesn't have is the ability to declare variables virtually anywhere in a program. This allows variables to be declared close to where they are used. Programmers looking at your code will be able to tell more easily what data type the variables are and what they're used for.

Let's take the `for` loop in Hands On 9.3 as an example. For convenience, it is repeated here in Example 9.1. Since we declare the loop counter variable `i` strictly for controlling the loop, we can declare it in the initialization section of the loop. This tells other programmers who look at our code that we are declaring the variable for use with the loop. It also makes the type of the variable easy to see.

EXAMPLE 9.1 Loop Counter Variable Declaration

```
for (int i=0;i<100;i++)
{
   cout << "i=" << i << ' ';
   if (i%5 == 0)
   {
      cout << '\n';
   }
}
```

A C++ `for` loop also allows us to initialize multiple variables in the initialization section. Example 9.2 illustrates this.

EXAMPLE 9.2 Multiple Initializations in a `for` Loop

```
int i,j;
for (i=0,j=100; i!=j; i++, j--)
{
   cout << "i=" << i << endl;
   cout << "j=" << j;
}
```

TRAP: A common mistake that new C++ programmers make is to try and separate multiple initializations with semicolons instead of commas. This will not work. The control portion of a `for` loop should contain exactly two semicolons, no more and no less.

The loop in Example 9.2 initializes `i` to 0 and `j` to 100. You can actually put more initializations in the initialization section. Each initialization must be separated by commas.

Example 9.2 also demonstrates that a `for` loop may have multiple increments and decrements. Like multiple initializations, multiple increments and decrements are separated by commas.

You may at this point be asking whether or not `for` loops can have multiple conditions. The answer is that you already know the answer. We saw in earlier chapters that logical conditions can be put together with the AND (&&) and the OR (||) operators. The condition on a `for` loop is no different than other logical conditions in C++. Example 9.3 shows two `for` loops with multiple conditions.

EXAMPLE 9.3 `for` Loops with Multiple Conditions

```
for (int i=0,j=100;(i<100) || (j>0);i++,j--)
{
   cout << "i=" << i << endl;
   cout << "j=" << j;
}
```

```
char aChar = ' ';
for (int k=0;(aChar!='q') && (aChar!='Q'); k++)
{
   cout << k << endl;
   cout << "Type in Q to quit :";
   cin >> aChar;
}
```

Compare the initialization sections of these two loops. The first loop declares and initializes two integers, i and j. The second loop contains just one initialization, an integer variable called k. Just before the second loop, the program declares a character variable called aChar. Could we have changed that loop to look like Example 9.4?

EXAMPLE 9.4 An Improper Initialization

```
for (int k=0,char aChar=' ';(aChar!='q') && (aChar!='Q');k++ )
{
   cout << k << endl;
   cout << "Type in Q to quit :";
   cin >> aChar;
}
```

The answer is no. The comma can't be used to separate the declaration of two variables of different types. Example 9.5 shows another initialization that won't work.

EXAMPLE 9.5 Multiple Declarations of the Same Variable

```
int j;
for (int i=0,j=100;(i<100) || (j>0);i++,j--)
{
   cout << "i=" << i << endl;
   cout << "j=" << j;
}
```

As the title of Example 9.5 suggests, these statements declare the variable j twice. That isn't allowed.

The sections of the control portion of a for loop are optional. The loop shown in Example 9.6 illustrates this.

EXAMPLE 9.6 A for Loop with No Increments or Decrements

```
for (char aChar=' '; (aChar!='q') && (aChar!='Q'); )
{
   cout << "Type in Q to quit :";
   cin >> aChar;
}
```

Notice that there is nothing between the second semicolon in the control portion of the loop and the final parenthesis. The C++ compiler has no problem with this. In fact, all three sections are optional. If the program omits the initialization or increments and decrements, nothing is done for those sections of the loop. If it leaves the condition off, the program always assumes that the condition is true. Example 9.7 illustrates this.

EXAMPLE 9.7 An Endless Loop

```
for ( ; ; )
{
   cout << "This is a loop that never ends" << endl;
}
```

Programmers have no real reason to create a loop like this. Doing so will only cause problems for you or whoever maintains your code.

Here's another pop quiz. So far, all the `for` loops presented in this chapter have used a postincrement or postdecrement. If we changed them to preincrement or predecrement (as Example 9.8 shows), what would happen?

EXAMPLE 9.8 Changing the Postincrement in a `for` Loop to Preincrement

```
for (int i=0; i<100; ++i)
{
   cout << "What value will be printed? :";
   cout << i << endl;
}
```

Usually people assume that by changing the postincrement to preincrement, the program will increment the loop before it executes the loop's code block. This is a logical assumption. It is also an incorrect assumption.

Changing the postincrement in a `for` loop to a preincrement makes absolutely no difference. Your C++ program will always perform the increment after it executes the code block, no matter what. As long as the code block is executed, any increments or decrements that you put into the increment/decrement section of the `for` loop will be performed after it.

Troubleshooting Guide

After reading this section, you should be able to:

- Prevent common problems with `while` loops.
- Prevent common problems with `for` loops.

Preventing Problems with `while` Loops

As with `if` statements, the indentation and use of curly braces in `while` loops can be confusing if not done properly. Example 9.9 illustrates this.

EXAMPLE 9.9 Confusing Indentation with a `while` Loop

```
#include <iostream.h>

int main()
{
   int userInput;
   cout << "Please enter a number greater than 0:" ;
   cin >> userInput;
   int i=0;
   while (i < userInput)
      cout << "i=" << i << endl ;
      i++;
   return (0);
}
```

Notice that the program in Example 9.9 is a slightly modified version of the program in Hands On 9.1. The program now increments the variable `i` on another line. But there's a problem here. A `while` loop can contain only one statement if the curly braces are left off. The indentation indicates that we want two statements in the `while` loop's code block. Of course, the compiler will not see it that way. It doesn't care about indentation, so it will see the `while` loop as containing one statement. Therefore, the only statement in the loop's code block is the statement that prints the value of `i`. The loop does not contain the increment. Because the loop does not contain the increment, the `while` loop will print out the number 0 forever. OK, maybe not forever, but for as long as you let the program run. This is called an **endless loop.**

By now you've probably anticipated the solution. We need to add curly braces onto the `while` loop. Example 9.10 shows the resolution of this problem.

EXAMPLE 9.10 Proper Form for while Loops

```
#include <iostream.h>

int main()
{
   int userInput;
   cout << "Please enter a number greater than 0:" ;
   cin >> userInput;
   int i=0;
   while (i < userInput)
   {
      cout << "i=" << i << '\n' ;
      i++;
   }
   return (0);
}
```

TIP: It's a good idea to put the curly braces around the block of code attached to a `while` loop, even if there is only one statement in the block.[1]

Sometimes programmers will intentionally create endless loops, as illustrated in Example 9.11.

EXAMPLE 9.11 An Intentional Endless Loop

```
#include <iostream.h>

int main()
{
   int userInput;
   cout << "Please enter a number greater than 0:" ;
   cin >> userInput;
   int i=0;
   while (1)
   {
      if (i >= userInput)
         break;
      cout << "i=" << i << '\n' ;
      i++;
   }
   return (0);
}
```

This loop demonstrates a poor grasp of basic programming principles. There is no functional difference between the programs in Examples 9.10 and 9.11, except that the program in Example 9.11 is harder to read. When the program encounters the `while` loop in Example 9.11, it tests the condition. In this example, the condition is 1 so it always evaluates to true. It can never evaluate to false. A maintenance programmer will look at this and think it's an endless loop because, at first glance, it appears to be.

I inserted an `if` statement into the code block of the `while` loop. It checks to see if the value in the variable `i` is greater than or equal to the value in the variable `userInput`. If it is, the program executes the `break` statement. This causes execution to break out of the loop. Program execution will continue with the next statement after the loop. This is an extremely bad way to use a `break` statement.

[1]This is a suggestion many longtime C and C++ practitioners give. See also David M. Collopy, *Introduction to C Programming: A Modular Approach* (Upper Saddle River, NJ: Prentice Hall, 1997), pp. 588–89.

By using an intentional endless loop combined with `break` statements, programmers often make it easy for themselves to create the desired path through the code. However, the easy way is not always the best way. That's especially true in this case.

Programmers who use this style of programming have no clear understanding of how to create high-quality programs. They usually don't employ just one combination of an endless loop and a `break` statement. There are often dozens of constructs such as this throughout their blocks of code.

What this means is that anyone reading their code has no clear idea of the conditions that will cause the loop to end. They must hunt through the entire code block to find the loop's termination conditions. If the loop is very long, the maintenance programmer will almost always miss one or more termination conditions.

TRAP: Don't create intentional endless loops. They are a nightmare for maintenance programmers and testers.

Remember, the condition at the beginning of a loop is there for a reason. You shoot yourself (or someone else) in the foot if you short-circuit your loops by moving the termination condition anywhere else.

TRAP: Never put the termination condition of a loop anywhere else but in the condition section of the loop.

In addition, intentional endless loops make testing code a painful process. The paths through the code are no longer clearly defined. We must hunt for them. Using intentional endless loops and `break` statements together multiplies the number of possible paths through the code. You don't need to use very many of them before you create so many paths through the block of code that it is literally impossible to test them all.

If you find that not all of your termination conditions can go in the condition portion of a loop, then at least use the technique shown in Example 9.12.

EXAMPLE 9.12 A Way to Avoid Endless Loops

```
int done=0;
while (!done)
{
    if (condition 1)
    {
        do some processing
        done=1;
    }
    else
    {
        do some more processing
    }

    if ((!done) && (condition 2))
    {
        done=1;
    }
    etc...
}
```

Example 9.12 does not show true C++ code, but it approximates what your C++ code would look like. The program sets the value of the variable `done` to 0, which is false. The test on the loop says that the loop should continue while it is not done (`!done`). In other words, the value of 0 in the variable `done` is made true by the logical NOT operator. The value of done is not actually changed, just the evaluation of it. `!0` is 1, or true.

As soon as the variable `done` becomes true (indicating that the loop is done), the test with the ! operator will make the true value in `done` false. Because the condition on the loop now evaluates to false, the loop exits. Execution continues with the next statement after the loop.

What is the advantage of this over using an `if` with a `break`? The primary difference is that it is more readable and maintainable. A maintenance programmer can search for the variable `done` to find all of the termination conditions of the loop. You might point out that the programmer could just as easily search for the word `break`. That's true, as far as it goes. However, there are other ways to exit a loop that don't involve the word `break`. Programmers who use an endless loop with `break` statements scattered throughout it will usually also use some of the other methods of exiting loops. Finding all possible combinations of exit conditions is a chore I don't wish on anyone. It's much much easier to use the technique shown in Example 9.12. It guarantees that a maintenance programmer who uses his or her text editor's search function can find all of the exit conditions you put in your loops just by searching for the variable `done`.

Another common error that we programmers all occasionally make when we use `while` loops is to accidentally put a semicolon after the condition. Example 9.13 illustrates this.

EXAMPLE 9.13 A `while` Loop with a Misplaced Semicolon

```
int i=0;
while (i<100);
{
   cout << i << endl;
   i++;
}
```

The semicolon after the `while` loop's condition terminates the loop. This will compile and run, usually with no errors or warnings. However, because the `while` loop ends at the semicolon, the statement that increments the variable `i` is not in the loop. Therefore, the value of `i` will never change. The result is an endless loop. The program will hang.

Preventing Problems with `for` Loops

Let's do some variations on the theme we saw in Hands On 9.3. First, you have probably already figured out that if there is only one statement in the `for` loop, we can leave out the open and closing curly braces. Example 9.14 illustrates this.

EXAMPLE 9.14 A `for` Loop with One Statement

```
#include <iostream.h>

int main()
{
   int i;
   for (i=0;i<100;i++)
      cout << "i=" << i << ' ';

   return (0);
}
```

The loop in Example 9.15 shows the same sort of problem we've seen with all C++ statements that have a code block. The indentation indicates that the `for` loop's code block contains more than one statement. However, the compiler doesn't see indentation because it ignores white space. Example 9.16 gives a corrected version of the loop.

EXAMPLE 9.15 A `for` Loop with Incorrect Indentation

```
#include <iostream.h>

int main()
{
   int i;
   for (i=0;i<100;i++)
      cout << "i=" << i << ' ';
      if (i%5 == 0)
      {
         cout << endl;
      }

   return (0);
}
```

TIP: It's wise to put the curly braces on a `for` loop, even if there is only one statement in its code block.

EXAMPLE 9.16 The Correction of Example 9.15

```
#include <iostream.h>

int main()
{
   int i;
   for (i=0;i<100;i++)
   {
      cout << "i=" << i << ' ';
      if (i%5 == 0)
      {
         cout << endl;
      }
   }

   return (0);
}
```

As with `while` loops, it is easy to accidentally put a semicolon after the control portion of a `for` loop. The code in Example 9.17 shows how this might look in a program.

EXAMPLE 9.17 A Misplaced Semicolon in a `for` Loop

```
for (int i=0;i<1000;i++);
{
   cout << i;
}
```

The indentation and placement of the code block indicates we want the statement

```
cout << i;
```

executed every time the loop executes. That's not what will happen. The semicolon after the `for` loop's control portion terminates the loop. The compiler determines that the code block is not attached to the `for` loop immediately before it. When the program runs, it faithfully executes the loop, doing nothing but incrementing the value of the variable `i`. Afterward, it unconditionally executes the statement in the code block after the `for` loop.

Summary

C++ programs are able to execute code blocks repetitively, based on the evaluation of a condition. In other words, C++ programs can have conditional loops.

Loops are either pre-test loops or post-test loops. A pre-test loop is one in which the condition is evaluated at the beginning of the loop. Therefore, programs execute pre-test loops zero or more times, depending on the condition. A post-test loop evaluates its condition at the end of the loop. Programs execute post-test loops one or more times. The C++ `for` and `while` loops are pre-test loops. The `do-while` loop is a post-test loop.

The `while` and `do-while` loops are the simplest to use. They execute their code blocks and evaluate their conditions. The `for` loop is more complex to use, but it is also more powerful and flexible.

Review Questions

1. What is a conditional loop in a C++ program?
2. What is a pre-test loop? What is a post-test loop?
3. If a `while` loop contains only one statement, the curly braces can be left off of it. What is the main pitfall with leaving them off?

4. How are endless loops created? What is wrong with endless loops?
5. What can you do to avoid creating an endless loop when all of your conditions will not fit in the condition portion of the loop you're creating?
6. What happens if you leave the initialization section of the control portion of a `for` loop blank? What happens if you leave the condition blank? What happens if you leave the increment/decrement section blank?
7. How is a `for` loop affected if you use a preincrement in the increment/decrement section rather than a postincrement?
8. C++ programs can declare variables anywhere in the program. What advantage does this give a C++ program?
9. How many semicolons are there in the control portion of a `for` loop? If multiple initializations are done, how many more semicolons should you add?
10. What logical operators can you use to concatenate conditions together into a complex condition for a loop?

Exercises

1. Write a program that uses a `while` loop to start at 0 and count to a number that the user enters from the keyboard. On each iteration of the loop, the program should output the value of the counter variable.
2. Write a program that uses a `do-while` loop to start at 0 and count to a number that the user enters from the keyboard. On each iteration of the loop, the program should output the value of the counter variable.
3. Write a program that uses a `for` loop to start at 0 and count to a number that the user enters from the keyboard. On each iteration of the loop, the program should output the value of the counter variable.
4. Write a program that uses a `for` loop. Inside the loop should be a statement asking the user to type in a character. If the character that the user types in is 'Q' or 'q,' exit the loop. Otherwise, continue prompting the user.
5. Write a program that uses a `while` loop to print all of the characters in the standard ASCII set. *Hint:* Character variables can be treated as `int` if they are typecast. They can be incremented and decremented. See Hands On 4.1 in Chapter 4. All of the characters in the standard ASCII set have a value of 0–127. When this program executes, don't be surprised if the computer beeps and there are some odd things printed to the screen. This is normal.
6. Write a program that uses a `for` loop and an `if` statement to print to the screen all of the characters in the ASCII set that are in the ranges 'A' to 'Z' and 'a' to 'z.'
7. Write a program that will repeatedly ask the user for the radius of a pizza. It should calculate the total square inches in a pizza using the formula πr^2 where π is 3.14159 and r^2 is the radius that the user typed in multiplied by itself (radius * radius). After the square inches of pizza are calculated, the program should ask the user if he/she wants to quit. If the user enters a 'Y' or a 'y,' exit the loop. Otherwise ask the user for another pizza radius and perform the calculation again.
8. Write a program that uses a `for` loop. It should ask the user for a number. The condition of the `for` loop should be

   ```
   aDouble > 0
   ```

   where `aDouble` is a variable of type `double`. The number that the user types in should be stored in the variable `aDouble`. The increment/decrement section of the `for` loop should read

   ```
   aDouble/=2.0
   ```

   Run this program. Describe what happens. Explain why.
9. Write a program that gets an integer greater than 3 from the user. Use a loop to repeatedly ask the user for input until he/she enters a number greater than 3. When your program has valid input, it should calculate and output all of the prime numbers from 1 to

the number that the user types in. A prime number is divisible only by 1 and itself. The first three prime numbers are 1, 2, and 3. *Hint:* The only way to tell if a number *n* is prime is to divide it by every number from 2 to *n – 1*. *Another hint:* It's easier to test to see if a number is NOT prime than to test if it's prime.

10. Optimize the program you wrote for Exercise 9. *Hint:* All even numbers are divisible by 2, so they don't need to be checked. *Another hint:* If you're checking a number *n* to see if it's prime, you need to divide it by the numbers in the range 2 to *n – 1*. This range can be optimized further.

Chapter Glossary

Endless Loop A loop with no termination condition, or a termination condition that is never false.

Iterate To do something repeatedly.

Post-test Loop A loop that tests its condition after it executes its block of code.

Pre-test Loop A loop that tests its condition before it executes its block of code.

10 Single-Dimensional Arrays

Objectives

After reading this chapter, you should be able to:

- Declare and initialize arrays in C++ programs.
- Access array elements.
- Define named constants to eliminate "magic numbers."

Preview

So far, we have looked at how to declare variables that contain single pieces of data. We have also examined some of the basic operations that can be performed on them. C++, like most programming languages, also provides a way to declare variables that store collections of data. This type of variable is called an **array**.

The purpose of an array is to give a single variable name to a **homogenous** collection of data. A collection of data is homogenous if all of the items in the collection are the same type.

Declaring Arrays

C++ programs declare arrays in nearly the same way that they declare other variables. Applications must declare the name and type of the array variable, just as they would any other variable. The difference is that an array is a collection of data, so programs must also specify the size of the data collection. Example 10.1 demonstrates how to declare arrays.

EXAMPLE 10.1 Declaring Arrays

```
int anIntegerArray[10];
char aCharacterArray[15];
double aDoubleArray[1000];
```

Example 10.1 shows that programs declare arrays by stating their type and name, followed by the number of array **elements** in square brackets ([]). The first line of code in Example 10.1 declares an array called `anIntegerArray`. The statement allocates space in memory for 10 integers. The second statement in the example declares the array `aCharacterArray`, which is an array of 15 characters. The array `aDoubleArray` can hold 100 elements of type `double`.

FIGURE 10.1 Accessing Array Elements

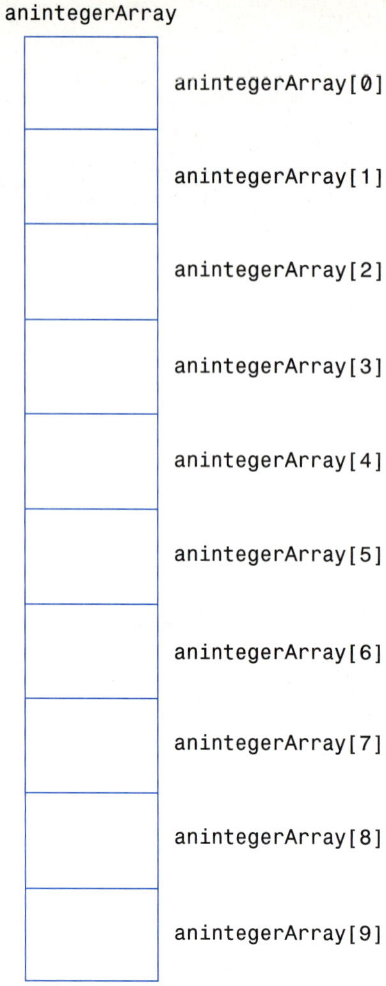

Accessing Array Elements

Each element in an array is numbered, starting with 0. Figure 10.1 illustrates the layout of the array `anIntegerArray`, which was declared in Example 10.1. Each element in the array is accessed by its number.

It's important to note that the **index numbers** of array elements of C++ arrays always begin with zero. Therefore, if an array has 10 elements in it, they are numbered 0 through 9.

Hands On 10.1 shows how arrays can be used in programs.

Hands On 10.1

Objective

Write a program that demonstrates the use of arrays.

Experiment

Type the following program into your text editor or IDE. Compile, link, and run it.

```
#include <iostream.h>

int main()
{
```

```
    int i;
    int anArray[100];

    // Fill the array.
    for (i=0;i<100;i++)
    {
        anArray[i]=i;
    }

    cout << endl << "Printing the array." << endl;
    for (i=0;i<100;i++)
    {
        cout << anArray[i] << ' ';
        if (i%10==0)
        {
            cout << endl;
        }
    }

    cout << endl << endl << "Printing the array backwards." << endl;
    for (i=99;i>=0;i--)
    {
        cout << anArray[i] << ' ';
        if (i%10==0)
        {
            cout << endl;
        }
    }

    return (0);
}
```

Results

```
Printing the array.
0
1 2 3 4 5 6 7 8 9 10
11 12 13 14 15 16 17 18 19 20
21 22 23 24 25 26 27 28 29 30
31 32 33 34 35 36 37 38 39 40
41 42 43 44 45 46 47 48 49 50
51 52 53 54 55 56 57 58 59 60
61 62 63 64 65 66 67 68 69 70
71 72 73 74 75 76 77 78 79 80
81 82 83 84 85 86 87 88 89 90
91 92 93 94 95 96 97 98 99

Printing the array backwards.
99 98 97 96 95 94 93 92 91 90
89 88 87 86 85 84 83 82 81 80
79 78 77 76 75 74 73 72 71 70
69 68 67 66 65 64 63 62 61 60
59 58 57 56 55 54 53 52 51 50
49 48 47 46 45 44 43 42 41 40
39 38 37 36 35 34 33 32 31 30
29 28 27 26 25 24 23 22 21 20
19 18 17 16 15 14 13 12 11 10
9 8 7 6 5 4 3 2 1 0
```

Analysis

In Hands On 10.1, we combined arrays, `for` loops, and `if` statements. The program declares an integer variable `i` for use as a loop counter. It also declares an array of 100 integers. Remember that, since array indexing begins at 0, the array elements are numbered 0 through 99.

The first `for` loop in the program stores the value in the variable `i` into the array. The program accesses each individual array element by its number. The first time through the loop, the variable `i` will contain the value 0. Therefore, the array element being accessed is `anArray[0]`. On the next iteration of the loop, the value in `i` will be 1, so `anArray[1]` will receive the value of `i`.

By the way, when we read the statement `anArray[1]` aloud, we read that as, "anArray sub 1". The square brackets indicate the array **subscript.**

The program in Hands On 10.1 executes its first loop 100 times. Each time it iterates, it increases the value of `i` by 1. So `i` will take on the values of 0 through 99. This corresponds exactly to the index numbers of the array elements. Therefore, these values can be used as array subscripts.

The program next prints a text label to make the output of the program more comprehensible. It enters a loop that prints the value in each array location, followed by a space character (character 32 in the ASCII set). This is done with the line

```
cout << anArray[i] << ' ';
```

This statement retrieves the value in `anArray[i]` and uses it as output to the screen.

The code block of an `if`, `switch`, `for`, `while`, or `do-while` statement is also called its *body*.

The program then executes an `if` statement. The condition on the `if` tests to see if the value of `i` is evenly divisible by 10. It uses the modulus operator to determine if the remainder of `i` divided by 10 is 0. If it is, `i` divides evenly by 10. The code block of the `if` statement prints an endline character.

The last loop in the sample program iterates through the array in reverse, printing the values stored in it. Notice that it initializes `i` to 99, not 100. The last element of the array has an index number of 99. The loop continues as long as the value in `i` is greater than or equal to 0.

In Hands On 10.2, we'll modify the program from Hands On 10.1 so that it uses characters. We'll also implement a simple type of document scrolling that we'll use in our text editor.

Hands On 10.2

Objective

Write a program that:

- Fills an array with 100 characters.
- Declares and initializes the variable **top** to keep track of the first character to be printed.
- While the user has not pressed 'Q' or 'q' to quit,
  - Prompts the user for input.
  - Gets input from the user.
  - If the user types 'U' or 'u',
    - Decrements **top** by 19 until it equals 0.
  - If the user types 'D' or 'd',
    - Increments **top** by 19 until it equals 100-20.
  - Prints each character in the array beginning with **top** and ending with **top**+20.

Experiment

Type the following program into your text editor or IDE. Compile, link, and run it.

```
#include <iostream.h>

int main()
{
   int i;
   char tempChar;
   char anArray[100];

   // Fill the array.
   for (i=0,tempChar=' ';i<100;i++)
   {
      anArray[i]=tempChar++;
   }

   int top=0;
   for (tempChar=' ';(tempChar!='q') && (tempChar!='Q');cin>>tempChar)
   {
      switch (tempChar)
      {
         case 'U':
         case 'u':
            top -= 20-1;
         break;

         case 'D':
         case 'd':
            top += 20-1;
         break;
      }

      if (top<0)
      {
         top=0;
      }
      else if (top >= 100)
      {
         top=100-20;
      }

      int j;
      for (i=top,j=0;(i < top+20) && (i < 100);i++,j++)
      {
         cout << "Display Line " << j;
         cout << ":  Array element " << i << ": ";
         cout << anArray[i] << endl;
      }
      cout << "\nCOMMAND:";
   }
   return (0);
}
```

Results

The initial display will resemble Figure 10.2. After a 'd' or 'D' is entered at the keyboard, the display will look like Figure 10.3.

FIGURE 10.2 **Initial Output of the Program in Hands On 10.2**

```
Display Line 0:  Array element 0:
Display Line 1:  Array element 1: !
Display Line 2:  Array element 2: "
Display Line 3:  Array element 3: #
Display Line 4:  Array element 4: $
Display Line 5:  Array element 5: %
Display Line 6:  Array element 6: &
Display Line 7:  Array element 7: '
Display Line 8:  Array element 8: (
Display Line 9:  Array element 9: )
Display Line 10:  Array element 10: *
Display Line 11:  Array element 11: +
Display Line 12:  Array element 12: ,
Display Line 13:  Array element 13: -
Display Line 14:  Array element 14: .
Display Line 15:  Array element 15: /
Display Line 16:  Array element 16: 0
Display Line 17:  Array element 17: 1
Display Line 18:  Array element 18: 2
Display Line 19:  Array element 19: 3

COMMAND:
```

FIGURE 10.3 **More Output of the Program in Hands On 10.2**

```
Display Line 19:  Array element 19: 3

COMMAND:d
Display Line 0:  Array element 19: 3
Display Line 1:  Array element 20: 4
Display Line 2:  Array element 21: 5
Display Line 3:  Array element 22: 6
Display Line 4:  Array element 23: 7
Display Line 5:  Array element 24: 8
Display Line 6:  Array element 25: 9
Display Line 7:  Array element 26: :
Display Line 8:  Array element 27: ;
Display Line 9:  Array element 28: <
Display Line 10:  Array element 29: =
Display Line 11:  Array element 30: >
Display Line 12:  Array element 31: ?
Display Line 13:  Array element 32: @
Display Line 14:  Array element 33: A
Display Line 15:  Array element 34: B
Display Line 16:  Array element 35: C
Display Line 17:  Array element 36: D
Display Line 18:  Array element 37: E
Display Line 19:  Array element 38: F

COMMAND:
```

Analysis

This program declares an array of characters and fills the array using a `for` loop. When the program enters the first loop, it assigns the variable `i` a value of 0. It also assigns the variable `tempChar` the value of space, which is ASCII character 32. The program then tests the variable `i` to see if it is less than 100. The value 100 was used because that is the size of the array. During the course of the loop, `i` will take on the values 0–99. When the last iteration occurs, `i` will be 100 and the loop will stop.

Each time through this loop, the program assigns the current value of `tempChar` into an array location. It also increments the variable `tempChar` to the next character.

The program next enters another loop. The control portion of this loop is a bit tricky. The initialization section is plain enough; it initializes `tempChar` back to space. The condition section says that the loop will continue for as long as `tempChar` is not equal to either 'q' or 'Q.' As soon as `tempChar` is 'q' or 'Q,' the loop will end.

The increment/decrement section of this loop looks strange. We're not doing an increment or a decrement. Instead, we've said that we want to get input from the keyboard at the end of each iteration of the loop and store it in `tempChar`. Although this may look odd, it is perfectly valid C++ programming.

When the program executes the code block of the `for` loop, it enters a `switch` statement. In Chapter 8, I specifically said that you should put a `break` after each `case`. I've used this example to show a situation where it might be valid to break that rule. However this is an exception that validates the rule. In this case, we put two `case` labels for each block of code we want executed. The result is that if the user types in 'U' or 'u,' the line

```
top -= 20-1;
```

will be executed. If the user types in 'd' or 'D', the line

```
top += 20-1;
```

will be executed.

We could have used an `if` statement to accomplish the same thing. It would have looked like Example 10.2.

EXAMPLE 10.2 An Alternative to the switch Statement of Hands On 10.2

```
if ((tempChar=='u') || (tempChar=='U'))
{
    top -= 20-1;
}
else if ((tempChar=='d') || (tempChar=='D'))
{
    top += 20-1;
}
```

The difference between the two is that the `switch` statement is slightly more efficient. Also, it's easier for the person writing the code to add cases to a `switch` than it is to add additional `if-else` clauses. For this reason, many C++ programmers use this technique.

To me, these are not strong justifications for using this style of `switch` statement rather than a set of chained `if-else` statements. In my opinion, the set of chained `if-else` statements is safer because it's much harder to accidentally execute the wrong code block. Also, it's harder for the maintenance programmer to misinterpret. Which you prefer is something you'll have to judge for yourself.[1]

Many programmers would not agree. They would say that this is a perfect example of a situation where the `break` can be left off of cases. Because this is a common technique you will see on the job, I have demonstrated it here.

The program in Hands On 10.2 uses the `switch` statement to increment or decrement a variable called `top`. This variable holds the index number in the array of the character that will be printed on the first line of the output. When the user presses a 'd' or 'D,' the program increments the variable `top` toward the end of the array. If we think of the array as a vertical collection of characters like Figure 10.4, we are scrolling toward the bottom of the array. If the user presses 'u' or 'U,' the

[1]You must judge many stylistic issues for yourself when you take up C++ programming. In most cases, the overriding criterion should be whether or not the maintenance programmer will understand the code you've written. Modern compilers can optimize your code for you. Optimization isn't generally the highest priority these days—maintenance is. That's where much of the money is spent on a program. See Chapter 12 for details.

FIGURE 10.4 An Array of Characters Depicted Vertically

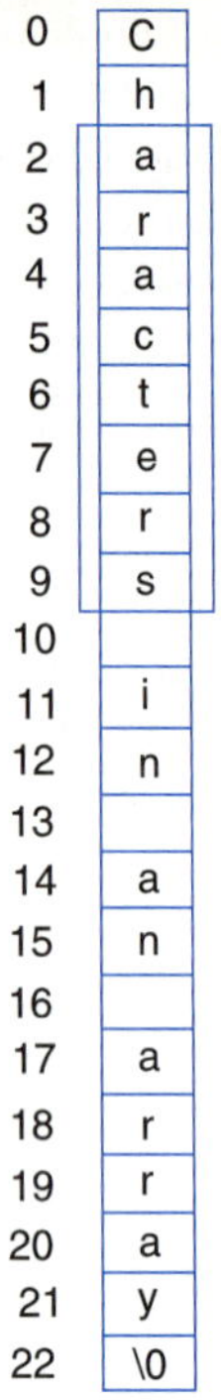

program decrements the variable `top` toward the beginning. This tells the program to scroll its output toward the top of the array. We define a display area, which is the portion of the array that will be displayed on the screen. This is also indicated in Figure 10.4 by the light green box.

It's important to remember that arrays in memory are neither horizontal nor vertical. They're just a collection of memory locations that are all together in a block. That is, they are **contiguous.** We just draw them vertically or horizontally so we can visualize them better. However, that is not how they are in the computer.

You may wonder why `top` is incremented and decremented by 20 – 1. Why don't we just write 19? This will become clearer later in this chapter when we cover named constants. However, the short explanation is that the portion of the array that we're displaying in this example is 20 lines long. When we scroll the display area up or down, we want to leave some overlap. By scrolling by the length of the display area minus one, the program will redisplay one of the lines that it displayed before scrolling. This helps users orient themselves within the context of our program's output.

After the program sets the variable `top`, it checks to see if `top` has been decremented to a position before the beginning of the array or after the end of it. If it has, the program adjusts `top` so that it is within the bounds of the array.

Next, the Hands On program enters a `for` loop. The `for` loop starts at the location indicated by `top` and prints characters. The loop prints each character on a single line. Before it outputs each character, it prints the display line number and the array index number. The program accomplishes this task using a `for` loop within a `for` loop. The outer `for` loop runs until the user presses 'q' or 'Q.' The inner `for` loop displays 20 lines of text each time the outer `for` loop iterates.

If you scroll up and down through the array, you'll see that it displays all characters in the array, 20 lines at a time. The program will not allow the user to go beyond the end of the array, nor before the beginning.

After it outputs a group of 20 lines to the screen, the program prints a prompt and waits for the user input. Note that the user must press a character and then press the Enter key for the program to work. It would be nice if we could just press 'u' or 'd' and not have to press Enter each time. That is one of the modifications we'll make to this program in the future.

Initializing Arrays

Like any other type of variable, an array can be initialized. When we initialize a variable, we set it to an initial, known value. Hands On 10.3 demonstrates array initialization.

Hands On 10.3

Objective

Write a program that demonstrates array initialization and usage.

Experiment

Type the following program into your text editor or IDE. Compile, link, and run it.

```
#include <iostream.h>

int main()
{
   int array1[10];
   double array2[10]={1.2};
   char array3[10]={'d'};
   unsigned array4[]={1,2,5,6,7};
   char aString[10]="A String.";
   int i;

   cout << "Array 1" << endl;
   for (i=0;i<10;i++)
   {
      cout << array1[i] << endl;
   }
   cout << endl;

   cout << "Array 2" << endl;
   for (i=0;i<10;i++)
   {
      cout << array2[i] << endl;
   }
   cout << endl;

   cout << "Array 3" << endl;
   for (i=0;i<10;i++)
   {
      cout << array3[i] << endl;
   }
   cout << endl;

   cout << "Array 4" << endl;
   for (i=0;i<10;i++)
   {
      cout << array4[i] << endl;
   }

   cout  << endl << aString << endl;

   return (0);
}
```

Results

```
Array 1
3338
-38
-32768
-26636
4595
-82
0
7906
3338
0

Array 2
1.2
0
0
0
0
0
0
0
0
0

Array 3
d









Array 4
1
2
5
6
7

A String.
```

Analysis

In Hands On 10.3, we declare and initialize a variety of arrays. The first, `array1`, is declared but not initialized. What does it contain?

TIP: Uninitialized memory must be assumed to contain garbage.

The answer is in the Results section of the Hands On. The array contains random values. Memory has been allocated, but not initialized. Therefore, it contains garbage.

The second array in the Hands On program, `array2`, is an array of 10 doubles. The program initializes only the first location in the array. The Results section shows us that the first location in `array2`, which is location number 0, was initialized to 1.2. All other elements in the array were initialized to 0. Even though we only initialized the first location, the other elements in the array were initialized as well.

FIGURE 10.5 The Contents of aString

0	1	2	3	4	5	6	7	8	9
A		S	t	r	i	n	g		\0

TRAP: Some C++ compilers will not initialize uninitialized data to 0 for you. You can't depend on it being done if you want your code to be portable. It is best to assume that data that you do not specifically initialize is garbage.

Most C++ compilers conform to this behavior. However, the C++ is a language that evolved (and is still evolving) out of C. The old C standard was to leave all data that was not specifically initialized in an uninitialized state. In a C program, `array2` would have contained 1.2, followed by garbage. Some C++ compilers will do this as well.

The next array, `array3`, is of type `char`. Like `array2`, element number 0 (the first element in the array) is initialized. The rest of the array is left uninitialized. When we print `array3`, the character 'd' is printed on a line by itself. The other 10 lines are blank. That is because, like `array2`, the uninitialized portions of `array2` are set to 0. For characters, 0 is the **null character.** The null character means that there is no character there. It is the only character with the ASCII value of 0.

The next array, `array4` has an unusual-looking declaration. We omitted the array size specifier in the square brackets. When the C++ compiler encounters an array declaration like this, it counts the number of array elements in the initialization. If there is no initialization, it will generate an error. In this case, we initialized five array locations, so that is how many unsigned integers are allocated to compiler memory.

TIP: In C++, all strings must be terminated by the null character.

TIP: The null character '\0' is one character, even though it looks like two.

The last array declared in the Hands On program, `aString`, demonstrates that character arrays can be used to store a string of characters. C++ compilers will allow character arrays to be initialized with a string in quote marks. When we do this, the C++ compiler will automatically put the null character (which is represented by '\0') after the last character in the string. So the contents of the array `aString` would look like Figure 10.5.

The array `aString` could also have been initialized like this:

```
char anArray = {'A',' ','S','t','r','i','n','g','.','\0'};
```

But who wants to do that?

Magic Numbers

Most of the programs we have written to this point contain what are commonly referred to in the software industry as **magic numbers.**[2] A magic number is a number that doesn't explain itself. Most numbers don't explain themselves. To illustrate the idea of magic numbers, let's take another look at the program we wrote for Hands On 10.2. It is repeated in Example 10.3 for convenience.

EXAMPLE 10.3 A Program with Magic Numbers

```
#include <iostream.h>

int main()
{
   int i;
   char tempChar;
   char anArray[100];

   // Fill the array.
```

[2]See Scott Meyers, *Effective C++* (Reading, MA: Addison Wesley Longman, 1992), pp. 10–12, 31.

```
    for (i=0,tempChar=' ';i<100;i++)
    {
        anArray[i]=tempChar++;
    }

    int top=0;
    for (tempChar=' ';(tempChar!='q') && (tempChar!='Q');cin>>tempChar)
    {
        switch (tempChar)
        {
            case 'U':
            case 'u':
                top -= 20-1;
            break;

            case 'D':
            case 'd':
                top += 20-1;
            break;
        }

        if (top<0)
        {
            top=0;
        }
        else if (top >= 100)
        {
            top=100-20;
        }

        int j;
        for (i=top,j=0;(i < top+20) && (i < 100);i++,j++)
        {
            cout << "Display Line " << j;
            cout << ":  Array element " << i << ": ";
            cout << anArray[i] << endl;
        }
        cout << "\nCOMMAND:";
    }
    return (0);
}
```

The program in Example 10.3 uses numbers such as 20 and 100. Twenty what? One hundred what? Why these numbers in particular? A person seeing this program for the first time would conclude that they must be important numbers because they are used repeatedly. But he/she would not know that they meant.

C++ allows us to make these numbers more self-documenting by creating what are called **named constants.** A named constant is a name that we assign a constant value. Programs can use the name wherever the value would be used.

There are two advantages to replacing magic numbers with named constants. The first is that programs become more self-documenting. That is, the name will hopefully explain what the number is being used for. Programs become easier to read.

The second advantage to using named constants is that they make a program easier to modify. Example 10.3 is a case in point. What if we decided to change the 20 to a 22? We would have to hunt through the program and find every 20 and replace it with a 22.

You may say, "That's OK, my text editor has a search and replace function. All I have to do is tell it to replace all 20s in the program with 22s." The problem with that is that a large, professional program will likely use the number 20 for other things unrelated to the value we want to change. Changing all 20s to 22s would undoubtedly have a bigger impact on the program than we want. If we define a named constant, we can just change the value assigned to the name. That changes the value in all of the appropriate places throughout the program.

Both of these advantages will become clearer in the next few examples.

You may be asking, "Are all numbers in programs magic numbers?" Strictly speaking, the answer is yes. However, most programmers will understand if you put the numbers –1, 0, or 1 in a program rather than a named constant. Those are just about the only magic numbers your program can safely use. If you do use them, use them sparingly. It is still better to use named constants, even for –1, 0, and 1.

A C++ program can create a named constant in two different ways. It can declare named constants using the keyword `const`, or it can define them by using the C++ preprocessor `#define` directive.

Declaring Constants Using const

Declaring named constants with the keyword `const` is the preferred method of declaring constants. When C++ programs declare named constants using the `const` keyword, they declare the constants very much like they declare variables. Example 10.4 illustrates this.

EXAMPLE 10.4 Declaring Constants with const

```
#include <iostream.h>

const int AN_INTEGER_CONSTANT = 20;

int main()
{
    const double A_LOCAL_CONSTANT = 2.3;

    cout << AN_INTEGER_CONSTANT << endl;
    cout << A_LOCAL_CONSTANT;

    return (0);
}
```

The program in Example 10.4 declares two constants. The declarations look almost like the declarations of variables. The only difference is the keyword `const` at the beginning of each declaration.

By convention, programmers capitalize all named constants. C++ does not force you to do this. It does not prevent you from using lowercase letters if you want to. However, other programmers will find your code more readable if you follow the convention of using all capital letters.

Notice also that constants can be declared outside of `main()`.[3] In this example, the constant `AN_INTEGER_CONSTANT` is declared before `main()`. Declaring a constant outside of a function (`main()` is a function) makes it a global constant.[4] That is often exactly

[3]Actually, the same can be done with variables. **Never** declare a variable outside a function. Doing so makes it a global variable. A global variable is one of the worst things you can put in your program. Using many global variables in a program demonstrates very clearly to other programmers that you don't know how to design professional programs. Technically speaking, global variables increase modular cohesion, which degrades program structure. See Edward Yourdon et al., *Yourdon Systems Method* (Englewood Cliffs, NJ: Yourdon Press, 1993), pp. 4–5, and Maureen Sprankle, *Problem Solving and Programming Concepts* (Upper Saddle River, NJ: Prentice Hall, 1998), pp. 64–65.

[4]Strictly speaking, a constant declared outside of a function with the `const` keyword has what is called *internal linkage*. That means it can be seen only in the file in which it is declared. To make it truly global, it must be put in a header file. For more information on header files, see Chapter 18.

what you want. A global constant can be seen anywhere in the program. It is initialized when the program is loaded.

The program in Example 10.4 declares the constant `A_LOCAL_CONSTANT` inside of the function `main()`. It can be accessed only in the `main()` function. C++ programs usually contain many functions. Whenever programs declare constants inside a function, as `A_LOCAL_CONSTANT` is, only the function that declares the constant can access it.

Now that we have a way to declare named constants in a program, let's go back and fix the program from Hands On 10.2 so that it uses named constants.

EXAMPLE 10.5 A Program with Named Constants

```
#include <iostream.h>

//---------------------------------------------------------------
// Constants
//---------------------------------------------------------------

const int ARRAY_LENGTH          = 100;
const int DISPLAY_AREA_SIZE     = 20;

//------------------------end Constants---------------------



int main()
{
   int i;
   char tempChar;
   char anArray[ARRAY_LENGTH];

   // Fill the array.
   for (i=0,tempChar=' ';i<ARRAY_LENGTH;i++)
   {
      anArray[i]=tempChar++;
   }

   int top=0;
   for (tempChar=' ';(tempChar!='q') && (tempChar!='Q');cin>>tempChar)
   {
      switch (tempChar)
      {
         case 'U':
         case 'u':
            top -= DISPLAY_AREA_SIZE-1;
         break;

         case 'D':
         case 'd':
            top += DISPLAY_AREA_SIZE-1;
         break;
      }

      if (top<0)
      {
         top=0;
      }
      else if (top >= ARRAY_LENGTH)
```

```
        {
            top=ARRAY_LENGTH-DISPLAY_AREA_SIZE;
        }

        int j;
        for (i=top,j=0;
              (i < top+DISPLAY_AREA_SIZE) && (i < ARRAY_LENGTH); i++,j++)
        {
            cout << "Display Line " << j;
            cout << ": Array element " << i << ": ";
            cout << anArray[i] << endl;
        }
        cout << "\nCOMMAND:";
    }
    return (0);
}
```

The program in Example 10.5 demonstrates not only the use of named constants, but some program documentation as well. In a professional program, named constants are put in labeled sections, which makes them easier to find. However, this leads to some differences of opinion.

Some say that the scope of constants should be strictly controlled. For example, since the constants in Example 10.5 were only used by the `main()` function, they should be declared in `main()`. As it is, other functions that we might add to this program would be able to access the constants `ARRAY_LENGTH` and `DISPLAY_AREA_SIZE`. Declaring these constants in `main()` declares them inside the code block that uses them. They should only be declared outside of a function if they are used by many functions in a program.

Others prefer to declare all constants outside of functions and make them global or nearly global. The advantage of this method is that it is easier for the programmer developing the program. You don't have to worry about whether or not a constant will be available to a particular function. All constants are available to all (or nearly all) functions. It is also easier to find a constant's value when you need it. They are always together in one place.

We can make the code even more self-documenting by changing `DISPLAY_AREA_SIZE-1` to `DISPLAY_AREA_SIZE-DISPLAY_AREA_OVERLAP`, where `DISPLAY_AREA_OVERLAP` is 1. This also gives the maintenance programmer the option of changing `DISPLAY_AREA_OVERLAP` to another value, such as 2.

Which style of organization you choose is up to you. Be aware, however, that the intent in C++ is to declare things close to where they are used, rather than in a single, global spot.

One last note on the program in Example 10.5. Now that the number 20 is replaced in the program with the constant `DISPLAY_AREA_SIZE`, it is easier to see why we didn't put the number 19 in the program. It was always written as 20–1. That has now become `DISPLAY_AREA_SIZE-1`. Techniques such as this make the programmer's intentions clearer. In this case, the program uses the value `DISPLAY_AREA_SIZE-1` to "scroll" the screen. By subtracting 1 from the `DISPLAY_AREA_SIZE`, we as the designers of the program indicate that we intend to repeat one line of the display. If the user scrolls the screen down, what used to be the bottom line of text is repeated as the top line. When the user scrolls the screen up, what used to be the top line is repeated as the bottom line.

Defining Constants Using `#define`

C++ programs can also create named constants by defining them with the preprocessor statement `#define`. The preprocessor can do some processing on our C++ programs just before they are compiled. In fact, every time you invoke the compiler, it calls the preprocessor first. When the preprocessor is finished, the compiler compiles the program.

We'll present more information about the preprocessor in Chapter 17. However, the important point here is that it allows us to define constants. Example 10.6 demonstrates the use of the `#define` directive.

EXAMPLE 10.6 Using #define

```
#include <iostream.h>

#define A_CONSTANT    20

int main()
{
   #define ANOTHER_CONSTANT = 2.3;

   cout << A_CONSTANT << endl;
   cout << ANOTHER_CONSTANT;

   return (0);
}
```

The program in Example 10.6 is very similar to the one in Example 10.4. However, the way in which it is compiled is quite different. Because the program creates constants with the preprocessor's `#define` statement, the preprocessor goes through the program and substitutes the value 20 everywhere it finds the constant A_CONSTANT. It substitutes the value 2.3 everywhere it finds ANOTHER_CONSTANT. Example 10.7 demonstrates this.

EXAMPLE 10.7 The Result of the Preprocessor

```
#include <iostream.h>

int main()
{
   cout << 20 << endl;
   cout << 2.3;

   return (0);
}
```

Some preprocessors produce what is called an *intermediate file.* It has an .i extension. The compiler then compiles the .i file.

Note that the preprocessor does not change the contents of your CPP file. It takes what you see in Example 10.6 and turns it into what you see in Example 10.7. It then feeds that result directly into your compiler without your ever seeing it, and without changing the your CPP file.

Another difference between creating constants with `const` and creating them with `#define` is that the preprocessor doesn't recognize functions. Because of that, any constant that you create with `#define` is accessible from the point it is defined to the end of the file. In Example 10.4, only the `main()` function can access the constant A_LOCAL_CONSTANT. If there were other functions after `main()`, they could not access A_LOCAL_CONSTANT.

That is not the case when constants are created with a `#define`. Any defined constant is visible from the point it is defined to the end of the file. Other functions that we might add to Example 10.6 after `main()` could access and use ANOTHER_CONSTANT.

As you can see, the use of `const` gives you much stricter control over the visibility of constants than `#define` does. That is one of the reasons that C++ programmers prefer to create constants with `const` rather than `#define`.

Troubleshooting Guide

After reading this section, you should be able to:

- Recognize array boundary errors.
- Fix array boundary errors.

Going Beyond Array Boundaries

In the Hands On examples throughout this chapter, we very carefully avoided going beyond the boundaries of the arrays. Some computer languages strictly enforce array boundaries. They absolutely won't let you access data before or after the array.

C++ is not one of the those languages. There's actually a very good reason for this, which we'll see when we discuss pointers. For now, however, let's examine what can happen when we do go outside the allocated boundaries of an array.

EXAMPLE 10.8 A Quick Way to Crash a Program

```
#include <iostream.h>

int main()
{
   int anIntegerArray[10];
   int i;

   for (i=-5; i<20; i++)
   {
      anIntegerArray[i]=i;
   }
   for (i=-5; i<20; i++)
   {
      cout << anIntegerArray[i];
   }

   return (0);
}
```

TRAP: Writing data outside the memory allocated for the array will yield unpredictable results. It may crash the program, or it may work fine—for a while.

As the example title suggests, this program is nothing but bad news. On my DOS PC, I got the output shown in Figure 10.6. After displaying what you see in the figure, my computer locked up completely. I had to turn it off and back on again to get it going. When I ran this in a DOS box under Windows 3.1, Windows shut the program right down. It told me that the program had violated system integrity. Other operating systems (Windows 95 and Linux) behaved in a similar manner.

TIP: Never try to store data outside the boundaries of an array. Never try to read data from outside the boundaries of an array.

The point here is that you should never try to access data beyond the boundaries of an array. Nothing in the C++ language prevents you from doing so. A program like this can actually work for a while, depending on how your compiler lays out memory for programs. It can run perfectly well for a long time. That is, until you change something in the program that is completely unrelated to your array. Suddenly, after a perfectly reasonable modification, your program no longer works and there is apparently no reasonable explanation. This is a sure sign of a **memory overwrite.** That is what happened in the program in Example 10.8. By writing data outside the boundaries of the array, it overwrote other important data.

More precisely, the program allocates memory from the stack when the program encounters the array declaration.

When you declare an array, your program sets aside enough memory for all of the elements in the array. It sets this memory aside, when the program is loaded. When a program sets aside memory for data, we call it a **memory allocation.** In particular, it is a **static memory allocation** because the amount of memory that the program allocates for the array does not change as the program runs.

When a program declares a variable of an atomic data type, it statically allocates enough memory for that variable. When it declares an array, it statically allocates memory for every element in the array.

FIGURE 10.6 A Crashed Program and Garbage for Output

Summary

An array is a homogenous collection of data. To declare an array in a program, you must declare its type, name, and the number of elements it holds.

If *n* represents the number of elements in the array, the individual elements are numbered 0 through $n - 1$.

Array elements are accessed using the square brackets ([]). This is known as *array notation* or *array subscripting*.

Programs can use array elements anywhere they can use an atomic data variable.

Programs can set arrays to initial values when they declare them. It is best to assume that all uninitialized data in an array is garbage.

C++ programs use character arrays as strings.

Array declarations need a size specifier. That size specifier is a magic number. It does not document itself. Therefore, magic numbers such as array size specifiers should be replaced with named constants. Create named constants with the keyword `const`, or with the preprocessor directive `#define`.

Review Questions

1. What is an array?
2. How is an array declared?
3. How is an array initialized?
4. How are array elements numbered? In other words, what is the range of numbers used for the array elements?
5. What is an array subscript? What is it used for?
6. What happens if you try to store data outside the boundaries of an array? Why? Does the C++ compiler prevent you from doing this?
7. What are the two ways that an array of characters can be initialized?
8. What does uninitialized memory contain?
9. What are magic numbers? Why are they so bad to use in C++ programs?
10. What are the two ways that named constants can be created in C++? What is the difference between these two methods?

Exercises

1. Explain why an array is a homogenous collection of data.
2. Demonstrate how arrays are declared and initialized. Give examples. These should include a variety of data types, with initializations for each. In particular, show at least one demonstration of an array in which not every element is initialized. Describe the contents of this array.
3. Explain what an array index number is. Demonstrate how array index numbers are used to access array elements.
4. Explain what a memory overwrite is. Describe how programs overwrite memory.
5. In your own words, define the terms *memory allocation* and *static memory allocation.*
6. Describe how to replace magic numbers with named constants in C++ programs.
7. Write a program that declares an array of 10 characters. Initialize the array to the string "This is a very, really, extremely, especially, truly long string that is definitely more than 10 characters." Compile your program and run it. Explain the results.
8. Write a program that contains an array of 100 integers. The integers can be any value. The program should print the contents of the array to the screen. Next, it should copy the array in reverse order into another array of 100 integers. It should then print the contents of the second array.

9. Type the following program into your text editor or IDE. It fills an array with 100 random integers. After you have typed in the program, insert a `for` loop that will search the array for the largest value. Use the comments as a guide.

```
//-----------------------------------------------------------------
// Include Files
//-----------------------------------------------------------------
#include <iostream.h>
#include <stdlib.h>

//End Include
Files-------------------------------------------------------------


//-----------------------------------------------------------------
// Constants
//-----------------------------------------------------------------

const int ARRAY_LENGTH = 100;

//End
Constants---------------------------------------------------------



int main()
{
   int i, integerArray[ARRAY_LENGTH];

   // Fill the array with random integers.
   // For each array element...
   for (i=0;i<ARRAY_LENGTH;i++)
   {
      integerArray[i]=rand();
   }

   int currentMax=0;

   // For each array element...
      // If the array element is greater than the current max...
          // Set the current max to the value in the array element.

   return (0);
}
```

10. Write a program that fills an array with 100 characters. It should print the first 20 characters on a single line of the display. When the user presses 'r' or 'R,' the display should be scrolled to the right 19 characters. That is, instead of displaying characters 0–19 in the array, it should display 19–39. The user should be able to scroll the screen all the way to the last 20 characters in the array. If the user presses 'l' or 'L,' the program should scroll the display of characters toward the beginning of the array. Do not use any magic numbers in your program.

Chapter Glossary

Array A homogenous collection of data that is given a single variable name and accessed using array subscript notation.

Contiguous A group of items that are all together. Each one is immediately adjacent to the other.

Element One data item in an array.

Homogenous A group of objects that are all of the same type.

Index Number The number that is used to access an array element. For instance, the first element in array always has an index number of 0. The second has an index number of 1, etc.

Magic Number A number in a program that doesn't explain itself. Most numbers in programs don't explain themselves. Magic numbers should be replaced by named constants.

Memory Allocation Setting aside memory for use by a program.

Memory Overwrite When a program writes data to an area of memory that hasn't been allocated or has been allocated for something else.

Named Constant A constant value that is given a name.

Null Character The character '\0'. It has an ASCII value of 0, and is used to terminate strings.

Static Memory Allocation A memory allocation that does not change size as the program runs.

Subscript The array element index number in square brackets.

11 Multidimensional Arrays

Objectives

After reading this chapter, you should be able to:

- Declare multidimensional arrays.
- Initialize multidimensional arrays.
- Use multidimensional arrays.

Preview

Multidimensional arrays are a straightforward extension of the single-dimensional arrays we covered in Chapter 10. Normally, they would not warrant a complete chapter by themselves. However, we're going to take this opportunity to practice many of the other C++ statements we've learned. In fact, it is in this chapter that we'll begin building what will become a text editor.

A single-dimensional array can be thought of as a row or a column of data. The elements in the single-dimensional arrays presented in Chapter 10 were atomic data. That is, they were arrays of integers, floating point numbers, or characters.

A multidimensional array in C++ is also an array. Unlike a single-dimensional array, a multidimensional array is an array of arrays. Figure 11.1 illustrates this. It shows a two-dimensional array, often abbreviated as "2-D array". We can think of each element in the array as a row of data in a table. Because each row is a single array element, the figure shows them with bold borders. Each of these elements, or rows, is an array. Each row array contains its own collection of elements. The elements in the row array can be thought of as columns in a table of data. In this example, each column contains an integer.

The array in the Figure 11.1 contains three elements, which are the rows. They are numbered 0–2. Each row, which is also an array, has seven elements. They are numbered 0–6. Each element in a row array is an integer.

3-D and 4-D arrays are used in computer graphics, engineering, and scientific computing.

It is possible to create 3-D arrays, 4-D arrays, and so forth. However, they are rarely encountered because most programmers find them hard to deal with.

FIGURE 11.1 A Two-Dimensional Array of Integers

	0	1	2	3	4	5	6
0	5	-32	81	6	0	66	4
1	21	958	-658	12	-357	159	654
2	91	73	48	29	62	38	48

Declaring Multidimensional Arrays

When programs declare multidimensional arrays, they use much the same syntax they do when they declare 1-D arrays. For each dimension you want to declare, you just add a size specifier in square brackets. Example 11.1 shows how this is done for 1-D, 2-D, and 3-D arrays.

EXAMPLE 11.1 Declaring Arrays of Various Dimensions

```
int aSingleDimensionalArray[10];
int a2DArray[3][7];
int a3DArray[5][10][15];
```

Accessing Array Elements

Programs access elements in multidimensional arrays essentially the same way that they access them in single-dimensional arrays. Hands On 11.1 shows a small program that uses a 2-D array.

Hands On 11.1

Objective

Write a program that:

Declares and initializes a 2-D array of integers.
Displays the contents of each array location.

Experiment

Type the following program into your IDE or text editor. Compile, link, and run it.

```
#include <iostream.h>

int main()
{
   int a2DArray[10][20];
   int i,j;
   for (i=0;i<10;i++)
   {
      for (j=0;j<20;j++)
      {
         a2DArray[i][j]=i+j;
      }
   }

   for (i=0;i<10;i++)
   {
      cout << "Row " << i << ": ";
      for (j=0;j<20;j++)
      {
         cout << a2DArray[i][j];
         if (a2DArray[i][j] < 10)
         {
            cout << "  ";
         }
         else if (a2DArray[i][j] < 100)
```

```
            {
                cout << "  ";
            }
        }
        cout << endl;
    }

    return (0);
}
```

Results

The output of this program is shown in Figure 11.2.

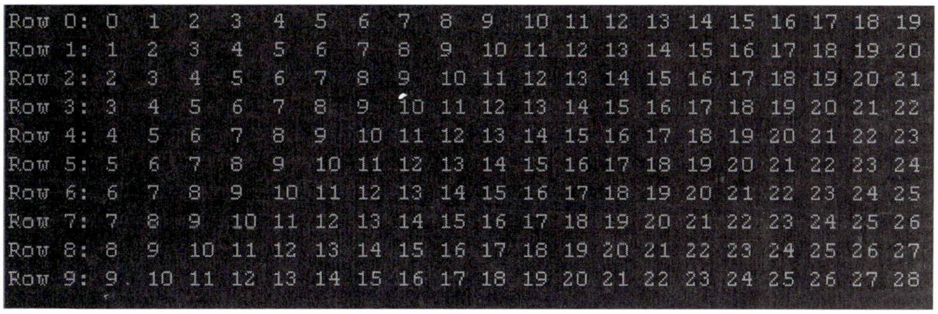

```
Row 0: 0  1  2  3  4  5  6  7  8  9  10 11 12 13 14 15 16 17 18 19
Row 1: 1  2  3  4  5  6  7  8  9  10 11 12 13 14 15 16 17 18 19 20
Row 2: 2  3  4  5  6  7  8  9  10 11 12 13 14 15 16 17 18 19 20 21
Row 3: 3  4  5  6  7  8  9  10 11 12 13 14 15 16 17 18 19 20 21 22
Row 4: 4  5  6  7  8  9  10 11 12 13 14 15 16 17 18 19 20 21 22 23
Row 5: 5  6  7  8  9  10 11 12 13 14 15 16 17 18 19 20 21 22 23 24
Row 6: 6  7  8  9  10 11 12 13 14 15 16 17 18 19 20 21 22 23 24 25
Row 7: 7  8  9  10 11 12 13 14 15 16 17 18 19 20 21 22 23 24 25 26
Row 8: 8  9  10 11 12 13 14 15 16 17 18 19 20 21 22 23 24 25 26 27
Row 9: 9  10 11 12 13 14 15 16 17 18 19 20 21 22 23 24 25 26 27 28
```

FIGURE 11.2 The Output of Hands On 11.1

Analysis

This program declares a 2-D array called `a2DArray`. It also declares some variables that are used as loop counters. It enters a set of two nested `for` loops. The outer `for` loop performs one iteration for each row in the array. The inner `for` loop iterates once for each column. So every time the program executes the outer loop, it executes the inner loop 20 times. This means that the statements in the inner `for` loop are performed once for each column in the current row. The variable `i` keeps track of the current row. The variable `j` keeps track of the current column. As the program iterates through the pair of loops for each row and column, it stores the value of `i+j` in each location in the array.

The program then enters another pair of nested `for` loops. It uses these `for` loops to iterate through each row and column in the 2-D array. For each element in the 2-D array, the program prints the value in each column to the screen. It also uses an `if` statement to add some blank space as padding between the values it prints. If the value is less than 10, the number being printed (0 through 9) is one digit long. Therefore, the program prints two spaces to the screen. If the number is not less than 10, the program tests to see if it is less than 100. Since the numbers 10–99 are all two digits long, the program prints only one space to the screen. This set of chained `if` statements makes sure that the columns of output line up when the program prints them on the display.

The program in Hands On 11.1 demonstrates how elements are accessed in a 2-D array. Each element is specified by the array name, followed by its row and column number.

Initializing Multidimensional Arrays

Like single-dimensional arrays, multidimensional arrays can be initialized when they are declared. Example 11.2 demonstrates how this is done.

EXAMPLE 11.2 Initializing Multidimensional Arrays

```
int a2DIntArray[3][4] = {{1,2,3,4},
                         {4,5,6,7},
                         {7,8,9,10} };
int a3DArray[2][2][2] = {{{1,2},{3,4}},
                         {{4,3},{2,1}}};
```

This example demonstrates how C++ programs initialize 2-D and 3-D arrays. Each row and column can be individually initialized. The initializations for each row are set off in curly brackets. The indentation I used in Example 11.2 is not required by C++. However, it helps us visualize a 2-D array as a table if we line up the rows and columns.

Looking at the initialization for the 3-D array indicates why it doesn't see much use. If we visualize it as a table, we must add a depth to it. It is as if we have placed a 2-D array on a desk in front of us, and then put another one over the top of it. The array has height, width, and depth. The initialization must reflect that.

Using Multidimensional Arrays in Programs

Let's get some experience with multidimensional arrays by using one in a program.

Hands On 11.2

Objective

Write a program that:

Creates a constant called DISPLAY_AREA_SIZE and sets it to 20.
Declares and initializes a 2-D array of characters.
Declares a character variable called **tempChar** and initializes it to a space.
Declares an integer variable called **top** and initializes it to 0.
While the user hasn't typed 'Q' or 'q,'
  If the user entered a 'U' or 'u,'
    Decrements the variable top by DISPLAY_AREA_SIZE.
  If the user entered a 'D' or 'd,'
    Increments the variable **top** by DISPLAY_AREA_SIZE.
  If **top** is now outside the boundaries of the array,
    Adjusts **top** to be inside the array boundaries.
  Clears the screen.
    Displays each row of the array starting with line **#top** and ending with `top+DISPLAY_AREA_SIZE`.
  Prompts the user for input.
  Gets input from the user.

Experiment

Type the following program into your text editor or IDE. Save it under the name EditV1.CPP. Compile, link, and run it.

```
//-----------------------------------------------------------------------
/*
File Name:    EditV1.CPP

Remarks: This is the first version of what will become a text editor. At
         this point, this file will contain the entire program.

*/
```

```
//--------------------------------------------------------------------------
// Include Files
//--------------------------------------------------------------------------

#include <iostream.h>

// End Include Files---------------------------------------------------------



//--------------------------------------------------------------------------
// Constants
//--------------------------------------------------------------------------

const int MAX_BUFFER_ROWS       = 100;
const int MAX_BUFFER_COLS       = 78;
const int DISPLAY_AREA_SIZE     = 20;
const int SCREEN_SIZE           = 25;

// End Constants-------------------------------------------------------------



int main()
{
   char textBuffer[MAX_BUFFER_ROWS][MAX_BUFFER_COLS];
   int i,j;
   char tempChar;

   // Fill the buffer with characters.
   // For each row...
   for (i=0,tempChar=' ';i<MAX_BUFFER_ROWS;i++)
   {
      // For each column...
      for (j=0;j<MAX_BUFFER_COLS-1;j++)   // The -1 is for the '\0'
      {
         // Store a character in the buffer.
         textBuffer[i][j]=tempChar++;

         // If tempChar was incremented past z...
         if (tempChar>'z')
         {
            // Reset tempChar to  space.
            tempChar=' ';
         }
      }
      textBuffer[i][MAX_BUFFER_COLS-1]='\0';
   }

   // While the user doesn't want to quit...
   int top=0;
   for (tempChar=' ';(tempChar!='q') && (tempChar!='Q');cin>>tempChar)
   {
      // Scroll the screen up or down based on user input.
      switch (tempChar)
      {
         case 'U':
```

```
         case 'u':
            top -= DISPLAY_AREA_SIZE-1;
         break;

         case 'D':
         case 'd':
            top += DISPLAY_AREA_SIZE-1;
         break;
      }

      /* If the index of the first line of text to be displayed is now
      outside the boundaries of the array, adjust it so that it is inside. */
      if (top<0)
      {
         top=0;
      }
      else if (top >= MAX_BUFFER_ROWS)
      {
         top=MAX_BUFFER_ROWS-DISPLAY_AREA_SIZE;
      }

      // Clear the screen.
      for (i=0;i<SCREEN_SIZE;i++)   // For each screen row...
      {
         // Print an endline.
         cout << endl;
      }

      // For each row of text...
      for (i=top,j=0;
           (i < top+DISPLAY_AREA_SIZE) && (i < MAX_BUFFER_ROWS);
           i++,j++)
      {
         cout << textBuffer[i] << endl;
      }

      // Display a status line.
      if (top==0)
      {
         cout << endl << "Beginning of buffer" << endl;
      }
      else if (top+DISPLAY_AREA_SIZE>=MAX_BUFFER_ROWS)
      {
         cout << endl << "End of buffer" << endl;
      }
      else
      {
         cout << endl << endl;
      }

      // Prompt the user for a command.
      cout << "COMMAND:";
   }


   return (0);
}

//----------------------------end EditV1.CPP----------------------------------
```

Results

When the program starts, it will display a screen like Figure 11.3. If the user presses 'd' or 'D' on the keyboard until the program gets to the end of the array, the screen will resemble Figure 11.4.

Analysis

The first thing you'll probably notice about this program is that it is more heavily commented than the programs presented so far. Now that we're beginning to write real programs, we need to document them like real programs. The name of this file is EditV1.CPP. The "Edit" part of the name is short for text editor. The V1 stands for version 1.

You'll see a comment banner at the beginning of EditV1.CPP. The banner lists the file name. It also provides a section for comments about what the file contains. Every C++ source file you create should have a banner like this. Many companies also insist you include a modification history in this banner.

FIGURE 11.3 **The Output of Hands On 11.2 at Program Startup**

FIGURE 11.4 **The Output of Hands On 11.2—User Presses 'd' or 'D'**

After the file banner, there are comments indicating where the `include files` should go. We'll discuss the details of include files in Chapter 16. The only `include file` we use in this program is the same one we have always used, `iostream.h`.

Next is a section for constants. As I mentioned in the last chapter, there are many programmers who prefer to declare constants close to where they are used. I declared them all together in one global area just to show what it looks like.

In this program, we use a 2-D array of characters. I've arbitrarily set the number of rows in the array to 100. The number of columns is set to 78. Most computer screens display 80 characters across in text mode. Some display more. If you want to, you can adjust the number of columns to whatever will fit on one line of your display.

The constant `SCREEN_SIZE` indicates the number of rows on the screen in text mode. The program uses this constant to clear the screen each time the user scrolls the display. Many computer screens display 24 rows. I set the screen size to one more than the actual number of rows on the screen to ensure that it was entirely blanked. If your computer displays more lines of text on your screen, adjust the constant `SCREEN_SIZE` to be one more than that number.

In the `main()` function, the program declares a 2-D array of characters called `textBuffer`. When a program sets aside a large chunk of memory to store data, we say that it has allocated a buffer. In this case, `textBuffer` holds the text that will be scrolled in the program.

TIP: Declare variables close to where they are used. If they are used through the entire function (`main()` is a function), then declare them at the beginning of the function.

You may wonder why the program declares some variables at the beginning of `main()` and others farther down. The variables declared at the beginning of `main()` are the ones that are used throughout `main()`. Variables that are used only in one spot are declared close to where they are used. This is the typical C++ programming style

The `main()` function uses two `for` loops to store characters into the array `textBuffer`. The outer loop iterates through each row. The inner loop iterates through every column. Each time through the inner loop, the program stores the value from the variable `tempChar` into `textBuffer[i][j]`. It then increments `tempChar`. It also checks the value in `tempChar` to ensure it doesn't go beyond lowercase `'z'`. If it does, it is reset to a space (ASCII character 32).

The inner `for` loop executes once for each column in a row. After the loop finishes, the program uses an assignment statement to store a null character in the last position in the current row. Remember that if there are 78 characters in the row, they are numbered 0 through 77. So in order to access the last position in the row, we use `MAX_BUFFER_COLS-1`, not `MAX_BUFFER_COLS`. This also explains why the condition on the inner `for` loop is `j<MAX_BUFFER_COLS-1`. If `MAX_BUFFER_COLS` is set to 78, then the loop quits when `j` equals 77. In other words, characters are stored in locations 0 through 76. When `j` becomes 77, the loop quits and the assignment statement that follows it will assign a null character into location 77.

I emphasize this behavior because it is often a source of confusion with programmers. In fact, it's very common for even experienced programmers to make mistakes on the boundary conditions of their loops. The boundary conditions are the initial and final values of the variables that control a loop.

After the text buffer has text in it, we want this program to display the text and allow the user to scroll it up and down. To accomplish this, we use another pair of `for` loops. This is similar to examples we saw in the last chapter. A `switch` statement is used to adjust the first line of the array that will be printed on the screen. If the user presses 'u' or 'U,' the program decrements the variable `top` by one less than the display area size. If the user presses 'd' or 'D,' the program increments `top` by one less than the display area size.

If the top line has been incremented or decremented to a value outside of the array boundaries, the program adjusts it so that it is inside the array. It then clears the screen by printing endlines. If a program prints enough endlines, whatever is currently on the screen will eventually scroll off of it.

You are probably wondering if there is a better way to clear a display. The answer is yes. There are many. In fact, there is at least one for each type of display, and they are not the same from display type to display type. The method we use here is the only one that works on any text mode display.

Once the screen is clear, `main()` is ready to display each row of text. Notice something significant here. Throughout this program, we've always used two subscripts with the array `textBuffer`. To access a single element in the array, we've used `textBuffer[i][j]`. However, in the `for` loop that prints each row, we only use one subscript. Why?

Remember that a 2-D array is an array of arrays. In other words, one row in `textBuffer` is an array. The row `textBuffer[0]` is an array of characters. So is `textBuffer[1]`, etc. The C++ compiler treats character arrays terminated by the null character as strings. Therefore, each row in `textBuffer` is a string. By leaving off one subscript, we access an entire string of characters rather than an individual character element. C++ programmers do this a lot with character arrays.

After it displays a portion of the text buffer on the screen, `main()` displays a status line. Programs commonly show some kind of status output line on the screen. Graphical user interfaces (GUIs) will typically have a status bar on the bottom of an application's window. It serves the same purpose that the status line does here. It allows us to give messages to the user based on the current state of the program.

In this case, `main()` utilizes a set of chained `if-else` statements that test to see if the user has scrolled to the beginning or the end of the text buffer. If the program encounters the beginning of the buffer, it prints the message "Beginning of buffer" to the screen. If it reaches the end of the buffer, it prints the message "End of buffer" to the status line. If neither of these conditions is true, the program leaves status line blank.

At the end of the loop, the program prompts the user for input. It retrieves the input in the increment/decrement section of the `for` loop.

With this example, we are beginning to build a text editor. However, we can't keep using letters like 'u' and 'd' to send scrolling commands to our program. If we did, users wouldn't be able to type 'u' or 'd' into their documents.

Traditionally, there are two ways to solve this problem. The first is to have the program run in two different modes, command mode and edit mode. When it is in command mode, it interprets all input from the keyboard as commands. One of the commands puts the program in edit mode. In this mode, the program stores all keyboard input as text in the text buffer. Usually, the user gets back to command mode by pressing the Escape key. The text editor vi, which is often included with the Unix operating system, works in this way.

The other traditional way to send user commands to the program is to assign commands to keys that users would never use for their documents. For example, instead of using 'u' and 'd' for scrolling up and down, we could use Ctrl+u and Ctrl+d. Ctrl+u is often abbreviated ^u or ^U. Ctrl+d is abbreviated ^d or ^D.

Both of these characters are in the ASCII set. However, there is no character representation for them. We can't put the statement `if (tempChar != '^u')` in our programs. This isn't a problem, though. We can define a named constant to represent these characters. Example 11.3 illustrates the way that constants can be declared to represent Ctrl+u and Ctrl+d. The values for Ctrl+u and Ctrl+d come from the ASCII set of characters shown in Table 4.2 in Chapter 4. In Example 11.3, we store the ASCII values for Ctrl+u and Ctrl+d into named constants of type `char`. To do this, we need a type cast to change the integer values into characters.

EXAMPLE 11.3 Declaring Character Constants

```
const char CTRL_U = (char)21;
const char CTRL_D = (char)4;
```

You may be wondering why we don't use the Page Up and Page Down keys on the keyboard to scroll up and down one screenful at a time. The answer is that these keys, as well as the arrow keys and the function keys, are not part of the ASCII set. C++ input and output classes only allow us to use characters in the ASCII set. If we want to get input from keys that are not represented in the ASCII set, we must use other methods that are often not portable.

Troubleshooting Guide

After reading this section, you should be able to:

- Find problems with declaring large arrays.
- Fix problems with declaring large arrays.

Declaring Large Arrays

Some compilers have trouble allocating and accessing large arrays. Just exactly how "large" is defined depends on the compiler.

Arrays larger than 64 kilobytes (64K) have traditionally been a problem for MS DOS–based compilers. When a PC is running MS DOS as its operating system, it uses a segmented memory architecture. That means that memory is accessible in 64K chunks. The result of this is that it is difficult for DOS-based PCs to allocate arrays larger than 64K. Typically, compiler manufacturers provide memory models of different sizes. We don't have to know the details of DOS memory models to use them. If you are declaring arrays that are larger than 64K, you need to use the Large or Huge memory model (whichever your compiler provides).

Windows 95, Windows NT, and the various varieties of Unix all use a flat memory architecture. This means that you should have no problems declaring large arrays. However, if your compiler gives you an error when declaring a large array, you may need to make your stack larger. Your compiler documentation will tell you how to do this.

Summary

Arrays can be declared with more than one dimension. Typically, arrays in commercial programs have no more than two dimensions. A 2-D array can be thought of as a table with rows and columns. In memory, it is actually an array of arrays.

Multidimensional arrays are initialized by indicating values for each element. The values for each row are in curly brackets; the sets of row values are separated from each other with commas.

Multidimensional array elements are accessed by specifying an index number for each dimension. A 2-D array would require the row and column number of an element to access that element.

Review Questions

1. What is a multidimensional array?
2. Why don't programmers normally use 4-D and 5-D arrays?
3. How are array elements initialized by default in a multidimensional array?
4. What is another name for an array of characters?
5. How can an entire row in an array of characters be printed to the screen at once?
6. In Hands On 11.2, the first pair of nested `for` loops stores characters in each row of the 2-D array. Why is a null character appended to the end of each row?
7. What does it mean to say that a 2-D array is an array of arrays?
8. Why didn't we use the Page Up and Page Down keys in the program in Hands On 11.2?

9. How can text editors tell whether the user's input is a command or text to store in the text buffer? What are the two traditional ways of solving this problem?
10. Where do you think named constants should appear—all together at the beginning of a program or close to where they are used? Why?

Exercises

1. Modify the program in Hands On 11.2 so that it uses the command Ctrl+U to scroll toward the beginning of the text buffer and Ctrl+D to scroll toward the end of the text buffer. Use named constants in your program.
2. Modify your program from Exercise 1 so that it prints the contents of the variable `top` onto the status line. Ensure that it prints this information each time the screen is scrolled.
3. Modify your program from Exercise 2. Replace the `switch` statement with an equivalent chained `if-else` statement.
4. Modify your program from Exercise 3. Make it scroll toward the beginning of the buffer one line at a time when the user types Ctrl+B. Make it scroll toward the end of the buffer one line at a time when the user enters Ctrl+E.
5. Modify your program from Exercise 4. Make it exit the program when the user types Ctrl+X.
6. Modify your program from Exercise 5. When the user types Ctrl+S, the status line is toggled on or off. That is, by default the status line should be displayed. When the user enters Ctrl+S, your program sets a variable indicating that the status line should not be displayed. If the user enters Ctrl+S again, the variable is set to indicate that the status line should be displayed.
7. Modify your program from Exercise 6 so that it uses `while` loops rather than `for` loops. Explain which you think is more appropriate for this program, the `while` loop or the `for` loop. Explain why.
8. Write a program that stores integer values in a 3-D array. The 3-D array should be 50 rows by 20 columns and 5 elements deep. The value that is stored in each array element should be the sum of the row number plus the column number plus the depth number. After the values are stored in the array, print them to the screen.
9. Demonstrate how a 3-D array is initialized by giving at least two examples.
10. Write a program that stores integer values in a 4-D array. The 4-D array should be 50 by 20 by 10 by 5. The value that is stored in each array element should be the sum of the four index numbers of each element. After the values are stored in the array, print them to the screen.

12 Structured Design with Functions

Objectives

After reading this chapter, you should be able to:

- Explain what a function is and what it does.
- Explain the essential principles of designing functions.
- Write functions.
- Pass information into functions.
- Get information from functions.
- Use function prototypes.

Preview

Professional programs are seldom as short as the example programs in this book. Most commercial application programs are hundreds of thousands of lines of source code. Some are millions of lines long. It is normal for programs to be written by large teams. In fact, their size makes it nearly impossible for one person to write them in a timely manner.

It would not be reasonable for a program that is hundreds of thousands of lines of source code to fit into `main()`. A program must be broken into manageable pieces. That is one of the primary reasons for functions.

It is not enough, however, to build programs from manageable pieces. The pieces must have a definite design to them, or they won't be worth creating.

This chapter introduces functions and describes the part they play in C++ programs. It also presents some fundamentals of software design.

Structured Design

Function oriented languages like C (you may remember that C++ is an extension of the C programming language) have been used for decades. Experience shows that building programs from functions is beneficial, particularly when structured design techniques are used.

Why Structured Design?

The most important reasons for structured software design are derived from the software life cycle.

The Software Life Cycle One of the most valuable tools to come into use in the 1970s was the concept of a **software life cycle** for dealing with the different tasks of the software development process. By isolating tasks and specifying areas of focus, it became

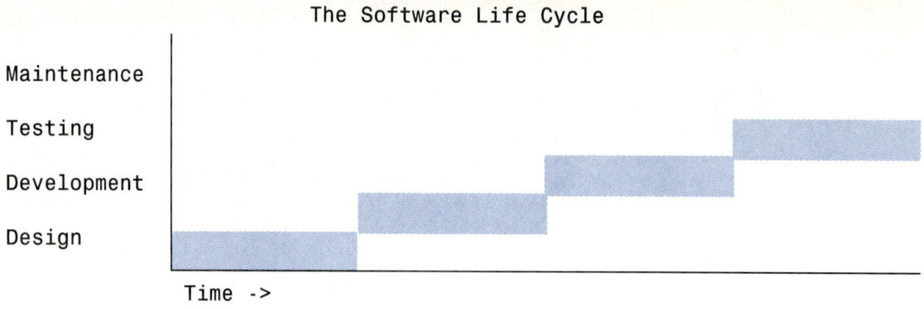

FIGURE 12.1 The Software Life Cycle

possible to do a more efficient and accurate job of producing software within budget and on time.[1]

Software has a given length of time that is its useful lifespan. The lifespan of some software is short. Most software for the CP/M operating system came and went rather quickly. Other pieces of software continue to be used for a long time. The vi editor for Unix is nearly as old as I am. The lifespan of software is called the *software life cycle*.

During the life cycle of a program, there are several distinct phases. First is usually analysis and design. Next comes development, testing, and then maintenance. The maintenance phase is when all bug fixes and enhancements are done. Figure 12.1 shows the software life cycle.

There are many views of just what phases the software life cycle should contain. The information here is not meant to reflect any one software design methodology. Instead, it is a generic summary of the main phases of the software life cycle. More information is available on the software life cycle than you could possibly want to know. However, the concepts presented here will help provide an understanding of the basics. That is enough to begin to design and develop robust and reusable software.

The Design Phase The design phase occurs first in the software life cycle. When software is well designed, it generally contains far fewer errors than if it is just thrown together.[2]

During the design phase, the designers gather a list of requirements from the people who will use or sell the software. They may examine competing products. They often do surveys of potential users. If they are writing the software to replace a paper-based system, they will look at the printed forms. This helps them find out what information the current system gathers and processes.

The overall goals of the design phase are to communicate accurately and completely with the users and to provide users with all the information they need to determine what they want from the software. You must then create a software model that accurately reflects the users' specifications. This model is usually a combination of diagrams that show the architecture of the software, and a text description of how the software works. The model must be easy to modify and maintain.

Specific goals of the software design phase are as follows:

- Determine what is and is not part of the system.
- Determine which parts of the system can be automated and/or computerized.
- Create a model of the existing system that includes both the data and the processes that manipulate the data.
- Design a specification document that reflects the ways the users of the system do business.
- Write the specification to enhance information hiding, code reusability, and independence from the operating environment.
- Eliminate as many design errors as possible before coding begins.
- Enhance the specification to reflect modular design.

[1]For references from the period, see Philip W. Metzger, *Managing a Programming Project* (Englewood Cliffs, NJ: Prentice Hall, 1981), as well as P. Bruce and S.M. Pederson, *The Software Development Project: Planning and Management* (John Wiley & Sons, 1981).

[2]This was recognized as far back as the 1960s. See C. Bohn and G. Jacopini, "Flow Diagrams, Turing Machines and Languages with Only Two Formation Rules," *Communications of the ACM,* Vol. 9, No. 5 (May 1966), pp. 366–71. See also Edgar Djikstra, "Go To Statement Considered Harmful," *Communications of the ACM,* Vol. 11, No. 3 (March 1968), pp. 147–48.

The Development Phase The overall goal of the programming phase is to create a software system that will be efficient, robust, and modifiable as well as meet all of the specifications. Specific goals include the following:

- Write the program according to the design specification and the model.
- Write the program in a way that makes the software robust (i.e., crash-proof) and modular. Also endeavor to eliminate errors and document any programmer assumptions.

The Testing Phase The overall goal of the testing phase is to be certain that the application is robust, runs correctly, and meets the specifications.

The Maintenance Phase The overall goal of this phase of the software life cycle is to quickly get the user up and running on the program. This includes getting the program installed and giving the user enough information or training so that he can quickly learn the software.

The software must then be maintained as needed. This requires fixing errors and adding new features when users request them. The code must be retested as it is maintained. The engineers who perform the maintenance must also modify the comments in the code to reflect the changes in the program.

Finding Problems Early Of the four phases shown in Figure 12.1, which do you think costs the most? Most of my students usually guess that development is the most expensive, but that's not correct. It's maintenance. Fixing bugs, adding new features, and other maintenance tasks are often where 75 to 85 percent of the money spent on a piece of software goes. In my experience, it's closer to 85 percent than to 75 percent. This means that anything we can do to bring down the cost of maintenance will save us money.

TIP: Don't be afraid to spend extra time designing software. It will pay off quickly in the other phases of the software life cycle.

Many large software companies have found that extra time and money spent in design can lead to huge savings during maintenance. Almost without exception, developers use the extra time in the early phases of the project to do structured design and development.

In software development projects, it's always true that the earlier you find a problem, the less expensive it is to fix it. If bugs are found in a piece of software after it is released (the maintenance phase), it is a very expensive problem. Companies have actually had to send out free versions of their software with fixes for serious bugs that users found. This is very costly, and it hurts a company's reputation.

If software errors are found during testing, the developers can typically fix them for less than one-tenth of what it would cost to fix during maintenance. If bugs are found during development, the cost of fixing them is usually less than one-tenth of what would be spent to fix them during testing. If problems are discovered during design, the price of fixing them is normally less than a tenth of the cost of fixing them during development.

TRAP: Rushing into development without adequate design can drive up the cost of software.

The result is that if it costs \$1 to fix a bug during the design phase, it will cost \$10 to fix during development. The same bug will cost at least \$100 to repair during testing and \$1,000 to fix during maintenance. Clearly, good design saves the most money.

Extending and Modifying Programs I was in computing for several years before I realized one basic fact: computer programs aren't written to be read by computers, they're written so humans can read them.[3]

Surprised? It's true. There's not a single computer on the market today that can read a C++ program directly. Every one of them needs a compiler or interpreter to translate C++ to binary.

TIP: Always try to make your programs easy for other programmers to read and understand.

If programs are meant to be read by humans, then we should make them as readable as possible. Programs that are easy for maintenance programmers to read are less expensive to maintain and enhance than programs that are hard to read. Structured design techniques assist us in creating readable programs.

Structured design will also help us build software modules that are easily integrated into a large variety of programs. And that's what I like—getting the most mileage out of my efforts. I tell my students that, in programming, laziness is a virtue. The more use they

[3]For a similar discussion, see Edward Yourdon and Carl Argila, *Case Studies in Object Oriented Analysis and Design* (Upper Saddle River, NJ: Prentice Hall, 1996), pp. 5–6.

can get out of a piece of code that they have written, the more successfully lazy they have been.

Another reason for using these techniques is that your success at a company is influenced by the quality of your code. Other people will at some point take over the maintenance of the program. If so, you'll have a much better reputation in the company if the program is well organized and easily maintainable.

Portability Successful software is often rewritten so that it can be easily moved to new operating systems or hardware. The process of making a program run on different hardware or under a different operating system is called **porting.**

Writing portable software can save the company you work for huge amounts of money. This is not an exaggeration. I have had actual job experiences where this has occurred. Structuring a program in the design phase can make writing highly portable programs a much simpler task.

Reliability Structured design naturally results in programs that are broken into small, reusable pieces. Each piece can be tested on its own. The benefit of this is that individual pieces of the program can be tested much sooner than the whole program. In fact, there can be (and should be) a lot of overlap between the development and testing phases of the software life cycle.

Because program pieces can be tested as development proceeds, testers can spend much more time testing them. The result is more reliable programs built from reliable, well-tested pieces.

Remember that well-designed programs tend to be more readable. Programs that are readable are easier for maintenance programmers to understand and modify in a reliable way.

Using Structured Design

At this point, I'll climb down off of my soapbox and stop preaching the benefits of structured design. Instead, let's take a look at how it's done.

Hitting the Bull's-Eye The three principal factors in a programming project are (1) quality, (2) cost, and (3) time. The main task when managing a programming project is optimizing these three factors. In practical experience, companies are too often extremely short-sighted and will sacrifice quality to optimize cost and time. Companies that take this approach do themselves no favors. Sacrificing quality to cost and time in the short term often leads to high costs and wasted time later.

Quality can be increased without adding significantly to cost and time by using what is known as a "bull's-eye" approach to software development. This approach is illustrated in Figure 12.2.

Figure 12.2 shows us that projects can be developed in stages. We start by implementing the core feature set. Once it's done, the testers can begin testing it. We can demonstrate it to the user and get feedback for additional design reviews.

As the project approaches the halfway point, many of the program's features should be up and running. We may even allow users to install the software and begin using it. That way, they can provide more feedback.

Based on the feedback from the previous two stages, we can target the software more accurately to the users' needs. We clean up any final bugs, write the documentation, and release the software.

Which features should be implemented in stage A depends on the situation. The following are some common priorities:

- Most "important" functions are finished first.
- Most quickly implemented functions are finished first.
- Most easily implemented functions are finished first.

Ways to implement the above priorities might include the following:

- Simulation of the user interface(s).
- Rapid prototyping of the potential product.
- Simulation of the software system using off-the-shelf components.

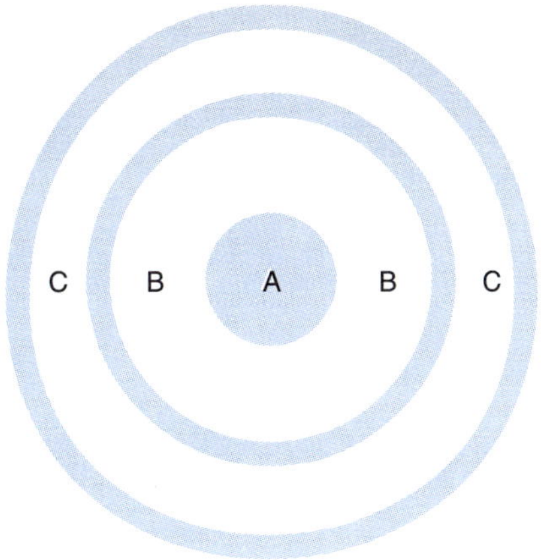

A—Early version of the program with only the essential features of the program completed.

B—Project nearing the halfway mark. Many features are in place. Fixes and enhancements of the early features are complete.

C—Project finished. The errors are corrected and the software is documented.

FIGURE 12.2 The Bull's-Eye Approach to Software Development

- Code the critical modules first.
- Top-down development.

Using the bull's-eye approach helps find errors early. The earlier an error is found, the less costly it is to fix it.

Top-Down Design There are many excellent books on structured design and development. Since the focus of this book is object oriented development in C++, we won't try to cover specific structured design methods. However, a simple and direct method of software design is **top-down design.**

The essence of this technique is to start with the most general statement of what a program does. From there, you break the general task into more specific tasks. Those tasks are broken down into subtasks, and so on until the lowest level is reached. When is the lowest level reached? There is no hard and fast rule for that. However, a good guideline to start you off is this: You're done when your design results in programs made up of functions that are shorter than one or two printed pages in length.

Let's look at an example. Let's say that we're building a computer game that we'll call Space Attackers. Space Attackers will be a game in which there are several rows of evil, mean, nasty, and incredibly bad-mannered attackers from outer space slowly moving back and forth across the screen together. When they reach either edge of the screen, every row will move down some and they'll start marching back the other way. Periodically, the attackers will fire their guns at the defender.

The defender will be drawn as a tank at the bottom of the screen. It will be able to move back and forth and shoot at the attackers. If any of the attackers' bullets hit the defender, or if any of the attackers reach the bottom of the screen, the defender dies. An attacker dies when it is hit by the defender's bullet.

Between the attackers and the defender are a few barriers that the defender can use for shelter. Figure 12.3 illustrates what Space Attackers might look like.

By describing the game, we've stated its **functional specification.** A functional specification lists everything that a program does. You must have this before you start writing the program or you won't know when it's finished.

Once we write a functional specification, we can start the design. First we draw a diagram that gives the most general statement of what the program does. The diagram for Space Attackers is shown in Figure 12.4.

FIGURE 12.3 **Space Attackers**

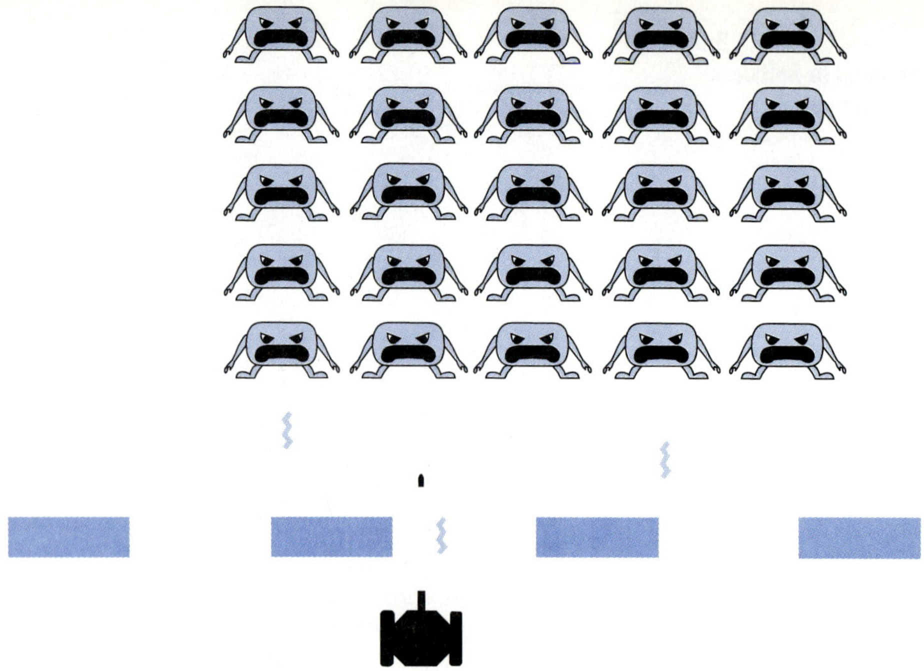

FIGURE 12.4 **The First-Level Design Diagram for Space Attackers**

There it is. Not much to look at, is it? However, its value becomes clearer when we start to break this task down. Figure 12.5 shows the first level or so of subtasks.

As you can see, the diagram is beginning to be helpful to a C++ programmer. The major tasks that are needed to perform the general task of running the Space Attacker game are now shown. All of them except *Init Game* are done repeatedly until the game ends.

Let's focus on the task of animating the evil horde of Space Attackers. If we were to draw the next level of subtasks for that task, it would resemble Figure 12.6.

This is top-down design in action. We start with a very general diagram of what the program does. Each successive diagram grows more and more specific. If we were doing a diagram for a game we really wanted to implement, we would need to break down each of the second-level tasks just the way we did with *Animate Attackers*.

FIGURE 12.5 **Space Attackers Diagram with Subtasks**

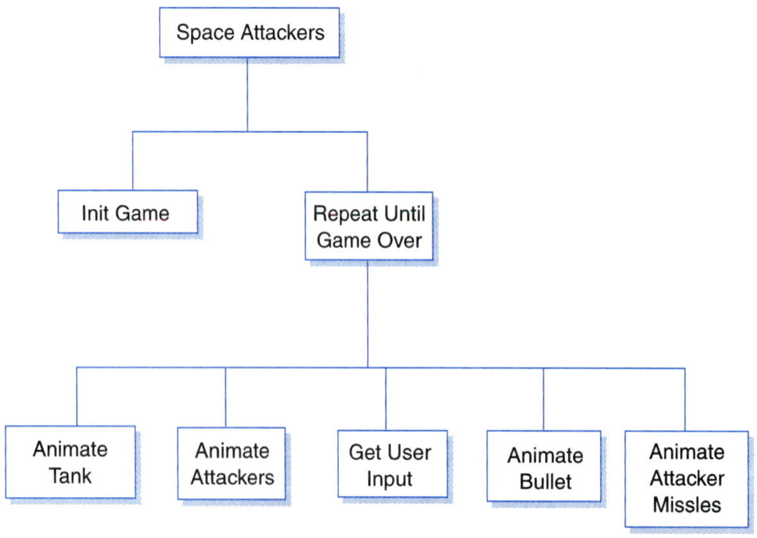

FIGURE 12.6 Space Attackers with More Subtasks

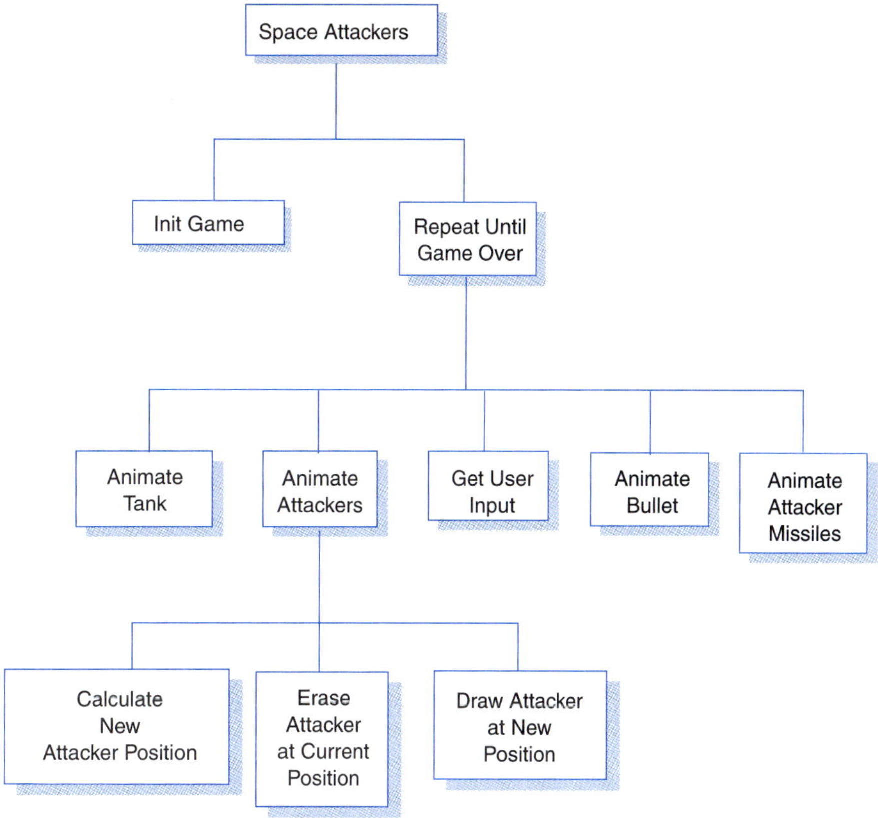

Modularizing Programs As you can see from the last few figures, top-down design means breaking a program down into more and more specific tasks. Breaking programs into small, reusable pieces is called **modularization.** Any computer program can be broken down into clearly defined modules.

Creating a Function

C++ functions give us a way to create C++ programs that are composed of modules. These modules correspond to the boxes in a top-down design diagram. If we were writing the Space Attackers program, we would create functions for each of the boxes in Figures 12.5 and 12.6.

You already know how to write functions in C++. We have been using a function in every program we've written. It's called `main()`.

Creating any C++ function is done in essentially the same way as creating `main()`. Hands On 12.1 illustrates this by showing a program that calls a function to clear the screen.

Hands On 12.1

Objective

Write a program that:

Calls a function to clear the screen.
Declares a 2-D array of integers.
Fills the integer array.
Displays the contents of the integer array.

Experiment

Type the following program into your IDE or text editor. Compile, link, and run it.

```
//-----------------------------------------------------------------------------
// Include Files
//-----------------------------------------------------------------------------

#include <iostream.h>
// End Include Files------------------------------------------------------------


//-----------------------------------------------------------------------------
// Prototypes
//-----------------------------------------------------------------------------

void ClearScreen(void);

// End Prototypes---------------------------------------------------------------



int main()
{
   // Local constants.
   const int MAX_ARRAY_ROWS = 10;
   const int MAX_ARRAY_COLS = 10;
   ClearScreen();

   int a2DArray[MAX_ARRAY_ROWS][MAX_ARRAY_COLS];
   int i,j;

   for (i=0;i<MAX_ARRAY_ROWS;i++)
   {
      for (j=0;j<MAX_ARRAY_COLS;j++)
      {
        a2DArray[i][j]=i*j+j;
      }
   }

   cout << "The current contents of the array are:" << endl;

   for (i=0;i<MAX_ARRAY_ROWS;i++)
   {
      for (j=0;j<MAX_ARRAY_COLS;j++)
      {
         cout << a2DArray[i][j];

         if (a2DArray[i][j] < 10)
         {
            cout << "  ";
         }
         else if (a2DArray[i][j] < 100)
         {
            cout << ' ';
         }
      }
      cout << endl;
   }
```

```
   int tempInt;
   for (i=0;i<MAX_ARRAY_ROWS;i++)
   {
      for (j=0;j<MAX_ARRAY_COLS;j++)
      {
         if (i<j)
         {
            tempInt=a2DArray[i][j];
            a2DArray[i][j]=a2DArray[j][i];
            a2DArray[j][i]=tempInt;
         }
      }
   }

   cout << "Press any character, then press Enter to continue.";
   char inputChar;
   cin >> inputChar;
   ClearScreen();

   cout << "The current contents of the array are:" << endl;

   for (i=0;i<MAX_ARRAY_ROWS;i++)
   {
      for (j=0;j<MAX_ARRAY_COLS;j++)
      {
         cout << a2DArray[i][j];

         if (a2DArray[i][j] < 10)
         {
            cout << "  ";
         }
         else if (a2DArray[i][j] < 100)
         {
            cout << ' ';
         }
      }
      cout << endl;
   }
   return (0);
}


void ClearScreen(void)
{
   // Local constant
   const int MAX_SCREEN_ROWS = 25;

   for (int i=0;i<MAX_SCREEN_ROWS;i++)
   {
      cout << endl;
   }
}
```

Results

When we run the program, it will first display a screen that looks like Figure 12.7.

After the user presses any character key and then presses Enter, the screen shown in Figure 12.8 will appear.

FIGURE 12.7 **First Screen of the Program in Hands On 12.1**

```
The current contents of the array are:
0  1  2  3  4  5  6  7  8  9
0  2  4  6  8  10 12 14 16 18
0  3  6  9  12 15 18 21 24 27
0  4  8  12 16 20 24 28 32 36
0  5  10 15 20 25 30 35 40 45
0  6  12 18 24 30 36 42 48 54
0  7  14 21 28 35 42 49 56 63
0  8  16 24 32 40 48 56 64 72
0  9  18 27 36 45 54 63 72 81
0  10 20 30 40 50 60 70 80 90
Press any character, then press Enter to continue.
```

FIGURE 12.8 **Subsequent Screen of the Program in Hands On 12.1**

```
The current contents of the array are:
0  0  0  0  0  0  0  0  0  0
1  2  3  4  5  6  7  8  9  10
2  4  6  8  10 12 14 16 18 20
3  6  9  12 15 18 21 24 27 30
4  8  12 16 20 24 28 32 36 40
5  10 15 20 25 30 35 40 45 50
6  12 18 24 30 36 42 48 54 60
7  14 21 28 35 42 49 56 63 70
8  16 24 32 40 48 56 64 72 80
9  18 27 36 45 54 63 72 81 90
```

Analysis

This program loads a 2-D array with integer values and prints them to the screen. It then swaps them to a different location in the array and prints them again.

Notice that this program declares all constants close to where they are used. If there was a global constant, its declaration would occur near the top of the program so that it would be visible to all functions.

Before it does anything else, the program calls the function `ClearScreen()`. As the name indicates, the function clears the screen. The function is called again after the contents of the array are printed for the first time.

The `ClearScreen()` demonstrates how a function is defined. Figure 12.9 shows the generic form of a function definition.

The first thing a function must have is a return type. The return type can be any valid C++ data type, such as `int` or `char`. In this case, the `ClearScreen()` function does not need a return type (some functions don't), so we use the type `void`.

All functions in a program must have a function name. The name is followed by a parameter list in parentheses. The parameter list can have any number of parameters, each with their own data type (`int`, `char`, `double`, and so forth). The `ClearScreen()` function doesn't use any parameters, so we put the word `void` in the parentheses.

Figure 12.9 shows that every function has a block of code associated with it. The block of code is contained in the curly brackets. The code block is executed when the function is called. The function is called when its name appears

```
return_type FunctionName(parameter1_type parameterName1,parameter2_type parameterName,... parameterN _type parameterName
{
    C++statements
}
```

FIGURE 12.9 The Generic Form of a Function Definition

A function's block of code is also called the function's *body*.

in another function. For example, in Hands On 12.1, the name `ClearScreen()` appears twice in `main()`. Each time the name `ClearScreen()` appears, program execution jumps to the `ClearScreen()` function and its code block is executed.

If a function declares a variable within its code block, the variable is visible only within that function. Take a look at the `main()` and `ClearScreen()` functions. They both have a variable called `i` declared inside them. The two different variables have the same name, but they are not accessible outside of the function in which they are declared.

The `main()` function also declares a variable named `j`. It is only accessible in `main()`. Example 12.1 has a version of the `ClearScreen()` function that tries to increment the variable `j`. If you tried to use the variable `j` in the `ClearScreen()` function, as the example shows, your compiler would tell you that the variable `j` is an undeclared identifier.

EXAMPLE 12.1 An Undeclared Identifier

```
void ClearScreen(void)
{
   for (int i=0;i<MAX_SCREEN_ROWS;i++)
   {
      // This is not allowed. j has not been declared in this function.
      j++;
      cout << endl;
   }
}
```

When a variable is declared in a function, it is accessible and usable from the point it is declared to the end of the code block it is declared in.

Naming Functions

There are a few simple rules for naming functions. First, function names must start with a letter. It can be uppercase or lowercase. The rest of the function name can contain numbers, letters, or the underscore character (_).

The ANSI C++ standard states that function names can be up to 1,024 characters long. However, not all compilers support such long function names. It's generally not convenient to make your function names longer than 30 or 40 characters anyway. They become too tedious to type.

When naming a function, uppercase letters are recognized by the compiler as being different than lowercase letters. That is, the function name `thisfunc()` is seen by the compiler as being different than the function names `ThisFunc()` or `thisFunc()`.

No spaces are allowed in function names. Table 12.1 shows some valid and invalid function names.

A function name should always describe the action that the function performs. Function names such as `DoStuff()` or `CalcValues()` are often useless to the maintenance programmer because they're too vague.

TABLE 12.1 Valid and Invalid Function Names

Valid Function Names	Invalid Function Names
CalculateInterestRate	Calculate Interest Rate
merge_text	merge-text
CleanupAndExit	Cleanup&Exit
Find100Ways	100Ways

TABLE 12.2 Good and Bad Function Names

Good Function Names	Bad Function Names
CalcInterestRate	DoStuff
TransferData	GP1toGP2CCDtaXfr4Rl
DisplayPicture	Picture
CloseWindow	FiniWin

Similarly, a function name should be understandable to most ordinary human beings. For instance, I once worked on a project where there was a function in the code named `GP1toGP2CCDtaXfr4Rl()`. Got any idea what that function does? Neither do most people from this planet.

However, if program code contains a function named `CalcInterestRate()`, what would you think that function does? That's right. It calculates the interest rate. Not only is the second name understandable to most people, it also gives the context that it is used in. You can expect that a function called `CalcInterestRate()` is for some sort of financial application.

Good function names describe what the function does. They do it in a way that is understandable to most maintenance programmers. They all contain a verb. Most contain a direct object in the name as well. The verb states what the function does. The direct object states the receiver of the verb's action.

If the function name does not contain an object, it must be well understood what the verb does. For instance, the function name `Print()` is acceptable because it is well understood that printing something sends output to the screen or printer. It would be better, however, to specify where the output is going—to the screen or the printer. The function name `Calculate()` is too vague to be useful. Calculate what? It is not well understood what is being calculated, even if you know the type of program for which the function is being written.

If a function name contains any abbreviations, they should be abbreviations that most people use and understand. For the most part, words in good function names should be completely written out. They should not contain cryptic abbreviations. A name like `GP1toGP2CCDtaXfr4Rl()` is gobbledygook and should be avoided. A function name like that doesn't do anyone any good.

Bad function names are vague, undescriptive, or contain too many abbreviations. They do not give any information about the context in which they are used. They do not contain verbs. Table 12.2 lists some good and bad function names.

What Happens When a Function Is Called?

When a function is called, we also say that it is invoked. Program execution jumps from the spot in the program where the function is invoked to the beginning of the function. At the end of the function, program execution returns to the point where the function was called.

For example, in Hands On 12.1, the first thing that happened was that the `main()` function called the function `ClearScreen()`. Whenever this happens, program execution jumps to the `ClearScreen()` function. All statements between the opening and closing curly brackets ({ and }) are executed. At the end of the `ClearScreen()` function, program execution returns to the point where `ClearScreen()` was invoked.

Parameters are actually passed to functions by copying them onto the program's stack. The stack is an area of memory used for passing parameters and for automatically allocated variables in functions. The number of parameters and variables a function may have depends on the amount of memory available for the stack.

Passing Information to a Function

We often need to pass information to functions. This is done through the parameter list. The parameter list may contain as many parameters as you like, within the limits of your computer's memory.

Example 12.2 demonstrates how parameters can be passed to a function through the parameter list. It shows the `ClearScreen()` function with one parameter. The parameter is the number of lines on the screen. Notice that the parameter has a name and a type, just like a variable. A parameter is visible only in the code block of the function to which it belongs.

EXAMPLE 12.2 A Version of `ClearScreen()` with a Parameter

```
void ClearScreen(int maxScreenRows)
{
   for (int i=0;i<maxScreenRows;i++)
   {
      cout << endl;
   }
}
```

When the `ClearScreen()` function is called, an integer value must be passed to it or the program will not compile. Example 12.3 demonstrates different ways the `ClearScreen()` function in Example 12.2 can be called.

EXAMPLE 12.3 Calling the `ClearScreen()` Function in Example 12.2

```
int main()
{
   ClearScreen(25);
   int rows=100;
   ClearScreen(rows);
   return (0);
}
```

In Example 12.3, the program calls the `ClearScreen()` function twice. The first time, it passes the function a literal integer value, 25. The second time the program calls `ClearScreen()`, it passes an integer variable called `rows` through the parameter list. The value in `rows` is 100. It makes no difference to the operation of the `ClearScreen()` function whether we pass it a literal integer value or an integer variable. Either way, `ClearScreen()` works correctly because it is getting an integer.

Example 12.4 demonstrates some problems that can occur if we use the `ClearScreen()` function improperly. In this example, the program calls `ClearScreen()` three times. The first time, the program tries to pass `ClearScreen()` a character. Even though this is an odd thing to do, it can work. C++ compilers will probably give an error. However, if we adjust the compiler settings, we can force it to change this error to a warning. This is never a good idea.

EXAMPLE 12.4 Calling `ClearScreen()` with Wrong Parameters

```
int main()
{
   ClearScreen('C');
   float badValue=25.25;
   ClearScreen(badValue);
   ClearScreen("If a function expects an int, never give it a string.");
   return (0);
}
```

One of the strengths of C++ is that it is a strongly typed language, which means that it enforces variable and parameter types. It doesn't allow us to use mixed-type expressions willy-nilly. We saw in earlier chapters that we can get around this to a certain extent by using type casting. Be very careful with type casting and mixed-type expressions. It is far better to always pass an integer to a function that expects an integer than it is to type cast the parameter to an `int`.

Example 12.4 also demonstrates an attempt to call `ClearScreen()` with a floating point number in its parameter list. This also can work if we adjust the compiler settings. By default, most compilers will report this as an error. If it does work, the fractional part of the floating point number will (hopefully) be truncated. Most C++ compilers follow this behavior. However, you can't depend on it.

TIP: Always pass data of the correct type to a function. If it expects an integer type, pass an integer. If it expects a character, pass it a character, and so on.

In the last attempt to call `ClearScreen()` in Example 12.4, the program tries to pass it a string. This is extremely bad programming practice. It should be reported as an error by your compiler.

If a function expects more than one parameter, the parameters are separated by commas. Each parameter must have a type declared for it, even if it is the same type as the parameter before it. For example, if a function has two integer parameters in its parameter list, the word `int` must appear before each parameter name. Each parameter declaration must have comma separating it from the next parameter declaration.

Example 12.5 demonstrates a program that calls a function expecting two parameters. The example illustrates that the parameters can be of different types. It also demonstrates that arrays can be passed as parameters. Notice that the size of the array is not specified in the parameter list. C++ allows this so we can use the same function on different-sized arrays. Remember that an array of characters is a string. In C++, strings are terminated by the null character. So we know how long the array of characters is by the position of the null character.

EXAMPLE 12.5 A Function That Takes Two Parameters

```
#include <iostream.h>

void RepeatString(int repetitionCount,char outputString[]);

int main()
{
   RepeatString(10,"This is a string");
   int count=100;
   char aString[]="This is another string";
   RepeatString(count,aString);
   return (0);
}


void RepeatString(int repetitionCount,char outputString[])
{
   for (int i=0;i<repetitionCount;i++)
   {
      cout << outputString << endl;
   }
}
```

I have repeatedly stated that `main()` is a function. It may occur to you that `main()` might be able to take parameters. That is true. It is possible to pass values to `main()`. These parameters are values that the user types in on the command line when she runs the program. Command line parameters are presented in Chapter 21.

I have been leaving the parameter list of `main()` empty. If you want to, you can put the word `void` into the parentheses for `main()`. You can also just leave them blank.

Returning a Value from a Function

Information is passed into a function through the parameter list. It is passed out of a function by using the return value. To send a value out of a function, you must use the C++ keyword `return`.

Hands On 12.2

Objective

Write a program that uses a function to find the maximum of two values.

Experiment

Type the following program into your IDE or text editor. Compile, link, and run it.

```
#include <iostream.h>

int Max(int value1,int value2);

int main()
{
   int inputValue1,inputValue2,maxValue;

   cout << "Please enter a number and press Enter: ";
   cin >> inputValue1;

   cout << "Please enter another number and press Enter: ";
   cin >> inputValue2;

   maxValue=Max(inputValue1,inputValue2);

   cout << endl;
   cout << "The maximum of the two values you typed ";
   cout << "in was: ";
   cout << maxValue;

   return (0);
}


int Max(int value1,int value2)
{
   int maxValue;

   if (value1 > value2)
   {
      maxValue=value1;
   }
   else
   {
      maxValue=value2;
   }

   return (maxValue);
}
```

Results

```
Please enter a number and press Enter: 10
Please enter another number and press Enter: 20
The maximum of the two values you typed in was: 20
```

Analysis

This program calls a function named `Max()`. It finds the maximum of two integers that are passed in as parameters and returns the maximum to the `main()` function.

When the program executes, it asks the user for two integer values. After the user types them in, the program calls the `Max()` function. `Max()` uses a simple `if-else` statement to determine which of the two is the maximum value. It returns the largest value by using the statement

```
return (maxValue);
```

TIP: It is helpful to put the value you are returning from a function in parentheses.

The data that the `Max()` function returns does not have to be put in parentheses as I do throughout this book. When I was first programming if C, I ran across a few compilers that wouldn't evaluate return values properly if they weren't in parentheses. I got into the habit of using them for return values and have never stopped. I continue this habit because I think it makes the code clearer. It eliminates the possibility of misunderstanding. The compiler can't misunderstand, and neither can the maintenance programmer.

REMINDER: An Rvalue is anything on the right side of an assignment operator (=). An Lvalue is anything that can be put on the left of an equal sign.

In the program in Hands On 12.2, `main()` calls `Max()`. As far as `main()` is concerned, the `Max()` function evaluates to a value. It can be treated just like any other value. Function calls can be used just the way an Rvalue would be used. Functions that return values cannot be used as Lvalues.

Since `main()` is a function, it can return a value. In all of the programs we wrote so far, we returned the value 0 from `main()`. This is because many operating systems expect your programs to return a value. Typically, they want a zero if the program terminates normally. Most operating systems want your programs to return a nonzero value if there was an error.

Function Prototypes

Every function that you write in your C++ programs, with the exception of `main()`, should have a prototype. A **prototype** is a declaration of a function's name, return type, and parameter list. It enables the C++ compiler to do type checking on the return type and parameter list whenever the function is called.

A function prototype looks exactly like the first line of the function. The only difference is that the prototype is terminated by a semicolon (;). Example 12.6 repeats the program that was given in Example 12.5. The prototype for the `RepeatString()` function appears before `main()`. It looks like this:

```
void RepeatString(int repetitionCount,char outputString[]);
```

EXAMPLE 12.6 A Program That Calls a Function

```
#include <iostream.h>

void RepeatString(int repetitionCount,char outputString[]);

int main()
{
   RepeatString(10,"This is a string");
   int count=100;
   char aString[]="This is another string";
   RepeatString(count,aString);
   return (0);
}
```

```
void RepeatString(int repetitionCount,char outputString[])
{
    for (int i=0;i<repetitionCount;i++)
    {
        cout << outputString << endl;
    }
}
```

By putting function prototypes at the beginning of program files, you enable the prototype to be visible from the point it is declared to the end of the file. The result is that any function in the program file can call any other function, and type checking will be done for all calls.

TIP: Create a prototype for every function that you write except `main()`. The prototypes should go at the beginning of your program files.

The `main()` function never needs a prototype. It is called by the operating system. Don't ever try to call `main()` yourself. That is a very quick way to crash your program.

The easiest way to create a function prototype is to use your text editor's copy function. Simply copy the first line of every function to the top of the program file. Terminate each prototype with a semicolon, as shown in Example 12.6.

Structured Design with Functions

To properly structure your programs, all of your functions should follow a few basic guidelines. They should be modular, and they should hide their implementation whenever possible.

Modular Functions

A modular function has a name that describes what it does. It may seem odd to mention such a small detail. However, if you can't give your function a short name that tells what the function does, it probably does too much. You may need to break it down into a group of smaller functions.

To be modular, all functions should have one entry point and one exit point. It is possible to put multiple return statements in a function. Avoid the temptation to do this. Multiple returns in a function make it harder to maintain. It unnecessarily increases the possible paths through the function. Example 12.7 demonstrates a function that has multiple exits.

EXAMPLE 12.7 A Function with Multiple Exits

```
int AFunction(int aParameter)
{
    if (aParameter > 0)
        return -1;
    return 1;
}
```

Multiple exits don't do much damage to a short function like this. However, real functions that you write in commercial applications tend to be longer than this. Multiple exits from a long function can very easily confuse a maintenance programmer or a tester.

Functions should always have clearly defined interfaces. All information that goes into a function should be passed in through the parameter list. All information that is passed out of a function should be passed out through the return value.[4]

All functions in a program should be no more than two printed pages of code in length. This is a general rule of thumb, not a law written in stone. There will always be a few functions in your program that are several pages long. However, if the majority of functions in your program are longer than two printed pages, you should think about redesigning your program.

[4]It is possible to pass information out of a function through the parameter list. There are very valid and logical reasons for doing so. See Chapter 21.

A Black Box

All functions should hide their implementation. Example 12.8 illustrates what I mean. It shows a program that we saw earlier in this chapter. The program calls a function named `ClearScreen()`.

EXAMPLE 12.8 A Function That Hides Its Implementation

```
int main()
{
    ClearScreen(25);
    int rows=100;
    ClearScreen(rows);
    return (0);
}
```

Let's say that you are writing a program that calls the `ClearScreen()` function. Let's also suppose that you and I are working on the same project, and that I wrote the `ClearScreen()` function for you.

Do you care about the internal workings of the `ClearScreen()` function? Probably not. You shouldn't have to. As long as it does its job of clearing the screen to your satisfaction, that's all that concerns you.

As much as possible, this is the way that all functions should be written. Each function should perform a task. Other programmers using functions that we've written should not have to know the algorithm of the function to use it. As long as it produces the correct results, they're happy.

When functions are written in this manner, we say that they are a **black box.** The name *black box* indicates that the function does its task without you and I knowing how.

You use many black boxes every day. For example, do you know all of the internal workings of your telephone? How about your microwave oven? You may know the inner workings of a computer in great detail, but have no idea how to fix a car. The black box approach helps us to simplify our world. That includes the programs that we write. We learn just enough about them to make them do what we want.

Troubleshooting Guide

After reading this section, you should be able to:

- Recognize and fix errors that are commonly made when creating functions.
- Use debugging programs.

Mistakes Programmers Commonly Make When Creating Functions

One common error that programmers encounter when creating functions is to accidentally put a semicolon (;) on the end of the first line of the function. If you do this, the compiler will think that you are declaring a prototype. It may tell you that it's found an unexpected curly bracket ({) in your program.

It is also easy to forget the closing curly bracket (}) on a function. If your compiler tells you that it has found an unexpected end of file in your program, it may be that a closing curly bracket is missing.

If you get an error that some code at the end of your function is unreachable, you've probably ignored my advice about not using multiple return statements. Take the extra `return` statements out of your function if you want that error to go away.

All functions must return a value if they do not have the `void` return type. Forgetting the `return` statement at the end of a function is quite common. You will know you have done this when your compiler tells you that your function must return a value.

Using Debugging Programs

Most commercial compilers today come with debugging programs. If your compiler does not have a debugging program, you should invest in one as soon as possible. Debugging programs will save you large amounts of time and effort.

Programmers often refer to debugging programs as "debuggers." Most debuggers allow you to set breakpoints, single-step through programs, set variable watches, alter the values of variables, and evaluate expressions.

Setting Breakpoints When you set a breakpoint in a program that you're debugging, the program will execute until it reaches the breakpoint. When it does, the debugger stops program execution and displays the source code of the program. You can then examine the state of the program.

Advanced debuggers will allow you to set conditional breakpoints. When the breakpoint is encountered, a condition is checked. If the condition is true, debugger halts program execution. If not, it just continues. For instance, you can set a breakpoint condition to stop the program on the tenth time the debugger encounters the breakpoint.

When you test your program and find that it crashes, the first thing you'll need to do is find the location in the code where the crash occurs. An easy way to do this is to set a breakpoint at a likely spot in the code; then run the program. If the program crashes before the debugger encounters the breakpoint, you must move the breakpoint toward the beginning of the program. You may set several breakpoints throughout the program and execute from breakpoint to breakpoint until the crash occurs. This helps track down the statement causing the crash.

Once you find where the program crashes, you set a breakpoint just before the problem statement and run the program again. When the breakpoint is encountered, you can examine the state of the program just before it crashes and look for clues as to why it fails.

Single-Stepping Through Programs Setting breakpoints enables us to skip over large sections of our programs that we know are working. It is often very beneficial, however, to step through our programs one line at a time. Debugging programs enable us to do exactly that.

As we step through the program, we can watch the changes in the variables. We can also view the program logic. It is not always what we expect it to be.

Setting Variable Watches To be valuable, debuggers must enable us to examine the state of program variables. This ability is crucial to being able to tell what state a program is in. Most program crashes are due to variables taking on wrong or unexpected values. Typically, our program sets a variable or group of variables to something we did not plan for. The incorrect or unexpected values put the program into an illegal state. The result is that the program doesn't function correctly.

To find the cause of the problem, we must be able to see how the values of variables change as the program executes. We do this by setting a watch. When we set a watch, we are telling the debugger that we want to watch the contents of a variable. It will usually display the variable and its current contents somewhere on the screen. As we step through the program, we can watch the variable's value change.

Altering Variable Values Advanced debuggers enable us to set the value of variables as a program executes. We can use this ability to force the program down a particular logic path. That is, we can use it to make loops start or stop, or to make a program execute an `if` or `else` statement. This is highly desirable when we are testing programs.

Evaluating Expressions We use conditions to control loops and program branches. Debuggers give us the ability to evaluate conditions. This enables us to see why a particular condition may evaluate to unexpected values. It also enables us to evaluate complex conditions a piece at a time.

Other Debugger Features Most debuggers can either step over or into a function. Stepping over a function means executing it without showing the code being executed. When you step into a function, the debugger displays each line of the function it executes. You step over a function when you know it works and you just want the results it produces. You step into a function when you want to debug it.

Many debuggers also automatically display the return value of a function. This is especially helpful when you do not have the source code for a function that you are using in your program. For example, if you link your program to a commercial library, you may have the object code for a function but not the source code.

C++ programming is based on objects. The objects contain data. To verify that an object is in a valid state, your debugger should allow you to inspect the object. That is, it should allow you to see the value of all of the member data. If any of the data members are objects, you should be able to inspect them. Without this ability, debugging C++ programs is extremely difficult.

Summary

Structured program design requires that we break programs down into sections or modules. Each module should perform a single task, or a group of highly related tasks. In C++, these program modules are called *functions*.

There are many reasons that a program must use functions for structure. Most of them are derived from the software life cycle. The software life cycle is the useful lifespan of a program. Research and experience have shown that maintenance is by far the most expensive phase of the software life cycle. Structured design helps reduce the cost and effort of maintenance.

Top-down design is a simple method of structured design that developers have used for many years. Top-down design is done by breaking a program down into subtasks. These subtasks are in turn broken down into smaller subtasks until the subtasks are small enough. Finding the point where they are small enough is mainly a matter of experience.

We use functions to create C++ program modules. Every function must have a name. It must also have a return type, a parameter list, and a function body. Information is input into a function through the parameter list. It is output from a function through the return type. You should create a prototype for every function that you write except `main()`.

In general, functions should follow the black box rule. That is, a programmer should not need to know the internal workings of a function to use it. If the interface is completely specified, any programmer should be able to invoke a function that you write.

Review Questions

1. What is structured design?
2. What is the software life cycle?
3. What are the phases of the software life cycle?
4. Which phase of the software life cycle is most expensive?
5. What is top-down design?
6. What is a function?
7. How can functions be used in structured design?
8. How is information passed to a function?
9. How do you get information out of a function?
10. What is a function prototype? How is it created? What does it do?

Exercises

1. Write a program that uses a function to square a number. Call the function `Squared()`. Your program should invoke `Squared()` to calculate the squares of 2, 10, and –5. The square of a number is that number times itself.
2. Write a program that uses a function called `Power()`. The `Power()` function should match the following prototype exactly:

   ```
   int Power(int aNumber,int thePower);
   ```

The `Power()` function should raise the number in the `aNumber` parameter to the power in the `thePower` parameter. Your program should demonstrate the `Power()` function by calculating the answers to the following: 2^5, 10^3, and -3^7. The `Power()` function only needs to handle positive powers. That is, the user should not be able to pass in a negative value for `thePower`. *Hint:* Use a `for` loop that starts from 0 and stops when the loop counter variable is equal to `thePower`.

3. Write a program that uses a function called `PrintPrimes()`. The `PrintPrimes()` function should calculate all of the prime numbers between 1 and the number that is passed in and print them to the screen. It should match the following prototype exactly:

```
int PrintPrimes(int upperLimit);
```

If `PrintPrimes()` is successful at finding some prime numbers, it should print them out and return the total number of prime numbers that it found. *Hint:* There is no easy way to find prime numbers. The most straightforward way is to iterate through every number between 2 and `upperLimit` inclusive. Divide each number by all of the numbers below it. This implies a `for` loop in a `for` loop.

4. Write a program that uses a function that calculates the area of a rectangle. The area is found by multiplying the length of the rectangle by its width. The function should match the following prototype:

```
int RectangleArea(int length, int width);
```

It should calculate the area using the parameters `length` and `width`, then return the answer. Demonstrate that your function works by having your program calculate the areas of the following rectangles:

Rectangle	Width	Length
1	10	12
2	81	3
3	9	9
4	50	21
5	11	183

5. Write a program that uses a function that calculates the area of a circle. The area of a circle is found using the formula πr^2, where π is the value 3.14159 and r is the radius of the circle. Your function should match the following prototype:

```
double CircleArea(double radius);
```

Demonstrate that the function works by having your program find and print the area of circles of the radius 10, 5.5, 0.453, and 20.

6. Modify the program in Example 12.6. Your program should get a string from the user. It should also ask the user how many times to repeat the string. It should then call the `RepeatString()` function to print the string the specified number of times.

7. Write a program that uses a function that calculates the total length of the sides of a rectangle. The total length is found by adding two times the length to two times the width ($2L + 2W$). The function should match the following prototype:

```
int RectangleEdgeLength(int length, int width);
```

It should calculate the total length of the sides using the parameters `length` and `width`, then return the answer. Demonstrate that your function works by having your program calculate the total edge lengths of the following rectangles:

Rectangle	Width	Length
1	10	12
2	81	3
3	9	9
4	50	21
5	11	183

8. Write a program that uses a function that calculates the circumference of a circle. The circumference of a circle is found using the formula $2\pi r$, where π is the value 3.14159 and r is the radius of the circle. Your function should match the following prototype:

```
double CircleCircumference(double radius);
```

   Demonstrate that the function works by having your program find and print the circumference of circles with the radius 10, 5.5, 0.453, and 20.

9. Write a program that calls a function to print a string in reverse order. The function should take any size character array in its parameter list. The program should demonstrate that the function works by invoking it at least three times with three different strings.

10. Write a program using a function named `StringLength()`. The `StringLength()` function should have the following prototype:

```
int StringLength(char inputString[]);
```

   This function should count the number of characters (excluding the null character) in the parameter `inputString`. It should return the total as the return value. Have your program demonstrate that the function works correctly by calling it at least three times with three different strings as input.

Chapter Glossary

Black Box A modular unit of program code, such as a function, that will perform a task without our knowing about how it is implemented.

Functional Specification A list of everything a program does.

Modularization Breaking programs into reusable blocks of code with clearly defined interfaces.

Porting Rewriting software so that it will run on another operating system and/or different kind of computer.

Prototype A declaration of a function's name, return type, and parameter list.

Software Life Cycle The useful lifespan of software.

Top-Down Design A design technique that starts with general statements and proceeds to more and more specific tasks.

13 Object Oriented Programming

Objectives

After reading this chapter, you should be able to:

- Understand and explain what a C++ object is.
- Understand and explain the concept of encapsulation.
- Understand and explain the concept of polymorphism.
- Understand and explain the concept of inheritance.

Preview

One of the primary purposes of this book is not just to teach C++, but to teach object oriented programming as well. These are not necessarily the same thing. During my time as a college professor and my employment in the software industry, I have seen many programs that were written in C++ but were not object oriented. Object oriented programming requires a specific way of thinking. This chapter introduces the concepts that are central to object oriented programming.

The Concept of an Object

An object in software is a representation or a model. The model is made up of data and functions. Together the data and functions model the way something behaves. I know that this is not the clearest of definitions, but it is accurate. **Software objects** represent things in the real world, things that don't exist, and ideas.

Modeling the Real World

An architectural design program might enable us to create a wall object. In software, we would want that wall object to behave exactly as a real wall does, or as close to it as possible. The wall object in software is not a real wall. It exists only in the computer.

Creating a software model of the real world enables us to manipulate the software objects as if we were manipulating a real object. In the preceding example, I might use several wall objects to build a house in the computer. I could look at the house, repaint it, possibly even navigate my way through it. All this can be done without actually building the house.

Modeling Ideas

Another example of a software object is a dragon. I spent part of my career in private industry writing computer games. I actually have had occasion to create a dragon object in software. Dragons don't exist, but you and I as software developers are not limited by that. We can easily create dragon objects in software.

It's also common in the business world to create objects that exist only as ideas. One example is a bank account. Surprisingly enough, a bank account is not a real thing. You can't paint it, you can't touch it, you can't take it home and put it in your closet. It doesn't really exist. A bank account is an idea that we all pretend exists. We have little bank books describing it, we get letters from our bankers about it. However, it is nothing more than an idea.

The idea of a bank account is very often modeled in software. In fact, a significant percentage of all of the software ever written is primarily for dealing with bank accounts.

Encapsulation

Why do we create objects? Software engineers successfully wrote programs for many years without software objects. One of the main reasons that object oriented languages became popular is that they encapsulate data. In other words, software objects group related data together and control access to it. This is called **encapsulation** or **data hiding.**

Data Hiding

Most function oriented languages, such as C or Pascal, provide some means of encapsulating data. However, it is not as strictly enforced as it is in object oriented languages like C++.

Encapsulation helps us write better software. With software objects, we have the opportunity to strictly control access to the data in an object. We can set limits on the values that the data can receive. We can validate the data in any way we need to as it is set. We can enforce control over which parts of the program can access the data, and which can't. All of this control helps us ensure that the object contains valid data at all times.

In our earlier example of a dragon object for a game, all of the information that the software needs about the dragon should be private to a dragon object. No other part of the software should have direct access to that data. Any access that is allowed is through a very well-defined interface. This ensures that the dragon object is properly initialized, and that it behaves in the way dragons should.

Data in objects is stored as **member data.** If a piece of data is a member of an object, access to the data is controlled through the object's interface of **member functions.**

Sending Messages to Objects with Member Functions

When we develop objects, we define an interface for them. The interface is a set of functions that can perform operations on the data. That is part of encapsulation. In C++, the interface functions are called *member functions*.

You can think of an object as a very exclusive club. Only members can get access to anything inside the clubhouse. In this case, the members are functions, and the clubhouse is the object. The only functions that can change member data in an object are the member functions. If there is an error in an object's data, the first place to look for software bugs is in the member functions.

When a program calls a member function, it sends a message to the object to instruct it to perform an action on itself. Member functions are the method by which we send that message. That's why member functions are also called **methods.**

By sending a message to an object, we tell it what operations to perform on its data. The rest of the program is unable to perform those operations directly. They must be done through the member functions. That's why we say that the member functions define an interface. They form the set of all operations that can be performed on the member data in an object.

Code Reuse Through Inheritance

If objects are created properly, they can be easily reused in a variety of programs. They can also be used as building blocks for other objects. For instance, we can create a generic car object in software. The generic car's member data describes its characteristics. We can perform specific operations on the car software object. These operations are defined by the member functions.

If you want to make a particular type of car object, a sports car for instance, you can use the generic car object as a building block. This technique is called **inheritance.** A sports car can do anything other types of cars can do. It can also do things other cars can't. We can use the member functions of the generic car object for most of what a sports car does. Features that are unique to the sports car can be introduced simply by adding a few member functions to the sports car object.

What if the sports car does something that other cars do, but it does that thing differently? An example is acceleration. A generic car doesn't accelerate very fast, but a sports car does (that's the whole reason for buying a sports car). They both do the same thing—accelerate. However, they do it differently.

In a case like this, software objects allow us to create a member function that replaces or enhances a function of the object that it was built from. An acceleration function can be added to the sports car object that replaces, or overrides, the acceleration function in the generic car.

Code Reuse Through Polymorphism

True software objects support a feature called **polymorphism.** The prefix *poly* means *many*. To *morph* something is to map it or change it from one form to another. So polymorphism is a one-to-many mapping. This means that we are able to create objects that can perform the same operation with many objects. Let's take the example of a string of characters. It makes sense for us to want to occasionally put one string onto the end of another. It also makes sense for us to want to add a single character on the end of a string. We want to perform the same operation, appending something onto the end of a string, with two different types, strings and characters. Objects allow us to create two member functions with the exact same name. So in this case, we could create two member functions called `Append`, one for appending single characters onto the end of strings and the other for appending strings onto the end of strings. This is polymorphism.

Through polymorphism, software objects can define a consistent set of operations for many different types of objects. That set of operations can be extended by other programmers to include objects that the original designer knew nothing about. Polymorphism makes it possible to add features to existing objects without having to completely rewrite them.

Summary

An object in software is a representation or model of something. It can model an idea, or something in the real world.

An object contains member data and member functions. Member functions are also called *methods*. All access to the member data is through the member functions. Therefore, the member functions form an interface for the object. They form the set of operations that can be performed on an object.

Because access to member data is through the member functions, we say that the data is encapsulated. Encapsulating data in objects helps us write better software because it helps us ensure that the data is in a valid state.

When a member function is called, we say that we are sending a message to the object. The purpose of sending a message to an object is to perform an operation on it or to ask it about its current state.

Objects help us reuse existing code. Through inheritance, we can use objects as the building blocks of other objects. Through polymorphism, we can extend the capabilities of existing objects.

Review Questions

1. What is a software object?
2. Why has object oriented programming become so important to the software industry?
3. What is encapsulation?
4. What is inheritance?
5. What is polymorphism?
6. What is member data? Why is it used?
7. What are member functions? Why are they used?
8. Why are member functions called *methods*?
9. Why is it that only an object's member functions have access to member data?
10. What can be modeled with software objects?

Exercises

1. Create the design for a car software object by making a list of the data that you think the car object should contain. Also list the operations that would need to be performed on the data.
2. Create the design for a sports car software object using the car object you created in Exercise 1. Indicate the data and operations that the car object would provide. Indicate the data and member functions you would add to make the generic car into a sports car.
3. Create the design for a family minivan using the car object you created in Exercise 1. Indicate the data and operations that the general car object would provide. Indicate the data and member functions you would add to make the generic car into a minivan.
4. Explain why you could use the generic car object as a building block for both the sports car and the minivan. What do you think the relationship between these three objects says about the thought processes you need to go through to do object oriented programming?
5. Look back at the partial design for the game Space Attackers in Chapter 12. Define the most important objects you think you would need to implement that game. Define at least three objects, and define the interface for each.
6. Using the partial design for the game Space Attackers in Chapter 12 as a starting point, create a set of top-down diagrams that details the design for the game. Be as complete as you can.
7. Using the object designs you created in Exercise 5 and the top-down design diagrams you created in Exercise 6, write a pseudocode version of the `main()` function for the Space Attackers game. Indicate what objects you would declare and the actions you would perform on them. Do not write C++ code. If you need help with writing pseudocode, look back at the Objective portions of the Hands On examples in the last several chapters. Most of them contain a pseudocode description of the Hands On program.
8. Continue creating the pseudocode program you started in Exercise 7. Select one of the objects you defined in Exercise 5. Write pseudocode versions of no more than five of the member functions that you defined for it.
9. Continue creating the pseudocode program you started in Exercise 8. Select another of the objects you defined in Exercise 5. Write pseudocode versions of no more than five of the member functions that you defined for it.
10. Continue creating the pseudocode program you started in Exercise 9. Select an object you defined in Exercise 5 for which you have not written any pseudocode. Write pseudocode versions of no more than five of the member functions that you defined for it.

Chapter Glossary

Data Hiding See **Encapsulation.**

Encapsulation Controlled access to data. In object oriented programming, data is encapsulated in an object and access to it is through the object's member functions.

Inheritance Using one object as the building block of another object. The new object can inherit the features and abilities of the old object.

Member Data Data in an object.

Member Functions Functions in an object. They form the set of operations that can be performed on the object.

Methods See **Member Functions.**

Polymorphism The ability to perform the same operation on many different types of objects. Polymorphism allows us to extend the features of existing objects.

Software Object A software representation of a thing or an idea. A software object must support encapsulation, inheritance, and polymorphism.

14 C++ Objects

Objectives

After reading this chapter, you should be able to:

- Write a program that uses C++ objects.
- Explain the use of constructors and destructors.
- Write constructors and destructors for C++ objects.
- Use `public` and `private` access specifiers appropriately.

Preview

Chapter 13 introduced to the concept of software objects. This chapter demonstrates the basics of how to create software objects in C++.

Objects Are Data Types

We saw in earlier chapters that C++ comes with built-in data types, such as `int` or `float`. When we as C++ programmers create an object, we create a new data type. In effect, objects are a way to extend the C++ language. We can add nearly any data type to C++ and define a set of operations that can be performed on the data type. By extending the C++ language in this way, we create data types that model the problem we want to solve.

Creating an Object

In C++, we create objects through the use of classes. Hands On 14.1 demonstrates the creation of a simple class.

Hands On 14.1

Objective

Define a timer object that contains:

Member Data:

The current number of clock ticks.

Member Functions:

A function that initializes a timer.
A function that performs any required clean-up on a timer object.
A function to make the timer tick.
A function to reset the timer to zero.
A function that returns the current number of clock ticks.

Experiment

Type the following program into your IDE or text editor. Compile, link, and run it.

```
#include <iostream.h>

class timer
{
public:
   timer(void);
   ~timer(void);

   void Tick(void);
   void Reset(void);
   int GetTime(void);

private:
   int currentTime;
};

timer::timer(void)
{
   currentTime = 0;
}

timer::~timer(void)
{
}

void timer::Tick(void)
{
   currentTime++;
}

void timer::Reset(void)
{
   currentTime = 0;
}

int timer::GetTime(void)
{
   return (currentTime);
}

int main()
{
   cout << "The timer is starting." << endl;
   for ( timer aTimer; aTimer.GetTime() < 100; aTimer.Tick() )
   {
      cout << aTimer.GetTime() << "    ";
      if ((aTimer.GetTime() % 10) == 0)
```

```
            cout << endl;
    }

    return (0);
}
```

Results

```
The timer is starting.
0
1     2     3     4     5     6     7     8     9     10
11    12    13    14    15    16    17    18    19    20
21    22    23    24    25    26    27    28    29    30
31    32    33    34    35    36    37    38    39    40
41    42    43    44    45    46    47    48    49    50
51    52    53    54    55    56    57    58    59    60
61    62    63    64    65    66    67    68    69    70
71    72    73    74    75    76    77    78    79    80
81    82    83    84    85    86    87    88    89    90
```

Analysis

This example program contains a class definition. All class definitions in C++ begin with the keyword `class`. Creating a new class creates a new data type. The class definition contains a list of all of the class's member functions and its member data. The member functions form the set of all operations that can be performed on an object of the class. We create the list of member functions by inserting their prototypes into the class definition.

In this example, we used a class definition to create a new data type called `timer`. If you look at the `main()` function, you'll see that we declared a variable of type `timer` at the beginning of the `for` loop. The only actions that can be performed on a timer are the actions given by the member functions. For instance, resetting a timer with the `Reset()` function is a valid action on a timer. If we were to type the statement

```
aTimer++;
```

somewhere in the `main()` function of our program, the C++ compiler would give an error. Postincrementing is not a valid operation on a timer variable.[1]

When you create a class, you must also list the member data. The member data in the timer class is an integer containing the current number of ticks that have occurred since the timer started.

Once a class is created, it can be used in a program just like any other data type. In Hands On 14.1, we are able to declare variables of type `timer` because we defined the `timer` type.

The member functions for the `timer` class appear after the definition of the class itself. The name of each member function must be preceded by the name of the class that the function is a member of, and the scope resolution operator. The scope resolution operator is the double colon (::). Attaching the class name to the function name with the scope resolution operator tells the C++ compiler that the function is a member of a class.

For instance, the first line of the `Reset()` function looks like this:

```
void timer::Reset(void)
```

This line says that the name of the function is `Reset`. The return type is `void`. The statement `timer::` tells us that the `Reset()` function is a member of the `timer` class. It is possible to have another `Reset()` function in the same program that is

[1]However, we can *make* postincrement a valid action on a varible of type timer. We just define a postincrement function for the timer class. See Chapter 16.

a member of another class. It is even possible to have a `Reset()` function that is not a member of any class. The C++ compiler (and the maintenance programmer) will not be confused if you use the scope resolution operator.

There are two functions in the `timer` class definition that look rather odd at first. Their prototypes are

```
timer(void);
~timer(void);
```

The first of these two functions is a constructor; the second is a destructor. C++ objects call constructors each time they create an object. The constructor initializes the object into a known state. Whenever a C++ program finishes with an object, it calls the object's destructor. The destructor function performs any necessary cleanup on the object before it is deleted. In this example program, no clean-up needed to be performed on the `timer` object. However, the destructor was included in the class definition for completeness.

Take a look at the `main()` function. Whenever it invokes a member function, it does so by stating the object name, followed by a period, followed by the member function name. For example, `main()` calls the `GetTime()` function of the `timer` object like this:

```
aTimer.GetTime()
```

public and private

Only member functions have direct access to the member data. Example 14.1 illustrates this by giving a slightly different version of the `main()` function from Hands On 14.1. Notice that an attempt is made in `main()` to access the member data. This will not compile. The C++ compiler will flag this as an error.

EXAMPLE 14.1 Trying to Access Private Member Data

```
int main()
{
   timer aTimer;

   aTimer.currentTime++;    // This is an error!
   cout << "The timer is starting." << endl;
   for ( ; aTimer.GetTime() < 100; aTimer.Tick())
   {
      cout << aTimer.GetTime() << "    ";
      if ((aTimer.GetTime() % 10) == 0)
         cout << endl;
   }

   return (0);
}
```

The reason that `main()` can't get access to `currentTime` is because `main()` isn't a member of the `timer` class. You might justifiably ask, "If `main()` isn't a member of the `timer` class, why can it get access to the member functions?"

The answer is that the member functions are defined as being public. Any function can have access to a public member of a class. The reason `main()` can't get access to the member data is that the data is defined as being private. Private members of a class can be accessed only by class members.

The next questions my students invariable ask is whether the member data can be public and the member functions can be private. The answer is yes to both. However, you should *never* define member data as being public. There is no reason to do so, and it completely undermines the purpose of having classes. The point of creating a class is to create a self-contained object that is reusable and easily modifiable. Whenever you define public data members, any function in the program can change the member data. If the data becomes corrupted or erroneous, you will have no idea where the problem is. Neither will the maintenance programmer. When you make a class's member data public, the class can become so difficult to reuse that most other programmers will just avoid it.

All data members should be private. Any access you give to member data should be through public member functions.[2]

Using the keyword `private` declares member data to be private. The keyword `public` declares member functions to be public. In Hands On 14.1, the program declares the member data `currentTime` to be `private`. It declares the member functions `timer()`, `~timer()`, `Tick()`, `Reset()`, and `GetTime()` to be `public`.

When programmers use an object, they are most interested in the object's interface. If you know what the interface is, you know how to use the object. Since the public member functions form the interface, it is common to put the public member functions first in your class. That way, you make it easy for other programmers to find out how to use your class. They simply look at the beginning of the class definition for its interface.

Member Data

The member data in a class can be of any type. That is, we can define member data as being of type `float`, `double`, `char`, or whatever else we want to use. We can even use other objects. Any data type that is valid in our program can be used to define the private data members of a class.

When we define a class, we are *only* defining it. All we do by creating a class is tell the C++ compiler what will be in the type. We also tell it what operations can be performed on the type. Defining a class does not allocate any memory for any variables. Therefore, no initializations can be done in a class. Example 14.2 shows an attempt to initialize the data member of the `timer` class in the class definition. This code will not compile. When a class is defined, no memory is allocated for it, so it can't be initialized.

EXAMPLE 14.2 An Attempt to Initialize Data in a Class Definition

```
class timer
{
public:
    timer(void);
    ~timer(void);

    void Tick(void);
    void Reset(void);
    int GetTime(void);

private:
    int currentTime=0;    // This won't work!
};
```

Programs only allocate memory when they declare a variable of the class type. In Hands On 14.1, the program allocates memory when it declares the variable `aTimer`. In technical terms, the variable `aTimer` is an **instance** of an object. Declaring a variable and allocating memory for it **instantiate** an object.

When a program instantiates an object, it allocates only enough memory for the member data of the object. For instance, when the variable `aTimer` is declared in Hands On 14.1, enough memory is allocated for one integer because that is the member data that the `timer` object contains.

All objects of the same type share the same member functions. Each one has its own private copy of its data. Example 14.3 shows another version of the `main()` function from

[2] Virtually everyone who writes a book about C++ will give you the same admonition. For instance, see Scott Meyers, *Effective C++* (Reading, MA: Addison Wesley Longman, Inc., 1992), pp. 71–72, and Stephen Prata, *The Waite Group's C++ Primer Plus* (Mill Valley, CA: Waite Group Press, 1991), pp. 356–57.

FIGURE 14.1 **All Objects of Type `timer` Share Member Functions**

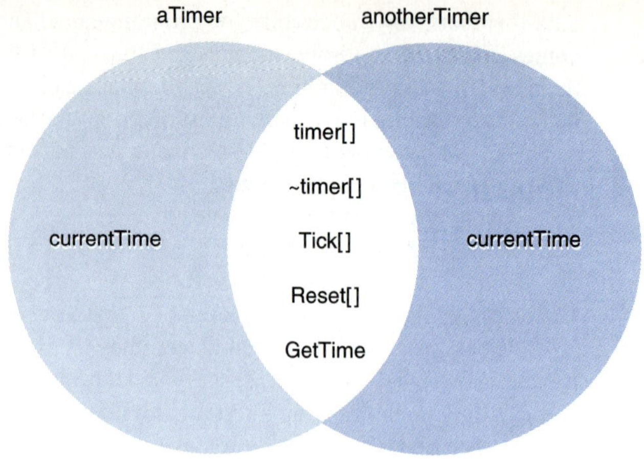

Hands On 14.1. In this version, we declare two variables of type `timer`. Each timer variable has its own copy of the data. Both share the same set of member functions. Figure 14.1 illustrates this.

EXAMPLE 14.3 Declaring Two Variables of Type `timer`

```
int main()
{
   timer aTimer, anotherTimer;
   cout << "The timer is starting." << endl;
   for ( ; aTimer.GetTime() < 100; aTimer.Tick())
   {
      cout << aTimer.GetTime() << "    ";
      if ((aTimer.GetTime() % 10) == 0)
         cout << endl;
      anotherTimer.Tick();
      anotherTimer.Tick();
   }
   cout << anotherTimer.GetTime();
   return (0);
}
```

The code in Example 14.3 demonstrates that we can create two (or more) variables of type `timer`. Memory is allocated for them when they are declared. They each have their own copy of the private data member `currentTime`. They both share the same member functions.

Member Functions

Member functions perform operations on member data. The names of member functions can be almost anything you want. The rules for naming member functions are the same as the rules for naming any other type of function.

Member functions are called through an object. That is, we must have a variable of the object to call a member function. In Hands On 14.1, the program declares a variable called `aTimer`. It uses the variable to call functions that are members of the `timer` class. It does this by stating the variable name, followed by a period, followed by the member function's name, like this:

```
aTimer.GetTime();
```

This C++ statement calls the `GetTime()` function. When `GetTime()` is called, it operates on the member data in the variable `aTimer`.

In Example 14.3, we declared two variables of type `timer`. C++ compilers are not confused when the same member functions are called for different `timer` variables. When a program invokes a member function, the member function always operates on the variable for which it was called. For example, the call

```
aTimer.GetTime();
```

calls the `GetTime()` function for the `aTimer` variable. Any references in `GetTime()` to the private data member `currentTime` refer to the `currentTime` in `aTimer`, not to the one in `anotherTimer`.

In the same manner, the call

```
anotherTimer.GetTime()
```

calls the `GetTime()` function for the variable `anotherTimer`. During that call, any reference to `currentTime` is to the `currentTime` in `anotherTimer`, not to the one in `aTimer`. All member functions work this way.[3]

Constructors and Destructors

The ~ character is called a *tilde.*

In Hands On 14.1, there is a function that has the same name as the class, `timer()`. There is also a function called `~timer()`.

When a member function has the same name as the class it is a member of, that function is called a *constructor*. A constructor is a special function that is called whenever an object of its class is created. In Hands On 14.1, the program calls the `timer()` function whenever it creates a variable of type `timer`. Constructors are used to initialize data members of a class into a known state. In Hands On 14.1, the constructor initializes the private data member `currentTime` to zero. That is its known state. In this implementation, we know that `timer` variables always start with the time set to zero.

TIP: Always write a constructor for every class that you create. Write the constructor so that it initializes all member data to a known state.

A common error in C is to use a variable before it is initialized. C++ constructors help fix that. One of the most important habits you can get into at this point is to always create a constructor for every class you write.

The other special function in the `timer` class is called `~timer()`. It is a destructor. C++ provides destructors so that our classes can clean up after themselves. In the case of the `timer` class, the destructor doesn't do anything. It could have been safely left out. When we look at dynamic memory allocation, we'll see that destructors are extremely important in some classes.

Destructors have no return type and they never have any parameters in their parameter lists. In fact, compilers will usually not even allow you to type the word `void` into a destructor's parameter list.

Default Parameter Values

Like any other function (except destructors), member functions can have parameters. Any member function in a class that has parameters can have default parameters. Let's suppose that we want to allow programmers using our `timer` class to set the initial time when a timer variable is created. One way we can do that is to add a parameter to the constructor.

Example 14.4 demonstrates a constructor with a parameter. It also has a default value for the parameter. This is shown in the prototype. Figure 14.2 shows the output of the program in Example 14.4.

EXAMPLE 14.4 A Constructor with a Default Parameter

```
#include <iostream.h>

class timer
{
public:
   timer(int startTime=0);
   ~timer(void);

   void Tick(void);
```

[3]There's an exception to almost every rule in C++. The exception to this is static member functions. See Chapter 23.

```
    void Reset(void);
    int GetTime(void);

private:
    int currentTime;
};

timer::timer(int startTime)
{
    currentTime = startTime;
}

timer::~timer(void)
{
}

void timer::Tick(void)
{
    currentTime++;
}

void timer::Reset(void)
{
    currentTime = 0;
}

int timer::GetTime(void)
{
    return (currentTime);
}


int main()
{
    timer timer1, timer2=5,timer3(100);

    cout << "The timers are starting." << endl;
    for ( ; timer1.GetTime() < 100; timer1.Tick())
    {
        cout << timer1.GetTime() << "    ";
        if ((timer1.GetTime() % 10) == 0)
            cout << endl;
        timer2.Tick();
        timer2.Tick();
        timer3.Tick();
    }
    cout << endl;
    cout << timer2.GetTime() << endl;
    cout << timer3.GetTime() << endl;

    return (0);
}
```

As you can see from Example 14.4, a function's default parameter appears only in the prototype, not in the function definition. In this case, the parameter `startTime` in the `timer` constructor has a default value of 0.

The program in Example 14.4 declares three timers. The constructor is called once for each variable declaration. Only two of them, `timer2` and `timer3`, have initial values.

FIGURE 14.2 The Output of the Program in Example 14.4

```
The timers are starting.
0
1  2  3  4  5  6  7  8  9  10
11   12   13   14   15   16   17   18   19   20
21   22   23   24   25   26   27   28   29   30
31   32   33   34   35   36   37   38   39   40
41   42   43   44   45   46   47   48   49   50
51   52   53   54   55   56   57   58   59   60
61   62   63   64   65   66   67   68   69   70
71   72   73   74   75   76   77   78   79   80
81   82   83   84   85   86   87   88   89   90
91   92   93   94   95   96   97   98   99
205
200
```

The program does not give the variable `timer1` an initial value when it is declared. Therefore, the constructor assigns the default value to `startTime` when it is called. The result is that the `currentTime` private member of the `timer1` variable is set to zero. The output from the program shows that this is so.

There is something else important to notice about this example. The program initializes both `timer2` and `timer3` to values. They use different notations. However, in both cases, the constructor is called. The declaration for `timer2` uses an equal sign (=). Because it is a variable declaration, the C++ compiler sees it as a call to the constructor. The example program declares the `timer3` variable using what is called *function notation*. It looks like a call to the constructor. For this reason, many C++ programmers prefer this style of variable initialization. However, there is no hard and fast rule about which to use. They both do the same thing.

A Simple String Object

Let's use what we have learned in the last several chapters to build a simple string object. This will become one of the fundamental objects that we will use in the text editor we'll write in this book.

The first thing we must do when designing an object is to decide what information it will contain. A string contains a sequence of characters. It may also contain the length of the character sequence—or it may not. This is where seemingly simple design considerations become slightly more complicated.

If we create a string object that contains an integer that holds the length of the character sequence, then every string in our program will take up a little extra memory. It won't be much extra memory, but it will be some. The alternative is to count the number of characters in the string every time we want to know its length. That takes processor time, which means the program is a bit slower. Not much slower, but slower nonetheless.

So what is more important, speed or size? The answer is, it depends. If speed is absolutely critical, then wasting a little memory is probably acceptable. If memory is scarce, then using a little extra CPU time is probably not important. The point here is that you must know something about the context in which the string class will be used to make the appropriate design decision. There is no one universal string class that will work in every single program. However, it is reasonable to expect that we can write a string class that will work in many or even most programs.

Many C++ compilers already come with a class called "string." Therefore, we'll call our class `cpp_string`, which stands for *C++ string*.

We know that our string class must contain a sequence of characters. That character sequence is one of the string's data items. All data members in classes should be kept private. To save memory, let's not store the length of the string. Instead, we'll use the null character to mark the end of the string. When we want to know the length of the string, we'll count the number of characters before the null character.

Hands On 14.2

Objective

Define an object named `cpp_string` that contains:

Member Functions

A constructor to initialize the object.
A destructor to perform clean-up.
A function that appends a character to the end of the string.
A function that gets a character in the string.
A function that returns the length of the string.

Member Data

An array of characters.

The program should do the following:

Prompt the user to enter characters, or ^E to end.
While the user has not entered ^E
{
Get a character from the user.
Append the character to the end of the string.
}
Print the string that the user typed in.

Experiment

Type the following program into your text editor or IDE. Compile, link, and run it.

```
#include <iostream.h>

const int STRING_LENGTH = 80;
class cpp_string
{
public:
   cpp_string(void);
   ~cpp_string(void);

   int AppendCharacter(char newCharacter);
   char GetCharacter(int characterIndex);

   int GetLength(void);

private:
   char charString[STRING_LENGTH];
};

cpp_string::cpp_string(void)
{
   for (int i=0; i<STRING_LENGTH; i++)
   {
      charString[i] = '\0';
   }
}
```

```
cpp_string::~cpp_string(void)
{
}


int cpp_string::AppendCharacter(char newCharacter)
{
   int newCharacterPosition;

   for (newCharacterPosition=0;
        charString[newCharacterPosition] != '\0';
        newCharacterPosition++)
   {
   }

   if (newCharacterPosition < STRING_LENGTH-1)
   {
      charString[newCharacterPosition] = newCharacter;
      charString[newCharacterPosition+1] = '\0';
   }
   else
   {
      newCharacterPosition = -1;
   }

   return (newCharacterPosition);
}


char cpp_string::GetCharacter(int characterIndex)
{
   char returnCharacter = '\0';

   if (characterIndex < STRING_LENGTH)
   {
      returnCharacter = charString[characterIndex];
   }

   return (returnCharacter);
}


int cpp_string::GetLength(void)
{
   int i=0;
   while (charString[i] != '\0')
   {
      i++;
   }

   return (i);
}



int main()
{
   cpp_string aString;
```

```
    char inputCharacter = '\0';
    int done = 0;

    cout << "Press Ctrl+E, then press Enter to stop entering the string.";
    cout << endl;
    while (!done)
    {
        cin>>inputCharacter;
        if ((int)inputCharacter == 5)
            done=1;
        else
        {
            aString.AppendCharacter(inputCharacter);
        }
    }

    cout << "The string you entered was :";
    for (int i = 0;i < aString.GetLength(); i++)
    {
        cout << aString.GetCharacter(i);
    }
    cout << endl;
    return (0);
}
```

Results

```
Press Ctrl+E, then press Enter to stop entering the string.
asdf das jkl;^E
The string you entered was: asdfdasjkl;
```

Analysis

Although this string class is not usable in a real application, such as the text editor we will write, it gives us a starting point for building a good string class.

The `cpp_string` class has five public member functions: a constructor, a destructor, `AppendCharacter()`, `GetCharacter()`, and `GetLength()`. It contains one private data member that is an array of 80 characters. The code for the member functions comes after the class definition.

Notice that the name of the class, followed by two colons, appears before the name of each one of the five member functions. As we mentioned earlier, the double colon (::) is called the *scope resolution operator*. It is used to state that these functions are members of the `cpp_string` class. The reason that this is necessary is because we can create functions in C++ that are not members of a class. For instance, it is possible for us to write a function in a program like this:

```
int AppendCharacter(char newCharacter)
{
    // Code for the function goes here.
}
```

This `AppendCharacter()` function is not a member of any class. We don't want the compiler to confuse this `AppendCharacter()` function with the one in the `cpp_string` class. By putting the class name and the scope resolution operator in front of the name, as we did in Hands On 14.2, we state that the function is a member of a class. The general form for class member functions is

```
return_type class_name::function_name(parameter_list)
{
    function code goes here
}
```

where return_type is the type of the data being returned, class_name is the name of the class of which this function is a member, function_name indicates the name of the function, and parameter_list is the list of parameters that is passed to the function.

The constructor for the class does not contain a declared return type such as int or void, because the constructor always returns the object that it constructs. Therefore, its name is also its return type.

The constructor uses a loop to initialize all 80 characters in the string to the null character. By doing this, it sets the string into a known state. Remember that a C++ compiler may or may not automatically initialize data that we don't initialize in our constructors. Therefore, we must assume that any uninitialized data members contain random values. All data members in a class should be initialized to a known state.

The destructor for this class doesn't do anything yet. We'll use it in later versions of the cpp_string class.

The AppendCharacter() function adds a single character onto the end of a string, if there is room. It returns the location in its array that the new character was stored in. If the function is unable to store the character in its array, it returns –1.

The first thing that the AppendCharacter() function does is use a loop to search for the position on which the character should be appended. This is necessary because the cpp_string class does not contain a data member that stores the position of the end of the string.

The loop searches for the null character at the end of the string. You might well ask, "What happens if there is no null character?" The answer is that the loop will continue marching through memory until it finds a zero, which is the ASCII value of the null character. This could cause serious problems, which is why we initialized the entire array to the null character in the constructor. That way, we guarantee that there is at least one null character in the array.

Notice that the if-else statement that follows the loop in the AppendCharacter() function checks to see if the new character position is less than STRING_LENGTH-1, or 79. Remember that arrays in C++ are numbered beginning with 0. Therefore, the locations in an 80-character array have the index numbers 0–79. The comparison in the if-else statement ensures that the last character position in the array that the AppendCharacter() function will write to is position 78. Position 79 in the array will never be written to. In the constructor for this class, all of the characters in the array were set to '\0' (the null character). Therefore, the character in array position 79 will never be anything but '\0'. Again, this ensures that we always have a '\0' terminating the string.

The GetCharacter() function retrieves a character from the string. It can be used to get any character in the range of 0–79. The if statement prevents this function from trying to get a character that is beyond the end of the array. If the index of the character is less than 80, the GetCharacter() function will return the character from the array. If it is greater than or equal to 80, the statement inside the if statement will be ignored. This function will simply return the value in the variable returnCharacter, which is '\0'.

The GetLength() function counts the number of characters in the string and returns that number.

All of the cpp_string functions are used in the main() function. It begins by declaring the variables it needs, and then prompting the user to enter a string.

The main() function then enters a while loop. The condition on the loop is !done. It initializes the variable done to zero when it is declared. Remember that in C++ truth is anything that evaluates to nonzero. Only the value 0 is false. In other words, the variable done is initialized to false when it is declared.

Recall that the logical NOT operator (!) inverts the logical value. So !done can be read, "NOT done." This is the C++ way of saying that we want the loop to continue while it's not done. In C++, !0 evaluates to one. One is true. The while loop will continue while its condition evaluates to true. As soon as the variable done is set to true, which is one, the loop will terminate.

Inside the loop, main() reads in a character and stores it in the variable inputCharacter. Next, an if-else statement checks the character to see if it has the ASCII value of 5. The character with the ASCII value of 5 is Ctrl+E. If the user typed in a Ctrl+E, the variable done is set to one. This will terminate the loop.

If the user types in any other character, the condition on the if-else statement will evaluate to false. This causes the else portion of the if-else statement to be executed. It contains a statement that appends the character onto the end of the string.

After the user enters characters and presses Ctrl+E followed by the Enter key, the while loop terminates.

The program prints a prompt to tell the user what the string was. The main() function begins a for loop that prints each character in the string. It uses the cpp_string's GetLength() function to get the number of characters in the string. As long as the variable i evaluates to less than the length of the string, the loop will continue.

For each iteration of the loop, one character from the string is output to cout. When the program finishes printing all of the characters in the string, the for loop ends. It sends an endline to the screen, and the main() function terminates by returning the value 0.

When you run this program, you will probably notice that it does not print back white space that you type in. That is, if you type in spaces or line feeds (by pressing the Enter key), the program will not print those back. We'll see why in the chapter on streams. We'll also see how we can change that and force the input streams to read in white space.

Improving the String Class

The string class in Hands On 14.2 is a reasonable start, but it has several problems. First, it can only store a maximum of 80 characters in a string. Our string class is also not very efficient. Every time we need to know its length, it must count all of the characters in the string. It would be faster to keep track of the length of the string and store it in a private data member.

It would also be more efficient to be able to set an entire string at once, rather than character-by-character. In addition, we will probably need to be able to copy one string into another like this:

```
cpp_string aString, anotherString;
aString.Set("As for Passepartout, he was a true Parisian of Paris.");
anotherString.Copy(aString);
```

Hands On 14.3 improves the string class introduced in Hands On 14.2.

Hands On 14.3

Objective

Define an object named cpp_string that contains:

Member Functions

A constructor to initialize the object.
A destructor to perform clean-up.
A function that sets the entire string.

A function that copies one string to another.
A function that appends a character to the end of the string.
A function that gets a character in the string.
A function that returns the length of the string.

Member Data

An array of characters.

The program should do the following:

Prompt the user to enter characters, or ^E to end.
While the user has not entered ^E
{
Get a character from the user.
Append the character to the end of the string.
}
Print the string that the user typed in.
Declare another string variable.
Initialize it to “The journey round the world in eighty days?”.
Print it.
Demonstrate the use of the `Copy()` member function in the string class.
Print the copied string.

Experiment

Type the program below into your IDE or text editor. Compile, link, and run it.

```
#include <iostream.h>

const int STRING_LENGTH = 80;

class cpp_string
{
public:
   cpp_string(void);
   ~cpp_string(void);

   void Set(char aCharArray[]);
   void Copy(cpp_string aCppString);

   int AppendCharacter(char newCharacter);
   char GetCharacter(int characterIndex);

   int GetLength(void);

private:
   char charString[STRING_LENGTH];
   int length;
};


cpp_string::cpp_string(void)
{
   length = 0;
   for (int i=0; i<STRING_LENGTH; i++)
   {
      charString[i] = '\0';
   }
}
```

```
cpp_string::~cpp_string(void)
{
   length = 0;
}


void cpp_string::Set(char aCharArray[])
{
   int i;
   for (i=0; (i<length) && (aCharArray[i]!='\0'); i++)
   {
      charString[i] = aCharArray[i];
   }
   length = i;
}


void cpp_string::Copy(cpp_string aCppString)
{
   int i;
   for (i=0; i<aCppString.length; i++)
   {
      charString[i] = aCppString.charString[i];
   }
   length = aCppString.length;
}


int cpp_string::AppendCharacter(char newCharacter)
{
   int newCharacterPosition = -1;

   if (length < STRING_LENGTH)
   {
      charString[length] = newCharacter;
      newCharacterPosition = length++;
   }
   return (newCharacterPosition);
}


char cpp_string::GetCharacter(int characterIndex)
{
   char returnCharacter = '\0';
   if (characterIndex < STRING_LENGTH)
   {
      returnCharacter = charString[characterIndex];
   }

   return (returnCharacter);
}


int cpp_string::GetLength(void)
{
   return (length);
}
```

```
int main()
{
   cpp_string aString;
   char inputCharacter = '\0';
   int done = 0;
   const char CONTROL_E = (char)5;

   cout << "Press Ctrl+E, then press Enter to stop entering the string.";
   cout << endl;
   while (!done)
   {
      cin >> (inputCharacter);
      if (inputCharacter == CONTROL_E)
      {
         done=1;
      }
      else
      {
         aString.AppendCharacter(inputCharacter);
      }
   }

   cout << "The string you entered was :";
   for (int i = 0;i < aString.GetLength(); i++)
   {
      cout << aString.GetCharacter(i);
   }

   aString.Set("The journey round the world in eighty days?");

   cout << endl << "aString = ";
   for (i = 0;i < aString.GetLength(); i++)
   {
      cout << aString.GetCharacter(i);
   }

   cpp_string anotherString;
   anotherString.Copy(aString);

   cout << endl << "anotherString = ";
   for (i = 0;i < anotherString.GetLength(); i++)
   {
      cout << anotherString.GetCharacter(i);
   }

   return (0);
}
```

Results

```
Press Ctrl+E, then press Enter to stop entering the string.
A short string^E
The string you entered was :Ashortstring

aString = The journey round the world in eighty days?
anotherString = The journey round the world in eighty days?
```

Analysis

Hands On 14.3 contains an implementation of two new functions, `Set()` and `Copy()`. It also uses a revised version of the `cpp_string` class, which keeps track of the length of its character string. If you compare this version of `main()` with the one in Hands On 14.2, you'll see that these changes did not affect the existing code in the `main()` function. We reused the same code in `main()` without alteration. All we did was add a few more statements onto the end of `main()` to demonstrate the new member functions. This is the great benefit of properly designed C++ programs. We can make major implementation changes inside objects, and yet the functions that use those objects do not need to be altered.

The first function in the `cpp_string` class that needed to be changed was the constructor. The statement

```
length = 0;
```

was added so that `length`, the new private data member, is initialized to a known state whenever a variable of type `cpp_string` is declared.

The destructor was also modified. It also contains a statement setting the length of the `cpp_string` to zero. This is not strictly necessary in this program. I put this in as a preventative measure. I've found that assignments in destructors such as this one can prevent problems when the code for the class is modified. If you're worried about efficiency, you should consider omitting such assignments in destructors. The maintenance programmer will just have to be more careful when updating the software.

There can be situations where we may need the null character at the end of the string. However, we'll handle those by appending it when it is needed, rather than by storing it at the end of the string.

The `Set()` function sets the entire string, rather than just one character at a time like `AppendCharacter()`. It does this by entering a `for` loop. The condition on the loop states that it will continue while the variable `i` is less than 80 and the character in `aCharArray[i]` is not the null character. Notice that we do not specify the length of the array `aCharArray` in the parameter list. This is just fine with C++. It allows you to pass arrays of unspecified length to functions.

There's an important point to note about the `Set()` function. It does not copy the null character onto the end of the character array in the `cpp_string`. The null character is no longer needed now that we're keeping track of the length of the string.

The `Copy()` function copies characters from one `cpp_string` object to another. It takes a `cpp_string` object as its parameter. If we look at the end of `main()`, we can see that program invokes the `Copy()` function by the object `anotherString`. The `aString` object is passed in as a parameter. All references in the `Copy()` function to private member data are to the member data of the object that invoked the function. In this case, the references to `charString[i]` and `length` are to the `charString[i]` and `length` members of `anotherString`.

To reference the members of the `cpp_string` object that is passed in through the parameter list, we must use the parameter name. In this case, the program passes the variable `aString` as the parameter. When `main()` calls the function, the contents of `aString` are automatically copied into the parameter `aCppString`. Therefore, `aCppString.length` is different than just `length`. The variable `aCppString.length` refers to the `length` member of the parameter `aCppString`. If we refer to just `length` by itself, it means the length member of the `cpp_string` that invoked the `Copy()` function.

We could add the statement

```
aString.Copy(anotherString);
```

into `main()`. If we did, the references in `Copy()` to the variable `length` would be to the `length` member of the `aString` object. The references to `aCppString.length` would refer to the `length` member of `anotherString`, which is the object that is passed in through the parameter list.

If you're wondering why the `Copy()` function can access the private members of two objects, just look back at the class definition. By declaring the member data as `private`, we tell the compiler that only objects of type `cpp_string` can access the private member data. The variables `aString` and `anotherString` are both of type `cpp_string`. Member functions of the `cpp_string` class can access the private data members of any `cpp_string` object that they "know about." In this example, the `Copy()` function knows about two `cpp_string` objects: the one that invoked the `Copy()` function and the one that was passed in through the parameter list.

As you might expect, the `Copy()` function copies the characters from one `cpp_string` object to another. It also sets the length of the `cpp_string` object to which the characters are copied.

The new version of the `AppendCharacter()` function is much simpler than the previous one. If the length of the string is less than 80 characters, the new character is added to the end of the string. The length is also incremented with a postincrement, which says that we are going to use the value in the variable length first, and then increment it. The result is that the value in `length` is assigned to the variable `newCharacterPosition`, and then `length` is incremented.

The `AppendCharacter()` function returns the index number of the position in the array where the character was stored. If it was not stored in the array, the function returns –1.

The `GetCharacter()` function did not need to be modified from the version in Hands On 14.2.

Like the `AppendCharacter()` function, the function `GetLength()` is simpler in this version. It just returns the value in `length`.

The first part of the `main()` function is unchanged from Hands On 14.2. However, we did add the statement

```
aString.Set("The journey round the world in eighty days?");
```

near the end. This calls the `Set()` function, which sets the private character array `charString` in the variable `aString` to the characters in the string "The journey round the world in eighty days?" We prove that the `Set()` function did its job by retrieving each of the characters from `aString` and printing them to the screen.

In addition, the `main()` function declares a variable of type `cpp_string` called `anotherString`. By using the `Copy()` function, `main()` copies the characters in the variable `aString` into `anotherString`. It also prints these two strings to demonstrate that the copy was done correctly.

Troubleshooting Guide

After reading this section, you should be able to:

- Recognize and solve constructor creation problems.
- Recognize and solve constructor parameter problems.

Omitting Constructors

What happens if you don't create a constructor for a class? Let's do a Hands On and find out.

Hands On 14.4

Objective

Define an object named `timer` that contains the following:

Member Functions:

A function that makes the timer tick.
A function that resets the timer.
A function that returns the current tick count.

Member Data

The current tick count.

Write a program that does the following:

Declares a timer variable.
While the timer has not ticked 100 times,

Output the current number of ticks.
Increment the timer.

Experiment

Type the following program into your text editor or IDE. Compile, link, and run it.

```
#include <iostream.h>

class timer
{
public:
   void Tick(void);
   void Reset(void);
   int GetTime(void);

private:
   int currentTime;
};

void timer::Tick(void)
{
   currentTime++;
}

void timer::Reset(void)
{
   currentTime = 0;
}

int timer::GetTime(void)
{
   return (currentTime);
}


int main()
{
   timer aTimer;


   cout << "The timer is starting." << endl;
   for ( ; aTimer.GetTime() < 100; aTimer.Tick())
   {
      cout << aTimer.GetTime() << "    ";
      if ((aTimer.GetTime() % 10) == 0)
         cout << endl;
   }

   return (0);
}
```

Results

```
The timer is starting.
12    13    14    15    16    17    18    19    20
21    22    23    24    25    26    27    28    29    30
31    32    33    34    35    36    37    38    39    40
41    42    43    44    45    46    47    48    49    50
51    52    53    54    55    56    57    58    59    60
61    62    63    64    65    66    67    68    69    70
71    72    73    74    75    76    77    78    79    80
81    82    83    84    85    86    87    88    89    90
```

Some compilers have an option that you can set to make the default constructor that the compiler creates initialize all data in an object to zero. This is very compiler-dependent. It is not portable, and you should not rely on it.

Analysis

The program in Hands On 14.4 appears to execute even without a constructor. Actually, it does have a constructor. If we do not provide a constructor for a class, the C++ compiler will create a default constructor when it compiles the program.

However, all the default constructor does is get an object created. It doesn't initialize the object into a known state. That's why the timer in this program started at 12. The 12 is a random value that was in the memory allocated for the private data member `currentTime`. The program faithfully performed its loop, printing the timer value and incrementing it each time. The fact that the timer didn't start at zero doesn't make a difference to the program.

For this reason, it is vital that you get into the habit of writing a constructor for every class that you create. Every data member of every class should be initialized into a known state.

TRAP: If we omit constructors from our classes, the data members of the classes will not be initialized into a known state.

Constructor Parameters

We saw earlier that constructors can have parameters. Example 14.5 shows a version of the `timer` class. Its constructor takes one parameter. However, if you type this program into your IDE or text editor and try to compile it, you'll get an error.

EXAMPLE 14.5 A Constructor with a Parameter

```
#include <iostream.h>

class timer
{
public:
   timer(int startTime);
   void Tick(void);
   void Reset(void);
   int GetTime(void);

private:
   int currentTime;
};


timer::timer(int startTime)
{
   currentTime=startTime;
}

void timer::Tick(void)
{
```

```
      currentTime++;
}

void timer::Reset(void)
{
      currentTime = 0;
}

int timer::GetTime(void)
{
      return (currentTime);
}



int main()
{
      timer aTimer;


      cout << "The timer is starting." << endl;
      for ( ; aTimer.GetTime() < 100; aTimer.Tick())
      {
            cout << aTimer.GetTime() << "    ";
            if ((aTimer.GetTime() % 10) == 0)
                  cout << endl;
      }

      return (0);
}
```

The problem in Example 14.5 is not exactly with the class but in how the `main()` function tries to use the class. The `main()` function declares a variable of type `timer` called `aTimer`. The constructor in the class requires that a parameter be passed to it. The variable declaration in `main()` did not pass a parameter. You might expect the compiler to solve this problem by generating the default constructor that takes no parameters. However, if you provide any constructors at all in your class, the compiler will not generate a default constructor.

If the statement in `main()` is changed to

```
timer aTimer = 0;
```

the compiler will not generate an error. The other alternative is to change the constructor so that it does not take a parameter. However, if we do this, we will not be able to initialize variables of type `timer` when they are declared.

One way to allow object declarations with or without an initialization is to use default parameters. When a constructor has a default parameter, variables of that type will be properly initialized whether or not an initialization is supplied when the variable is declared. For an illustration of this, take a look back at Example 14.4.

Summary

The rules of C++ enable us to extend the language by creating new types. The primary way of doing this is through the use of objects. A C++ object is created using a class.

C++ classes provide a method of modeling things in software. Anything can be modeled, including both things in the real world and ideas that exist only in our minds.

Classes have member data, which should always be private. They also have member functions, which can be public. Each variable of a class type has its own memory for its private member data. The member functions are shared between all objects of the same class type. Member functions can access private member data.

Classes have constructors and destructors. Constructors are used to initialize objects into known states. Destructors are used to do any clean-up that must be performed on objects when they are being deallocated.

Member functions, except for destructors, may have parameters. The parameters may have default values. A default value is the value that the parameter will have if no value is passed in the function call.

Review Questions

1. What is a C++ class? Describe its use.
2. What is member data?
3. Why is member data declared as private? What functions in a program can access them?
4. What does it mean when member functions are declared as public? What functions in a program can access them?
5. What is a constructor? Describe its use.
6. What is a destructor? Describe its use.
7. What is a default parameter? Describe its use.
8. How do the Hands On examples in this chapter demonstrate the ability of C++ to minimize the impact of change on programs?
9. What happens when we do not write constructors for our classes?
10. What potential problem can be encountered when a class contains a constructor that has a parameter, but no default value is defined for the parameter?

Exercises

1. Take a look at the `cpp_string` class in Hands On 14.2. In particular, explain what would happen if the `GetCharacter()` function was passed a value of –1. Name two ways that this class can be modified to solve this problem.
2. Using the `cpp_string` class given in Hands On 14.3, add a member function to the `cpp_string` class called `StringToCharArray()` that has the following prototype:

   ```
   void StringToCharArray(char charArray[]);
   ```

   The new function should copy the characters in the `cpp_string` object into the array of characters that is passed in through the parameter list. Write a program that uses this function and demonstrate that the function works.
3. Compare the `cpp_string` class in Hands On 14.2 to the one in Hands On 14.3. The primary difference between the two implementations is that the first keeps track of the length of a string using the null character, while the second uses an integer to store a length count. Explain the advantages and disadvantages of each implementation.
4. Write a program that uses the `cpp_string` class you enhanced in Exercise 2. The program should declare an array of `cpp_string` objects, like this:

   ```
   cpp_string allStrings[50];
   ```

   Your program should load every string in the array with strings of text. The text can be anything you want as long as it is 80 characters in length. Your program should enter a loop and print each string in the array of `cpp_string` objects to the screen.
5. Use the program you wrote for Exercise 4. Using the program in Hands On 11.1 (in Chapter 11) as a guide, write a program called *EditV2.cpp*. It should load an array of 100 `cpp_string` objects with text, and then display the first 20 lines of text. Your program should prompt the user for input. When the user presses Ctrl+U, your program should scroll up toward the beginning of the array 19 lines. If the user presses Ctrl+D, your program should scroll down 19 lines toward the end of the array.
6. Modify your program from Exercise 5. When the user presses Ctrl+B, your program should scroll up one line toward the beginning of the array. When the user presses Ctrl+E, your program should scroll down one line toward the end of the array.

7. Change your program from Exercise 6. When the user presses Ctrl+X, your program should exit.
8. Demonstrate that your program from Exercise 7 can be easily modified by changing the number of lines of text it displays to 23. Change the number of lines it scrolls when the user presses Ctrl+U or Ctrl+D to 22.
9. Add the ability to copy strings to the program you wrote in Exercise 8. When the user presses Ctrl+K, your program should copy the first line on the display to all of the currently displayed strings. Redisplay the screenful of strings.
10. Use the program you wrote for Exercise 9. Add the ability to set an entire string at once. When the user presses Ctrl+S, your program should clear the screen, prompt the user to enter a string, and store that string in the `cpp_string` object that is currently set as the top line of the screen (e.g., store it in `allStrings[top]`). It should then clear the screen and redisplay one screenful of text.

Chapter Glossary

Instance When a variable is declared in a program, that variable is said to be an instance of the type.

Instantiate To declare an instance of an object or type.

15 Designing Objects

Objectives

After reading this chapter, you should be able to:

- Determine the essential attributes of an object and their types.
- Determine the essential functions for an object's public interface.

Preview

This chapter deals with the skills that we need to acquire to design and develop robust, useful C++ objects. Be sure to attempt as many of the exercises at the end of the chapter as you can. They will walk you through the process of designing objects.

Identifying Essential Objects

Before we start designing objects in the software we write, we must determine what the objects are. That is, we must identify the objects that we use to build our software. Many books expounding a large variety of object oriented software design methods are currently available. Each has its own unique way of identifying objects that are essential to a software system. However, most of them share some common ideas.

The first is that objects must usually react to an **event.** An event is something that triggers a response from the software. Think about living things, like the person sitting next to you. If you poke that person, you will probably produce a reaction. The act of poking your neighbor (not a suggested activity) is an event. What your neighbor does when the event occurs is the reaction (you may need to duck).

Events come from a variety of sources. The person using the software triggers most of the events to which the software will respond. For example, when a user selects an item from a menu, that action is an event. The software must respond to that event. Pressing keys on the keyboard, moving the mouse, and clicking mouse buttons all cause events that the software may need to handle. Events can be caused by the passage of time (a timed backup, for instance). Sometimes events are generated by other objects in the system.

When you design objects, temporarily pretend that you are the object. Make it justify its existence. Say, "I am a *object_name.* My function is to *object_function.* The events that I react to are *event_list.*" If you have trouble stating the primary function of an object, or find that it does not react to any events, you probably don't need the object in the system.

The top-down design techniques presented in Chapter 12 identify the tasks that a program must perform. Knowing the tasks a program must accomplish helps us determine what events the software must respond to. It is often helpful to use a spreadsheet program and make a worksheet of all of the tasks that the program must handle. From this, generate a list of events that would cause each task to begin.

For instance, a text editor must save a document to a file. That is one of its tasks. It performs that task when particular events occur. One of the events would be the user selecting Save from the File menu. Another might be the user clicking a mouse button on a Save icon in a toolbar.

Once you identify the tasks and events, you select the appropriate object to handle the event. Here again, the worksheet can be useful. Start with a list of tasks in a column. In the next column, list the events that cause the task to be performed. In another column, list the objects that handle the event.

The primary function of an object is to encapsulate data and perform operations on it. If an object in your system doesn't store any data, you should strongly question whether you need the object.

You may also find it helpful to try and imagine your system without the object you are designing. Would it make a difference in the software if the object was eliminated? The larger the impact, the more likely that the object should be in the software.

As you are designing, you periodically encounter object operations and attributes that naturally cluster together. For instance, if an object contains a list, and the list length, and special functions that just operate on the list, then you probably need to create a separate object for the list itself. Operations and attributes that go together sometimes indicate that a new object needs to be created.

Object Attributes

In C++ terminology, *objects* are composed of member data and member functions. The data describes an object. An object's data is its attributes. You and I have attributes (height, weight, hair color, etc.) that describe us. All objects have attributes as well. Once we determine that an object is required in the software we are writing, we must ask ourselves what attributes are important for the object to have.

Finding Essential Attributes

The essential attributes an object requires depends entirely on the context of the object. For instance, a customer record object in a database program for a software store would probably include attributes such as name and address. It would probably not include shoe size. However, shoe size might be an important attribute in a customer record object in a database for a shoe store. Both databases need a customer record object. However, the important attributes are different for each context.

The events an object responds to can also help you determine what attributes an object requires. For instance, if you are writing a simulation of a hockey game, you will undoubtedly need a puck object in the software. The primary event that a puck object must respond to is coming into contact with another object (hockey sticks, goal nets, wall, player's faces, etc.). The puck must react by changing position, speed, or direction. Therefore, the puck must keep track of its current position, speed, and direction.

Another helpful way to isolate the important attributes of objects is to describe them. Several object oriented software design methodologies require a written description of each object in the software. You may or may not want to be that formal. However, it can still be helpful to sit down with another software engineer on the project and describe your software objects to her. As you do, she can write down a list of the important attributes. See how well your list agrees with your colleague's. Conducting design reviews such as this can help every member of your team design a better set of objects.

Choosing Attribute Types

After you've identified what attributes (member data) an object needs, you must choose a type for each attribute. This is not always straightforward. This also very often depends on the context.

For instance, if you are writing a 3-D aircraft simulation, you will need to keep track of the aircraft's current position as it flies through the 3-D simulated world. For a military or commercial jet simulation, you would probably store the aircraft's position as floating point numbers. This normally results in greater accuracy. Accuracy can be very important for a simulator that is used to train military or commercial airline pilots. However, for a game that people play on their personal computers, accuracy is often not as important as smooth animation. To get the performance you need on a personal computer, you may choose to sacrifice accuracy for speed. Tracking the user's position using integers is typically faster on microcomputers because they don't have the capability for processing floating point numbers that high-end hardware does. This example demonstrates how context can influence attribute data types.

As you select the type of each attribute, you must strive to be as flexible as possible. For instance, many designers of databases forget that people have a wide variety of names. I have a friend whose last name is Vander Hooven. He often complains to me about computer systems for businesses and government agencies that choke on his name. They were designed for people with a single last name, and they can't handle it when users enter two words for a last name. Often, he gets mail addressed to Vanderhooven, which makes him angry, or Van Derhooven, which he usually just throws away. If you have a hyphenated name, such as Blythington-Smith, you can probably relate to my friend's plight.

Unfortunately, systems designers often don't account for non-English punctuation in names. For instance, many punctuation marks are used in Spanish, French, and German names that are not used in English names. The same is true of names from many other nationalities. When we select or create types for object attributes, they must account for all possibilities.

In actual practice, it's next to impossible to account for all future possibilities when you select object attributes. Therefore, you must design your objects in such a way that you can change the type of attributes without impacting other objects in the system.

Object Operations

A class's set of public member functions form the set of all operations that can be performed on the object. Another way to say this is that they form the object's public interface.

TIP: Object interfaces should be both minimal and complete.

Designing the interface for a class can be difficult. Our task as object designers is to create an interface that is minimal but complete.

Designing a Minimal Interface

It's easy to create too many functions in an object's interface. We want our objects to be convenient and powerful to use. So we tend to add more functions than we really need.

On most projects, other programmers will use our objects. They may find our objects difficult to understand if the objects' interfaces are overburdened with extra functions. They tend to get lost in a maze of detail.

In addition, it's not up to us as programmers to try and determine all possible future uses of our objects. That doesn't mean we should disregard all future needs. However, C++ provides us with ways to extend the functionality of existing objects.[1] Using these methods, we can enhance or alter the functionality of existing objects. If our objects employ a well-designed, minimal set of functions for their interfaces, enhancing them later is generally straightforward.

TIP: An object's public member functions should not contain extra or duplicate functions.

Suppose, for example, we create an object that contains a public member function called `Copy()`. Some users may prefer the name of the function to be `Duplicate()`. Others might want it to be `Clone()`. We can accommodate them all by creating `Duplicate()` and `Clone()` functions that call the `Copy()` function. However, we are not creating a minimal interface. Some users will inevitably wonder what the difference is between `Duplicate()`, `Clone()`, and `Copy()`. Having three functions in an interface that do the exact same thing will generate more confusion than is worthwhile.

[1]One of the primary ways of doing this is through inheritance. See Chapter 19.

Designing a Complete Interface

> **TIP:** When designing and developing objects, look for repetitive tasks that you perform on objects that require large chunks of code. Consider making these tasks member functions.

> **TIP:** When designing and developing objects, add functions that reduce the likelihood of programmer errors.

Object interfaces should also be complete. That is, they must allow programmers to do anything with the object that they might reasonably expect to do. The definition of *reasonable* is very subjective. However, there are a few guidelines that you can follow that will help.

As you design and develop your software, look for tasks that you perform on objects repetitively. Are these tasks simple function calls? Or do you repeatedly need to write many lines of code to complete the task? If it's the latter, you might think about including a function in the object's interface that performs the task.

Here's something else we should notice as we design and create objects: Do programmers repeatedly make the same errors whenever they use our objects? If so, we may need to look at what they are trying to get our objects to do. If they are using our objects in unexpected ways, we may need to add member functions to accommodate them.

Troubleshooting Guide

After reading this section, you should be able to:

- Recognize and fix problems with object attributes.
- Recognize and fix problems with object interfaces.

Troubles with Attributes

When determining object attributes, it's easy to create problems as we try to solve them. Let's take a look at some of the most common types of errors novice C++ programmers make as they choose object attributes.

Too Few Attributes Let's face it, no matter how much memory is installed on a computer, it's never enough. As developers, we're constantly looking for ways to reduce the amount of memory our programs use. We call this reducing the program's "memory footprint." One of the easiest ways to do this is to reduce the amount of data that each object stores. While this is generally a good goal, it can sometimes lead to problems.

One way to tell that you've packaged too little information in an object is if you are constantly calculating values that you will use with it.

For instance, let's say that I create a string object that does not store the length of the string. Let's also suppose that I don't provide a function that calculates the length of the string. If you are using my string object, you will repeatedly need to write loops that get each character in the object and count the number of characters in the string. This indicates that I have a problem with my design. If memory is so tight that I don't think it best to store the length of the string in the object, then I should provide a member function that performs that calculation. If the memory requirements for my application are not that stringent, I should store the length in my string object.

When other programmers on our current project can't seem to use our objects without adding more attributes to them, we probably need to take a look at our object design. It may be that there are many different uses for the objects we designed. It's possible that it is most efficient for other programmers to extend our design in ways that suit them. However, we can ask ourselves if there is common information that most of the other programmers are adding. If there is, it's a strong indicator that we've left something out.

Too Many Attributes Imagine I'm writing the Space Attackers game from Chapter 12. I determine that I need an object to represent attackers in software. Example 15.1 shows one possible version of that class.

EXAMPLE 15.1 An `attacker` Class

```
class attacker
{
public:
    // Member functions go here.
```

```
private:
    int upLeftX,upLeftY,lowRigthX,lowRightY;
    int height, width;
    bitmap attackerImage;
    int speed, acceleration;
    movement_direction currentDirection;
};
```

I've omitted the member functions in Example 15.1 so that we can focus on the private member data.

A *pixel* is an abbreviation for **pi**cture **el**ement. I don't know where the *x* came from. A pixel is one tiny dot on your computer screen. Your program can turn it on and set its color.

This `attacker` class contains four integers that define a rectangle for the attacker's image. Positions on computer screens are commonly defined by pixel locations. Each pixel location has an x and y number associated with it. These represent the column and row number of each pixel. This `attacker` class keeps track of the pixel location of the upper left and lower right corners of the attacker's image.

The `attacker` class also contains the height and width, in pixels, of the attacker's image. This is redundant information. My `attacker` class takes up more memory than it needs to. If the `attacker` class contains the two corner positions, I can calculate the height and width when it is needed. If it contains the height and width, I can leave out one of the corner positions. With one corner and the height and width, I can calculate the position of the other corner.

You might justifiably ask if having both the corner positions and the height and width would save some time. After all, it would decrease the number of calculations that my program needs to perform. To a certain extent, this is correct. However, there is overhead associated with passing information to functions. In this case, the extra overhead incurred when I pass attacker objects to functions would probably decrease performance enough to make up for any increase I might get in not calculating the information.

This example may seem to conflict with the previous section. Situations such as this are common. As you design objects, you are constantly pulled in two directions. You want the object to contain all the information it should. However, you don't want to put so much information into it that it degrades performance. Much of programming ends up being a balancing act between how much memory and how much microprocessor time a program uses.

Irrelevant Attributes One common way that some programmers use to get rid of global variables is to package them all together into an object and pass the object to functions in the program. The resulting object contains attributes that are not related to the object itself or to each other. Packaging the global variables into an object allows programmers to turn global variables into local variables. They can then pass the object to all functions that would reference a global variable. Unfortunately, this technique doesn't solve the problem of global variables.

TIP: All of an object's attributes should have a strong connection to the object and to each other. They should describe the object.

Global variables create too strong of a connection between program modules.[2] It's hard to use or enhance any one piece of the program without the rest. Often, programmers who enhance a program find that they must throw away and rewrite large parts of it because it depends on global variables. Simply combining unrelated global variables into a single object doesn't remove the connection between the program modules.

Poor Attribute Names Object attributes are variables. Like all variables, they should be well named. Avoid cryptic abbreviations. In general, programmers looking at your code will not find one-letter variable names helpful. The exceptions to this are when you are writing an extremely trivial application, or when you are declaring loop counter variables. Most programmers will understand what variables with names like *i*, *j*, and *k* are for. These are common names for loop counters. Another exception is in computer graphics. If you declare variables with names like *x* and *y*, most programmers will understand that this usually indicates a column and row location on the screen.

[2]They create too much cohesion between program modules. See Maureen Sprankle, *Problem Solving and Programming Concepts* (Upper Saddle River, NJ: Prentice Hall, 1992), pp. 66–67.

TIP: Make attribute names self-documenting.

For the most part, variables with names like *q, r,* or *dx* don't communicate enough information to maintenance programmers to be useful. Choose names that document themselves. Instead of *dx,* try *deltaX* to indicate a change in *x* position. Rather than a variable named *r,* use one named *radius* to store the radius of a circle.

Trouble with Operations

The operations, or member functions, of an object can suffer from the same difficulties as the attributes. The same general rules apply. We mentioned earlier in this chapter that we should try to create objects with interfaces that contain enough member functions, but not too many. All of the member functions should relate directly to the object itself. They should also relate to one another. The name of each member function should be a short but specific description of what the function does.

Summary

When designing object oriented software, we must identify the tasks that the software must perform. We also need to identify and design the software objects. This includes identifying what objects are needed, what data they contain, and what operations can be performed on the data.

Well-designed objects contain a minimal but complete set of attributes. They support a minimal but complete set of interface functions. The interface is appropriate for the object. It provides the set of operations that programmers would reasonably expect from the object.

Objects that are easy to use are well named. So are their member data and member functions.

Review Questions

1. How do you identify the essential objects in a software system?
2. How can you identify objects that may not be needed in the software?
3. How do you go about selecting the most important attributes for an object?
4. What guidelines are important to remember when selecting types for member data?
5. What are some ways you can determine whether your object's set of interface functions is minimal?
6. What are some ways you can determine whether your object's set of interface functions is complete?
7. How can you tell when you have too many or too few attributes in an object?
8. What guidelines should you keep in mind to ensure your object's attributes and operations are relevant?
9. How do you go about picking good names for your objects, member data, and member functions?
10. What should be your primary goals when designing software objects?

Exercises

1. The top-down design diagram in Figure 15.1 shows a partial design of a simple text editor. Continue this design by filling in greater detail.
2. Table 15.1 contains a list of all of the things the text editor should do. Use this list to create a list of all events to which the text editor should respond.
3. Make a list of all of the objects that you think are necessary for the text editor.
4. Use the list of events from Exercise 2 and the list of objects from Exercise 3. Make a list of each event and the object that will respond to it.
5. Use the list of objects you created for Exercise 3. Write down a brief justification for the existence of each object in your system.

FIGURE 15.1 A Partial Design of the Text Editor

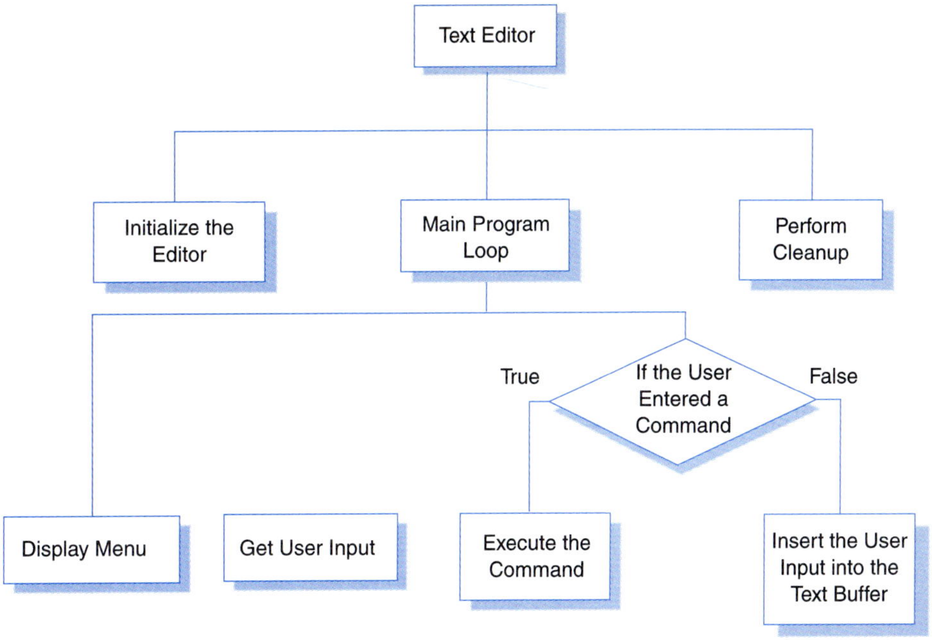

TABLE 15.1 The Text Editor's Task List

Task	Comment
Load a file.	Load an ASCII text file from the disk into the text buffer.
Save a file.	Save ASCII text from the buffer onto the disk.
Display a menu.	Display a list of commands that the editor recognizes.
Get user input.	Get input from the keyboard.
Interpret keyboard input.	Distinguish between user commands and text for the buffer.
Insert text.	If the user types in text for the buffer, insert it into the text buffer.
Delete text.	Delete text from the buffer when the user presses the backspace key.

6. Use the list of objects that you created for Exercise 3. Select the member data for each object. Choose the type of each object attribute. Explain why you chose the types that you did.
7. Use the list of objects you created for Exercise 6. Create a set of member functions for each object. Explain why you think each object needs the functions you included.
8. Select an object from the list of objects you created for Exercise 6. Explain why you think that object's interface of public member functions is both minimal and complete.
9. Select an object from the list of objects you created for Exercise 6. Explain how you chose the attribute names that you did. Make a list of alternate names for each of the object's attributes. Explain how these names are better or worse.
10. Select an object from the list of objects you created for Exercise 6. Explain how you chose the member function names that you did. Make a list of alternate names for each of the object's member functions. Explain how these names are better or worse.

Chapter Glossary

Event A stimulus to which the software reacts.

16 Polymorphism Through Overloading

Objectives

After reading this chapter, you should be able to:

- Make your classes look and act in a manner similar to the C++ built-in types.
- Overload member operators functions.
- Overload friend functions.

Preview

One of the fundamental concepts of the C++ philosophy is to be able to extend the C++ language. You can do this by creating new types and defining the set of operations for the new types. The new types can look and act very much like the built-in types. This helps other programmers use your classes in an intuitive way.

This chapter describes polymorphism through function overloading. It demonstrates how function overloading can be used to create types that behave similarly to the built-in types.

Overloading Functions

Overloading functions means that you can have two or more functions with the same name. The C++ compiler can tell which function is being called because the parameter lists are different. When you create classes, you can overload constructors, member functions, and operators.

Overloading Constructors

It is common to overload constructors of classes. Programs often declare objects in many different ways. Whenever you write a new class, you should provide constructors that accommodate the various ways that programs can declare objects.

Hands On 16.1 illustrates this concept. In it, we'll develop a class called `logical`. In programming, logical (also called *boolean*) variables can only have two values, true or false. Your C++ compiler probably provides a type called `bool` or `boolean` that does this. A boolean and a logical value are the same thing.

Hands On 16.1

Objective

Define a class that implements a logical, or boolean, type. The class should contain:

Member Functions

A constructor that takes no parameters.
A constructor that takes one parameter.
A function that sets the logical value.
A function that gets the logical value.

Member Data

The logical value. This can be either true or false.

Write a program that demonstrates the use of the logical class.

Experiment

Type the following program into your IDE or text editor. Compile, link, and run it.

```
#include <iostream.h>

const int FALSE = 0;
const int TRUE = 1;

class logical
{
public:
   logical(void);
   logical(int newValue);

   int Get(void);
   void Set(int newValue);

private:
   int logicalValue;
};


logical::logical(void)
{
   logicalValue = FALSE;
}


logical::logical(int newValue)
{
   logicalValue = newValue;
}


int logical::Get(void)
{
   return (logicalValue);
}


void logical::Set(int newValue)
```

```
{
   logicalValue = newValue;
}



main()
{
   logical aVulcan;
   int inputValue = -1;

   for (int i=0; i<5; i++)
   {
      cout << endl << "Enter a logical value (0 or 1):";
      cin >> inputValue;

      if ((inputValue == 0) || (inputValue==1))
      {
         aVulcan.Set(inputValue);

         cout << endl << "The logical value = ";
         if (aVulcan.Get() == TRUE)
         {
            cout << "TRUE" << endl;
         }
         else
         {
            cout << "FALSE" << endl;
         }
      }
      else
      {
         cout << endl << "That is not logical" << endl;
      }
   }

   logical aLogicalValue;
   logical anotherLogicalValue(TRUE);

   cout << endl << "aLogicalValue = ";
   if (aLogicalValue.Get() == TRUE)
   {
      cout << "TRUE" << endl;
   }
   else
   {
      cout << "FALSE" << endl;
   }

   cout << endl << "anotherLogicalValue = ";
   if (anotherLogicalValue.Get() == TRUE)
   {
      cout << "TRUE" << endl;
   }
   else
   {
      cout << "FALSE" << endl;
   }
```

```
    aLogicalValue = anotherLogicalValue;

    cout << endl << "aLogicalValue = ";
    if (aLogicalValue.Get() == TRUE)
    {
       cout << "TRUE" << endl;
    }
    else
    {
       cout << "FALSE" << endl;
    }
    cout << endl << "anotherLogicalValue = ";
    if (anotherLogicalValue.Get() == TRUE)
    {
       cout << "TRUE" << endl;
    }
    else
    {
       cout << "FALSE" << endl;
    }

    return (0);
}
```

Results

```
Enter a logical value (0 or 1):0
The logical value = FALSE

Enter a logical value (0 or 1):1
The logical value = TRUE

Enter a logical value (0 or 1):2
That is not logical

Enter a logical value (0 or 1):-5
That is not logical

Enter a logical value (0 or 1):1
The logical value = TRUE

aLogicalValue = FALSE

anotherLogicalValue = TRUE

aLogicalValue = TRUE

anotherLogicalValue = TRUE
```

Analysis

The `logical` class in this example has two constructors: one that takes a parameter and one that doesn't. The compiler uses the parameter lists of the two constructors to differentiate between which one the program calls. The `main()` function declares a `logical` variable called `aVulcan`. Because the variable has no initialization, the C++ compiler knows to call the constructor with no parameters. Further into the program, the variable `anotherLogicalValue` is declared with a parameter. This results in the constructor that takes a parameter being called. This call uses function notation, but we also could have written the same call as

```
logical anotherLogicalValue = TRUE;
```

This class also provides two member functions: `Get()` and `Set()`. They are used to get the logical value and set it. However, they result in a very unsatisfactory style of code. Take a look at the `main()` function. Notice the statements

```
if (aVulcan.Get() == TRUE)
```

and

```
if (aLogicalValue.Get() == TRUE)
```

These don't look much like the built-in types. We'd like to be able to rewrite these as

```
if (aVulcan == TRUE)
```

and

```
if (aLogicalValue == TRUE)
```

We'll make this modification to future versions of the `logical` class in this chapter.

Like most Alert Readers, you probably realized that the two constructors in the `logical` class can be combined by using a constructor with a default parameter. You are right. You will find in many cases that you must choose between overloading a constructor and providing a constructor with default parameters.

In general, it is better to provide constructors with default parameters than to overload constructors. Providing default parameters results in fewer versions of the constructor. There is less code to test and maintain.

You may be wondering if it is also possible to overload a destructor. The answer is no. Destructors can never take any parameters. Therefore, no class may have more than one destructor.

Overloading Member Functions

In addition to overloading constructors, it is possible to overload any other member function. Hands On 16.2 illustrates overloading member functions.

Hands On 16.2

Objective

Define a class that represents a point in a Cartesian coordinate system. It should contain the following:

Member Functions

- A constructor that takes no parameters.
- A constructor that takes two parameters.
- A function that sets the X value of the point.
- A function that gets the X value of the point.
- A function that sets the Y value of the point.
- A function that gets the Y value of the point.

Member Data

- The x and y locations of the point.

Write a program that demonstrates the use of the point class.

Experiment

Type the following program into your IDE or text editor. Compile, link, and run it.

```
#include <iostream.h>

class point
{
public:
   point(void);
   point(int newXValue,int newYValue);

   void X(int newXValue);        // Set the value.
   int X(void);                  // Get the value.

   void Y(int newYValue);        // Set the value.
   int Y(void);                  // Get the value.

private:
   int x,y;
};


point::point(void)
{
   x=0;
   y=0;
}


point::point(int newXValue,int newYValue)
{
   x=newXValue;
   y=newYValue;
}

void point::X(int newXValue)
{
   x=newXValue;
}


int point::X(void)
{
   return (x);
}

void point::Y(int newYValue)
{
   y=newYValue;
}


int point::Y(void)
{
   return (y);
}
```

```
int main()
{
   point p1;
   point p2(10,20);

   cout << "p1 = (" << p1.X() << "," << p1.Y() << ")";
   cout << endl;

   cout << "p2 = (" << p2.X() << "," << p2.Y() << ")";
   cout << endl;

   p1.X(p2.X());
   p1.Y(p2.Y());
   cout << "p1 = (" << p1.X() << "," << p1.Y() << ")";
   cout << endl;

   return (0);
}
```

Results

```
p1 = (0,0)
p2 = (10,20)
p1 = (10,20)
```

Analysis

The `point` class in this example is very useful whenever you need Cartesian coordinates to create a graph. Such classes are also commonly used in computer graphics.

Like the `logical` class in the last section, the `point` class has two constructors. When we're designing classes such as this, it is wise to ask ourselves if we can get rid of one of the constructors by using default parameters. In this case, the answer is no.

If we added a constructor with default parameters to the class, it would have a prototype like this:

```
point (int newXValue = 0, int newYValue=0);
```

When declaring a variable using this constructor, a programmer using our `point` class could make a declaration like the following:

```
point aPoint(10);
```

This declares the variable `aPoint`, and sets its `X` value to 10. The `Y` value is initialized to zero because it was omitted. This is almost never what the programmer intends. Usually, this is a mistake. If the programmer specifies an `X` value, he should also specify a `Y` value. Therefore, by having two constructors, one that takes no parameters and one that takes two parameters, we specify the usage of the `point` object. Programmers using this class *must* declare variables of type `point` with either no parameters or a pair of X,Y coordinates. The class definition does not allow any other style of declaration.

The class contains the declarations for two overloaded functions called `X()`. Since a point on an x,y graph has an `X` value and a `Y` value, the function name `X()` makes sense. It indicates the `X` value of the point. Because we have two overloaded functions, the `X()` function can be used to set or get the point's `X` value. If a program calls the `X()` function with an integer parameter, the C++ compiler knows that the program is calling the first overloaded `X()` function. If a program calls `X()` with no parameters, it is trying to retrieve the `X` value. Therefore, the C++ compiler knows the program is calling the second overloaded function.

The class definition also provides a pair of overloaded `Y()` functions that follow the same pattern.

The `main()` function demonstrates the use of the `point` class. It declares two variables of type `point`: `p1` and `p2`. The program does not initialize the variable `p1`, so the constructor with no parameters is called. The constructor initializes the private data members `x` and `y` to zero.

The program passes parameters to the constructor when it initializes the variable `p2`, so the constructor with two parameters is called. If you want to see what happens when you pass just one parameter to the constructor, type this program into your text editor or IDE, delete the 10 or the 20 in this declaration, and compile. The compiler won't like it.

The `main()` function prints the values in `p1` by calling the `X()` and `Y()` functions with no parameters. As mentioned previously, these functions retrieve the values of `x` and `y`. We can see from the output in the Results section that `p1` was indeed initialized to (0,0). A similar statement prints the values of `x` and `y` for `p2`.

The program next sets the values of `x` and `y` for the point `p1`. It fetches the value of `x` from `p2` by calling the overloaded `X()` function with no parameters. The program stores that value in `p1` by passing it as the parameter value to the `X()` function. This is equivalent to

```
int temp = p2.X();
p1.X(temp);
```

The statement

```
p1.X(p2.X());
```

demonstrates that the return value of one function can be passed as the parameter value to another function. The value of `y` for `p1` is set in this same way. The program prints the `X` and `Y` values to the screen and terminates by returning zero.

When overloading any function, it is important to remember that the C++ compiler uses the parameter list to differentiate between overloads. Therefore, the parameter lists of all overloaded functions must be different. As a result, two overloaded functions may not differ only in return type (though this is likely to change in the future). For instance, if the two functions

```
int GetValue();
float GetValue();
```

are in the same class definition, the C++ compiler will not be able to tell which to use, since only the return types are different.

Also, no two overloaded functions may differ only by their default parameters. For example, if the functions

```
void SetValue(int newValue);
void SetValue(int newValue=10);
void SetValue(int newValue=20);
```

are in the same class definition, the C++ compiler will not be able to tell which to use when.

Overloading Operators

Earlier in this chapter, we looked at a class called `logical`. It is repeated in Example 16.1 for convenience.

EXAMPLE 16.1 The `logical` Class

```
const int FALSE = 0;
const int TRUE = 1;

class logical
```

```
{
public:
   logical(void);
   logical(int newValue);

   int Get(void);
   void Set(int newValue);

private:
   int logicalValue;
};


logical::logical(void)
{
   logicalValue = FALSE;
}


logical::logical(int newValue)
{
   logicalValue = newValue;
}


int logical::Get(void)
{
   return (logicalValue);
}


void logical::Set(int newValue)
{
   logicalValue = newValue;
}
```

One of the shortcomings of this class is that it requires the use of the functions `Get()` and `Set()`. For instance, in `if` statements, we must write code along the lines of the following:

```
if (aLogicalValue.Get() == TRUE)
{
   // Do something
}
```

Similarly, when we assign values to variables of type `logical`, we must use statements like this:

```
aLogicalValue.Set(FALSE);
```

Ideally, we want to make the types that we create look and act like the built-in types. If we do, their use will be more intuitive for anyone using the class. If the preceding statements could be changed to

```
if (aLogicalValue == TRUE)
{
 // Do something
}
```

and

```
aLogicalValue = FALSE;
```

our `logical` class would be much more like the C++ built-in types. In fact, the C++ language provides us with a way to achieve this by overloading operators for a class.

Creating Overloaded Operator Functions Hands On 16.3 demonstrates a revised version of the `logical` class with two overloaded operators. This class contains an overloaded `operator` = function that returns a reference[1] to an object of type `logical`. All `operator` = functions should follow this form.

Hands On 16.3

Objective

Define a class that implements a logical, or boolean, type. The class should contain:

Member Functions

A constructor that takes no parameters.
A constructor that takes one parameter.
A function that sets the logical value.
A function that gets the logical value.

Member Data

The logical value. This can be either true or false.

Write a program that demonstrates the use of the logical class.

Experiment

Type the following program into your IDE or text editor. Compile, link, and run it.

```
#include <iostream.h>

const int FALSE = 0;
const int TRUE = 1;

class logical
{
public:
   logical(void);
   logical(int newValue);

   logical &operator = (int newValue);
   operator int();
private:
   int logicalValue;
};


logical::logical(void)
{
   logicalValue = FALSE;
}


logical::logical(int newValue)
{
   logicalValue = newValue;
}


logical &logical::operator = (int newValue)
```

[1]For a closer look at references, see Chapter 21.

```
{
   logicalValue = newValue;
   return (*this);
}


logical::operator int()
{
   return (logicalValue);
}



main()
{
   logical aVulcan;
   int inputValue = -1;

   for (int i=0; i<5; i++)
   {
      cout << endl << "Enter a logical value (0 or 1):";
      cin >> inputValue;

      if ((inputValue == 0) || (inputValue==1))
      {
         aVulcan = inputValue;

         cout << endl << "The logical value = ";
         if (aVulcan == TRUE)
         {
            cout << "TRUE" << endl;
         }
         else
         {
            cout << "FALSE" << endl;
         }
      }
      else
      {
         cout << endl << "That is not logical" << endl;
      }
   }

   logical aLogicalValue, anotherLogicalValue(TRUE);

   cout << endl << "aLogicalValue = ";
   if (aLogicalValue == TRUE)
   {
      cout << "TRUE" << endl;
   }
   else
   {
      cout << "FALSE" << endl;
   }

   cout << endl << "anotherLogicalValue = ";
   if (anotherLogicalValue == TRUE)
   {
```

```
      cout << "TRUE" << endl;
   }
   else
   {
      cout << "FALSE" << endl;
   }

   aLogicalValue = anotherLogicalValue;

   cout << endl << "aLogicalValue = ";
   if (aLogicalValue == TRUE)
   {
      cout << "TRUE" << endl;
   }
   else
   {
      cout << "FALSE" << endl;
   }

   cout << endl << "anotherLogicalValue = ";
   if (anotherLogicalValue == TRUE)
   {
      cout << "TRUE" << endl;
   }
   else
   {
      cout << "FALSE" << endl;
   }

   return (0);
}
```

Results

```
Enter a logical value (0 or 1):0
The logical value = FALSE

Enter a logical value (0 or 1):1
The logical value = TRUE

Enter a logical value (0 or 1):2
That is not logical

Enter a logical value (0 or 1):-1
That is not logical

Enter a logical value (0 or 1):0
The logical value = FALSE

aLogicalValue = FALSE

anotherLogicalValue = TRUE

aLogicalValue = TRUE

anotherLogicalValue = TRUE
```

Analysis

All overloaded operator functions have the keyword `operator` before the name of the operator. When a program calls the overloaded operator function, it uses only the operator name or symbol.

The `logical` class now has two overloaded operators: `operator =` and `operator int()`. To call the `operator =` function, we just need to use an assignment operator in the program. The left-hand argument of the assignment must be a variable of type `logical`. The right-hand argument must be an integer.

The other overloaded function, `operator int()`, is a type cast. It is used like this:

```
logical aLogicalValue(TRUE);
int anInteger = (int)aLogicalValue;
```

As you can see, it is just as normal type casts are used. These two statements declare a `logical` variable, set it to true, and then convert it to an `int` with the type cast function. They then assign it to an integer variable.

If you look at the program in Hands On 16.3, you will not see the type cast operator used. However, you may notice that the statement

```
if (aVulcan.Get() == TRUE)
```

has been changed to

```
if (aVulcan == TRUE)
```

Remember that in an `if` statement, the expression must evaluate to either zero or nonzero. This means the variable `aVulcan` must evaluate to a value. When the C++ compiler compiles this program, it looks in the class for a function that will convert the `logical` variable to a value. This is exactly the purpose of the type cast operator function. The compiler has enough smarts built into it to recognize that fact. Therefore, it will insert a call to the function `operator int()`. This call converts the `logical` value to an integer. The program then compares the integer value to TRUE.

This means that you can create types that can be used in conditions just like the built-in types. Just insert a type cast operator in the class. It also illustrates that the compiler will sometimes call type cast functions without telling us. The type cast operators can be a good thing, but you should use them sparingly because you can't always control when they will be called.

Rules for Overloading Operators Most, but not all, of the C++ operators can be overloaded. Figure 16.1 lists the operators that can't be overloaded.

We haven't discussed some of these operators yet, but we will see how they are used as we go along.

The operators that can be overloaded are shown in Figure 16.2.

FIGURE 16.1 C++ Operators That Can't Be Overloaded

```
.    .*    ::    ?:
```

FIGURE 16.2 C++ Operators That Can Be Overloaded

```
new       delete     new[]      delete[]
+(unary)  -(unary)   *(unary)   /   %   ^   &(unary)   |   ~
!   =   <   >   +=   -=   *=   /=   %=
^=   &=   |=   <<   >>   >>=   <<=   ==   !=
<=   >=   &&   ||   ++   --   ,   ->*   ->
()   []  +(binary)   –(binary)   *(binary)   &(binary)
```

Some operators have both a unary and a binary form. That is, they have a form that takes one argument or two. The – operator is a good example. The statement

```
thisInteger = -anInteger;
```

uses the unary form of the – operator. This form takes one argument. If the value in `anInteger` is positive, the negative of the same number will be stored in `thisInteger`. If the value in `anInteger` is negative, the positive of the same number will be stored in `thisInteger`. The – operator also has a binary form. It is used for subtraction.

Binary operators such as +, –, *, or / can be called using infix notation or function notation. Infix notation is the notation that we normally use to write binary operators. For instance, the statement

```
anInteger + anotherInteger
```

uses the + operator with infix notation. C++ also lets us use function-style notation. For example, the `operator = ()` function in the `logical` class in Hands On 16.3 is a binary operator. In the program, we called the `operator = ()` function with infix notation in statements like

```
aVulcan = inputValue;
```

However, we could have used function notation, like this:

```
aVulcan.=(inputValue);
```

This uses the style of call we have seen for other types of member functions. It is the standard C++ function call style. So with overloaded binary operators, you may use either infix or function call style of notation.

With a Little Help from My Friends

The overloaded operator functions presented so far have a weakness that is illustrated by Hands On 16.4.

Hands On 16.4

Objective

Define a vector class that contains the following:

Member Functions

A constructor with two parameters.
A multiplication operator.
A function to print the vector to the screen.

Member Data

The vector magnitude.
The vector direction.

Write a program to demonstrate the use of the vector class.

Experiment

Type the following program into your IDE or text editor. Compile, link, and run it.

```
#include <iostream.h>
#include <math.h>


class vector
{
public:
```

```
    vector(double vectorMagnitude=0,double directionInRadians=0);

    vector operator *(double scalar);
    void Print(void);

public:
    double magnitude;
    double direction;
};


vector::vector(double vectorMagnitude,double directionInRadians)
{
    magnitude = vectorMagnitude;
    direction = directionInRadians;
}


vector vector::operator *(double scalar)
{
    return (vector(magnitude * scalar, direction));
}


void vector::Print(void)
{
    cout << "(" << magnitude;
    cout << "," << direction << ")";
}


int main()
{
    vector v1, v2(5.9,M_PI/2);

    cout << endl<< "v2 = ";
    v2.Print();
    cout << endl;

    v1=v2*3.0;

    cout << endl<< "v1 = ";
    v1.Print();
    cout << endl;

    return (0);
}
```

When we discus pointers, we'll see that the `operator =()` function generated by the compiler is not always appropriate for our classes.

In general, the technique of returning nameless temporary variables created by calling a constructor is a good one to use. Many compilers can optimize the nameless temporary variable right out of existence. By a strict interpretation of the C++ rules, the compiler would have to create a nameless temporary variable, then call the constructor again to copy the values in that into a variable on the stack. That would be two calls to the constructor. Instead, many C++ compilers are able to recognize that nameless temporary variables are just a return value, so they create the return value directly. The result is just one call to the variable's constructor.

Results

```
v2 = (5.9,1.5708)

v1 = (17.7,1.5708)
```

Analysis

The program in Hands On 16.4 creates a `vector` class. Vectors have magnitude (how "big" the vector is) and direction. This `vector` class has only the operators and functions that are needed by this particular program.

To be specific, the `main()` function uses two operators on the `vector` class and one function. The operators are `operator *()` and `operator =()`. However, in the class definition, only the function `operator *` is provided. The C++ compiler automatically generates the `operator =()` function if you don't provide it.

The `operator *()` function for the `vector` class returns a `vector`. The `vector` is a nameless temporary `vector` object created by calling the `vector` constructor. The parameters to the constructor are the magnitude of the `vector` multiplied by the scalar quantity that was passed into the `operator *()` function, and the direction of the current `vector`. Multiplying a `vector` by a scalar only changes the magnitude of a `vector`, not the direction.

The other `vector` function that this program uses is `Print()`.

The program in Hands On 16.4 simply multiplies a `vector` by a scalar and prints the result. But let's think a moment. By the rules of math, we should be able to multiply a `vector` by a scalar, and a scalar by a `vector`. That is, both the statements

```
v1=v2*3.0;
```

and

```
v1=3.0*v2;
```

should be valid in our programs. However, because of the rules of C++ and the way our `vector` class is currently defined, the second statement will not work in a program. Every member function of an object must be invoked by an object. Remember that the statement

```
v1=v2*3.0;        // Infix notation.
```

is the same as

```
v1=v2.*(3.0);        // Function notation.
```

Using function notation makes it clear that the `operator *()` function in the `vector` class is being invoked by the variable `v2`.

Looking at the statement

```
v1=3.0*v2;
```

forces us to ask the question, "What object is invoking the `operator *()` function?" The answer is that no object is invoking that function. That's the reason this statement will not work in our program. The number 3.0 is of type `double`, not `vector`. We must have a `vector` object to invoke the `operator *()` function for the `vector` class.

The only way to fix this problem is to modify the `double` type to accept `vector` objects. As radical as that sounds, C++ gives us a way to essentially do just that by using friend functions.

Friend Functions A friend function is a function that is not a member of the class. However, it can still access the class's private data members. Functions are made friends of classes by putting their prototypes into the class, preceded by the word `friend`. Hands On 16.5 demonstrates how a function can be made a friend of a class.

Hands On 16.5

Objective

Define a vector class that contains the following:

Member Functions

A constructor with two parameters.
A multiplication operator that multiplies a vector by a scalar.
A multiplication operator that multiplies a scalar by a vector.
A function to print the vector to the screen.

Member Data

The vector magnitude.
The vector direction.

Write a program to demonstrate the use of the vector class.

Experiment

Type the following program into your IDE or text editor. Compile, link, and run it.

```
#include <iostream.h>
#include <math.h>

class vector
{
public:
   vector(double vectorMagnitude=0,double directionInRadians=0);

   vector operator *(double scalar);
   friend vector operator *(double scalar, vector theVector);

   void Print(void);

public:
   double magnitude;
   double direction;
};

vector::vector(double vectorMagnitude,double directionInRadians)
{
   magnitude = vectorMagnitude;
   direction = directionInRadians;
}


vector vector::operator *(double scalar)
{
   return (vector(magnitude * scalar, direction));
}


vector operator *(double scalar, vector theVector)
{
   return (vector(theVector.magnitude * scalar, direction));
}


void vector::Print(void)
{
   cout << "(" << magnitude;
   cout << "," << direction << ")";
}

int main()
{
   vector v1, v2(5.9,M_PI/2);

   cout << endl<< "v2 = ";
   v2.Print();
```

```
    cout << endl;

    v1 = v2 * 3.0;

    cout << endl << "v1 = ";
    v1.Print();
    cout << endl;

    v1 = 5.0 * v2;

    cout << endl << "v1 = ";
    v1.Print();
    cout << endl;

    return (0);
}
```

Results

```
v2 = (5.9,1.5708)

v1 = (17.7,1.5708)

v1 = (29.5,1.5708)
```

Analysis

In this example, we added another `operator *()` function to the class. The function is declared a friend of the `vector` class, so it is not a member. If we look at the code for the new `operator *()` function, we can verify this. Every function that is a member of the `vector` class has `vector::` before the function name. This function does not. It is therefore not a member of the `vector` class.

The `vector` class now has access to two different `operator *()` functions. How does the compiler know which to call? We can get the answer by looking in the `main()` function.

As before, the `main()` function contains the line

```
v1 = v2 * 3.0;
```

In this case, the object `v2` invokes the `operator *()` function. Because it is invoked by the object `v2`, which is of type `vector`, the compiler must call the `operator *()` function that is a member of the `vector` class. This function takes one parameter, a scalar quantity.

However, later on in the program, we see the line

```
v1 = 5.0 * v2;
```

In this case, the `operator *()` function can't be invoked by the object `v2` because `v2` is the right-hand operand. For binary operators, the operator function must always be called by the left-hand operand. In this case, the left-hand operand is 5.0, which is a `double`.

Variables of type `double` are not implemented as classes. To resolve this function call, the compiler looks in the program's *global namespace* to see if there is an `operator *()` function that takes a `double` as the left-hand operator and a `vector` as the right-hand operator. It finds the other `operator *()` function. The compiler can also see that it is a friend of the `vector` class, so the `operator *()` function can access the private data members of the `vector` class.

The `friend` version of the `operator *()` function takes two parameters. When we create a binary operator function that is a member of a class, the left-hand operand is the object that invokes the function. Therefore, it doesn't need to be specified in the parameter list. However, when we create binary operator functions that are not members of classes, both operands must be passed in through the parameter list in the order that they occur. Therefore, this `operator *()` function has two parameters: the scalar quantity and the `vector` that it is being multiplied by.

Since the `operator *()` function can access the private data members of the `vector` class, it is OK to refer to `theVector.magnitude` in the `friend` function. If this function were not a member or a `friend`, the compiler would not allow that statement in the function.

There is a way to make this function simpler. Example 16.2 shows the simpler version. The `friend` version of the `operator *()` function just swaps the order of the parameters and calls the `operator *()` that is a member of the vector class.

EXAMPLE 16.2 A Simpler Version of the `friend operator *()` Function

```
vector operator *(double scalar, vector theVector)
{
   return (vector(theVector * scalar, direction));
}
```

Overloading the Insertion and Extraction Operators

One important property of all built-in types is that they can be read directly in from the keyboard with the insertion operator. They can also be printed to the screen with the extraction operator. We would like to be able to do this for the types that we create as well.

To accomplish this, we use operator overloading and friend functions. The program in Hands On 16.6 illustrates how this is done.

Hands On 16.6

Objective

Define a class called `logical`. It should contain:

Member Functions

- A constructor that takes no parameters.
- A constructor that takes one parameter.
- An extraction operator function.
- An insertion operator function.

Member Data

- The logical value.

Write a program that demonstrates the use of the class.

Experiment

Type the following program into your IDE or text editor. Compile, link, and run it.

```
#include <iostream.h>

const int FALSE = 0;
const int TRUE = 1;


class logical
{
```

```
public:
   logical(void);
   logical(int newValue);

   friend istream &operator >> (istream &inputStream,logical &inputValue);
   friend ostream &operator << (ostream &outputStream,logical &outputValue);

private:
   int logicalValue;
};


logical::logical(void)
{
   logicalValue = FALSE;
}


logical::logical(int newValue)

   logicalValue = newValue;
}

istream &operator >> (istream &inputStream,logical &inputValue)
{
   int temp;

   inputStream >> temp;
   if (temp==0)
   {
      inputValue.logicalValue = FALSE;
   }
   else
   {
      inputValue.logicalValue = TRUE;
   }

   return (inputStream);
}

ostream &operator << (ostream &outputStream,logical &outputValue)
{
   if (outputValue.logicalValue==FALSE)
   {
      outputStream << "FALSE";
   }
   else
   {
      outputStream << "TRUE";
   }

   return (outputStream);
}

main()
{
   logical aVulcan;
```

```
    for (int i=0; i<5; i++)
    {
       cout << endl << "Enter a logical value (zero or nonzero):";
       cin >> aVulcan;

       cout << endl << "The logical value = ";
       cout << aVulcan;
       cout << endl;
    }

    logical aLogicalValue, anotherLogicalValue(TRUE);

    cout << endl << "aLogicalValue = ";
    cout << aLogicalValue;

    cout << endl << "anotherLogicalValue = ";
    cout << anotherLogicalValue;

    aLogicalValue = anotherLogicalValue;
    cout << endl << "aLogicalValue = anotherLogicalValue";

    cout << endl << "aLogicalValue = ";
    cout << aLogicalValue;

    cout << endl << "anotherLogicalValue = ";
    cout << anotherLogicalValue;

    return (0);
}
```

Results

```
Enter a logical value (zero or nonzero):-1
The logical value = TRUE

Enter a logical value (zero or nonzero):0
The logical value = FALSE

Enter a logical value (zero or nonzero):1
The logical value = TRUE

Enter a logical value (zero or nonzero):2
The logical value = TRUE

Enter a logical value (zero or nonzero):a
The logical value = TRUE

aLogicalValue = FALSE
anotherLogicalValue = TRUE
aLogicalValue = anotherLogicalValue
aLogicalValue = TRUE
anotherLogicalValue = TRUE
```

Analysis

This is a modified version of the `logical` class that we saw earlier in this chapter. For this version, the insertion and extraction operators have been overloaded.

They are `friend` functions, not member functions. They must be `friend` functions because they are invoked by stream objects, not logical objects.[2]

Adding the insertion and extraction operator functions to the `logical` class also results in a simpler `main()` function. Using a `logical` variable is now much more like using one of the built-in types.

Troubleshooting Guide

After reading this section, you should be able to:

- Make each overloaded function different enough for the compiler to be able to distinguish them.
- Do defensive design on overloaded operators.
- Avoid too many overloaded functions.
- Choose between overloading functions and using default parameters.

Differentiating Overloaded Functions

As of this writing, the ANSI C++ committee is considering changing the standard so that overloaded functions may differ only by return type.

At present, a C++ compiler differentiates between overloaded functions strictly on the basis of their parameter lists. If the parameter lists are not different enough, the compiler will be unable to pick which overloaded version of a function your code refers to. Sometimes, parameter lists may appear different to you and me, but look the same to a compiler.

For instance, Example 16.3 shows a class with two constructors. One of the constructors takes no parameters; the other takes an integer as a parameter. If you compiled this program, the C++ compiler would not be able to determine which constructor to use when a variable is declared with no parameters. It could use the constructor with the empty parameter list, or it could use the constructor that takes one parameter and use the default parameter value. One is just as good a candidate as the other. Therefore, the compiler throws up its hands, so to speak, and says, "I don't know which one you want."

EXAMPLE 16.3 Constructors That Can't Be Differentiated

```
class an_object
{
public:
   an_object(void);
   an_object(int param=0);

private:
   int aDataMember;
};

an_object::an_object(void)
{
   aDataMember = 0;
}


an_object::an_object(int param)
{
   aDataMember=param;
}

int main()
{
```

[2]For more on stream objects, see Chapter 20.

```
    // Which constuctor will be used?
    an_object anObject;

    return(0);
}
```

The way we avoid this is to choose between function overloading and default parameters, which will be presented shortly.

Defensive Operator Design

Since they are functions, overloaded operators can be made to do anything. If you wanted to, you could overload the + operator of a class to do division. However, that doesn't make much sense. To help ensure that your classes are used in the way they are intended, you need to do the programming equivalent of "defensive driving." That is, you need to make your operators do what most programmers expect them to do.

The general rule is that you want to make your types look and act as much like the C++ built-in types as possible. If you overload an operator for one of your classes, it should do conceptually the same thing that the operator would do for a built-in type.

As an example, we created a class called `cpp_string` in Chapter 14. If I wanted to create a function that concatenated one string onto the end of another, it would be logical to overload the + operator for that class. As the user of my class, you would expect that the statement

```
aCppString = anotherCppString + yetAnotherCppString;
```

to result in the contents of the variable `aCppString` receiving the contents of the variable `anotherCppString` followed by the contents of the variable `yetAnotherCppString`. If the + operator is overloaded to do this for the `cpp_string` class in this way, it does conceptually the same thing as the + operator for the built-in types.

Too Many Overloads

One source of confusion for programmers who want to look at your classes is too many overloaded functions. For instance, suppose I were writing a computer graphics application that manipulated colors. Most PC display adaptors specify their colors as red, green, blue, and alpha levels. For my application, I decide to create a class, such as the one in Example 16.4.

In this case, the alpha level can be thought of as the level of brightness. It is also used for transparency.

EXAMPLE 16.4 A `color` Class

```
class color
{
public:
    // What member functions are needed?

private:
    int red, green,blue,alpha;
};
```

In creating this class, I want to design it for flexibility. To accomplish this, I may overload the constructors so that a variety of initializations are possible. Example 16.5 demonstrates this.

EXAMPLE 16.5 A `color` Class with Overloaded Constructors

```
class color
{
public:
    color(void);
    color(int redValue);
    color(int redValue,int greenValue);
    color(int redValue,int greenValue,int blueValue);
```

```
    color(int redValue,int greenValue,int blueValue,int alphaValue);

private:
    int red,green,blue,alpha;
};


color::color(void)
{
    red=green=blue=alpha=0;
}


color::color(int redValue)
{
    red=redValue;
    green=blue=alpha=0;
}

color::color(int redValue,int greenValue)
{
    red=redValue;
    green=greenValue;
    blue=alpha=0;
}

color::color(int redValue,int greenValue,int blueValue)
{
    red=redValue;
    green=greenValue;
    blue=blueValue;
    alpha=0;
}

color::color(int redValue,int greenValue,int blueValue,int alphaValue)
{
    red=redValue;
    green=greenValue;
    blue=blueValue;
    alpha=alphaValue;
}
```

This implementation contains constructors that let a programmer decide how many of the `color` values to initialize. Any that are not initialized are set to zero.

While this kind of flexibility is commendable, it can lead to confusion. With only four parameters, the `color` class has five overloaded constructors. If it were any more complex and had more possible parameters, the number of constructors would quickly get out of hand. Programmers using the class would never quite know what was needed to get the object properly initialized.

Another problem is maintenance. When any one of the constructors in this class changes, it's a sure bet that all of them will need to change. However, Murphy's Law being what it is, one of the constructors probably won't get changed when all the others do. The result will be that an object will sometimes get into an erroneous state for no apparent reason. Bugs like that are simple to create, but hard to track down.

A better approach would be to use default parameters, as in Example 16.6. This version of the `color` class uses only one constructor with default parameters. It does exactly what the class in Example 16.5 does. However, it is much more understandable and maintainable.

EXAMPLE 16.6 A Better `color` Class

```
class color
{
public:
   color(int redValue=0,int greenValue=0,int blueValue=0,int alphaValue=1);

private:
   int red,green,blue,alpha;
};

color::color(int redValue,int greenValue,int blueValue,int alphaValue)
{
   red=redValue;
   green=greenValue;
   blue=blueValue;
   alpha=alphaValue;
}
```

Overloading and Default Parameters

At this point, we can't help but say a few words about when to overload functions and when to use default parameters. From previous examples throughout this chapter, you've seen good reasons for using both techniques. Choosing between them boils down to two questions:

1. Is there a reasonable default value?
2. How many versions of the function do you want to maintain?

If there are no reasonable defaults, you will probably need to overload the function. If there are, it's better to have one version with default parameters. Ideally, it would be nice if we had to maintain only one version of each function in our programs. However, if you find you must overload a function, try to create as few overloads as you think are reasonable.

Summary

This chapter presented techniques we can use in our C++ programs to make our user-defined types look and act more like the built-in types. Specifically, we overloaded constructors, operator functions, other member functions, and friend functions.

As software component designers, we must try to provide intuitive ways of creating and initializing objects. Overloading a class's constructor does just that by providing multiple methods of initializing the object.

Destructors cannot be overloaded. Multiple destructors in a class are not allowed.

Any function that is a member of a class (except a destructor) can be overloaded. The parameter lists of the various versions of the overloaded function must each be different from the others.

Operators can also be overloaded. Providing overloaded operators simplifies code considerably. Almost all C++ operators can be overloaded for any class. It is wise to make the overloaded operators do the same basic task that the same operators do for the C++ built-in types. This will make classes more intuitive for other programmers to use.

Friend functions are functions that are not members of a class, but they can access the private members of a class. Some operators, such as the insertion and extraction operators, must be implemented as friend functions. It is generally not wise to use too many friend functions. They tend to break down the modularity of programs if they are overused.

Review Questions

1. What does it mean to overload a function?
2. Why does C++ allow overloaded functions?

3. Which of the following cannot be overloaded?
   a. Constructors
   b. Destructors
   c. Member functions
   d. Operators
4. What parameters are required for destructors?
5. How does the C++ compiler tell which version of an overloaded function is being called?
6. How do you choose between function overloading and functions with default parameters?
7. Which operators can't be overloaded?
8. What is a unary operator? What is a binary operator?
9. What is a friend function?
10. In what ways are friend functions helpful? In what ways are they not good?

Exercises

1. Use the cpp_string class in Hands On 14.3 (see Chapter 14). Rewrite the class so that an object of type cpp_string can be declared in the following two ways:

```
cpp_string aString;
cpp_string anotherString = "The quick brown fox";
```

   The variable aString should be initialized to null characters and its length set to zero. The variable anotherString should be set to the string "The quick brown fox" and its length set appropriately. Write a short program to demonstrate that your class works. Tell which you used—two overloaded constructors or one constructor with a default parameter. Explain why you chose the method you did.
2. Rewrite the cpp_string class so that it contains two overloaded String functions. The first one should take an array of characters as its only parameter. The second one should take an object of type cpp_string as its only parameter. The two functions should allow code such as the following:

```
cpp_string aString, anotherString;
aString.String("This string");
anotherString.String(aString);
```

   Delete the Set() and Copy() functions from the class. Write a program demonstrating that your overloaded string() functions work.
3. Overload the + operator for the cpp_string class. It should take a cpp_string as a parameter and return the concatenation of the left- and right-hand operands. That is, it should allow code such as the following:

```
cpp_string string1, string2 = "So long, and thanks ";
cpp_string string3 = "for all the fish.";
string1 = string2 + string3;
```

   The preceding source code should not modify string2 or string3. It should result in string1 being set to "So long, and thanks for all the fish." Write a program to demonstrate that this version of your cpp_string class works.
4. Overload the + function that you wrote for Exercise 3. Make a version that takes an array of characters as its parameter. That is, the new overloaded version should have a prototype that matches this:

```
cpp_string operator +(char charArray[]);
```

   The new operator +() function must allow code such as the following:

```
cpp_string string1;
cpp_string string2 = "So long, and thanks ";
char aCharArray[] = "for all the fish.";
string1 = string2 + aCharArray;
```

The preceding source code should not modify `string2`. It should result in `string1` being set to "So long, and thanks for all the fish." Write a program to demonstrate that this version of your `cpp_string` class works.

5. Overload the + function that you wrote for Exercises 3 and 4. Make a friend function that takes an array of characters as its left-hand parameter. The new overloaded version should have a prototype that matches this:

```
friend cpp_string operator +(char aCharArray[],cpp_string aString);
```

The new `operator +()` function must allow code such as the following:

```
cpp_string string1;
char aCharArray[] = "So long, and thanks ";
cpp_string string2 = "for all the fish.";
string1 = aCharArray + string2;
```

The preceding source code should not modify `string2`. It should result in `string1` being set to "So long, and thanks for all the fish." Write a program to demonstrate that this version of your `cpp_string` class works.

6. Modify the `cpp_string` class. Rename the `GetCharacter()` function to `Character()`. Overload the `Character()` function with another version that sets a character. That is, create another `Character()` function with the following prototype:

```
int Character(int characterIndex,char newCharacter);
```

This new version should set a character in the array `charString` to the character that is passed in through the parameter `newCharacter`. It should return the index number of the new character's position in the array. For example, if the character is put in array position 3, the function should return 3. Do not let the programmer put a character beyond the end of the string. For instance, it should not let a programmer do this:

```
cpp_string aString = "cat";
aString.Character(10,'x');
```

If a programmer attempts to insert characters beyond the length of the string, your `Character()` function should return –1. Write a program to prove that your `Character()` functions work.

7. Write a `SubString()` function for your `cpp_string` class. It should have the following prototype:

```
int SubString(cpp_string searchString);
```

The `SubString()` function should search the character array in a `cpp_string` object for the characters in the search string. If they are found, then the `SubString()` function must return the index number in the character array where the substring begins. Here's an example of how it should work:

```
cpp_string string1 = "So long, and thanks";
cpp_string string2 = "long";
// This statement should result in index being set to 3.
int index = string1.SubString(string2);
```

If the substring is not found in the string, your `SubString()` function will return –1. Write a program to demonstrate that your `SubString()` function works.

8. Overload the `SubString()` function you wrote for Exercise 7. This version should set a portion of a string in a `cpp_string` object to the characters in the substring. For example, the following code should set the variable `string1` to "So long".

```
cpp_string string1 = "So gnol";
cpp_string string2 = "long";
string1.SubString(string2,3);
```

This overload of the `SubString()` function will match the following prototype:

```
int SubString(cpp_string newSubString,int startPosition);
```

The `SubString()` function must not modify the length of the string. That is, inserting the substring cannot increase or decrease the current length of the string. The substring may not be inserted after the end of the string. Write a program to prove that your function works.

9. Overload the `SubString()` function for the `cpp_string` class again. It should behave exactly as described in Exercise 7. However, this version of the `SubString()` function will take an array of characters as its parameter instead of a `cpp_string`. Its prototype will be:

   ```
   int SubString(char searchString[]);
   ```

   Helpful hint: Your `SubString()` function can use an old C (not C++) library function named `strlen()` to find the length of `searchString`. However, you must put the statement

   ```
   #include <string.h>
   ```

   at the beginning of your program.
10. Overload the `SubString()` function for the `cpp_string` class again. It should behave exactly as described in Exercise 8. However, this version of the `SubString()` function will take an array of characters as its parameter instead of a `cpp_string`. Its prototype will be

   ```
   int SubString(char newSubString[],int startPosition);
   ```

17 Preprocessor Directives

Objectives

After reading this chapter, you should be able to:

- Use preprocessor directives to define constants.
- Use preprocessor directives to define macros.
- Use preprocessor directives to perform conditional compilation.
- Use preprocessor directives to control compilation options.

Preview

In this chapter, we'll discuss the use of the C++ preprocessor. The preprocessor is an extremely powerful tool that programmers use to write professional-caliber C++ programs. Surprisingly, it is often overlooked in discussions of C++ programming.

In this chapter, we'll first look at what the C++ preprocessor is and what it's used for. We'll then discuss the commands, or directives, that the preprocessor understands.

What Is the Preprocessor?

In Chapter 2, I said that we develop C++ programs by compiling source code into object code. We then link the object code into executable code. This process was illustrated in Figure 2.1, which is repeated here in Figure 17.1.

What's shown in Figure 17.1 is *not quite* a complete picture of the process of creating a computer program. In fact, there is one more step. Before your compiler ever sees the source file, it is automatically processed by the C++ preprocessor, as shown in Figure 17.2.

The preprocessor executes any preprocessor directives that you put into your code. For instance, we saw in Chapter 10 that we can create named constants with the `#define` directive. The `#define` directive is not a C++ command. It is a preprocessor directive. Example 17.1 shows a named constant created with the `#define` directive.

EXAMPLE 17.1 Creating a Named Constant with `#define`

```
#define MAX_STUDENTS_PER_CLASS 100
```

FIGURE 17.1 Creating a Computer Program

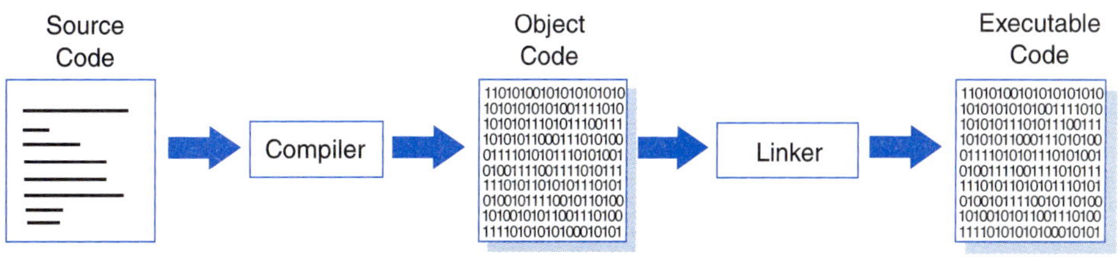

FIGURE 17.2 A More Detailed Look at Creating a Computer Program

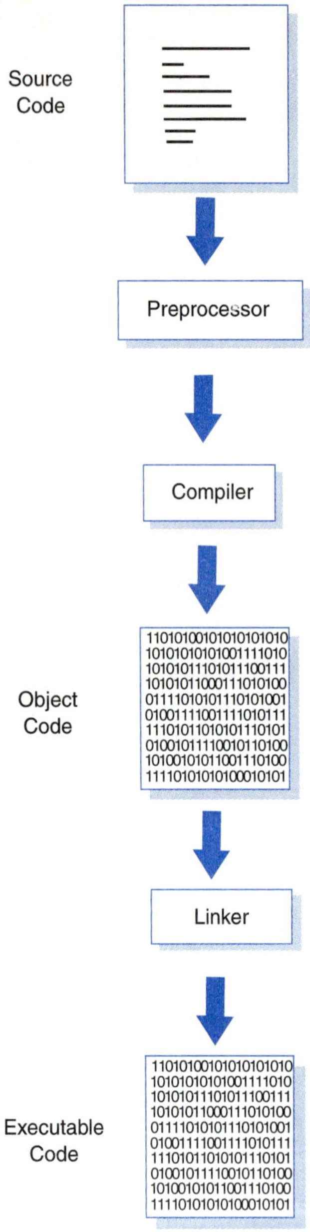

In this example we create a named constant called `MAX_STUDENTS_PER_CLASS`. When we compile the program, the compiler automatically invokes the C++ preprocessor. Everywhere the preprocessor finds the constant `MAX_STUDENTS_PER_CLASS`, it will substitute the value 100. The output of the preprocessor goes directly into the compiler. The preprocessor does not change your source files in any way.

Some preprocessors create an intermediate file with an .i extension. The compiler then compiles the .i file.

The C++ preprocessor supports quite a number of directives. The most commonly used are shown in Table 17.1. These are the directives that we'll cover in this chapter.

TABLE 17.1 Commonly Used C++ Directives

Directive	Meaning
`#define`	Defines named constants and macros.
`#ifdef-#else-#endif`	Provides conditional compilation capabilities.
`#ifndef-#else-#endif`	Provides conditional compilation capabilities.
`#if defined()`	Same as `#ifdef`.
`#if !defined()`	Same as `#ifndef`.
`#include`	Includes a header file.
`#pragma`	Compiler-dependent directives.

#define

As we've seen from previous examples, the `#define` directive can be used to create named constants. It can also be used to create macros. A macro looks like a function, and usually acts like one. Hands On 17.1 demonstrates how to create a macro.

Hands On 17.1

Objective

Write a program that uses a macro to square a number.

Experiment

Type the following program into your IDE or text editor. Compile, link, and run it.

```
#include <iostream.h>

#define Squared(aNumber) aNumber*aNumber

int main()
{
   cout << "Did you know that 25 squared is ";
   cout << Squared(25) << '?' << endl;

   int anIntegerVariable = 35;
   cout << "Did you know that 35 squared is ";
   cout << Squared(anIntegerVariable) << '?' << endl;

   return (0);
}
```

Results

```
Did you know that 25 squared is 625?
Did you know that 35 squared is 1225?
```

Analysis

This program creates a macro that squares the number passed to it. The macro looks like a function. However, it is not. Instead of program execution jumping to the macro code, as it does with a function, the macro code is substituted into the program. Everywhere the `Squared()` macro appears, the preprocessor substitutes the macro's source code. When the preprocessor finds the call

```
Squared(25)
```

it substitutes

```
25*25
```

instead. Wherever it sees

```
Squared(anIntegerVaraible)
```

it substitutes

```
anIntegerVaraible*anIntegerVaraible
```

in its place.

Using macros has definite advantages. Whenever program execution jumps to a function, it incurs a slight amount of overhead. Macros do not require that overhead. However, because the macro's code is substituted throughout the program, it increases the size of the program. Using macros heavily can greatly increase your program's memory footprint. So you must decide which is more important, size or speed.

Macros also have another advantage: they don't do type checking on their parameters. For instance, Example 17.2 shows a macro named `Max()`. This macro finds the maximum of two values. The values can be integers, unsigned, floats, or any other numeric data type.

EXAMPLE 17.2 The Macro `Max()`

```
#define Max(value1,value2) (value1>value2) ? value1:value2
```

Defining this macro for use with numeric data types can save us much effort. Example 17.3 shows the equivalent functions that you would need to do the same thing that the `Max()` macro does.

EXAMPLE 17.3 `Max()` Functions

```
short Max(short value1,short value2)
{
   return ((value1>value2) ? value1:value2);
}

int Max(int value1,int value2)
{
   return ((value1>value2) ? value1:value2);
}

long Max(long value1,long value2)
{
   return ((value1>value2) ? value1:value2);
}

unsigned short Max(unsigned short value1,unsigned short value2)
{
   return ((value1>value2) ? value1:value2);
}

unsigned Max(unsigned value1,unsigned value2)
{
   return ((value1>value2) ? value1:value2);
}

unsigned long Max(unsigned long value1,unsigned long value2)
{
   return ((value1>value2) ? value1:value2);
}

float Max(float value1,float value2)
{
   return ((value1>value2) ? value1:value2);
}

double Max(double value1,double value2)
{
   return ((value1>value2) ? value1:value2);
}
```

```
long double Max(long double value1,long double value2)
{
   return ((value1>value2) ? value1:value2);
}
```

As you can see, this a quite a bit of code to accomplish the same thing as the Max() macro.

Not doing type checking on parameters is also one of the disadvantages of macros. To see why, look at Example 17.4. This program fragment declares an array of characters and passes it to the Squared() macro we saw in Hands On 17.1. It then defines an integer array and passes the integer array and the character array to the Max() macro. The preprocessor has no problem with this because it doesn't do any type checking on the parameters of a macro. No matter how ridiculous it is to try and square an array, the preprocessor will not stop us from doing so.

EXAMPLE 17.4 One Weakness of Macros

```
char aCharArray[100];
char aChar;
aChar=Squared(aCharArray);
int anIntArray[10];
aChar=Max(anIntArray,aCharArray);
```

You'll usually find this behavior only in compilers written for highly specialized hardware. It is not fully compatible with ANSI C++, but it makes compilers so much easier to write that some companies will do it just to be able to ship a compiler with their hardware. When you complain to them about the incompatibilities, they usually try to convince you that you need to upgrade to the new version of the compiler (for a fee).

What makes matters worse is that there is an outside possibility that the compiler will not catch this error as well. Both of these array names are treated as pointers.[1] Although it is rare, there are actually some compilers that treat all pointers as unsigned integers. Therefore, they allow you to do bizarre math such as this on pointers.

The long and short of this is that the lack of type checking can be both a strength and a weakness for macros.

Example 17.5 illustrates another common problem with macros. In this program, we repeat the Squared() macro from Hands On 17.1.

EXAMPLE 17.5 A Precedence Problem

```
#include <iostream.h>

#define Squared(aNumber) aNumber*aNumber

int main()
{
   int anIntegerVariable = 35;
   cout << Squared(anIntegerVariable+3) << '?' << endl;

   return (0);
}
```

As the title of Example 17.5 indicates, there is a precedence problem here. When the preprocessor performs its substitution on the Squared() macro, it will change

```
Squared(anIntegerVariable+3)
```

to

```
anIntegerVariable+3*anIntegerVariable+3
```

which will not give us the answer we expect. The rules of precedence say that the multiplication is performed before both of the additions on the line. Therefore, the program will first multiply 3*anIntegerVariable. It will then add anIntegerVariable. Finally, it will add 3. This does not give us the answer we are seeking.

[1]See Chapter 21.

The solution to precedence problems in macros is to put parentheses around your parameter names nearly everywhere they occur in macros. Example 17.6 demonstrates this technique with the `Squared()` macro.

EXAMPLE 17.6 Fixing the Precedence Problem in the `Squared()` Macro

```
#define Squared(aNumber) (aNumber)*(aNumber)
```

If we use this version of the macro as we did in Example 17.5, the preprocessor will change

```
Squared(anIntegerVariable+3)
```

to

```
(anIntegerVariable+3)*(anIntegerVariable+3)
```

which will give the correct answer.

Macros can span more than one line if you use the continuation character, which is the backslash (\). For instance, Example 17.7 shows a macro version of the `ClearScreen()` function we saw in earlier chapters. This macro spans more than one line. In fact, it even defines an entire code block, just like a function. C++ allows macros to do this.

EXAMPLE 17.7 A Macro That Spans More Than One Line

```
#define ClearScreen(totalScreenLines)           \
   {                                            \
      for (int i=0;i<totalScreenLines;i++)      \
      {                                         \
         cout<<endl;                            \
      }                                         \
   }
```

Remember that the preprocessor substitutes all of the macro code wherever the macro name appears. Using large, multiline macros can rapidly increase the memory footprint of your program.

`#ifdef`, `#else`, and `#endif`

C++ preprocessor directives enable us to define blocks of code that are conditionally compiled. The `#ifdef` directive tells the preprocessor to conditionally include a block of code for compilation if a particular named constant is defined. All of the code that is being conditionally compiled must occur between the `#ifdef` and `#endif` statements. Hands On 17.2 demonstrates a block of code that compiles conditionally.

Hands On 17.2

Objective

Write a program that conditionally compiles a block of code.

Experiment

Type the following program into your `IDE` or text editor. Make sure that you define the constant `COMPILE_THIS_CODE` in the program. Then compile, link, and run the program. After you view the results, delete the definition of the named constant `COMPILE_THIS_CODE`. Compile, link, and run the program again.

```
#include <iostream.h>

int main()
```

```
{
   #define COMPILE_THIS_CODE

   #ifdef COMPILE_THIS_CODE
   cout << "This code is conditionally ";
   cout << "compiled and executed." << endl;
   #endif

   cout << "This code is always compiled ";
   cout << "and executed." << endl;

   return (0);
}
```

Results

```
First Run:
This code is conditionally compiled and executed.
This code is always compiled and executed.

Second Run, after recompilation:
This code is always compiled and executed.
```

Analysis

This is also true of the `#ifndef`, `#if defined()`, and `#if !defined()` statements.

For the first run, the named constant `COMPILE_THIS_CODE` was defined, as shown in the code in the Experiment section. Because the preprocessor detected that the constant `COMPILE_THIS_CODE` was defined in the program, it included the block of code between the `#ifdef` and the `#endif` for compilation. Those lines of the program were compiled and executed.

It does not matter that the constant `COMPILE_THIS_CODE` is not defined to a value. If we define a constant and put nothing after it, the C++ preprocessor still sees it as being defined. Wherever it encounters the constant `COMPILE_THIS_CODE`, it substitutes nothing. An exception to this is in `#ifdef` statements. It does not perform the substitution in that case. Instead, it tests to see if the constant is defined.

Before the second run of the program, I deleted the line

```
#define COMPILE_THIS_CODE
```

so that the constant was no longer defined. When the preprocessor checked this source file, it did not find the constant `COMPILE_THIS_CODE`. The condition of the `#ifdef` evaluated to false. Therefore, the preprocessor did not pass the code between the `#ifdef` and the `#endif` to the compiler. As far as the compiler could detect, that code did not exist. The output for the second run in the Results section demonstrates that those lines of code did not become part of the final executable program.

As with C++ language `if` statements, preprocessor `#ifdef` directives can have `else` clauses. An `else` clause for an `#ifdef` directive uses the `#else` directive. Example 17.8 demonstrates an `#ifdef` directive with an `#else` clause.

EXAMPLE 17.8 An `#ifdef` with an `#else` Clause

```
#ifdef COMPILE_THIS_CODE
cout << "This code is conditionally ";
cout << "compiled and executed in the #ifdef." << endl;
#else
```

```
cout << "This code is conditionally ";
cout << "compiled and executed in the #else." << endl;
#endif
```

If the constant `COMPILE_THIS_CODE` is defined in the program before this `#ifdef` statement, the preprocessor sends the statements in the `#ifdef` block to the compiler. If it is not defined, the preprocessor sends the statements in the `#else` block to the compiler.

#ifndef, #else, and #endif

In addition to the `#ifdef` directive, the preprocessor uses an `#ifndef` directive. It is an abbreviation of "if not defined." The `#ifndef` directive works in exactly the opposite way that `#ifdef` does. If the constant that it is testing for is *not* defined, then preprocessor sends the code block of the `#ifndef` to the compiler. If it *is* defined, none of that code is compiled. Hands On 17.3 demonstrates the use of `#ifndef`, along with `#else` and `#endif`.

Hands On 17.3

Objective

Write a program that demonstrates the use of `#ifndef`, `#else`, and `#endif`.

Experiment

Type the following program into your IDE or text editor. Make sure that you do *not* define the constant `DONT_COMPILE_THIS_CODE` in the program. Then compile, link, and run the program. After you view the results, add the definition of the named constant `DONT_COMPILE_THIS_CODE`. Compile, link, and run the program again.

```
#include <iostream.h>

int main()
{
   #ifndef DONT_COMPILE_THIS_CODE
   cout << "This code is conditionally ";
   cout << "compiled and executed in the #ifndef." << endl;
   #else
   cout << "This code is conditionally ";
   cout << "compiled and executed in the #else." << endl;
   #endif

   return (0);
}
```

Results

```
First Run:
This code is conditionally compiled and executed in the #ifndef.

Second Run:
This code is conditionally compiled and executed in the #else.
```

Analysis

For the first run of this program, I did not define the named constant `DONT_COMPILE_THIS_CODE`. Because the preprocessor did not find the constant

`DONT_COMPILE_THIS_CODE` in the program, it included the block of code between the `#ifndef` and the `#else` for compilation. Those lines of the program were compiled and executed.

Before the second run of the program, I added the line

```
#define DONT_COMPILE_THIS_CODE
```

to the program before the `#ifndef`. When the preprocessor checked this source file, it found the constant `DONT_COMPILE_THIS_CODE`. The condition of the `#ifndef` evaluated to false. Therefore, the preprocessor passed the code between the `#else` and the `#endif` to the compiler. The output for the second run in the Results section demonstrates that those lines of code became part of the final executable program.

#if defined() and #if !defined()

Originally, the preprocessor directives were created for the C language. Early versions of C limited the length of identifiers and keywords to eight characters. That's why directives such as `#ifdef` and `#ifndef` are so terse.

Over time, C compilers became able to handle longer identifiers and keywords. Programmers wanted preprocessor directives that were easier to read and more self-documenting. Therefore, the ANSI C committee added the preprocessor directives `#if defined()` and `#if !defined()`, which do exactly the same thing as `#ifdef` and `#ifndef`. The code fragments in Example 17.9 demonstrate their use.

EXAMPLE 17.9 Using `#if defined()` and `#if !defined()`

```
#if defined(COMPILE_THIS_CODE)
cout << "This code is conditionally ";
cout << "compiled and executed in the #if defined()." << endl;
#else
cout << "This code is conditionally ";
cout << "compiled and executed in the #else." << endl;
#endif

#if !defined(DONT_COMPILE_THIS_CODE)
cout << "This code is conditionally ";
cout << "compiled and executed in the #if !defined()." << endl;
#else
cout << "This code is conditionally ";
cout << "compiled and executed in the #else." << endl;
#endif
```

#elif

The C++ preprocessor also provides an `#elif` directive, which is short for "else if." You can use it with `#ifdef`, `#ifndef`, `#if defined()`, and `#if !defined()`. With `#elif`, you can create a series of chained `if` conditions. Example 17.10 demonstrates one possible use of a series of code blocks that are conditionally compiled.

EXAMPLE 17.10 Using `#elif`

```
#ifdef OS_MSDOS
#define ClearScreen() system("cls")
#elif defined(OS_UNIX)
#define ClearScreen() system("clear")
#elif defined(OS_BRACKENBUSH)
#define ClearScreen() system("clrscr")
```

```
#else
#define ClearScreen()                    \
   {                                     \
      for (int i=0;i<25;i++)             \
         cout << endl;                   \
   }
#endif
```

Example 17.10 demonstrates a way to write macros that are portable across any operating system. In this case, the `#elif` directive enables us to create a definition of the `ClearScreen()` macro for any operating system.

The `#ifdef` in this code fragment tests to see if the constant `OS_MSDOS` is defined. If it is, the fragment defines the `ClearScreen()` macro as a call to the C `system()` function. This function is part of the C Standard Library, which is included with C++ compilers. It executes a command that the current operating system recognizes. The format of these commands is completely dependent on the operating system. In the case of MS DOS, the command to clear the screen is *cls*.

If the constant `OS_MSDOS` is not defined, the code fragment uses the `#elif` and `defined()` directives to test to see if `OS_UNIX` is currently defined. If it is, it defines the `ClearScreen()` macro as a call to the C `system()` function. In this case, it passes the string "clear" to the operating system because that is the command to clear the screen under Unix.

If the constant `OS_UNIX` is not defined, the fragment tests to see if the constant `OS_BRACKENBUSH` is defined. For the sake of generality, I often use a made-up computer and operating system in my examples called the "Brackenbush 5000." The command to clear the screen on this imaginary system is *clrscr*. If this code fragment detects that the constant `OS_BRACKENBUSH` is defined, then it defines the `ClearScreen()` macro as a call to the C `system()` function with the string "clrscr" to clear the screen.

If the none of the constants tested by this code fragment are currently defined, the fragment creates a `ClearScreen()` macro that clears the screen by printing 25 endlines. This is a reasonable default action.

#include

We have been using the `#include` directive in every C++ program so far. This directive instructs the preprocessor to read a file into the current file. This ability enables us to create definitions that we can use in many C++ files. The preprocessor reads in all of the definitions in the file that it includes. It is as if we typed the definitions into the C++ file at the point where the `#include` directive occurs.

As you know, C++ files have the extension .CPP on the end. The files that we include are called **header files.** Header files have traditionally used an .H extension. This is currently changing. The new standard is to have no extension on the file name. We have not been using the new standard in our examples because not all compilers support it yet. However, if your compiler does support the new standard, you should use the directive

```
#include <iostream>
```

instead of

```
#include <iostream.h>
```

in all of your programs.

This is done for portability. The actual implementation of the iostream class is different for each type of hardware and each operating system. However, the interface to the iostream class is the same for all computers and operating systems.

The C++ Standard Library comes with a set of header files for you to use. They contain definitions that are widely used. For instance, the file *iostream.h* (or *iostream* under the new standard) contains the class definition of an `iostream` object. The header files also declare global variables (in this case, that's OK) called `cin` and `cout`. Input from the keyboard and output to the screen is not actually part of the C++ language itself. It is added through objects defined in the C++ Standard Library. That's why we needed to include *iostream.h* (or *iostream*) in all of our programs.

For information on what goes in header files and what goes in CPP files, see Chapter 18.

When you include header files from the C++ Standard Library, you need to put the name of the header file in angle brackets (< and >). Since we have only been using the C++ Standard Library file *iostream.h,* that's what we have been doing. This tells the C++ compiler to search in its standard include directory for the header file. The path to this directory is compiler-dependent. Most compilers will let you set it manually if you need to.

If we create our own header files (we will), we should not try to put them in the compiler's standard include directory. We don't want to get our header files mixed up with those that come with the compiler. Usually, we keep the header files that we create in the current directory for the project we are working on. To get the compiler to check the current directory for the header file, we simply put the header file name in quotes, like this:

```
#include "MyFile.h"
```

#pragma

No matter what type of product a company manufactures, they always want to distinguish themselves from the competition. One way to do this is to add features that the competition doesn't have. Companies that manufacture C++ compilers are no different.

Using the `#pragma` directive, the C++ preprocessor enables us to access compiler-specific features in a compiler-independent way. The compiler ignores any `#pragma` directives that it doesn't recognize.

When you use the `#pragma` directive, you put the compiler-specific command or directive immediately after the `#pragma`. See Example 17.11.

EXAMPLE 17.11 Using the `#pragma` Directive

```
#pragma auto_inline
```

The compiler directive in Example 17.11 is specific to Microsoft's Visual C++. Other compilers may or may not support the `auto_inline` directive. If they don't, they just ignore the entire `#pragma` statement.

Troubleshooting Guide

After reading this section, you should be able to:

- Use preprocessor directives to keep header files from being included more than once.
- Use preprocessor directives to help you debug your programs.

Header Files That Include Header Files

In C++ programming, you often define an object for use with another object. For instance, many games use sprites. A sprite is an animated object that moves on the screen. A sprite has a bitmap image and a current position. The `sprite` object in Example 17.12 follows this pattern.

EXAMPLE 17.12 A `sprite` Object

```
class sprite
{
public:
    sprite();
    sprite(bitmap spriteImage,int initialX,int initialY);
    sprite(point upperLeftCorner);
    void Image(bitmap spriteImage);
    bitmap Image(void);
    void UpperLeftX(int xValue);
    int UpperLeftX(void);
```

```
    void UpperLeftY(int yValue);
    int UpperLeftY(void);
  private:
    bitmap bitmapImage;
    point upperLeft;
};
```

In a professional program, this definition of the `sprite` class would go into a file called *Sprite.h* (or *Sprite,* if you follow the new style). Notice that it uses a `bitmap` object and a `point` object. These would most likely be defined in the files *Bitmap.h* (or *Bitmap*) and *Point.h* (or *Point*). That means *Sprite.h* would need to include those two files.

It is possible that another file might need to include *Sprite.h*. The programmer using the `sprite` class, for very good reasons, might also include *Bitmap.h* and *Point.h* in her header file. The result is that *Bitmap.h* and *Point.h* would get included twice. Figure 17.3 illustrates this problem.

The compiler will definitely not like this situation. It will see the definitions of the `bitmap` and `point` classes twice in the file *MyFile.h.*

The way we resolve this problem is to use preprocessor directives to keep track of when a header file has already been included. Example 17.13 illustrates this technique.

EXAMPLE 17.13 Preventing Multiple Definitions

```
// This is the file Bitmap.h
#if !defined(BITMAP_H)
#define BITMAP_H

class bitmap
{
  // Class definition details go here.
};

#endif
```

The first line of the header file *Bitmap.h* contains the preprocessor directive

```
#if !defined(BITMAP_H)
```

FIGURE 17.3 A Problem with Header Files

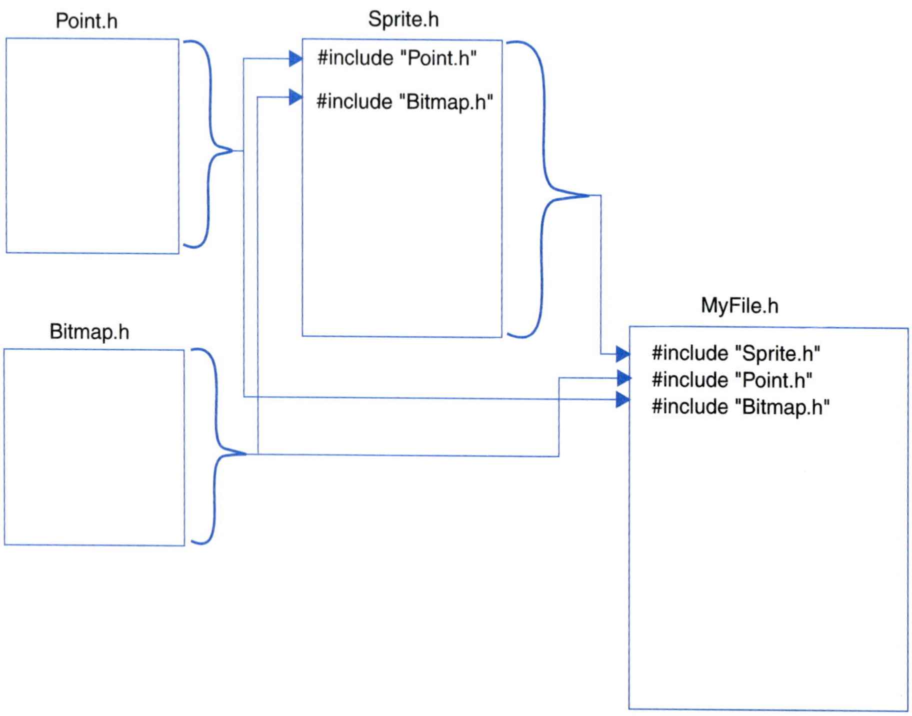

When I was learning C programming in college, I worked this technique out for myself. I actually thought I was the first to invent it, and spent about three weeks congratulating myself on what a clever programmer I was. Then I found the technique explained in a C programming book that had been written years prior to that time. That experience taught me that it's sometimes better to be well read than clever.

This tells the preprocessor to send the code block of the `#if !defined` directive to the compiler if the named constant `BITMAP_H` is not defined. The very first item in the `#if !defined` directive's code block is the statement

```
#define BITMAP_H
```

That means that when the header file *Bitmap.h* has been included once, the constant `BITMAP_H` is defined. If *Bitmap.h* is accidentally included again, the preprocessor will process each statement in the file again. The first statement is, of course, the

```
#if !defined(BITMAP_H)
```

directive. This time, the constant `BITMAP_H` is defined. Therefore, nothing between the `#if !defined()` directive and the `#endif` directive is sent to the compiler. The preprocessor prevents all of the definitions in *Bitmap.h* from appearing more than once in a file.

Using Preprocessor Directives for Debugging

Debugging programs aren't always available for the environment in which we're working. Even if they are, there are ways to ease our debugging burdens using the C++ preprocessor.

Marking Code for Debug One common debugging strategy is to define code as being for debugging purposes only. For instance, suppose you create a function that writes the current status of a program out to a log file. This enables you to, among other things, print the log file and review it together with co-workers. In the version of the program that you release to the public, you don't want the program to save its status in a log file. That will slow it down considerably. In this scenario, you can use the preprocessor to conditionally compile code only in the debug version. Example 17.14 demonstrates this technique.

EXAMPLE 17.14 Defining Code for Debug

```
#if defined(DEBUG)
SaveProgramStatusToLogFile();
#endif
```

As you can see, the preprocessor will pass the call to the function `SaveProgramStatusToLogFile()` to the compiler only if the constant DEBUG is defined. As long as you are working on your program, you can have the definition of the constant DEBUG in your program. As soon as you are ready for release, delete (or comment out) the definition of DEBUG and recompile. The preprocessor will not pass the call to `SaveProgramStatusToLogFile()` to the compiler.

Simulating Breakpoints If a debugger isn't available for the hardware or operating system you're using, you can still put breakpoints in your program using the preprocessor. Example 17.15 shows a macro called `Breakpoint()`. This macro will cause a program to display a message and pause until the user presses the Enter key on the keyboard. The message can be any string that contains program status information. This enables you to print the contents of variables, for instance. The program will wait until you are done looking at the status message. When you press Enter, the program continues.

Notice also that Example 17.15 uses the technique described in the previous section. That is, if the constant DEBUG is defined, the preprocessor defines the `Breakpoint()` macro with the code block shown in the example. If it isn't, the preprocessor defines the `Breakpoint()` macro as nothing. Everywhere the call to the `Breakpoint()` macro occurs in the source code, the preprocessor substitutes nothing. The compiler never sees the macro or the call.

EXAMPLE 17.15 Simulating Breakpoints

```
#if defined(DEBUG)
#define Breakpoint(msgstr)                          \
      {                                             \
       cout << msgstr;                              \
       cout << endl;                                \
```

```
        cout << "Press any key to continue...";    \
        char aChar;                                 \
        cin >> achar;                               \
    }
#else
#define Breakpoint(msgstr)
#endif
```

Summary

Every time you compile a program, it is automatically processed by the C++ preprocessor before it is compiled. We can put the C++ preprocessor directives in our programs to control the preprocessor's behavior.

We can use the preprocessor to define named constants, define macros, and perform conditional compilation. Create named constants and macros using the `#define` directive. Perform conditional compilation with the `#ifdef`, `#ifndef`, `#else`, `#elif`, `#if defined()`, and `#if !defined()` directives.

C++ programmers put the class and constant definitions that are used in more than one file into header files. This allows them to include the header file in another file that needs the definitions. Use the `#include` directive to include a header file.

The `#pragma` directive enables us to access compiler-specific features in a portable way. If a compiler doesn't support a particular `#pragma` option, it ignores the option.

Review Questions

1. What is the C++ preprocessor? Describe its use.
2. How do you define a named constant with the `#define` directive? Where is the constant visible in the file? *Hint:* You might want to look back at Chapter 10.
3. How do you define a macro with the `#define` directive?
4. What are some of the advantages of macros when compared to functions? What are some of the disadvantages?
5. What preprocessor directives are used to perform conditional compilation?
6. What are three reasons you might want to do conditional compilation?
7. What does the `#include` directive do?
8. Why do we use header files?
9. What is one potential problem with the `#include` directive? How do you solve this problem?
10. How can you use preprocessor directives to aid you in debugging your programs?

Exercises

1. Define a macro called `Cube()` that cubes any number that you pass to it. In other words, if you pass it 5, it should evaluate to 5*5*5. Write a program demonstrating that your macro works.
2. Change the program that you wrote for Exercise 1. Declare an integer variable called `anInteger`. Initialize `anInteger` to 5. Your program should call the `Cube()` macro you wrote in Exercise 1 and pass it `anInteger+2`. If it does not give the correct answer, fix it so that it does.
3. Explain how you can write highly portable macros using conditional compilation.
4. Define a macro called `Max2()` that finds the maximum of two values. Write a program that demonstrates the macro.
5. Write a macro called `Max3()` that finds the maximum of three values. *Hint:* This is easier if you use the `Max2()` macro from Exercise 4.
6. Write a program that uses a `for` loop to count from 0 to 999. Inside the loop, call a function called `PrintCounter()` that prints the current value of the loop counter

variable to the stream `cout`. Make the call to the function conditionally compiled. If the constant `PRINT_COUNTER` is defined, then the call to the `PrintCounter()` function should be compiled. If it is not defined, the compiler should not compile the call to `PrintCounter()`.

7. Look in your compiler's documentation and find three `#pragma` options that are specific to your compiler. Briefly explain each.
8. Write a program that uses the `Breakpoint()` macro defined in this chapter to simulate breakpoints.
9. Write a program that uses conditional compilation to define a named constant called `ARRAY_LENGTH`. If the constant `SMALL_ARRAY` is defined, the value of `ARRAY_LENGTH` should be 20. If the constant `BIG_ARRAY` is defined, the value of `ARRAY_LENGTH` should be 1000. If neither of these constants are defined, the value of `ARRAY_LENGTH` should be 100. Your program should declare an array of characters of length `ARRAY_LENGTH`. It should use a `for` loop to fill the array with characters, and then print the characters to the screen.
10. Look in your compiler's online documentation or a book about the C/C++ Standard Library for information about a function called `abort()`. Use the `abort()` function in a macro called `DebugAbort()` that prints an error message to the stream `cout`, and then aborts the program. The macro should only be included in the compiled program if the constant DEBUGGING is defined. Write a program that demonstrates your macro works.

Chapter Glossary

Header File A file that contains definitions that are used in more than one CPP file.

18 Organizing Programs

Objectives

After reading this chapter, you should be able to:

- Organize programs composed of multiple files.
- Explain what goes into a header file.
- Explain what goes into a CPP file.

Preview

Most commercial programs are composed of a large number of files. Part of being able to design and develop an application is knowing what goes where. This skill is basic to building working systems in a team environment. This chapter introduces some common organizational conventions used by C++ programmers.

Organizing Files

It is a fact of life in most development environments that programs must be divided into many files. When you are working as part of a development team, working in the same file or files as other developers is generally too difficult to be worthwhile. You often end up overwriting each other's work.

Development teams ordinarily divide up the program and assign each team member to write an object or a group of objects. They agree on the interface to each object. Each team member then goes to his computer and begins implementing his part of the program. When the team members finish their portions of the program, all of the pieces must fit together. Therefore, they must all agree on and use the same method of organizing their files.

The most common method is to put the definition of shared objects into header files. The member functions for the objects go into a CPP file. Using this style, objects tend to stand on their own better. It is more likely that they can be used in other programs. (Technically speaking, they have low cohesion.)

Header Files

Header files are the most common method of sharing information between CPP files. Used properly, they can be a tremendous aid in writing portable, reusable objects.

What to Put in a Header File What goes into a header file?

Remember that one of the goals of object oriented programming is encapsulation. No object should need to "know" how any other object is implemented. If you and I are working on a project together, I should be able to change the implementation of any of my

TABLE 18.1 The Contents of a Header File

Item	Explained In
Include Files	Chapter 17
Global Constants	Chapter 10, Chapter 17
Type Definitions	Chapter 25
Enumerated Types	Chapter 25
Classes, Structures, and Unions	Chapter 13, Chapter 14, Chapter 25
Inline Functions*	Chapter 24
Macros	Chapter 17
Prototypes	Chapter 12

*Many programmers prefer to put their inline functions in a separate file with the .inl extension. See the Troubleshooting Guide in Chapter 25 for a discussion of the advantages and disadvantages of this approach.

objects without making you change the implementation of any of yours. As long as the interfaces to my objects stay the same, it should make no difference to you.

Using this philosophy, a header file should only contain the things that need to be shared between two or more CPP files. Any time we put something into a header file, we should ask ourselves if it is needed in more than one CPP file. If not, it should not go into a header file.

Table 18.1 contains a list of everything that normally goes into a header file. In general, programmers also follow the order of arrangement shown in the table. That is, include files come before global constants, global constants come before types, and so on.

Header files often include other header files. All `#include` directives generally go together at the beginning of the header file. The purpose of including a header file in a header file is because the definitions that one header file uses are also used in the other. Therefore, you generally want the header files to come first so that their definitions are available to everything else in the header file.

Keep in mind that we're not setting anything in stone here, just discussing common practice. If you've got a good reason to use a different style than the one shown here, by all means discuss it with your team members.

As you may recall, the C++ philosophy is to declare variables and constants close to where they are used. However, if constants are widely used in a program, programmers often declare them together in a header file. Constants that are only used in one spot should be declared close to where they are used.

Sometimes the value of a constant depends on the value of a constant in another header file. Therefore, the section for the global constants usually comes after the `#include` directives. It's also not unusual for type definitions, enumerations, class definitions, and other header file items to use the global constants. Therefore, programmers often put global constants before any of those header file items.

Type definitions, enumerated types, classes, structures, and unions are all ways of creating your own types. Your types form the building blocks of a program and its functions, so programmers generally insert these items next.

For very good reasons, you may or may not choose to put inline functions in a header file. Inline functions are a way of making class member functions into macros. If you do put inline functions in your header file, they will need to come after the definition of the class to which they belong.

As we saw in Chapter 17, macros do not check the types of their parameters. They can occur virtually anywhere in the header file. Since they do not depend on any type definitions, many programmers put them together with the global constants. Usually the other members of your team will not mind if you choose to use that style.

It is not unusual for even very object oriented programs to contain functions that are not members of any class. Their prototypes commonly depend on the definitions of the constants and types, so they usually come last in a header file.

What Not to Put in a Header File The one thing that header files should not contain is functions.[1] If you put a function into a header file, it will undoubtedly be included in more

[1]The exception to this in inline functions. See Chapter 25.

TIP: Never include a CPP file—compile and link them. Never compile or link a header file—always include them.

than one CPP file. When you compile your program, the linker will detect two (or more) identical versions of your functions. It will not know which one to link to, so your link will fail.

For this same reason, you should also never include a file with a .cpp extension.

CPP Files

Header files contain the definitions a program needs. CPP files contain the program's implementation. A CPP file can contain anything that a header file contains. It also contains functions.

Table 18.2 displays the contents of a CPP file in the order that items typically occur. Notice that the only difference here is that the CPP files also contain functions.

How do you know when a class definition, for instance, goes into a header file and when it goes into a CPP file? I'll answer that question with a question: Is it shared? If the information (1) is not a function and (2) must be shared between two or more CPP files, it goes into a header file. If not, it goes into a CPP file.

Typically, programmers organize their header and CPP files around their objects. That is, for each shared object, they create a header file to hold the class definition. They also make a CPP file containing the class's member function.

Let's suppose that we're working on a text editor together. The text editor uses a text buffer. Each line of the text buffer contains a string. We decide that you will implement a string class called `text_string`, and I will use that to implement a `text_buffer` class. You will need to create a file called *Tstring.h* (or just *Tstring,* if you're following the newer convention). You also should make a file called *Tstring.cpp*.

The file *Tstring.h* (or *Tstring*) will hold the class definition of the `text_string` class. It will also contain any other types, constants, and so on that may be needed to use the `text_string` class.

Tstring.cpp will have the member functions of the the `text_string` class. There may also be other types, constants, functions, and so on that you need for the `text_string` class. However, I will not need to know that to use your `text_string` class.

I will include your header file in my file, *Tbuffer.h* (or *Tbuffer*). This file has the class definition of the `text_buffer` class. I will also need to write a file called *Tbuffer.cpp*. It will hold the member functions of the `text_buffer` class.

In addition, we will also need to create a file for the `main()` function of our program. It will declare and manipulate a `text_buffer` object, get user input, and interpret user commands. In addition to `main()`, this file may contain functions that are not members of any class.

Figure 18.1 shows the organization of the text editor.

This style of organization affords several advantages. It helps hide the implementation of the object by sharing only the class definition in the header file. The implementation stands alone in a CPP file. It lessens the dependence between object implementations and increases encapsulation. It helps other programmers figure out how the program works and it enables programmers to quickly find object implementations.

TABLE 18.2 The Contents of a CPP File

Item	Explained In
Include Files	Chapter 17
Global Constants	Chapter 10, Chapter 17
Type Definitions	Chapter 25
Enumerated Types	Chapter 25
Classes, Structures, and Unions	Chapter 13, Chapter 14, Chapter 25
Inline Functions	Chapter 24
Macros	Chapter 17
Prototypes	Chapter 12
Class Member Functions	Chapter 12, Chapter 14
Nonmember Functions	

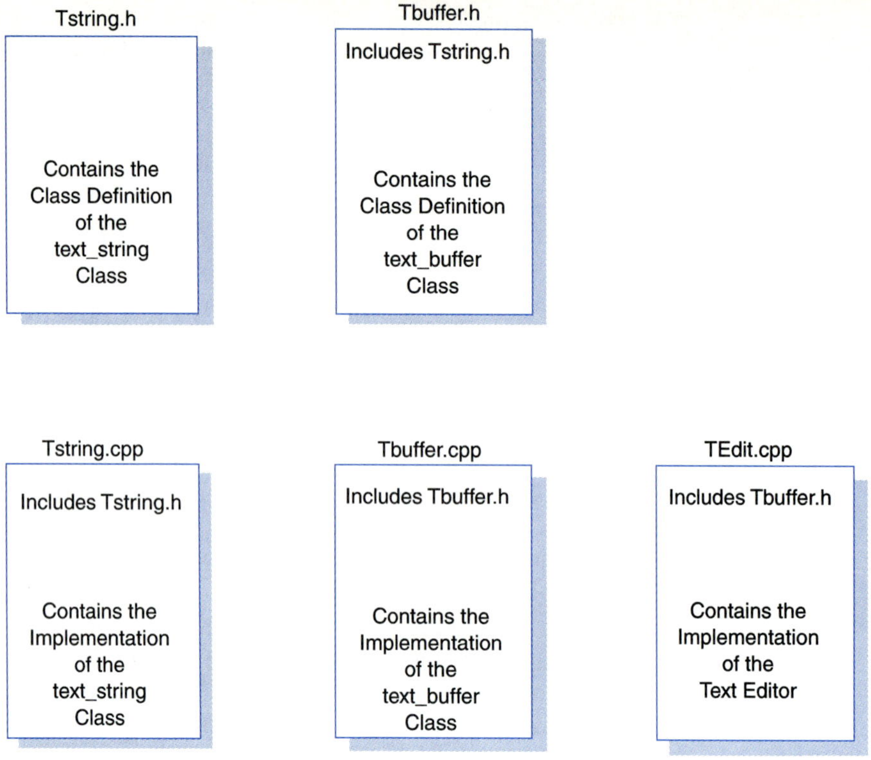

FIGURE 18.1 One Possible Organization of a Text Editor Program

Troubleshooting Guide

After reading this section, you should be able to:

- Find and fix circular inclusions.
- Understand the advantages and disadvantages of using one central include file.

Circular Inclusions

When you follow the file organization style described in this chapter, you will find that it has one characteristic that is either an advantage or a disadvantage, depending on your point of view.

Suppose we have three header files, *A.h, B.h,* and *C.h.* Figure 18.2 shows fragments of these three files. Notice that the file *B.h* includes *A.h. C.h* includes *B.h. A.h* includes *C.h.*

C++ compilers don't allow this. By separating every class definition of each object into its own header file, C++ compilers make it hard to keep track of which file includes what. You've got to expect that programmers using your objects may run into this problem.

This is not necessarily a bad thing. In my personal experience, circular inclusions always indicate a design flaw. Every time I've run into this, I've found that my objects were too interdependent. Sometimes I just had to redesign their interfaces. Other times, I needed

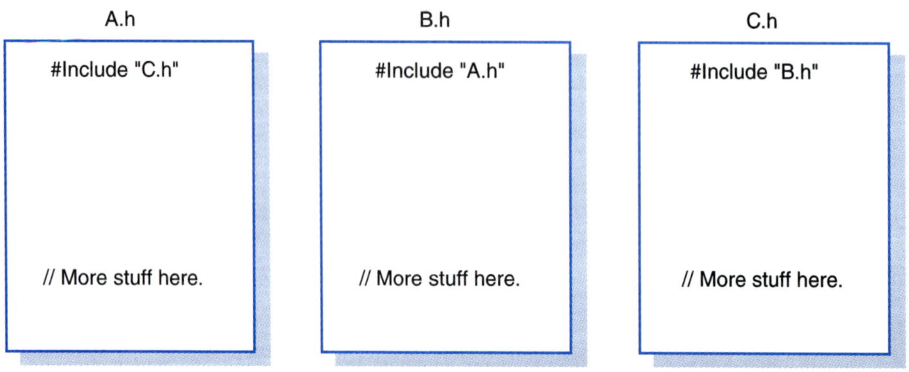

FIGURE 18.2 Circular Inclusion

FIGURE 18.3 An All-Inclusive Include File

to create additional objects in the program. At times, I had to combine two or more objects into one. In each instance, I was able to come up with a better design that did not suffer the circular inclusion problem.

For this reason, I think of circular inclusions as a benefit, not a disadvantage. They tell me when I have a design problem. I know many other programmers, however, see circular inclusions as a serious disadvantage.

One Big Inclusion

Some programmers include all of their header files into one file. Figure 18.3 demonstrates this technique. It uses the header files from Figure 18.1 and adds an additional header file called *Tedit.h*. This file includes all other header files created for the program. All CPP files include the header file *Tedit.h*. They do not include any other header file.

You can extend this technique to solve the problem of circular includes. Example 18.1 shows the contents of the three header files from Figure 18.2. It also adds a fourth header file, *D.h*.

EXAMPLE 18.1 Solving the Circular Inclusion Problem

```
// Beginning of A.h
#define A_H
#if !defined(D_H)
#include D.h
#endif

// More stuff here.

// End of A.h


// Beginning of B.h
#define B_H
#if !defined(D_H)
#include D.h
```

```
#endif

// More stuff here.

// End of B.h
```

```
// Beginning of C.h
#define C_H
#if !defined(D_H)
#include D.h
#endif

// More stuff here.

// End of C.h
```

```
// Beginning of D.h
#define D_H

#if !defined(A_H)

#include A.h

#endif

#if !defined(B_H)

#include B.h

#endif

#if !defined(C_H)

#include C.h

#endif

// End of D.h
```

Let's suppose that the preprocessor is currently working on the file *A.h*. The file *A.h* defines the constant A_H. Since the constant D_H is not defined, it includes the file *D.h*. The first thing that *D.h* does is to define the constant D_H. Next, it tests to see if A_H is defined. Since A_H is defined at this point, *D.h* does not include *A.h*. It does include *B.h* and *C.h*. The files *B.h* and *C.h* will not include *D.h* because D_H is currently defined.

The processing of *B.h* and *C.h* follow the same pattern. Using this technique, you can include one header file in every other header file and every CPP file in a program. It will automatically include every other header file. There can never be a circular inclusion in your program.

The disadvantage of this, however, is that your program grows by leaps and bounds. This technique causes *everything* (classes, types, constants, etc.) to be defined in *every* CPP file. Your compiler might optimize away things that are not used. Or it might not.

Using an all-inclusive include file also increases the time it takes to compile your program. For a large professional program, compilation can literally take hours. Adding more overhead to an already long compile time may simplify your coding effort. However, you pay a price for it.

Summary

C++ programmers normally put the class definition of an object into a header file. The member functions go into a CPP file. Together, the header file and the CPP file form the definition and implementation of an object.

Header files should contain information that needs to be shared between two or more CPP files. Anything that is required by only one CPP file should go into that CPP file.

Following this style of implementation can lead to circular inclusions. This usually indicates a design problem. You can eliminate the circular inclusion problem by using one all-inclusive include file. However, it may make your program larger. It *will* make your program compile slower.

Review Questions

1. What does a header file contain?
2. What does a CPP file contain?
3. How do you decide whether something should go in a header file or a CPP file?
4. What is circular inclusion?
5. How might circular inclusion be a benefit?
6. How does the possibility of circular inclusion place a burden on the programmer?
7. How does an all-inclusive include file ease the burden on the programmer?
8. What penalty is paid for using an all-inclusive include file?
9. Why should your header files never include CPP files?
10. Why should your CPP files never include CPP files?

Exercises

1. Explain how the sample organization of the text editor in this chapter helps program development.
2. Look back at the diagrams for the Space Attackers game in Chapter 12. Name at least three objects you would create for this game. Describe how you would organize the files for these three objects. Explain your reasons for organizing the files the way you did.
3. Suppose you are designing a customer database program for a software store. Name at least three objects you would create for this program. Describe how you would organize the files for these three objects. Explain your reasons for organizing the files the way you did.
4. Some programmers organize their files around the tasks a program performs, rather than the objects it uses. Tell what you think of this technique. Explain your reasons for your viewpoint.
5. Go to the library at your school (or your local library) and find at least three books that deal with software design and development. Find at least two magazine articles on software design and development. List the sources you found.

19 Inheritance

Objectives

After reading this chapter, you should be able to:

- Design and develop reusable objects with inheritance.
- Extend object functionality by overriding member functions.
- Appropriately use inheritance and containership.

Preview

It's generally not a good idea for programmers to work hard. I often tell my students that they should strive to be successfully lazy. A hardworking programmer, when he's given the assignment to write a program, goes directly to his keyboard and starts coding objects. That's not the best approach to the job of programming.

A successfully lazy programmer, when given an assignment to write a program, designs her objects, then consults her reference books to see if she can find something to use. She may also check programming magazines, code repositories on the Internet, and other public-domain sources. If she can't find objects there, she'll probably look though advertisements in programming magazines for object class libraries. If all else fails, she'll write her own objects.

Even when we do try to be successfully lazy, we seldom find objects that fit our needs exactly. The objects that someone else has written invariably are *almost,* but not quite, what we need. In these instances, C++ provides us with a powerful language feature called *inheritance,* which enables us to extend and modify the functionality of objects without changing any of their source code.

This chapter introduces inheritance and explains how to apply it to reuse and extend the functionality of objects.

Base Classes and Derived Classes

The essential concepts of object oriented programming were first introduced in the overview in Chapter 13. To introduce the idea of inheritance, I used the example of a automobile software object.

Suppose once again that we work for a company, and our boss gives us the task of writing a car simulation. You and I decide that we should create a generic car object in software. The generic car's member data describe its characteristics. Its member functions form the set of operations that our program can perform on a car.

Object oriented programming literature also calls the base class the *parent* class and the derived class the *child* class.

Our program should model particular types of cars. For instance, it needs a sports car object. With inheritance, we can use the generic car object as a building block for the

FIGURE 19.1 **An Inheritance Relationship**

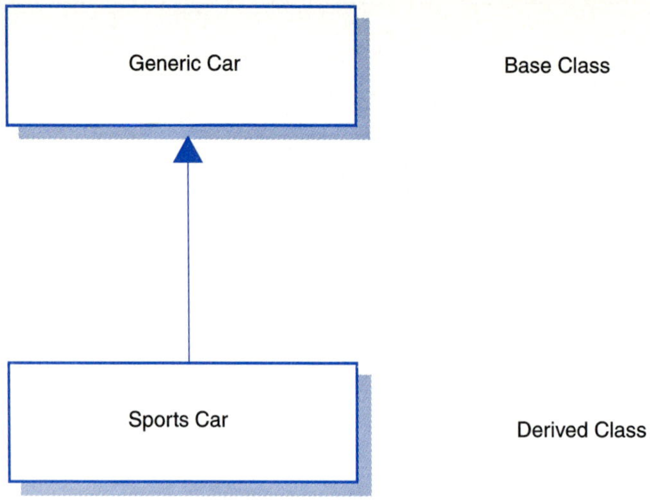

sports car. The generic car object forms the **base class** for the sports car object. Since we're deriving the sports car from the generic car, the sports car is called a **derived class.**

Figure 19.1 illustrates the relationship between the generic car and the sports car. The lines in this type of diagram are usually drawn to show which are the derived classes and which are the base classes. Therefore, the arrow is drawn pointing from the sports car class to the generic car class.

Because the sports car object is derived from the generic car object, it inherits all of the characteristics of the generic car. That is, a sports car can do anything other types of cars can do. Real sports cars can also do things other cars can't. We can use the member functions of the car object for most of what a sports car does. Anything that the sports car does that a regular car doesn't do can be added by just adding a few member functions to the sports car object.

What if the sports car does something that other cars do, but it does that thing differently? An example is acceleration. A generic car doesn't accelerate very fast. However, a sports car does. They both do the same thing—accelerate—but they do it differently.

In the inheritance relationship, we can **override** the member functions of the base class. C++ enables us to create a function that replaces a function in an object's base class. We can add an acceleration function to the sports car object that replaces, or overrides, the acceleration function in the generic car.

The advantage of using a generic base class to create specific derived classes is that we can create many different derived classes from the same base class. We write and debug the code in the base class only once. This decreases the amount of work that we need to do to get our job done.

Some object oriented programming literature would refer to the minivan and sports car objects as *peer* or *sibling* objects since they are both derived from the generic car object.

For instance, suppose our boss tells us to add a minivan to our car simulation. We can reuse the generic car object that we already wrote. With inheritance, we build a minivan software object on the generic car software object. As it did for the sports car, the generic car object performs most of the functionality of the minivan object. We just add specific characteristics and functionality to customize the generic car object into a minivan object. This does not alter the generic car object in any way. Figure 19.2 illustrates this relationship.

FIGURE 19.2 **Reusing the Generic Car Object**

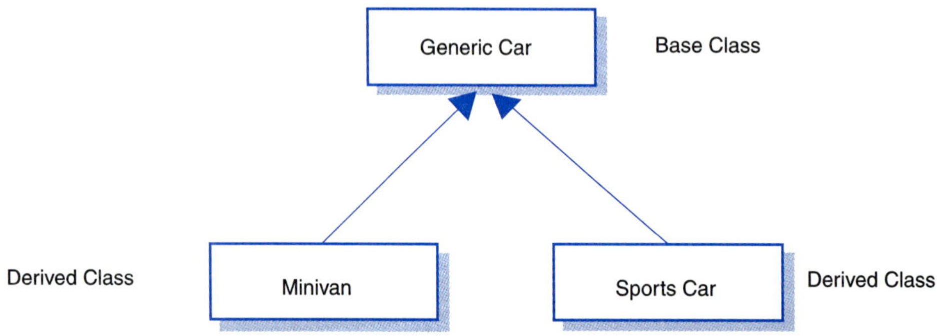

FIGURE 19.3 The Instantiation of a sports_car Object

When we declare an object of a derived type, that object also contains an object of the base type. Figure 19.3 depicts an object called `sports_car`. It is derived from a base class called `generic_car`.

A program creates a `sports_car` object in just the same way it creates any variable of any other type. That is, the program contains a statement like this:

```
sports_car aCar;
```

Derived Constructors

Constructors in a derived class should do two things. First, they should call the constructor of the base class from which they inherit. Second, they should initialize the data that is specific to the derived class.

As much as possible, objects in a program should initialize themselves into a known state. Since a derived object contains an embedded object of its base class, the derived object calls the base class constructor to initialize the embedded object. The embedded base object must be initialized before the derived object because the attributes of the derived object may depend on the attributes of the base object.

Once a derived object calls the base class constructor, it should initialize its own data members into a known state.

Hands On 19.1 demonstrates inheritance.

Hands On 19.1

Objective

Write a program that demonstrates inheritance.

Experiment

Type the following program into your IDE or text editor. Compile, link, and run it.

```
#include <iostream.h>

class base_class
```

```
{
public:
    base_class(void);

    void PrintBaseDataMember(void);

private:
    int baseClassDataMember;
};



base_class::base_class(void)
{
    cout << "base_class constructor" << endl;
    baseClassDataMember = 10;
}


void base_class::PrintBaseDataMember(void)
{
    cout << baseClassDataMember << endl;
}


class derived_class : public base_class
{
public:
    derived_class(void);

    void PrintDerivedDataMember(void);

private:
    int derivedClassDataMember;
};


derived_class::derived_class(void) : base_class()
{
    cout << "derived_class constructor" << endl;
    derivedClassDataMember=20;
}


void derived_class::PrintDerivedDataMember(void)
{
    cout << derivedClassDataMember<< endl;
}



int main()
{
    base_class baseClassObject;
    derived_class derivedOjbect;

    baseClassObject.PrintBaseDataMember();
```

```
    derivedOjbect.PrintDerivedDataMember();

    return (0);
}
```

Results

```
base_class constructor
base_class constructor
derived_class constructor
10
20
```

Analysis

This program defines two objects: `base_class` and `derived_class`. The `base_class` object contains an integer data member, as does the `derived_class` object.

Take a look at the definition of the `derived_class` object. The first line looks like this:

```
class derived_class : public base_class
```

This is how you indicate inheritance in your programs.

Note that the first line of the constructor for the derived class uses a similar notation. The line

```
derived_class::derived_class(void) : base_class()
```

states that this function is a member of the class `derived_class`. Its function name specifies it as the constructor. The addition of `: base_class()` tells the program to call the constructor for `base_class` whenever it creates an object of type `derived_class`.

If you look at the program output in the Results section, you'll see that the `base_class` constructor gets called twice. It's called the first time when the `main()` function declares a variable of type `base_class`. The second call occurs when the `main()` function declares an object of type `derived_class`.

Parameters are also called *arguments* in much of the C++ programming literature.

TIP: When you create a derived class, make its constructor explicitly call the base class's constructor.

If your derived class does not define a constructor, the C++ compiler will automatically create one with no parameters. It will even automatically call the constructor from the base class that has no parameters.

However, if you later decide that your derived class needs a constructor with one parameter and add it, the C++ compiler will not automatically call the constructor of the base class. You must explicitly call it in the manner shown in Hands On 19.1.

For this and many other reasons, it's best to get into the habit of always creating at least one constructor for every class you write. If the class inherits from another class, call the constructor explicitly.

You do not have similar worries when it comes to destructors. The C++ compiler automatically generates a call to the base object's destructor.[1]

Overriding Member Functions

Member functions in derived classes can override the member functions in base classes. This capability enables us to create functions in the derived class that replace or enhance functions in the base class. It does so without forcing us to modify the base class in any

[1]The exception to this is discussed in Chapter 24 in the section titled "Virtual Destructors."

way. Hands On 19.2 demonstrates a function named `Print()` in the derived class that enhances the `Print()` function in the base class.

Hands On 19.2

Objective

Write a program that demonstrates how a member function in a derived class can override a member function in a base class.

Experiment

Type the following program into your IDE or text editor. Compile, link, and run it.

```
#include <iostream.h>


class base_class
{
public:
    base_class(void);

    void Print(void);

private:
    int baseClassDataMember;
};



base_class::base_class(void)
{
    cout << "base_class constructor" << endl;
    baseClassDataMember = 10;
}


void base_class::Print(void)
{
    cout << baseClassDataMember << endl;
}


class derived_class : public base_class
{
public:
    derived_class(void);

    void Print(void);

private:
    int derivedClassDataMember;
};


derived_class::derived_class(void) : base_class()
```

```
{
    cout << "derived_class constructor" << endl;
    derivedClassDataMember=20;
}


void derived_class::Print(void)
{
    base_class::Print();
    cout << derivedClassDataMember<< endl;
}



int main()
{
    base_class baseClassObject;
    derived_class derivedOjbect;

    baseClassObject.Print();
    derivedOjbect.Print();

    return (0);
}
```

Results

```
base_class constructor
base_class constructor
derived_class constructor
10
10
20
```

Analysis

This variation of the program from Hands On 19.1 uses a member function called `Print()` in both the base and derived classes. When the `Print()` function in the derived class executes, it first calls the `Print()` function from the base class.

Notice that the call to `Print()` in the base class is preceded by the scope resolution operator. If you leave this out, the C++ compiler will assume that you are trying to call the `Print()` function in the derived class, not the `Print()` function in the base class. The `Print()` function in the derived class can call itself. The rules of the C++ language allow this.

This technique is called *recursion.*

Because the `Print()` function in the derived class calls the `Print()` function in the base class, it adds to the functionality of the base class's `Print()` function. It does not change the `Print()` function in the base class at all. This powerful feature of the C++ language enables us to easily build new functionality on objects that others provide for us.

The program in Hands On 19.2 showed how a member function in a derived class can enhance the functionality of a member function in a base class. If you want to completely replace a function in the base class, you use the same technique. The difference is that you don't call the function in the base class that you're overriding.

Public and Private Inheritance

Inheritance can be public or private. So far, the examples in this chapter have demonstrated only public inheritance. That is by far the most common. However, we can also use private inheritance.

What is meant by *public* and *private inheritance*?

With public inheritance, all of the public member functions of the base class can be called using an object in the derived class. Example 19.1 demonstrates this idea. The implementation of the member functions is omitted from the example for brevity.

EXAMPLE 19.1 Calling the Member Functions of a Base Class

```
class B
{
public:
   void ThisFunction(void);
};

class D : public B
{
public:
   void ThatFunction(void);
};

int main()
{
   D dObject;

   // This is ok because it's inherited publicly.
   dObject.ThisFunction();

   // This is ok too.
   dObject.ThatFunction();
}
```

The `main()` function declares an object of the derived class. The function `ThisFunction()`, which is a member of the base class, can be called by `main()`. The derived class `D` inherits the function `ThisFunction()` from the base class `B`. In other words, through inheritance, `D` acquires all of the attributes and operations of `B`.

Private inheritance restricts access to the interface of the base class. Functions in the base class can't be accessed through the derived class. Example 19.2 shows a derived class that uses private inheritance.

EXAMPLE 19.2 Private Inheritance

```
class B
{
public:
   void ThisFunction(void);
};

class D : private B
{
public:
 void ThatFunction(void);
};

int main()
```

```
{
    D dObject;

    // This is not allowed.
    dObject.ThisFunction();

    // This is ok.
    dObject.ThatFunction();
}
```

The attempt by the `main()` function to access `ThisFunction()` using an object of the derived class will not work. Functions that are members of the derived class can access functions in the base class. However, nonmembers cannot get access to the interface in the derived class when you use private inheritance.

Specify private inheritance by inserting the keyword `private` after the colon on the first line of the derived class, as shown in Example 19.2.

Using Inheritance in Programs

Hands On 19.3 implements an example of inheritance that is more like what you would encounter in a real program. The application itself is not a common C++ programming task. There are not very many car simulation programs on the market today. However, the way that the application is implemented is how you will implement many of the C++ programs that you will write in your professional career. Each object is defined in its own header file. The implementation is defined in a corresponding CPP file. The `main()` function uses the objects to declare variables and perform the highest-level tasks of the program.

Hands On 19.3

Objective

Define a generic car class.
Derive a sports car class from the generic car class.
Derive a minivan class from the generic car class.
Write a program that demonstrates the car classes.

Experiment

This program consists of four CPP files and three header files. Type all of them separately into your IDE or text editor. Compile and link all of the CPP files together in one project or make file. See your compiler's documentation for information on creating project or make files. After you link the program, run it.

```
//-----------------------------------------------------------------------
/*
File Name:     GCar.h
Comments:      Contains the definition of the generic_car class.
*/
//-----------------------------------------------------------------------

#if !defined(GCAR_H)
#define GCAR_H


class generic_car
{
```

```
// Public member functions.
public:
   generic_car(void);
   ~generic_car();

   int Speed(void);          // Get the current speed.
   int TopSpeed(void);
   void Accelerate(void);

// Protected member functions.
protected:
   void Speed(int newSpeed);   // Set the current speed.

// Private member data.
private:
   int currentSpeed;
};


#endif
// End GCar.h
//---------------------------------------------------------------------------



//---------------------------------------------------------------------------
/*
File Name:      GCar.cpp
Comments:       Contains the member functions of the generic_car class.
*/
//---------------------------------------------------------------------------



//---------------------------------------------------------------------------
// Include Files

#include "GCar.h"

// End Include Files
//---------------------------------------------------------------------------



//---------------------------------------------------------------------------
/*
Function Name:          generic_car
Member of:              generic_car
Input Parameters:       None.
Output Parameters:      None.
Return Value:           Constructed generic_car object.
Comments:               Constructor for the generic_car class.
*/

generic_car::generic_car()
{
   currentSpeed=0;
}
```

```
//------------------------------------------------------------------------------
/*
Function Name:          ~generic_car
Member of:              generic_car
Input Parameters:       None.
Output Parameters:      None.
Return Value:           None.
Comments:               Destructor for the generic_car class.
*/

generic_car::~generic_car()
{
}


//------------------------------------------------------------------------------
/*
Function Name:          Speed
Member of:              generic_car
Input Parameters:       None.
Output Parameters:      None.
Return Value:           Current speed.
Comments:               Use this function to get the value of the current speed.
*/

int generic_car::Speed(void)
{
   return (currentSpeed);
}



//------------------------------------------------------------------------------
/*
Function Name:          Speed
Member of:              generic_car
Input Parameters:       None.
Output Parameters:      None.
Return Value:           Current speed.
Comments:               Use this function to get the value of the current speed.
*/

void generic_car::Speed(int newSpeed)
{
   currentSpeed=newSpeed;
}


//------------------------------------------------------------------------------
/*
Function Name:          TopSpeed
Member of:              generic_car
Input Parameters:       None.
Output Parameters:      None.
Return Value:           Maximum speed of the car object.
```

```
Comments:                Use this function to get the value of the top speed.
*/

int generic_car::TopSpeed(void)
{
   return (0);
}



//----------------------------------------------------------------------------
/*
Function Name:          Accelerate
Member of:              generic_car
Input Parameters:       None.
Output Parameters:      None.
Return Value:           Constructed generic_car object.
Comments:               Use this function to make the car accelerate.
*/

void generic_car::Accelerate(void)
{
   currentSpeed++;
}


// End GCar.cpp
//----------------------------------------------------------------------------



//----------------------------------------------------------------------------
/*
File Name:       Minivan.h
Comments:        Contains the definition of the minivan class.
*/
//----------------------------------------------------------------------------

#if !defined(MINIVAN_H)
#define MINIVAN_H



//----------------------------------------------------------------------------
// Include Files

#include "GCar.h"

// End Include Files
//----------------------------------------------------------------------------



//----------------------------------------------------------------------------
// Class Definitions
class minivan : public generic_car
{
```

```
// Public member functions.
public:
   minivan(void);

   int TopSpeed(void);
};

// End Class Definitions
//-----------------------------------------------------------------------------



#endif
// End Minivan.h
//-----------------------------------------------------------------------------



//-----------------------------------------------------------------------------
/*
File Name:   Minivan.cpp
Comments:    Implements the minivan class.
*/
//-----------------------------------------------------------------------------



//-----------------------------------------------------------------------------
// Include Files

#include "Minivan.h"

// End Include Files
//-----------------------------------------------------------------------------



//-----------------------------------------------------------------------------

Function Name:         minivan
Member of:             minivan
Input Parameters:      Nonc.
Output Parameters:     Nonc.
Return Value:          Constructed minivan object.
Comments:              Constructor for the minivan class.
*/

minivan::minivan(void) : generic_car()
{
}



//-----------------------------------------------------------------------------
/*
Function Name:         TopSpeed
Member of:             minivan
```

```
Input Parameters:       None.
Output Parameters:      None.
Return Value:           The top speed for the minivan.
Comments:               Use this function to get the maximum speed of a minivan
                        object.
*/

int minivan::TopSpeed(void)
{
   const int TOP_SPEED = 100;
   return (TOP_SPEED);
}


// End Minivan.cpp
//------------------------------------------------------------------------------




//------------------------------------------------------------------------------
/*
File Name:   SportCar.h
Comments:    Contains the definition of the sports_car class.
*/
//------------------------------------------------------------------------------
#ifndef SPORTCAR_H
#define SPORTCAR_H



//------------------------------------------------------------------------------
// Include Files

#include "GCar.h"

// End Include Files
//------------------------------------------------------------------------------




//------------------------------------------------------------------------------
// Class Definitions

class sports_car : public generic_car
{
// Public member functions.
public:
   sports_car(void);

   void Accelerate(void);
   int TopSpeed(void);
   bool ShouldShift(void);
   void ShiftUp(void);

// Private member functions.
```

```
private:
   void DoAcceleration(int currentGearMaxSpeed);

// Private member data.
private:
   int currentGear;
   bool shouldShift;
};

// End Class Definitions
//-----------------------------------------------------------------------------



#endif
// End SportCar.h
//-----------------------------------------------------------------------------



//-----------------------------------------------------------------------------
/*
File Name:   SportCar.cpp
Comments:    The member functions in this file implement the sports_car
             class.
*/
//-----------------------------------------------------------------------------



//-----------------------------------------------------------------------------
// Include Files

#include "SportCar.h"
// End Include Files
//-----------------------------------------------------------------------------



//-----------------------------------------------------------------------------
// Constants

const int NEUTRAL = 0;
const int FIRST_GEAR = 1;
const int SECOND_GEAR = 2;
const int THIRD_GEAR = 3;
const int FOURTH_GEAR = 4;
const int FIFTH_GEAR = 5;

// End Constants
//-----------------------------------------------------------------------------



//-----------------------------------------------------------------------------
/*
Function Name:         sports_car
Member of:             sports_car
```

```
Input Parameters:       None.
Output Parameters:      None.
Return Value:           Constructed sports_car object.
Comments:               Constructor for the sports_car class.
*/

sports_car::sports_car(void) : generic_car()
{
   currentGear = NEUTRAL;
   shouldShift = false;
}



//------------------------------------------------------------------------
/*
Function Name:          Accelerate
Member of:              sports_car
Input Parameters:       None.
Output Parameters:      None.
Return Value:           None.
Comments:               This function makes the sports car increase its speed.
*/

void sports_car::Accelerate(void)
{
   const int FIRST_GEAR_MAX_SPEED = 30;
   const int SECOND_GEAR_MAX_SPEED = 60;
   const int THIRD_GEAR_MAX_SPEED = 90;
   const int FOURTH_GEAR_MAX_SPEED = 120;

   switch (currentGear)
   {
       case NEUTRAL:
          Speed(0);
       break;

       case FIRST_GEAR:
          DoAcceleration(FIRST_GEAR_MAX_SPEED);
       break;

       case SECOND_GEAR:
          DoAcceleration(SECOND_GEAR_MAX_SPEED);
       break;

       case THIRD_GEAR:
          DoAcceleration(THIRD_GEAR_MAX_SPEED);
       break;

       case FOURTH_GEAR:
          DoAcceleration(FOURTH_GEAR_MAX_SPEED);
       break;

       case FIFTH_GEAR:
          DoAcceleration(TopSpeed());
       break;
       };
}
```

```
//------------------------------------------------------------------
/*
Function Name:          TopSpeed
Member of:              sports_car
Input Parameters:       None.
Output Parameters:      None.
Return Value:           The maximum speed of the sports car.
Comments:               Use this function to get the sports car's top speed.
*/

int sports_car::TopSpeed(void)
{
   const int TOP_SPEED = 150;
   return (TOP_SPEED);
}



//------------------------------------------------------------------
/*
Function Name:          ShouldShift
Member of:              sports_car
Input Parameters:       None.
Output Parameters:      None.
Return Value:           If the sports car needs to shift gears, this function
                        returns true. If not, it returns false.
Comments:               Use this function to detect when to shift.
*/
bool sports_car::ShouldShift(void)
{
   return (shouldShift);
}


//------------------------------------------------------------------
/*
Function Name:          ShiftUp
Member of:              sports_car
Input Parameters:       None.
Output Parameters:      None.
Return Value:           None.
Comments:               This function shifts the sports car's current gear up
                        one.
*/

void sports_car::ShiftUp(void)
{
   if (currentGear<FIFTH_GEAR)
   {
      currentGear++;
   }
   shouldShift=false;
}



//------------------------------------------------------------------
/*
```

```
Function Name:        DoAcceleration
Member of:            sports_car
Input Parameters:     currentGearMaxSpeed - The maximum speed for the current
                      gear.
Output Parameters:    None.
Return Value:         None.
Comments:             This function is only called by sports_car::Accelerate().
                      Using the maximum speed for the current gear, it
                      determines whether the car needs to shift. If it does,
                      it sets the state of the sports car appropriately. If the
                      car doesn't need to shift, this function accelerates it.
*/

void sports_car::DoAcceleration(int currentGearMaxSpeed)
{
   const int SPORTS_CAR_ACCELERATION_FACTOR = 2;

   if (Speed() < currentGearMaxSpeed)
   {
      int currentSpeed = Speed();
      currentSpeed += SPORTS_CAR_ACCELERATION_FACTOR;
      Speed(currentSpeed);
   }
   else
   {
      shouldShift = true;
   }
}

// End SportCar.cpp
//-----------------------------------------------------------------------



/*
File Name:    Cars.cpp
Comments:     Program that uses the generic_car, minivan, and sports_car
              classes.
*/
//-----------------------------------------------------------------------



//-----------------------------------------------------------------------
// Include Files

#include <iostream.h>
#include "Minivan.h"
#include "SportCar.h"

// End Include Files
//-----------------------------------------------------------------------



int main()
{
   minivan aVan;
```

```
    sports_car aFastCar;

    while (aVan.Speed() < aVan.TopSpeed())
    {
       cout << "The current speed of the minivan is: ";
       cout << aVan.Speed() << endl;
       aVan.Accelerate();
    }

    aFastCar.ShiftUp();       // Put the car in gear.
    while (aFastCar.Speed() < aFastCar.TopSpeed())
    {
       cout << "The current speed of the sports car is: ";
       cout << aFastCar.Speed() << endl;
       aFastCar.Accelerate();
       if (aFastCar.ShouldShift())
       {
          aFastCar.ShiftUp();
       }
    }

    return (0);
}

// End Cars.cpp
//-----------------------------------------------------------------------------
```

Results

The results of the program run have been abbreviated to save space:

```
The current speed of the minivan is: 0
The current speed of the minivan is: 1
The current speed of the minivan is: 2
The current speed of the minivan is: 3
The current speed of the minivan is: 4
The current speed of the minivan is: 5
.
.
.
The current speed of the minivan is: 95
The current speed of the minivan is: 96
The current speed of the minivan is: 97
The current speed of the minivan is: 98
The current speed of the minivan is: 99
The current speed of the sports car is: 0
The current speed of the sports car is: 2
The current speed of the sports car is: 4
The current speed of the sports car is: 6
The current speed of the sports car is: 8
The current speed of the sports car is: 10
.
.
.
The current speed of the sports car is: 130
The current speed of the sports car is: 132
The current speed of the sports car is: 134
The current speed of the sports car is: 136
```

```
The current speed of the sports car is: 138
The current speed of the sports car is: 140
The current speed of the sports car is: 142
The current speed of the sports car is: 144
The current speed of the sports car is: 146
The current speed of the sports car is: 148
```

Analysis

The program in this example is made up of the files *Gcar.h, Gcar.cpp, Minivan.h, Minivan.cpp, SportCar.h, SportCar.cpp,* and *Cars.cpp.*

The file *Gchar.h* contains the definition of the `generic_car` object. The statements

```
#if !defined(GCAR_H)
#define GCAR_H
```

along with the `#endif` at the end of the file, keep this header file from being included more than once in any other file.

The `generic_car` object implements most of the functionality of a car. For instance, it keeps track of the current speed of the car using the `currentSpeed` data member. Your program can query a car for its speed using the `Speed()` function.

Notice also that there is a `Speed()` function in a section labeled `protected`. Protected member functions are accessible only to derived classes.[2] Any class derived from `generic_car` can use the `protected` version of the `Speed()` function to set the car's current speed. Classes and functions that are not derived from `generic_car` can't access this protected function.

The `generic_car` class also provides a function called `TopSpeed()`. Functions use `TopSpeed()` to get the maximum speed at which the car can travel. If you look in the file *GCar.cpp*, you'll see that the implementation of the `TopSpeed()` function just returns zero. We do this as a way of specifying what the interface of all objects derived from `generic_car` should be. If the derived objects don't override `TopSpeed()`, then their maximum speed will be zero. That doesn't make for a very useful car. Therefore, any time anyone uses `generic_car` as a base class, they are encouraged to write a `TopSpeed()` function that overrides the one in `generic_car`.[3]

You may sensibly ask why we don't just define a constant for each class derived from `generic_car` that specifies its top speed. That is a reasonable and efficient approach. Its only drawback is that it forces programmers to look up several different constants spread across several different files. Each of these constants *must* have a unique name. Using a function that each derived class must override means that we only need to learn one name to get the top speed of any kind of car. Using constants results in faster code; using an overridden function with a uniform name makes it easier for the maintenance programmer. It's up to you to decide which of these is the higher priority for the particular software you're developing.

The `generic_car` class also contains a public function called `Accelerate()`. This function increases the speed of a car by one.

The program uses the `generic_car` class as the base class for the `minivan` class in *Minivan.h.* It uses public inheritance, so all of the functions of the `generic_car` class can be called using a `minivan` object.

The `minivan` class does not add any new characteristics to the `generic_car` class. It does override the `TopSpeed()` function to provide an appropriate maximum speed for a minivan.

---

[2] For details, see Chapter 23.

[3] For information on how to *require* that other developers override a member function in a base class, see the section entitled "Base Classes and Virtual Functions" in Chapter 24.

Like the minivan class, the sports_car class inherits from generic_car. Although the sports_car class does use the functionality of generic_car, it also adds some enhancements. For instance, the sports_car class contains attributes that keep track of what gear the sports car is in and when it should shift (this sports car has a manual transmission). It includes a public member function that allows the program to ask a sports car if it is time to shift gears. In addition, the interface provides a public function that shifts up one gear.

The sports_car class overrides the Accelerate() and TopSpeed() functions in the generic_car class. There is also a private member function that helps implement the sports_car class's Accelerate() function.

If we look at the implementation of the sports_car class in *SportCar.cpp*, we'll see that it is more complex than the minivan class. For instance, the implementation defines a set of constants near the beginning of *SportCar.cpp*. The class uses these to keep track of what gear the car is in.[4]

The sports_car constructor calls the generic_car constructor. It then initializes the data members that are specific to the sports_car class. It sets the initial gear to NEUTRAL and sets the status variable shouldShift to false.

By the way, you may notice that the sports_car class uses a type called bool. This is a new type that most (but not all) C++ compilers support. Variables of type bool can be set to the values true or false. If your compiler does not yet support the bool type, put the statement

I've deliberately left off the units of speed. Whether the car is going 30 miles per hour or 30 kilometers per hour is not important to this example.

```
enum bool {false,true};
```

on line 22 of *SportCar.h*. That will fix the problem.

A sports car accelerates much faster (hopefully) than a minivan. Its acceleration also depends on what gear it is in. The Accelerate() function in the sports_car class defines a group of constants to use as the upper speed limit for each individual gear. When the sports car is in neutral, its maximum speed is zero. If it is in first gear, it can't go any faster than 30.

At this point, it's reasonable to ask why these constants are defined in the function, and the previous constants were defined at the top of the file. The answer lies in where the constants are used. The sports_car class uses the constants that specify the current gear (NEUTRAL, FIRST_GEAR, etc.) throughout most of the file *SportCar.cpp*. They are defined at the top of the file so that they will be visible to all functions in the file. The constants that define the maximum speed for each gear (FIRST_GEAR_MAX_SPEED, SECOND_GEAR_MAX_SPEED, etc.) are used only by the Accelerate() function. Therefore, they are defined at the beginning of the Accelerate() function.

The Accelerate() function uses a switch statement to determine what gear the sports car is in. For each gear, it calls the function DoAcceleration() and passes in the maximum speed for the particular gear.

The DoAcceleration() function increases the speed of the car. It defines a constant that it uses as the acceleration factor for a sports_car object. It calls the public Speed() function that it inherits from the generic_car class to get the current speed. It also calls its own TopSpeed() function to get the maximum speed of a sports_car object.

Notice that an object's member functions do not need an object to call its own member functions. The main() function, for instance, must declare variables of type sports_car to get access to the sports_car member functions, like this:

```
sports_car aFastCar;
aFastCar.ShiftUp();       // Put the car in gear.
```

[4]If you're thinking that there must be a better way to define a long list of integer constants than this, you're right. See "Enumerated Types" in Chapter 26.

This is not necessary in an object's member functions. Remember that when a member function is invoked, it is invoked for an object. For example, the statement

```
aFastCar.ShiftUp()
```

calls the `ShiftUp()` function for the object `aFastCar`. When `ShiftUp()` is finished, the object `aFastCar` will be in a higher gear if it is not already in its highest gear. Member functions such as `ShiftUp()`, `Accelerate()`, and `DoAcceleration()` can call any other `sports_car` member function. The member functions that they call operate on the current object. So when `Accelerate()` calls `DoAcceleration()`, the `DoAcceleration()` function will increase the speed of the object on which `Accelerate()` was invoked.

The `DoAcceleration()` function compares the current speed to the maximum speed for the current gear. If the current speed is less than the maximum, the function increases the speed of the car by the amount specified in the constant `SPORTS_CAR_ACCELERATION_FACTOR`. It increases the speed by calling the protected member function `Speed()` from the `generic_car` class. If the car has reached its maximum speed, the `DoAcceleration()` function sets the `sports_car` class's private data member `shouldShift` to true. The function then exits.

Each time the program accelerates a `sports_car` object, it should check to see if it is time to shift by calling the public member function `ShouldShift()`.

If we look in the file *Cars.cpp* at the program that uses the minivan and `sports_car` objects, we see that it includes the files *Minivan.h* and *SportCar.h*. Both of these files include *GCar.h*. However, the definitions in *GCar.h* are not done twice because the program uses the `#if !defined()` trick presented in Chapter 17.

The `main()` function declares a variable of type `minivan` and one of type `sports_car`. It enters a loop that prints the current speed of the `minivan`, accelerating the `minivan` each time through the loop. Remember that the only function that the `minivan` class overrides is the `TopSpeed()` function. The rest of the functions that `main()` calls using the variable `aVan` are functions from the `generic_car` class. When `aVan` reaches the top speed for a `minivan`, the loop terminates.

Next, the `main()` function puts the sports car into gear by calling the function `ShiftUp()` for the object `aFastCar`. It enters another loop, which prints the current speed of the sports car. It accelerates the car and tests to see if it is time to shift. If it is, `main()` calls `ShiftUp()`.

Note that the `sports_car` class overrides the `TopSpeed()` and `Accelerate()` functions of the `generic_car` class. When the `main()` function calls the `TopSpeed()` and `Accelerate()` functions for the object `aFastCar`, it calls the `TopSpeed()` and `Accelerate()` functions in the `sports_car` class, not the `generic_car` class.

The same is not true of the public `Speed()` function. The `sports_car` class inherits the `Speed()` function from the `generic_car` class. Every time `main()` calls the `Speed()` function for the `aFastCar` object, it calls the public `Speed()` function in the `generic_car` class.

Multiple Inheritance

The C++ language specification allows objects to inherit from more than one base class. This is called **multiple inheritance.** Hands On 19.4 illustrates the process of multiple inheritance.

Hands On 19.4

Objective

Write a program that demonstrates multiple inheritance.

Experiment

Type the following program into your IDE or text editor. Compile, link, and run it.

```
#include <iostream.h>

class base1
{
public:
    base1(int newValue);

    void PrintValue1(void);

private:
    int value1;
};


base1::base1(int newValue)
{
    value1=newValue;
}

void base1::PrintValue1(void)

    cout << value1 << endl;
}



class base2
{
public:
    base2(int newValue);

    void PrintValue2(void);

private:
    int value2;
};


base2::base2(int newValue)
{
    value2=newValue;
}

void base2::PrintValue2(void)
{
    cout << value2 << endl;
}


class derived : public base1, public base2
{
public:
    derived(int value1,int value2, int value3);

    void PrintValue3(void);
```

```
    void PrintAll(void);

private:
    int value3;
};


derived::derived(int newValue1,
                 int newValue2,
                 int newValue3) : base1(newValue1), base2(newValue2)
{
    value3=newValue3;
}

void derived::PrintValue3(void)
{
    cout << value3 << endl;
}

void derived::PrintAll(void)
{
    PrintValue1();
    PrintValue2();
    PrintValue3();
}


int main()
{
    derived derivedObject(1,2,3);

    derivedObject.PrintValue1();
    derivedObject.PrintValue2();
    derivedObject.PrintValue3();
    derivedObject.PrintAll();
}
```

Results

```
1
2
3
1
2
3
```

Analysis

Here, the class `derived` inherits from `base1` and `base2`. Each of these three classes has its own data member, as well as some member functions.

The `derived` class indicates that it inherits from multiple base classes with the statement

```
class derived : public base1, public base2
```

on the first line of the class definition. In this case, it inherits both `base1` and `base2` publicly. It could also inherit one or both privately.

The constructor for the `derived` class takes three parameters. Whenever a constructor takes parameters, it may pass those parameters (or any other value, for that matter) to the constructors of its base classes. When the constructor for the `derived` class is called, it calls the constructors for both of its base classes. It passes the parameter `newValue1` to the constructor for the `base1` class. The parameter `newValue2` is passed to the constructor for the `base2` class. The `derived` class constructor uses `newValue3` to initialize its own private data member, `value3`.

The `main()` program in this example declares an object of type `derived`. It initializes the constructor's three parameters to the values 1, 2, and 3, respectively.

Next, `main()` uses the variable `derivedObject` to call the `PrintValue1()` function. Objects of type `derived` inherit the `PrintValue1()` function from `base1`. The `main()` function also uses `derivedObject` to call `PrintValue2()`, which derived inherits from `base2`. In addition, the `main()` function invokes the `PrintValue3()` and `PrintAll()` functions. These are both members of the `derived` class.

Whenever we derive an object from another object, the derived object inherits the member data and the interface of functions from the base class. If it is derived from more than one base class, it inherits the data and functions of all base classes from which it is derived. If the object uses public inheritance, the public member functions essentially become part of the derived class's set of interface functions.

Troubleshooting Guide

After reading this section, you should be able to:

- Distinguish between when it is appropriate to use inheritance and when it is appropriate to use containership.
- Distinguish between when it is appropriate to use public inheritance and when it is appropriate to use private inheritance.
- Recognize and solve potential problems with multiple inheritance.

Inheritance and Containership

C++ objects can either contain an object or inherit from it. In the code fragment in Example 19.3, the class `container_object` has a data member of type `contained_object` in it. Any time we define an object having a data member that is itself an object, we are using containership.

EXAMPLE 19.3 An Object That Uses Containership

```
class contained_object
{
public:
   // Public member functions go here.
private:
   // Private data members go here.
};

class container_object
{
public:
   // Public member functions go here.
private:
   contained_object containedObject;
};
```

When we use containership, we create the contained object inside the container object. When we use inheritance, we create the base object inside the derived object.

The question is, when should we use containership and when should we use inheritance? To find the answer, we need to ask another question: What do inheritance and containership mean?

When an object contains another object, it uses the contained object as one of its building blocks. This is another way of saying that, if object A contains a data member of object B, then A *is implemented in terms of* B, or A *has a* B.

For example, suppose that your boss gives you an assignment to enhance the car simulation from Hands On 19.3 so that it actually displays pictures of the vehicles it simulates. To keep track of the information that the graphics system needs, you decide that the `generic_car` object must have a data member of type `car_body`. The `car_body` object holds the information needed to draw a 3-D simulation of the car's body. You decide that you will also have an array of four `car_wheel` objects in `generic_car`.

TIP: Use containership when object A is composed of B, is implemented in terms of B, or has a B.

If you were to translate the class definition of the `generic_car` into English, you could say that a `generic_car` has a `car_body` and four `car_tires`. Another way to say this is that a car is implemented in terms of a body and four wheels.[5]

TIP: Use inheritance if object A is a specialized kind of B.

Inheritance, on the other hand, tells us that the derived object *is a kind of* the base object, but not the other way around. The derived object is a more specialized kind of the base object.

For instance, in Hands On 19.3, the `sports_car` object inherits from `generic_car`. In English, we say that a sports car is a kind of car.[6] However, not all cars are sports cars. A sports car is a specialized kind of car.

These two relationships tell us when to use containership and when to use inheritance. If object A is composed of B, is implemented in terms of B, or has a B, then we need to use containership. If object A is a specialized kind of B, then we should probably use inheritance.

Private Inheritance: Approach with Caution

Recall that derived objects that use private inheritance do not allow nonmember functions to access the public member functions of the base class. Under public inheritance, derived objects inherit the attributes and operations of the base class. The base class's member functions essentially become part of the public interface of the derived class.

TIP: Prefer containership to private inheritance.

The same cannot be said of private inheritance. Since the base class's member functions are not visible to functions outside the derived class, the base class's functions are not part of its public interface. So derived classes that use private inheritance do not follow the rule that derived classes should be specializations of base classes. Instead, private inheritance means that the derived class is implemented in terms of the base class, much like containership.

In general, use containership instead of private inheritance. It specifies a clearer relationship. Containership is also typically easier to implement.

Ambiguity in Multiple Inheritance

Another reason to avoid multiple inheritance is the numerous complications it causes when using virtual functions from two objects derived from the same class. Also, some compilers use pointers to pure virtual base classes rather than instances. In a situation where an object multiply inherits from two objects that, in turn, inherit from the same base class, this can lead to unexpected side effects.

There are many reasons to avoid multiple inheritance. One important reason is that it can quickly lead to confusion. The classes in Example 19.4 illustrate the problem.

EXAMPLE 19.4 Bad News in Multiple Inheritance

```
class ultimate_base
{
public:
    ultimate_base(void);
```

[5]Much of the C++ literature calls this relationship the *Whole-Part Structure*. The contained object is a part of the container object. See Edward Yourdon and Carl Argila, *Case Studies in Object Oriented Analysis and Design* (Upper Saddle River, NJ: Prentice Hall, 1996), pp. 11–12.

[6]Object oriented design literature calls this relationship the *Generalization-Specialization (Gen-Spec) Structure*. See Edward Yourdon and Carl Argila, *Case Studies in Object Oriented Analysis and Design* (Upper Saddle River, NJ: Prentice Hall, 1996), pp. 11–12.

```
    void Set(int dataValue);
    void PrintData(void)
private:
    int dataMember;
};

class derived_base1 : public ultimate_base
{
public:
    derived_base1(void);

    void Set(int dataValue);
    void PrintData(void);

private:
    int anotherDataMember;
};

class derived_base2 : public ultimate_base
{
public:
    derived_base2(void);

    void Set(int dataValue);
    void PrintData(void);

private:
    int anotherDataMember;
};

class derived : public derived_base1, public derived_base2
{
public:
    derived(void);
};

int main()
{
    derived derivedObject;

    // Houston, we have a problem.
    derivedObject.Set(5);
    derivedObject.PrintData();

    return(0);
}
```

The inheritance hierarchy in Example 19.4 has multiple problems. The first is that it is diamond-shaped, as illustrated in Figure 19.4.

Any time your objects inherit multiple times from the same base class, you've got problems. And the problem with multiple inheritance is that this is so easy to do. In complex object hierarchies, it can be difficult (bordering on impossible) to keep your objects from inheriting more than once from the same class.

Inheriting from the same class through more than one object means that the C++ compiler may not be able to resolve which inherited member function is being called. It also results in more than one copy of the same object "hidden" inside the derived object. It is seldom clear to maintenance programmers which copy your code operates on at any given time.

FIGURE 19.4 Not a Programmer's Best Friend

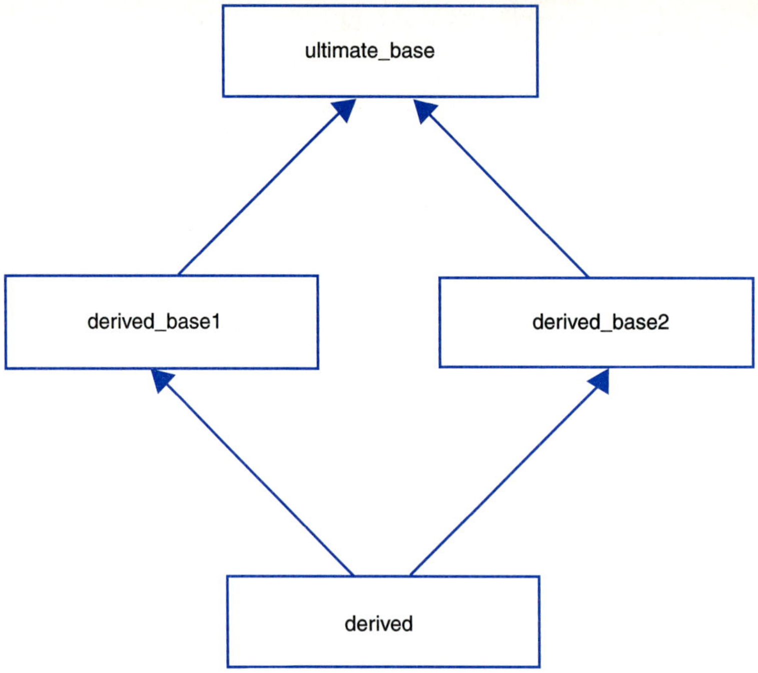

In the program in Example 19.4, try to figure out which `Set()` function and which `PrintData()` function is being called. I didn't show the implementation of these functions because it wouldn't help. Let's assume that the `Set()` and `PrintData()` functions in the `derived_base1` and `derived_base2` classes completely override the functions in the `ultimate_base` class. We still don't know which `Set()` and `PrintData()` functions `main()` calls. Neither does the compiler. It will flag this as an error.

Example 19.5 shows the same program, but uses the scope resolution operator to clarify which function is being called.

EXAMPLE 19.5 Resolving the Ambiguity

```
class ultimate_base
{
public:
   ultimate_base(void);

   void Set(int dataValue);
   void PrintData(void)
private:
   int dataMember;
};

class derived_base1 : public ultimate_base
{
public:
   derived_base1(void);

   void Set(int dataValue);
   void PrintData(void);

private:
   int anotherDataMember;
};

class derived_base2 : public ultimate_base
{
```

```
public:
    derived_base2(void);

    void Set(int dataValue);
    void PrintData(void);

private:
    int anotherDataMember;
};

class derived : public derived_base1, public derived_base2
{
public:
    derived(void);
};

int main()
{
    derived derivedObject;

    // This will compile
    derivedObject.derived_base1::Set(5);
    derivedObject.derived_base2::Set(10);
    derivedObject.derived_base1::PrintData();
    derivedObject.derived_base2::PrintData();

    return(0);
}
```

TIP: Use multiple inheritance sparingly.

TIP: Resolve ambiguity problems in multiple inheritance with the scope resolution operator.

Note that this solution will not work for virtual functions. They stop acting virtual.

Although this looks clumsy (it is), it works. Using the scope resolution operator tells the compiler exactly which `Set()` and `PrintData()` functions to call.

There is one more complication (isn't there always?). What do we do if we want to call the `Set()` and `PrintData()` functions in the `ultimate_base` class? Since there are two objects of type `ultimate_base` inside of the `derived` class, we must also specify which copy we're dealing with. The `main()` function in Example 19.6 gives the solution to this problem. For this example, I have omitted the rest of the program since it is the same as Example 19.5.

EXAMPLE 19.6 Selecting an `ultimate_base` Object

```
int main()
{
    derived derivedObject;

    // This will compile (frighteningly enough!).
    derivedObject.derived_base1::Set(5);
    derivedObject.derived_base2::Set(10);
    derivedObject.derived_base1::ultimate_base::Set(20);
    derivedObject.derived_base2::ultimate_base::Set(20);
    derivedObject.derived_base1::PrintData();
    derivedObject.derived_base2::PrintData();
    derivedObject.derived_base1::ultimate_base::PrintData();
    derivedObject.derived_base2::ultimate_base::PrintData();
    return(0);
}
```

Again, the scope resolution operator solves the problem. By specifying, for instance, the `derived_base1` class and then the `ultimate_base` class, we tell the compiler to call the `Set()` function or `PrintData()` function for the `ultimate_base` object that is inside the `derived_base1` object. Likewise, by specifying the `derived_base2` class and then the `ultimate_base` class, we tell the compiler to call the `Set()` function or `PrintData()` function for the `ultimate_base` object that is inside the `derived_base2` object.

Sound confusing? It is.

Having said all of this, please don't get the impression that you should never use multiple inheritance. In fact, the C++ Standard Library uses it quite effectively. However, to avoid the problems associated with multiple inheritance, you should plan on downloading the C++ specification from the Internet and becoming *very* familiar with it.

Summary

When programming in C++, we can use classes as a basis for other classes. Through inheritance, we can create specializations of a class.

Constructors of a derived class should call the constructors of the base class.

Member functions in a derived class can override the member functions of a base class. This technique can be used to enhance or completely replace functions in the base class.

Derived classes can inherit publicly or privately from base classes.

Under public inheritance, the member functions of the base class can be called using an object of the derived class. They essentially become part of the public interface of functions of the derived class.

When using private inheritance, the member functions of the base class are accessible to the member functions of the derived class. However, they cannot be called by nonmember functions using an object of the derived class.

Objects can inherit from multiple base classes. Multiple inheritance is a powerful tool. However, it increases program complexity and may result in many types of ambiguity.

Review Questions

1. What is inheritance in C++?
2. Why do you think the C++ language provides inheritance?
3. Why do constructors in derived classes need to call the constructors in base classes?
4. What does it mean to use a function in a derived class to override a member function in a base class?
5. How can you enhance the utility of a member function in a base class by overriding it in a derived class?
6. How can you replace a member function in a base class by overriding it in a derived class?
7. What is public inheritance?
8. What is private inheritance?
9. What is containership?
10. When do you use inheritance? When do you use containership?

Exercises

1. Write a program that defines an object called `insect`. Give the `insect` object a member function called `Name()` that prints the word "Insect". Also, include a function in the class definition called `Fly()`. When the `Fly()` function is invoked, it should print the words "Look, Ma! I'm flying!" Create a class called `bee` that inherits from `insect`. Override the `Name()` function for the `bee` class so that it prints the word "Bee" instead. Override the `Fly()` function so that it adds to the functionality of the `insect::Fly()` function. In addition to printing "Look, Ma! I'm flying!", it should print "Bzzzzzz." Write a program demonstrating that these classes and functions work.
2. Write a program that uses the `insect` class from Exercise 1. Derive an `ant` class from `insect`. Override the `Name()` function so that it prints the word "Ant." Write a

program demonstrating that these classes and functions work. Explain what you think about this class hierarchy. Specifically, the `ant` object inherits the `Fly()` function. However, an ant doesn't fly. Explain how you would fix this class hierarchy.

3. Write a program that creates and demonstrates a `person` object. The `person` object should have member data to store a person's name and address. It should have member functions that get the name and address from the user. It should also have a member function that prints a person's information.
4. Write a program that uses the `person` object in Exercise 3. Define an `employee` object. The `employee` object should contain the employee's salary and employee number. Write member functions to get and set this data. Your program should allow a user to input an employee's name, address, employee number, and salary. It should then print the information.
5. Write a program that uses the `employee` object you created for Exercise 4. Define a `manager` object and a `worker` object. In addition to the attributes it inherits from the `employee` object, a `manager` object should have a data member for golfing fees. It also needs member functions to get and set this data. In addition to the attributes that a `worker` object inherits from `employee`, it should also have a data member for overtime pay. The `worker` object needs functions to get and set this data. Your program must demonstrate that these objects and functions work.
6. Write a program that defines a class called `machine`. Objects of type `machine` should have an attribute that stores their battery life. The `machine` class also needs functions to get and set this attribute. Your program should demonstrate that this object and its member functions work properly.
7. Write a program that uses the `machine` class you created for Exercise 6. Define a class called `robot`. An object of type `robot` should have data members that store its number of arms and legs. It should also have member functions to get and set the data. Your program should demonstrate that the `robot` class and its member functions work properly.
8. Write a program that uses the `robot` class you created for Exercise 7. Define an `intelligent_robot` class with a data member that stores the robot's I.Q. Your `intelligent_robot` class needs member functions to get and set the I.Q. Your program should demonstrate that the `intelligent_robot` class works properly.
9. Write a program that defines a class called `customer`. The `customer` class should inherit from the `person` class in Exercise 3. It should also have data members for a phone number and credit card information. It needs member functions to get and set these attributes. Define a class called `phone_number`. It should contain a phone number with its area code. Define a class called `credit_card_info`. It should store credit card information, including the name on the card, the card number, and the expiration date. Both the `phone_number` and `credit_card_info` classes need member functions to get and set their data. Your program should demonstrate that the objects and member functions work properly.
10. Write a program that defines a class called `software_store_customer`. This class should inherit from the `customer` class you created for Exercise 9. The `software_store_customer` class should also store the type of the user's computer and the name of the user's operating system. The `software_store_customer` class will need member functions to get and set its data. Your program should demonstrate that the `software_store_customer` class and its member functions work properly.

Chapter Glossary

Base Class A class from which another class inherits or is derived.

Derived Class A class that inherits from another class.

Multiple Inheritance Inheriting from more than one class.

Override To replace a member function of a base class with a member function of a derived class that has the same prototype.

20 Input and Output with Streams

Objectives

After reading this chapter, you should be able to:

- Name and use the standard C++ streams.
- Read and write formatted data.
- Read data from files.
- Write data to files.

Preview

Most of the topics presented so far in this book have dealt with C++ language tools that help us process data. However, processing data is only one-third of what a computer does. It must also read data in from various sources and send data out. Data input and output are the topics of this chapter.

The Standard Streams

It is sometimes surprising to programmers with experience in languages such as Basic or Pascal, but there are no statements in the C++ language to do data input and output (data I/O). The C++ Standard Library adds data I/O through the use of streams.

Streams are a standardized set of classes. Every compiler manufacturer implements them for the hardware and the operating system for which their compiler compiles programs. The underlying details of that implementation are normally different for every type of computer and operating system. However, the interface of public member functions to the stream classes is the same on all computers and operating systems. Streams help us write portable C++ code.

C++ I/O streams are conceptually like streams of water. They can be input streams, output streams, or both. When you insert data into a stream, it flows out to some device. The devices are typically hardware such as disks or monitors. When you extract data from a stream, it flows from a device into the memory allocated for your program's data. Devices that data flows in from include the keyboard, disks, and serial ports.

The C++ Standard Library defines eight standard streams: `cin`, `cout`, `cerr`, `clog`, `wcin`, `wcout`, `wcerr`, and `wclog`. We've already used `cin` and `cout` in many of the programs in this book.

The stream `cerr` (pronounced *see-err*) is, by default, connected to the display. You use it to send error messages to the user. The C++ standard defines this special stream for error messages because it is possible to redirect the flow of a stream. For instance, you can redirect the `cout` stream to send its output into another program. Since the output no longer flows to

FIGURE 20.1 Data Buffers

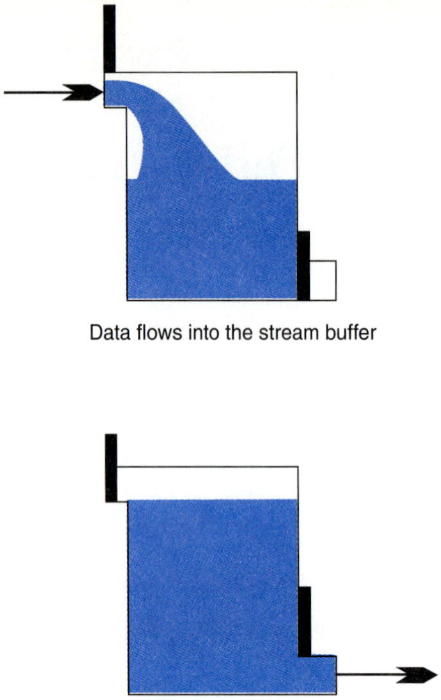

Data flows into the stream buffer

When the buffer flushes, the data flows out byte by byte

the screen, the user will not see any error messages sent to `cout`. If you send error messages to `cerr` instead, the user will see them even if `cout` is redirected.

The `clog` (pronounced *see-log*) stream essentially performs the same task as the `cerr` stream. The difference is that output to the `clog` stream is buffered. Output to the `cerr` stream is unbuffered.

I/O streams can be buffered or unbuffered. Streams that perform unbuffered input make data immediately available to the program. Likewise, unbuffered output goes directly to its destination device.

On the other hand, data from a buffered input stream goes into a data buffer. Figure 20.1 illustrates how data buffers work. Data in a buffer is not available to the program until something flushes the buffer. Line buffers are flushed each time the stream receives an endline character. Other buffers flush only when they are full. The C++ I/O streams provide a function called `flush()` that you can use at any time to manually flush a stream buffer.

In addition to the types `char`, `unsigned char`, and `signed char`, the C++ specification also provides a wide character type called `wchar`. Programmers primarily use the `wchar` types to access non-English character sets. Use the `wchar` type with the `wcin`, `wcout`, and `wcerr` streams to perform I/O with wide characters.

The Stream Class Hierarchy

The input and output streams are actually part of a class hierarchy. That is, the stream classes that programmers commonly use inherit many of their member data and member functions from other classes. Figure 20.2 shows a simplified version of the stream class hierarchy.

The `istream` class in Figure 20.2 defines streams for input only. The `cin` object is of type `istream`. The `ostream` class defines streams for output only. The objects `cout` and `cerr` are of type `ostream`. Objects of type `iostream` can be used for both input and output.

The stream class hierarchy also provides objects for input and output with files. Objects of type `ifstream` and `ofstream` are for input from files and output to files, respectively. Programs can use `fstream` objects for both input from and output to files.

FIGURE 20.2 **The Stream Class Hierarchy**

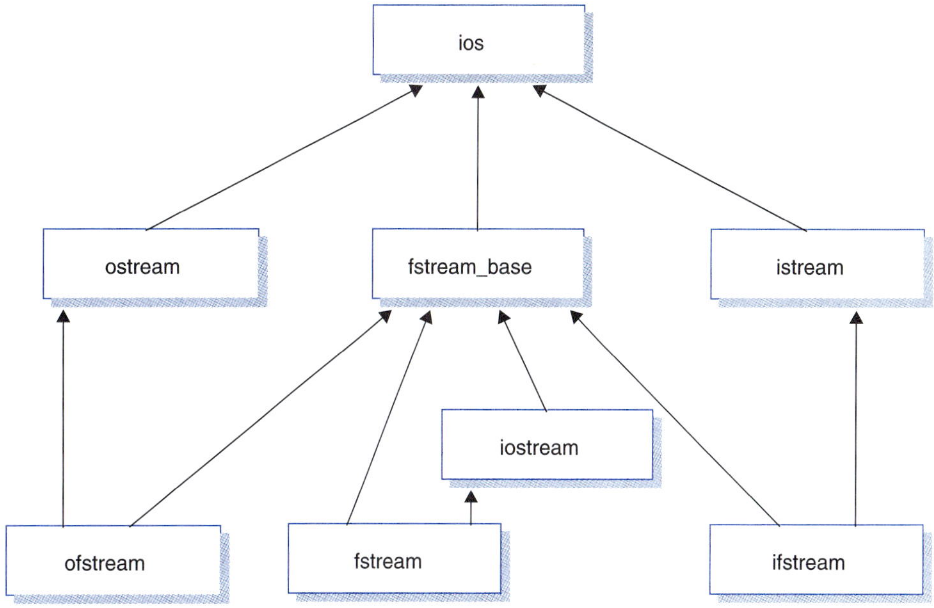

It is common to refer to member functions using the notation `class_name::FunctionName()`. The notations `ios::flags()` and `ios::setf()` refer to the `flags()` function and the `setf()` function, which are members of `ios`. Stream classes inherit from `ios`, so these functions will be available to you when you are using `istream`, `ostream`, `iostream`, `fstream`, `ifstream`, and `ofstream` objects.

Stream Functions

The stream classes provide a variety of functions for formatting the input and output of your programs. The base class of the stream functions, `ios`, contains a set of formatting flags. Programs control most of the I/O formatting options using these flags. You set the flags by invoking either the `ios::flags()` or `ios::setf()` functions. Hands On 20.1 shows the effects of some of these flags.

Hands On 20.1

Objective

Write a program that demonstrates the ios formatting flags.

Experiment

Type the following program into your IDE or text editor. Compile, link, and run it.

```
#include <iostream.h>

int main()
{
   int aNumber = -1;
   do
   {
      cout << endl << "Please input an integer greater than zero :";
      cin >> aNumber;
   } while (aNumber <= 0);

   cout << endl << "Here's the number you entered in";
   cout.flags(ios::oct);
   cout << endl << "Octal format: " << aNumber;
   cout.flags(ios::hex);
   cout << endl << "Hexadecimal format: " << aNumber;
   cout.flags(ios::dec);
   cout << endl << "Decimal format: " << aNumber;
```

```
    cout.flags(ios::showpos);
    cout.flags(ios::showpoint);
    cout << endl << endl << "Here's a floating-point number";
    cout << endl << 5.00987;
    cout << endl << "And its negative";
    cout << endl << -5.00987;

    cout.flags(ios::scientific);
    cout << endl << endl << "Here's a floating-point number ";
    cout << "in scientific notation.";
    cout << endl << 5000.00987;
    cout << endl << "And its negative";
    cout << endl << -5000.00987;

    return (0);
}
```

Results

```
Please input an integer greater than zero :45

Here's the number you entered in
Octal format: 55
Hexadecimal format: 2d
Decimal format: 45

Here's a floating-point number
+5.00987
And its negative
-5.00987

Here's a floating-point number in scientific notation.
+5.000010e+03
And its negative
-5.000010e+03
```

Analysis

This program begins by declaring an integer variable and initializing it to –1. It enters a loop that continues for as long as the variable contains a value less than or equal to zero. Inside the `do-while` loop, the program prompts the user for an integer greater than zero. It then reads the number in from the keyboard.

The program uses the `cout` object to call the `ios::flags()` function. By passing it the constant `ios::oct`, the program sets the stream to display integer output in octal (base 8). C++ enables us to define constants called *enumerated values* in classes.[1] To access the constant, we must use the scope resolution operator with the name of the class that it's defined in.

After setting integer output so that it will be displayed in octal format, the program executes the statement

```
cout << endl << "Octal format: " << aNumber;
```

This outputs the number. As you can see from the Results section, it is indeed displayed in octal format.

Next, the program passes the constant `ios::hex` to the `ios::flags()` function. That sets the `cout` stream so that displays output in hexadecimal (base 16). The

[1]For details, see Chapter 26.

example program prints the number that the user typed in. It also sets `cout` to display numeric output in decimal format. The Results section shows that it worked correctly.

Using the `ios::flags()` function again, the program sets floating point output so that it will be printed with a plus sign if it is greater than or equal to zero. It also sets the `cout` stream to add a decimal point to all floating point output. It then prints a floating point number and its negative.

The last part of the program sets the `cout` stream to display all floating point numbers in scientific notation. It finishes by printing a floating point number and its negative.

Not all of the formatting flags are demonstrated in Hands On 20.1. Table 20.1 lists all of the `ios` formatting flags. Unfortunately, not all compilers support all of the flags yet. See your compiler documentation for the list of what it supports.

Note that for many years, C and C++ programmers have traditionally defined all constants in their programs in uppercase. The C++ Standard Library shows that the trend seems to be going the other way these days. Whether you choose to use uppercase or lowercase is entirely a matter of your personal taste. However, it will help maintenance programmers if you are consistent in your usage. That is, choose one or the other. Don't use both uppercase and lowercase constants in your programs.

Hands On 20.1 used the `ios::flags()` function to set the `ios` flags. It could have just as easily used the `ios::setf()` function instead. Your program can clear the `ios` flags by calling the `ios::unsetf()` function.

File Input and Output

Computer programs store data in files. To process data, our programs must be able to read from and write to data files.

There are two basic types of files: text and binary files. You can use the C++ stream classes to read from and write to either type of file.

Reading Data from Files

To read data from a file, your program must create a stream object and connect it to the file by opening the file. It uses the stream input functions to read data. When it is finished, it should close the file.

TABLE 20.1 The `ios` Formatting Flags

Flag	Meaning
`ios::boolalpha`	Read and write boolean values (type `bool`) as the strings `false` or `true`.
`ios::dec`	Format numeric input and output in decimal (base 10).
`ios::fixed`	Use fixed point notation for floating point input and output.
`ios::hex`	Format numeric input and output in hexadecimal (base 16).
`ios::internal`	Add fill characters between the sign or base indicator and the value.
`ios:left`	Left-align values. Pad space on the right with the fill character.
`ios::oct`	Format numeric input and output in octal (base 8).
`ios::right`	Right-align values. Pad space on the left with the fill character. This is the default alignment.
`ios::scientific`	Use scientific notation for floating point output.
`ios::showbase`	Generate a prefix for integer output, which indicates the base.
`ios::showpoint`	Add the decimal point to all floating point output.
`ios::showpos`	Display a + sign for all floating point data greater than or equal to zero.
`ios::skipws`	Skip white space (spaces, tabs, etc.) in the input.
`ios::unitbuf`	Flush the output buffer after each output operation.
`ios::uppercase`	Display uppercase A through F for hexadecimal values and E for floating point values in scientific notation.

There is actually a third method, but it is an advanced topic that is not discussed in this book. You normally only use it when you want to provide your own custom file buffers that your program manages itself.

There are two ways of creating a stream and opening a file. The first is to declare a variable of type `ifstream`, and call the `ifstream::open()` function. The code fragment in Example 20.1 demonstrates this method.

EXAMPLE 20.1 One Way to Open a File

```
// Declare an ifstream variable.
ifstream anInputStream;
anInputStream.open("filename");
```

When your program calls the `open()` function, it must pass in a string containing the name of the file as the first parameter. The file name must be in a format that is particular to the operating systems the program runs on. For example, MS DOS and MS Windows programs use the backslash character (\) in file names. Unix programs use the forward slash (/).

The second way to create a stream and open a file is to declare an `ifstream` variable and pass the file name to the constructor. Example 20.2 illustrates this technique.

EXAMPLE 20.2 Opening a File with the `ifstream` Constructor

```
ifstream anInputStream("filename");
```

Reading from Text Files The default file type when you open files for input or output is a text file. To open a text file, you use the methods demonstrated in Examples 20.1 and 20.2. These are both shown in the next two Hands On examples.

Hands On 20.2

Objective

Write a program that opens a text file and reads data from it.

Experiment

Type the following program into your IDE or text editor. Compile, link, and run it. On the CD that comes with this book, you'll find a directory called *Examples*. In the Examples directory is a subdirectory called *Chapt20*. The directory Chapt20 contains a file called *testfile.txt*. Copy that file into the same directory that contains this program.

```
#include <fstream.h>
#include <iostream.h>


int main()
{
   // Declare and open a stream.
   ifstream inputStream("testfile.txt");


   const int INPUT_STRING_LENGTH = 80;
   char inputString[INPUT_STRING_LENGTH];

   while (!inputStream.eof())
   {
      inputStream >> inputString;
      cout << inputString;
   }
```

```
    inputStream.close();
    return (0);
}
```

Results

Figure 20.3 shows the output of this program.

FIGURE 20.3 The Output of the Program in Hands On 20.2

Analysis

This program reads text from a text file and writes it to the screen. It first declares an object of type `ifstream`. Programs use `ifstream` objects for read-only access to files. The term *read-only access* means that our program can read data from the file, but it may not write data to the file. Attempting to do so will cause an error.

When the program creates the `ifstream` object, it passes the name of the file to open to the constructor. The Hands On program declares an array and then enters a `while` loop. The loop continues while the program has not reached the end of the file. It uses the `eof()` member function to test for the end of the file.

Inside the `while` loop, the program reads a string from a file using the extraction operator. It stores the string in the array of characters. It then uses the insertion operator to send the string to the stream `cout`.

The program in Hands On 20.2 illustrated how we can read data from a text file. However, its output is not exactly what most people would call readable. By default, the extraction operator skips white space. The result is that the input text loses any spaces and endlines it may contain.

REMINDER: The newline and the endline are essentially different names for the same thing. The word *newline* comes from C programming terminology. The word *endline* is the preferred C++ programming term.

The C++ stream classes provide a function called `getline()` that reads one line of characters from a file. When you call the `getline()` function, you must pass it an array of characters to read text into. You must also pass in the size of the array. Let's use the letter n to represent the size of the array. The `getline()` function will read from the text file until it reads $n - 1$ characters. It will also stop reading if it encounters a newline[1] character, which is '\n'. In a text file, each line is terminated by a newline character. As it reads data in, the `getline()` function preserves white spaces.

Hands On 20.3 demonstrates the use of the `getline()` function. It also shows how to open a text file with the `open()` function.

Hands On 20.3

Objective

Write a program that opens a text file and reads data from it.

Experiment

Type the following program into your IDE or text editor. Compile, link, and run it. On the Tools and Examples CD that comes with this book, you'll find a directory called *Examples*. In the Examples directory is a subdirectory called *Chapt20*. The directory Chapt20 contains a file called *testfile.txt*. Copy that file into the same directory that contains this program.

```
#include <fstream.h>
#include <iostream.h>


int main()
{
   // Declare and open a stream.
   ifstream inputStream;
   inputStream.open("testfile.txt");

   const int INPUT_STRING_LENGTH = 80;
   char inputString[INPUT_STRING_LENGTH];

   while (!inputStream.eof())
   {
      inputStream.getline(inputString,INPUT_STRING_LENGTH);
      cout << inputString;
   }

   inputStream.close();
   return (0);
}
```

Results

```
As several of its eyes meandered in other directions, it gazed
at me with its primary eye and asked, "Are you hungry?""Well,
yes," I replied. "A bit peckish I suppose.""Perhaps you would
like to have a piece of my leg," it offered. A tentacle
gestured toward one of its many legs."Wha?" I answered
politely. I continued, "Huh?"It shifted its features into what
I later learned was its equivalent of a hopeful smile. "It's
quite tender. I have been soaking it in the finest mud. I see
you don't have the fangs required to help yourself. Would you
like me to cut some off for you?" So saying, it grabbed a
machete-sized knife off the wall and wacked off its leg.
"Don't feel you're being rude if you're not able to eat it
all," it said casually. "I can see that you're quite small. I
can always give some to my Foremothers. I need to make a
Respect Offering anyway."This was just more than I could
take."Look," I said. "I was just mowing my lawn. The next
thing I know, I'm heaven knows where, I'm almost eaten by what
looks like a minivan with an oversized mouth and flippers, and
now you're offering me pieces of yourself." I sat, flopping
```

```
down onto the dirt floor like a wet sack of potatoes.It
hesitated, withdrawing the leg a bit. "I apologize for saying
so, but your speech is strange. I do not know what this Laahn
is that you speak of. However, I can see that it has deep
spiritual significance for you. Perhaps your Laahn will allow
you to do mooweeng here while you are with us. Our ancestors
often give us permission to do our oblations to them while we
travel to other lands. Tomorrow, I can take you to our village
Thinkers. I'm sure they too will be moved by your predicament.
Somehow, we will help you do your mooweeng. In the meantime,
you must eat. As your host, it is only polite that I feed you
the best I have." It extended the severed leg again.The
bleeding had already stopped. It didn't seem to be in any
pain. I would soon learn the amazing speed at which these
creatures grew limbs. "I, uh. I usually eat meat cooked," I
told it. Instantly it grabbed what looked like a large wok off
the wall and tossed the leg in. "Many of our people prefer
cooked foods these days as well. Although it is not humble of
me to say so, I have been told that I am an excellent cook.
Please relax, your meal will be ready shortly."It was. And the
creature was right. It was an excellent cook.
```

Analysis

This is essentially the same program that appeared in Hands On 20.2. The primary differences are that it uses the `open()` member function to open the file, and it uses the `getline()` function rather than the extraction operator to read input.

Notice that the output of this Hands On program is more readable, but it is still not what appears in the input file. In particular, all of the paragraphs in the output run together. The cause of this lies in how the `getline()` function reads input.

Remember that each line in a text file is terminated by a newline character. The `getline()` function reads characters until the string is full or until it encounters the newline character. When it finds the newline character, it does not store the newline in the array of characters. Instead, it puts a null character in the array to mark the end of the string.

When the Hands On program writes the string to the `cout` stream, it does not send a newline character because there is no newline in the string. If we want the newline characters to go to the `cout` stream, we must send them explicitly. Hands On 20.4 demonstrates this.

Hands On 20.4

Objective

Write a program that opens a text file and reads data from it.

Experiment

Type the following program into your IDE or text editor. Compile, link, and run it. On the CD that comes with this book, you'll find a directory called *Examples*. In the Examples directory is a subdirectory called *Chapt20*. The directory Chapt20 contains a file called *testfile.txt*. Copy that file into the same directory that contains this program.

```
#include <fstream.h>
#include <iostream.h>
#include <string.h>
```

```
int main()
{
   // Declare and open a stream.
   ifstream inputStream;
   inputStream.open("testfile.txt");

   const int INPUT_STRING_LENGTH = 80;
   char inputString[INPUT_STRING_LENGTH];

   while (!inputStream.eof())
   {
      inputStream.getline(inputString,INPUT_STRING_LENGTH);
      if (strlen(inputString)>0)
      {
         cout << inputString;
      }
      else
      {
         cout << endl;
      }
      cout << endl;
   }


   inputStream.close();
   return (0);
}
```

Results

```
As several of its eyes meandered in other directions,
it gazed at me with its primary eye and asked, "Are
you hungry?"


"Well, yes," I replied. "A bit peckish I suppose."


"Perhaps you would like to have a piece of my leg," it
offered. A tentacle gestured toward one of its many legs.


"Wha?" I answered politely. I continued, "Huh?"


It shifted its features into what I later learned was
its equivalent of a hopeful smile. "It's quite tender. I
have been soaking it in the finest mud. I see you don't
have the fangs required to help yourself. Would you like
me to cut some off for you?" So saying, it grabbed a
machete-sized knife off the wall and wacked off its leg.


"Don't feel you're being rude if you're not able to eat
it all," it said casually. "I can see that you're quite
small. I can always give some to my Foremothers. I need
to make a Respect Offering anyway."
```

```
This was just more than I could take.


"Look," I said. "I was just mowing my lawn. The next thing
I know, I'm heaven knows where, I'm almost eaten by what
looks like a minivan with an oversized mouth and flippers,
and now you're offering me pieces of yourself." I sat,
flopping down onto the dirt floor like a wet sack of
potatoes.


It hesitated, withdrawing the leg a bit. "I apologize for
saying so, but your speech is strange. I do not know what
this Laahn is that you speak of. However, I can see that
it has deep spiritual significance for you. Perhaps your
Laahn will allow you to do mooweeng here while you are
with us. Our ancestors often give us permission to do our
oblations to them while we travel to other lands. Tomorrow,
I can take you to our village Thinkers. I'm sure they too
will be moved by your predicament. Somehow, we will help
you do your mooweeng. In the meantime, you must eat. As
your host, it is only polite that I feed you the best I
have." It extended the severed leg again.


The bleeding had already stopped. It didn't seem to be in
any pain. I would soon learn the amazing speed at which
these creatures grew limbs.


"I, uh. I usually eat meat cooked," I told it.


Instantly it grabbed what looked like a large wok off the
wall and tossed the leg in. "Many of our people prefer cooked
foods these days as well. Although it is not humble of me to
say so, I have been told that I am an excellent cook. Please
relax, your meal will be ready shortly."

It was. And the creature was right. It was an excellent cook.
```

The `strlen()` function is a C Standard Library function. Since C++ is a superset of C, all of the C Standard Library functions are available to C++ programs. To use the C `strlen()` function, you must include `string.h` in your program.

Analysis

To get the appropriate paragraphing, this version of the program uses an `if-else` statement. It calls the `strlen()` function to test if the length of the input string is greater than zero. If it is, the program writes the string to the `cout` stream. If the input string is empty, the program sends an `endline` to the `cout` stream.

In addition, the program sends an `endline` to the `cout` stream after each line of text. Each line in the input file is terminated by an `endline`. The program sends an `endline` to the `cout` stream to make the output appear exactly the way the input did in the text file. Text editors sometimes do this. Word processing programs almost never do.

An important feature that's missing from all of the Hands On examples in this chapter is error checking. These programs do not check to make sure that the input file is actually open before trying to read from it. You do that by checking the stream itself. If the stream variable evaluates to a nonzero value, there is no error. A value of zero indicates an error on the last operation. The rest of the Hands On examples will use this technique.

Reading from Binary Files Text files can only contain text data from the ASCII set of characters. Binary files, on the other hand, can contain any valid binary number. All data in computers can ultimately be stored as binary numbers. Therefore, a binary file may contain any type of data.

Your programs use the same techniques to open binary files that they use to open text files. The only difference is that programs must specify binary mode. To do this, they pass the `ios::binary` constant as the second parameter to the stream constructor or the `open()` function.

If a program calls a stream constructor to open a file, like this

```
ifstream inputStream("binfile.dat",ios::binary);
```

to open a stream, the second parameter specifies the mode. The same is true if it uses the `open()` function to open a file. For instance, the statements

```
ifstream inputStream;
inputStream.open("binfile.dat",ios::binary);
```

also open a file in binary mode.

The C++ streams also provide other mode constants. Table 20.2 lists the rest of the constants that can be passed through the second parameter.

Bitwise operations are an advanced topic not discussed in this book.

If you want to combine these mode constants, you can. Use an operator called bitwise OR, which is a single vertical line (|). For instance, the statement

```
ofstream outputStream("file.bin", ios::binary | ios::app);
```

opens a file for output. If the file already exists, the new data is appended onto the end of the file.

Once a file is open, your program can retrieve data from it by calling the `read()` function.

Binary files are often used for **random access.** Users seldom want to start at the beginning of a data file and read byte by byte until the end. They typically want access to specific data scattered throughout the file.

The C++ stream classes provide random access through the use of **current location pointers.** The current location pointers mark the position where the next read or write operation will take place. These pointers are maintained by the stream classes. However, your program can manipulate them by calling stream class member functions.

The stream classes keep two pointers: one for reading and the other for writing data. The current location pointer used for reading is called the **get pointer.**

You control the get pointer with the functions `seekg()` and `tellg()`. The `seekg()` function moves the get pointer to a specific location in the file. The `tellg()` function reports the get pointer's current location.

When your program calls `seekg()`, it must pass the number of bytes to move as the first parameter. The second parameter is the point from which to start moving. Example 20.3 demonstrates some calls to the `seekg()` function.

TABLE 20.2 The `openmode` Constants

Constant	Meaning
`ios::app`	Append data onto the end of the file.
`ios::ate`	Open and seek to end of the file immediately after opening.
`ios::binary`	Open a binary file.
`ios::in`	Open a file for input. This is the default for the `istream` and `ifstream` classes.
`ios::out`	Open a file for output. This is the default for the `ostream` and `ofstream` classes.
`ios::trunc`	Open a file and truncate (erase) any existing data in it.

EXAMPLE 20.3 Using seekg()

```
inputStream.seekg(100,ios::beg);
inputStream.seekg(-5,ios::beg);
inputStream.seekg(350,ios::cur);
inputStream.seekg(-10,ios::cur);
inputStream.seekg(20,ios::end);
inputStream.seekg(-50,ios::end);
```

According to the recent ANSI C++ specification, the `seekg()` function is actually specified in a class called `ios_base`. However, `ios` inherits from `ios_base`, so this code will work. The `ios_base` class is an abstract base class. Programmers should avoid referencing it directly.

Example 20.3 assumes that there is a valid input stream object called `inputStream`. The first call to `seekg()` moves the current location pointer 100 bytes from the beginning of the file. The constant `beg` is specified in the `ios` class, so we need the scope resolution operator to get access to it. Table 20.3 shows the three constants that can be used as the second parameter to `seekg()`.

The second call to `seekg()` in Example 20.3 attempts to move the current location pointer to a position 5 bytes before the beginning of the file. Your program can execute a call like this, but the call will fail. You can't move the current location pointer before the beginning of the file.

When we use `seekg()`, we can move the current location pointer relative to its current position. Example 20.3 shows a call that moves the current location pointer 350 bytes forward in the file from the current location. If the `seekg()` function encounters the end of the file before it moves 350 bytes, it will point the current location pointer at the end of the file. There is no way to move the current location pointer beyond the end of the file using the `seekg()` function.

We can also move the current location pointer backward toward the beginning of the file. Example 20.3 illustrates this with the call

```
inputStream.seekg(-10,ios::cur);
```

This tells the `seekg()` function to move the current location pointer 10 bytes toward the beginning of the file. If it encounters the beginning of the file before it moves 10 bytes, it stops at the beginning of the file.

Your program can also use the end of the file as its starting point for `seekg()`. The call

```
inputStream.seekg(20,ios::end);
```

tells the `seekg()` function to move the current location pointer 20 bytes past the end of the file. Since `seekg()` can't move past the end of the file, passing a number greater than zero as the first parameter when using `ios::end` as the second parameter has no real effect. It just sets the current location pointer to the end of the file.

The statement

```
inputStream.seekg(-50,ios::end);
```

tells the `seekg()` function to move the current location pointer 50 bytes before the end of the file.

Use the `tellg()` function to get the position of the current location pointer. It returns the offset in bytes where the next read operation will take place. Example 20.4 illustrates the use of the `tellg()` function.

EXAMPLE 20.4 Calling the tellg() Function

```
int currentLocation = inputStream.tellg();
```

TABLE 20.3 The Seek Direction Constants

Constant	Meaning
`ios::beg`	Seek from the beginning of the file.
`ios::cur`	Begin seeking from the current location in the file.
`ios::end`	Seek from the end of the file.

The program in Hands On 20.5 pulls together many of the ideas presented so far into a program that reads objects from a binary file.

Hands On 20.5

Objective

Write a program that defines a customer object and an index object. The program should store customer names and identification numbers. It should read an index from a file that is sorted by customer number. The program should allow the user to type in customer numbers. It should then read the appropriate customer record in from a file and display the customer's name.

Experiment

Type the following program into your IDE or text editor. Compile, link, and run it. On the CD that comes with this book, you'll find a directory called *Examples*. In the Examples directory is a subdirectory called *Chapt20*. The directory Chapt20 contains the files *binfile.dat* and *cust.ndx*. Copy these files into the directory that contains this program.

```
#include <fstream.h>
#include <iostream.h>
#include <string.h>


const MAX_CUSTOMER_NAME_LENGTH=40;

class customer
{
public:
   customer(void);

   void Name(char customerName[]);
   char *Name(void);

   void CustomerNumber(int customerIDNumber);
   int CustomerNumber(void);

private:
   int customerNumber;
   char name[MAX_CUSTOMER_NAME_LENGTH];
};


customer::customer(void)
{
   customerNumber=0;
   name[0]='\0';
}


void customer::Name(char customerName[])
{
   int length=strlen(customerName);

   if (length > 0)
```

```
   {
      for (int i=0;customerName[i];i++)
      {
         name[i]=customerName[i];
      }
      name[i]='\0';
   }
   else
   {
      name[0]='\0';
   }
}


char *customer::Name(void)
{
   return (name);
}


void customer::CustomerNumber(int customerIDNumber)
{
   customerNumber=customerIDNumber;
}


int customer::CustomerNumber(void)
{
   return (customerNumber);
}


class index_entry
{
public:
   index_entry(void);

   void CustomerNumber(int customerIDNumber);
   int CustomerNumber(void);

   void RecordNumber(int customerRecordNumber);
   int RecordNumbcr(void);

private:
   int customerNumber;
   int recordNumber;
};



index_entry::index_entry(void)
{
   customerNumber=0;
   recordNumber=0;
}


void index_entry::CustomerNumber(int customerIDNumber)
```

```
{
   customerNumber=customerIDNumber;
}


int index_entry::CustomerNumber(void)
{
   return (customerNumber);
}


void index_entry::RecordNumber(int customerRecordNumber)
{
   recordNumber=customerRecordNumber;
}


int index_entry::RecordNumber(void)
{
   return (recordNumber);
}


const int MAX_INDEX_SIZE=100;


class index
{
public:
   index(void);

   bool Full(void);
   void Insert(int customerIDNumber,int CustomerRecordNumber);
   int Find(int customerIDNumber);

private:
   void Sort(void);

private:
   index_entry customerIndex[MAX_INDEX_SIZE];
   int totalEntries;
};



index::index(void)
{
   totalEntries=0;
}


bool index::Full(void)
{
   bool isFull=false;

   if (totalEntries==MAX_INDEX_SIZE)
   {
```

```
      isFull=true;
   }

   return (isFull);
}


void index::Insert(int customerIDNumber,int customerRecordNumber)
{
   if (!Full())
   {
      index_entry theEntry;

      theEntry.CustomerNumber(customerIDNumber);
      theEntry.RecordNumber(customerRecordNumber);

      customerIndex[totalEntries++]=theEntry;

      Sort();

   }
}


int index::Find(int customerIDNumber)
{
   int recordNumber = -1;
   int top,middle,bottom;
   bool found=false;

   for (top=0,bottom=totalEntries-1,middle=top+((bottom-top)/2);
        (top<=bottom) && (!found);
        middle=top+((bottom-top)/2))
   {
      if (customerIDNumber==customerIndex[middle].CustomerNumber())
      {
         found=true;
         recordNumber=customerIndex[middle].RecordNumber();
      }
      else if (customerIDNumber<customerIndex[middle].CustomerNumber())
      {
         bottom=middle-1;
      }
      else   // customerIDNumber>customerIndex[middle].CustomerNumber()
      {
         top=middle+1;
      }
   }

   return (recordNumber);
}


void index::Sort(void)
{
   int i,j;
   index_entry temp;
```

```
    for (i=1;i<totalEntries;i++)
    {
       for (j=0;j<i;j++)
       {
          if (customerIndex[i].CustomerNumber() <
              customerIndex[j].CustomerNumber())
          {
             temp=customerIndex[i];
             customerIndex[i]=customerIndex[j];
             customerIndex[j]=temp;
          }
       }
    }
}



int main()
{
    ifstream inputStream("binfile.dat",ios::binary);
    ifstream indexStream("cust.ndx",ios::binary);

    if ((inputStream) && (indexStream))
    {
       index theIndex;
       customer theCustomer;
       char continueChar;

       indexStream.read((char *)(&theIndex),sizeof(index));

       int customerNumber;

       for (continueChar='y';
            (continueChar!='n') && (continueChar!='N') &&
            (inputStream.good());
            /* No increment or decrement */)
       {

          cout << "Enter a customer number: ";
          cin >> customerNumber;

          int recordNumber;
          recordNumber=theIndex.Find(customerNumber);

          if (recordNumber>=0)
          {
             inputStream.seekg(recordNumber*sizeof(customer),ios::beg);
             inputStream.read((char *)(&theCustomer),sizeof(customer));
             cout << theCustomer.Name() << endl;
             cout << theCustomer.CustomerNumber() << endl;
             cout << endl;
          }
          else
          {
             cout << endl << "Not found" << endl;
          }
```

```
            cout << endl << "Continue? Y/N: ";
            cin>>continueChar;
            cin.ignore(1,'\n');
            cout << endl << endl;
        }

        inputStream.close();
        indexStream.close();
    }

    return (0);
}
```

Results

```
Enter a customer number: 987065
Paki Tonomaipe'a
987065


Continue? Y/N: y


Enter a customer number: 432432
Jane Jones
432432


Continue? Y/N: y


Enter a customer number: 123456
Mariko Tanaka
123456


Continue? Y/N: y


Enter a customer number: 234234
Bob Smith
234234


Continue? Y/N: y


Enter a customer number: 111111
Not found

Continue? Y/N: n
```

Analysis

This program contains more code than it currently uses. Some of the functions will be used in Hands On 20.7, which demonstrates writing to binary files.

Essentially, this is a small portion of a database program. Like most database programs, this example program uses a data file and an index file. The customer information is stored in the data file. Each entry, or **record,** in the data file contains information about one customer. Each piece of information in a record is called a **field.** In this program, there are two fields in each record: one for the customer name and one for the customer number.

The customer records are stored one after another in the data file. They are not sorted. In the early days of programming, database program developers quickly learned that database records often hold large amounts of information. Sorting that information can require a huge amount of time. It's normally much faster to use index files.

The index file contains entries also. Each entry contains a customer identification number and a record number. The information in the index file is sorted. This program searches through entries in the index file to find a customer number that the user is seeking. If it finds the customer number, it retrieves the record number. It then uses the record number to find the record for that customer in the data file.

The first thing the program does is define a `customer` object, which contains a name and a customer number. The `customer` object contains member functions to get and set both the name and the customer number.

Next, the program defines an `index_entry` object. Each object of this type contains a customer number and a record number in the data file. The `index_entry` object has member functions for getting and setting the customer number and record number.

C++ developers often call classes such as index *list classes* or *container classes.*

The program also defines an `index` object. It contains an array of `index_entry` objects. Because the `index` object has a fixed size, it needs a member function that tests whether the `index` is full. It also uses a member function to insert `index_entry` objects into the `index`.

The list in the `index` object must be sorted at all times. Therefore, the `index` object contains a private member function that sorts the index each time an entry is inserted. The `index::Sort()` function uses an algorithm called the *Bubble Sort.* It is one of the simplest and least efficient types of sorts available.

In addition, the `index` object has a member function that searches the list. The `index::Find()` function uses a Binary Search. This is an easy and efficient algorithm for searching.

The `main()` function opens streams for the data file and the index file. Be sure you copy these two files from the CD that came with this book into the directory that contains this program. If you don't, the program won't work.

If the program successfully opens both streams, it calls the `read()` function to read in the entire index. The invocation of the `read()` function looks like this:

```
indexStream.read((char *)(&theIndex),sizeof(index));
```

All calls to `read()` follow this pattern. This is because the first parameter of the `read()` function must be type cast to a character pointer.[2] The general form of the syntax that does this is

```
(char *)(&object_name)
```

where *object_name* is the name of the variable that you are reading data into.

The second parameter of the `read()` function tells it how many bytes of information to read in from the file. Whenever we read in a single object from the disk, we set this parameter to

```
sizeof(object_type)
```

where *object_type* is the type name of the object we are reading from the file. If we were reading multiple objects from the disk, we could set this parameter to

```
numberOfObjects * sizeof(object_type)
```

[2]For more information on pointers, see Chapter 21.

where the variable `numberOfObjects` is equal to the number of objects that we want to read from the disk.

The program next enters a loop that continues until the user tells it to quit, or until some type of stream error occurs. In the loop, it prompts the user for a customer number. It passes that number to the `index::Find()` function, which gets the record number of that customer's record in the data file.

If it found the record, it uses the `seekg()` function to position the file's current location pointer to the beginning of the record. It then calls the `read()` function to read in the customer's record. The program prints the customer information from the record on the screen.

This assumes line-buffered keyboard input, which is true for the most common types of computers.

At the end of the loop, the program asks the user whether or not to continue looping. Typically, the user will type in a 'y' or a 'Y'. Because stream input from the keyboard will continue until the Enter key is pressed, the user will also press the Enter key. However, the statement

```
cin>>continueChar;
```

will read only one character. The user has probably pressed two: the 'y' (or 'Y') and the Enter key. The Enter key is read in as a '\n'. We want the program to throw away the extra character. Therefore, the program calls the `ignore()` function. The first parameter tells it how many characters to throw away. The second tells it to stop ignoring input when it encounters the '\n'. This technique clears out any extraneous keyboard input.

When the user indicates that he/she is finished looking up customer information in the data file, the program exits the loop. It closes both of the streams attached to the input files and then exits.

Writing Data to Files

Writing data to files is similar to reading it. Your program must create a stream object and connect it to a file. It writes either text or binary data. When it is finished, it should close the file.

When your program reads data from files, it uses a current location pointer, called the *get pointer,* to keep track of where the next read will take place. The `seekg()` function controls where the get pointer points. The `tellg()` function reports its location to your program.

In the same way, programs use a current location pointer to keep track of where the next write will take place. This pointer, called the **put pointer,** can be controlled with the `seekp()` function. Calling `seekp()` works exactly like calling the `seekg()` function. They both take the same parameters. Similarly, there is a `tellp()` function that reports the location of the put pointer.

Writing to Text Files Use the insertion operator (<<) or the `put()` function to write text to a stream object. Example 20.5 shows that using the insertion operator to write text to a file is essentially the same as writing it to the `cout` stream. Hands On 20.6 demonstrates the `put()` function.

EXAMPLE 20.5 Writing Text to a Text File

```
int main()
{
   ofstream outputFile("output.txt");

   if (outputFile)
   {
      outputFile << "Writing text to the file." << endl;
      outputFile.close();
   }
   return (0);
}
```

Hands On 20.6

Objective

Write a program that opens a text file and writes data to it.

Experiment

Type the following program into your IDE or text editor. Compile, link, and run it.

```
#include <fstream.h>
#include <iostream.h>


int main()
{
   ofstream outputFile;

   outputFile.open("outfile.txt");

   if (outputFile)
   {
      char quitChar='N';
      const int INPUT_LINE_LENGTH = 40;
      char inputText[INPUT_LINE_LENGTH];

      while ((quitChar != 'y') && (quitChar != 'Y'))
      {
         cout << "Enter a string of no more than 40 characters" << endl;
         cout << ">>> ";
         cin.getline(inputText,INPUT_LINE_LENGTH);
         for (int i=0;inputText[i];i++)
         {
            outputFile.put(inputText[i]);
         }
         outputFile << endl;

         cout << endl << "Quit? Y/N: ";
         cin>>quitChar;
         cin.ignore(1,'\n');
         cout << endl << endl;

      }

      outputFile.close();
   }

   return (0);
}
```

Results

This program displays the following on the screen:

```
Enter a string of no more than 40 characters
>>> Little boy blue
Quit? Y/N: n
```

```
Enter a string of no more than 40 characters
>>> Come blow your horn
Quit? Y/N: y
```

The contents of the output file are:

```
Little boy blue
Come blow your horn
```

Analysis

This program reads character input from the keyboard and writes it to a text file. It begins by declaring a stream object and connecting to a file. If the object `outputFile` is able to open the stream, the program prompts the user to enter a string of no more than 40 characters. It reads the characters in from the keyboard by calling the `getline()` function. To send the characters out to the file, it invokes the `put()` function. Because the `put()` function can send only one character at a time, the program uses a loop to send all characters in the string. The statements

```
for (int i=0;inputText[i];i++)
{
   outputFile.put(inputText[i]);
}
```

cause the program to initialize the integer variable `i` to zero. The program accesses each character in the array to see whether it evaluates to zero or nonzero. The only character that evaluates to zero is the null character ('\0'). So when the character that the loop is examining is the null character, the condition of the loop evaluates to zero and the loop terminates.

This program could have used the insertion operator instead. The entire loop could be replaced with the statement

```
outputFile << inputText;
```

and the program would do exactly the same thing.

After the user types in a line of text, the program prints a prompt on the screen asking whether to continue or not. Because the user must type in a character and then press the Enter key, the program uses the `ignore()` function to throw away the endline character.

When the loop terminates, the program calls the `close()` function to close the file.

Writing to Binary Files One of the great advantages of using binary files is that your program can read or write the entire contents of an object. It can even read or write groups of objects. To write binary data to a file, programs must call the `write()` function. It uses exactly the same parameters as the `read()` function. The only difference is the direction that the data flows.

Hands On 20.7 contains a program that writes the binary data file we used for Hands On 20.5.

Hands On 20.7

Objective

Write a program that defines a customer object and an index object. The program should store customer names and identification numbers. The program should allow the user to type in customer names and customer identification numbers. It should then write the customer record to a file. Next, the program must create an index that is sorted by customer number. Finally, it should write the index to a file.

Experiment

Type the following program into your IDE or text editor. Compile, link, and run it.

```
#include <fstream.h>
#include <iostream.h>
#include <string.h>



const MAX_CUSTOMER_NAME_LENGTH=40;

class customer
{
public:
   customer(void);

   void Name(char customerName[]);
   char *Name(void);

   void CustomerNumber(int customerIDNumber);
   int CustomerNumber(void);

private:
   int customerNumber;
   char name[MAX_CUSTOMER_NAME_LENGTH];
};


customer::customer(void)
{
   customerNumber=0;
   name[0]='\0';
}


void customer::Name(char customerName[])
{
   int length=strlen(customerName);
   if (length > 0)
   {
      for (int i=0;customerName[i];i++)
      {
         name[i]=customerName[i];
      }
      name[i]='\0';
   }
   else
   {
      name[0]='\0';
   }
}


char *customer::Name(void)
```

```
{
   return (name);
}


void customer::CustomerNumber(int customerIDNumber)
{
   customerNumber=customerIDNumber;
}


int customer::CustomerNumber(void)
{
   return (customerNumber);
}



class index_entry
{
public:
   index_entry(void);

   void CustomerNumber(int customerIDNumber);
   int CustomerNumber(void);

   void RecordNumber(int customerRecordNumber);
   int RecordNumber(void);

private:
   int customerNumber;
   int recordNumber;
};



index_entry::index_entry(void)
{
   customerNumber=0;
   recordNumber=0;
}


void index_entry::CustomerNumber(int customerIDNumber)
{
   customerNumber=customerIDNumber;
}


int index_entry::CustomerNumber(void)
{
   return (customerNumber);
}


void index_entry::RecordNumber(int customerRecordNumber)
{
```

```
   recordNumber=customerRecordNumber;
}


int index_entry::RecordNumber(void)
{
   return (recordNumber);
}



const int MAX_INDEX_SIZE=100;

class index
{
public:
   index(void);

   bool Full(void);
   void Insert(int customerIDNumber,int CustomerRecordNumber);
   int Find(int customerIDNumber);

private:
   void Sort(void);

private:
   index_entry customerIndex[MAX_INDEX_SIZE];
   int totalEntries;
 };



index::index(void)
{
   totalEntries=0;
}


bool index::Full(void)
{
   bool isFull=false;

   if (totalEntries==MAX_INDEX_SIZE)
   {
      isFull=true;
   }

   return (isFull);
}


void index::Insert(int customerIDNumber,int customerRecordNumber)
{
   if (!Full())
   {
      index_entry theEntry;
      theEntry.CustomerNumber(customerIDNumber);
      theEntry.RecordNumber(customerRecordNumber);
```

```
      customerIndex[totalEntries++]=theEntry;

      Sort();

   }
}


int index::Find(int customerIDNumber)
{
   int recordNumber = -1;
   int top,middle,bottom;
   bool found=false;

   for (top=0,bottom=totalEntries-1,middle=top+((bottom-top)/2);
        (top<=bottom) && (!found);
        middle=top+((bottom-top)/2))
   {
      if (customerIDNumber==customerIndex[middle].CustomerNumber())
      {
         found=true;
         recordNumber=customerIndex[middle].RecordNumber();
      }
      else if (customerIDNumber<customerIndex[middle].CustomerNumber())
      {
         bottom=middle-1;
      }
      else   // customerIDNumber>customerIndex[middle].CustomerNumber()
      {
         top=middle+1;
      }
   }

   return (recordNumber);
}


void index::Sort(void)
{
   int i,j;
   index_entry temp;


   for (i=1;i<totalEntries;i++)
   {
      for (j=0;j<i;j++)
      {
         if (customerIndex[i].CustomerNumber() <
             customerIndex[j].CustomerNumber())
         {
            temp=customerIndex[i];
            customerIndex[i]=customerIndex[j];
            customerIndex[j]=temp;
         }
      }
   }
}
```

```
int main()
{
   ofstream outputStream;

   outputStream.open("binfile.dat",ios::binary);
   if (outputStream)
   {
      char customerName[MAX_CUSTOMER_NAME_LENGTH];
      int customerNumber;
      customer theCustomer;
      int recordNumber;
      index theIndex;
      char continueChar;

      for (continueChar='y',recordNumber=0;
           (continueChar!='n') && (continueChar!='N') &&
           (!theIndex.Full());
           recordNumber++)
      {
         cout << "Enter customer name: ";
         cin.getline(customerName,MAX_CUSTOMER_NAME_LENGTH);
         cout << "Enter customer number: ";
         cin >> customerNumber;

         theCustomer.Name(customerName);
         theCustomer.CustomerNumber(customerNumber);

         outputStream.write((char *)(&theCustomer),sizeof(customer));

         theIndex.Insert(customerNumber,recordNumber);

         cout << endl << "Continue? Y/N: ";
         cin>>continueChar;
         cin.ignore(1,'\n');
         cout << endl << endl;
      }

      ofstream indexStream("cust.ndx",ios::binary);
      if (indexStream)
      {
         indexStream.write((char *)(&theIndex),sizeof(index));
      }

      outputStream.close();
      indexStream.close();

   }


   return (0);
}
```

Results

Enter customer name: **Jane Jones**
Enter customer number: **432432**

```
Continue? Y/N: y


Enter customer name: Bob Smith
Enter customer number: 234234

Continue? Y/N: y


Enter customer name: Mariko Tanaka
Enter customer number: 123456

Continue? Y/N: y


Enter customer name: Paki Tonomaipe'a
Enter customer number: 987065

Continue? Y/N: n
```

Analysis

This program uses the same set of objects that were defined for Hands On 20.5. The `main()` function begins by declaring an output stream for the data file. If it can open the output stream, it declares the temporary variables it needs. The program then enters a loop that continues while the user has not indicated that he/she wants to quit. Since we are using an array with a fixed size in the `index` object, the loop must also stop when the `index` object is full.

Inside the loop, the program prompts the user for the customer name and identification number. It stores those in an object of type `customer` and writes the object to a binary data file.

The program inserts the customer information into the index by calling the `index::Insert()` function. This function tests to see whether the index is full. If not, the function puts the customer identification number and the record number into an `index_entry` object. It stores the `index_entry` object in the first available spot in the array.

The function invokes the private member function `index::Sort()` to sort the index by customer identification number. The `index::Sort()` function uses the Bubble Sort. You'll see the Bubble Sort quite a bit in your programming classes. It is one of the easiest, but least efficient, sorts to implement. It gets used quite a bit as an introduction to sorting, but you don't see it much in actual commercial programs.

When the `index::Sort()` function finishes, the program returns to `index::Insert()`. At this point, the `index::Insert()` function is also done, so the program returns to the `for` loop in the `main()` function.

At the end of the `for` loop, the program asks the user if she wants to continue entering information. If the user types 'n' or 'N', the loop terminates. The program opens a binary file and writes the entire contents of the `index` object out to it. It then closes the data file and the index file.

Adding File I/O to the Text Editor

Now it's time to pull together many of the ideas that we've discussed throughout this book and write the text editor.

Hands On 20.8

Objective

Write a text editor that enables a user to load, edit, and save a text file.

Experiment

Type the following program into your IDE or text editor. Compile, link, and run it. This program is composed of five files: *TEdit.cpp*, *Tstring.h*, *Tstring.cpp*, *Tbuffer.h*, and *Tbuffer.cpp*. When you run this text editor, be sure you copy the file *test.txt* from the CD that comes with this book into the directory that contains the executable program file.

This is the file `TEdit.cpp`*:*

```
//-----------------------------------------------------------------------
/*
File Name:      TEdit.cpp
Comments:       This is the main file of the text editor.
*/
//-----------------------------------------------------------------------



//-----------------------------------------------------------------------
// Include Files

#include "TString.h"
#include "TBuffer.h"
#include "stdlib.h"

// End Include Files
//-----------------------------------------------------------------------



//-----------------------------------------------------------------------
// Prototypes

void ClearScreen(void);
void DisplayMenu(void);

// End Prototypes
//-----------------------------------------------------------------------



int main()
{
   const int TOTAL_TEXT_AREA_LINES = 20;
   const char SCROLL_UP_COMMAND = (char)21;     // Ctrl+U
   const char SCROLL_DOWN_COMMAND = (char)4;    // Ctrl+D
   const char SAVE_COMMAND = (char)1;           // Ctrl+A
   const char LOAD_COMMAND = (char)12;          // Ctrl+L
   const char EDIT_COMMAND = (char)5;           // Ctrl+E
   const char QUIT_COMMAND = (char)17;          // Ctrl+Q
   const char BEEP_CHARACTER = (char)7;
```

```
static text_buffer textBuffer;  // Uses static because it's large.
bool done=false;
int i,top;
text_string inputText;

// While the user doesn't want to quit...
while (!done)
{
   // Clear the screen.
   ClearScreen();
   text_string outputString;

   // Display one screenful of text.
   for (i=0,top=textBuffer.TopLine();
        (i<TOTAL_TEXT_AREA_LINES) && (top+i<TEXT_BUFFER_LENGTH);
        i++)
   {
      cout << (top+i) << ": ";
      outputString = textBuffer.Line(top+i);
      cout << outputString;
      cout << endl;
   }

   // Display the menu.
   DisplayMenu();

   // Get a character from the user.
   cin >> inputText;

   text_string fileName;

   switch (inputText.Get(0))
   {
      // If the user wants to scroll up one screenful...
      case SCROLL_UP_COMMAND:
         // Scroll up.
         textBuffer.ScrollUp(TOTAL_TEXT_AREA_LINES-1);
      break;

      // If the user wants to scroll down one screenful...
      case SCROLL_DOWN_COMMAND:
         // Scroll down.
         textBuffer.ScrollDown(TOTAL_TEXT_AREA_LINES-1);
      break;

      // If the user wants to save the buffer to a file...
      case SAVE_COMMAND:
         // Save to file.
         cout << "Enter File Name: ";
         cin >> fileName;
         if (textBuffer.Save(fileName)!=NO_BUFFER_ERROR)
         {
            cout << BEEP_CHARACTER;
         }
      break;

      // If the user wants to load from a file...
      case LOAD_COMMAND:
```

```
            // Load from file.
            cout << "Enter File Name: ";
            cin >> fileName;
            if (textBuffer.Load(fileName)!=NO_BUFFER_ERROR)
            {
               cout << BEEP_CHARACTER;
            }
         break;

         // If the user wants to edit text...
         case EDIT_COMMAND:
         {
            cout << "Enter Line Number: ";
            cin >> inputText;

            // Convert the line number to a number.
            char tempString[MAX_TEXT_STRING_LENGTH];
            inputText.Get(tempString);
            int lineNumber=atoi(tempString);

            // If the line number is displayed on the screen...
            if ((lineNumber >= top) &&
                (lineNumber < top+TOTAL_TEXT_AREA_LINES))
            {
               // Prompt the user for input.
               cout << lineNumber << ": ";

               // Get the new line of text.
               cin >> inputText;

               // Insert the new line of text into the buffer.
               textBuffer.Line(lineNumber,inputText);
            }
         }
         break;

         // If the user wants to quit...
         case QUIT_COMMAND:
            done=true;
         break;

         // Else the input is not recognized...
         default:
            // Beep the speaker.
            cout << BEEP_CHARACTER;
         break;
      }
   }
   return (0);
}


//-----------------------------------------------------------------------
/*
Function Name:      ClearScreen
Member of:          N/A
Input Parameters:   None.
Output Parameters:  None.
```

```
Return Value:       None.
Comments:           A function that clears any screen that is 24 lines of text
                    or less. If your screen displays more than 24 lines,
                    change SCREEN_SIZE to one more than the number of lines it
                    displays.
*/

void ClearScreen(void)
{
   const int SCREEN_SIZE = 25;
   for (int i=0;i<SCREEN_SIZE;i++)
   {
      cout << endl;
   }
}

// End ClearScreen
//-------------------------------------------------------------------------------



//-------------------------------------------------------------------------------
/*
Function Name:      DisplayMenu
Member of:          N/A
Input Parameters:   None.
Output Parameters:  None.
Return Value:       None.
Comments:           Displays a menu for the text editor.
*/

void DisplayMenu(void)
{
   cout << "To enter a command, press one of the following, ";
   cout << "then press Enter" << endl;
   cout << "Edit text: Ctrl+E  ";
   cout << "Scroll Up: Ctrl+U  ";
   cout << "Scroll Down: Ctrl+D"  << endl;
   cout << "Load File: Ctrl+L  ";
   cout << "Save File: Ctrl+A  ";
   cout << "Quit: Ctrl+Q";
   cout << "    Command :";
}

// End DisplayMenu
//-------------------------------------------------------------------------------


// End TEdit.cpp
//-------------------------------------------------------------------------------
```

This is the file `Tstring.h`:

```
//-------------------------------------------------------------------------------
/*
File Name:   TString.h
Comments:    This file contains the definition of the text_string class. It
             also defines the constants needed to use the text_string class.
```

```
/*
//--------------------------------------------------------------------------

#ifndef TSTRING_H
#define TSTRING_H



//--------------------------------------------------------------------------
// Include Files

#include <iostream.h>

// End Include Files
//--------------------------------------------------------------------------


//--------------------------------------------------------------------------
// Constants

const int MAX_TEXT_STRING_LENGTH = 60;

// End Constants
//--------------------------------------------------------------------------



//--------------------------------------------------------------------------
// Class Definitions

class text_string
{
public:
   text_string(void);
   text_string(char textString[]);
   ~text_string(void);

   int Set(int characterIndex,char newCharacter);
   int Set(char sourceCharArray[]);
   int Set(text_string sourceString);

   char Get(int characterIndex);
   void Get(char textString[MAX_TEXT_STRING_LENGTH+1]);

   int Length(void);

   friend istream &operator >> (istream &inputStream,
                                text_string &inputString);
   friend ostream &operator << (ostream &outputStream,
                                text_string &outputString);

private:
   char charString[MAX_TEXT_STRING_LENGTH];
   int length;
};

// End Class Definitions
//--------------------------------------------------------------------------
#endif
```

```
// End text_string
//-----------------------------------------------------------------------
```

This is the file `Tstring.cpp`*:*

```
//-----------------------------------------------------------------------
/*
File Name:   TString.cpp
Comments:    This file contains the member functions for the text_string
             class.
*/
//-----------------------------------------------------------------------



//-----------------------------------------------------------------------
// Include Files

#include "TString.h"

// End Include Files
//-----------------------------------------------------------------------



//-----------------------------------------------------------------------
/*
Function Name:      text_string
Member of:          text_string
Input Parameters:   None.
Output Parameters:  None.
Return Value:       Initialized text_string object.
Comments:           This function is the default, or no-argument,
                    constructor for the text_string class.
*/

text_string::text_string(void)
{
   // Set the length of the string to zero.
   length = 0;

   // Set all of the characters in the string to the null character.
   for (int i=0; i<MAX_TEXT_STRING_LENGTH; i++)
   {
      charString[i] = '\0';
   }
}

// End text_string
//-----------------------------------------------------------------------



//-----------------------------------------------------------------------
/*
Function Name:      text_string
Member of:          text_string
Input Parameters:   textString - An array of characters that the string will
                        be initialized to.
```

```
Output Parameters:  None.
Return Value:       Initialized text_string object.
Comments:           This function is an overloaded constructor for the
                    text_string class.
*/

text_string::text_string(char textString[])
{
   int i;

   // Copy the characters from the input string into this object.
   for (i=0;
        (i < MAX_TEXT_STRING_LENGTH) && (textString[i]);
        i++)
   {
      charString[i]=textString[i];
   }

   // Set the length.
   length=i;
}

// End text_string
//---------------------------------------------------------------------------



//---------------------------------------------------------------------------
/*
Function Name:      ~text_string
Member of:          text_string
Input Parameters:   None.
Output Parameters:  None.
Return Value:       None.
Comments:           This is the destructor for the text_string class.
*/

text_string::~text_string(void)
{
   length = 0;
}

// End ~text_string
//---------------------------------------------------------------------------



//---------------------------------------------------------------------------
/*
Function Name:      Set
Member of:          text_string
Input Parameters:   characterIndex - The index number of the character in the
                        string to set. Index numbering begins with zero.
                    newCharacter - The new character to store in the string.
Output Parameters:  None.
Return Value:       If this function is successful it returns the index
                    number of the location in the string where it stored the
                    new character. If not, it returns -1.
```

```
Comments:           This function stores a character in a text_string object.
*/

int text_string::Set(int characterIndex,char newCharacter)
{
   int insertLocation = -1;

   if (characterIndex<length)
   {
      charString[characterIndex]=newCharacter;
      insertLocation=characterIndex;
   }

   return (insertLocation);
}

// End Set
//-----------------------------------------------------------------------------



//-----------------------------------------------------------------------------
/*
Function Name:      Set
Member of:          text_string
Input Parameters:   sourceCharArray - An array of characters which this
                        function will copy into the text_string object.
Output Parameters:  None.
Return Value:       This function returns the length of the string it stored
                    in this object.
Comments:           This overloaded version of the Set() function copies an
                    array of characters in a text_string object.
*/


int text_string::Set(char sourceCharArray[])
{
   int i;
   for (i=0;
        (i<MAX_TEXT_STRING_LENGTH) && (sourceCharArray[i]!='\0');
        i++)
   {
      charString[i] = sourceCharArray[i];
   }
   length = i;
   return (length);
}

// End Set
//-----------------------------------------------------------------------------



//-----------------------------------------------------------------------------
/*
Function Name:      Set
Member of:          text_string
```

```
Input Parameters:   sourceString - A text_string object which this
                        function will copy.
Output Parameters:  None.
Return Value:       This function returns the length of the string it stored
                    in this object.
Comments:           This overloaded version of the Set() function copies
                    another text_string into the current text_string object.
*/

int text_string::Set(text_string sourceString)
{
   for (int i=0;i<sourceString.length;i++)
   {
      charString[i] = sourceString.charString[i];
   }
   length = sourceString.length;
   return (length);
}

// End Set
//-----------------------------------------------------------------------------



//-----------------------------------------------------------------------------
/*
Function Name:      Get
Member of:          text_string
Input Parameters:   characterIndex - Index number of the character to get.
                        Character index numbers begin with zero.
Output Parameters:  None.
Return Value:       On success, this function returns the requested
                    character. On failure, or if the string is empty, it
                    returns a null character.
Comments:           This function retrieves a character from the current
                    text_string object.
*/

char text_string::Get(int characterIndex)
{
   char returnCharacter = '\0';

   if ((characterIndex>=0) && (characterIndex < length))
   {
      returnCharacter = charString[characterIndex];
   }

   return (returnCharacter);
}

// End Get
//-----------------------------------------------------------------------------



//-----------------------------------------------------------------------------
/*
```

```
Function Name:      Get
Member of:          text_string
Input Parameters:   None.
Output Parameters:  textString - An array of character that the characters
                        from this object will be copied into.
Return Value:       None.
Comments:           This function retrieves all of the characters in the
                    current text_string object and stores them in a
                    character array. Note that the character array must be
                    one character longer than the maximum length of the
                    text_string object. This allows room for the null
                    character, which must be on the end of a C++ string.
*/

void text_string::Get(char textString[MAX_TEXT_STRING_LENGTH+1])
{
   int i;
   for (i=0;(i<length) && (i<MAX_TEXT_STRING_LENGTH);i++)
   {
      textString[i] = charString[i];
   }
   textString[i] = '\0';
}

// End Get
//-----------------------------------------------------------------------------



//-----------------------------------------------------------------------------
/*
Function Name:      Length
Member of:          text_string
Input Parameters:   None.
Output Parameters:  None.
Return Value:       Returns the length of the string.
Comments:           The Return Value section says it all.
*/

int text_string::Length(void)
{
   return (length);
}

// End Length
//-----------------------------------------------------------------------------



//-----------------------------------------------------------------------------
/*
Function Name:      operator >>
Friend of:          text_string
Input Parameters:   inputStream - The stream that the input will be extracted
                        from.
                    inputString - The text_string object that the input will
                        be stored in.
```

```
Output Parameters:  None.
Return Value:       Returns a reference to a stream.
Comments:           This function overloads the extraction operator for the
                    text_string class. It is not a member of text_string
                    class, it is a friend function.

                    WARNING: This extraction operator uses the
                    istream::getline() function for input. This deviates
                    from the normal behavior of an insertion operator
                    function. This is done in this example only for
                    code brevity. It is not generally a good practice.
*/

istream &operator >> (istream &inputStream,
                      text_string &inputString)
{
   inputStream.getline(inputString.charString,
                       MAX_TEXT_STRING_LENGTH);
   inputString.length = strlen(inputString.charString);
   return (inputStream);
}

// End operator >>
//---------------------------------------------------------------------------



//---------------------------------------------------------------------------
/*
Function Name:      operator <<
Friend of:          text_string
Input Parameters:   outputStream - The stream that the output will be
                        inserted into.
                    outputString - The text_string object that the output
                        will come from.
Output Parameters:  None.
Return Value:       Returns a reference to a stream.
Comments:           This function overloads the insertion operator for the
                    text_string class. It is not a member of text_string
                    class, it is a friend function.
*/

ostream &operator << (ostream &outputStream,
                      text_string &outputString)
{
   for (int i=0;i<outputString.length;i++)
   {
      outputStream << outputString.charString[i];
   }

   return (outputStream);
}

// End operator <<
//---------------------------------------------------------------------------

// End TString.cpp
//---------------------------------------------------------------------------
```

This is the file `Tbuffer.h`*:*

```
//---------------------------------------------------------------------------
/*
File Name:  TBuffer.h
Comments:   This file contains the definition of the text_buffer class. It
            also defines the constants needed to use the text_buffer class.
*/
//---------------------------------------------------------------------------


#if !defined (TBUFFER_H)
#define TBUFFER_H


//---------------------------------------------------------------------------
// Constants

const int TEXT_BUFFER_LENGTH = 100;

// Buffer error status values.
const int NO_BUFFER_ERROR = 0;
const int CANT_LOAD_FILE = -1;
const int CANT_SAVE_FILE = -2;

// End Constants
//---------------------------------------------------------------------------



//---------------------------------------------------------------------------
// Class Definitions

class text_buffer
{
public:
   text_buffer(void);

   int TopLine(void);

   int ScrollUp(int linesToScroll);
   int ScrollDown(int linesToScroll);

   int Load(text_string fileName);
   int Save(text_string fileName);

   void Line(int lineToSet,text_string newText);
   text_string Line(int lineToGet);

private:
   text_string textBuffer[TEXT_BUFFER_LENGTH];
   int topLine;
   int linesUsed;
};

// End Class Definitions
//---------------------------------------------------------------------------

#endif
```

```
// End TBuffer.h
//-----------------------------------------------------------------------
```

This is the file `Tbuffer.cpp`:

```
//-----------------------------------------------------------------------
/*
File Name:  TBuffer.cpp
Comments:   This file contains the implementation of the member functions for
            the text_buffer class.
*/
//-----------------------------------------------------------------------



//-----------------------------------------------------------------------
// Include Files

#include <fstream.h>
#include "TString.h"
#include "TBuffer.h"
// End Include Files
//-----------------------------------------------------------------------



//-----------------------------------------------------------------------
/*
Function Name:      text_buffer
Member of:          text_buffer
Input Parameters:   None.
Output Parameters:  None.
Return Value:       Initialized text_buffer object.
Comments:           This function is the default constructor for the
                    text_buffer class.
*/

text_buffer::text_buffer(void)
{
   topLine=0;
   linesUsed=0;
}

// End text_buffer
//-----------------------------------------------------------------------



//-----------------------------------------------------------------------
/*
Function Name:      TopLine
Member of:          text_buffer
Input Parameters:   None.
Output Parameters:  None.
Return Value:       The top line of the buffer
Comments:
*/

int text_buffer::TopLine(void)
```

```
{
   return (topLine);
}

// End TopLine
//-----------------------------------------------------------------------------



//-----------------------------------------------------------------------------
/*
Function Name:      ScrollUp
Member of:          text_buffer
Input Parameters:   linesToScroll - Integer number of lines to scroll toward
                        the beginning of the text buffer.
Output Parameters:  None.
Return Value:       Returns the number of lines actually scrolled.
Comments:           This function moves the current top line of the buffer
                    that is displayed on the screen toward the beginning of
                    the buffer. It prevents the top line from being moved
                    before the beginning of the buffer.

                    If, for instance, the current top line is 5, and the
                    input parameter specifies that the function should
                    scroll the buffer up 20 lines, it will only scroll 5
                    lines to the beginning of the buffer. The return value
                    reports the number of lines the function actually
                    scrolls.
*/

int text_buffer::ScrollUp(int linesToScroll)
{
   int linesScrolled;

   // If the top line is less than the number of lines to scroll...
   if (topLine <= linesToScroll)
   {
      /* The first screenful of the buffer is currently displayed.
      Display the buffer from the beginning. */
      linesScrolled = topLine;
      topLine=0;
   }
   // Else scroll the screen toward the beginning of the buffer.
   else
   {
      topLine -= linesToScroll;
      linesScrolled = linesToScroll;
   }
   return (linesScrolled);
}

// End ScrollUp
//-----------------------------------------------------------------------------



//-----------------------------------------------------------------------------
/*
Function Name:      ScrollDown
```

```
Member of:           text_buffer
Input Parameters:    linesToScroll
Output Parameters:   None.
Return Value:        Returns the number of lines actually scrolled.
Comments:            This function moves the current top line of the buffer
                     that is displayed on the screen toward the end of
                     the buffer. It prevents the top line from being moved
                     after the end of the buffer.

                     Suppose, for instance, that the buffer is 100 lines of
                     text in length. If current top line is 95, and the
                     input parameter specifies that the function should
                     scroll the buffer down 20 lines, it will only scroll 5
                     lines toward the end of the buffer. The return value
                     reports the number of lines the function actually
                     scrolls.
*/

int text_buffer::ScrollDown(int linesToScroll)
{
   int linesScrolled;
   int newTopLine = topLine+linesToScroll;

   // If the last few lines of the buffer are currently displayed...
   if (newTopLine >= TEXT_BUFFER_LENGTH-linesToScroll)
   {
      // Set the top line to display the last few lines of the buffer.
      topLine = TEXT_BUFFER_LENGTH-linesToScroll;
      linesScrolled = newTopLine-topLine;
   }
   // Else the end of the buffer is not currently displayed...
   else
   {
      // Scroll down the requested number of lines.
      topLine = newTopLine;
      linesScrolled = linesToScroll;
   }
   return (linesScrolled);
}

// End ScrollDown
//---------------------------------------------------------------------------



//---------------------------------------------------------------------------
/*
Function Name:       Load
Member of:           text_buffer
Input Parameters:    fileName - Name of the file to load.
Output Parameters:   None.
Return Value:        If the file is loaded successfully, this function
                     returns NO_BUFFER_ERROR. If not, it returns
                     CANT_LOAD_FILE.
Comments:            This function loads the specified file into the
                     text buffer. Any file error will generate a
                     CANT_LOAD_FILE error. A text_buffer object for a
                     professional application would need to provide more
```

```
                    specific feedback to the function that calls this
                    routine.
*/

int text_buffer::Load(text_string fileName)
{
   char tempFileName[MAX_TEXT_STRING_LENGTH];
   int errorStatus = NO_BUFFER_ERROR;

   // If the file name string is not empty...
   if (fileName.Length() > 0)
   {
      text_string tempString;

      // Get the file name into an array of characters.
      fileName.Get(tempFileName);

      // Open the file.
      ifstream inputStream(tempFileName);

      // If the file could be opened...
      if (inputStream)
      {
         // Read in each line of text.
         int i;
         for (i=0;
              (i<TEXT_BUFFER_LENGTH) && (!inputStream.eof());
              i++)
         {
            /* If the line of text in the file is longer than
            MAX_TEXT_STRING_LENGTH, it is truncated. */
            inputStream >> tempString;
            textBuffer[i].Set(tempString);
         }
         linesUsed = i;
      }
      // Else the file could not be opened...
      else
      {
         errorStatus = CANT_LOAD_FILE;
      }
   }
   // Else the file name string was empty...
   else
   {
      errorStatus = CANT_LOAD_FILE;
   }
   return (errorStatus);
}

// End Load
//---------------------------------------------------------------------------



//---------------------------------------------------------------------------
/*
Function Name:      Save
```

```
Member of:          text_buffer
Input Parameters:   fileName - The name of the file to save.
Output Parameters:  None.
Return Value:       This function returns NO_BUFFER_ERROR if it successfully
                    saves the specified file. If there is any kind of file
                    error, it returns CANT_SAVE_FILE.
Comments:           This function saves the text buffer into the
                    specified file. Any file error will generate a
                    CANT_SAVE_FILE error. A text_buffer object for a
                    professional application would need to provide more
                    specific feedback to the function that calls this
                    routine.
*/
int text_buffer::Save(text_string fileName)
{
   char tempString[MAX_TEXT_STRING_LENGTH];
   int errorStatus=NO_BUFFER_ERROR;

   // If the file name string is not empty...
   if (fileName.Length() > 0)
   {
      // Store the file name into an array of characters.
      fileName.Get(tempString);

      // Open the file.
      ofstream outputStream(tempString);

      // If the file could be opened...
      if (outputStream)
      {
         // Write each line of the buffer to the file.
         for (int i=0;
              (i<linesUsed) && (outputStream.good());
              i++)
         {
            outputStream << textBuffer[i] << endl;
         }
      }
      // Else the file could not be opened...
      else
      {
         errorStatus = CANT_SAVE_FILE;
      }
   }
   // Else the file name string is empty...
   else
   {
      errorStatus = CANT_SAVE_FILE;
   {
   return (errorStatus);
}

// End Save
//-----------------------------------------------------------------------------



//-----------------------------------------------------------------------------
/*
```

```
Function Name:      Line
Member of:          text_buffer
Input Parameters:   lineToSet - Line number of the line in the text buffer
                        to set.
                    newText - The text that will be stored in the specified
                        line of the buffer.
Output Parameters:  None.
Return Value:       None.
Comments:           This function stores characters in the specified line.
                    Line numbering begins with zero. If the text string is
                    too long for the line of text in the buffer, the extra
                    characters are truncated.

                    If the specified line to set is before the beginning or
                    beyond the end of the buffer, this function does
                    nothing.
*/

void text_buffer::Line(int lineToSet,text_string newText)
{
   // If the line to set is in the proper range for the buffer...
   if ((lineToSet>=0) && (lineToSet<TEXT_BUFFER_LENGTH))
   {
      // Set the text of the specified line.
      textBuffer[lineToSet].Set(newText);

      /* If the specified line is beyond the end of the part of the
      buffer that is currently in use... */
      if (lineToSet>linesUsed)
      {
         /* Mark the new line as the last line of the buffer that is
         being used. */
         linesUsed=lineToSet;
      }
   }
}

// End Line
//---------------------------------------------------------------------------



//---------------------------------------------------------------------------
/*
Function Name:      Line
Member of:          text_buffer
Input Parameters:   lineToGet - The line in the buffer that this function
                        will retrieve.
Output Parameters:  None.
Return Value:       The requested line of text.
Comments:           This function gets a text string from the buffer. Line
                    numbering begins with zero. If the specified line is
                    before the beginning or after the end of the buffer,
                    this function does nothing.
*/

text_string text_buffer::Line(int lineToGet)
{
   text_string line;
```

```
    if ((lineToGet>=0) && (lineToGet<TEXT_BUFFER_LENGTH))
    {
       line = textBuffer[lineToGet];
    }

    return (line);
 }

 // End Line
 //---------------------------------------------------------------------------



 // End TBuffer.cpp
 //---------------------------------------------------------------------------
```

Results

When the program starts, the screen will resemble Figure 20.4.

Press Ctrl+L, and then press Enter. When prompted, type the file name test.txt. Your screen will resemble Figure 20.5.

FIGURE 20.4 **Initial Program Output**

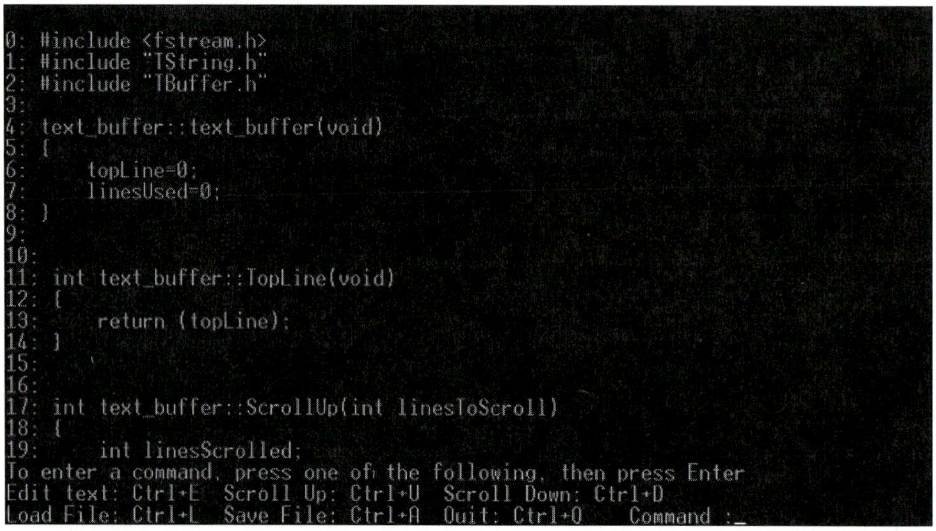

FIGURE 20.5 **Editing the File `test.txt`**

Analysis

Congratulations! You have just created a working text editor that loads and saves files. As you run this program, test each of the commands. Notice that the layout of the files follows the design ideas we covered in previous chapters. Following those design guidelines helps up produce a text editor that is easy for maintenance programmers to understand and enhance.

This text editor functions very much like some of the first text editors that programmers commonly used. However, it is more limited in its functionality than most of them were. It makes some of the same design compromises that were common back then, and it makes them for the same reasons.

There were actually commercial text editors that truncated files in the past. That's why I got into the habit of marking the end of my files with a comment. If the comment was ever missing, I knew that something in my file got thrown away by the editor.

For instance, this text editor only uses commands that are in the ASCII set of characters. This helps ensure portability across multiple hardware and operating system platforms. The text buffer that holds the text to edit is only 100 lines long. If the file you load into the editor is longer than 100 lines, it quietly truncates the rest of the file. This is not a good feature.

Also, the length of each line of text in the buffer is limited. That is something else we can improve upon.

The program begins in the file *Tedit.cpp* by including the header files that it needs. It defines the prototypes for some general-purpose functions that are not members of any class.

The `main()` function defines the constants it will need. Most of these are constants that represent the commands that the text editor will recognize.

The program next declares some variables. One of them is the actual text buffer. Notice that the variable declaration begins with the word `static`. This declaration is required on some operating systems, depending on how your compiler lays out program memory. Using the word `static` will help ensure that the program gets the memory it needs for the buffer.[3] For more information on the keyword `static`, see Chapter 23.

The program enters a loop that continues until the user enters the Quit command. Inside the loop, it clears the screen and displays a screenful of text. The loop that displays the text begins displaying at the current top line of the buffer. It continues while it has not displayed the number of lines indicated by the constant `TOTAL_TEXT_AREA_LINES`, and while it has not reached the end of the buffer. The `for` loop gets each line of text from the `text_buffer` object, and then outputs it to the `cout` stream.

This means, of course, that the program completely redraws the screen each time the user enters a command. Users generally don't care for that. However, it gives us an easy and portable way to implement the text editor.

Astute readers may wonder whether the inside of the `for` loop could be shortened to

```
cout << (top+i) << ": ";
cout << textBuffer.Line(top+i) << endl;
```

The answer is maybe. It depends on your compiler. Some compilers will not give the expected results.[4]

After the program displays a screenful of text, it calls a function to display the menu. Next, it waits for input from the user. Like many programs, the text editor uses a `switch` statement to interpret the input.

[3]The more precise explanation is that your stack may not be big enough. If you try to allocate the `text_buffer` object on the stack, which is where the memory for local variables comes from, you may wind up overwriting another area of memory. Using the keyword `static` puts the `text buffer` object into a global area (but it does not become a global variable!) that is allocated and initialized when the program loads. This avoids stack problems. We'll discuss a better way to handle the stack problem when we cover dynamic memory allocation in Chapter 22.

[4]Some compilers don't give the results you'd expect because we should be returning a reference to a `text_string` object, not a `text_string` object itself. References to objects are presented in Chapter 21.

The user can enter the Scroll Up command (Ctrl+U), the Scroll Down command (Ctrl+D), the Save command (Ctrl+A), the Load command (Ctrl+L), the Edit command (Ctrl+E), or the Quit command (Ctrl+Q). All other input causes the default case of the `switch` statement to be executed. The default case beeps the speaker so that the user knows the input was incorrect.

Notice that the case for the Edit command has opening and closing curly brackets, while the other cases do not. If you remove them, some compilers will issue a warning when you compile this program. The case for the Edit command declares and uses variables that the other cases don't. Programs that do this often contain errors. Therefore, the compiler points it out to you. By putting the entire code block for the `case` inside curly brackets, you tell the compiler that this is a unique block of code that is intended to stand separately from the other `case` statements. Therefore, it won't issue a warning when you compile this program.

The cases for the Scroll Up and Scroll Down commands simply call the appropriate `text_buffer` member functions. The Save and Load commands must prompt the user for the name of a file. Like the Scroll Up and Scroll Down commands, they then call `text_buffer` member functions to save or load the file. If, for any reason, the file could not be saved or loaded, the program beeps the speaker by sending character 7 in the ASCII set to the `cout` stream.

If the user selects the Edit command, the program displays a prompt asking for the number of the line to edit. The program gets the line number from the user as a string and converts it to a number. That way, if the user types in anything other than a number, the program can do error checking on the input.

In this case, the text editor program uses the Standard Library function `atoi()` to convert the string of ASCII characters to an integer. If the user enters data that is not an integer, the function will simply return zero. You'll add more error checking here in one of the exercises at the end of this chapter.

After the user enters the line number, the program displays a prompt indicating that the user can enter new text for that line. Although there were actually text editors that functioned this way, users find it annoying. Even if they only want to change one character on the line, they must reenter the entire line of text.

Modern text editors enable users to move the cursor to a particular line on the screen and edit that line. Remember that the arrow keys are not in the ASCII set. For portability, we are only using ASCII characters. Many text editors in the past have used characters in the ASCII set for cursor movement. We could do the same. However, cursor movement often depends on the hardware, operating system, and compiler you are using. Is there a portable way to perform hardware-dependent operations such as clearing the screen and moving the cursor?

Well, no and yes. There is no standard, portable way built into C++ to do these operations. However, we can use preprocessor directives to conditionally compile macros that perform these tasks.

The file *Tstring.h* contains the class definition of the `text_string` class. It's similar in some ways to the `cpp_string` we class created for earlier chapters. However, it is more specialized toward use in the text editor.

Notice that the `text_string` class declares a private data member that is an array of characters. This holds the character data. The `length` member keeps track of the number of characters in the string.

The implementation of the `text_string` class is in the file *Tstring.cpp*. The first overloaded constructor not only initializes the length of the string to zero, it sets all characters in the private data member `charString` to the null character. The second overloaded constructor copies the contents of a character array into the current `text_string` object.

The destructor for the `text_string` class simply sets the length to zero. This is not strictly necessary.

The `text_string` class provides three overloaded `Set()` functions. Use the first overload to set a single character in the string.

The second overloaded `Set()` function enables programs to set the entire text string at once. It copies the contents of an array of characters into the text_string object. Note that the array of characters passed in through the sourceCharArray parameter must have a null character at the end.

The final overloaded Set() function copies the contents of a text_string object into the current text_string object.

The text_string class also contains two overloaded Get() functions. One retrieves a single character from the text_string object. The other copies the characters from a text_string object into an array of characters. Note that the array of characters must be one character longer than the maximum length of a text_string object. This ensures that there is enough room for a null character, which the Get() function puts onto the end of the array.

In addition, the text_string object provides a function for getting the length of the string, and it overloads the insertion and extraction operators for the text_string class.

Note that the extraction operator is implemented in terms of the istream::getline() function. This produces nonstandard behavior for the extraction operator. It's generally not advisable. I did it here to make a point. I've seen this style of overloaded extraction operator in programs. If you look at the code, it's a very simple way to implement the behavior you want for a string class. Programmers may find this simplicity enticing when they're writing code. However, if you do this, other programmers on your project may not appreciate your taking the easy road, so to speak. Since the extraction operator now has a nonstandard behavior, it does not do what everyone expects an extraction operator to do.

An alternative to using this style is to derive a new class from the istream class. This enables you to override the istream::getline() function so that it handles the text_string object. The disadvantage of this is that it results in slightly more code. The advantages are that everyone on your team can override any of the istream functions for their objects. All of the overridden functions can be implemented in a standard, intuitive way.

In the file *TBuffer.h*, the text_buffer object is implemented in as an array of text_string objects. The buffer keeps track of the top line that is currently displayed on the screen. It also has a data member that stores the number of lines in the buffer that contain text.

The file *Tbuffer.cpp* contains the implementation of the text_buffer member functions. The constructor sets the topLine and linesUsed members to zero. It does not need to call the constructor for the array of text_string objects. When it compiles your source code, the compiler automatically inserts calls to the text_string constructor for each text_string object in the textBuffer array. Remember that the text_string constructor initializes each character in the text_string object to the null character and sets its length to zero. Because each text_string object takes care of initializing itself, the text_buffer constructor doesn't need to deal with that.

The text_buffer class provides a function for retrieving the index number of the first line of text that is currently displayed on the screen. It also contains functions for scrolling the buffer up and down. Both the ScrollUp() and ScrollDown() functions scroll by adjusting the top line of the buffer.

The Load() function reads a text file from a disk into the text_buffer object. After declaring the variables it needs, it tests to ensure that the file name in the input parameter is not empty. If it is not, the function attempts to open the file. If the file name is empty, or if the Load() function can't find the file, Load() sets the variable errorStatus to CANT_LOAD_FILE. In a professional application, it would be advisable to have more error codes. That way, you could be much more specific about why the file can't be loaded. Programmers using your objects always appreciate it when you give them detailed information.

If the Load() function is able to open the input stream, it enters a for loop and reads in each line of text. The for loop reads a string into a temporary text_string object, then copies that into an element in the array of the text_string object.

After the for loop finishes, the Load() function stores the value of the variable i into the data member linesUsed. This indicates the last line in the buffer that contains text.

The `Save()` function operates in a manner that is similar to the `Load()` function. They are nearly identical. The primary difference is the direction that the data flows.

In addition, the `text_buffer` object provides two overloaded `Line()` functions. The first copies the contents of a `text_string` object into one line of the buffer. The second gets the contents of the specified line of the buffer.

Troubleshooting Guide

After reading this section, you should be able to:

- Detect and handle errors that occur during file I/O.
- Use file I/O as a debugging tool.

Error Handling in File I/O

We saw earlier in this chapter that we can test the stream variable itself for errors. The `ios` class keeps error status information for stream objects. It provides the functions `good()`, `clear()`, `bad()`, and `fail()` for detecting errors. The `ios::good()` function returns `true` if the stream operations have not caused an error. The `ios::clear()` function clears the indicators for any errors that have occurred. If the stream classes encounter an error that is not bad enough to cause stream I/O to stop, the `ios::fail()` function will return `true`. If the error is so bad that stream I/O can't continue, `ios::bad()` returns `true`.

Hands On 20.9 illustrates the use of these functions.

Hands On 20.9

Objective

Write a program that opens a text file and reads data from it.

Experiment

Type the following program into your IDE or text editor. Compile, link, and run it. On the CD that comes with this book, you'll find a directory called *Examples*. In the Examples directory is a subdirectory called *Chapt20*. The directory Chapt20 contains a file called *testfile.txt*. Copy that file into the same directory that contains this program.

```
#include <fstream.h>
#include <iostream.h>
#include <string.h>


int main()
{
    // Declare and open a stream.
    ifstream inputStream;
    inputStream.open("testfile.txt");

    const int INPUT_STRING_LENGTH = 80;
    char inputString[INPUT_STRING_LENGTH];

    while ((!inputStream.eof()) && (inputStream.good()))
    {
```

```
      inputStream.getline(inputString,INPUT_STRING_LENGTH);
      if ((inputStream.fail()) && (!inputStream.eof()))
      {
         inputStream.clear();
      }
      else if (!inputStream.bad())
      {
         if (strlen(inputString)>0)
         {
            cout << inputString;
         }
         else
         {
            cout << endl;
         }
      }
      cout << endl;
   }

   return (0);
}
```

Results

```
As several of its eyes meandered in other directions,
it gazed at me with its primary eye and asked, "Are
you hungry?"


"Well, yes," I replied. "A bit peckish I suppose."


"Perhaps you would like to have a piece of my leg," it
offered. A tentacle gestured toward one of its many legs.


"Wha?" I answered politely. I continued, "Huh?"


It shifted its features into what I later learned was
its equivalent of a hopeful smile. "It's quite tender. I
have been soaking it in the finest mud. I see you don't
have the fangs required to help yourself. Would you like
me to cut some off for you?" So saying, it grabbed a
machete-sized knife off the wall and whacked off its leg.


"Don't feel you're being rude if you're not able to eat
it all," it said casually. "I can see that you're quite
small. I can always give some to my Foremothers. I need
to make a Respect Offering anyway."


This was just more than I could take.


"Look," I said. "I was just mowing my lawn. The next thing
I know, I'm heaven knows where, I'm almost eaten by what
```

looks like a minivan with an oversized mouth and flippers, and now you're offering me pieces of yourself." I sat, flopping down onto the dirt floor like a wet sack of potatoes.

It hesitated, withdrawing the leg a bit. "I apologize for saying so, but your speech is strange. I do not know what this Laahn is that you speak of. However, I can see that it has deep spiritual significance for you. Perhaps your Laahn will allow you to do mooweeng here while you are with us. Our ancestors often give us permission to do our oblations to them while we travel to other lands. Tomorrow, I can take you to our village Thinkers. I'm sure they too will be moved by your predicament. Somehow, we will help you do your mooweeng. In the meantime, you must eat. As your host, it is only polite that I feed you the best I have." It extended the severed leg again.

The bleeding had already stopped. It didn't seem to be in any pain. I would soon learn the amazing speed at which these creatures grew limbs.

"I, uh. I usually eat meat cooked," I told it.

Instantly it grabbed what looked like a large wok off the wall and tossed the leg in. "Many of our people prefer cooked foods these days as well. Although it is not humble of me to say so, I have been told that I am an excellent cook. Please relax, your meal will be ready shortly."

It was. And the creature was right. It was an excellent cook.

Analysis

Unlike the program in Hands On 20.4, this version of the program does error checking. After it attempts to open the file, it checks the stream to see if it was successful.

The primary loop in this version of the example program iterates until it encounters the end of the file, or until the `ios::good()` function returns `false`. This indicates that an error of some kind has happened.

The program also checks to see if each read from the file is successful. The `ios::fail()` function returns true when a nonfatal error occurs. Specifically, it returns `true` if any attempt to read or write data fails. One of the causes of a nonfatal read failure is when the program reaches the end of the file. The statements

```
if ((inputStream.fail()) && (!inputStream.eof()))
{
   inputStream.clear();
}
```

cause the program to clear the stream error status if any nonfatal error occurs. The exception is when the program reaches the end of the file. If we were to read these statements in English, they would be, "If a nonfatal error occurs, but the end of the file has not yet been encountered, clear the error status information."

If no nonfatal errors occur, the program tests for fatal errors. If there are no fatal errors, the program outputs the string it read from the file. If a fatal error does occur, the program does not output the string. The loop iterates and the program tests the loop condition. The fatal error makes the loop stop.

Using Error Log Files to Debug Programs

Many programmers find log files to be a handy debugging aid. A log file is a file that a program writes status information to as it executes. Log files supplement the use of debugging programs. They can also be used in situations where debugging programs are not available or not desirable.

For instance, many game programmers use log files to debug their games. Typically, games take over the entire screen. If you use a debugging program while developing games, the debugging program will pop up its window to show status information while the game is executing. This can interfere with the color palette or obscure a critical part of the screen image. Writing program status information to a log file provides a way to get debugging information without disturbing the images on the screen.

A Simple Debugging System

Hands On 20.10 demonstrates one simple approach to a debugging system that uses log files.

Hands On 20.10

Objective

Write a debugging system that logs errors to files. Write a program to demonstrate the log file routines.

Experiment

Type the following program into your IDE or text editor. Compile, link, and run it. This program consists of two files: *main.cpp* and *debugger.h*.

This is the file `main.cpp`.

```
#define DEBUGGING
#define EXTERN
#include "Debugger.h"

int main()
{
   OpenLogFile("log.txt");

   WriteToLogFile("Entering for loop");
   WriteToLogFile(endl);

   for (int i=0;i<100;i++)
   {
      WriteToLogFile("i=");
      WriteToLogFile(i);
      WriteToLogFile(endl);
   }
```

```
   CloseLogFile();

   return (0);
}
```

This is the file `debugger.h`

```
#ifndef DEBUGGER_H
#define DEBUGGER_H

#ifdef DEBUGGING
#include <fstream.h>
#include <stdlib.h>

#if !defined(EXTERN)
#define EXTERN extern
#else
#define EXTERN
#endif

EXTERN ofstream logFile;


#define OpenLogFile(logFileName)                          \
        {                                                 \
            logFile.open(logFileName);                    \
            if (!logFile)                                 \
            {                                             \
               abort();                                   \
            }                                             \
        }

#define WriteToLogFile(data)    logFile << data

#define CloseLogFile()  logFile.close()

#else

#define OpenLogFile(logFileName)
#define WriteToLogFile(data)
#define CloseLogFile()

#endif  // end #ifdef DEBUGGING

#endif  // end #ifndef DEBUGGER_H
```

Results

Note: The output of this program has been shortened to save space. All of the values between 10 and 90 have been omitted.

```
Entering for loop
i=0
i=1
i=2
i=3
i=4
i=5
```

```
i=6
i=7
i=8
i=9
i=10
.
.
.
i=90
i=91
i=92
i=93
i=94
i=95
i=96
i=97
i=98
i=99
```

Analysis

You'll undoubtedly notice some odd-looking `#define` statements at the beginning of this program. I'll explain what those are for shortly.

The program that demonstrates the log file system uses three macros. The first, `OpenLogFile()`, does just what the name suggests. The log file must be open before program status information can be written to it. You can use this debugging system in a program made up of many CPP files. The only requirement is that they include the file *Debugger.h*. The `OpenLogFile()` macro needs to be called only once at the beginning of the program. After that, the log file debugging system is available to all functions and all files in your program.

Programs use the second debugging macro, `WriteToLogFile()`, for writing information to the error log file. Notice that the program uses the `WriteToLogFile()` macro to write a string, some integers, and some endline characters to the file. This macro can output any streamable data type to the log file. Simply put, a streamable data type is one that can be written to a stream with the insertion operator.

When the program finishes with the error logging system, it uses the `CloseLogFile()` macro to close the log file.

You'll find the implementation of the log file debugging system in the file *Debugging.h*. It begins with the standard method of using `#ifndef` (or `#if !defined()`) to keep this header file from defining its contents more than once in any single CPP file. It also contains a statement that reads

```
#ifdef DEBUGGING
```

This statement forms one of the key aspects of the log file debugging system. If the constant `DEBUGGING` is defined, this file defines all of the debugging macros. If it is not defined, the `#else` clause is processed by the preprocessor. It looks like this:

```
#else

#define OpenLogFile(logFileName)
#define WriteToLogFile(data)
#define CloseLogFile()

#endif  // end #ifdef DEBUGGING
```

The `#else` clause defines all of the debugging macros as nothing. Because these macros are defined as being nothing but a blank line, the preprocessor removes the macros from the source code when it does a pass over a CPP file. When the constant DEBUGGING is not defined in a CPP file, the preprocessor substitutes blank lines where the debugging macros appear in the CPP file. This effectively turns off the debugging system. When you want to use it again, simply define DEBUGGING in your CPP file before the #include "Debugging.h" statement.

That's exactly what the sample program does. Right at the beginning of the file *Main.cpp,* the program contains the statement

```
#define DEBUGGING
```

just before the statement

```
#include "Debugging.h"
```

This effectively turns on the debugging system.

If the constant DEBUGGING is defined, the debugging system includes some needed files from the Standard Library. It then contains a set of statements that reads

```
#if !defined(EXTERN)
#define EXTERN extern
#else
#define EXTERN
#endif
```

These statements perform an old programmer's trick for handling global variables. The statement that follows these actually declares a global stream variable for the debugging system. This is one of the few situations in which a global variable is useful in a program. That is primarily because it is removed automatically from the final version of the program. Under most circumstances, global variables cause far more problems than they solve.

This set of statements tells the preprocessor that if the constant EXTERN is not defined, define EXTERN as the C++ keyword extern. When you use a global variable, only one file in your program can actually declare the variable. The other files use the extern keyword to tell the compiler that they are referencing a global variable declared in another file. The preceding set of statements automatically use the extern keyword to indicate that the global variable is declared in another CPP file.

One of the CPP files in the program must have the constant EXTERN declared in it. You'll see that declaration at the beginning of the file *Main.cpp* in the sample program. If EXTERN is declared, the program redefines EXTERN as blank. This effectively declares the global variable in the CPP file.

If all of this seems somewhat complicated, that's only because it is. This is one of the many reasons that global variables should generally not find their way into released versions of a program.

The OpenLogFile() macro uses the global stream variable to open the log file. If it can't open the log file, the program calls the Standard Library abort() function to halt execution.

The macro WriteToLogFile() uses the insertion operator to insert into the log file stream whatever data the programmer passes into the macro. For this reason, the data must be streamable.

Finally, the CloseLogFile() macro calls the close() function for the global log file stream variable.

Summary

C++ programs use streams to write data to and read data from devices. These devices include the keyboard, the screen, disks, and tapes. The C++ Standard Library provides the streams cin, cout, cerr, clog, wcin, wcout, wcerr, and wclog.

Streams can be buffered or unbuffered. Unbuffered streams make data immediately available to the device or program. Buffered streams do not make the data available until the buffer is flushed.

Streams can be for input, output, or both. The C++ stream classes provide a `flags()` function for formatting data. Programs control data formatting with the `ios` formatting flags.

For long-term storage, data is stored in files. These typically reside on disks, but they can exist on any valid data storage device. Files contain either text or binary data.

All files must be opened before programs can read from them or write to them. Programs can retrieve data from files using the extraction operator, the `getline()` function, or the `read()` function. Write data to files using the insertion operator, the `put()` function, or the `write()` function.

The C++ streams use current location pointers to keep track of where the next read or write will occur in a file. Your program can control the position of the get pointer with the `seekg()` function. It can find the location of the get pointer in a file with the `tellg()` function. Also, it can control where the put pointer is by calling the `seekp()` function. It can get the location of the put pointer using the `tellp()` function.

After a C++ stream is open, the stream variable itself can be used to report errors. If it evaluates to a nonzero value, the stream variable has no errors. As soon as it evaluates to zero, an error has occurred. This can include reaching the end of the file.

In addition, the C++ stream classes provide the `good()`, `bad()`, `clear()`, and `fail()` functions to detect and clear the error status.

Review Questions

1. What do the streams `cin`, `cout`, `cerr`, `clog`, `wcin`, `wcout`, `wcerr`, and `wclog` do?
2. What is buffered I/O? What is unbuffered I/O? What is line buffered input? How can a program manually flush a stream buffer?
3. What do the `ios` formatting flags do?
4. How do you open a stream to read from a text file? How do you open a stream to read from a binary file?
5. What is the difference between reading text from a file using the extraction operator and reading it using the `getline()` function?
6. What do the openmode constants do?
7. How do you control the get and put pointers?
8. How do you use the `read()` function to read data from a binary file?
9. What is the difference between writing data to files with the insertion operator, the `put()` function, and the `write()` function?
10. How can your program detect read or errors?

Exercises

1. Write a program that gets input from the keyboard, writes it to a text file, and prints it on the screen. If the output file already exists, the program should overwrite any text that it contains.
2. Write a program that gets input from the keyboard, writes it to a text file, and prints it on the screen. If the file exists, do not overwrite the existing data. Append the new text to it.
3. Use the programs in Hands On 20.5 and Hands On 20.7 to write a program that reads and writes customer records. The program should first present the user with a menu that displays three options: read a customer record, write a customer record, and list customer numbers. If the user chooses to read a customer record, your program should prompt for a customer number. When the user enters the customer ID number, your program should display the customer's record. When the user selects to write a customer record from the main menu, your program should prompt the user for the customer data. The program should then write the data to a binary file. If the user inputs a customer number that matches an existing customer record, your program should overwrite the existing record. *Hint:* Use the `seekp()` function. If the user chooses to list the customer numbers from the main menu, your program should list all customer numbers.

4. Modify the program from Exercise 3. Add fields to the customer class that contain the customer's street address, city, state, and ZIP code. Add the appropriate functions to get and set this information. Make sure your program displays this information when the user chooses to read a record from the main menu. Ensure that the user can enter this information when he/she chooses to write a record from the main menu.
5. The program in Hands On 20.8 contains a `switch` statement in the `main()` function that is used to determine which command a user entered. The section of the `switch` statement labeled `case EDIT_COMMAND:` contains the statement

```
if ((lineNumber >= top) &&
    (lineNumber < top+TOTAL_TEXT_AREA_LINES))
```

   Explain what would happen in this `if` statement if the user entered a number less than zero (such as –5) as the line number to edit. Write a new version of the text editor that fixes this problem.
6. Once again, examine the `if` statement from Exercise 5. Explain what would happen if the user input a line number greater than `TEXT_BUFFER_LENGTH`. Write a version of the text editor that fixes this problem.
7. The program in Hands On 20.8 contains a group of overloaded functions called `text_string::Set()` in the file *Tstring.cpp*. The first overloaded version of this function requires the index number of the character in the string to set. Explain what happens if this number is less than zero. Write a version of the text editor that fixes this problem.
8. The program in Hands On 20.8 contains a function called `text_buffer::ScrollUp()` in the file *TBuffer.cpp*. Explain what would happen if the parameter `linesToScroll` is less than zero. Write a version of the text editor that fixes this problem.
9. The program in Hands On 20.8 contains a function called `text_buffer::Load()` in the file *Tbuffer.cpp*. Locate the `for` loop in the function. Notice that it does not check to see whether errors occurred while it was reading data from the file. Note also that the `text_buffer::Save()` function also does not check for errors when it writes data to the text file. Write a version of the text editor that uses the `ios` error checking functions to fix this problem.
10. Modify the text editor program from Hands On 20.8 so that it scrolls up one line of text when the user inputs the command Ctrl+H. Also, modify it so that it scrolls one line down when the user enters the command Ctrl+T. These are intended to indicate movement toward the head and tail of the file. Explain why using control keys for commands might be nonintuitive to the user.

Chapter Glossary

Current Location Pointer A pointer in a file that indicates where the next read or write will take place.

Field One piece of information in a database record.

Get Pointer The current location pointer that keeps track of where the next read will take place.

Put Pointer The current location pointer that tracks where the next write operation will take place.

Random Access The ability to read or write any piece of data at any time without searching sequentially through the file.

Record A collection of information that describes one object in a database. For instance, a customer record contains information that describes one customer.

21 Pointers and References

Objectives

After reading this chapter, you should be able to:

- Explain what a pointer is and what it is for.
- Declare pointers and use them to point at data.
- Dereference pointers with pointer or array notation.
- Create dynamically allocated arrays.
- Explain and use references.
- Use `const` with pointers and references.

Preview

C++ is a flexible and efficient programming language. Much of its flexibility comes from its use of pointers and references. However, because these two features are such powerful and flexible tools, they are also a constant source of programmer errors. This is particularly true of pointers. If you look in any software development magazine that is oriented toward C++ programmers, you'll see many advertisements for products that detect memory leaks. The primary source of memory leaks is the improper use of pointers.

This chapter presents essential techniques for using pointers. It also contains warnings about ways to help prevent pointer errors. Nearly anything you can do to reduce the likelihood of pointer errors is worth doing. Pointer problems are sometimes notoriously difficult to find and often excruciatingly difficult to fix. Nevertheless, pointers and references are such powerful tools that they are two of the key features of the C++ language.

What Is a Pointer?

A pointer is a variable that does not contain data. It contains the address of data. Remember that every location in a computer's memory has an address. Normally, we give names to memory locations by declaring variables. That way, we don't need to know or deal with absolute addresses in memory. Pointers enable us to use and manipulate memory addresses in a generic way. We can use addresses to locate data without knowing the address itself.

Computer hardware relies heavily on the use of addresses. Because pointers enable us to utilize addresses in our programs, we have the ability to communicate with the computer in a manner that is close to the way it "thinks." It is often said that pointers take us "closer to the hardware." This feature of pointers makes our programs both more efficient and more powerful.

Declaring and Initializing Pointers

We declare pointer variables in programs in nearly the same way we declare any other variable. Example 21.1 shows how this is done.

EXAMPLE 21.1 Declaring Pointer Variables

```
int *anIntegerPointer;
char *aCharacterPointer;
unsigned long *anotherPointer;
double *aPointerToDouble;
customer_record *customerPointer;
void *aPointerToAnything;
```

You cannot dereference void pointers without type casting them.

Whenever we declare pointer variables, we must declare the type of the data to which the pointer points. The only exception to this is when we declare a pointer to the type `void`. Pointers to `void` can point at any type of data. That gives us a way to create and use a generic pointer. However, there are special restrictions on `void` pointers that make them somewhat more complex to use. In general, it's safer to avoid `void` pointers.

The first declaration in Example 20.1 declares a pointer to integers. The pointer may point at one single integer, or a group of them. In fact, we'll see in this chapter that array names are really just pointers.

Most of the other declarations in Example 20.1 declare pointers to atomic data types. However, the declaration

```
customer_record *customerPointer;
```

declares a pointer to a `customer_record` object, not one of the built-in types. Pointers can point at any type of data, whether that data type is built into the compiler or created by you.

Whenever you declare a pointer, it is wise to initialize it immediately. Never let a pointer contain an unknown value. Because pointers are so powerful, accidentally using an uninitialized pointer can be a disastrous error. What makes it so bad is that it can actually work for quite a while, then suddenly not work. Or it can work sometimes but not others. This type of error is very difficult to track down. Modern debugging tools can help, but it's a whole lot easier to just get into the habit of initializing every pointer.

Pointer variables should be initialized to the value NULL, as shown in Example 21.2.

EXAMPLE 21.2 Initializing Pointer Variables

TIP: Always initialize all pointers.

```
int *anIntegerPointer = NULL;
char *aCharacterPointer = NULL;
unsigned long *anotherPointer = NULL;
double *aPointerToDouble = NULL;
customer_record *customerPointer = NULL;
void *aPointerToAnything = NULL;
```

Pointing Pointers at Data

The purpose of pointer variables is to contain the address of data. You can get the address of data using the ampersand operator (&). Example 21.3 demonstrates the use of the ampersand operator.

EXAMPLE 21.3 Pointers to Atomic Data

```
int anInteger;
int *anIntegerPointer = &anInteger;
char aCharacter = 'C';
char *aCharacterPointer = &aCharacter;
unsigned long anUnsignedLongValue = 10000;
unsigned long *anotherPointer = &anUnsignedLongValue;
double aDouble = 0;
```

```
double *aPointerToDouble = &aDouble;
customer_record aCustomer;
customer_record *customerPointer = &aCustomer;
```

By the way, when we read a statement such as `&aCharacter` aloud, we read it as, "The address of the character variable `aCharacter`" or just "The address of `aCharacter`".

Example 21.3 shows that getting the address of any piece of data is essentially the same, no matter what the data type is. For instance, the example declares an integer variable and an integer pointer. The integer pointer does not contain integers. It contains the address of integer data. Using the & operator, Example 21.3 gets the address of the integer variable. That is, it gets the address in memory of where the variable stores its data. The example then assigns the address into the pointer variable.

The other data types work exactly the same way. Each of them is set to point at a location in memory that can store data. The location may or may not contain data when the pointer value is assigned. An example is the statement

```
char aCharacter = 'C';
char *aCharacterPointer = &aCharacter;
```

The first statement declares a character variable and stores the letter 'C' in it. The second declares a variable that is a pointer to a character. The pointer variable contains an address; the character variable contains a character. These are two different types of data that are typically two different sizes. The size of the pointer is not determined by the type of the data at which it points. Figure 21.1 illustrates the relationship between the character and character pointer variables.

Characters are often 8 or 16 bits. Pointers are usually 16 or 32 bits, but they may be 64 or even 128 bits.

FIGURE 21.1 A Character and a Character Pointer

This figure shows that the character variable contains the character 'C'. The character pointer variable contains the address of where in memory the character variable is located. Rather than show the actual address in binary or hexadecimal, I've followed the convention of most C and C++ literature and depicted the pointer with an arrow. However, let me emphasize that nothing magic, mysterious, or even symbolic is stored in pointer variables. They contain a memory address in binary.

Note here that initializing the pointer does not initialize the data. Initializing the data does not initialize the pointer. These are two separate operations. The character variable can be set to any character. That does not change the contents of the character pointer variable. The pointer variable can be set to point at any other character anywhere else in memory. That does not change the contents of the character variable.

Dereferencing Pointers

One of the purposes of setting pointers to point at data is to look at and manipulate data. When we examine the contents of the memory location to which a pointer points, we are **dereferencing** the pointer.

Look again at Figure 21.1. When we dereference the pointer `aCharacterPointer`, we are examining the contents of the memory location to which it points. In this case, it points at a memory location that contains the letter 'C'. Example 21.4 shows how to dereference a pointer.

EXAMPLE 21.4 Dereferencing Pointers

```
int anInteger = 5;
int *anIntegerPointer = &anInteger;
```

```
cout << *anIntegerPointer;
*anIntegerPointer = 20;
cout << *anIntegerPointer;
cout << anInteger;
anInteger = 30;
cout << *anIntegerPointer;
cout << anInteger;
anIntegerPointer = 20;        // This is probably an error!
```

This example declares an integer and initializes it to 5. It then declares an integer pointer and stores the address of the integer variable in it. The statement

```
cout << *anIntegerPointer;
```

sends the contents of the memory location that `anIntegerPointer` points to out to the standard stream `cout`. The variable `anIntegerPointer` contains the address of the variable `anInteger`. The contents of `anInteger` is 5. Therefore, the 5 gets printed to the screen.

What makes this somewhat confusing is that C and C++ programmers read statements such as `*anIntegerPointer` as "The contents of `anIntegerPointer`." However, that's not really what the dereference operation gets. The contents of the variable `anIntegerPointer` is an address. In this case, it's the address of the variable `anInteger`. The statement `*anIntegerPointer` really gets the contents of what `anIntegerPointer` points at, not the contents of the variable `anIntegerPointer`.

In Example 21.4, the statement

```
*anIntegerPointer = 20;
```

stores the value 20 in the memory location to which `anIntegerPointer` points. Since `anIntegerPointer` points at the variable `anInteger`, it also changes the contents of `anInteger`. Therefore, the statements

```
cout << *anIntegerPointer;
cout << anInteger;
```

both do exactly the same thing. They print the value 20 to the screen.

Because `anIntegerPointer` points at the variable `anInteger`, changing the value in `anInteger` changes the value `anIntegerPointer` points to. It doesn't change where `anIntegerPointer` points. Only the data `anIntegerPointer` points at is changed. Therefore, making the assignment

```
anInteger = 30
```

causes the value 30 to be printed out when the statements

```
cout << *anIntegerPointer;
cout << anInteger;
```

are executed.

Some operating systems present programs with a virtual address space, which they then map to physical addresses. This enables the operating system to convince programs that they have much more memory than is physically installed. The extra memory is supplied by swapping portions of programs and data out to the disk. The upshot of this is that assigning an absolute address on an OS like this may not cause the program to crash. However, it is probably not correct because it doesn't enable you to set a pointer to an actual hardware address.

Assigning a value to `*anIntegerPointer` is not the same as assigning a value to `anIntegerPointer`. The difference is illustrated in Figure 21.2. The statement

```
*anIntegerPointer = 20;
```

in Example 21.4 assigns the value 20 to the memory location where `anIntegerPointer` points. The statement

```
anIntegerPointer = 20;        // This is probably an error!
```

at the end of Example 21.4 assigns the value 20 into `anIntegerPointer`. That means that the variable `anIntegerPointer` now points to memory location 20 in your computer. If you're using MS DOS, you've just pointed the pointer to a section of memory called the *Interrupt Vector Table*. If you then assign a value into `*anIntegerPointer`, you'll probably discover that your computer will stop working rather quickly. If you're using another operating system, this may or may not work.

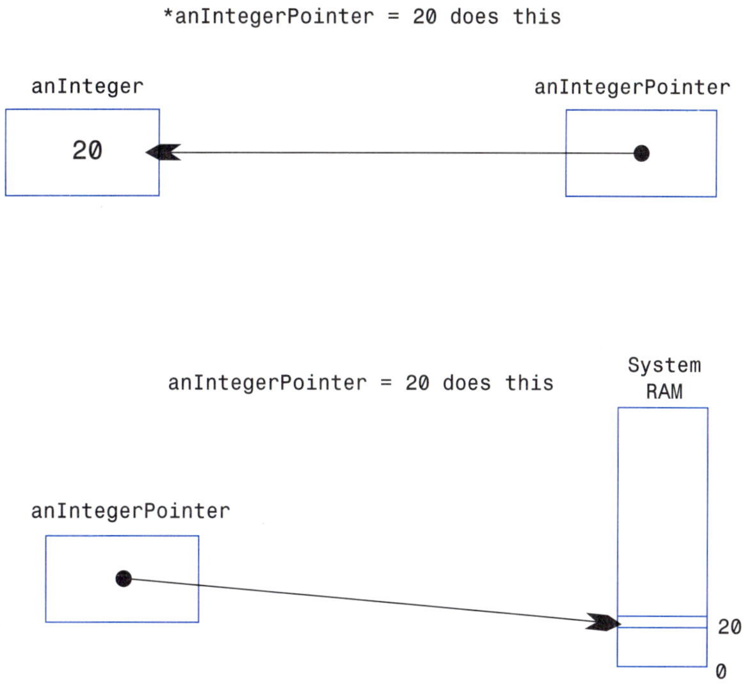

FIGURE 21.2 Assigning a Value to a Dereferenced and Undereferenced Pointer

TRAP: It is usually a mistake to assign an absolute numeric value to a pointer variable.

Usually, you don't want to try to point a pointer at an absolute address in memory. Most of the time, assigning a numeric value to a pointer (instead of the contents of the location where it points) is a mistake.

Pointers to Objects

We've already seen that pointers can be used to point at virtually any type of data, including objects. However, when we access an object, we're (hopefully) not accessing the object's data directly. We generally want to call member functions.

We access the data that a pointer points at with the dereference operator (`*`). If we have a pointer called `anObjectPointer` that points at an object, the statement

```
*anObjectPointer
```

evaluates to an object. Recall that if we have an object, we can call its member functions with a notation like this:

```
anObject.MemberFunction();
```

Therefore, to access an object through a pointer, we just need to combine the two notations. Accessing an object's member functions through a pointer uses the notation

```
*anObjectPointer.MemberFunction();
```

However, there is a shorthand version of this. We can accomplish exactly the same thing with the notation

```
anObjectPointer->MemberFunction();
```

Almost all C++ programmers use this arrow notation.

Pointers and Arrays

Pointers can point at a single piece of data or at a collection of data. If a pointer variable points at a collection of data, the data must all be of the same type. In other words, a pointer can be used as an array.

In C++, array names are pointers in disguise. Every array name contains the address of the first byte of the first element in the array. When you leave the subscript operator (the square brackets) off of an array, the array name evaluates to a pointer.

There are two primary differences between an array and a pointer that points at a block of data:

1. The array points at a fixed location in memory. The pointer can point to any memory location.
2. The amount of memory allocated for the array is fixed, or static. It is determined when you write the program and it does not change as the program runs. Pointers can point to memory blocks of varying sizes.

Another way to say this is that the array memory is statically allocated.

Example 21.5 demonstrates some basics of pointers and arrays.

EXAMPLE 21.5 Pointing to an Array

```
int *anIntPointer = NULL;
int anIntArray[100],anotherIntArray[50];
anIntPointer = anIntArray;
anIntPointer = anotherIntArray;
```

This example code fragment declares an integer pointer called `anIntPointer`. It also declares two arrays of integers: `anIntArray` and `anotherIntArray`. Next, it points the pointer at each array, one after the other. There are some important things to notice in these few simple statements.

First, when we point a pointer at an array, we do not need to use the ampersand operator (&) to get the address of the data. Array names are really pointers. They contain the address of the beginning of the array. Therefore, when you leave the array subscript off the array name, the ampersand operator is not needed. Since an array name points to the first byte of the first element in the array, an equivalent way to find this address is to use a statement like this:

```
anIntPointer = &anIntArray[0];
```

Here we take the address of the first element in the array and store it in the pointer. Early C compilers used to require this style. However, some no longer support it.

Another important thing to note in this example is that the pointer can point at any array of integers. It can also point at a single integer. Array names can't do that. In fact, the statement

```
anIntArray = anotherIntArray;
```

will not work. The compiler will flag this as an error. Array names can only point to the memory that is allocated when they are declared.

Dereferencing Notation

Recall that when we get the data a pointer points at, we are dereferencing the pointer. The asterisk operator (*) is used to dereference pointers. A logical question to ask is, "If an array is really a pointer, can array notation be used with pointers?" The answer is yes. Hands On 21.1 demonstrates pointer dereferencing with pointer notation and array notation.

Hands On 21.1

Objective

Write a program that demonstrates dereferencing with pointer and array notation.

Experiment

Type the following program into your IDE or text editor. Compile, link, and run it.

```
#include <iostream.h>

int main()
```

```
{
    const int ARRAY_SIZE = 100;
    int anArray[100];
    int *anIntPointer = NULL;
    int i;

    anIntPointer = anArray;

    // Array notation with the pointer name.
    for (i=0;i<100;i++)
    {
        anIntPointer[i] = i;
    }

    // Pointer notation with the array name.
    for (i=0;i<100;i++)
    {
        cout << *(anArray+i) << endl;
    }

    return (0);
}
```

Results

The output of this program has been shortened to save space.

```
0
1
2
3
4
5
6
7
8
9
10
.
.
.
90
91
92
93
94
95
96
97
98
99
```

Analysis

This sample program begins by declaring an array of integers and a pointer to integers. It then points `anIntPointer` at the array.

Using a `for` loop, the program loads integer values into the array. However, it does not use the array name. Rather, it uses the pointer name to store data. In addition, the loop treats the pointer name exactly as if it is an array name. That's because it *is* an array name for as long as it points at the array.

When our programs dereference pointers to blocks of data (which is what an array is), they must resolve the address of each data item in the block. For instance, let's say that the program in Hands On 21.1 executes the statement

```
anIntPointer[i] = i;
```

where `i` equals 3. To store the value of 3 in `anIntPointer[3]`, the C++ compiler must generate executable code that gets the address in the variable `anIntPointer` and adds `(3 * sizeof(int))` to it. This is permissible under the rules of C++. If you add an integer to an address, you get another address. You can also subtract an integer from an address, but you can't multiply or divide addresses. Those operations make no sense for pointers.

It's the fourth integer because array numbering always starts with zero.

Remember that the pointer is pointing at integer data. If we are setting the value of `anIntPointer[3]`, we are setting the value of the fourth integer in the array. If the executable program just added 3 to the address in `anIntPointer`, it would be accessing the memory location starting 3 bytes after the beginning of the array. If integers are 4 bytes long, as they are on many computers today, the program will definitely *not* be accessing the fourth element in the array. Therefore, the program must multiply the array element number by the total number of bytes in each array element. In this example, the statement

```
anIntPointer[i] = i;
```

is the same as

```
*(anIntPointer + (i*sizeof(int))) = i;
```

TIP: You can always find an array element using the formula

```
ArrayElementAddress =
    ArrayBaseAddress + Offset
```

Find the offset using the formula

```
Offset = ElementIndexNumber
    * sizeof (element_type)
```

This statement first multiplies `i` times the `sizeof(int)`. That finds the number of bytes from the beginning of the array where array element `i` is stored. We call this an **offset.** It then takes the address in `anIntPointer` and adds the offset to the address. The address in the pointer is called the **base address** of the array.

Any element in an array can be found by adding an offset to the base address. The offset can always be found by multiplying the array element number times the `sizeof()` an array element. Figure 21.3 illustrates how this works.

FIGURE 21.3 Array Indexing with a Base Address and Offset

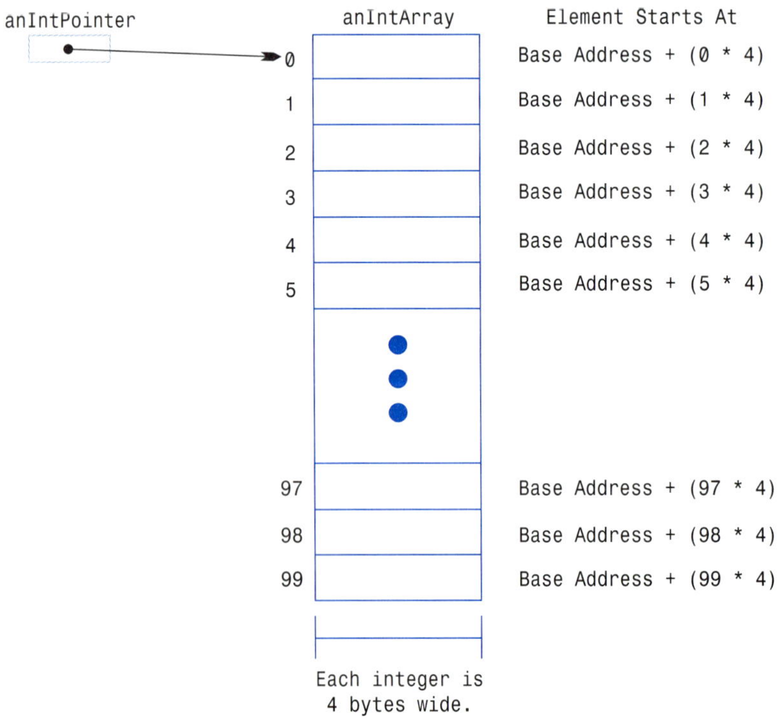

Note: This figure assumes a 4-byte integer. Integers on your computer may not be that size.

When compilers see array notation in programs, they convert it to pointer notation internally. The final binary executable contains pointers and offsets. Essentially, the compiler invisibly converts all array notation to pointer notation in the executable code.

The second loop doesn't need the `sizeof()` operator because the compiler "knows" that `anIntPointer` points to integers.

The second loop in Hands On 21.1 demonstrates that not only can we use array notation with pointers, we can use pointer notation with arrays. This is not something programmers generally do. For the most part, developers find array notation easier to deal with than pointer notation. Therefore, many programmers use it rather than pointer notation when they can.

Strings

We saw in previous chapters that C++ uses arrays of characters as strings. The fact that pointers and arrays are essentially the same thing implies that a pointer to characters is equivalent to a string. This also means that an array of character pointers can be used as an array of strings. Hands On 21.2 shows one way we can use this equivalence to our advantage.

Hands On 21.2

Objective

Write a program that sorts an array of strings using an array of pointers to characters.

Experiment

Type the following program into your IDE or text editor. Compile, link, and run it.

```
#include <string.h>
#include <iostream.h>


int main()
{
   const int ARRAY_SIZE = 30;
   const int CHARS_PER_STRING = 40;
   static char a2DCharArray[ARRAY_SIZE][CHARS_PER_STRING];
   char far *charPointerArray[ARRAY_SIZE];
   int i,j;
   char tempChar;

   for (i=0,tempChar = 'A';i<ARRAY_SIZE;i++)
   {
      for (j=0;j<CHARS_PER_STRING-1;j++)
      {
         if (tempChar > 'z')
         {
            tempChar = 'A';
         }

         a2DCharArray[i][j] = tempChar++;
      }
      a2DCharArray[i][CHARS_PER_STRING-1] = '\0';
   }

   for (i=0;i<ARRAY_SIZE;i++)
   {
      charPointerArray[i] = a2DCharArray[i];
   }

   cout << endl << "The unsorted array..." << endl;
   for (i=0;i<ARRAY_SIZE;i++)
```

```
   {
      cout << charPointerArray[i] << endl;
   }

   char *tempPointer = NULL;
   for (i=1;i<ARRAY_SIZE;i++)
   {
      for (j=0;j<i;j++)
      {
         if (strcmp(charPointerArray[i],charPointerArray[j]) < 0)
         {
            tempPointer = charPointerArray[i];
            charPointerArray[i] = charPointerArray[j];
            charPointerArray[j] = tempPointer;
         }
      }
   }

   cout << endl << "The sorted array..." << endl;
   for (i=0;i<ARRAY_SIZE;i++)
   {
      cout << charPointerArray[i] << endl;
   }

   return (0);
}
```

Results

```
The unsorted array...
ABCDEFGHIJKLMNOPQRSTUVWXYZ[\]^_`abcdefg
hijklmnopqrstuvwxyzABCDEFGHIJKLMNOPQRST
UVWXYZ[\]^_`abcdefghijklmnopqrstuvwxyzA
BCDEFGHIJKLMNOPQRSTUVWXYZ[\]^_`abcdefgh
ijklmnopqrstuvwxyzABCDEFGHIJKLMNOPQRSTU
VWXYZ[\]^_`abcdefghijklmnopqrstuvwxyzAB
CDEFGHIJKLMNOPQRSTUVWXYZ[\]^_`abcdefghi
jklmnopqrstuvwxyzABCDEFGHIJKLMNOPQRSTUV
WXYZ[\]^_`abcdefghijklmnopqrstuvwxyzABC
DEFGHIJKLMNOPQRSTUVWXYZ[\]^_`abcdefghij
klmnopqrstuvwxyzABCDEFGHIJKLMNOPQRSTUVW
XYZ[\]^_`abcdefghijklmnopqrstuvwxyzABCD
EFGHIJKLMNOPQRSTUVWXYZ[\]^_`abcdefghijk
lmnopqrstuvwxyzABCDEFGHIJKLMNOPQRSTUVWX
YZ[\]^_`abcdefghijklmnopqrstuvwxyzABCDE
FGHIJKLMNOPQRSTUVWXYZ[\]^_`abcdefghijkl
mnopqrstuvwxyzABCDEFGHIJKLMNOPQRSTUVWXY
Z[\]^_`abcdefghijklmnopqrstuvwxyzABCDEF
GHIJKLMNOPQRSTUVWXYZ[\]^_`abcdefghijklm
nopqrstuvwxyzABCDEFGHIJKLMNOPQRSTUVWXYZ
[\]^_`abcdefghijklmnopqrstuvwxyzABCDEFG
HIJKLMNOPQRSTUVWXYZ[\]^_`abcdefghijklmn
opqrstuvwxyzABCDEFGHIJKLMNOPQRSTUVWXYZ[
\]^_`abcdefghijklmnopqrstuvwxyzABCDEFGH
IJKLMNOPQRSTUVWXYZ[\]^_`abcdefghijklmno
pqrstuvwxyzABCDEFGHIJKLMNOPQRSTUVWXYZ[\
```

```
]^_`abcdefghijklmnopqrstuvwxyzABCDEFGHI
JKLMNOPQRSTUVWXYZ[\]^_`abcdefghijklmnop
qrstuvwxyzABCDEFGHIJKLMNOPQRSTUVWXYZ[\]
^_`abcdefghijklmnopqrstuvwxyzABCDEFGHIJ

The sorted array...
ABCDEFGHIJKLMNOPQRSTUVWXYZ[\]^_`abcdefg
BCDEFGHIJKLMNOPQRSTUVWXYZ[\]^_`abcdefgh
CDEFGHIJKLMNOPQRSTUVWXYZ[\]^_`abcdefghi
DEFGHIJKLMNOPQRSTUVWXYZ[\]^_`abcdefghij
EFGHIJKLMNOPQRSTUVWXYZ[\]^_`abcdefghijk
FGHIJKLMNOPQRSTUVWXYZ[\]^_`abcdefghijkl
GHIJKLMNOPQRSTUVWXYZ[\]^_`abcdefghijklm
HIJKLMNOPQRSTUVWXYZ[\]^_`abcdefghijklmn
IJKLMNOPQRSTUVWXYZ[\]^_`abcdefghijklmno
JKLMNOPQRSTUVWXYZ[\]^_`abcdefghijklmnop
UVWXYZ[\]^_`abcdefghijklmnopqrstuvwxyzA
VWXYZ[\]^_`abcdefghijklmnopqrstuvwxyzAB
WXYZ[\]^_`abcdefghijklmnopqrstuvwxyzABC
XYZ[\]^_`abcdefghijklmnopqrstuvwxyzABCD
YZ[\]^_`abcdefghijklmnopqrstuvwxyzABCDE
Z[\]^_`abcdefghijklmnopqrstuvwxyzABCDEF
[\]^_`abcdefghijklmnopqrstuvwxyzABCDEFG
\]^_`abcdefghijklmnopqrstuvwxyzABCDEFGH
]^_`abcdefghijklmnopqrstuvwxyzABCDEFGHI
^_`abcdefghijklmnopqrstuvwxyzABCDEFGHIJ
hijklmnopqrstuvwxyzABCDEFGHIJKLMNOPQRST
ijklmnopqrstuvwxyzABCDEFGHIJKLMNOPQRSTU
jklmnopqrstuvwxyzABCDEFGHIJKLMNOPQRSTUV
klmnopqrstuvwxyzABCDEFGHIJKLMNOPQRSTUVW
lmnopqrstuvwxyzABCDEFGHIJKLMNOPQRSTUVWX
mnopqrstuvwxyzABCDEFGHIJKLMNOPQRSTUVWXY
nopqrstuvwxyzABCDEFGHIJKLMNOPQRSTUVWXYZ
opqrstuvwxyzABCDEFGHIJKLMNOPQRSTUVWXYZ[
pqrstuvwxyzABCDEFGHIJKLMNOPQRSTUVWXYZ[\
qrstuvwxyzABCDEFGHIJKLMNOPQRSTUVWXYZ[\]
```

Analysis

The underlying concept behind this program is the same technique that database programs use. Like database programs, this sample program sorts an index of data without moving the data itself.

The program begins by declaring some constants, two arrays, and some temporary working variables that it needs. One of the arrays is a 2-D array of characters. Each row in this array is a string. The other array is a one-dimensional array of pointers to characters. Recall that, in C++, a pointer to characters is another form of a string.

The program enters a pair of nested `for` loops that fill the array `a2DCharArray` with characters. Since strings in C++ must be terminated by a null character, it puts a null character on the end of each row.

Next, the program uses another `for` loop to point each of the pointers in the array `charPointerArray` to the beginning of a row in `a2DCharArray`. Notice that the statement

```
charPointerArray[i] = a2DCharArray[i];
```

omits one dimension of the array `a2DCharArray`. When you leave the second set of square brackets off of a two-dimensional array, it evaluates to a pointer. The pointer points to the first item in the row. So the preceding statement gets the address of the first character in each row and stores that address in the array of pointers. The statement

```
charPointerArray[i] = &a2DCharArray[i][0];
```

is another way to do the same thing.

The program in Hands On 21.2 prints each string using the array `charPointerArray`. This proves that the strings are not in sorted order. It then enters a pair of nested `for` loops that sort the strings using the Bubble Sort we saw previously. The program makes use of the Standard C Library string function `strcmp()`, which is pronounced *string comp*. This function compares two strings. If the first string is less than the second string, `strcmp()` returns a number that is less than zero. If they are equal, it returns zero. If the string in the first parameter is greater than the string in the second parameter, `strcmp()` returns a number greater than zero. The order that the `strcmp()` function uses is based on the ASCII chart. That is, it uses the ASCII values of the characters in the string to order the strings. Any string beginning with uppercase letters will come before any string beginning with lowercase letters. Uppercase letters occur before lowercase letters in the ASCII chart.

If `strcmp()` detects that the string indicated by `charPointerArray[i]` is less than the string pointed at by `charPointerArray[j]`, the body of the `if` statement swaps them by swapping the pointers. The strings themselves are never moved. This is exactly the same concept that is used in index files in database programs. It's generally much more efficient and more flexible to sort an index than to sort data.

The program finishes by printing the sorted array of pointers.

Pointers and Functions

One of the great advantages of pointers is that you can pass them as parameters to functions and use them as the return value of functions. When you pass a pointer as a parameter to a function, the function can change the data. When the function returns, the data remains changed.

Example 21.6 shows a program that passes a pointer to an integer as a parameter to a function. Figure 21.4 displays the output of this program.

EXAMPLE 21.6 A Pointer as a Parameter

```
#include <iostream.h>


void AFunction(int intParameter,int *intPointerParameter);

int main()
{
   int anInteger = 10;
   int anotherInteger = 20;

   cout << "anInteger = " << anInteger << endl;
   cout << "anotherInteger = " << anotherInteger << endl;

   AFunction(anInteger,&anotherInteger);

   cout << "anInteger = " << anInteger << endl;
   cout << "anotherInteger = " << anotherInteger << endl;

   return (0);
}
```

```
void AFunction(int intParameter,int *intPointerParameter)
{
   intParameter = 50;
   *intPointerParameter = 60;
   cout << "intParameter = " << intParameter << endl;
   cout << "intPointerParameter = " << *intPointerParameter << endl;
}
```

Notice that the function `AFunction()` in Example 21.6 expects two parameters. It defines one as an integer and the other as a pointer to an integer. `AFunction()` assigns the value of 50 to `intParameter`. It assigns a value of 60 to the memory location where `intPointerParameter` points. Those values *both* remain while the program executes `AFunction()`. When the program returns to `main()`, you can see from the output that the value in `anInteger` did not change.

When you pass a value as a parameter to a function, the function can change the value of the parameter, but it is not changed once the function has ended. Essentially, all parameters transmit data *into* a function only. They can't transmit data out of it.

Pointers enable us to get around that rule. When the program in Example 21.6 calls `AFunction()`, it passes the address of `anotherInteger` as the second parameter. That address is copied into the parameter `intPointerParameter`. Therefore, `intPointerParameter` points at `anotherInteger`. When the statement in `AFunction()` assigns the value 60 into `*intPointerParameter`, it stores the 60 into the location where `intPointerParameter` points. Since `intPointerParameter` points at `anotherInteger`, the value in `anotherInteger` gets changed. Figure 21.5 illustrates this.

FIGURE 21.4 Program Output of Example 21.6

```
anInteger = 10
anotherInteger = 20
intParameter = 50
intPointerParameter = 60
anInteger = 10
anotherInteger = 60
```

FIGURE 21.5 An Integer Parameter and an Integer Pointer Parameter

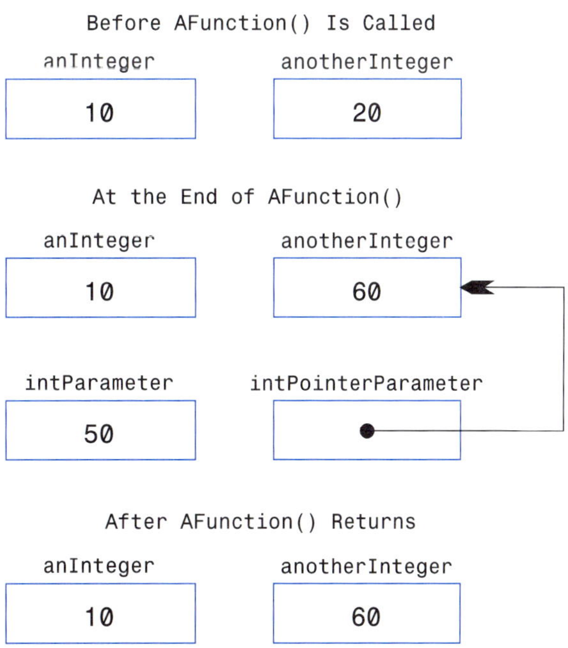

TIP: Normally, parameters pass data into functions. Pointer parameters enable you to pass data out of functions through the parameter list.

When programs pass pointers as parameters to functions in the way shown in Example 21.6, the function can change the data. It doesn't matter what data type you're using. If you pass a function a pointer to an object, the function can change the object and the object will remain changed when the function finishes. If you just pass the object, the changes in the function will not be reflected in the object. Let's use Hands On 21.3 to demonstrate this idea.

Hands On 21.3

Objective

Write a program that passes a function an object and a pointer to an object.

Experiment

Type the following program into your IDE or text editor. Compile, link, and run it.

```
#include <iostream.h>


class an_object
{
public:
   an_object(void);

   void IntData(int dataValue);
   int IntData(void);

private:
   int integerData;
};


an_object::an_object(void)
{
   integerData=0;
}


void an_object::IntData(int dataValue)
{
   integerData = dataValue;
}


int an_object::IntData(void)
{
   return (integerData);
}



void AFunction(an_object objectParameter,
               an_object *objectPointerParameter);


int main()
{
```

```
    an_object anObject;
    an_object anotherObject;

    anObject.IntData(10);
    anotherObject.IntData(20);

    cout << "anObject = " << anObject.IntData() << endl;
    cout << "anotherObject = " << anotherObject.IntData() << endl;

    AFunction(anObject,&anotherObject);

    cout << "anObject = " << anObject.IntData() << endl;
    cout << "anotherObject = " << anotherObject.IntData() << endl;

    return (0);
}


void AFunction(an_object objectParameter,
               an_object *objectPointerParameter)
{
    objectParameter.IntData(50);
    objectPointerParameter->IntData(60);

    cout << "objectParameter = " << objectParameter.IntData() << endl;
    cout << "objectPointerParameter = " ;
    cout << objectPointerParameter->IntData() << endl;
}
```

Results

```
anObject = 10
anotherObject = 20
objectParameter = 50
objectPointerParameter = 60
anObject = 10
anotherObject = 60
```

Analysis

This program is very much like Example 21.6, except that it uses a simple type of object. Like the program in Example 21.6, it calls `AFunction()` and passes it two parameters. The first is an object. The second is a pointer to an object. Changing the value in the object that `objectPointerParameter` points at causes it to remain changed after `AFunction()` returns.

In addition to pointers to atomic data types and objects, programs can also use pointers to pass strings as parameters to functions. In previous chapters, we've seen that strings can be passed to functions as arrays. Since arrays are really pointers in disguise, you can also use character pointers as string parameters.

Example 21.7 shows a program that passes a string to a function. The function counts the number of characters in the string, and returns that count. Notice that the parameter is an array with empty square brackets. You may recall that this is one way in C++ to indicate a string of unknown length.

Another way to indicate the same thing is shown in Example 21.8. It contains the same program as Example 21.7. The only difference is that the parameter to the `StringLength()` function is specified as a pointer, not an array. Functionally, there is no difference between these two definitions of this parameter.

EXAMPLE 21.7 Passing an Array as a Parameter

```
#include <iostream.h>


int StringLength(char aString[]);


int main()
{
   char tempString[] = "A short string.";

    cout << "The length of the string is ";
    cout << StringLength(tempString);

    return (0);
}


int StringLength(char aString[])
{
   int i;
    for (i=0;aString[i]!='\0';i++)
       /* Empty loop body */  ;
    return (i);
}
```

EXAMPLE 21.8 Passing a Pointer as a Parameter

```
#include <iostream.h>


int StringLength(char *aString);


int main()
{
   char tempString[] = "A short string.";

    cout << "The length of the string is ";
    cout << StringLength(tempString);

    return (0);
}


int StringLength(char *aString)
{
   int i;
    for (i=0;aString[i]!='\0';i++)
       /* Empty loop body */  ;
    return (i);
}
```

Passing a two-dimensional array to a function is somewhat more complex. You can define the array in different ways. Each method that you use accomplishes essentially the same task. However, the variations have slightly different limitations.

For instance, your program can pass a 2-D array to a function by using array notation. Table 21.1 contains some sample function prototypes for a function called

TABLE 21.1 Methods of Passing 2-D Arrays

Prototype	Comments
`void FunctionName( int arrayName[TOTAL_ROWS],[TOTAL_COLS]);`	Uses array notation. Specifies the size of both dimensions.
`void FunctionName( int arrayName[],[TOTAL_COLS],int rows);`	Uses array notation. Specifies the number of columns. The array can have any number of rows.
`void FunctionName(int *arrayName[], int rows,int cols);`	Uses both array and pointer notation. There can be any number of columns and rows.
`void FunctionName(int **arrayName, int rows,int cols);`	Uses pointer notation. There can be any number of columns and rows.

If you're wondering whether you can also leave off the number of columns from the array specification, the answer is no. If you use array notation for multi-dimensional arrays in parameter lists, you can only leave off the first size specifier.

`FunctionName()`. For the sake of example, the return type of `FunctionName()` is `void`. However, it can be anything you want.

All versions of the function `FunctionName()` expect an array as the first parameter. Some versions also take parameters that specify the number of rows or columns in the array.

The first version of the function in Table 21.1 specifies a 2-D array as its only parameter. Both the number of columns and the number of rows are known at compile time. This function can only be passed an array that has `TOTAL_ROWS` rows and `TOTAL_COLS` columns. If you try to pass it anything else, the compiler will flag it as an error. This version of the function is easiest for programmers to work with. However, it is also the most restrictive.

In the second version of the function, the number of rows is omitted. This means that `FunctionName()` can take an array with any number of rows, but every row can be no longer than the number of columns specified by `TOTAL_COLS`. This version of the function is somewhat more flexible. It is still easy for programmers to use because you always know how many columns each row contains. The function also takes a second parameter. It is normal practice when using this style to pass in the number of rows in the array. The function usually needs to have that information.

The third version of this function uses a mixture of pointer and array notation. It specifies an array of pointers of unknown length. You could put `TOTAL_ROWS` in the square brackets if you wanted. This is a very flexible method of passing an array. The array can have any number of rows. Each row can be any length.

Strictly speaking, each row can be a different length. However, in most situations, all of the rows in the array will be the same length. Therefore, it is also typical to pass in parameters that tell the function how many rows and columns the row contains.

The fourth method of passing arrays is exactly equivalent to the third method. It just uses pure pointer notation rather than a mixture of pointer and array notation.

Functions can use pointers as return types, just as they do any other type. For instance, suppose I wanted to declare a function called `MyFunction()` that returns a pointer to characters. Its prototype would look something like this:

```
char *MyFunction(void);
```

Your functions can return pointers to atomic data types, pointers to objects, or strings (pointer to character).

References

In addition to pointers, the C++ programming language also defines references. A reference is very similar to a pointer. The primary difference is that you don't use pointer notation. You declare a reference using the ampersand (&) instead of the asterisk (*). You do not need pointer notation to dereference a reference. Hands On 21.4 demonstrates a function that uses a reference to an integer in its parameter list.

Hands On 21.4

Objective

Write a program that defines a function that uses a reference to an integer in its parameter list.

Experiment

Type the following program into your IDE or text editor. Compile, link, and run it.

```
#include <iostream.h>


void ChangeTheInt(int &intReference);


int main()
{
   int anInteger = 5;

   cout << anInteger << endl;
   ChangeTheInt(anInteger);
   cout << anInteger << endl;

   return (0);
}


void ChangeTheInt(int &intReference)
{
   intReference = 10;
}
```

Results

```
5
10
```

Analysis

As you can see from the Results section, a function can change the value of a reference parameter. Just like a pointer, the change remains after the function returns. However, a reference does not use pointer notation. The `main()` function does not need to pass `&anInteger` to the `ChangeTheInt()` function as it would if the function used a pointer parameter. The `ChangeTheInt()` function does not need to use the `*` notation inside the function body to store a value in the reference parameter.

As with pointers, your functions can return a reference to data. The data can be atomic types or classes.

Pass by Value, Pass by Address, and Pass by Reference

C++ provides us with three ways to pass data to a function in its parameter list. Chapter 12, which discussed functions, presented the first method. That is, we simply pass the value.

When we pass a value to a function, the C++ compiler generates executable code that copies the value into the parameter. In Example 21.9, the code fragment calls the function `ThisFunction()`. When program execution jumps to `ThisFunction()`, the value in the variable `anInteger` is copied into the parameter `anIntParameter`. Because `anIntParameter` contains a copy of the value, changing the copy does not change the original value in `anInteger`.

EXAMPLE 21.9 Pass by Value

```
int main()
{
    int anInteger = 5;
    ThisFunction(anInteger);

    // More program code here.

    return (0);
}

void ThisFunction(int anIntParameter)
{
    anintParameter=20;
}
```

Pass by value is very similar to going to a copy machine and making a copy of this page. If you write on the copy, it does not change anything on this page. You can change the copy without changing the original. When we pass parameters by value, we do the same thing. The program makes a copy of the value that we pass in and stores the copy in the parameter. Changes to the parameter do not change the original. Figure 21.6 illustrates passing parameters by value.

We can also pass parameters by address. Passing by address means that we pass a pointer to the data. When we pass by address, the address of the data is copied into the pointer parameter. If we change the value in the memory location where the pointer points, we change the original data. Example 21.6, Figure 21.5, and Hands On 21.3 all illustrate functions that pass by address.

Passing a parameter by reference is similar to passing by address. The primary difference is that you don't need to use pointer notation.

So when should you use pass by value, pass by address, and pass by reference? Each of these methods has its advantages and disadvantages.

For instance, pass by value makes a copy of the data we pass to functions. Passing by value prevents functions from accidentally changing data when they should not. However, pass by value is very inefficient when we pass large pieces of data. Objects in particular can grow to be quite large if an object's private data members are also objects. Passing large amounts of data by value forces the program to spend a lot of time creating multiple copies of the data.

Passing by address is more efficient. Only the address is copied into the parameter. The program does not make a new copy of the data as it does when using pass by value. However, passing the address of data a function means that the function can change the data. This leaves your program open to unintended side effects.

There are times when we *want* functions to change the values we pass as parameters. In fact, the C++ language would be hobbled if it *didn't* provide pass by address. It is one of the techniques that enable us to get more than one value out of a function when it returns.

FIGURE 21.6 Pass by Value

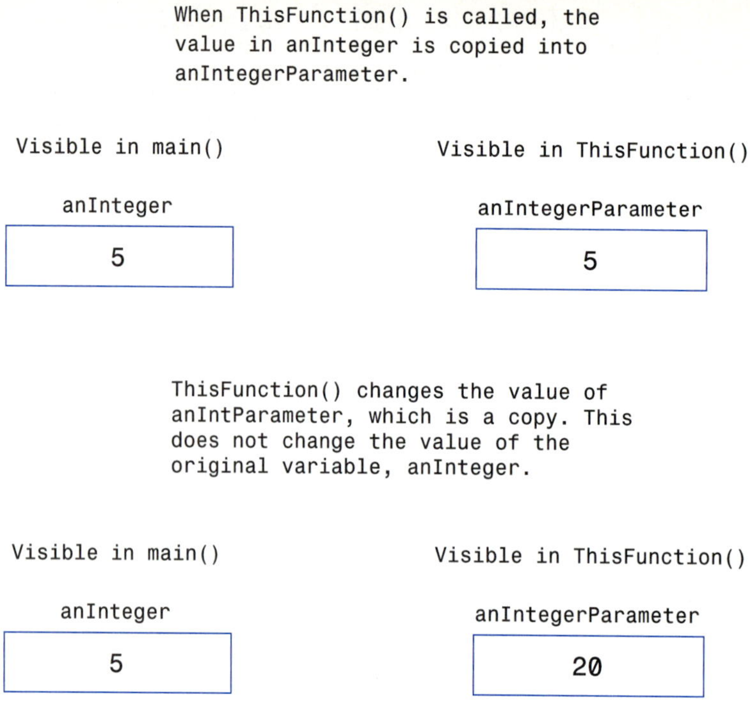

It is actually possible to return two values from a C++ function. However, this is not widely used in industry because so many programmers are unfamiliar with the technique. Even if you know how to do it, the maintenance programmer probably won't. So it's best just to avoid returning multiple values.

Recall that a function can return only one value at a time. If we want a function to pass back more than one value when it ends, we must pass those values through the parameter list using pass by address or pass by reference.

Passing by reference is also more efficient than passing by value. Since the reference refers to the original data, the program does not copy the data when it calls the function. However, like pointers, that means the function can change the data.

It would be nice if C++ provided us a way to get the efficiency of pass by address and pass by reference while preventing functions from changing data when they shouldn't. In fact, the C++ language does exactly that. We can apply the `const` keyword to pass by address and pass by reference parameters that we don't want changed. The compiler will prevent functions from changing the value of `const` parameters. Hands On 21.5 demonstrates the use of `const` with pass by address and pass by reference parameters.

Hands On 21.5

Objective

Write a `text_string` object with the following member functions:

A constructor that takes no parameters.
A constructor that takes a `text_string` as a parameter.
A constructor that takes a C++ string as a parameter.
= (Assign a `text_string` to another `text_string`)
= (Assign a C++ string to a `text_string`)
+ (Concatenate one `text_string` onto another)
+ (Concatenate a C++ string onto a `text_string`)
+= (Append one `text_string` onto another)
+= (Append one character onto a `text_string`)
+= (Append a C++ string onto a `text_string`)
>>
<<
`CppString()` (Convert the `text_string` to a C++ string)

Write a program that demonstrates each of these functions.

Experiment

Type the following program into your IDE or text editor. Compile, link, and run it. This program is composed of three files: *StrTest.cpp*, *TString.h*, and *TString.cpp*.

This is the file `StrTest.cpp`*:*

```
#include "TString.h"

int main()
{
   text_string string1; // Call the no-arg constructor.
   text_string string2 = "This is ";  // Call the one-arg constructor.
   text_string string3 = "a string."; // Call the one-arg constructor.

   string1 = string2 + string3;
   cout << string1 << endl;

   string2 = "Is this";
   string1 = string2 + " also a string?";
   cout << string1 << endl;

   string1 = "That is ";
   string1 += "also a string";
   cout << string1 << endl;

   string1 = "Here is ";
   string2 = "another string.";
   string1 += string2;
   cout << string1 << endl;

   string1 += 's';
   cout << string1 << endl;

   cout << "The length of the string is ";
   cout << strlen(string1.CppString()) << endl;

   cout << "The length of the string is ";
   cout << string1.Length() << endl;

   cout << "Please type in a string and press Enter" << endl;
   cin >> string1;

   cout << "The string you typed in was:" << endl;
   cout << string1;

   return (0);
}
```

This is the file `TString.h`*:*

```
#if !defined(TSTRING_H)
#define TSTRING_H

#include <iostream.h>

const int MAX_TEXT_STRING_LENGTH = 81;

class text_string
{
public:
```

```
   text_string(void);
   text_string(const char * const charArray);

   text_string &operator = (const text_string &textString);
   text_string &operator = (const char * const charArray);

   text_string operator + (const text_string &textString);
   text_string operator + (const char * const charArray);

   text_string &operator += (const text_string &textString);
   text_string &operator += (const char * const charArray);
   text_string &operator += (char oneChar);

   friend istream &operator >> (istream &inputStream,
                                text_string &destinationString);
   friend ostream &operator << (ostream &outputStream,
                                const text_string &sourceString);

   const char *CppString(void);

   int Length(void);

private:
   text_string &Copy(const text_string &sourceString);
   text_string &Copy(const char * const charArray);

private:
   char charString[MAX_TEXT_STRING_LENGTH];
};

#endif
```

This is the file `TString.cpp`*:*

```
#include "TString.h"


text_string::text_string(void)
{
   for (int i=0;i<MAX_TEXT_STRING_LENGTH;i++)
   {
      charString[i] = '\0';
   }
}


text_string::text_string(const char * const charArray)
{
   Copy(charArray);
}


text_string &text_string::operator = (const text_string &textString)
{
   return (Copy(textString));
}


text_string &text_string::operator = (const char * const charArray)
```

```
{
   return (Copy(charArray));
}


text_string text_string::operator + (const text_string &textString)
{
   text_string tempString;
   int i,j;

   tempString.Copy(charString);

   for (i=tempString.Length(),j=0;
        (i<MAX_TEXT_STRING_LENGTH) && (textString.charString[j]);
        i++,j++)
   {
      tempString.charString[i]=textString.charString[j];
   }

   if (i==MAX_TEXT_STRING_LENGTH)
   {
      tempString.charString[MAX_TEXT_STRING_LENGTH-1] = '\0';
   }
   else
   {
      charString[i] = '\0';
   }

   return (tempString);
}


text_string text_string::operator + (const char * const charArray)
{
   return (*this+text_string(charArray));
}


text_string &text_string::operator += (const text_string &textString)
{
   *this = *this + textString;
   return (*this);
}


text_string &text_string::operator += (const char * const charArray)
{
   *this = *this + charArray;
   return (*this);
}

text_string &text_string::operator += (char oneChar)
{
   int length = Length();

   if (length < MAX_TEXT_STRING_LENGTH-1)
   {
      charString[length]=oneChar;
```

```
        charString[length+1]='\0';
    }
    return (*this);
}


istream &operator >> (istream &inputStream,
                      text_string &destinationString)
{
    inputStream >> destinationString.charString;
    return (inputStream);
}


ostream &operator << (ostream &outputStream,
                      const text_string &sourceString)
{
    outputStream << sourceString.charString;
    return (outputStream);
}


const char *text_string::CppString(void)
{
    return (charString);
}


int text_string::Length(void)
{
    int i;
    for (i=0;
         (i<MAX_TEXT_STRING_LENGTH) && (charString[i]);
         i++)
    {
        // Empty loop body. The stuff in the () does the counting.
    }
    return (i);
}


text_string &text_string::Copy(const text_string &sourceString)
{
    int i;

    for (i=0;
         (i<MAX_TEXT_STRING_LENGTH) &&
         (sourceString.charString[i]);
         i++)
    {
        charString[i] = sourceString.charString[i];
    }

    if (i==MAX_TEXT_STRING_LENGTH)
    {
        charString[MAX_TEXT_STRING_LENGTH-1] = '\0';
    }
    else
```

```
    {
        charString[i] = '\0';
    }

    return (*this);
}


text_string &text_string::Copy(const char * const charArray)
{
    int i;

    for (i=0;
         (i<MAX_TEXT_STRING_LENGTH) &&
         (charArray[i]);
         i++)
    {
        charString[i] = charArray[i];
    }

    if (i==MAX_TEXT_STRING_LENGTH)
    {
        charString[MAX_TEXT_STRING_LENGTH-1] = '\0';
    }
    else
    {
        charString[i] = '\0';
    }

    return (*this);
}
```

Results

```
This is a string.
Is this also a string?
That is also a string
Here is another string.
Here is another string.s
The length of the string is 24
The length of the string is 24
Please type in a string and press Enter
ThisIsAStringWithoutSpaces
The string you typed in was:
ThisIsAStringWithoutSpaces
```

Analysis

The program begins by calling the no-argument constructor to create a `text_string` object. It also calls the constructor that takes one parameter to create two `text_string` variables. The one-argument constructor sets each object to the characters contained in the array that the program passes in through the parameter list.

REMINDER: In this book, the terms *argument* and *parameter* are taken to mean the same thing.

Notice that the parameter of the one-argument constructor is a constant character pointer to constant data. This means that inside the function, the constructor cannot change the data that `charArray` points to. It also prevents the constructor from changing where `charArray` points. This is done strictly as a defensive programming measure. It tells the maintenance programmer that nothing should change the parameter in any way.

Most of the rest of the member functions of the `text_string` class follow this style. Their parameters are usually constant references, constant pointers, or constant pointers to constant locations. When a function takes a constant reference as a parameter, it can't change the data to which the reference refers. If it takes a constant pointer, it can't change the data to which the pointer points. Functions that take constant pointers to constant memory locations can't change the data or the pointers.

Next, the program uses the addition operator and the assignment operator. When we call the addition operator with numeric data types, the operator adds the value of one number to another. It doesn't change either value. The `operator +()` function for `text_string` objects does conceptually the same thing. It concatenates one string onto the end of another. It does this without changing either of the strings. The `main()` function in this example program uses the assignment operator to store the result of the `operator +()` function into the object `string1`.

There is also a version of the `operator +()` function that concatenates a `text_string` object and a character string. The `main()` function demonstrates this as well.

The `main()` function stores the results of both versions of the `operator +()` functions in variables. To do this, it uses two different versions of the assignment operator. One takes a `text_string` object as its parameter. The `main()` function demonstrates this version with the statement

```
string1 = string2 + string3;
```

Since the `operator +()` function returns a reference to a `text_string` object, the C++ compiler determines that it must generate a call to the version of the assignment operator that takes a reference to a `text_string` object as its parameter.

The statement

```
string2 = "Is this";
```

demonstrates the other version of the assignment operator for `text_string` objects. It takes a pointer to a character as its parameter.

The `text_string` class contains overloaded `operator +=()` functions that append strings. The `main()` function demonstrates one of these with the statement

```
string1 += "also a string";
```

This version appends a character string onto the end of the characters in the `text_string` object `string1`. Unlike the `operator +()` function, the `operator +=()` function changes the object that invokes it.

The `main()` function calls the other version of the `operator +=()` function with the statement

```
string1 += string2;
```

This version appends the characters in the `string2` object onto the end of the `string1` object. It changes `string1` in the process.

The `text_string` class also contains a version of the `operator +=()` function that appends a single character onto the end of a `text_string` object. The `main()` function demonstrates this function as well.

Before C++ was invented, the C programming language used character arrays as strings. The C Standard Library contains many extremely useful functions for manipulating strings. Since C++ is an extension of C, the C++ language must support all of the C functions. When you create a string object class using C++, it is possible that you (or other programmers on your project) will want to call C Standard Library string functions and pass them your string object. To do this, you must have a way to convert your string objects into C/C++ character strings.

There are two common methods for providing the conversion. One is to include a type cast operator in your string class. For example, we could define the function

```
operator char *();
```

in the text_string class. If we did, anyone could convert a text_string object to a character pointer by a type cast. However, there are several potential problems with this. Providing a type cast operator enables programmers to put statements like the following into their programs:

```
char *charPointer;
text_string string1 = "This is a string";
charPointer = (char *)string1;
*charPointer = 'Q';
```

These statements provide programmers with direct access to the data in the text_string object. Any part of the program can change the contents of a text_string object without ever calling a member function. This completely defeats the purpose of using C++.

The other method of converting string objects to character strings is demonstrated in the text_string class. The function CppString() returns the name of the character array charString. Earlier in this chapter, we saw that array names without the square brackets ([]) evaluate to pointers to the array data. So this function essentially does the same thing as a type cast operator. However, there are some differences.

First, the CppString() function returns a const pointer. That means programmers can use the pointer to view the contents of a text_string object. However, they cannot use the const pointer to change the contents of the text_string object. The statements

```
char *charPointer;
text_string string1 = "This is a string";
charPointer = string1.CppString();
*charPointer = 'Q';
```

will cause an error when they are compiled.

Type cast operators can cause other problems as well. If the C++ compiler sees a type cast operator in your class, it will sometimes call the type cast to perform a conversion without telling you. This can lead to errors that are hard to track down. By providing a function that performs the conversion, but does not have the same name as the type cast operator, you prevent the compiler from silent conversions. It forces the programmer using your class to explicitly decide if a conversion is appropriate.

In the case of the example program in Hands On 21.5, main() uses the CppString() function to convert the text_string object to a character pointer. It then passes that pointer to the C Standard Library function strlen() to find the length of the string.

Of course, the text_string class provides a Length() function that does the same thing. The point here is to demonstrate the CppString() function, and to show that the Length() function returns the same thing as strlen().

You may remember that the text_string object in Chapter 20 contained a private data member that tracked the length of the string. Just to show a different implementation, I created this version of the text_string class such that it requires a null character on the end of every string. Therefore, when the Length() function is called, it must count the number of printable characters (not including the null character) in the string.

For efficiency, Hands On 21.5 makes heavy use of pointers and references. There are very few functions that pass objects through parameter lists or use objects as return values. We see this if we look at the implementation of the text_string class in the file *TString.cpp*.

In addition, most of the work of the text_string class is done by just a few functions. The two private member functions called Copy(), and one of the operator + functions, contain most of the code for the text_string class. By looking at each of the text_string functions in turn, we can see how this helps.

The class contains two overloaded constructors. The no-argument constructor initializes its private member data to the null character. The one-argument constructor calls the Copy() function to store the character array in its parameter into the private array charString. This means that if the Copy() function works correctly, so does the constructor.

There are two versions of the Copy() function. One copies the characters in the source object into the current object. The other version copies the characters in a C++ string (a character array) into the current object. The two versions of the operator =() function in the text_string class each call one of the versions of the Copy() function. If the two Copy() functions perform their job correctly, then both of the assignment operators do as well.

The first versions of the operator +() function calls one of the Copy() functions to copy characters from the current object into a temporary text_string object. Again, if the Copy() function works properly, so does this part of the operator +() function.

The concatenation function then uses a for loop to copy the characters from the text_string object that was passed in as a parameter. It stores them in the temporary object. If there are too many characters, this function just ignores them. It will not try to copy more characters than can fit in the array charString.

Notice that this function returns a text_string object. Most of the rest of the operator functions return a reference to a text_string. What is the difference?

When a function returns any piece of data, it returns the data by value. It makes a copy of the data and returns the copy. A function that returns a reference or a pointer does not return a copy of the data. If it returns a pointer, it returns the address of the data. Since references allow direct access to data, functions that return them also do not return a copy of the data.

A function that returns a pointer or a reference must point or refer to data that will still exist after the function ends. Variables declared inside a function (local variables) do not exist after the function ends. Therefore, functions that return pointers or references cannot return pointers or references to local variables. If a function must return the value in a local variable, it should return the variable by value. It should not return a reference or a function. That way, the program will copy the value in the local variable and return the copy.

The operator +() function must return the value in the local variable tempString. It can't return a pointer or a reference to tempString because tempString will cease to exist after the function returns. The operator +() function must return a text_string object so that a copy of tempString will be made and passed back to main().

The second version of the operator +() function takes a character array as its parameter. It returns a text_string object. This operator +() function uses the other overloaded operator +() to do all of its work.

This operator +() function contains some statements that may look odd at first, but they are a handy shorthand. The statement *this specifies the object that called this function. Every member function has an extra implied parameter called the **this pointer.**[1] The this pointer points to the object that called the member function. The operator +() function uses the this pointer to access the current object. Since *this is a text_string object, the statement

```
*this+text_string(charArray)
```

calls the operator +() function that takes a text_string object as its parameter. The array charArray is converted to a text_string object by calling the text_string constructor and passing the array. The constructor returns a text_string object, which is immediately passed as the parameter to the other operator +() function. In effect, this function creates a nameless temporary variable.

This practice of creating and using nameless temporary variables is very efficient. Many C++ compilers recognize this and will optimize the variable right out of existence.

Instead of allocating memory for another variable, they use the registers on the microprocessor.

[1]The exception to this is static member functions. See Chapter 23 for details.

The operator +() function that takes a character array as its parameter turns the character array into a text_string object. It then calls the *other* operator +() function (the one that takes a text_string as its parameter) to do the actual work. When the work is done, it returns the value that it got from the other operator +() function. So if the other operator +() function works properly, so does this one.

The first overload of the operator +=() function uses the same sort of trick. It uses the current object, specified by *this, to call the + function (the one that takes a text_string object as its parameter). It uses the assignment operator to store the result in *this, which is the current object. So if the operator =() and operator +() function do what they should, so will this one.

The operator +=() function returns a reference to a text_string. Of course, returning references is generally more efficient than returning an object. It's good to return a reference whenever you can. Recall that references must refer to an object that will still exist after the current function returns. For that reason, the operator +=() function returns a reference to *this. Whenever a member function is executing, you know that the object pointed to by the this pointer will still exist after the function ends. It has to. It called the member function in the first place. Since it existed before the function started, it will exist after the function ends. Therefore, it is safe to return a reference to *this. If a member function needs to return a pointer to an object, it is safe to return the this pointer.

Returning a reference to *this also allows statements such as

```
string1 += string2 += string3;
```

or

```
string1 = string2 = string3;
```

This makes a very concise way to write complex operations.

The text_string object also provides a version of the operator +=() function that appends a single character onto a text_string object. Since it appends only one character, it is more efficient just to append it in this function than to call other member functions to perform the task.

To make input and output of text_string objects easier, the text_string class provides overloads of the insertion and extraction operators. These call the insertion and extraction operators for character strings. Therefore, they behave exactly the way C++ programmers expect.

The overloaded insertion and extraction operators are friend functions. They return a reference to the stream that was passed in through the parameter list. This enables you to write statements like

```
cout << string1 << "A string";
```

The cout object calls the overloaded insertion operator that is a friend of the text_string class. The overloaded insertion operator outputs the characters in the string1 object, then returns a reference to a stream.

Sometimes references seem very much like pointers. In this case, the reference to the stream behaves more like an object than a pointer. It calls the insertion operator for character strings to output "A string" to the screen.

For reasons explained previously, the text_string class provides a member function called CppString() that returns a const pointer to the character array inside a text_string object.

The text_string class defines a Length() function, which counts the number of characters in the character array. All of the counting is done in the control portion of the for loop, so the body of the loop is empty.

As mentioned previously, the text_string class contains two versions of a private member function called Copy(). One of these takes a text_string object as its parameter. The other takes a character array. Each copies the characters in its parameter into the current object.

In general, it is good design practice to base the functionality of a class on a few workhorse functions. It decreases the amount of code that must be maintained and tested. Once you get a few functions working properly, most of the functionality of the class is up and running.

The Equivalence of Pointers and Arrays Revisited

The StringCopy() function is modeled on a C/C++ Standard Library function called strcpy().

The fundamental equivalence of pointers and arrays means that you can choose which notation you want to use based on your needs. You can select the notation that's fastest, or the one that easiest to read.

Example 21.10 shows a function called StringCopy(). The StringCopy() function uses array notation. It is easy and straightforward for most programmers to read.

EXAMPLE 21.10 The StringCopy() Function

```
char *StringCopy(char destinationString[],char sourceString[])
{
   int i;

   for (i=0;sourceString[i]!='\0';i++)
   {
      destinationString[i]=sourceString[i];
   }
   destinationString[i]='\0';

   return (destinationString);
}
```

The for loop in Example 21.10 copies characters from the source array to the destination array. The condition on the for loop prevents the function from copying the null character to the destination string. When the loop finds the null character in the source string, the condition evaluates to false. That means the body of the loop and the increment are not executed. To ensure that the destination string has a null character on the end, the StringCopy() function explicitly puts one there before it returns.

Example 21.11 contains a version of the StringCopy() function that takes pointers for its parameters instead of arrays. This does not affect how the function works. Pointers can be treated as arrays.

EXAMPLE 21.11 StringCopy() with Pointer Parameters

```
char *StringCopy(char *destinationString,char *sourceString)
{
   int i;

   for (i=0;sourceString[i]!='\0';i++)
   {
      destinationString[i]=sourceString[i];
   }
   destinationString[i]='\0';

   return (destinationString);
}
```

The StringCopy() function can use equivalent pointer notation if we want it to. Example 21.12 demonstrates StringCopy() with pointer notation.

EXAMPLE 21.12 StringCopy() with Pointer Notation

```
char *StringCopy(char *destinationString,char *sourceString)
{
   int i;
```

```
    for (i=0;*(sourceString+i)!='\0';i++)
    {
       *(destinationString+i) = *(sourceString+i);
    }
    *(destinationString+i)='\0';

    return (destinationString);
}
```

You may be wondering why we need to enclose the base address and offset in parentheses. For example, the statement

```
*(destinationString+i) = *(sourceString+i);
```

puts the pointer names and the variable `i` into parentheses. The reason has to do with precedence. If we wrote the statement

```
*(destinationString+i)
```

without the parentheses, like this:

```
*destinationString+i
```

it would not give us the answer we want. The pointer dereference operator has higher precedence than addition. Leaving the parentheses out of the statement means that the compiler will generate code that dereferences the pointer, then adds the value in `i` to the contents of memory at that location. What we want is to add `i` to the base address of the array to get another address. We then want to access the contents of *that* location.

Note that we can use pointer notation inside the `StringCopy()` function whether we declare the parameters as pointers or arrays.

If we do use pointer parameters for the `StringCopy()` function, we can eliminate the integer variable `i` by incrementing the pointers. Example 21.13 demonstrates this technique.

EXAMPLE 21.13 Eliminating `i` from `StringCopy()`

```
char *StringCopy(char *destinationString,char *sourceString)
{
   for ( ;*sourceString != '\0';sourceString++,destinationString++)
   {
      *destinationString = *sourceString;
   }
   *destinationString='\0';

   return (destinationString);
}
```

Although this version of the function looks quite different, it does exactly the same thing as previous versions. When a program calls this function, it passes `StringCopy()` two pointers to characters.

Let's suppose that a program calls the `StringCopy()` function with the statement

```
StringCopy(string1,string2);
```

The character strings `string1` and `string2` are passed by address. *The pointers themselves are passed by value.* That's an important detail to remember. The variables `string1` and `string2` are pointers. The addresses in those two pointers are copied into the parameters `destinationString` and `sourceString` when the `StringCopy()` function begins. The variables `destinationString` and `sourceString` contain *copies* of the addresses in `string1` and `string2`. You can change the copies of the addresses if you want to, but that doesn't change the addresses that `string1` and `string2` contain.

The `for` loop in Example 21.13 does not need anything in its initialization section, so it performs its test. Each time the test on the `for` loop evaluates to true, it executes the body of the loop. Inside the loop's body, the statement

```
*destinationString = *sourceString;
```

copies a character from the memory location that `sourceString` points to and stores it in the memory location pointed to by `destinationString`.

After the function executes the loop's body, it performs the increments. The `for` loop increments the addresses in the parameters `destinationString` and `sourceString`. This does not change the addresses in the calling program (`string1` and `string2` in our example). The parameters `destinationString` and `sourceString` are copies of the original pointers that were passed in.

Example 21.14 also shows a version of the `StringCopy()` function. This time, the test in the `for` loop has been made more efficient. This version still tests for the null character. However, it performs the test by evaluating the character itself. Since the null character evaluates to zero, the test will evaluate to false when it encounters the null character.

EXAMPLE 21.14 Eliminating the Comparison from `StringCopy()`

```
char *StringCopy(char *destinationString,char *sourceString)
{
   for ( ;*sourceString;sourceString++,destinationString++)
   {
      *destinationString = *sourceString;
   }
   *destinationString='\0';

   return (destinationString);
}
```

We can make this function even more efficient. An assignment statement evaluates to a value. The value of the assignment statement is the value that is assigned. We can use this fact to make our loop even more concise, as shown in Example 21.15.

EXAMPLE 21.15 A Terse Version of `StringCopy()`

```
char *StringCopy(char *destinationString,char *sourceString)
{
   for ( ;*destinationString = *sourceString;
        sourceString++,destinationString++)
   {
   }

   return (destinationString);
}
```

The body of the `for` loop is now empty. All of the work is done in the control portion. The assignment statement

```
*destinationString = *sourceString
```

assigns the value in the memory location that `sourceString` points at to the memory location `destinationString` points at. The value of that assignment is the character that was assigned. If the character is the null character, the assignment evaluates to zero, or false. If it is anything else, it evaluates to true.

Because the assignment statement is now in the test portion of the `for` loop, the null character is copied to the destination string. We no longer need the extra assignment of the null character just before the return statement.

It is actually possible to make this function even more efficient and concise. Example 21.16 shows how.

EXAMPLE 21.16 A Bare Bones `StringCopy()` Function

```
char *StringCopy(char *destinationString,char *sourceString)
{
    while (*destinationString++ = *sourceString++)
    {
        // Nothing in here. It's all done in the test.
    }

    return (destinationString);
}
```

In this version, the `for` loop becomes a `while` loop. The increments are done in the test. The C++ compiler will not see anything wrong with that. Since the function uses a `postincrement`, the dereference and the assignment operations are performed first. Each time the function executes this loop, it performs the test. To evaluate the test, it must perform the assignment. To do the assignment, the function must dereference the pointers. So it gets the character in the memory location at which `sourceString` points. It assigns the character into the memory location where `destinationString` points. The value of the assignment is the value of the character. As long as the null character is not assigned, the loop continues.

After the function performs the assignment and the test, it increments the pointers to the next location in memory.

There are trade-offs to using pointer notation this way. Programmers may find it hard to read. Many more programmers are familiar and comfortable with array notation than with this style of pointer notation. The version of `StringCopy()` in Example 21.16 is extremely efficient. However, some programmers may not understand how it works. Therefore, you must decide what's more important, code readability or efficiency.

If you do choose to use these pointer techniques, it's a good idea to include plenty of comments explaining what you did. Adding comments goes a long way toward helping new programmers on the project understand the code they're reading.

Using Pointers and References in the Text Editor

Hands On 21.5 showed ways to incorporate pointers, references, and the `const` keyword into the `text_string` object. Hands On 21.6 demonstrates the same techniques for the rest of the text editor.

Hands On 21.6

Objective

Write a text editor that uses the techniques presented in this chapter.

Experiment

Type the following program into your IDE or text editor. Compile, link, and run it. This program is composed of five files: *TEdit.cpp*, *TString.h*, *TString.cpp*, *TBuffer.h*, and *TBuffer.cpp*.

This is the file `TEdit.cpp`

```
//---------------------------------------------------------------------------
/*
File Name:   TEdit.cpp
Comments:    This is the main file of the text editor.
*/
//---------------------------------------------------------------------------
```

```
//-----------------------------------------------------------------------------
// Include Files

#include "TString.h"
#include "TBuffer.h"
#include "stdlib.h"
// End Include Files
//-----------------------------------------------------------------------------



//-----------------------------------------------------------------------------
// Prototypes

void ClearScreen(void);
void DisplayMenu(void);

// End Prototypes
//-----------------------------------------------------------------------------


int main()
{
   const int TOTAL_TEXT_AREA_LINES = 20;
   const char SCROLL_UP_COMMAND = (char)21;    // Ctrl+U
   const char SCROLL_DOWN_COMMAND = (char)4;   // Ctrl+D
   const char SAVE_COMMAND = (char)1;          // Ctrl+A
   const char LOAD_COMMAND = (char)12;         // Ctrl+L
   const char EDIT_COMMAND = (char)5;          // Ctrl+E
   const char QUIT_COMMAND = (char)17;         // Ctrl+Q
   const char BEEP_CHARACTER = (char)7;

   static text_buffer textBuffer;  // Uses static because it's large.
   bool done=false;
   int i,top;
   text_string inputText;

   // While the user doesn't want to quit...
   while (!done)
   {
      // Clear the screen.
      ClearScreen();
      text_string outputString;

      // Display one screenful of text.
      for (i=0,top=textBuffer.TopLine();
           (i<TOTAL_TEXT_AREA_LINES) && (top+i<TEXT_BUFFER_LENGTH);
           i++)
      {
         cout << (top+i) << ": ";
         outputString = textBuffer[top+i];
         cout << outputString;
         cout << endl;
      }

      // Display the menu.
      DisplayMenu();
```

```
// Get input from the user.
char inputString[MAX_TEXT_STRING_LENGTH];
cin.getline(inputString,MAX_TEXT_STRING_LENGTH);
inputText = inputString;

text_string fileName;

switch (inputText[0])
{
   // If the user wants to scroll up one screenful...
   case SCROLL_UP_COMMAND:
      // Scroll up.
      textBuffer.ScrollUp(TOTAL_TEXT_AREA_LINES-1);
   break;

   // If the user wants to scroll down one screenful...
   case SCROLL_DOWN_COMMAND:
      // Scroll down.
      textBuffer.ScrollDown(TOTAL_TEXT_AREA_LINES-1);
   break;

   // If the user wants to save the buffer to a file...
   case SAVE_COMMAND:
      // Save to file.
      cout << "Enter File Name: ";
      cin.getline(inputString,MAX_TEXT_STRING_LENGTH);
      fileName = inputString;
      if (textBuffer.Save(fileName)!=NO_BUFFER_ERROR)
      {
         cout << BEEP_CHARACTER;
      }
   break;

   // If the user wants to load from a file...
   case LOAD_COMMAND:
      // Load from file.
      cout << "Enter File Name: ";
      cin.getline(inputString,MAX_TEXT_STRING_LENGTH);
      fileName = inputString;
      if (textBuffer.Load(fileName)!=NO_BUFFER_ERROR)
      {
         cout << BEEP_CHARACTER;
      }
   break;

   // If the user wants to edit text...
   case EDIT_COMMAND:
   {
      cout << "Enter Line Number: ";
      cin >> inputString;

      // Convert the line number to a number.
      int lineNumber=atoi(inputString);

      // If there is a '\n' still left in the input stream...
      if (cin.peek()=='\n')
      {
```

```
            // Pull it out.
            cin.ignore(1,'\n');
         }

         // If the line number is displayed on the screen...
         if ((lineNumber >= top) &&
             (lineNumber < top+TOTAL_TEXT_AREA_LINES))
         {
            // Prompt the user for input.
            cout << lineNumber << ": ";

            // Get the new line of text.
            cin.getline(inputString,MAX_TEXT_STRING_LENGTH);

            // Insert the new line of text into the buffer.
            textBuffer[lineNumber] = inputString;
         }
      }
      break;

      // If the user wants to quit...
      case QUIT_COMMAND:
         done=true;
      break;

      // Else the input is not recognized...
      default:
         // Beep the speaker.
         cout << BEEP_CHARACTER;
      break;
   }
  }
  return (0);
}



//-----------------------------------------------------------------------
/*
Function Name:      ClearScreen
Member of:          N/A
Input Parameters:   None.
Output Parameters:  None.
Return Value:       None.
Comments:           A function that clears any screen that is 24 lines of text
                    or less. If your screen displays more than 24 lines,
                    change SCREEN_SIZE to one more than the number of lines it
                    displays.
*/

void ClearScreen(void)
{
   const int SCREEN_SIZE = 25;
   for (int i=0;i<SCREEN_SIZE;i++)
   {
      cout << endl;
```

```
   }
}

// End ClearScreen
//---------------------------------------------------------------------------



//---------------------------------------------------------------------------
/*
Function Name:      DisplayMenu
Member of:          N/A
Input Parameters:   None.
Output Parameters:  None.
Return Value:       None.
Comments:           Displays a menu for the text editor.
*/

void DisplayMenu(void)
{
   cout << "To enter a command, press one of the following, ";
   cout << "then press Enter" << endl;
   cout << "Edit text: Ctrl+E  ";
   cout << "Scroll Up: Ctrl+U  ";
   cout << "Scroll Down: Ctrl+D"  << endl;
   cout << "Load File: Ctrl+L  ";
   cout << "Save File: Ctrl+A  ";
   cout << "Quit: Ctrl+Q";
   cout << "    Command :";
}

// End DisplayMenu
//---------------------------------------------------------------------------


// End TEdit.cpp
//---------------------------------------------------------------------------
```

This is the file `TString.h`

```
//---------------------------------------------------------------------------
/*
File Name:  TString.h
Comments:   This file contains the constants and class definition needed to
            use the text_string class.
*/
//---------------------------------------------------------------------------


#if !defined(TSTRING_H)
#define TSTRING_H

//---------------------------------------------------------------------------
// Include Files

#include <iostream.h>
```

```
// End Include Files
//------------------------------------------------------------------------


//------------------------------------------------------------------------
// Constants

const int MAX_TEXT_STRING_LENGTH = 60;

// End Constants
//------------------------------------------------------------------------



//------------------------------------------------------------------------
// Class Definitions

class text_string
{
// Public member functions.
public:
   text_string(void);
   text_string(const char * const charArray);

   text_string &operator = (const text_string &textString);
   text_string &operator = (const char * const charArray);

   text_string operator + (const text_string &textString);
   text_string operator + (const char * const charArray);

   text_string &operator += (const text_string &textString);
   text_string &operator += (const char * const charArray);
   text_string &operator += (char oneChar);

   char &operator [](const int index);

   friend istream &operator >> (istream &inputStream,
                                text_string &destinationString);
   friend ostream &operator << (ostream &outputStream,
                                const text_string &sourceString);

   const char *CppString(void);

   int Length(void);

// Private member functions.
private:
   void Initialize(void);
   text_string &Copy(const text_string &sourceString);
   text_string &Copy(const char * const charArray);

// Private member data.
private:
   char charString[MAX_TEXT_STRING_LENGTH];
};

// End Class Definitions
//------------------------------------------------------------------------
```

```
#endif

// End TString.h
//---------------------------------------------------------------------------
```

This is the file `TString.cpp`

```
//---------------------------------------------------------------------------
/*
File Name:  TString.cpp
Comments:   This file contains the implementation of the text_string class.
*/
//---------------------------------------------------------------------------




//---------------------------------------------------------------------------
// Include Files

#include "TString.h"

// End Include Files
//---------------------------------------------------------------------------



//---------------------------------------------------------------------------
/*
Function Name:      text_string
Member of:          text_string
Input Parameters:   None.
Output Parameters:  None.
Return Value:       Constructed text_string object.
Comments:           No-arg constructor. Calls the private member function
                    Initialize() to set the text_string object into a known
                    state.
*/

text_string::text_string(void)
{
   Initialize();
}

// End text_string
//---------------------------------------------------------------------------



//---------------------------------------------------------------------------
/*
Function Name:      text_string
Member of:          text_string
Input Parameters:   charArray - A pointer to characters. These chars are
                       copied into the object.
Output Parameters:  None.
Return Value:       Constructed text_string object.
Comments:           One-arg constructor. Calls the private member function
```

```
                    Initialize() to set the text_string object into a known
                    state. It then calls the private member function
                    Copy() to copy the characters from charArray into the
                    private member data array charString.
*/

text_string::text_string(const char * const charArray)
{
   Initialize();
   Copy(charArray);
}

// End text_string
//-----------------------------------------------------------------------------



//-----------------------------------------------------------------------------
/*
Function Name:      operator =
Member of:          text_string
Input Parameters:   textString - The object the characters will be copied
                       from.
Output Parameters:  None.
Return Value:       Returns a reference to *this.
Comments:           This function copies characters from a text_string
                    object into the current text_string object. It calls
                    the private member function Copy() to perform the
                    copy.
*/

text_string &text_string::operator = (const text_string &textString)
{
   return (Copy(textString));
}

// End operator =
//-----------------------------------------------------------------------------



//-----------------------------------------------------------------------------
/*
Function Name:      operator =
Member of:          text_string
Input Parameters:   charArray - The array from which the characters will be
                       copied.
Output Parameters:  None.
Return Value:       Returns a reference to *this.
Comments:           This function copies characters from a character array
                    into the current text_string object. It calls the private
                    member function Copy() to perform the copy.
*/

text_string &text_string::operator = (const char * const charArray)
{
   return (Copy(charArray));
}
```

```
// End operator =
//-----------------------------------------------------------------------



//-----------------------------------------------------------------------
/*
Function Name:        operator +
Member of:            text_string
Input Parameters:     textString - The object containing characters to
                         concatenate onto the end of the current object.
Output Parameters:    None.
Return Value:         Returns the concatenated text_string object.
Comments:             This function concatenates the string in the textString
                      parameter onto the end of the current text_string. If
                      the combined length of the strings is greater than
                      the maximum allowable string length, the resulting
                      string is truncated. This function does not change the
                      textString object or the current object.
*/

text_string text_string::operator + (const text_string &textString)
{
   text_string tempString;
   int i,j;

   tempString.Copy(charString);

   for (i=tempString.Length(),j=0;
        (i<MAX_TEXT_STRING_LENGTH) && (textString.charString[j]);
        i++,j++)
   {
      tempString.charString[i]=textString.charString[j];
   }

   if (i==MAX_TEXT_STRING_LENGTH)
   {
      tempString.charString[MAX_TEXT_STRING_LENGTH-1] = '\0';
   }
   else
   {
      charString[i] = '\0';
   }

   return (tempString);
}

// End operator +
//-----------------------------------------------------------------------



//-----------------------------------------------------------------------
/*
Function Name:        operator +
Member of:            text_string
Input Parameters:     charArray - The array containing characters to
                         concatenate onto the end of the current object.
```

```
Output Parameters:   None.
Return Value:        Returns the concatenated text_string object.
Comments:            This function concatenates the string in the array
                     charArray onto the end of the current text_string. If
                     the combined length of the strings is greater than
                     the maximum allowable string length, the resulting
                     string is truncated. This function does not change the
                     character array or the current object.
*/


text_string text_string::operator + (const char * const charArray)
{
   return (*this+text_string(charArray));
}
// End operator +
//-----------------------------------------------------------------------------




//-----------------------------------------------------------------------------
/*
Function Name:       operator +=
Member of:           text_string
Input Parameters:    textString - A text_string object containing characters
                        to append onto the end of the current object.
Output Parameters:   None.
Return Value:        Returns a reference to *this.
Comments:            This function appends characters onto the end of a
                     text_string object. It uses the text_string::operator +()
                     function to do most of its work. This function modifies
                     the current object (*this).
*/

text_string &text_string::operator += (const text_string &textString)
{
   *this = *this + textString;
   return (*this);
}

// End operator +=
//-----------------------------------------------------------------------------




//-----------------------------------------------------------------------------
/*
Function Name:       operator +=
Member of:           text_string
Input Parameters:    charArray - An array of characters that this function
                        will append onto the end of the current object.
Output Parameters:   None.
Return Value:        Returns a reference to *this.
Comments:            This function appends characters onto the end of a
                     text_string object. It uses the text_string::operator +()
                     function to do most of its work. This function modifies
                     the current object (*this).
```

```
*/

text_string &text_string::operator += (const char * const charArray)
{
   *this = *this + charArray;
   return (*this);
}

// End operator +=
//-----------------------------------------------------------------------------



//-----------------------------------------------------------------------------
/*
Function Name:       operator +=
Member of:           text_string
Input Parameters:    oneChar - An character that this function will append
                        onto the end of the current object.
Output Parameters:   None.
Return Value:        Returns a reference to *this.
Comments:            This function appends a single character onto the end
                     of a text_string object. If the resulting string is too
                     long, this function does nothing. This function modifies
                     the current object (*this).
*/

text_string &text_string::operator += (char oneChar)
{
   int length = Length();

   if (length < MAX_TEXT_STRING_LENGTH-1)
   {
      charString[length]=oneChar;
      charString[length+1]='\0';
   }
   return (*this);
}

// End operator +=
//-----------------------------------------------------------------------------



//-----------------------------------------------------------------------------
/*
Function Name:       operator []
Member of:           text_string
Input Parameters:       index - The index number of the character to set.
                        Numbering starts with zero.
Output Parameters:   None.
Return Value:        If the index is in range, this function returns a
                     reference to the requested character. If not, it returns
                     a reference to the last printable character.
Comments:            The intent of this function is to enable developers to
                     get and set individual characters in a text_string
                     object. It provides bounds checking on the index value.
*/
```

```
char &text_string::operator [](const int index)
{
   if ((index >= 0) && (index<MAX_TEXT_STRING_LENGTH-1))
   {
      return charString[index];
   }
   else
   {
      return charString[MAX_TEXT_STRING_LENGTH-2];
   }
}

// End operator []
//---------------------------------------------------------------------------



//---------------------------------------------------------------------------
/*
Function Name:       operator >>
Member of:           None. Friend of text_string.
Input Parameters:    inputStream - The stream from which the input will be
                        read.
Output Parameters:   destinationString - The string that will contain the
                     input when this function completes.
Return Value:        Returns a reference to the input stream.
Comments:            This friend function overloads the insertion operator
                     for the text_string class.
*/

istream &operator >> (istream &inputStream,
                      text_string &destinationString)
{
   inputStream >> destinationString.charString;
   return (inputStream);
}

// End operator >>
//---------------------------------------------------------------------------



//---------------------------------------------------------------------------
/*
Function Name:       operator <<
Member of:           None. Friend of text_string.
Input Parameters:    sourceString - The string from which characters will be
                        read.
Output Parameters:   outputStream - The stream to which output will be
                        written.
Return Value:        Returns a reference to the output stream.
Comments:            This friend function overloads the extraction operator
                     for the text_string class.
*/

ostream &operator << (ostream &outputStream,
                      const text_string &sourceString)
{
```

```
   outputStream << sourceString.charString;
   return (outputStream);
}

// End operator <<
//-----------------------------------------------------------------------------



//-----------------------------------------------------------------------------
/*
Function Name:       CppString
Member of:           text_string
Input Parameters:    None.
Output Parameters:   None.
Return Value:        Returns a constant reference to the character array that
                     this text_string object contains.
Comments:            See Return Value section.
*/

const char *text_string::CppString(void)
{
   return (charString);
}

// End CppString
//-----------------------------------------------------------------------------



//-----------------------------------------------------------------------------

/*
Function Name:       Length
Member of:           text_string
Input Parameters:    None.
Output Parameters:   None.
Return Value:        Returns the length of the string. This is the same as the
                     number of printable characters (excluding the null
                     character).
Comments:            See Return Value section.
*/

int text_string::Length(void)
{
   int i;
   for (i=0;
        (i<MAX_TEXT_STRING_LENGTH) && (charString[i]);
        i++)
   {
      // Empty loop body. The stuff in the () does the counting.
   }
   return (i);
}

// End Length
//-----------------------------------------------------------------------------
```

```
//---------------------------------------------------------------------------
/*
Function Name:      Initialize
Member of:          text_string
Input Parameters:   None.
Output Parameters:  None.
Return Value:       None.
Comments:           This function sets all of the characters in the private
                    member data to the null character.
*/

void text_string::Initialize(void)
{
   for (int i=0;i<MAX_TEXT_STRING_LENGTH;i++)
   {
      charString[i] = '\0';
   }
}

// End Initialize
//---------------------------------------------------------------------------



//---------------------------------------------------------------------------
/*
Function Name:      Copy
Member of:          text_string
Input Parameters:   sourceString - The string from which the characters will
                       be copied.
Output Parameters:  None.
Return Value:       Returns a reference to the current object (*this).
Comments:           This private member function copies characters from a
                    text_string object into the current object. If the length
                    of the combined string is too long, the extra characters
                    are truncated.
*/

text_string &text_string::Copy(const text_string &sourceString)
{
   int i;

   for (i=0;
        (i<MAX_TEXT_STRING_LENGTH) &&
        (sourceString.charString[i]);
        i++)
   {
      charString[i] = sourceString.charString[i];
   }

   if (i==MAX_TEXT_STRING_LENGTH)
   {
      charString[MAX_TEXT_STRING_LENGTH-1] = '\0';
   }
   else
```

```
   {
      charString[i] = '\0';
   }

   return (*this);
}

// End Copy
//-----------------------------------------------------------------------------



//-----------------------------------------------------------------------------
/*
Function Name:      Copy
Member of:          text_string
Input Parameters:   charArray - The character array from which the characters
                       will be copied.
Output Parameters:  None.
Return Value:       Returns a reference to the current object (*this).
Comments:           This private member function copies characters from a
                    character array into the current object. If the length
                    of the combined string is too long, the extra characters
                    are truncated.
*/

text_string &text_string::Copy(const char * const charArray)
{
   int i;

   for (i=0;
        (i<MAX_TEXT_STRING_LENGTH) &&
        (charArray[i]);
        i++)
   {
      charString[i] = charArray[i];
   }

   if (i==MAX_TEXT_STRING_LENGTH)
   {
      charString[MAX_TEXT_STRING_LENGTH-1] = '\0';
   }
   else
   {
      charString[i] = '\0';
   }

   return (*this);
}

// End Copy
//-----------------------------------------------------------------------------

// End TString.cpp
//-----------------------------------------------------------------------------
```

This is the file `TBuffer.h`

```
//-------------------------------------------------------------------------
/*
File Name:  TBuffer.h
Comments:   This file contains the definition of the text_buffer class. It
            also defines the constants needed to use the text_buffer class.
*/
//-------------------------------------------------------------------------


#if !defined (TBUFFER_H)
#define TBUFFER_H


//-------------------------------------------------------------------------
// Constants

const int TEXT_BUFFER_LENGTH = 100;

// Buffer error status values.
const int NO_BUFFER_ERROR = 0;
const int CANT_LOAD_FILE = -1;
const int CANT_SAVE_FILE = -2;

// End Constants
//-------------------------------------------------------------------------



//-------------------------------------------------------------------------
// Class Definitions

class text_buffer
{
public:
   text_buffer(void);

   text_string &operator [](const int index);

   int TopLine(void);

   int ScrollUp(int linesToScroll);
   int ScrollDown(int linesToScroll);

   int Load(text_string fileName);
   int Save(text_string fileName);

private:
   text_string textBuffer[TEXT_BUFFER_LENGTH];
   int topLine;
   int linesUsed;
};

// End Class Definitions
//-------------------------------------------------------------------------

#endif
```

```
// End TBuffer.h
//-----------------------------------------------------------------------
```

This is the file `TBuffer.cpp`

```
//-----------------------------------------------------------------------
/*
File Name:   TBuffer.cpp
Comments:    This file contains the implementation of the member functions for
             the text_buffer class.
*/
//-----------------------------------------------------------------------



//-----------------------------------------------------------------------
// Include Files

#include <fstream.h>
#include "TString.h"
#include "TBuffer.h"

// End Include Files
//-----------------------------------------------------------------------



//-----------------------------------------------------------------------
/*
Function Name:       text_buffer
Member of:           text_buffer
Input Parameters:    None.
Output Parameters:   None.
Return Value:        Initialized text_buffer object.
Comments:            This function is the default constructor for the
                     text_buffer class.
*/

text_buffer::text_buffer(void)
{
   topLine=0;
   linesUsed=0;
}

// End text_buffer
//-----------------------------------------------------------------------



//-----------------------------------------------------------------------
/*
Function Name:       operator []
Member of:           text_buffer
Input Parameters:    index - The line number of the line being accessed.
Output Parameters:   None.
Return Value:        If index is valid, this function returns a reference to
                     the specified line. If not, it returns a reference to the
                     last line used.
```

```
Comments:           This function enables you to get or set a line of text in
                    the buffer. It does this by returning a reference to the
                    specified line. If the line specified is less than 0 or
                    greater than the length of the buffer, this function
                    returns a reference to the last line of the buffer.
*/

text_string &text_buffer::operator [](int index)
{
   text_string line;
   if ((index>=0) && (index<TEXT_BUFFER_LENGTH))
   {
      if (index>linesUsed)
      {
         linesUsed = index+1;
      }
      return textBuffer[index];
   }
   else
   {
      return (textBuffer[linesUsed]);
   }
}

// End operator []
//-----------------------------------------------------------------------------



//-----------------------------------------------------------------------------
/*
Function Name:      TopLine
Member of:          text_buffer
Input Parameters:   None.
Output Parameters:  None.
Return Value:       The top line of the buffer
Comments:           This function returns the line number of the line that
                    will be displayed at the top of the screen when the
                    contents of the buffer are displayed.
*/

int text_buffer::TopLine(void)
{
   return (topLine);
}

// End TopLine
//-----------------------------------------------------------------------------



//-----------------------------------------------------------------------------
/*
Function Name:      ScrollUp
Member of:          text_buffer
Input Parameters:   linesToScroll - Integer number of lines to scroll toward
                        the beginning of the text buffer.
```

```
Output Parameters:  None.
Return Value:       Returns the number of lines actually scrolled.
Comments:           This function moves the current top line of the buffer
                    that is displayed on the screen toward the beginning of
                    the buffer. It prevents the top line from being moved
                    before the beginning of the buffer.

                    If, for instance, the current top line is 5, and the
                    input parameter specifies that the function should
                    scroll the buffer up 20 lines, it will only scroll 5
                    lines to the beginning of the buffer. The return value
                    reports the number of lines the function actually
                    scrolls.
*/

int text_buffer::ScrollUp(int linesToScroll)
{
   int linesScrolled;

   // If the top line is less than the number of lines to scroll...
   if (topLine <= linesToScroll)
   {
      /* The first screenful of the buffer is currently displayed.
      Display the buffer from the beginning. */
      linesScrolled = topLine;
      topLine=0;
   }
   // Else scroll the screen toward the beginning of the buffer.
   else
   {
      topLine -= linesToScroll;
      linesScrolled = linesToScroll;
   }
   return (linesScrolled);
}

// End ScrollUp
//-----------------------------------------------------------------------------



//-----------------------------------------------------------------------------
/*
Function Name:      ScrollDown
Member of:          text_buffer
Input Parameters:   linesToScroll
Output Parameters:  None.
Return Value:       Returns the number of lines actually scrolled.
Comments:           This function moves the current top line of the buffer
                    that is displayed on the screen toward the end of
                    the buffer. It prevents the top line from being moved
                    after the end of the buffer.

                    Suppose, for instance, that the buffer is 100 lines of
                    text in length. If current top line is 95, and the
                    input parameter specifies that the function should
                    scroll the buffer down 20 lines, it will only scroll 5
                    lines toward the end of the buffer. The return value
```

```
                    reports the number of lines the function actually
                    scrolls.
*/

int text_buffer::ScrollDown(int linesToScroll)
{
   int linesScrolled;
   int newTopLine = topLine+linesToScroll;

   // If the last few lines of the buffer are currently displayed...
   if (newTopLine >= TEXT_BUFFER_LENGTH-linesToScroll)
   {
      // Set the top line to display the last few lines of the buffer.
      topLine = TEXT_BUFFER_LENGTH-linesToScroll;
      linesScrolled = newTopLine-topLine;
   }
   // Else the end of the buffer is not currently displayed...
   else
   {
      // Scroll down the requested number of lines.
      topLine = newTopLine;
      linesScrolled = linesToScroll;
   }
   return (linesScrolled);
}

// End ScrollDown
//-----------------------------------------------------------------------------



//-----------------------------------------------------------------------------
/*
Function Name:      Load
Member of:          text_buffer
Input Parameters:   fileName - Name of the file to load.
Output Parameters:  None.
Return Value:       If the file is loaded successfully, this function
                    returns NO_BUFFER_ERROR. If not, it returns
                    CANT_LOAD_FILE.
Comments:           This function loads the specified file into the
                    text buffer. Any file error will generate a
                    CANT_LOAD_FILE error. A text_buffer object for a
                    professional application would need to provide more
                    specific feedback to the function that calls this
                    routine.
*/

int text_buffer::Load(text_string fileName)
{
   int errorStatus = NO_BUFFER_ERROR;

   // If the file name string is not empty...
   if (fileName.Length() > 0)
   {
      char tempString[MAX_TEXT_STRING_LENGTH];

      // Open the file.
      ifstream inputStream(fileName.CppString());
```

```
      // If the file could be opened...
      if (inputStream)
      {
         // Read in each line of text.
         int i;
         for (i=0;
              (i<TEXT_BUFFER_LENGTH) && (!inputStream.eof());
              i++)
         {
            /* If the line of text in the file is longer than
            MAX_TEXT_STRING_LENGTH, it is truncated. */
            inputStream.getline(tempString,MAX_TEXT_STRING_LENGTH,'\n');
            textBuffer[i] = tempString;
         }
         linesUsed = i;
      }
      // Else the file could not be opened...
      else
      {
         errorStatus = CANT_LOAD_FILE;
      }
   }
   // Else the file name string was empty...
   else
   {
      errorStatus = CANT_LOAD_FILE;
   }
   return (errorStatus);
}

// End Load
//---------------------------------------------------------------------------



//---------------------------------------------------------------------------
/*
Function Name:       Save
Member of:           text_buffer
Input Parameters:    fileName - The name of the file to save.
Output Parameters:   None.
Return Value:        This function returns NO_BUFFER_ERROR if it successfully
                     saves the specified file. If there is any kind of file
                     error, it returns CANT_SAVE_FILE.
Comments:            This function saves the text buffer into the
                     specified file. Any file error will generate a
                     CANT_SAVE_FILE error. A text_buffer object for a
                     professional application would need to provide more
                     specific feedback to the function that calls this
                     routine.
*/
int text_buffer::Save(text_string fileName)
{
   int errorStatus=NO_BUFFER_ERROR;

   // If the file name string is not empty...
   if (fileName.Length() > 0)
   {
      // Open the file.
```

```
         ofstream outputStream(fileName.CppString());

         // If the file could be opened...
         if (outputStream)
         {
            // Write each line of the buffer to the file.
            for (int i=0;
                 (i<linesUsed) && (outputStream.good());
                 i++)
            {
               outputStream << textBuffer[i] << endl;
            }
         }
         // Else the file could not be opened...
         else
         {
            errorStatus = CANT_SAVE_FILE;
         }
      }
      // Else the file name string is empty...
      else
      {
         errorStatus = CANT_SAVE_FILE;
      }
      return (errorStatus);
   }

   // End Save
   //--------------------------------------------------------------------


   // End TBuffer.cpp
   //--------------------------------------------------------------------
```

Results

Figure 21.7 shows the output of this program after executing the Load command to load the file `test.txt`.

FIGURE 21.7 Output of the Text Editor

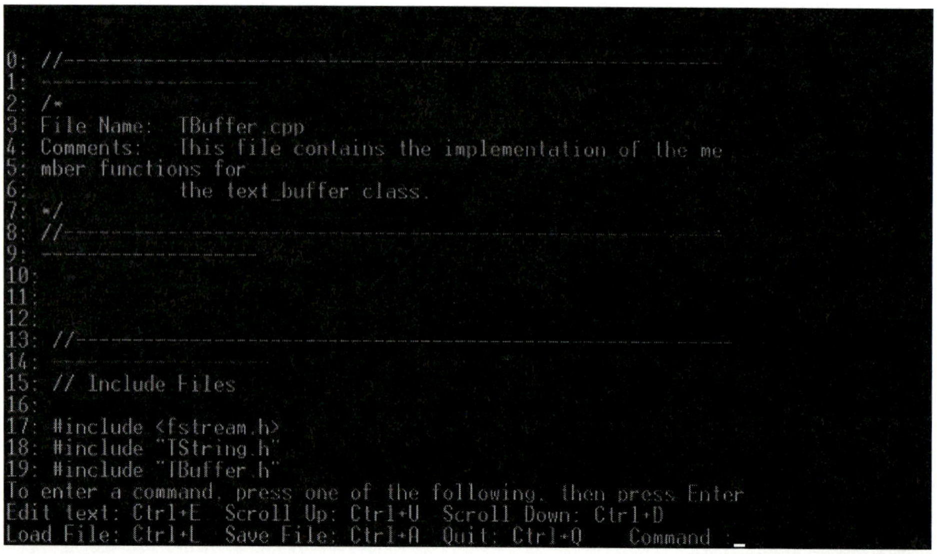

Analysis

This version of the text editor uses the `text_string` class developed in Hands On 21.5. Although the implementation of the `text_string` class has changed radically since the previous version of the text editor, it doesn't impact the functions in the other file very much.

The interface of the `text_buffer` class was also redesigned for this Hands On 21.6. Instead of `Get()` and `Set()` functions, the interface of public member functions defines an `operator []` function. This operator gives you the ability to make any class appear as if it is an array. The sample program uses the subscript operator function to access the contents of the text buffer. This simplifies the code in the `main()` function somewhat.

The `main()` function no longer uses the extraction operator for the `text_string` class to read in text from the keyboard. You may remember that the previous implementation of the extraction operator depended on the `istream::getline()` function. Since that implementation is counterintuitive for most C++ programmers, we've eliminated it. The technique shown here is slightly better. In statements such as

```
char inputString[MAX_TEXT_STRING_LENGTH];
cin.getline(inputString,MAX_TEXT_STRING_LENGTH);
inputText = inputString;
```

the `main()` function declares a string variable, gets text input into it, and then stores it in a `text_string` object.

Because the `main()` function uses a combination of the extraction operator and the `istream::getline()` function for input, it is possible that an unwanted '\n' character can remain in the input stream. A solution to this problem is in the switch statement in `main()`. If you look in the `case` that deals with the edit command, you'll see the statements

```
if (cin.peek()=='\n')
{
   cin.ignore(1,'\n');
}
```

This `if` statement uses the `istream::peek()` function to look at the input stream `cin`. If there is a '\n' left in the stream, the `if` statement calls the `istream::ignore()` function to pull it out.

With the exception of these changes, the `main()` function really doesn't differ much from our previous implementation of the text editor.

There is one difference between the `text_string` class in this example program and the one in Hands On 21.5. This version contains an `operator []()` function. It enables us to treat the `text_string` object more like a character array.

Implementing the `operator []()` function is not as straightforward as it might seem. Whenever the `text_string` object allows a programmer to access its character data, it should check to ensure that the index number the programmer passes in is within the bounds of the array. The `text_string` object should not allow the programmer to access memory outside of its private character array. The `operator []()` function does this with an `if` statement.

You could avoid this by using the `assert()` function or by using exception handling.

Notice, however, that there are `return` statements inside the `if`. This is not a good idea. In this case, however, it is unavoidable. The `operator []()` function must return a reference to a character. Functions should never return references to local variables, so the reference must be to data that exists after the `operator []()` function ends. That means `operator []()` must return a reference to a character inside the current object. Since the `if` statement creates two paths through the code, there must be two `return` statements.

Also, adding an `operator []()` function to the string class forces some other changes in it. The `operator []()` function is called whenever a programmer tries to access one single character in a `text_string` object. The previous version of the text_string class contained a Get() and a Set() function to get and set individual characters. The Get() function was only called when retrieving a character. The Set() function was only called to set a character value in the object. Whenever a programmer called the Set() function, it could check whether the user set a character beyond the end of the string. If she did, the Set() function adjusted the end of the string to accommodate the programmer.

However, programs call the operator []() function for *all* access to characters in the text_string object. From inside the function, there is no way to tell whether operator []() is being called to get a character or to set it. Therefore, we can't include code that adjusts the end of the string like the Set() function did in the previous version of the text_string object. The text_string object must make sure that every unused character in every text_string object is initialized to the null character. It must also prevent the programmer from ever storing any character value in the last position of the private character array. By doing this, it always preserves the null character at the end of the string. If you compare this version of the text_string object to the one in Hands On 21.5, you'll see that it does both of these tasks.

Parsing Command-Line Arguments

Through the use of pointers, C++ supports a rich set of very powerful programming techniques. For example, pointers enable programmers to pass a variable number of parameters to a function. This technique is commonly used to pass parameters to the main() function in a program.

When we run a C++ program, the operating system calls its main() function. We can pass arguments (parameters) from the operating system to main(). The main() function can take two set parameters, called argc and argv. Example 21.17 shows a main() function with arguments.

EXAMPLE 21.17 A main() Function with Arguments

```
int main(int argc,char *argv[])
{
    // Program statements go here.
}
```

The parameter name argc is short for *argument count.* It contains the number of items on the command line, including the program name itself. The parameter name argv stands for *argument vector*. It programming terminology, an array is sometimes referred to as a vector. The parameter argc contains the number of items in the array argv. The argv parameter is an array of pointers to characters. Since each pointer to a character is a string, that means argv is an array of strings. Each string is one item that was typed on the command line.

Let's suppose that I type the program name MyProg at my operating system's prompt, then press Enter. When the program starts, the operating system will pass the string "MyProg" in argv[0]. The parameter argc will contain a one. It will set argv[1] to NULL.

Example 21.18 demonstrates another command line. At the operating system prompt, the user has entered the program name

```
c:\mydir\myprog
```

The user also typed three file names. Whatever the program myprog does, the user wants it done to these three files.

EXAMPLE 21.18 Entering Arguments at the Command Prompt

```
d:\ >>c:\mydir\myprog this.txt that.txt those.txt
```

When myprog starts, argc contains the value 4. The string in argv[0] is "c:\mydir\myprog"; while argv[1] contains the string "this.txt". The string "that.txt" will be stored in argv[2], and "those.txt" will be stored in argv[3]. A NULL will be in argv[4].

You can treat argv like any other array of strings. You can parse it, pass it to other functions, or whatever. If you don't want your program to support command-line arguments, just leave the parameter list of main() empty.

Example 21.19 demonstrates how you might use command-line arguments. It is a version of the main() function for the text editor in Hands On 21.6. The version of main() in this example allows the user to enter a file name when he/she invokes the program. If the user types in a file name, the text editor will load the file. The program allows only one file name to be entered on the command line. If too many file names are entered, the program prints an error message for the user. The changes to the main() function are shown in bold.

EXAMPLE 21.19 The Text Editor with Command-Line Arguments

```
int main(int argc,char *argv[])
{
   const char BEEP_CHARACTER = (char)7;
   const int MAX_COMMAND_LINE_ARGUMENTS = 2;

   if (argc > MAX_COMMAND_LINE_ARGUMENTS)
   {
      ClearScreen();
      cout << BEEP_CHARACTER;
      cout << "Error: Too many command-line arguments." << endl;
      cout << "Usage:" << endl << "tedit <filename>" << endl;
   }
   else
   {
      const int TOTAL_TEXT_AREA_LINES = 20;
      const char SCROLL_UP_COMMAND = (char)21;      // Ctrl+U
      const char SCROLL_DOWN_COMMAND = (char)4;     // Ctrl+D
      const char SAVE_COMMAND = (char)1;            // Ctrl+A
      const char LOAD_COMMAND = (char)12;           // Ctrl+L
      const char EDIT_COMMAND = (char)5;            // Ctrl+E
      const char QUIT_COMMAND = (char)17;           // Ctrl+Q

      static text_buffer textBuffer;  // Uses static because it's large.
      bool done=false;
      bool fileLoaded=false;
      int i,top;
      text_string inputText;

      // While the user doesn't want to quit...
      while (!done)
      {
         // Clear the screen.
         ClearScreen();
         text_string outputString;

         // Display one screenful of text.
         for (i=0,top=textBuffer.TopLine();
              (i<TOTAL_TEXT_AREA_LINES) && (top+i<TEXT_BUFFER_LENGTH);
              i++)
         {
            cout << (top+i) << ": ";
            outputString = textBuffer[top+i];
```

```
        cout << outputString;
        cout << endl;
    }

    // Display the menu.
    DisplayMenu();

    text_string fileName;
    char inputString[MAX_TEXT_STRING_LENGTH];

    /* If the user specified a file name to load on the command line,
    and if the file has not already been loaded...*/
    if ((argc>1) && (!fileLoaded))
    {
        // Select the Load File command.
        inputText[0] = LOAD_COMMAND;
        inputText[1] = '\0';

        // Set the name of the file.
        fileName = argv[1];

        fileLoaded = true;
    }
    else
    {
        // Get input from the user.
        cin.getline(inputString,MAX_TEXT_STRING_LENGTH);
        inputText = inputString;
    }

    switch (inputText[0])
    {
        // If the user wants to scroll up one screenful...
        case SCROLL_UP_COMMAND:
            // Scroll up.
            textBuffer.ScrollUp(TOTAL_TEXT_AREA_LINES-1);
        break;

        // If the user wants to scroll down one screenful...
        case SCROLL_DOWN_COMMAND:
            // Scroll down.
            textBuffer.ScrollDown(TOTAL_TEXT_AREA_LINES-1);
        break;

        // If the user wants to save the buffer to a file...
        case SAVE_COMMAND:
            // Save to file.
            cout << "Enter File Name: ";
            cin.getline(inputString,MAX_TEXT_STRING_LENGTH);
            fileName = inputString;
            if (textBuffer.Save(fileName)!=NO_BUFFER_ERROR)
            {
                cout << BEEP_CHARACTER;
            }
        break;

        // If the user wants to load from a file...
        case LOAD_COMMAND:
```

```
            // If the file name is empty...
            if (fileName.Length()==0)
            {
               // Get the file name from the user.
               cout << "Enter File Name: ";
               cin.getline(inputString,MAX_TEXT_STRING_LENGTH);
               fileName = inputString;
            }

            // Load the file
            if (textBuffer.Load(fileName)!=NO_BUFFER_ERROR)
            {
               cout << BEEP_CHARACTER;
            }
         break;

         // If the user wants to edit text...
         case EDIT_COMMAND:
         {
            cout << "Enter Line Number: ";
            int lineNumber;
            cin >> lineNumber;

            if (cin.peek()=='\n')
            {
               cin.ignore(1,'\n');
            }
            // If the line number is displayed on the screen...
            if ((lineNumber >= top) &&
                (lineNumber < top+TOTAL_TEXT_AREA_LINES))
            {
               // Prompt the user for input.
               cout << lineNumber << ": ";

               // Get the new line of text.
               cin.getline(inputString,MAX_TEXT_STRING_LENGTH);

               // Insert the new line of text into the buffer.
               textBuffer[lineNumber] = inputString;
            }
         }
         break;

         // If the user wants to quit...
         case QUIT_COMMAND:
            done=true;
         break;

         // Else the input is not recognized...
         default:
            // Beep the speaker.
            cout << BEEP_CHARACTER;
         break;
      }
   }
 }
 return (0);
}
```

Troubleshooting Guide

After reading this section, you should be able to:

- Recognize and fix errors caused by uninitialized pointers.
- Recognize and fix errors with unterminated strings.
- Read complex pointer declarations.

Uninitialized Pointers

Forgetting to initialize pointers is a common source of pointer problems in C++. In Example 21.20, the program fragment declares a pointer to an integer. It also assigns a value to the location that the pointer points to. We can't tell where that is just by looking at these statements.

EXAMPLE 21.20 An Assignment to an Uninitialized Pointer

```
int *anIntegerPointer;
*anIntegerPointer = 5;
```

If you accidentally do this (we all do eventually), you may be lucky enough to have a compiler that will catch this error. If it doesn't, your compiler may automatically initialize all uninitialized data to zero. If that is the case, then you'll get an error when you run the program. The text for the run time error will probably be "Null pointer assignment" or something similar. The operating system may generate an error. Typically it will display a message telling you that your program caused a "General Protection Fault" or an "Unrecoverable Error."

If your compiler doesn't automatically initialize uninitialized data to zero, your program can actually work just fine for a while. The pointer will contain a random value. The value might by chance be a memory valid address. If so, the program will work. The random value may also point to an area of memory that already stores data. In that case, you'll overwrite memory. Literally anything can happen to your program when it encounters a memory overwrite. The result is completely unpredictable.

The easy way to eliminate many pointer errors is to always initialize every pointer to NULL when you declare it. If you do, you'll get either a compiler error or a run time error when you try to assign a value to an uninitialized pointer.

Unterminated Strings

When using strings, it's easy to accidentally leave the null character off of the end. Example 21.21 shows a string with no null character at the end.

EXAMPLE 21.21 An Unterminated String

```
char anUnterminatedString[] = {'n', 'o', ' ', 'n', 'u', 'l', 'l'};
cout << anUnterminatedString;
```

When the insertion operator sends the string to the `cout` stream, it literally doesn't know when to quit. It will keep marching through memory until it encounters the value 0. As it goes through memory, it will print whatever it finds there. So if your program suddenly starts printing garbage at the end of a string, you probably need to add a terminating null character to the string.

Complex Pointer Declarations

Pointers enable programmers to accomplish very complex tasks in very efficient ways. That sometimes necessitates pointer declarations that are not very straightforward. For example, Example 21.22 shows some declarations that some programmers will not find easy to read.

EXAMPLE 21.22 Complex Pointer Declarations

```
int **anArray[];
int *AFunction();
int **AFunction();
int (*aFunctionPointer)();
int **(*aFunctionPointer)();
```

The key to being able to read statements like these is to follow precedence. You start with the identifier name and end with the type name. In between, you use the precedence chart to determine what is being declared.

Note that this can be one way of declaring a three-dimensional array.

To read the first statement in Example 21.22, we start with the name `anArray`. If we check a precedence chart, we can see that the array subscript operator (`[]`) has higher precedence than the pointer declaration (`*`). Therefore `anArray` is an array, as the name of the variable suggests. Each element in `anArray` is a pointer to a pointer to an integer.

Reading the second declaration in Example 21.22 uses the same technique. The identifier is `AFunction`. Since the parentheses have higher precedence than the asterisk, `AFunction` is a function. `AFunction()` returns a pointer to an integer. What we are looking at here is a function prototype. The same is true of the third declaration in Example 21.22. It is a function that returns a pointer to a pointer to an integer.

One of the really amazing things about pointers in C++ is that they can point at program code as well as data. The last two statements in Example 21.22 declare pointers to functions.

In the fourth declaration, the identifier is the variable `aFunctionPointer`. The declaration uses the parentheses to force the `*` to be associated with `aFunctionPointer` before anything else. Inserting parentheses around the name `aFunctionPointer` and the `*` makes `aFunctionPointer` a pointer. The parentheses at the end of the declaration have the next highest precedence. Therefore, `aFunctionPointer` points to functions. The functions to which `aFunctionPointer` points must return integers.

We haven't discussed pointers to functions. However, you can still read declarations of them using the same technique you use to read any other declaration. Start with the identifier name, end with the type name, and follow precedence in between. You don't have to know how to use them to be able to read their declarations.

I threw in the last declaration in Example 21.22 just to make things really hard to read. It declares that `aFunctionPointer` is a pointer to a function that returns a pointer to a pointer to integers. It's not very common to need complex variables like this one. However, if you do need it, you can declare it. Because others may declare them in programs you are maintaining, you need to be able read declarations like this.

Summary

Pointers and references are powerful and flexible features of C++. They are also a source of many programmer errors.

A pointer is a variable that contains an address. Declare a pointer in a program by inserting an asterisk into the declaration between the type name and the identifier name.

When programs dereference pointers, they access the contents of the memory location where the pointer points. To dereference a pointer, put the asterisk in front of the variable name. If the pointer points to an object, we call the object's member functions using the arrow notation (`->`).

Just passing a variable to a function is termed pass by value. Pointers can be passed to functions as parameters. This technique enables functions to pass values out through their parameter lists. Passing a pointer to a function passes the data by address.

References are similar to pointers. If you pass a function parameter by reference, the function can change the data. However, you don't need to use pointer notation for dereferencing when you pass a parameter by reference.

One common source of errors in C++ programs is to attempt to store data to uninitialized pointers. For this reason, it is wise to get into the habit of always initializing all uninitialized pointers to NULL.

Pointers to characters are treated as strings in C++. All strings must be terminated by a null character.

It is sometimes necessary to make complex pointer declarations in C++ programs. To read such declarations, start with the identifier name, end with the type name, and follow precedence in between.

Review Questions

1. What is a pointer?
2. How do you declare pointers to atomic data types? How do you declare pointers to objects?
3. How do you initialize pointers?
4. How do you point pointers at atomic data? How do you point them at objects?
5. How do you access the memory location pointed to by a pointer?
6. How do you use pointers to call an object's member functions?
7. In what ways are pointers and arrays similar? In what ways are they different?
8. What is a reference? What is the difference between a pointer and a reference? In what ways are they similar?
9. What are some ways to prevent pointer problems in programs?
10. How do you read complex pointer declarations?

Exercises

1. Explain the difference between parameters that are passed by value, passed by address, and passed by reference.
2. Make a chart showing the advantages and disadvantages of passing data by value, by address, and by reference.
3. Explain how and why the keyword `const` is used with pointer and reference parameters.
4. Modify the program in Hands On 21.2. Currently, the program sorts an array of strings by declaring an array of pointers. It sorts the pointers into ascending order. Add another array of pointers. Sort them into descending order. Print the sorted strings.
5. Write a function that swaps two integers. Write a program demonstrating that your swap function works.
6. Write a function that swaps two strings. Write a program demonstrating that your swap function works. Your program must not move the characters themselves. *Hint:* A string is a pointer to characters. To swap strings, you must pass the swap function pointers to strings. A pointer to a string is a pointer to a pointer to characters.
7. Write a program that copies a file. The easiest way to copy a file from one file name to another is to open the source file in binary mode. Read each byte of the source file and write it to the destination file. Your program must take the source file name and the destination file name as parameters on the command line.
8. Write a `StringReverse()` function that takes two character arrays as parameters. The function should copy the characters in the first string parameter into the second string parameter in reverse order. It should match the following prototype *exactly:*

```
char *StringReverse(char sourceString[],
                    char destinationString[]);
```

   Access the characters using array notation. The function should return a pointer to the destination string. Write a program to demonstrate that your function works.
9. Write a function called `StringCopy()`. The function should copy the characters from the first string parameter into the second string parameter. It should match the following prototype *exactly:*

```
char *StringCopy(char sourceString[],
                 char destinationString[]);
```

Access the characters using array notation. The function should return a pointer to the destination string. Write a program to demonstrate that your function works.

10. Write a `StringReverse()` function that takes two character arrays as parameters. The function should copy the characters in the first string parameter into the second string parameter in reverse order. It should match the following prototype *exactly:*

```
char *StringReverse(char sourceString[],
                    char destinationString[]);
```

Access the characters using pointers only. Do not use array notation. Set a pointer to the end of the source string. Copy characters into the destination string using pointers. Increment or decrement the pointers as appropriate. Do not use a base address and an offset to access the characters. Write a program to demonstrate that your function works.

Chapter Glossary

Base Address The beginning address of an array. The address of the first byte of data.

Dereference To access data using a pointer. Accessing the contents of the memory location to which a pointer points.

Offset The distance in bytes from the beginning of an array where an array element resides in memory.

`this` Pointer A pointer to the object that invoked the currently executing member function.

22 Dynamic Memory Allocation

Objectives

After reading this chapter, you should be able to:

- Allocate and deallocate memory as a program runs.
- Dynamically allocate memory for atomic data.
- Dynamically allocate arrays.
- Dynamically allocate memory for objects.

Preview

Pointers are powerful tools in C++. However, their real strength becomes available to us as programmers when we combine pointers with dynamic memory allocation. When a program does dynamic allocation, it allocates memory as it runs. So far, we've only examined static allocation. When a program uses static allocation, the amount of memory it requires is determined when it loads and doesn't change as it runs.

This chapter examines how dynamic memory allocation is done. It presents techniques for growing and shrinking the data areas in memory according to how much memory the program needs. At the end of the chapter, you'll find a version of the text editor that can grow a text buffer to the limits of memory.

Allocation and the Heap

A computer's memory is a limited resource. No matter what computer your program is running on, there is a physical limit to the amount of memory the program can use. Often, programs must share the available memory with other programs running on the system. The free memory that is not being used by any program is called the **heap.**

As programs run, they may need an increasing or decreasing amount of memory. To get more memory, they allocate it from the heap. When they are finished using it, they deallocate it so that it can go back to the heap.

Allocation and Deallocation

In C++, programs dynamically allocate memory using the keyword `new`. They do deallocation with the C++ keyword `delete`. When your program allocates memory, it must store the address of the memory it allocates in a pointer variable.

Allocating and Deallocating Atomic Data

To allocate any atomic data type, simply declare a pointer to contain the address of the data. Use the keyword new and specify the type you are allocating. Hands On 22.1 illustrates how programs dynamically allocate atomic data types.

Hands On 22.1

Objective

Write a program that demonstrates how to allocate and deallocate atomic data types.

Experiment

Type the following program into your IDE or text editor. Compile, link, and run it.

```
#include <iostream.h>


int main()
{
   int *anIntPointer = NULL;
   double *aDoublePointer = NULL;

   anIntPointer = new int;
   *anIntPointer = 50;
   cout << endl;
   cout << "The memory at location ";
   cout << anIntPointer;
   cout << " contains the value ";
   cout << *anIntPointer << '.';

   aDoublePointer = new double;
   *aDoublePointer = 123.45;
   cout << endl;
   cout << "The memory at location ";
   cout << aDoublePointer;
   cout << " contains the value ";
   cout << *aDoublePointer << '.';

   delete anIntPointer;
   delete aDoublePointer;

   return (0);
}
```

Results

```
The memory at location 0x211d0004 contains the value 50.
The memory at location 0x211e0004 contains the value 123.45.
```

Analysis

This short program declares two pointers to atomic data types. It allocates memory for an `int` and a `double`. The program assigns the address of the memory it allocates into the pointer variables `anIntPointer` and `aDoublePointer`. It also assigns values into the allocated memory. Notice that, when we store data into dynamically allocated memory, we use the pointer dereference operator.

TIP: Programs must deallocate all of the memory that they dynamically allocate.

If you want to, you can print the address in a pointer. The C++ stream classes print the address as a hexadecimal number. This program prints both the address in each pointer and the data to which the pointers point.

Just before it ends, the program uses the keyword `delete` to deallocate the memory that it allocated. Your program must deallocate all memory that it dynamically allocates.

Allocating and Deallocating Arrays

Chapter 21 stated that we can point a pointer at a group of data elements. Once we do, we can treat the group of data as an array. C++ enables us to dynamically allocate arrays. After they are allocated, dynamically allocated arrays are no different than statically allocated arrays in most ways.

The main advantage of dynamically allocated arrays is that they can change size. An array that we allocate statically, such as this one:

```
char anArray[100];
```

may never change size. However, dynamically allocated arrays can shrink or grow as the program runs. The amount of memory they use can be different each time the program runs.

Allocating an array is similar to allocating one item. However, when we allocate an array, we must specify the number of items in the array. Hands On 22.2 illustrates the process of allocating an array.

Hands On 22.2

Objective

Write a program that allocates an array of characters. The program should fill the array with characters, and then print them to the screen. It should then allocate a larger array of characters, fill the array, and print its contents.

Experiment

Type the following program into your IDE or text editor. Compile, link, and run it.

```
#include <iostream.h>


int main()
{
   const int ARRAY_SIZE1 = 40;
   const int ARRAY_SIZE2 = 60;
   char *charArray;

   charArray = new char [ARRAY_SIZE1];

   int i;
   char tempChar;
   for (i=0,tempChar='z';
        i < ARRAY_SIZE1-1;
        i++)
   {
      charArray[i]=tempChar--;
```

```
    }
    charArray[ARRAY_SIZE1-1]='\0';

    cout << charArray << endl;

    delete charArray;

    charArray = new char [ARRAY_SIZE2];
    for (i=0,tempChar='A';
         i < ARRAY_SIZE2-1;
         i++)
    {
       charArray[i]=tempChar++;
    }
    charArray[ARRAY_SIZE2-1]='\0';

    cout << charArray << endl;

    delete [] charArray;
    return (0);
}
```

Results

```
zyxwvutsrqponmlkjihgfedcba`_^]\[ZYXWVUT
ABCDEFGHIJKLMNOPQRSTUVWXYZ[\]^_`abcdefghijklmnopqrstuvwxyz{
```

Analysis

The sample program in Hands On 22.2 declares a character pointer and some constants that it needs. It uses the `new` statement to allocate memory for an array of characters.

Whenever you dynamically allocate an array in a C++ program, you put the data type after the `new` statement. This must be followed by the number of elements in the array. If you want to, you can put a variable in the square brackets. C++ gives your program the ability to calculate the amount of memory it needs as it runs. It can then allocate exactly that amount of memory.

After the program in Hands On 22.2 allocates memory for an array, it enters a `for` loop to fill the array with characters. It then appends a null character at the end of the array and prints the string.

TIP: Whenever you delete an array, put the square brackets between the keyword `delete` and the array name.

The program uses the `delete` statement to free the memory it allocated dynamically. It uses the same character pointer to allocate a larger array. As before, it fills the array with characters and prints the contents of the array.

At the end of the program, the program deletes the memory it allocated. When you delete a dynamically allocated array, you must put the array subscript operator between the `delete` statement and the array name. This tells the `delete` operator to deallocate an array and not just one array element.

Allocating and Deallocating Multidimensional Arrays

In addition to dynamically allocating single-dimensional arrays, your program can allocate arrays that have two or more dimensions.

Recall that a one-dimensional array name is a pointer to the first element in the array. For 2-D arrays, the array name is a pointer to a group of pointers. Each of the pointers in the group points to the first element of one row in the 2-D array. To dynamically allocate a 2-D array, we need to declare a pointer to pointers. Hands On 22.3 demonstrates this technique.

Hands On 22.3

Objective

Write a program that dynamically allocates a 2-D array.

Experiment

Type the following program into your IDE or text editor. Compile, link, and run it.

```
#include <iostream.h>

int main()
{
   const int TOTAL_ROWS = 10;
   const int COLS_PER_ROW = 20;

   int **a2DArray;
   int i,j;

   a2DArray = new int * [TOTAL_ROWS];

   for (i=0;i<TOTAL_ROWS;i++)
   {
      a2DArray[i] = new int [COLS_PER_ROW];
   }

   for (i=0;i<TOTAL_ROWS;i++)
   {
      for (j=0;j<COLS_PER_ROW;j++)
      {
         a2DArray[i][j] = i*j;
      }
   }

   for (i=0;i<TOTAL_ROWS;i++)
   {
      for (j=0;j<COLS_PER_ROW;j++)
      {
         cout << a2DArray[i][j] << ' ';
      }
      cout << endl;
   }

   for (i=0;i<TOTAL_ROWS;i++)
   {
      delete [] a2DArray[i];
   }
   delete [] a2DArray;

   return (0);
}
```

Results

```
0 0 0 0 0 0 0 0 0 0 0 0 0 0 0 0 0 0 0 0
0 1 2 3 4 5 6 7 8 9 10 11 12 13 14 15 16 17 18 19
```

```
0 2 4 6 8 10 12 14 16 18 20 22 24 26 28 30 32 34 36 38
0 3 6 9 12 15 18 21 24 27 30 33 36 39 42 45 48 51 54 57
0 4 8 12 16 20 24 28 32 36 40 44 48 52 56 60 64 68 72 76
0 5 10 15 20 25 30 35 40 45 50 55 60 65 70 75 80 85 90 95
0 6 12 18 24 30 36 42 48 54 60 66 72 78 84 90 96 102 108 114
0 7 14 21 28 35 42 49 56 63 70 77 84 91 98 105 112 119 126 133
0 8 16 24 32 40 48 56 64 72 80 88 96 104 112 120 128 136 144 152
0 9 18 27 36 45 54 63 72 81 90 99 108 117 126 135 144 153 162 171
```

Analysis

By declaring a pointer to a pointer to integers, this program creates a variable that it can use as a 2-D array. It first allocates an array of pointers to integers. Each of the integer pointers in the array will point at one row of integers. The program uses a `for` loop to allocate each row of integers. After the rows are allocated, the program can treat the variable the same as it would treat a statically allocated 2-D array.

This technique for allocating 2-D arrays may not work in some instances. For example, you could allocate the array of pointers in one function, then pass that to another function. If you then allocate each row in the second function, you may find that you get memory errors.

REMINDER: Contiguous memory is memory that is all together in an uninterrupted block.

You can also allocate the array of pointers, and then allocate some memory that is not used for the array. You could then allocate a few rows, and then allocate more memory that is not used for the array. The result could cause your program to access the array incorrectly.

TRAP: If your allocation isn't in contiguous memory, this technique for allocating 2-D arrays may not work.

The problem is that statically allocated 2-D arrays are laid out in contiguous memory. That's the way C++ programs generally expect to find them. If you do allocations that cause your array to not be contiguous in memory, it may not work correctly.

TIP: When allocating multidimensional arrays, allocate contiguous memory for all dimensions.

Allocating and Deallocating Objects

C++ programs dynamically allocate objects exactly the same way they allocate the built-in data types. When an object is allocated, the program automatically calls its constructor. The destructor is called when the object is deallocated.

Example 22.1 shows a program that allocates and deallocates an object. It stores the address of the allocated object in a pointer. All calls to the object's member functions must be made through the pointer.

EXAMPLE 22.1 Allocating an Object

```
class an_object
{
public:
   an_object(void);
   ~an_object();

   void ThisFunction(void);
   int ThatFunction(int aParameter);

private:
   int privateData;
};

/* The implementation of the member functions is omitted
for brevity. */
```

```
int main()
{
   an_object *theObject = new an_object;

   theObject->ThisFunction();
   int theAnswer = theObject->ThatFunction(42);
   cout << theAnswer;

   return (0);
}
```

TIP: Always call base constructors in derived constructors.

If an object inherits from another object, the constructors of both the derived and the base object must be called before the object is valid. There are some instances where the compiler automatically inserts calls to the base constructor for us. However, it is good practice to explicitly call the base constructor.

Hands On 22.4 shows allocation and deallocation for a derived class.

Hands On 22.4

Objective

Write a program that defines a derived class that inherits from a derived class. The program must allocate an object of the derived class, use it, and deallocate it.

Experiment

Type the following program into your IDE or text editor. Compile, link, and run it.

```
#include <iostream.h>

class base_object
{
public:
   base_object(int data=0);
   ~base_object();

   void SetIntData(int data);
   int GetIntData(void);

private:
   int intData;
 };


base_object::base_object(int data)
{
   cout << "Called base_object::base_object" << endl;
   intData = data;
}

base_object::~base_object()
{
   cout << "Called base_object::~base_object" << endl;
}

void base_object::SetIntData(int data)
{
```

```
   cout << "Called base_object::SetIntData" << endl;
   intData = data;
}

int base_object::GetIntData(void)
{
   return (intData);
}

class derived_object : public base_object
{
public:
   derived_object(int data=0,float moreData=0.0);
   ~derived_object();

   void SetData(int data,float moreData);
   float GetFloatData(void);

private:
   float floatData;
 };


derived_object::derived_object(
                    int data,
                    float moreData) : base_object(data)
{
   cout << "Called derived_object::derived_object" << endl;
   floatData = moreData;
}


derived_object::~derived_object()
{
   cout << "Called derived_object::~derived_object" << endl;
}


void derived_object::SetData(int data,float moreData)
{
   cout << "Called derived_object::SetData" << endl;
   SetIntData(data);
   floatData = moreData;
}


float derived_object::GetFloatData(void)
{
   return (floatData);
}


int main()
{
   derived_object *derivedObject;

   derivedObject = new derived_object;
```

```
    cout << derivedObject->GetIntData() << endl;
    cout << derivedObject->GetFloatData() << endl;

    derivedObject->SetIntData(5);
    derivedObject->SetData(10,3.14159);

    cout << derivedObject->GetIntData() << endl;
    cout << derivedObject->GetFloatData() << endl;

    delete derivedObject;

    return (0);
}
```

Results

```
Called base_object::base_object
Called derived_object::derived_object
0
0
Called base_object::SetIntData
Called derived_object::SetData
Called base_object::SetIntData
10
3.14159
Called derived_object::~derived_object
Called base_object::~base_object
```

Analysis

The `main()` function of this program declares a pointer to a `derived_object`. Objects of type `derived_object` inherit from the `base_object` class. As the `main()` function demonstrates, all of the public functions of the `base_object` class are available through the `derived_object` variable.

The program allocates a `derived_object` and stores the address of the new object in the pointer variable. Each function in the program prints its name when it is called. The Results section of Hands On 22.4 demonstrates that the program calls the constructor for the `base_object` class whenever it calls the constructor for the `derived_object`. The program explicitly specifies the call at the beginning of the `derived_object` constructor. The statement

```
derived_object::derived_object(
                     int data,
                     float moreData) : base_object(data)
```

calls the `base_object` constructor before the body of the `derived_object` constructor is executed.

Developers of derived classes should make every effort to ensure that the constructors of base classes get called before they execute statements in the derived class constructors. The derived object will probably depend on the base object being in a known state. Explicit calls to the base object's constructor ensure that's the case.

After the program allocates a `derived_object`, it prints the current state of the object. The program sets the object's data, and then prints the values the object contains. We can see from the Results section of Hands On 22.4 that the program deletes the `derived_object` when it finishes. Calling the destructor for the `derived_object` automatically calls the `base_object` destructor as well.

Dynamic Allocation in the Text Editor

Prior versions of the text editor all statically allocated memory to hold the characters. The editor created a `text_buffer` object. The `text_buffer` object in turn created an array of `text_string` objects. Each `text_string` object contained 80 characters.

With dynamic memory allocation, we can modify the `text_string` class so that it does not actually allocate space for characters until an attempt is made to store them. The text editor then requires only the memory it actually uses. Hands On 22.5 shows how dynamic allocation can be used in the text editor.

Hands On 22.5

Objective

Write a version of the text editor that uses dynamic allocation. Each `text_string` object in the text buffer should only allocate memory when the program stores characters in the string.

Experiment

Type the following program into your IDE or text editor. Compile, link, and run it. This program consists of five files: *TEdit.cpp*, *TString.h*, *TString.cpp*, *TBuffer.h*, and *TBuffer.cpp*.

This is the file `TEdit.cpp`.

```
//-------------------------------------------------------------------------
/*
File Name:  TEdit.cpp
Comments:   This is the main file of the text editor.
*/
//-------------------------------------------------------------------------


//-------------------------------------------------------------------------
// Include Files

#include "TString.h"
#include "TBuffer.h"
#include <stdlib.h>
#include <ctype.h>

// End Include Files
//-------------------------------------------------------------------------


//-------------------------------------------------------------------------
// Prototypes

void ClearScreen(void);
void DisplayMenu(void);

// End Prototypes
//-------------------------------------------------------------------------


int main()
{
  const int TOTAL_TEXT_AREA_LINES = 20;
```

```
const char SCROLL_UP_COMMAND = (char)21;     // Ctrl+U
const char SCROLL_DOWN_COMMAND = (char)4;    // Ctrl+D
const char SAVE_COMMAND = (char)1;           // Ctrl+A
const char LOAD_COMMAND = (char)12;          // Ctrl+L
const char EDIT_COMMAND = (char)5;           // Ctrl+E
const char QUIT_COMMAND = (char)17;          // Ctrl+Q
const char BEEP_CHARACTER = (char)7;

text_buffer textBuffer;  // Uses static because it's large.
bool done=false;
int i,top;
text_string inputText;

// While the user doesn't want to quit...
while (!done)
{
   // Clear the screen.
   ClearScreen();
   text_string outputString;

   // Display one screenful of text.
   for (i=0,top=textBuffer.TopLine();
        (i<TOTAL_TEXT_AREA_LINES) && (top+i<TEXT_BUFFER_LENGTH);
        i++)
   {
      cout << (top+i) << ": ";
      outputString = textBuffer[top+i];
      cout << outputString;
      cout << endl;
   }

   // Display the menu.
   DisplayMenu();

   // Get input from the user.
   char inputString[MAX_INPUT_STRING_LENGTH];
   cin.getline(inputString,MAX_INPUT_STRING_LENGTH);
   inputText = inputString;

   text_string fileName;

   switch (inputText[0])
   {
      // If the user wants to scroll up one screenful...
      case SCROLL_UP_COMMAND:
         // Scroll up.
         textBuffer.ScrollUp(TOTAL_TEXT_AREA_LINES-1);
      break;

      // If the user wants to scroll down one screenful...
      case SCROLL_DOWN_COMMAND:
         // Scroll down.
         textBuffer.ScrollDown(TOTAL_TEXT_AREA_LINES-1);
      break;

      // If the user wants to save the buffer to a file...
      case SAVE_COMMAND:
         // Save to file.
         cout << "Enter File Name: ";
```

```
      cin.getline(inputString,MAX_INPUT_STRING_LENGTH);
      fileName = inputString;
      if (textBuffer.Save(fileName)!=NO_BUFFER_ERROR)
      {
         cout << BEEP_CHARACTER;
      }
   break;

   // If the user wants to load from a file...
   case LOAD_COMMAND:
      // Load from file.
      cout << "Enter File Name: ";
      cin.getline(inputString,MAX_INPUT_STRING_LENGTH);
      fileName = inputString;
      if (textBuffer.Load(fileName)!=NO_BUFFER_ERROR)
      {
         cout << BEEP_CHARACTER;
      }
   break;

   // If the user wants to edit text...
   case EDIT_COMMAND:
   {
      cout << "Enter Line Number: ";
      cin >> inputString;

      bool inputError = false;
      for (i=0;(inputString[i]) && (!inputError);i++)
      {
         if (!isdigit(inputString[i]))
         {
            inputError=true;
         }
      }

      if (cin.peek()=='\n')
      {
         cin.ignore(1,'\n');
      }

      if (inputError)
      {
         cout << BEEP_CHARACTER;
      }
      else
      {
         // Convert the line number to a number.
         int lineNumber=atoi(inputString);

         // If the line number is displayed on the screen...
         if ((lineNumber >= top) &&
             (lineNumber < top+TOTAL_TEXT_AREA_LINES))
         {
            // Prompt the user for input.
            cout << lineNumber << ": ";

            // Get the new line of text.
            cin.getline(inputString,MAX_INPUT_STRING_LENGTH);
```

```
                    // Insert the new line of text into the buffer.
                    textBuffer[lineNumber] = inputString;
                }
            }
        }
        break;

        // If the user wants to quit...
        case QUIT_COMMAND:
            done=true;
        break;

        // Else the input is not recognized...
        default:
            // Beep the speaker.
            cout << BEEP_CHARACTER;
        break;
    }
  }
  return (0);
}



//-----------------------------------------------------------------------------
/*
Function Name:       ClearScreen
Member of:           N/A
Input Parameters:    None.
Output Parameters:   None.
Return Value:        None.
Comments:            A function that clears any screen that is 24 lines of text
                     or less. If your screen displays more than 24 lines,
                     change SCREEN_SIZE to one more than the number of lines it
                     displays.
*/

void ClearScreen(void)
{
   const int SCREEN_SIZE = 25;
   for (int i=0;i<SCREEN_SIZE;i++)
   {
      cout << endl;
   }
}

// End ClearScreen
//-----------------------------------------------------------------------------




//-----------------------------------------------------------------------------
/*
Function Name:      DisplayMenu
Member of:          N/A
Input Parameters:   None.
Output Parameters:  None.
```

```
Return Value:       None.
Comments:           Displays a menu for the text editor.
*/

void DisplayMenu(void)
{
   cout << "To enter a command, press one of the following, ";
   cout << "then press Enter" << endl;
   cout << "Edit text: Ctrl+E  ";
   cout << "Scroll Up: Ctrl+U  ";
   cout << "Scroll Down: Ctrl+D"  << endl;
   cout << "Load File: Ctrl+L  ";
   cout << "Save File: Ctrl+A  ";
   cout << "Quit: Ctrl+Q";
   cout << "    Command :";
}

// End DisplayMenu
//-----------------------------------------------------------------------------


// End TEdit.cpp
//-----------------------------------------------------------------------------
```

This is the file `TString.h`

```
//-----------------------------------------------------------------------------
/*
File Name:  TString.h
Comments:   This file contains the constants and class definition needed to
            use the text_string class.
*/
//-----------------------------------------------------------------------------


#if !defined(TSTRING_H)
#define TSTRING_H

//-----------------------------------------------------------------------------
// Include Files

#include <iostream.h>

// End Include Files
//-----------------------------------------------------------------------------



//-----------------------------------------------------------------------------
// Constants

const int MAX_INPUT_STRING_LENGTH = 256;

// End Constants
//-----------------------------------------------------------------------------



//-----------------------------------------------------------------------------
// Class Definitions
```

```
class text_string
{
// Public member functions.
public:
   text_string(void);
   text_string(const char * const charArray);
   text_string(const text_string &sourceString);
   ~text_string();

   text_string &operator = (const text_string &textString);
   text_string &operator = (const char * const charArray);

   text_string operator + (const text_string &textString);
   text_string operator + (const char * const charArray);

   text_string &operator += (const text_string &textString);
   text_string &operator += (const char * const charArray);
   text_string &operator += (const char oneChar);

   char &operator [](const int index);

   friend istream &operator >> (istream &inputStream,
                                text_string &destinationString);
   friend ostream &operator << (ostream &outputStream,
                                const text_string &sourceString);

   const char *CppString(void);

   int Length(void);

// Private member functions.
private:
   void Allocate(const int totalChars);
   text_string &Copy(const text_string &sourceString);
   text_string &Copy(const char * const charArray);

// Private member data.
private:
   char *charString;
};

// End Class Definitions
//-----------------------------------------------------------------------

#endif

// End TString.h
//-----------------------------------------------------------------------
```

This is the file `TString.cpp`*.*

```
//-----------------------------------------------------------------------
/*
File Name:  TString.cpp
Comments:   This file contains the implementation of the text_string class.
*/
//-----------------------------------------------------------------------
```

```
//------------------------------------------------------------------------
// Include Files

#include "TString.h"
#include "string.h"
#include <assert.h>

// End Include Files
//------------------------------------------------------------------------



//------------------------------------------------------------------------
/*
Function Name:       text_string
Member of:           text_string
Input Parameters:    None.
Output Parameters:   None.
Return Value:        Constructed text_string object.
Comments:            No-arg constructor. Sets the object to a known state.
*/

text_string::text_string(void)
{
   charString = NULL;
}

// End text_string
//------------------------------------------------------------------------



//------------------------------------------------------------------------
/*
Function Name:       text_string
Member of:           text_string
Input Parameters:    charArray - A pointer to characters. These chars are
                        copied into the object.
Output Parameters:   None.
Return Value:        Constructed text_string object.
Comments:            One-arg constructor. Allocates the memory for the
                     character string. It then calls the private member
                     function Copy() to copy the characters from charArray
                     into the private member data array charString.
*/

text_string::text_string(const char * const charArray)
{
   // Allocate the memory for the characters.
   Allocate(strlen(charArray));
   Copy(charArray);
}

// End text_string
//------------------------------------------------------------------------



//------------------------------------------------------------------------/*
Function Name:       text_string
```

```
Member of:            text_string
Input Parameters:     sourceString - A text_string that will be copied into
                         the object.
Output Parameters:    None.
Return Value:         Constructed text_string object.
Comments:             Copy constructor.
*/

text_string::text_string(const text_string &sourceString)
{
   Allocate(sourceString.Length());
   Copy(sourceString);
}

// End text_string
//-----------------------------------------------------------------------------



//-----------------------------------------------------------------------------
/*
Function Name:        text_string
Member of:            ~text_string
Input Parameters:     None.
Output Parameters:    None.
Return Value:         None.
Comments:             Deletes the character array in this object. Sets the
                      private data member charString to NULL just to be safe.
*/

text_string::~text_string()
{
   if (charString)
   {
      delete [] charString;
   }

   charString = NULL;
}

// End ~text_string
//-----------------------------------------------------------------------------



//-----------------------------------------------------------------------------
/*
Function Name:        operator =
Member of:            text_string
Input Parameters:     textString - The object the characters will be copied
                         from.
Output Parameters:    None.
Return Value:         Returns a reference to *this.
Comments:             This function copies characters from a text_string
                      object into the current text_string object. It calls
                      the private member function Copy() to perform the
                      copy.
*/

text_string &text_string::operator = (const text_string &textString)
```

```
{
   assert(&textString != this);

   if (charString!=NULL)
   {
      delete [] charString;
   }

   Allocate(textString.Length());
   Copy(textString);
   return (*this);
}

// End operator =
//-----------------------------------------------------------------------------



//-----------------------------------------------------------------------------
/*
Function Name:       operator =
Member of:           text_string
Input Parameters:    charArray - The array from which the characters will be
                        copied.
Output Parameters:   None.
Return Value:        Returns a reference to *this.
Comments:            This function copies characters from a character array
                     into the current text_string object. It calls the private
                     member function Copy() to perform the copy.
*/

text_string &text_string::operator = (const char * const charArray)
{
   if (charString!=NULL)
   {
      delete [] charString;
   }

   Allocate(strlen(charArray));
   Copy(charArray);
   return (*this);
}

// End operator =
//-----------------------------------------------------------------------------




//-----------------------------------------------------------------------------
/*
Function Name:       operator +
Member of:           text_string
Input Parameters:    textString - The object containing characters to
                        concatenate onto the end of the current object.
Output Parameters:   None.
Return Value:        Returns the concatenated text_string object.
Comments:            This function concatenates the string in the textString
                     parameter onto the end of the current text_string. This
                     function does not change the textString object or the
                     current object.
*/
```

```
text_string text_string::operator + (const text_string &textString)
{
   text_string tempString;
   int i,j;
   int leftStringLength,rightStringLength;

   leftStringLength = Length();
   rightStringLength = textString.Length();

   tempString.Allocate(leftStringLength+rightStringLength);
   tempString.Copy(charString);

   for (i=tempString.Length(),j=0;
        (i<leftStringLength+rightStringLength) && (textString.charString[j]);
        i++,j++)
   {
      tempString.charString[i]=textString.charString[j];
   }
   charString[i] = '\0';

   return (tempString);
}

// End operator +
//-----------------------------------------------------------------------------



//-----------------------------------------------------------------------------
/*
Function Name:       operator +
Member of:           text_string
Input Parameters:    charArray - The array containing characters to
                        concatenate onto the end of the current object.
Output Parameters:   None.
Return Value:        Returns the concatenated text_string object.
Comments:            This function concatenates the string in the array
                     charArray onto the end of the current text_string. This
                     function does not change the character array or the
                     current object.
*/


text_string text_string::operator + (const char * const charArray)
{
   return (*this+text_string(charArray));
}

// End operator +
//-----------------------------------------------------------------------------



//-----------------------------------------------------------------------------
/*
Function Name:       operator +=
Member of:           text_string
Input Parameters:    textString - A text_string object containing characters
                        to append onto the end of the current object.
```

```
Output Parameters:   None.
Return Value:        Returns a reference to *this.
Comments:            This function appends characters onto the end of a
                     text_string object. It uses the text_string::operator +()
                     function to do most of its work. This function modifies
                     the current object (*this).
*/

text_string &text_string::operator += (const text_string &textString)
{
   assert(&textString != this);
   *this = *this + textString;
   return (*this);
}

// End operator +=
//-----------------------------------------------------------------------------



//-----------------------------------------------------------------------------
/*
Function Name:       operator +=
Member of:           text_string
Input Parameters:    charArray - An array of characters that this function
                        will append onto the end of the current object.
Output Parameters:   None.
Return Value:        Returns a reference to *this.
Comments:            This function appends characters onto the end of a
                     text_string object. It uses the text_string::operator +()
                     function to do most of its work. This function modifies
                     the current object (*this).
*/

text_string &text_string::operator += (const char * const charArray)
{
   *this = *this + charArray;
   return (*this);
}

// End operator +=
//-----------------------------------------------------------------------------



//-----------------------------------------------------------------------------
/*
Function Name:       operator +=
Member of:           text_string
Input Parameters:    oneChar - An character that this function will append
                        onto the end of the current object.
Output Parameters:   None.
Return Value:        Returns a reference to *this.
Comments:            This function appends a single character onto the end
                     of a text_string object. This function modifies
                     the current object (*this).
*/

text_string &text_string::operator += (const char oneChar)
```

```
{
   int length = Length();

   char *tempString = charString;   // Save the current chars.
   Allocate(length);   // Allocate a new array of characters.
   Copy(tempString);   // Copy the chars into the new array.

   // Append the new character.
   tempString[length]=oneChar;
   tempString[length+1]='\0';

   // Delete the old array.
   delete tempString;

   return (*this);
}

// End operator +=
//---------------------------------------------------------------------------



//---------------------------------------------------------------------------
/*
Function Name:        operator []
Member of:            text_string
Input Parameters:     index - The index number of the character to set.
                         Numbering starts with zero.
Output Parameters:    None.
Return Value:         If the index is in range, this function returns a
                      reference to the requested character.
Comments:             The intent of this function is to enable developers to
                      get and set individual characters in a text_string
                      object.
                      It provides bounds checking on the index value. If the
                      developer tries to access a character that is out of
                      bounds, this function uses the assert() macro to abort
                      the program.
*/

char &text_string::operator [](const int index)
{
   assert((index >= 0) && (index<Length()));
   return charString[index];
}

// End operator [
//---------------------------------------------------------------------------



//---------------------------------------------------------------------------
/*
Function Name:        operator >>
Member of:            None. Friend of text_string.
Input Parameters:     inputStream - The stream from which the input will be
                         read.
Output Parameters:    destinationString - The string that will contain the
                         input when this function completes.
```

```
Return Value:        Returns a reference to the input stream.
Comments:            This friend function overloads the extraction operator
                     for the text_string class.
*/

istream &operator >> (istream &inputStream,
                      text_string &destinationString)
{
   char tempString[MAX_INPUT_STRING_LENGTH];

   // Read the string into a temp variable.
   inputStream >> tempString;

   // If the object's char array is not empty...
   if (destinationString.charString)
   {
      // Delete it.
      delete destinationString.charString;
   }

   // Allocate space for the input string.
   destinationString.Allocate(strlen(tempString));

   // Copy the input string into the object's char array.
   destinationString.Copy(tempString);

   return (inputStream);
}

// End operator >>
//-----------------------------------------------------------------------------



//-----------------------------------------------------------------------------
/*
Function Name:       operator <<
Member of:           None. Friend of text_string.
Input Parameters:    sourceString - The string from which characters will be
                        read.
Output Parameters:   outputStream - The stream to which output will be
                        written.
Return Value:        A reference to the output stream.
Comments:            This function overloads the insertion operator for the
                     text_string class.
*/

ostream &operator << (ostream &outputStream,
                      const text_string &sourceString)
{
   if (sourceString.Length() > 0)
   {
      outputStream << sourceString.charString;
   }

   return (outputStream);
}
// End operator <<
//-----------------------------------------------------------------------------
```

```
//-----------------------------------------------------------------------------
/*
Function Name:      CppString
Member of:          text_string
Input Parameters:   None.
Output Parameters:  None.
Return Value:       Returns a constant reference to the character array that
                    this text_string object contains.
Comments:           See Return Value section.
*/

const char *text_string::CppString(void)
{
   return (charString);
}

// End CppString
//-----------------------------------------------------------------------------



//-----------------------------------------------------------------------------
/*
Function Name:      Length
Member of:          text_string
Input Parameters:   None.
Output Parameters:  None.
Return Value:       Returns the length of the string. This is the same as the
                    number of printable characters (excluding the null
                    character).
Comments:           See Return Value section.
*/

int text_string::Length(void)
{
   int length=0;

   if (charString)
   {
      for (length=0;charString[length];length++)
      {
         // Empty loop body. The stuff in the () does the counting.
      }
   }

   return (length);
}

// End Length
//-----------------------------------------------------------------------------



//-----------------------------------------------------------------------------
/*
Function Name:      Allocate
Member of:          text_string
Input Parameters:   totalChars - An integer number of printable characters to
                       allocate space for.
```

```
Output Parameters:   None.
Return Value:        None.
Comments:            To accommodate the null character at the end of a string,
                     this function allocates totalChars+1. It also initializes
                     the memory it allocates to null characters.
*/

void text_string::Allocate(const int totalChars)
{
   if (totalChars>0)
   {
      charString = new char [totalChars+1];
      for (int i=0;i<totalChars+1;i++)
      {
         charString[i]='\0';
      }
   }
   else
   {
      charString = NULL;
   }
}

// End Allocate
//------------------------------------------------------------------------------



//------------------------------------------------------------------------------
/*
Function Name:       Copy
Member of:           text_string
Input Parameters:    sourceString - The string from which the characters will
                        be copied.
Output Parameters:   None.
Return Value:        Returns a reference to the current object (*this).
Comments:            This private member function copies characters from a
                     text_string object into the current object.
*/

text_string &text_string::Copy(const text_string &sourceString)
{
   if (sourceString.charString)
   {
      int i;

      for (i=0;sourceString.charString[i];i++)
      {
         charString[i] = sourceString.charString[i];
      }
      charString[i] = '\0';
   }
   else
   {
      if (charString)
      {
         delete [] charString;
      }
```

```
      charString=NULL;
   }

   return (*this);
}
// End Copy
//-----------------------------------------------------------------------------


//-----------------------------------------------------------------------------
/*
Function Name:       Copy
Member of:           text_string
Input Parameters:    charArray - The character array from which the characters
                        will be copied.
Output Parameters:   None.
Return Value:        Returns a reference to the current object (*this).
Comments:            This private member function copies characters from a
                     character array into the current object.
*/

text_string &text_string::Copy(const char * const charArray)
{
   int i;

   if (charArray)
   {
      for (i=0;charArray[i];i++)
      {
         charString[i] = charArray[i];
      }
      charString[i] = '\0';
   }
   else
   {
      if (charString)
      {
         delete [] charString;
      }

      charString=NULL;
   }

   return (*this);
}

// End Copy
//-----------------------------------------------------------------------------

// End TString.cpp
//-----------------------------------------------------------------------------
```

This is the file `TBuffer.h`.

```
//-----------------------------------------------------------------------------
/*
File Name:   TBuffer.h
Comments:    This file contains the definition of the text_buffer class. It
             also defines the constants needed to use the text_buffer class.
```

```
*/
//---------------------------------------------------------------------------


#if !defined (TBUFFER_H)
#define TBUFFER_H

//---------------------------------------------------------------------------
// Constants

const int TEXT_BUFFER_LENGTH = 100;

// Buffer error status values.
const int NO_BUFFER_ERROR = 0;
const int CANT_LOAD_FILE = -1;
const int CANT_SAVE_FILE = -2;

// End Constants
//---------------------------------------------------------------------------



//---------------------------------------------------------------------------
// Class Definitions

class text_buffer
{
public:
   text_buffer(void);

   text_string &operator [](const int index);

   int TopLine(void);

   int ScrollUp(const int linesToScroll);
   int ScrollDown(const int linesToScroll);

   int Load(const text_string &fileName);
   int Save(const text_string &fileName);

private:
   text_string textBuffer[TEXT_BUFFER_LENGTH];
   int topLine;
   int linesUsed;
};

// End Class Definitions
//---------------------------------------------------------------------------

#endif

// End TBuffer.h
//---------------------------------------------------------------------------
```

This is the file `TBuffer.cpp`*.*

```
//---------------------------------------------------------------------------
/*
```

```
File Name:  TBuffer.cpp
Comments:   This file contains the implementation of the member functions for
            the text_buffer class.
*/
//--------------------------------------------------------------------------




//--------------------------------------------------------------------------
// Include Files

#include <fstream.h>
#include "TString.h"
#include "TBuffer.h"
#include <assert.h>

// End Include Files
//--------------------------------------------------------------------------




//--------------------------------------------------------------------------
/*
Function Name:       text_buffer
Member of:           text_buffer
Input Parameters:    None.
Output Parameters:   None.
Return Value:        Initialized text_buffer object.
Comments:            This function is the default constructor for the
                     text_buffer class.
*/

text_buffer::text_buffer(void)
{
   topLine=0;
   linesUsed=0;
}

// End text_buffer
//--------------------------------------------------------------------------




//--------------------------------------------------------------------------
/*
Function Name:       operator []
Member of:           text_buffer
Input Parameters:    index - The line number of the line being accessed.
Output Parameters:   None.
Return Value:        If index is valid, this function returns a reference to
                     the specified line. If not, it returns a reference to the
                     last line used.
Comments:            This function enables you to get or set a line of text in
                     the buffer. It does this by returning a reference to the
                     specified line.
*/

text_string &text_buffer::operator [](int index)
```

```
{
   assert((index>=0) && (index<TEXT_BUFFER_LENGTH));

   text_string line;

   if (index>linesUsed)
   {
      linesUsed = index+1;
   }
   return textBuffer[index];
}

// End operator []
//------------------------------------------------------------------------------


//------------------------------------------------------------------------------
/*
Function Name:       TopLine
Member of:           text_buffer
Input Parameters:    None.
Output Parameters:   None.
Return Value:        The top line of the buffer
Comments:            See Return Value section.
*/

int text_buffer::TopLine(void)
{
   return (topLine);
}

// End TopLine
//------------------------------------------------------------------------------



//------------------------------------------------------------------------------
/*
Function Name:       ScrollUp
Member of:           text_buffer
Input Parameters:    linesToScroll - Integer number of lines to scroll toward
                        the beginning of the text buffer.
Output Parameters:   None.
Return Value:        Returns the number of lines actually scrolled.
Comments:            This function moves the current top line of the buffer
                     that is displayed on the screen toward the beginning of
                     the buffer. It prevents the top line from being moved
                     before the beginning of the buffer.

                     If, for instance, the current top line is 5, and the
                     input parameter specifies that the function should
                     scroll the buffer up 20 lines, it will only scroll 5
                     lines to the beginning of the buffer. The return value
                     reports the number of lines the function actually
                     scrolls.
*/

int text_buffer::ScrollUp(const int linesToScroll)
{
```

```
   int linesScrolled;

   // If the top line is less than the number of lines to scroll...
   if (topLine <= linesToScroll)
   {
      /* The first screenful of the buffer is currently displayed.
      Display the buffer from the beginning. */
      linesScrolled = topLine;
      topLine=0;
   }
   // Else scroll the screen toward the beginning of the buffer.
   else
   {
      topLine -= linesToScroll;
      linesScrolled = linesToScroll;
   }
   return (linesScrolled);
}

// End ScrollUp
//-----------------------------------------------------------------------------



//-----------------------------------------------------------------------------
/*
Function Name:       ScrollDown
Member of:           text_buffer
Input Parameters:    linesToScroll
Output Parameters:   None.
Return Value:        Returns the number of lines actually scrolled.
Comments:            This function moves the current top line of the buffer
                     that is displayed on the screen toward the end of
                     the buffer. It prevents the top line from being moved
                     after the end of the buffer.

                     Suppose, for instance, that the buffer is 100 lines of
                     text in length. If current top line is 95, and the
                     input parameter specifies that the function should
                     scroll the buffer down 20 lines, it will only scroll 5
                     lines toward the end of the buffer. The return value
                     reports the number of lines the function actually
                     scrolls.
*/

int text_buffer::ScrollDown(const int linesToScroll)
{
   int linesScrolled;
   int newTopLine = topLine+linesToScroll;

   // If the last few lines of the buffer are currently displayed...
   if (newTopLine >= TEXT_BUFFER_LENGTH-linesToScroll)
   {
      // Set the top line to display the last few lines of the buffer.
      topLine = TEXT_BUFFER_LENGTH-linesToScroll;
      linesScrolled = newTopLine-topLine;
   }
   // Else the end of the buffer is not currently displayed...
   else
```

```
   {
      // Scroll down the requested number of lines.
      topLine = newTopLine;
      linesScrolled = linesToScroll;
   }
   return (linesScrolled);
}

// End ScrollDown
//-----------------------------------------------------------------------------



//-----------------------------------------------------------------------------
/*
Function Name:         Load
Member of:             text_buffer
Input Parameters:      fileName - Name of the file to load.
Output Parameters:     None.
Return Value:          If the file is loaded successfully, this function
                       returns NO_BUFFER_ERROR. If not, it returns
                       CANT_LOAD_FILE.
Comments:              This function loads the specified file into the
                       text buffer. Any file error will generate a
                       CANT_LOAD_FILE error. A text_buffer object for a
                       professional application would need to provide more
                       specific feedback to the function that calls this
                       routine.
*/

int text_buffer::Load(const text_string &fileName)
{
   int errorStatus = NO_BUFFER_ERROR;

   // If the file name string is not empty...
   if (fileName.Length() > 0)
   {
      char tempString[MAX_INPUT_STRING_LENGTH];

      // Open the file.
      ifstream inputStream(fileName.CppString());

      // If the file could be opened...
      if (inputStream)
      {
         // Read in each line of text.
         int i;
         for (i=0;
              (i<TEXT_BUFFER_LENGTH) && (!inputStream.eof());
              i++)
         {
            /* If the line of text in the file is longer than
            MAX_TEXT_STRING_LENGTH, it is truncated. */
            inputStream.getline(tempString,MAX_INPUT_STRING_LENGTH,'\n');
            textBuffer[i] = tempString;
         }
         linesUsed = i;
      }
      // Else the file could not be opened...
```

```
        else
        {
            errorStatus = CANT_LOAD_FILE;
        }
    }
    // Else the file name string was empty...
    else
    {
        errorStatus = CANT_LOAD_FILE;
    }
    return (errorStatus);
}

// End Load
//----------------------------------------------------------------------------



//----------------------------------------------------------------------------
/*
Function Name:       Save
Member of:           text_buffer
Input Parameters:    fileName - The name of the file to save.
Output Parameters:   None.
Return Value:        This function returns NO_BUFFER_ERROR if it successfully
                     saves the specified file. If there is any kind of file
                     error, it returns CANT_SAVE_FILE.
Comments:            This function saves the text buffer into the
                     specified file. Any file error will generate a
                     CANT_SAVE_FILE error. A text_buffer object for a
                     professional application would need to provide more
                     specific feedback to the function that calls this
                     routine.
*/
int text_buffer::Save(const text_string &fileName)
{
    int errorStatus=NO_BUFFER_ERROR;

    // If the file name string is not empty...
    if (fileName.Length() > 0)
    {
        // Open the file.
        ofstream outputStream(fileName.CppString());

        // If the file could be opened...
        if (outputStream)
        {
            // Write each line of the buffer to the file.
            for (int i=0;
                 (i<linesUsed) && (outputStream.good());
                 i++)
            {
                outputStream << textBuffer[i] << endl;
            }
        }
        // Else the file could not be opened...
        else
        {
            errorStatus = CANT_SAVE_FILE;
```

```
        }
    }
    // Else the file name string is empty...
    else
    {
        errorStatus = CANT_SAVE_FILE;
    }
    return (errorStatus);
}

// End Save
//-----------------------------------------------------------------------



// End TBuffer.cpp
//-----------------------------------------------------------------------
```

Results

The output of this program is shown in Figure 22.1.

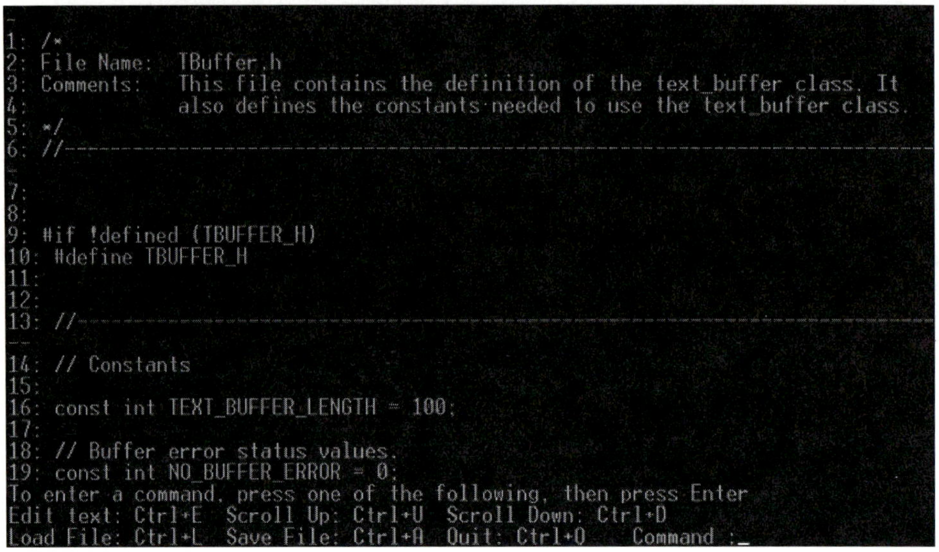

FIGURE 22.1 Output of the Text Editor Program

Analysis

Hands On examples in previous chapters demonstrated that we can change the implementation of the `text_string` class significantly without making large changes to the other classes. This new version of the text editor presents a `text_string` class that uses dynamic allocation. However, there is only one difference in the public interface of the class. Strings in the editor can now be longer than 80 characters. They can be virtually any length within the limits of memory. Therefore, references to the constant `MAX_TEXT_STRING_LENGTH` are gone.

The text editor now includes additional error checking. Take, for example, the `switch` statement in `main()`. The `case` that processes the Edit command prompts the user to input the number of the line to edit. It contains the loop

```
bool inputError = false;
for (i=0;(inputString[i]) && (!inputError);i++)
{
    if (!isdigit(inputString[i]))
```

```
        {
            inputError=true;
        }
    }
```

This loop checks each character that the user types in to see if any of them are not numeric digits. If they are not, the variable `inputError` is set to true. This indicates that the user entered incorrect input. The program beeps the speaker and continues.

The file *TString.h* contains only one public change. The constant `MAX_TEXT_STRING_LENGTH` was renamed `MAX_INPUT_STRING_LENGTH`. It is now set to 256 rather than 60.

There are some changes in the private interface of the `text_string` class. The private data member `charString` is now a pointer to characters. The `Initialize()` function was replaced with a function called `Allocate()`.

The implementation of the `text_string` class shows why these changes were necessary. The constructors no longer call `Initialize()`. The no-argument constructor sets `charString` to NULL. The one-argument constructor invokes the `Allocate()` function to dynamically allocate enough memory to hold the characters in the parameter `charArray`. It uses the old familiar `Copy()` function to copy characters from the parameter `charArray` into the private data member `charString`.

TIP: All classes using dynamic allocation must have a destructor.

The `text_string` class now requires a destructor. All classes that have one or more members that point to dynamically allocated memory *must* have a destructor. Whenever a `text_string` object goes out of scope, the destructor must deallocate the memory the object allocated.

The destructor for the `text_string` class sets the private data member `charString` to NULL. Strictly speaking, that is not necessary. However, it is a bit of preventive programming that can help.

The first overloaded version of the `text_string::operator =()` function now uses the `assert()` function from the C/C++ Standard Library. The `assert()` function takes a condition as a parameter. If the condition is false, the `assert()` function aborts the program.

This style of error handling should only be used to check programmer assumptions. If there are certain values that a parameter should never have, it is the responsibility of the programmer calling the function to ensure that it doesn't. Sometimes, however, programmers accidentally write code that calls a function with an invalid parameter value. In that situation, you can use an assertion to stop the program. Programmers who use your objects should discover the problem when they test their code.

TIP: Use the `assert()` function liberally.

Assertions are a very "in-your-face" way of helping other programmers use your objects correctly. I mean that in the most positive way possible. Assertions are a very good tool for producing robust programs. As a general rule of thumb, you should use assertions on most or all of your functions to check for programmer errors.

TIP: Use assertions to handle programmer errors. Use `if` or `switch` statements to handle user input and other runtime errors.

You should not use assertions to check for runtime errors. If, for instance, the user tries to load a file that doesn't exist into the text editor, your program should not use an assertion to handle the error. Imagine trying to use a text editor that aborted every time you typed in an incorrect file name. Not much fun.

The assertion in the first overloaded version of the `operator =()` function asserts that the `text_string` object that is passed in through the parameter list is not equal to the current object. It prevents a programmer from assigning a `text_string` object to itself. For example, if the statements

```
text_object s = "A string";
s=s;
```

occur in a program, the call to the `assert()` function in `text_string::operator =()` will make the program crash.

FIGURE 22.2 **Assignment to Self**

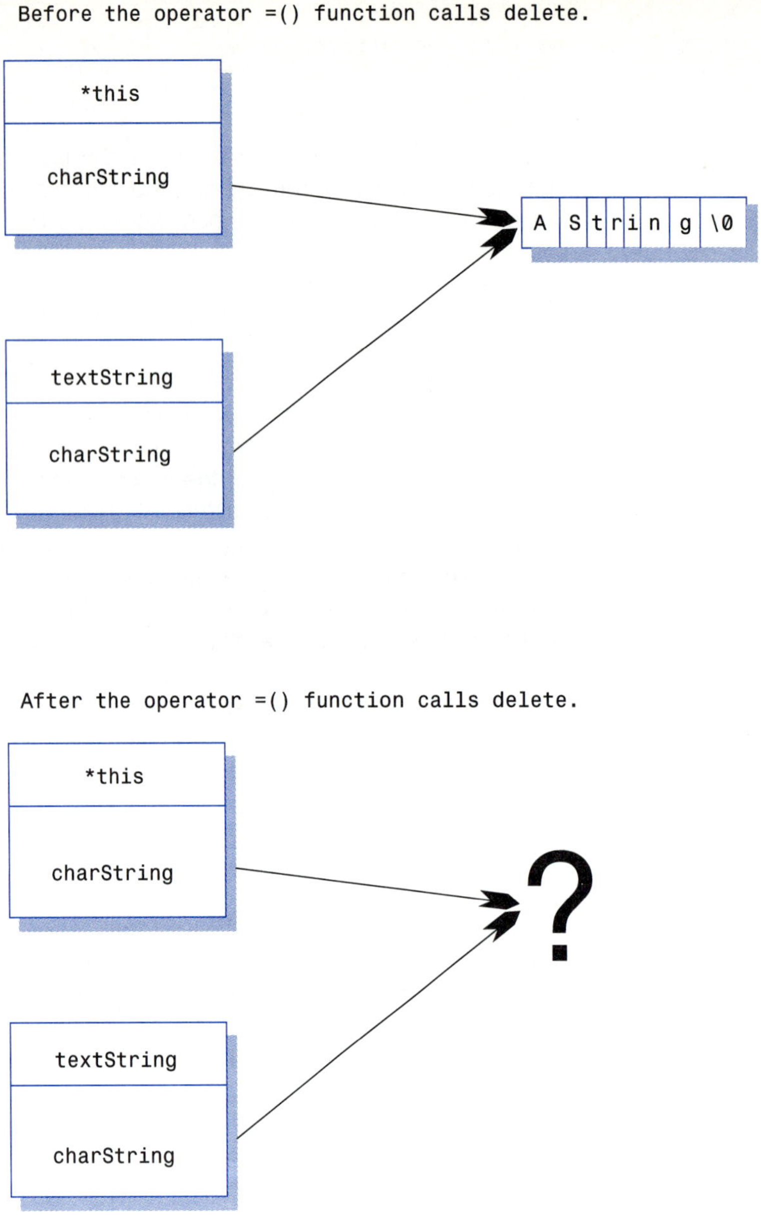

Strictly speaking, it is not syntactically incorrect to assign an object to itself. However, it doesn't make much sense and it usually indicates a programmer error. If you decide that you want to allow assignments to self, your objects must still check for it. Figure 22.2 shows why. In the `text_string::operator =()` function, the `if` statement deletes the memory allocated to the current `text_string` object. The rest of the function allocates memory and copies characters from the source object. If the object on the right of the equal sign is the same as the object on the left, the `operator =()` function will delete the character string that serves as the source from which to copy. The result will be a program crash.

To allow assignments to self, rewrite the `operator =()` function as shown in Example 22.2.

EXAMPLE 22.2 Allowing Assignment to Self

```
text_string &text_string::operator = (const text_string &textString)
{
   if (&textString != this)
   {
       if (charString!=NULL)
```

```
        {
            delete [] charString
        }

        Allocate(textString.Length());
        Copy(textString);
    }
    return (*this);
}
```

TIP: Most assignment operators should check for assignment to self.

This version of the `operator =()` function does nothing if the function is called for an assignment to self.

The second overload of the `text_string::operator =()` function does not assign a `text_string` object to a `text_string` object. It enables programmers to assign a character string to a `text_string` object. Therefore, this version of the assignment operator does not need to check for assignment to self.

As in the previous version of the `text_string` class, the first overloaded `operator +()` function contains much of the class's code. This function concatenates a `text_string` object onto the end of another `text_string` object. It does not change the objects on the left or right of the + sign.

The second overload of the `operator +()` object enables programmers to concatenate a character string onto the end of a `text_string` object. It creates a temporary `text_string` object, stores the character string in it, and uses the other `operator =()` function to perform the concatenation.

This check is not strictly necessary. The `operator +=()` function uses `operator =()` to do part of its work. The `operator =()` function checks for assignment to self. Therefore, the `operator +=()` function doesn't need to. I put it in to make the point that all forms of assignment may need to check for assignment to self.

The `operator +=()` function uses the `operator +()` function to append one string onto the end of the other. Unlike the `operator +()` function, `operator +=()` changes the object on the left of the += sign. Since the += operation is a form of assignment, this function must check for assignment to self. In this case, I've disallowed assignment to self. If you want to allow it, you must modify the `operator +=()` function to do nothing when it detects an assignment to self.

Programmers can append a character string onto the end of a `text_string` object using the second version of the `operator +=()` function. It uses the `operator +()` and `operator =()` functions to do its work. It does not need to check for assignment to self because it is not assigning a `text_string` to a `text_string`.

The final version of the `operator +=()` function enables programmers to append characters onto the end of a `text_string`.

The `operator []()` function uses the `assert()` function. It tests to see if the index number that is passed in is valid. If not, it is a programmer error, and the `assert()` function aborts the program.

The insertion, extraction, `CppString()`, and `Length()` functions required little or no change from previous versions of the `text_string` object.

The `Allocate()` function performs all of the dynamic memory allocation needed by the `text_string` class. It checks to ensure that the parameter `totalChars` is greater than zero. You could logically argue that this also is a programmer mistake and should be handled with an assertion rather than an `if` statement.

Since the `text_string` class now uses dynamic allocation, the `Copy()` function must check to ensure that the `text_string` it is copying from is not empty. If it is, the `Copy()` function deletes the characters in the destination string. This implementation allows programmers to assign an empty `text_string` object to other `text_string` objects. Some designers do not care for such assignments. If you want to disallow them, change the outer `if` statement to an assertion.

The `text_buffer` class is almost identical to the one in the previous version of the text editor. The only real changes are in the `text_buffer::operator[]` function, the `text_buffer::Load()` function, and the `text_buffer::Save()` function.

The `operator []()` function uses an assertion to check that the index number the programmer passes in is valid. The `Load()` and `Save()` functions both check for empty strings.

Troubleshooting Guide

After reading this section, you should be able to:

- Verify whether a dynamic allocation was successful.
- Perform "safe" pointer comparisons.
- Prevent memory leaks.

Checking the Allocation

TIP: Every time you allocate memory, check to make sure the allocation was successful.

Computers have a limited amount of memory installed. It seems that no matter how much memory is available, programs want more. Therefore, it is likely that, at some point, your program will try to allocate more memory than the operating system can give it. If you don't check for allocation failures, your program will crash.

If the operating system can't give your program the memory it's trying to allocate, the `new` operator will return the value `NULL`. So whenever you allocate memory, you should use an `if` statement to test for a `NULL` value.

Example 22.3 contains a version of the `text_string::Allocate()` function we used in Hands On 22.5. This version of the function checks the allocation it performs.

EXAMPLE 22.3 Checking Dynamic Memory Allocation

```
void text_string::Allocate(const int totalChars)
{
    if (totalChars>0)
    {
        charString = new char [totalChars+1];
        if (charString!=NULL)
        {
            for (int i=0;i<totalChars+1;i++)
            {
                charString[i]='\0';
            }
        }
    }
    else
    {
        charString = NULL;
    }
}
```

If the allocation fails, this version of the `Allocate()` function will not try to initialize anything to the null character. Doing so when there is an allocation failure would cause the program to crash.

Developers should never use assertions to check for memory allocation failures. Allocation failures are not a programmer error. They are one possible runtime error over which a programmer has no control. As a developer, the only thing you can do is write your software so that it will recover gracefully from a memory allocation failure.

Pointer Comparisons

A pointer is an integer memory address. C++ enables us to manipulate the addresses in pointers directly. For instance, we can add integers to pointers. We can also subtract integers from pointers. It is sometimes tempting to try and compare the addresses in pointers. For instance, it is possible in some circumstances to test for the end of a string using pointers. Example 22.4 demonstrates this technique.

EXAMPLE 22.4 Comparing Pointers

```
char *aString = new char [80];
strcpy(aString,"This is a string.");
```

```
char *pointer1, *pointer2;
pointer1 = &aString[0];
pointer2 = &aString[17];
char outputCharacter;
while (pointer1 < pointer2)
{
   outputCharacter = *pointer1;
   cout << outputCharacter;
   pointer1++;
}
```

The program fragment in this example declares two pointers: `pointer1` and `pointer2`. It sets `pointer1` to the beginning of a string. The program fragment uses the C/C++ Standard Library function `strcpy()` to copy characters into the string it allocates dynamically. It points `pointer2` at the end of the string. The program uses a `while` loop to iterate through the string and print each character to the screen. Syntactically, there is no reason why this program fragment should not work. However, that won't prevent it from crashing in some circumstances. The potential problem is in the way memory is organized on some computers.

Recall that programs allocate memory dynamically from the heap. The operating system may allocate heap memory with addresses that increase or decrease. The C++ languages definition does not specify whether successive blocks of memory have addresses that get larger or smaller. In programming terms, we say that the heap can grow up (toward larger addresses) or down (toward smaller addresses).

Look again at the program fragment in Example 22.4. If this program runs on a computer that allocates memory in increasing order, it will run just fine. It will increment `pointer1` until it gets to the same address as `pointer2`. However, what do you think will happen if the program runs on a computer that allocates memory in decreasing order?

The answer is that the program fragment won't work. It increments the pointer through memory, expecting to eventually encounter `pointer2`. If memory is allocated in decreasing order, the address in `pointer2` will be smaller than the address in `pointer1`. Each time the `while` loop increments the address in `pointer1`, `pointer1` points at a location that is increasingly distant from `pointer2`. The `while` loop will continue until the user manually terminates the program, reboots the computer, or until the program crashes.

Since you can't tell by looking at program code whether pointer comparisons are safe or not, you must assume they are not. The only absolutely safe pointer comparisons are shown in Table 22.1. Table 22.2 contains pointer comparisons that are usually safe.

Under most circumstances, you can compare two pointers to see if they equal or not equal. Most computers these days present a program with **normalized memory addresses.** When memory addresses are normalized, there is only one way to represent an address. A normalized memory addressing architecture is also referred to as a *flat memory architecture*.

On the other hand, some computers use **segmented memory addressing.** Computers that run MS DOS use segmented memory addressing. They represent memory addresses with segment:offset pairs. The segment and offset are combined to form a single

TABLE 22.1 Safe Pointer Comparisons

Comparison	Example
Pointer equal to NULL. Pointer not equal to NULL.	`thisPointer == NULL` `thisPointer != NULL`

TABLE 22.2 Mostly Safe Pointer Comparisons

Comparison	Example
Pointer equal to pointer. Pointer not equal to pointer.	`thisPointer == thatPointer` `thisPointer != thatPointer`

memory address. One drawback to segmented memory architectures is that many different segment:offset pairs can refer to given memory address. Under MS DOS, a pointer comparison like

```
if (thisPointer == thatPointer)
```

may not work because the variables `thisPointer` and `thatPointer` can use two different sets of numbers to refer to the same location in memory.

Computers that use segmented memory addressing are increasingly rare. Popular commercial operating systems such as Windows 95/98, Windows NT, Windows 2000, MacOS, NextStep, and Unix all use normalized, or flat, memory addressing. All of the pointer comparisons listed in Tables 22.1 and 22.2 are safe under these operating systems.

Memory Leaks

Another term for this is *memory orphaning.*

In programs that perform many dynamic allocations, any easy mistake to make is to set a pointer to a new address before deallocating the memory to which it points. Figure 22.3 shows a pointer that points to a dynamically allocated block of memory. Without deleting the dynamically allocated block, the program sets the pointer to point at something else.

FIGURE 22.3 A Memory Leak

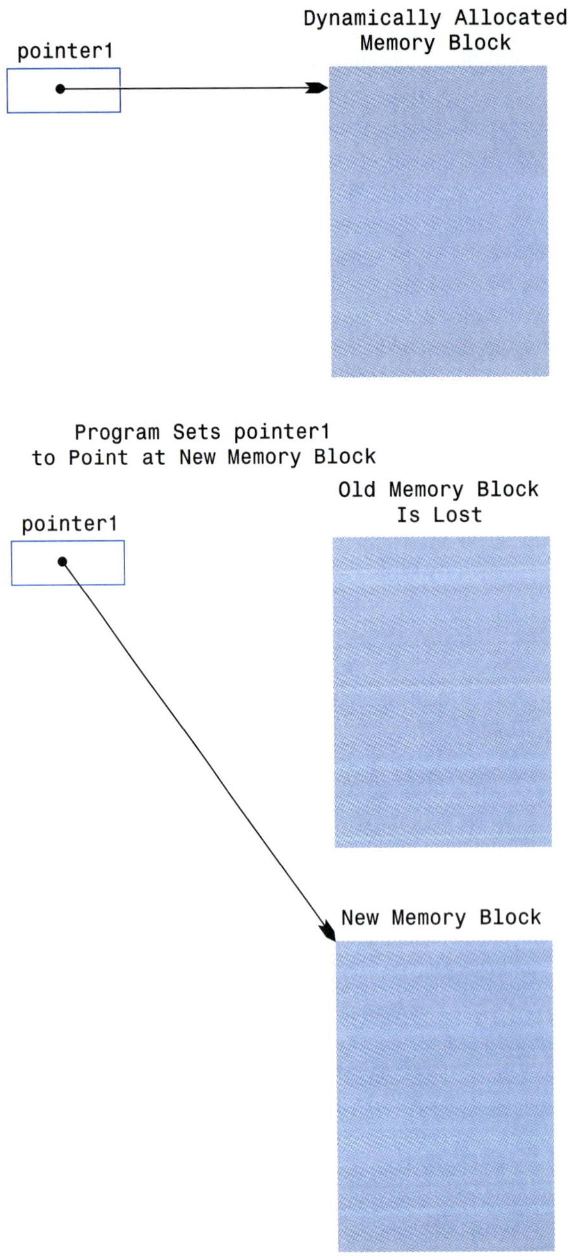

Since the address of the memory block is lost, the program can't use or deallocate the block. It becomes unusable until the program terminates. This is called a *memory leak*.

The only absolute way to prevent memory leaks is to be sure to deallocate every block of memory you allocate. That's very easy to say, but not so easy to do. This is especially true in large, complex programs. Memory leaks are one of the most common errors in C++ programming.

Currently, many companies produce programs that test for memory leaks and other types of pointer errors. If such a program doesn't come with your compiler, it is wise to invest in one.

In addition, some companies produce libraries that implement smart pointers. Smart pointer libraries create objects that look and act just like pointers. When you are using smart pointers, you can't tell the difference between them and normal pointers unless you know that the smart pointer library is linked into the program. Smart pointers automatically deallocate the memory to which they point. Strictly speaking, you never need to use the `delete` keyword if you have a smart pointer library.

Good smart pointer class libraries can be linked with any existing code. They can even be linked with other libraries provided by other companies. They will control all allocations in the program and prevent memory leaks.

Summary

Programs can allocate and free memory as they run. This is called *dynamic memory allocation*. Dynamically allocated memory comes from a program's heap.

Programs allocate memory using the keyword `new`. They deallocate with the C++ keyword `delete`. If the keyword `new` cannot give a program the requested memory, it returns NULL. Functions must declare pointers to store the address that they get from `new`.

You can allocate memory for atomic data types, objects, and arrays.

Review Questions

1. What is dynamic memory allocation? What is static memory allocation?
2. How do you use the keywords `new` and `delete`?
3. How do you dynamically allocate atomic data types?
4. How do you dynamically allocate a single-dimensional array?
5. How do you dynamically allocate a multidimensional array?
6. How do you dynamically allocate objects?
7. When objects inherit from other objects, in what order are their constructors called? Why would this be important? In what order are their destructors called? Why would that be important?
8. Why does every class that contains a pointer to dynamically allocated memory require a destructor? What would happen if you left the destructor out of the class?
9. Why is it important for objects that use dynamic allocation to check for assignment to self?
10. How do you check a memory allocation to see if it was successful? Why is it important to check every memory allocation?

Exercises

1. Write a program that allocates an array of 1,000 integers. It should fill the array with random integers, sort them, and then print them out.
2. Write a program that allocates a 2-D array of integers. It should fill each row of the array with random integers. The program should sort the integers in each individual row into ascending order. It should then print out the contents of the entire array.
3. Write a program that defines an `xy_point` object. It should contain the following private data members:

```
int x,y;
```

The `xy_point` class should have member functions for getting and setting the values of the private data members. Also define an object called `shape`. The `shape` object should contain the following private data member:

```
xy_point origin;
```

The `shape` object should have member functions for setting and getting its origin point. Your program should dynamically allocate an array of `shape` objects. It should assign random values to the *x* and *y* coordinates of each shape's origin. Sort the shapes by their *x* coordinate in ascending order. Print the *x,y* location of each shape.

4. Use the `shape` object you created for Exercise 3. Write a program that defines a `rectangle` object. A `rectangle` should inherit from a `shape`. It should add the following private data members:

```
int height, width;
```

Dynamically allocate an array of rectangles. Assign random values to the *x* and *y* coordinates of each rectangle. Also assign random values to the height and width of each rectangle. Sort the rectangles by height. Print the *x, y,* height, and width values of each rectangle in the array.

5. Use the rectangle object you created for Exercise 4. Define an object called `square`. The `square` object should be a special case of a rectangle that forces the height and width of the rectangle to be equal. Dynamically allocate an array of 100 pointers to squares. For each pointer in the array, dynamically allocate an array of ten squares. Assign random integers to the *x, y,* and height of each square. Write a loop that iterates through all of the squares and prints their *x, y,* and height values.
6. Write a program that dynamically allocates a 2-D array of 200 strings. Each string should be 80 characters in length. Your program should also dynamically allocate an array of 200 pointers to characters. Fill the strings with random characters. Set each pointer to point at one row in the 2-D array. Sort the strings by sorting the array of pointers. Do not move the strings around in memory. Print the strings in unsorted and sorted order.
7. Use the program you wrote for Exercise 6. Declare another array of pointers. Set each pointer to the beginning of a row in the 2-D array. Sort the strings in descending order by sorting the second array of pointers. Print the strings in descending order.
8. Use the text editor in Hands On 22.5. Write a version of the text editor that declares an array of five pointers to `text_buffer` objects called `allBuffers`. Allow the user to open up to five text files at once. Dynamically allocate a `text_buffer` object for each file the user wants to edit. Add a command to the menu to enable the user to select the current text file to edit. In other words, if the user selects text file 3, your program should display the text in `allBuffers[3]`. Be sure that your program checks every dynamic allocation that it does.
9. Use the program you wrote for Exercise 8. Enable the user to type in the names of up to five text files on the command line. Dynamically allocate a `text_buffer` object for each file the user wants to open.
10. Use the program you wrote for Exercise 9. Add a `text_string` member to the `text_buffer` object called `fileName`. After the first time the user saves the buffer to a file, the `text_buffer` object should store the name of the file in `fileName`. When the user chooses to save the file again, display the file name as a default. If the user just presses the Enter key, save the file to the current file name.

Chapter Glossary

Heap A pool of free memory that a program can use for dynamic allocation.

Normalized Memory Addressing Addressing memory in such a way that there is only one unique address number for each location in memory.

Segmented Memory Addressing A memory addressing scheme that uses segment: offset pairs to address each location in memory. Many different setment:offset pairs can be used to access any particular memory address.

23 Encapsulating Data

Objectives

After reading this chapter, you should be able to:

- Understand and explain the concept of data encapsulation.
- Understand and explain the concept of scope.
- Understand and explain the concept of persistence.
- Use scope and persistence to control encapsulation.
- Use storage classes to control scope and persistence.
- Use `const` to increase data encapsulation.
- Use the `public`, `protected`, and `private` access specifiers to control encapsulation.
- Use the scope resolution operator to control scope.

Preview

A great strength of C++ is that it provides programmers with very exact methods of encapsulating and controlling access to data. Good encapsulation helps us ensure that our data maintains its integrity. It also helps keep our programs in valid operational states.

This chapter introduces some advanced methods of data encapsulation. In particular, it presents techniques for overseeing access to data by controlling its scope and persistence.

Scope and Persistence

As we've seen in previous chapters, a variable's scope is defined as the portion of the code where the variable can be accessed. For example, we know that local variables can be accessed only in the function that declares them. In other words, the scope of a local variable is limited to the body of the function.

The persistence of a variable is the time of its existence. Local variables exist only in the function in which they are declared. Their scope and persistence are both limited to the function. A variable's scope and persistence aren't necessarily the same. Later in this chapter, we'll discuss how we can create variables that exist for as long as the program runs, but can only be seen by certain functions.

`const`

In addition to scope and persistence, we as developers of C++ objects need to control access to data. The `const` keyword provides us with one method that we can use to restrict changes to data.

This is not strictly true. It is the intent of const pointers. However, in actual practice, there are ways to get rid of the "const-ness" of a pointer variable. Casting away the "const-ness" of a pointer is usually not desirable.

Of course, const can be used to declare constants. We can apply it to function parameters to ensure that they are not changed inside the function. We can declare the return value of a function to be const.

For example, the text_string class we developed for the text editor has a function called CppString(). This function returns a const pointer. Even if a programmer uses the CppString() function to get a pointer to the characters in a text_string object, she can't use that pointer to change the characters because the pointer is const.

The const keyword can also be applied to objects and even functions. A const object can't be changed. If the class includes functions that change the data in an object (most do), then it should not be possible to call one of those functions on a const object. If C++ allowed us to do so, it could result in data being changed when it shouldn't be. Example 23.1 shows a program that declares a constant object.

EXAMPLE 23.1 A const Object

```
class an_object
{
public:
   an_object(int dataValue=0);

   void DoSomething(void);

private:
   int data;
};

an_object::an_object(int dataValue)
{
   data = dataValue;
}

void an_object::DoSomething(void)
{
   data = 5;
}

int main()
{
   const an_object thisObject=10;
   thisObject.DoSomething();
   return (0);
}
```

The function DoSomething() sets the value of the private data member to 5. Because this function changes the data in the object, you would expect that the C++ compiler would complain. In fact, it does.

Only const member functions can be called on const objects. Example 23.2 illustrates how member functions can be declared const. The const function, PrintData(), is shown in bold.

EXAMPLE 23.2 A Class with a const Member Function

```
#include <iostream.h>

class an_object
{
public:
   an_object(int dataValue=0);
```

```
    void DoSomething(void);
    void PrintData(void) const;

private:
    int data;
};

an_object::an_object(int dataValue)
{
    data = dataValue;
}

void an_object::DoSomething(void)
{
    data = 5;
}


void an_object::PrintData(void) const
{
    cout << data;
}


int main()
{
    const an_object thisObject=10;
    thisObject.PrintData();
    return (0);
}
```

If your compiler conforms to the latest ANSI C++ specification, it is possible to have functions that differ *only* in their "`const`-ness." The prototypes of the two functions can be identical except that one is `const` and one is not. This enables you to handle `const` and non-`const` objects differently.

Scope in Objects

We control scope inside objects by using the keywords `public`, `protected`, and `private`. Public members of an object are accessible to any function that can declare the object. Protected members are visible to object member functions. They are also visible to the member functions of objects that are derived from that class. Private members of an object are accessible only to that class's member functions.

Storage Classes

The C++ language provides us with multiple storage classes. A variable's storage class tells the compiler what the variable's scope and persistence is. There are six different storage classes: `auto`, `static`, `register`, `extern`, `mutable`, and `volatile`.

auto

The `auto` storage class specifies automatic variables. Automatic variables are the easiest type of storage class to deal with. We can completely ignore their storage class. Automatic variables are local variables.

We've already demonstrated the scope of automatic variables. They can be seen only in the function that declares them. We've also seen their persistence. They exist only for as long as the function that declares them is running.

Local variables have the storage class `auto` by default. So we don't need to put the keyword `auto` anywhere in our programs. However, you can insert it if you want to. Example 23.3 shows how.

EXAMPLE 23.3 An `auto` Variable

```
void MyFunction(void)
{
    auto int aVariable = 10;

    // More C++ statements here.
}
```

Automatic variables are recreated every time the function is called again. Example 23.3 shows an `auto` variable with an initial value. Each time this function begins to execute, it creates the automatic variable `aVariable`. It also initializes the variable to 10 every time `MyFunction()` is called.

static

The `static` storage class is the most complex. Using the `static` keyword has a different effect on different C++ program elements. You can use the `static` storage class on variables, functions, object data members, and object member functions.

`static` Variables Local variables with the `static` storage class have the same scope as automatic variables. They can be seen only in the function in which they are declared. However, they do not have the same persistence.

An automatic variable ceases to exist when the function that declares it finishes executing. Variables with the storage class `static` don't. They still exist, but no other function can get access to them. Example 23.4 demonstrates a `static` local variable in a function.

EXAMPLE 23.4 A `static` Variable

```
void MyFunction(void)
{
    static bool beenCalled = false;

    if (!beenCalled)
    {
        // C++ statements that do something go here.
    }
    beenCalled = true;
}
```

The function in Example 23.4 declares a `static` variable named `beenCalled`. This variable can be seen only in the function `MyFunction()`. No other function can access it.

`MyFunction()` sets `beenCalled` to `false`. However, this initialization is done only once. No matter how many times the program calls `MyFunction()`, the initialization is never done again. (Of course, it *is* done again if you exit the program and start it again.)

Just before it ends, `MyFunction()` sets `beenCalled` to true. When `MyFunction()` finishes executing, `beenCalled` will not go away. It will not lose its value. The next time the program calls `MyFunction()`, the variable `beenCalled` will still contain the value `true`.

In addition to `static` local variables, you can also use the `static` keyword to declare **module global variables.** The scope of a module global variable is limited to the CPP file in which it is declared. It can't be seen outside of that one CPP file.

Module global variables are a double-edged sword. They can be used to increase data encapsulation. However, like global variables, they can also seriously undermine a program's encapsulation. It all depends on how you use them.

Let's suppose, for example, that we're creating a windowing system for a program that's running on an operating system that doesn't come with a graphical user interface. Figure 23.1 shows how part of that program might look.

In the figure, you see a file called *Win.h*. It contains the prototypes of functions that create, destroy, and manipulate windows on the screen. The file *Win.cpp* contains the implementations of those functions. It also declares a static variable at the beginning of the file. This variable is not declared inside a function. It is visible to every function in the file *Win.cpp*. However, it is not visible to any function outside that file, so it is a module global variable. It is not global to the entire program.

Note that the initialization on `static` module global variables is performed when the operating system loads the program. It is not done again until the program is restarted.

The variable in this example is a dynamically allocated array of windows. Whenever a program calls `CreateWindow()`, a window is created and added to the array. The window functions perform various tasks on windows in the array. When the program is done with a window, it calls `DeleteWindow()`.

If it seems as if this is a way of doing object oriented programming without classes, that's correct. It is. This style of programming was, and still is, common in C. The C programming language doesn't have the object oriented extensions that C++ does. You can achieve much of the same level of encapsulation that classes provide by using module global variables.

The use of module global variables is more common in C programming than C++ programming. However, you'll undoubtedly find times when they are useful in C++ programs as well.

`static` Functions Like `static` module variables, `static` functions cannot be seen outside of the file in which they are defined. In this respect, a `static` function is similar to a class's private member function. They are support functions that are used to hide implementation.

```
//---------------------------------------
// Win.h
//---------------------------------------
void window *CreateWindow(int height,int width);
void MoveWindow(window *theWindow);
void ResizeWindow(window *theWindow,int newHeight,
                  int newWidth);
void DrawWindow(window *theWindow);
void DeleteWindow(window *theWindow);
```

```
//-----------------------------------
// Win.cpp
//-----------------------------------
static window *windowList = NULL;

window *CreateWindow(int height,int width)
{
  // Function body goes here
}
void MoveWindow(window *theWindow)
{
  // Function body goes here
}
void ResizeWindow(window *theWindow,
                  int newHeight,
                  int newWidth)
{
  // Function body goes here
}
void DrawWindow(window *theWindow)
{
  // Function body goes here
}
void DeleteWindow(window *theWindow)
{
  // Function body goes here
}
```

FIGURE 23.1 A Module Global Variable

```
//-------------------------------------
// Win.h
//-------------------------------------
void window *CreateWindow(int height,int width);
void MoveWindow(window *theWindow);
void ResizeWindow(window *theWindow,int newHeight,
                  int newWidth);
void DrawWindow(window *theWindow);
void DeleteWindow(window *theWindow);
```

```
//-------------------------------------
// Win.cpp
//-------------------------------------
static window *windowList = NULL;

static void RecalcWindowSize(window *theWindow);

window *CreateWindow(int height,int width)
{
  // Function body goes here
}

void MoveWindow(window *theWindow)
{
  // Function body goes here
}

void ResizeWindow(window *theWindow,
                  int newHeight,
                  int newWidth)
{
  // Function body goes here
}

void DrawWindow(window *theWindow)
{
  // Function body goes here
}

void DeleteWindow(window *theWindow)
{
  // Function body goes here
}

static void RecalcWindowSize(window *theWindow)
{
  // Function body goes here
}
```

FIGURE 23.2 A `static` Function

For example, Figure 23.2 shows the same pair of files that appeared in Figure 23.1. The file *Win.cpp* now contains a function called `RecalcWindowSize()`. This is a function that can be called only by other functions in *Win.cpp*. Functions in other files cannot get access to `RecalcWindowSize()`. The scope of this function is limited to the file in which it is defined. If necessary, any function in *Win.cpp* can call `RecalcWindowSize()`.

The `RecalcWindowSize()` function is completely dependent on the current implementation. If we change how windows are implemented, this function will likely change or disappear entirely. That's why we used the `static` keyword to prevent other files from accessing this function.

TIP: Use `static` module global variables sparingly.

It's important not to overuse module global variables. Because all functions in a file can access them, it can be difficult to track down problems with the data that they store. This is especially true if there are a large number of functions in the file.

`static` Data Members Objects can contain `static` data. Normally, each object contains its own private member data. All objects of the same class share the same set of member functions. If you declare a private data member as `static`, all objects of a class will share that data member. It will be created and initialized when the program loads. Hands On 23.1 demonstrates `static` member data.

Hands On 23.1

Objective

Write a program that defines a timer object. The timer class should allow the program to create only one instance of itself.

Experiment

Type the following program into your IDE or text editor. Compile, link, and run it.

```
#include <iostream.h>
#include <assert.h>


class timer
{
public:
   timer(int startTime=0);

   void Tick(void);
   int CurrentTime(void);

private:
   int currentTime;
   static int objectCount;
};



int timer::objectCount = 0;



timer::timer(int startTime)
{
   objectCount++;

   assert(objectCount==1);

   currentTime=startTime;
}

void timer::Tick(void)
{
   currentTime++;
}

int timer::CurrentTime(void)
{
   return (currentTime);
}


int main()
{
   timer aTimer;
```

```
    for (int i=0;i<1000;i++)
    {
       aTimer.Tick();
    }

    cout << aTimer.CurrentTime() << endl;

    timer anotherTimer;
    anotherTimer.Tick();
    return (0);
}
```

Results

```
1000
Assertion failed: objectCount==1, file ho23_1.cpp, line 28
Abnormal program termination
```

Analysis

The `timer` class in this Hands On program contains a `static` data member called `objectCount`. All objects of type `timer` share the same `objectCount` member. Any one of them can change it. When they do, they alter the value of `objectCount` for *every* `timer` object in the program.

When a class has a `static` data member, the `static` data member is created when the program loads. That is, its persistence is the entire time that the program is running. Its scope is limited to class members. If there is an initialization, it is done when the program loads. In this program, the statement

```
int timer::objectCount = 0;
```

initializes the `objectCount` data member to zero.

When the program creates a `timer` object, the `timer` constructor increments the `objectCount` member. The `timer` object constructor prevents the program from creating more than one `timer`. If the `objectCount` data member is anything other than one, the assertion fails. This crashes the program. It lets the programmer who is using the `timer` class know in no uncertain terms that there can never be more than one `timer` object in the program. This is demonstrated in `main()`.

The `main()` function declares and uses a timer called `aTimer`. However, when it tries to declare the variable `anotherTimer`, the assertion crashes the program.

TIP: Don't overuse `static` data members.

Because all objects of a class share `static` data members, `static` data members can seriously undermine the robustness of a program. If the information in the `static` data member becomes incorrect, you may have a difficult time tracking down which member function needs debugging. In general, use `static` data members very sparingly.

`static` Member Functions An object's member functions can also be `static`. However, `static` member functions can only access the `static` data members in a class. Functions that are declared `static` can be called without using an object. Example 23.5 demonstrates how.

EXAMPLE 23.5 Calling a `static` Member Function

```
#include <iostream.h>

class generic_object
{
public:
   // Various member functions.
```

```
    // This is a static member function.
    static void AFunction(void);

};

void generic_object::AFunction(void)
{
   cout << "Called AFunction()" << endl;
}


int main()
{
   generic_object::AFunction();

   generic_object anObject;
   anObject.AFunction();

   return (0);
}
```

The program in Example 23.5 defines the `generic_object` class, which has a member function named `AFunction()`. It is a `static` member function. It obeys the rules of C++ scope. It is visible in `main()` because it is declared `public`. If it were a `private` function, it would not be visible in `main()`.

The `static` function `AFunction()` can be called at any time during the program's execution. Your program does not need to declare a variable of type `generic_object` to invoke `AFunction()`.

TIP: `static` functions can't access non-`static` data in a class. They can only use the `static` data members.

`static` member functions can access their own parameters. They can use local variables. They may also access `static` member data. However, they cannot access non-`static` member data. If a class does not declare its private data member as `static`, then `static` functions may not access the member data.

The reason for this is that `static` member functions can be called without an object of their class. As shown in Example 23.5, a `static` function can be called before an object is declared in the program. If there are no objects, there are no non-`static` data members. Normal data members don't exist until the program creates an object.

`static` data members come into existence when the program starts running. `static` member functions can be called as soon as the program starts executing. `static` member functions can't access the normal, non-`static` data members of a class.

register

The storage class `register` declares that a variable has the same scope and persistence as automatic variables. Actually, the keyword `register` is just a hint to the compiler that a variable will be heavily used. The compiler may ignore the `register` storage class entirely.

REMINDER: CPU stands for *central processing unit.* It is the part of the microprocessor that executes instructions.

If it does not, the compiler will try, as much as possible, to keep `register` variables in the microprocessor's on-chip registers. Doing so will increase the speed at which the CPU can access the variables. The CPU has very fast access to its registers. Any time the CPU must access a device (such as RAM) that is not on board the microprocessor chip, the CPU must wait. By declaring often-used variables as having the storage class `register`, you might increase the speed of your program.

Example 23.6 contains the declaration of a `register` variable.

EXAMPLE 23.6 Declaring a `register` Variable in a Function

```
void AFunction(void)
{
   register int i;
```

```
        for (i=0;i<10000;i++)
        {
            // Do some processing here.
        }
    }
```

TRAP: If you declare *all* of your local variables as `register` variables, you get very much the same results as if you declared *none* of them as `register` variables.

Be aware, however, that microprocessors have only a limited number of registers to use. If your function declares many `register` variables, it is likely that the compiler will ignore the suggestion on at least some of them.

How do you know if you've declared too many `register` variables? Basically, you don't. If you have a background in Assembly Language programming, you can look at the executable code that your compiler generates for your program. This will tell you how the program uses the CPU's registers. There is no way, when looking at C++ source code, to tell which `register` variables are being kept in the CPU's registers and which are being kept in RAM.

`extern`

The `extern` keyword is used for declaring global variables. It tells the compiler that memory is allocated elsewhere for a variable being referred to in the current file. Figure 23.3 shows two files. The file *This.cpp* declares a global variable. A function in the file *That.cpp* accesses the global variable.

Using a global variable in many files is bad because *all* of the files depend on the presence of *This.cpp* in the program. None of the other files can be used in another program unless we also use *This.cpp*. It is very likely that we won't be able to use *any* of these 1,000 files in another program. That equates to a lot of wasted effort.

To make the global variable visible to the functions in *That.cpp,* you must declare the variable as `extern` in *That.cpp*. Doing so tells the compiler that you are allowing access to the global variable, but the compiler should not allocate memory for it in *That.cpp*. Memory for the global variable is allocated elsewhere. When you link the program, the linker will check to ensure that memory is allocated for the global variable somewhere in the program's code.

Notice in Figure 23.3 that there are multiple declarations of `aGlobalVariable`. Let's suppose that the program our team of developers is working on is made up of 1,000 files (which would not be at all unusual in professional programs). Let's also suppose that all 1,000 files must access the global variable. That means that there will be 1,000 declarations of `aGlobalVariable`.

TRAP: Using global variables generally complicates your program code.

Now let's suppose that, for some reason, we find that `aGlobalVariable` should be a `long` rather than an `int`. We must now go back and change all 1,000 declarations of `aGlobalVariable`. Maintenance difficulties such as this are typical when you use global variables. The Troubleshooting Guide at the end of this chapter contains some techniques that will help lessen this problem.

`mutable`

When your program declares an object variable to be `const`, none of the member functions can change the values of private member data. This is known as *bitwise* `const`*-ness*. None of the bits of a `const` object may change.

Another type of `const`-ness, called *conceptual* `const`*-ness,* allows your program to change the value of private data members as long as it is undetectable outside the class. Example 23.7 demonstrates conceptual `const`-ness.

FIGURE 23.3 Using `extern` to Declare a Global Variable

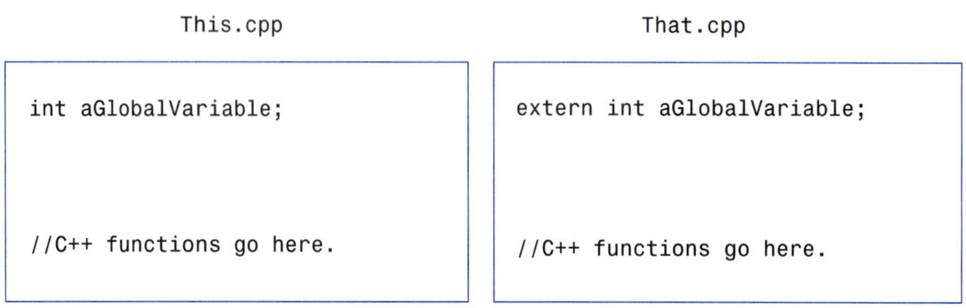

EXAMPLE 23.7 Conceptual `const`-ness

```
#include <iostream.h>

class an_object
{
public:
   an_object(int dataValue=0);

   void PrintData(void) const;

private:
   int data1;
   mutable int currentStatus;
};


an_object::an_object(int dataValue)
{
   data1 = dataValue;
}


void an_object::PrintData(void) const
{
   cout << data1;
   currentStatus = 10;
}


int main()
{
   const an_object thisObject= 50;

   thisObject.PrintData();

   return (0);
}
```

The example defines a class that contains two data members: `data1` and `currentStatus`. The private data member `currentStatus` uses the storage class `mutable`. Because `currentStatus` is `mutable`, it can be changed even though `my_object` is declared `const` in `main()`.

To everything outside the `my_object` class, a `my_object` appears to be `const` when it should be. However, inside the object's member functions, `currentStatus` can be changed. Since this is undetectable by any program code outside the `my_object` class, the variable `thisObject` in `main()` is conceptually `const`. It is not bitwise `const` because some of the bits in the object change.

Programs typically use the storage class `mutable` to declare a private data member that keeps track of an object's status. This is intended to be for internal use by the object. The information in a `mutable` data member should not be made available to functions that are not members of the class. Programs can apply the `mutable` keyword only to class data members.

`volatile`

If you develop operating systems or device drivers, you may find occasion to use the storage class `volatile`. Declaring a variable as `volatile` means that something besides the software can change the value of the variable.

When you write operating systems and device drivers, your compiler may allow you to map variables in your program to specific locations in memory. Developers use this ability to declare a variable name for I/O ports, hardware registers, and other hardware devices that may reside in the microprocessor's memory space. They can treat the port (or other hardware device) as if it is a variable in memory.

Unless you are developing a program that interacts with computer hardware directly, you will probably not find a use for the `volatile` keyword.

Troubleshooting Guide

After reading this section, you should be able to:

- Correctly define global variables in a header file.
- Understand problems with protected data.

Defining Global Variables

Let's look back at Figure 23.3. Because we need to declare a global variable in every file that accesses it, we end up with multiple declarations of every global variable. If you are like many alert readers, you may realize that we could use one declaration if we put it in a header file. Figure 23.4 demonstrates this technique.

There's a problem here, however. We can't include the header file in *This.cpp*. If we did, it would result in two declarations of `aGlobalVariable` in the same file. This will cause an error.

We can move the declaration of `aGlobalVariable` into the header file *and* include the header file in all of the CPP files (such as *This.cpp*) if we use a conditional compilation trick. Example 23.8 illustrates how this is done.

EXAMPLE 23.8 One Definition for a Global Variable

```
// MyProg.cpp
#define DEBUGGING
#define EXTERN
#include "Debugger.h"
#include "AFile.h"


int main()
{
   OpenLogFile("log.txt");

   WriteToLogFile("Entering for loop");
   WriteToLogFile(endl);

   for (int i=0;i<100;i++)
   {
      WriteToLogFile("i=");
```

This.cpp

```
#include "Those.h"
int aGlobalVariable;


//C++ functions go here.
```

That.cpp

```
#include "Those.h"


//C++ functions go here.
```

Those.h

```
extern int aGlobalVariable;


//Other header file stuff goes here.
```

FIGURE 23.4 A Global Variable in a Header File

```
      WriteToLogFile(i);
      WriteToLogFile(endl);
   }

   AnotherFunction();
   CloseLogFile();

   return (0);
}


// Debugger.h
#ifndef DEBUGGER_H
#define DEBUGGER_H

#ifdef DEBUGGING
#include <fstream.h>
#include <stdlib.h>

#if !defined(EXTERN)
#define EXTERN extern
#else
#define EXTERN
#endif

EXTERN ofstream logFile;


#define OpenLogFile(logFileName)                        \
        {                                               \
           logFile.open(logFileName);                   \
           if (!logFile)                                \
           {                                            \
              abort();                                  \
           }                                            \
        }

#define WriteToLogFile(data)    logFile << data

#define CloseLogFile()  logFile.close()

#else

#define OpenLogFile(logFileName)
#define WriteToLogFile(data)
#define CloseLogFile()

#endif  // end #ifdef DEBUGGING

#endif  // end #ifndef DEBUGGER_H


// AFile.h
void AnotherFunction(void);


// AFile.cpp
#include "Debugger.h"
void AnotherFunction(void)
```

```
{
   int i;
   for (int i=0;i<2000;i++)
   {
      WriteToLogFile("i=");
      WriteToLogFile(i);
      WriteToLogFile(endl);
   }
}
```

This is the debugging system we saw back in Chapter 20. I've made certain lines of text bold in Example 23.8 for emphasis. In the file *MyProg.cpp,* the line that reads

```
#define EXTERN
```

defines a constant named EXTERN. This constant has no value. However, as far as the C++ preprocessor is concerned, it is still defined. Everywhere the preprocessor finds the named constant EXTERN in a file, it will substitute a blank. In other words, it will remove EXTERN from the file wherever it occurs.

Next, *MyProg.cpp* includes the file *Debugger.h*. In *Debugger.h,* the statements

```
#if !defined(EXTERN)
#define EXTERN extern
#else
#define EXTERN
#endif
```

check to see if the named constant EXTERN is defined. It is, so the preprocessor processes all statements between the `#else` and the `#endif`. In this case, there is only one. It defines the constant EXTERN as blank. Isn't that redundant?

Well, yes and no. If the programmer using the debugging system put the statement

```
#define EXTERN 5
```

in *MyProg.cpp* instead of

```
#define EXTERN
```

then all occurrences of EXTERN would be replaced by 5. That's not what we want. If EXTERN is defined, we need it to be defined as blank.

The C++ preprocessor next encounters the statement

```
EXTERN ofstream logFile;
```

The constant EXTERN is currently defined as blank. Therefore, the preprocessor removes the constant EXTERN and doesn't substitute anything in its place. The result is that the global variable `logFile` is declared in the file *MyProg.cpp* and memory is allocated for the variable.

Let's suppose there's a file in the program called *AFile.cpp*. It contains a function named `AnotherFunction()`. Also, the program uses a header file called *AFile.h,* which contains the prototype for `AnotherFunction()`. Notice that *AFile.cpp* includes *Debugger.h.* However, it does not define the constant EXTERN. When the preprocessor includes *Debugger.h* in *AFile.cpp,* the constant EXTERN is not defined. When it processes the statement

```
#if !defined(EXTERN)
#define EXTERN extern
#else
#define EXTERN
#endif
```

it will process the `#define` statement between the `#if` and the `#else`. This statement defines the constant EXTERN to be the C++ keyword `extern`. When the preprocessor encounters the statement

```
EXTERN ofstream logFile;
```

it will substitute the keyword `extern` for the constant `EXTERN`. The result is that the global variable `logFile` is declared in *AFile.cpp*. However, memory is not allocated for it because it has an external storage class. Instead, the linker links all references to `logFile` in *AFile.cpp* to the `logFile` in *MyProg.cpp*. Recall that memory was allocated for the `logFile` in *MyProg.cpp*.

This example should demonstrate that using global variables is a lot of work. They cause numerous maintenance headaches that you can only get around with tricky code. Even then, they are still hard to debug when something goes wrong.

Problems with Protected Data

All protected members of a class are visible to the class's member functions and to all of the object's derived classes. Example 23.9 shows a class called `base_class`. It contains a `protected` data member. The class `derived_class` inherits from `base_class`. The object `base_class` encapsulates its data. It provides a `protected` data member, which `derived_class` uses. See any problems here?

EXAMPLE 23.9 Inheriting Protected Data

```
#include <iostream.h>


class base_class
{
public:
   base_class(int dataValue=0);

   void PrintData(void);

protected:
   int data1;
};


base_class::base_class(int dataValue)
{
   data1 = dataValue;
}


void base_class::PrintData(void)
{
   cout << data1 << endl;
}


class derived_class : public base_class
{
public:
   derived_class(int dataValue=0);

   int *GetAccess(void);
};


derived_class::derived_class(int dataValue) : base_class(dataValue)
{
}
```

```
int *derived_class::GetAccess(void)
{
   return (&data1);
}


int main()
{
   derived_class derivedObject = 10;
   derivedObject.PrintData();

   int *anIntPointer;
   anIntPointer = derivedObject.GetAccess();
   *anIntPointer = 50;
   derivedObject.PrintData();

   return (0);
}
```

TRAP: Derived classes can change the scope of protected data members they inherit from the base class.

Let's face it, not every programmer on every project you'll be part of will be as careful about object oriented design as you. You may carefully use the features of C++ to encapsulate data and control access to it. However, as Example 23.9 demonstrates, `protected` data gives anyone at any time the ability to come along behind you and create a derived object that permits access to your object's `protected` data. The function `derived_class::GetAccess()` returns a pointer to the protected data member `data1`. Any function that calls `derived_class::GetAccess()` can modify the protected data in a `base_class` object without calling any of the `base_class` member functions.

TIP: Make all data private. Instead of using protected data members, provide protected member functions in the base class.

To prevent this, make all member data `private`. If you want only inherited classes to be able to modify the data, provide `protected` member functions. Example 23.10 demonstrates this technique. All classes derived from `base_class` can get and set the value of `data1`. However, none of them can enable functions to access `data1` without calling `base_class` member functions.

EXAMPLE 23.10 Private Data and Protected Functions

```
#include <iostream.h>


class base_class
{
public:
   base_class(int dataValue=0);

   void PrintData(void);

protected:
   int GetDataValue(void);
   void SetDataValue(int dataValue);

private:
   int data1;
};


base_class::base_class(int dataValue)
{
   data1 = dataValue;
}
```

```
void base_class::PrintData(void)
{
   cout << data1 << endl;
}


class derived_class : public base_class
{
public:
   derived_class(int dataValue=0);

   int *GetAccess(void);
};


derived_class::derived_class(int dataValue) :
         base_class(dataValue)
{
}


int *derived_class::GetAccess(void)
{
   /* This function no longer compiles. The private data
member data1 is now out of scope. */
   return (&data1);
}



int main()
{
   derived_class derivedObject = 10;
   derivedObject.PrintData();

   int *anIntPointer;
   /* The following statements will no longer work.
   The member functions in derived_class can't get access
   to the private data in base_class. */
   anIntPointer = derivedObject.GetAccess();
   *anIntPointer = 50;
   derivedObject.PrintData();

   return (0);
}
```

Summary

One of the primary purposes of object oriented programming is data encapsulation. Encapsulating data controls access to it. This enables software modules to control how data changes.

We encapsulate data by controlling its scope and persistence. Scope is the visibility of data in a program. Persistence can be thought of as the "lifetime" of the data.

In addition to scope and persistence, we can control changes to data with the keyword `const`. C++ allows `const` variables, `const` parameters, `const` return values, and `const` functions.

Programmers can use storage classes to control the scope and persistence of data. Most variables in a C++ program are automatic variables declared locally in a function. Local variables have `auto` storage class by default. Automatic variables are created at the point they are declared in a function. They go out of scope when the function terminates.

The storage class `static` changes both scope and persistence. We can apply it to variables declared in functions, to variables declared outside of functions, to functions, to object data members, and to object member functions.

The `register` storage class has the same scope and persistence that automatic does. Variables declared with the storage class `register` are kept in the CPU's on-chip registers as much as possible. The use of the `register` storage class may speed up programs.

The `external` storage class is used for global variables.

Mutable data must be members of classes. A data member with the storage class `mutable` can be changed even if the object itself is declared `const`.

The `volatile` storage class tells the compiler that something other than the software can change the value in a variable. This is primarily provided for programming directly to the hardware.

We can control the scope of data and member functions in objects using the keywords `public`, `protected`, and `private`. Public members are available to the entire program. Protected members can be seen by the class's member functions and by those of any class derived from the object. Private members are available only to the class's member functions.

Review Questions

1. What is scope?
2. What is persistence?
3. What is data encapsulation?
4. Is data encapsulation a consideration in software development? Why or why not?
5. How can the keyword `const` be used to control changes to data?
6. What are automatic variables? What scope and persistence do they have?
7. What scope and persistence do the following have?
   a. `static` local variables
   b. `static` module global variables
   c. `static` nonmember functions
   d. `static` member data
   e. `static` member functions
8. What scope and persistence do the storage classes `register`, `extern`, `mutable`, and `volatile` have?
9. How do the following keywords affect the scope of object members?
   a. `public`
   b. `protected`
   c. `private`
10. What are three problems associated with global variables?

Exercises

1. Explain the pros and cons of module global variables. *Hint:* Can they suffer from any of the problems of global variables that have the storage class `extern`?
2. Some software designers think that `private` data members should not be declared in classes. They assert that you can hide and encapsulate the data more completely if you define all object data members as `static` module global variables. Explain why you think this approach is or is not a good design idea.
3. Explain the pros and cons of using `protected` data members in objects. Explain the pros and cons of using `protected` member functions.

4. If a parameter is passed by value to a function, is it really necessary to make it a `const` parameter when the function should not change its value? Explain why or why not. *Hint:* From the calling function, pass by value and pass by reference look the same.
5. Name three possible uses for `static` object data members and `static` object member functions.
6. It would be nice if we could associate constants with a class by declaring `const` variables in the class's public section. Write a program that declares a `const` data member in a class's public section. Be sure to initialize the `const` member. Explain what happened.
7. Modify the text editor program from Hands On 22.5 in Chapter 22. All member functions that do not modify the data of the object that invoked them should be declared `const`. Explain any exceptions to this rule that you discover. *Hint:* You must have a non-`const` `operator []` function in both of these classes. However, it's possible to also have a `const operator []` function as well.
8. The text editor in Hands On 22.5 contains the functions `ClearScreen()` and `DisplayMenu()` in the file *TEdit.cpp*. Should these functions be `static`? Explain the reasons for your answer.
9. The `text_string` class in Hands On 22.5 contains two `private` member functions. Explain any advantages and disadvantages that you can think of to making these functions `static` nonmember functions in the file *TString.cpp*. Some designers think that all private member functions should be converted into `static` nonmember functions. Do you agree? Explain why or why not.
10. In Hands On 22.5, some of the parameters of the member functions of `text_string` and `text_buffer` are not `const`. Look at each one and explain why it should or should not be `const`. *Hint:* If you have trouble figuring it out, modify the program so that the parameters are `const`. Compile, link, and test the program. Explain what happens.

Chapter Glossary

Module Global Variables Variables that can be seen by all functions in a CPP file.

24 Pointers and Inheritance

Objectives

After reading this chapter, you should be able to:

- Use pointers to base classes to access derived objects.
- Use virtual functions to design base classes.
- Create and use virtual destructors.
- Design abstract base classes using pure virtual functions.

Preview

The combination of pointers and inheritance in C++ is extremely powerful. This chapter examines these ideas in greater depth.

Designing with Base Classes

One goal of C++ is to enable programmers to create base classes that indicate the design of derived classes. For example, we could create a set of classes for a graphics application. The graphics our program displays on the screen can be based on software objects. The graphics program would display circles, rectangles, squares, triangles, and other shapes.

This description already indicates the basic design of the software. Since the program displays a variety of shapes, we should think about defining a base class called `shape`. The `shape` class should contain all of the information that is common to all shapes. Classes to implement circles, rectangles, and so on can be derived from the `shape` class. The `shape` class serves as a design guide for all of the derived classes.

In situations such as this one, we often need to store all of the different types of shapes in a single collection. In the graphics program example, it would be nice if we could define an array of pointers to the shapes. As the user creates more shapes, the program would dynamically allocate whatever shape the user wants. Each dynamically allocated shape would be pointed at by a pointer in the array.

The problem is, what data type do we declare the array?

C++ provides us with an easy answer. Pointers to base classes are type compatible with pointers to derived classes. Simply put, we can use pointers to base classes to point at objects from derived classes. Hands On 24.1 demonstrates this technique.

Hands On 24.1

Objective

Define a shape class. It should keep track of the current position of the shape on the screen. Derive a circle class from the shape class. Also derive a rectangle class from it. Derive a square class from the rectangle class. Write a program that demonstrates the functionality of these classes.

Experiment

Type the following program into your IDE or text editor. Compile, link, and run it. This program consists of the files *ShpProg.cpp, Point.h, Point.cpp, Shape.h, Shape.cpp, Circle.h, Circle.cpp, Rect.h, Rect.cpp, Square.h, Square.cpp, ShapeLst.h,* and *ShapeLst.cpp.*

This is the file `ShpProg.cpp`.

```
#include "Point.h"
#include "Shape.h"
#include "Circle.h"
#include "Rect.h"
#include "Square.h"
#include "Shapelst.h"
#include <iostream.h>


void ClearScreen(void);
void DisplayMenu(void);
void Pause(void);
void EatNewline(void);


int main()
{
   const int DEFAULT_SHAPE_LIST_LENGTH = 10;
   const char BEEP_CHARACTER = (char)7;

   char choice;
   bool programError = false;
   shape_list allShapes(DEFAULT_SHAPE_LIST_LENGTH);
   shape *currentShape;

   for (bool done=false; !done; )
   {
      ClearScreen();
      DisplayMenu();
      cin >> choice;
      EatNewline();
      if ((choice == 'D') || (choice == 'd'))
      {
         done = true;
      }
      else
      {
         cout << endl << "Please enter the X ";
         cout << "location of the shape's origin :";
         int originX;
         cin >> originX;
```

```
cout << endl << "Please enter the Y ";
cout << "location of the shape's origin :";
int originY;
cin >> originY;
point shapeOrigin(originX,originY);

if ((choice == 'C') || (choice == 'c'))
{
   circle *circlePointer = new circle;
   if (circlePointer)
   {
      *circlePointer = shapeOrigin;

      int radius;
      cout << endl << "Please enter ";
      cout << "the circle's radius :";
      cin >> radius;

      *circlePointer = radius;
      currentShape = circlePointer;
   }
   else
   {
      programError = true;
   }
}
else if ((choice == 'R') || (choice == 'r'))
{
   rectangle *rectPointer;
   rectPointer = new rectangle;
   if (rectPointer)
   {
      *rectPointer = shapeOrigin;

      int height;
      cout << endl << "Please enter ";
      cout << "the rectangle's height :";
      cin >> height;
      rectPointer->Height(height);

      int width;
      cout << endl << "Please enter ";
      cout << "the rectangle's width :";
      cin >> width;
      rectPointer->Width(width);

      currentShape = rectPointer;
   }
   else
   {
      programError = true;
   }
}
else if ((choice == 'S') || (choice == 's'))
{
   square *squarePointer;
   squarePointer = new square;
   if (squarePointer)
```

```
            {
               *squarePointer = shapeOrigin;

               int edgeLength;
               cout << endl << "Please enter ";
               cout << "the length of the square's edge :";
               cin >> edgeLength;
               squarePointer->EdgeLength(edgeLength);

            }
            else
            {
               programError = true;
            }

            currentShape = (shape *)squarePointer;
         }
         else
         {
            cout << BEEP_CHARACTER;
         }

         if ((programError) ||
             (allShapes.Insert(currentShape) != NO_ERROR))
         {
            programError = true;
            cout << endl << "There is not enough memory to ";
            cout << "create the shape you selected.";
            Pause();
         }
      }
   }

   for (int i=0;(!programError) && (i<allShapes.ListLength());i++)
   {
      allShapes[i]->Display();
   }

   return (0);
}


void ClearScreen(void)
{
   const int LINES_ON_SCREEN = 25;

   for (int i=0;i<LINES_ON_SCREEN;i++)
   {
      cout << endl;
   }
}

void DisplayMenu(void)
{
   cout << "Please enter one of the following:" << endl;
   cout << "C  Create Circle" << endl;
   cout << "R  Create Rectangle" << endl;
   cout << "S  Create Square" << endl;
```

```
   cout << "D  Display Shapes and Quit" << endl;
   cout << "Enter Selection: ";
}


void Pause(void)
{
   cout << endl << "Press Enter to continue...";
   char inputChar;
   cin >> inputChar;
   EatNewline();
}


void EatNewline(void)
{
   if (cin.peek() == '\n')
   {
      cin.ignore(1,'\n');
   }
}
```

This is the file `Point.h`.

```
#ifndef POINT_H
#define POINT_H

class point
{
public:
   point(void);
   point(const int xCoordinate,const int yCoordinate);

   void X(const int newX);
   int X(void) const;

   void Y(const int newY);
   int Y(void) const;

private:
   int x,y;
};

#endif
```

This is the file `Point.cpp`.

```
#include "Point.h"

point::point(void)
{
   x=y=0;
}


point::point(const int xCoordinate,const int yCoordinate)
{
   x=xCoordinate;
   y=yCoordinate;
}
```

```
void point::X(const int newX)
{
   x=newX;
}


int point::X(void) const
{
   return (x);
}


void point::Y(const int newY)
{
   y=newY;
}


int point::Y(void) const
{
   return (y);
}
```

This is the file `Shape.h`*.*

```
#ifndef SHAPE_H
#define SHAPE_H

#include <iostream.h>
#include "Point.h"

class shape
{
public:
   shape(void);
   shape(const point shapeOrigin);

   shape &operator =(const point shapeOrigin);

   void Origin(const point shapeOrigin);
   point Origin(void) const ;

   void Display(void) const;

// Private member data.
private:
   point origin;
};

#endif
```

This is the file `Shape.cpp`*.*

```
#include "Shape.h"

 shape::shape(void)
{
```

```
   origin.X(0);
   origin.Y(0);
}

shape::shape(const point shapeOrigin)
{
   origin = shapeOrigin;
}


shape &shape::operator =(const point shapeOrigin)
{
   origin = shapeOrigin;
   return (*this);
}


void shape::Origin(const point shapeOrigin)
{
   origin = shapeOrigin;
}


point shape::Origin(void) const
{
   return (origin);
}


void shape::Display(void) const
{
   cout << endl << "This is a shape." << endl;
   cout << "Origin = (" << origin.X() << ',';
   cout << origin.Y() << ')';
}
```

This is the file `Circle.h`.

```
#ifndef CIRCLE_H
#define CIRCLE_H

#include "shape.h"
#include "point.h"


class circle : public shape
{
public:
   circle(void);
   circle(const point &circleCenter,const int circleRadius);

   void Radius(const int circleRadius);
   int Radius(void) const;

   circle &operator =(const point &circleCenter);
   circle &operator =(const int circleRadius);
   void Display(void) const;
```

```
private:
   int radius;
};
#endif
```

This is the file `Circle.cpp`.

```
#include "Circle.h"


circle::circle(void) : shape()
{
   radius = 0;
}


circle::circle(const point &circleCenter,const int circleRadius)
{
   Origin(circleCenter);
   radius = circleRadius;
}


void circle::Radius(const int circleRadius)
{
   radius = circleRadius;
}


int circle::Radius(void) const
{
   return (radius);
}


circle &circle::operator =(const point &circleCenter)
{
   Origin(circleCenter);
   return (*this);
}


circle &circle::operator =(const int circleRadius)
{
   radius = circleRadius;
   return (*this);
}


void circle::Display(void) const
{
   cout << "This is a circle." << endl;
   cout << "Center = (" << Origin().X() << ',';
   cout << Origin().Y() << ')';
   cout << endl << "Radius = ";
   cout << radius;

}
```

This is the file `Rect.h`.

```
#ifndef RECT_H
#define RECT_H

class rectangle : public shape
{
public:
   rectangle(void);
   rectangle(const int rectHeight,const int rectWidth);
   rectangle(const int rectHeight,const int rectWidth,const point &upLeft);

   rectangle &operator =(const point &upLeft);

   void Height(const int rectHeight);
   int Height(void) const;

   void Width(const int rectWidth);
   int Width(void) const;

   void Display(void) const;

private:
   int height,width;
};

#endif
```

This is the file `Rect.cpp`.

```
#include "Rect.h"

rectangle::rectangle(void) : shape()
{
   height=width=0;
}


rectangle::rectangle(const int rectHeight,
                     const int rectWidth) : shape()
{
   height = rectHeight;
   width = rectWidth;
}


rectangle::rectangle(const int rectHeight,
                     const int rectWidth,
                     const point &upLeft) : shape(upLeft)
{
   height = rectHeight;
   width = rectWidth;
}


rectangle &rectangle::operator =(const point &upLeft)
{
   Origin(upLeft);
   return (*this);
}
```

```
void rectangle::Height(const int rectHeight)
{
   height = rectHeight;
}


int rectangle::Height(void) const
{
   return (height);
}


void rectangle::Width(const int rectWidth)
{
   width = rectWidth;
}


int rectangle::Width(void) const
{
   return (width);
}


void rectangle::Display(void) const
{
   cout << "This is a rectangle." << endl;
   cout << "Upper Left Corner = (" << Origin().X() << ',';
   cout << Origin().Y() << ')';
   cout << endl << "Height = ";
   cout << height << endl;
   cout << "Width = " << width;
}
```

This is the file `Square.h`.

```
#ifndef SQUARE_H
#define SQUARE_H

class square : private rectangle
{
public:
   square(const int edgeLength = 0);
   square(const int edgeLength,const point &upLeft);

   square &operator =(const point upLeft);
   square &operator =(const int edgeLength);

   void Origin(const point upLeft);
   point Origin(void) const ;

   void EdgeLength(int const edgeLength);
   int EdgeLength(void) const;

   void Display(void) const;
};

#endif
```

This is the file `Square.cpp`.

```
#include "Square.h"

square::square(const int edgeLength) : rectangle(edgeLength,
                                                 edgeLength)
{
}


square::square(const int edgeLength,
               const point &upLeft) : rectangle(edgeLength,
                                                edgeLength,
                                                upLeft)
{
}


square &square::operator =(const point upLeft)
{
   rectangle::Origin(upLeft);
   return (*this);
}


square &square::operator =(const int edgeLength)
{
   Height(edgeLength);
   Width(edgeLength);
   return (*this);
}


void square::Origin(const point upLeft)
{
   rectangle::Origin(upLeft);
}


point square::Origin(void) const
{
   return (rectangle::Origin());
}


void square::EdgeLength(int const edgeLength)
{
   Height(edgeLength);
   Width(edgeLength);
}


int square::EdgeLength(void) const
{
   return (Height());
}


void square::Display(void) const
```

```
{
   cout << "This is a square." << endl;
   cout << "Upper Left Corner = (" << Origin().X() << ',';
   cout << Origin().Y() << ')';
   cout << endl << "Edge Length = ";
   cout << EdgeLength();
}
```

This is the file `ShapeLst.h`.

```
#ifndef SHAPELST_H
#define SHAPELST_H

#include "shape.h"

const int DEFAULT_LIST_LENGTH = 10;

const int NO_ERROR = 0;
const int OUT_OF_MEMORY = -1;
const int UNKNOWN_ERROR = -2;



class shape_list
{
public:
   shape_list(int initialListLength=0);
   ~shape_list(void);

   int Insert(shape *aShape);

   const shape *operator [](const int index) const;

   int ListLength(void);

// Private member functions.
private:
   int FindEmptySpot(void);
   int GrowList(void);
   int AllocateList(int listLength);

private:
   shape **allShapes;
   int totalShapes,shapeArrayLength;
};


#endif
```

This is the file `Shapelst.cpp`

```
#include "shapelst.h"
#include "assert.h"


shape_list::shape_list(int initialListLength)
{
   shapeArrayLength = initialListLength;
   allShapes = NULL;
```

```
    totalShapes = 0;
}


shape_list::~shape_list(void)
{
    // If the array is not empty...
    if (allShapes)
    {
        // For each pointer in the array...
        for (int i=0;i<shapeArrayLength;i++)
        {
            // If the pointer points to a shape...
            if (allShapes[i])
            {
                // Delete it.
                delete allShapes[i];
            }
        }

        // Delete the array of pointers.
        delete [] allShapes;

        // Not necessary, but still a good idea.
        allShapes = NULL;
        shapeArrayLength = 0;
    }
}


int shape_list::Insert(shape *aShape)
{
    int index, returnStatus = NO_ERROR;

    // If the shape list is not empty...
    if (allShapes)
    {
        index = FindEmptySpot();
        // If an empty spot was found...
        if (index >= 0)
        {
            // Insert the new shape.
            allShapes[index] = aShape;
            totalShapes++;
        }
        // Else if there's no room in the array...
        else
        {
            // Reallocate the array.
            returnStatus = GrowList();

            // If the array could be reallocated...
            if (returnStatus == NO_ERROR)
            {
                index = FindEmptySpot();

                // If no spot was found...
                if (index < 0)
                {
```

```
                // Something's really wrong.
                returnStatus = UNKNOWN_ERROR;
             }
             // Else an empty spot was found...
             else
             {
                // Put the shape into the array.
                allShapes[index] = aShape;
                totalShapes++;
             }
          }
          // Else the array could not be reallocated...
          else
          {
             returnStatus = OUT_OF_MEMORY;
          }
       }
    }
    // Else the list is empty...
    else
    {
       returnStatus = GrowList();

       if (returnStatus == NO_ERROR)
       {
          index = FindEmptySpot();

          // If no spot was found...
          if (index < 0)
          {
             // Something's really wrong.
             returnStatus = UNKNOWN_ERROR;
          }
          // Else an empty spot was found...
          else
          {
             // Put the shape into the array.
             allShapes[index] = aShape;
             totalShapes++;
          }
       }
    }

    return (returnStatus);
 }


 const shape *shape_list::operator [](const int index) const
 {
    shape *temp = NULL;

    if ((index >= 0) && (index < totalShapes))
    {
       temp = allShapes[index];
    }

    return (temp);
 }
```

```
int shape_list::ListLength(void)
{
   return (totalShapes);
}


int shape_list::FindEmptySpot(void)
{
   int index;

   // Find an empty spot in the list.
   if (totalShapes<shapeArrayLength)
   {
      index = totalShapes;
   }
   else
   {
      index = -1;
   }

   return (index);
}


int shape_list::GrowList(void)
{
   int errorStatus = NO_ERROR;
   int listLength = shapeArrayLength;

   // If the list is not empty...
   if (allShapes)
   {
      // Set the new size.
      listLength += DEFAULT_LIST_LENGTH;

      errorStatus = AllocateList(listLength);
   }
   // Else the list is empty...
   else
   {
      // If the list is empty but we're doing a delayed allocation...
      if (shapeArrayLength > 0)
      {
         /* The requested list size is stored in listLength,
         so we can set shapeArrayLength to zero to match the list's
         real size. */
         shapeArrayLength = 0;
      }

      // If the list is empty and we're NOT doing a delayed allocation...
      if (listLength == 0)
      {
         listLength = DEFAULT_LIST_LENGTH;
      }

      /* listLength should now be non-zero. Because the list is empty,
      shapeArrayLength should be zero. */
      errorStatus = AllocateList(listLength);
   }
```

```
   return (errorStatus);
}



int shape_list::AllocateList(int listLength)
{
   assert(listLength!=0);
   assert((shapeArrayLength > 0) ? (allShapes!=NULL):true);

   int errorStatus = NO_ERROR;
   shape **temp;

   temp = new shape * [listLength];

   // If the new array could not be allocated...
   if (!temp)
   {
      errorStatus = OUT_OF_MEMORY;
   }
   // Else the array was allocated...
   else
   {
      int i;

      // Copy the contents of the current list into the new list.
      // If the current list is empty, this loop won't execute.
      for (i=0;i<shapeArrayLength;i++)
      {
         temp[i]=allShapes[i];
      }

      // Set unused spots in the new array to NULL.
      for (i=shapeArrayLength;i<listLength;i++)
      {
         temp[i]=NULL;
      }

      // Delete the current array.
      if (allShapes)
      {
         delete [] allShapes;
      }

      // Set the new array as the current array.
      allShapes = temp;
      shapeArrayLength = listLength;
   }

   return (errorStatus);
}
```

Results

```
Please enter one of the following:
C  Create Circle
R  Create Rectangle
S  Create Square
```

```
D  Display Shapes and Quit
Enter Selection: c

Please enter the X location of the shape's origin :10

Please enter the Y location of the shape's origin :20

Please enter the circle's radius :30

Please enter one of the following:
C  Create Circle
R  Create Rectangle
S  Create Square
D  Display Shapes and Quit
Enter Selection: r

Please enter the X location of the shape's origin :20

Please enter the Y location of the shape's origin :30

Please enter the rectangle's height :40

Please enter the rectangle's width :50

Please enter one of the following:
C  Create Circle
R  Create Rectangle
S  Create Square
D  Display Shapes and Quit
Enter Selection: s

Please enter the X location of the shape's origin :30

Please enter the Y location of the shape's origin :40

Please enter the length of the square's edge :60

Please enter one of the following:
C  Create Circle
R  Create Rectangle
S  Create Square
D  Display Shapes and Quit
Enter Selection: d

This is a shape.
Origin = (10,20)
This is a shape.
Origin = (20,30)
This is a shape.
Origin = (30,40)
```

Analysis

This example program utilizes many of the concepts presented in the last few chapters. It makes heavy use of dynamic allocation, pointers, and inheritance. Although it merely prints the attributes of each shape rather than drawing them, this program illustrates a design style that could easily be applied to a wide range of graphics applications.

The main() function in the file *ShpPrg.cpp* begins by declaring some constants and variables. Next, it enters a for loop, which runs until the user decides to print the contents of a shape list. It displays a menu asking the user to select the type of shape to create. Each time the user creates a shape, the program adds it to the shape list. From the main menu, the user can also choose to display the shapes and quit the program.

Whenever the user creates a shape, the main() function displays a series of prompts. It asks for the *X* and *Y* coordinates of the shape's origin. The origin of a shape is different for each type of shape. For example, the origin of a circle is its center. The origin for rectangles and squares is the upper left corner.

If the user chooses to create a circle, main() dynamically allocates a circle object. It stores the origin into the circle object and prompts the user for the radius. It saves the response into the object and sets the variable currentShape to point at the dynamically allocated circle object. Note that currentShape is a pointer to a shape object, not a circle object. This is OK because pointers to base objects are type-compatible with pointers to derived objects.

In the Results section of this Hands On example, I chose to create a circle, a rectangle, and a square. As you can see from the main() function, the program uses the second if statement in the series of chained if statements to handle this case. Whenever the user tells the program to create a rectangle, it dynamically allocates a rectangle object. The program prompts the user for the height and width of the rectangle and stores the information in the rectangle object. Finally, the program stores the address of the rectangle object in the variable currentShape. As with circle objects, rectangle objects are derived from shape objects in this program. Therefore, we can use a pointer to a shape to point at a rectangle.

If the user selects 'S' or 's', the main() function dynamically allocates a square object. It prompts the user for the length of the square's edges, and stores the information in the square object.

Some C++ programming literature would call the square class a "child" class and the rectangle class a "parent" class. Under this naming scheme, the shape class would be a "grandparent" class.

Next the program points currentShape at the square object. Notice that a type cast is necessary here, while it was not needed with the previous shapes. The square class is derived from the rectangle class, not the shape class. Some compilers will issue a warning about this if you don't put in a type cast. However, since square is derived from rectangle and rectangle is derived from shape, the C++ language specification allows us to use a shape pointer to point at a square.

If there is no error creating the shape the user wants, the program inserts the shape into a list of shape objects. When the user chooses to display the contents of the shape list, the for loop terminates. The program enters a short for loop near the end of the main() function. It prints the information in each graphical shape in the shape list.

Every different type of shape requires an origin that gives it a position in an *X,Y* space. This program implements the origin as a point object, which is defined in *Point.h*. Its member functions appear in *Point.cpp*.

The point class has a very simple design. It uses two constructors, one with no arguments and one with two arguments. Alert Readers may notice that we could have used default parameter values on the constructor with two arguments, like this:

```
point(const int xCoordinate = 0,const int yCoordinate = 0);
```

This would allow us to eliminate the constructor with no arguments. It would also enable us to make variable declarations like the ones shown in Example 24.1.

EXAMPLE 24.1 Variable Declarations

```
point aPoint;
point thisPoint(10);
point thatPoint(20,30);
```

As you can see from Example 24.1, default parameter values allow us to declare variables with zero, one, or two arguments. However, declaring a variable with only an *X* coordinate would not have fit well with the concept of a point in an *X,Y* space. A point must have both an *X* and a *Y* coordinate. It doesn't make sense to have just an *X* coordinate. It should either have no location, or a location with both *X* and *Y* values. Therefore, the `point` class in this program does not use default parameter values.

The `point` class is primarily used by the `shape` class, which is defined in *Shape.h* and implemented in *Shape.cpp*.

The `shape` class also uses two constructors. One takes no arguments. The other requires that a `point` object be passed to it. The `shape` class also defines an overloaded assignment operator. It allows a `point` to be assigned to the `shape`. This sets the `shape`'s origin.

The other member functions in the `shape` class enable you to set value of the origin, get the value of the origin, or display the information that a `shape` object contains.

This program uses the `shape` class as the basis for all of the graphical shapes it defines. For example, the `circle` class derives from the `shape` class. You'll find the definition of the `circle` class in the file *Circle.h*. All of the `circle` class's member functions are defined in *Circle.cpp*. The `circle` class defines two constructors. The first takes no parameters. The second requires an *X,Y* position and a radius. It also defines two `operator =()` functions. One can be used to set the origin of a `circle`, which is its center. You can use the other to set a `circle`'s radius. In addition, the `circle` class provides a `Display()` function that prints a `circle` object's information.

Like the `circle` class, the `rectangle` class derives from the `shape` class. So the design of the `rectangle` class resembles the design of the `circle` class.

The `rectangle` class defines three constructors. The first takes no arguments. The second requires the `rectangle`'s height and width. The third constructor has parameters for the height, width, and origin. The origin of a `rectangle` is its upper left corner.

As with the `circle` class, the `rectangle` class defines an assignment operator function for setting the `rectangle`'s origin. It also defines functions to get and set the height and width. In addition, it has a `Display()` function.

Both the `circle` and `rectangle` classes contain functions that set or get the *X,Y* location of the graphical shape's origin. All of them call the `Origin()` function, which they inherit from the `shape` class. If you think that the maintenance programmer might not be able to easily find the `Origin()` function, you could use the scope resolution operator to specify that `Origin()` is a member of `shape`. That is, you could change all calls to `Origin()` to `shape::Origin()`.

TIP: Some C++ software designers believe that a liberal use of the scope resolution operator to show where inherited functions are defined will help clarify your code.

Doing this is not any more or less efficient than just using the name `Origin()`. However, it does clarify the code. Some software designers assert that programmers should always use the scope resolution operator to show which classes define inherited member functions. Getting into this habit is only a little more work. However, it can help maintenance programmers when you use complex inheritance schemes.

Unlike the `circle` and `rectangle` classes, the `square` class does not derive directly from the `shape` class. Instead, it inherits from the `rectangle` class. After all, a square is just a rectangle whose sides all have equal length.

Also, the `square` class uses private inheritance, not public. Chapter 19 stated that when using private inheritance, all of the inherited member functions are accessible only by member functions. This means that functions that are not members of the `square` class can't call the inherited `rectangle` and `shape` functions using a `square` object. Example 24.2 shows a function that is not a member of a class. It declares a `square` object and tries to call the `Height()` and `Width()` functions in the `rectangle` class. However, because `square` uses private inheritance, the function `DoSomething()` can't call `rectangle` functions using a `square` object.

EXAMPLE 24.2 An Attempt to Call a `rectangle` Function

```
void DoSomething(void)
{
    square aSquare;
    aSquare.Height(10);   // This will not compile!
    aSquare.Width(20);    // This will not compile!
}
```

This behavior is just what we want. Since a square is a rectangle whose height and width are the same length, we don't want programmers to call the `rectangle::Height()` and `rectangle::Width()` functions on a `square` object. If they could, they would be able to set the height and width to different values. Then the square would no longer be square!

The `square` class defines two constructors. The first takes one parameter, but it has a default value. Therefore, it can be used anywhere a no-arg constructor would be used. The second constructor requires the edge length and the `square`'s origin be passed in. The origin of a `square` is its upper left corner.

Notice that there is no actual code inside the body of the `square` constructors. They both simply call the `rectangle` constructors, setting the height and width to the same value.

The `square` class also offers an assignment operator to set the origin of a `square` object. If we had not used private inheritance, we could just call the first assignment operator function defined for the `rectangle` class. However, since it is not visible, we must define one for the `square` class.

Notice that the `square::operator =()` function calls the `rectangle::Origin()` function. However, the `rectangle` class does not define an `Origin()` function. It inherits one from the `shape` class. The `square` class cannot tell the difference. It sees all member functions and inherited functions in the `rectangle` class as if they were simply `rectangle` member functions.

Private inheritance prevents programmers from calling any `rectangle` or `shape` functions using a `square` object. However, we want programmers to call the `Origin()` functions on a `square`. Therefore, we must define the `Origin()` functions in the square class. They just call the `Origin()` functions that the rectangle class inherits from `shape`.

The technique of a function calling itself has many valid uses. It is called *recursion*.

By the way, the scope resolution operator must be used inside both of the `square::Origin()` functions. If we change the calls to `rectangle::Origin()` to just `Origin()`, the `square::Origin()` functions will just call themselves. That's not what we want here.

The `square` class provides a function to get the edge length and one to set the edge length. In addition, it defines a `Display()` function.

The `shape_list` class is important for several reasons. First, it encapsulates all of the functionality of maintaining the list of shapes. Operating on the shape list is one of the most complex parts of this Hands On program. It's much easier to debug this code if it is together in a single class.

Common types of container classes are classes that implement linked lists, queues, and various types of information trees.

Second, The `shape_list` class demonstrates the concept of a **container class.** Container classes do nothing but create, maintain, and destroy lists of information. The lists can take many forms. However, they all are intended to store information for efficient update and retrieval. It is extremely common to use container classes in your programs, so it's a good idea to get familiar with them.

The `shape_list` class creates a dynamically allocated array of pointers to shapes. That is, each element in the dynamically allocated array is a pointer to a `shape` object. The `shape` pointers can be used to point at any class derived from `shape`.

The `shape_list` class defines a single constructor. It takes one parameter that has a default value of 0. Therefore, you can declare `shape_list` variables with no constructor parameters if you want to.

The `shape_list` class uses a technique called **lazy memory allocation**. The constructor parameter enables the programmer using the `shape_list` class to specify an initial size for the shape list. However, the memory for the list is not allocated in the constructor. Instead, it's put off until an item is actually inserted into the list.

Why might this be a good idea? Put simply, lazy memory allocation makes error handling *much* easier. Suppose we were to allocate memory in the `shape_list` constructor. Now suppose that the allocation fails. How do we handle the error? We can't return an error code from the constructor. Calling the `assert()` function would make the program *very* unpopular.

We could declare a private data member to store an error code. However, our program would need to query the error status of every shape every time it called any function on any object. Also, every kind of shape would need to carry around the error status data member. So we'd end up with a program that is both slower and larger.

C++ supports a type of error handling called *exceptions*. However, there are problems with using exceptions in constructors.

There aren't a whole lot of options left. One way to handle this problem is to just not do anything in the constructor that might cause a serious error. That's where lazy memory allocation comes in.

By delaying the allocation of the memory for the `shape` list until we actually insert something into the list, we move the allocation out of the constructor. The `shape_list` class allocates memory in the `Insert()` function. Unlike a constructor, the `Insert()` function can return an error status value. However, before we look at the `Insert()` function, let's examine the `shape_list` class's destructor.

Actually, the `Insert()` function calls the function that calls the function that does the allocation. But the effect is the same.

All classes that perform dynamic memory allocation must define a destructor. The destructor needs to delete all of the memory that the object dynamically allocates. That's exactly what `shape_list::~shape_list()` does. For every pointer in the array of `shape` pointers, the destructor deletes the object pointed to by the array element. When all of the objects are gone, the destructor deletes the array of pointers.

TIP: When you use a container class written by someone else, find out if it takes ownership of the objects it contains.

Because the `shape_list` container class deletes the objects it contains, we say that it *assumes ownership* of the objects. The concept of object ownership is an important one to programmers. Some container classes do not take ownership of the objects they store. The assumption is that you, the programmer, will delete any object that you dynamically allocate. You take complete responsibility for preventing memory leaks. When you use a container class someone else wrote, it's a good idea to find out whether or not the container class takes ownership of the objects it stores.

The `shape_list::Insert()` function requires one parameter, a pointer to the shape to be inserted. The `Insert()` function does not allocate memory for the shape. It assumes that the memory is already allocated. If you look back at the `main()` function, you'll see that's exactly what it does.

If the shape list is already allocated, the `Insert()` function calls the private member function `FindEmptySpot()`. This function searches for an unused location in the array of `shape` pointers. If it finds one, the `Insert()` function copies the address of the `shape` into that array location.

If there are no empty spots in the array, `Insert()` invokes the `GrowList()` function. `GrowList()` is a private member function that reallocates the array of pointers to shapes. If there is enough available memory, the `GrowList()` function makes the array larger. `Insert()` then calls `FindEmptySpot()` again to search for the first unused location in the shape list array. When it finds one, it puts the `shape` into the list by storing its address in the array. If the `GrowList()` function can't allocate a larger array, `Insert()` sets an error status value and returns it.

The first time the program calls the `Insert()` function, the list will be empty. The `Insert()` function calls `GrowList()` to allocate the list to a default size. If the programmer specified an initial size for the list, the `shape_list` object uses lazy memory allocation. As we'll soon see, the `GrowList()` function handles that as well.

The next function in *ShapeLst.cpp* is `operator []()`. This function enables programs to access a `shape_list` object as if the object itself were an array. One nice thing about adding an `operator []()` function to a class is that the class can use any kind of container (array, linked list, binary tree, etc.) and it will still look like an array. Other programmers using the `shape_list` class are not affected if you change the internal representation of the list from an array to another data structure.

The `shape_list` class also defines the `ListLength()` function, which returns the number of shapes in the list. The list might actually be longer. That is, the program may have allocated many more locations in the list array than it uses. The `ListLength()` function reports the actual number of array locations the list is using.

`FindEmptySpot()` is also a relatively straightforward function. It checks to see whether the first available spot is less than or equal to the number of spots allocated. If it is, it sets the return value to the first available spot. If not, it sets the return value to –1. Other `shape_list` functions, such as `Insert()`, can test the return value to see if it found an empty location in the list array.

The `GrowList()` function begins by testing to see whether the list is currently empty or not. If it is not, then the `GrowList()` function needs to allocate a new, longer array. It must also copy all existing pointer addresses in the current array into a longer array that it allocates. It must delete the old array and set the longer array as the current list.

Most of the work of growing the list is performed in the private member function `Allocate()`. The `GrowList()` primarily tests the list to see if whether is empty or not. It also checks to determine if the program is using lazy allocation.

If memory is currently allocated for the list array, `GrowList()` sets the desired number of list elements to a larger size. It then calls `Allocate()`.

If there is no memory allocated for the list, `GrowList()` determines whether the program is performing lazy memory allocation. If it is, the requested list size is stored in the private data member `shapeArrayLength`. `GrowList()` saves that value in the local variable `listLength` and passes it to the `Allocate()` function. It sets the `shapeArrayLength` to zero so that the `Allocate()` function will know that the list is empty. If the list is empty but `GrowList()` is not doing lazy allocation, then it needs to set the list to a default size. Once all of these conditions are tested for and the proper adjustments made, `GrowList()` can call `Allocate()`.

The `Allocate()` function uses assertions to verify that the information it needs is correct. The first call to `assert()` ensures that the programmer does not try to call `Allocate()` to allocate a list with no elements in it. The second call to `assert()` checks to see whether the private data member `shapeArrayLength` is greater than zero. If it is, it makes sure that `allShapes` is not equal to NULL. This helps ensure that the list size contained in `shapeArrayLength` is accurate. If `shapeArrayLength` is equal to zero, the assertion just evaluates to `true`.

`Allocate()` next tries to allocate memory for the larger array. If it can't allocate the memory, it sets an error status value and returns it. If there is enough memory available for the new array, it will be allocated. The `Allocate()` function enters a `for` loop to copy all of the shape pointers in `allShapes` into the newly allocated array. Next, it uses another `for` loop to initialize all of the unused array locations to NULL.

When this program runs, it enables us to create as many circles, rectangles, and squares as we want. The only limit imposed on the size of the list is how much memory you have on your computer. There is one problem, though. When it enters the last `for` loop in `main()`, the program calls the `Display()` function in the `shape` class. We would like it to call the `Display()` function for each of the derived classes. To do that, we need to use virtual functions, which are presented next.

Base Classes and Virtual Functions

Whenever we use a pointer to a base class to point at a derived object, the C++ compiler generates the executable code so that it uses the type of the pointer. The compiler assumes that the pointer points at a base class object. In Hands On 24.1, the pointers in the shape list were all of type shape. When the compiler compiled and linked the program, it assumed that the objects to which the pointers pointed were all of type shape. The last for loop in the main() function contains a call to Display(). Because the compiler assumes the array pointers are pointing at shape objects, it calls the shape::Display(). What we really want is for it to call the Display() functions in the derived classes.

The C++ language specification provides the keyword virtual, which can be used on class member functions. Making a function virtual tells the C++ compiler to use the contents of a pointer, not its type. If the base class pointer points at an object of a derived class and the function being called is virtual, the program examines the contents of the pointer. Enough information is kept in the pointer for the program to know that it points to a derived object. It will call the function in the derived class instead of the base class.

Hands On 24.2 demonstrates the use of virtual functions. It repeats the program from Hands On 24.1. However, it declares the Display() function in the shape class to be virtual.

Hands On 24.2

Objective

Define a shape class. It should keep track of the current position of the shape on the screen. Derive a circle class from the shape class. Also derive a rectangle class from it. Derive a square class from the rectangle class. Write a program that demonstrates the functionality of these classes.

Experiment

Use the files you created for Hands On 24.1. Add the word virtual to the definition of the shape::Display() function as shown in the bold type below:

```
class shape
{
public:
   shape(void);
   shape(const point shapeOrigin);

   shape &operator =(const point shapeOrigin);

   void Origin(const point shapeOrigin);
   point Origin(void) const ;

   virtual void Display(void) const;

// Private member data.
private:
   point origin;
};
```

Results

```
Please enter one of the following:
C  Create Circle
R  Create Rectangle
S  Create Square
D  Display Shapes and Quit
Enter Selection: c

Please enter the X location of the shape's origin :10
```

```
Please enter the Y location of the shape's origin :20

Please enter the circle's radius :30


Please enter one of the following:
C  Create Circle
R  Create Rectangle
S  Create Square
D  Display Shapes and Quit
Enter Selection: r

Please enter the X location of the shape's origin :20

Please enter the Y location of the shape's origin :30

Please enter the rectangle's height :40

Please enter the rectangle's width :50


Please enter one of the following:
C  Create Circle
R  Create Rectangle
S  Create Square
D  Display Shapes and Quit
Enter Selection: s

Please enter the X location of the shape's origin :30

Please enter the Y location of the shape's origin :40

Please enter the length of the square's edge :50


Please enter one of the following:
C  Create Circle
R  Create Rectangle
S  Create Square
D  Display Shapes and Quit
Enter Selection: d

This is a circle.
Center = (10,20)
Radius = 30
This is a rectangle.
Upper Left Corner = (20,30)
Height = 40
Width = 50
This is a square.
Upper Left Corner = (30,40)
Edge Length = 50
```

TIP: Whenever you think a function in a base class might be overridden in a derived class, make the base class function virtual.

Analysis

As you can see from the Results section, making the `shape::Display()` function virtual causes the program to use the contents of each pointer in the pointer array, not the type. Since the first pointer in the shape list points at a `circle`, the program calls the `circle::Display()` function rather than `shape::Display()`. Likewise, the second and third shapes are a `rectangle` and `square`, respectively. The program calls `rectangle::Display()` and `square::Display()` in that order.

Virtual Destructors

Since a derived object calls the constructor of its base class, it should also call the base class's destructor. Calling the base class's destructor ensures that your program performs all of the cleanup it needs to when it is finished with an object.

The C++ compiler will not automatically generate a call to the base class's destructor if you are using a base class pointer to point at a derived object. You must specify the call yourself. However, you do not use the same notation that you do to call the constructor.

You can get your compiler to generate a call to the base object's destructor by specifying that the base class's destructor is a virtual destructor. The program in Hands On 24.3 shows how to create and use a virtual destructor.

Hands On 24.3

Objective

Write a program that uses a virtual destructor.

Experiment

Type the following program into your IDE or text editor. Compile, link, and run it.

```
#include <iostream.h>

class base_class
{
public:
   base_class(void);
   virtual ~base_class();

   void PrintBaseDataMember(void);

private:
   int baseClassDataMember;
};



base_class::base_class(void)
{
   cout << "base_class constructor" << endl;
   baseClassDataMember = 10;
}



base_class::~base_class()
{
   cout << "base class destructor" << endl;
}
```

```
void base_class::PrintBaseDataMember(void)
{
   cout << baseClassDataMember << endl;
}


class derived_class : public base_class
{
public:
   derived_class(void);
   ~derived_class();
   void PrintDerivedDataMember(void);

private:
   int derivedClassDataMember;
};


derived_class::derived_class(void) : base_class()
{
   cout << "derived_class constructor" << endl;
   derivedClassDataMember=20;
}


derived_class::~derived_class(void)
{
   cout << "derived class destructor" << endl;
}


void derived_class::PrintDerivedDataMember(void)
{
   cout << derivedClassDataMember<< endl;
}



int main()
{
   base_class *derivedClassObject;

   derivedClassObject = new derived_class;

   derivedClassObject->PrintBaseDataMember();
   derivedClassObject->PrintDerivedDataMember();

   return (0);
}
```

Results

```
base_class constructor
derived_class constructor
10
20
derived class destructor
base class destructor
```

Analysis

This program uses the keyword `virtual` on the prototype of the destructor for the `base_class` object. Notice that the word `virtual` does not need to appear on the function itself. Whenever the program creates a `derived_class` object, it calls both the `base_class` constructor and the `derived_class` constructor. Making the `base_class` destructor virtual tells the compiler to call the `base_class` destructor when the program destroys a `derived_class` object. It will call the `base_class` destructor even if the program is pointing to a `derived_class` object with a `base_class` pointer.

The concept demonstrated in Hands On 24.3 can and should be applied to the program in Hands On 24.1 and 24.2. The `shape` destructor should be virtual. If it isn't, there may be a memory leak. Hands On 24.4 repeats the program from Hands On 24.2. However, it makes the `shape` destructor virtual.

Hands On 24.4

Objective

Define a shape class. It should keep track of the current position of the shape on the screen. Derive a circle class from the shape class. Also derive a rectangle class from it. Derive a square class from the rectangle class. Write a program that demonstrates the functionality of these classes.

Experiment

Use the .CPP and .H files you used in Hands On 24.2. A new version of the files *Shape.h* and *Shape.cpp* is given below. Use these versions rather than the ones you used in Hands On 24.2. The changes to the files are shown in bold type.

This is the file `Shape.h`*.*

```
#ifndef SHAPE_H
#define SHAPE_H

#include <iostream.h>
#include "point.h"

class shape
{
public:
   shape(void);
   shape(const point shapeOrigin);
                     virtual~shape();

   shape &operator =(const point shapeOrigin);

   void Origin(const point shapeOrigin);
   point Origin(void) const ;

   virtual void Display(void) const;

// Private member data.
private:
   point origin;
```

```
};

#endif
```

This is the file Shape.cpp.

```
#include "Shape.h"

shape::shape(void)
{
   origin.X(0);
   origin.Y(0);
}

shape::shape(const point shapeOrigin)
{
   origin = shapeOrigin;
}


shape::~shape()
{
}

shape &shape::operator =(const point shapeOrigin)
{
   origin = shapeOrigin;
   return (*this);
}


void shape::Origin(const point shapeOrigin)
{
   origin = shapeOrigin;
}


point shape::Origin(void) const
{
   return (origin);
}
```

Results

```
Please enter one of the following:
C  Create Circle
R  Create Rectangle
S  Create Square
D  Display Shapes and Quit
Enter Selection: c

Please enter the X location of the shape's origin :10

Please enter the Y location of the shape's origin :20

Please enter the circle's radius :30


Please enter one of the following:
C  Create Circle
R  Create Rectangle
```

```
S  Create Square
D  Display Shapes and Quit
Enter Selection: r

Please enter the X location of the shape's origin :20

Please enter the Y location of the shape's origin :30

Please enter the rectangle's height :40

Please enter the rectangle's width :50


Please enter one of the following:
C  Create Circle
R  Create Rectangle
S  Create Square
D  Display Shapes and Quit
Enter Selection: s

Please enter the X location of the shape's origin :30

Please enter the Y location of the shape's origin :40

Please enter the length of the square's edge :50


Please enter one of the following:
C  Create Circle
R  Create Rectangle
S  Create Square
D  Display Shapes and Quit
Enter Selection: d

This is a circle.
Center = (10,20)
Radius = 30
This is a rectangle.
Upper Left Corner = (20,30)
Height = 40
Width = 50
This is a square.
Upper Left Corner = (30,40)
Edge Length = 50
```

Analysis

Although the output of this program is no different than the version in Hands On 24.2, this program now uses a virtual destructor in the `shape` class. It will perform all of the necessary deallocation.

Abstract Base Classes Using Pure Virtual Functions

The examples in this chapter demonstrate that the technique of using inheritance and base class pointers provides C++ class designers with flexibility and power. In the Hands On programs that define the `shape` class, all of the classes derived from `shape` have common characteristics. These are implemented by the `shape` class itself. Using inheritance, we can specify the general interface design of the derived classes. With pointers to the `shape` class, we can call functions that follow the interface design. However, the implementation of the functions is specific to each derived class.

Inheritance, base class pointers, and virtual functions enable C++ programmers to separate the design of a class's interface from its implementation. We can specify the interface in a base class. We can then implement the functionality in a derived class. The ability to separate design and implementation enables us to specify how groups of related objects should operate.

The advantage of this is that it helps lower the learning curve for new programmers. In the graphics shapes examples in this chapter, you can get a general idea of how each of the derived classes work by knowing how the `shape` class works. Once they see how the Hands On programs implement `shape`, `circle`, and `rectangle`, most programmers should have no trouble figuring out how `square` works. Now that you've seen how these programs implement `shape`, `circle`, `rectangle`, and `square`, would it be hard for you to create your own `triangle` class?

The previous Hands On programs in this chapter each provided a default implementation for the `Display()` function. The `shape` class contained code for `Display()`. However, in actual practice, there would be no reason to call `shape::Display()`. In fact, if your program did call it, it would probably be an error.

If it is a mistake to call a virtual function in a base class, you may just want to eliminate the default implementation. The C++ language specification enables you to define just prototypes for virtual functions. Derived classes must implement the virtual functions. However, it is impossible to call the virtual function in the base class since there is no code for it in the program. This type of function is called a **pure virtual function.** It specifies the interface for a function in a derived class without specifying the implementation.

Hands On 24.5 shows another version of the graphics shapes program. This version uses a pure virtual function in the `shape` class.

Hands On 24.5

Objective

Define a shape class. It should keep track of the current position of the shape on the screen. Derive a circle class from the shape class. Also derive a rectangle class from it. Derive a square class from the rectangle class. Write a program that demonstrates the functionality of these classes.

Experiment

Use the .CPP and .H files you used in Hands On 24.4. A new version of the file *Shape.h* is given below. Use this version rather than the one you used in Hands On 24.4. The changes to the file are shown in bold type. In addition to the changes in *Shape.h,* you will need to delete the function `shape::Display()` from the file *Shape.cpp.*

This is the file `Shape.h`.

```
#ifndef SHAPE_H
#define SHAPE_H

#include <iostream.h>
#include "point.h"

class shape
{
public:
    shape(void);
    shape(const point shapeOrigin);
```

```
    ~shape();

    shape &operator =(const point shapeOrigin);

    void Origin(const point shapeOrigin);
    point Origin(void) const ;

    virtual void Display(void) const = 0;

// Private member data.
private:
    point origin;
};

#endif
```

Results

```
Please enter one of the following:
C  Create Circle
R  Create Rectangle
S  Create Square
D  Display Shapes and Quit
Enter Selection: c

Please enter the X location of the shape's origin :10

Please enter the Y location of the shape's origin :20

Please enter the circle's radius :30


Please enter one of the following:
C  Create Circle
R  Create Rectangle
S  Create Square
D  Display Shapes and Quit
Enter Selection: r

Please enter the X location of the shape's origin :20

Please enter the Y location of the shape's origin :30

Please enter the rectangle's height :40

Please enter the rectangle's width :50


Please enter one of the following:
C  Create Circle
R  Create Rectangle
S  Create Square
D  Display Shapes and Quit
Enter Selection: s

Please enter the X location of the shape's origin :30

Please enter the Y location of the shape's origin :40
```

```
Please enter the length of the square's edge :50

Please enter one of the following:
C  Create Circle
R  Create Rectangle
S  Create Square
D  Display Shapes and Quit
Enter Selection: d

This is a circle.
Center = (10,20)
Radius = 30
This is a rectangle.
Upper Left Corner = (20,30)
Height = 40
Width = 50
This is a square.
Upper Left Corner = (30,40)
Edge Length = 50
```

Analysis

If you look in the definition of the `shape` class, you'll see that the prototype of the function `shape::Display()` has the statement `= 0` on the end. This does not assign a value to anything. It tells the C++ compiler that the program does not provide the body of the function. The function is pure virtual.

The definition of the pure virtual `shape::Display()` function does not affect the operation of the program at all. However, if another programmer were to add a `triangle` class, he/she would find that the program would not compile if the `triangle` class called `shape::Display()`. By making `shape::Display()` a pure virtual function, we tell other programmers that all classes derived from `shape` must have a `Display()` function. We specify what the prototype of the `Display()` function is. However, we do not allow them to call `shape::Display()` since we don't provide code for it. We leave it to others to create the implementation of `Display()` for their particular class.

Summary

Base class pointers are type compatible with pointers to derived classes. Programs can use base class pointers to point at derived objects. This gives C++ programmers the ability to define a generic pointer to related objects.

Using base class pointers for derived objects usually means that you'll also need to use virtual functions. Both member functions and destructors can be virtual. Virtual constructors are not allowed.

All functions that will be overridden in a derived class should be defined as virtual in the base class. Any class that will be used as a base class should have a virtual destructor.

You can use pure virtual functions to define class interfaces, and at the same time avoid providing an implementation. Classes with pure virtual functions are typically referred to as *abstract base classes*.

Review Questions

1. What are base classes? What are derived classes?
2. What does the keyword `virtual` tell the C++ compiler? Why are virtual functions important to programming with derived classes?

3. What is a virtual destructor? Why do base classes need to make their destructors virtual?
4. What is a pure virtual function? What capabilities do pure virtual functions give programmers?
5. Why do you think C++ provides you with the ability to specify only the interface in a base class, without specifying the implementation?
6. In what ways do inheritance, pointers, and virtual functions simplify the process of designing C++ programs? Can you think of ways that these features might make C++ programs more complex?
7. What does it mean to say that base class pointers are type compatible with pointers to derived objects? How can this help you simplify your C++ programs?
8. What is a container class? Why are container classes important in C++ programming?
9. What does it mean when we say that a container class assumes ownership of an object?
10. What is lazy memory allocation? How can it be helpful to you when you're creating C++ objects?

Exercises

1. Explain why the ideas of container classes and object ownership might be important to your C++ programs.
2. In C++, pointers to base classes are type compatible with pointers to derived classes. Explain any advantages you might see to this. Also explain what design changes you need to make in your base classes to safely allow programmers to use base class pointers to point at derived objects.
3. Use the `text_string` class in Hands On 22.5 (see Chapter 22) as the base class for a class called `formatted_string`. The `formatted_string` class should have a data member that is set to true when the string will be displayed in bold type, and false when it will be displayed in normal type. It should have a similar data member for displaying in italics. It should also have two overloaded member functions called `Bold()` that can be used to get and set the data member controlling bold formatting. In addition, provide two overloaded `Italics()` functions that can be used to get and set the data member controlling italics formatting. Write a program demonstrating that your `text_string` and `format_string` classes work. *Note:* Your program does not actually need to display text in bold or italics. It should just prove that all of the member functions of the `format_string` class work.
4. Explain what changes you had to make to the `text_string` class in Exercise 3 to make it work properly as a base class. Tell which functions in `text_string` you needed to override in `formatted_string`. Explain why.
5. The `text_string` class in Hands On 22.5 (see Chapter 22) provides a function called `CppString()`. Explain what this function does. Name another function that can be used to do this same thing. Explain why the other function isn't provided in the `text_string` class.
6. Suppose you are writing a game called *Revenge of the Birds*. This game will implement many different types of birds. Design a base class called `bird`. The `bird` class needs a private data member of type `animated_bird_image`. This will be used by the game to display animated images of the birds. Indicate the other data members the `bird` class needs. Explain why you chose those data members. Also indicate the `bird` class member functions and explain why you think the design class requires those functions. Tell which functions you made virtual and which you made pure virtual. Explain why.
7. Use the `bird` class you created for Exercise 6 as the base class for a class called `flying_bird`. Explain why you think the `flying_bird` class needs the private member data and the member functions that you included in the class design. If you needed to make changes to your `bird` class so that it could be used as the base for `flying_bird`, explain what the changes were and why you needed to make them.
8. Use the `flying_bird` class you created for Exercise 7 as the base class for two classes, one called `eagle` and the other called `sparrow`. Explain why you think the `eagle` and `sparrow` classes need the private member data and the member functions

that you included in the class designs. If you needed to make changes to your `flying_bird` class so that it could be used as a base class, explain what the changes were and why you needed to make them. *Hint:* The primary differences between these two types of birds will be their speed and the maximum height they can achieve. These items could be constants if you wanted them to be.

9. Use the `bird` class you created for Exercise 6 as the base class for a class called `flightless_bird`. Explain why you think the `flightless_bird` class needs the private member data and the member functions that you included in the class design. If you needed to make changes to your `bird` class so that it could be used as the base for `flightless_bird`, explain what the changes were and why you needed to make them.
10. Use the `flightless_bird` class you created for Exercise 9 as the base class for two classes, one called `ostrich` and the other called `chicken`. Explain why you think the `ostrich` and `chicken` classes need the private member data and the member functions that you included in the class designs. If you needed to make changes to your `flightless_bird` class so that it could be used as a base class, explain what the changes were and why you needed to make them. *Hint:* The primary differences between these two types of birds will be their running speed. These items could be constants if you wanted them to be.

Chapter Glossary

Container Class A class that creates, maintains, and destroys a list or collection of information of objects.

Lazy Memory Allocation Delaying memory allocation until the program actually tries to store data in memory.

Pure Virtual Function A virtual function in a base class that all derived classes must implement. However, the base class provides only the prototype for the function, not an implementation.

25 Member Functions Revisited

Objectives

After reading this chapter, you should be able to:

- Use inline functions.
- Understand and use various implementation techniques associated with assignment operators and copy constructors.
- Perform type conversions between objects and built-in data types.
- Perform type conversions between object types.

Preview

This chapter presents some of the subtleties of defining and using object member functions. In particular, it discusses inline member functions, copy constructors, assignment operators, and type cast functions.

Inline Functions

Chapter 17 described how to use the C++ preprocessor to create macros. One of the primary advantages of macros is that the preprocessor substitutes a macro's code directly into the program code. Although a macro may look like a function, program execution doesn't jump to a macro's code like it does to a function's code. There is only one copy of a function's code in a program. A macro's code is copied into many spots in a program.

A primary disadvantage of macros is their inability to check the types of their parameters. C++ provides a way to create macro-like functions, called **inline functions**. Like macros, the code from inline functions is copied directly into a program's code. However, because inline functions are functions, the C++ compiler can check the types of their parameter values and return values.

There are two ways of defining inline functions. One is to write the function's code into a class definition. Hands On 25.1 illustrates how to do this. The other way is to define the function as you normally would, but add the keyword `inline`. Hands On 25.2 demonstrates this method.

Hands On 25.1

Objective

Define a class that uses inline functions. Write a program that demonstrates the class.

Experiment

Type the following program into your IDE or text editor. Compile, link, and run it.

```
#include <iostream.h>

class timer
{
public:
   timer(int startTime=0)
   {
      currentTime=startTime;
   }

   timer &operator ++(int)
   {
      currentTime++;
      return (*this);
   }

   void Reset(void)
   {
      currentTime=0;
   }

   int CurrentTime(void)
   {
      return (currentTime);
   }

private:
   int currentTime;
};

int main()
{
   timer aTimer;


   cout << "The timer is starting." << endl;
   for ( ; aTimer.CurrentTime() < 100; aTimer++)
   {
   cout << aTimer.CurrentTime() << "    ";
      if ((aTimer.CurrentTime() % 10) == 0)
      {
         cout << endl;
      }
   }

   return (0);
}
```

Results

```
The timer is starting.
0
1   2   3   4   5   6   7   8   9   10
11   12   13   14   15   16   17   18   19   20
21   22   23   24   25   26   27   28   29   30
31   32   33   34   35   36   37   38   39   40
41   42   43   44   45   46   47   48   49   50
51   52   53   54   55   56   57   58   59   60
61   62   63   64   65   66   67   68   69   70
71   72   73   74   75   76   77   78   79   80
81   82   83   84   85   86   87   88   89   90
91   92   93   94   95   96   97   98   99
```

Analysis

We've used various versions of the `timer` class in our examples throughout this book. This variation defines inline functions in the class definition. The constructor initializes the timer to a starting value that is passed in as a parameter. If no value is passed in, it sets the timer to zero.

Chapter 16 introduced the idea of overloading operators. The `timer` class uses an overloaded ++ operator. Recall that there are two kinds of ++ operators: preincrement and postincrement. When you write an `operator ++()` function, you must be able to tell the C++ compiler which you are overloading, preincrement or postincrement. The way you distinguish the two versions is by the parameter list. If you put the word `int` in the parameter list of a ++ (or --) operator function, you are overloading the postincrement (or postdecrement). However, if the parameter list of the ++ (or --) operator function is empty, you are overloading the preincrement (or predecrement) operator.

The `timer` class provides two more member functions. The `Reset()` function reinitializes the value of `currentTime` to zero. The function `CurrentTime()` returns the current number of ticks.

Hands On 25.2

Objective

Define a class that uses out-of-line inline functions. Write a program that demonstrates the class.

Experiment

Type the following program into your IDE or text editor. Compile, link, and run it.

```
#include <iostream.h>

class timer
{
public:
   timer(int startTime=0);
   timer &operator ++(int);
   void Reset (void);
   int CurrentTime (void);
```

```
private:
   int currentTime;
};


inline timer::timer(int startTime)
{
   currentTime=startTime;
}

inline timer &timer::operator ++(int)
{
   currentTime++;
   return (*this);
}

inline void timer::Reset(void)
{
   currentTime=0;
}

inline int timer::CurrentTime(void)
{
   return (currentTime);
}


int main()
{
   timer aTimer(10);
   cout << aTimer.CurrentTimer() << endl;

   cout << "The timer is starting." << endl;
   for (aTimer.Reset(); aTimer.CurrentTime()<100; aTimer++)
   {
      cout << aTimer.CurrentTime() << "    ";
      if ((aTImer.CurrentTime() % 10) == 0)
      {
         cout << endl;
      }
   }

return (0);
}
```

Results

```
10
The timer is starting.
0
1    2    3    4    5    6    7    8    9    10
11   12   13   14   15   16   17   18   19   20
21   22   23   24   25   26   27   28   29   30
31   32   33   34   35   36   37   38   39   40
41   42   43   44   45   46   47   48   49   50
51   52   53   54   55   56   57   58   59   60
```

```
61   62   63   64   65   66   67   68   69   70
71   72   73   74   75   76   77   78   79   80
81   82   83   84   85   86   87   88   89   90
91   92   93   94   95   96   97   98   99
```

Analysis

The only difference between this version of the timer class and the version in Hands On 25.1 is that this version defines out-of-line inline functions. This sounds rather like a contradiction, but the rules of C++ allow it.

A member function whose body doesn't appear in the class definition is always an out-of-line function. Adding the keyword `inline` makes it an inline function even though it is defined out of line.

Like inline functions that appear in a class definition, out-of-line inline functions are inserted into the program's code as if they were macros. However, they have full return type and parameter type checking.

There is a limit to how complex inline functions can be. The ANSI C++ specification allows compiler manufacturers to determine the level of complexity of inline functions.

Assignment Operators and Copy Constructors

Previous chapters briefly mentioned assignment operators and copy constructors. The default assignment operator and the copy constructor functions for any class that you create have the generic forms shown in Example 25.1.

EXAMPLE 25.1 The Generic Form of the Default Assignment Operator and Copy Constructor Functions

```
class_name &class_name::operator =(class_name &sourceObject);
class_name::class_name(class_name &sourceObject);
```

In this example, `class_name` represents the name of the class that defines the assignment operator and copy constructor. In many classes, you do not need to provide a default assignment operator or copy constructor. The compiler will generate them both for you. However, this is sometimes undesirable. In particular, any class containing a data member that points to dynamically allocated memory must provide an assignment operator and a copy constructor.

The assignment operator and copy constructor that the C++ compiler generate do a byte-by-byte copy of an object. When an object does dynamic allocation, the dynamically allocated memory is outside the object. The object contains a pointer to the dynamically allocated memory. A byte-by-byte copy will copy only the pointer, not the dynamically allocated memory.

The `text_string` class in Chapter 22 was an example of this kind of object. It contains a pointer to characters. The member functions dynamically allocate an array of characters for the object. They store the address of the array in the private data member `charString`, which is the pointer to characters. Figure 25.1 shows what happens if we assign one `text_string` object to another using the default assignment operator function that the compiler generates.

Notice that the pointer is copied from `string1` to `string2`. The default assignment operator had no way to copy the dynamically allocated array of characters pointed to by `charString`. The result is that both the `string1` and `string2` objects now point to the same array of characters. If we change `string1`, we change `string2`. The reverse is also true. This is generally not what we want in our programs.

FIGURE 25.1 Dynamic Allocation and the Default Assignment Operator

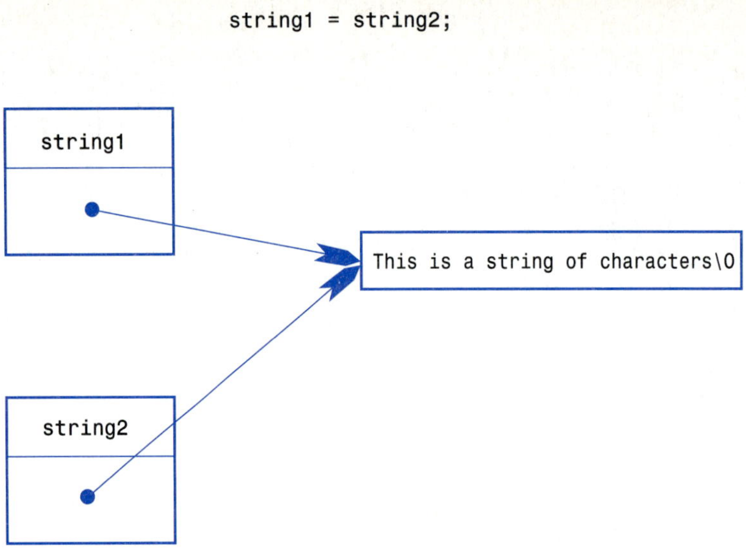

We saw the solution to this problem in Hands On 22.5 in Chapter 22. That version of the `text_string` class defines a default assignment operator function. In a statement like this:

```
string1 = string2;
```

the `operator =()` function dynamically allocates memory for the destination character array (the array in `string1`). It copies the characters from the array in the source object (`string2`).

The copy constructor has the same problem and the same solution. A copy constructor is a constructor that copies the contents of one object of a class into another object of that same type.

Every time you pass an object by value, it creates a copy of the object in the parameter. Your program calls the copy constructor to initialize the copy. Example 25.2 shows a function that passes an object by value. Whenever a program calls this function, it must call the copy constructor to copy the contents of the argument into the local function parameter.

EXAMPLE 25.2 A Function That Generates a Call to the Copy Constructor

```
void DoSomething(an_object objectParameter)
{
    // Function body goes here.
}
```

As with the assignment operator, a copy constructor performs a byte-by-byte copy of an object. This is generally not good for objects using dynamic allocation.

Example 25.3 contains the files *TString.h* and *TString.cpp* from Chapter 22. The prototype and implementation of the default assignment operator and the copy constructor are highlighted with bold type.

EXAMPLE 25.3 Tstring.h and Tstring.cpp

This is the file `TString.h`.

```
//---------------------------------------------------------------------
/*
File Name:  TString.h
Comments:   This file contains the constants and class definition needed to
            use the text_string class.
*/
//---------------------------------------------------------------------
```

```
#if !defined(TSTRING_H)
#define TSTRING_H

//-----------------------------------------------------------------------------
// Include Files

#include <iostream.h>

// End Include Files
//-----------------------------------------------------------------------------


//-----------------------------------------------------------------------------
// Constants

const int MAX_INPUT_STRING_LENGTH = 256;

// End Constants
//-----------------------------------------------------------------------------



//-----------------------------------------------------------------------------
// Class Definitions

class text_string
{
// Public member functions.
public:
   text_string(void);
   text_string(const char * const charArray);

   // Copy constructor.
   text_string(const text_string &sourceString);

   ~text_string();

   // Default assignment operator.
   text_string &operator = (const text_string &textString);

   text_string &operator = (const char * const charArray);

   text_string operator + (const text_string &textString);
   text_string operator + (const char * const charArray);

   text_string &operator += (const text_string &textString);
   text_string &operator += (const char * const charArray);
   text_string &operator += (const char oneChar);

   char &operator [](const int index);

   friend istream &operator >> (istream &inputStream,
                                text_string &destinationString);
   friend ostream &operator << (ostream &outputStream,
                                const text_string &sourceString);

   const char *CppString(void);

   int Length(void);
```

```
// Private member functions.
private:
   void Allocate(const int totalChars);
   text_string &Copy(const text_string &sourceString);
   text_string &Copy(const char * const charArray);

// Private member data.
private:
   char *charString;
};

// End Class Definitions
//-----------------------------------------------------------------------------

#endif

// End TString.h
//-----------------------------------------------------------------------------
```

This is the file `TString.cpp`.

```
//-----------------------------------------------------------------------------
/*
File Name:  TString.cpp
Comments:   This file contains the implementation of the text_string class.
*/
//-----------------------------------------------------------------------------



//-----------------------------------------------------------------------------
// Include Files

#include "TString.h"
#include "string.h"
#include <assert.h>

// End Include Files
//-----------------------------------------------------------------------------



//-----------------------------------------------------------------------------
/*
Function Name:      text_string
Member of:          text_string
Input Parameters:   None.
Output Parameters:  None.
Return Value:       Constructed text_string object.
Comments:           No-arg constructor. Sets the object to a known state.
*/

text_string::text_string(void)
{
   charString = NULL;
}

// End text_string
//-----------------------------------------------------------------------------
```

```
//---------------------------------------------------------------------------
/*
Function Name:       text_string
Member of:           text_string
Input Parameters:    charArray - A pointer to characters. These chars are
                        copied into the object.
Output Parameters:   None.
Return Value:        Constructed text_string object.
Comments:            One-arg constructor. Allocates the memory for the
                     character string. It then calls the private member
                     function Copy() to copy the characters from charArray
                     into the private member data array charString.
*/

text_string::text_string(const char * const charArray)
{
   // Allocate the memory for the characters.
   Allocate(strlen(charArray));
   Copy(charArray);
}

// End text_string
//---------------------------------------------------------------------------



//---------------------------------------------------------------------------
/*
Function Name:       text_string
Member of:           text_string
Input Parameters:    sourceString - A text_string that will be copied into the
                        object.
Output Parameters:   None.
Return Value:        Constructed text_string object.
Comments:            Copy constructor.
*/

text_string::text_string(const text_string &sourceString)
{
   Allocate(sourceString.Length());
   Copy(sourceString);
}

// End text_string
//---------------------------------------------------------------------------



//---------------------------------------------------------------------------
/*
Function Name:       text_string
Member of:           ~text_string
Input Parameters:    None.
Output Parameters:   None.
Return Value:        None.
Comments:            Deletes the character array in this object. Sets the
                     private data member charString to NULL just to be safe.
*/

text_string::~text_string()
```

```
{
   if (charString)
   {
      delete [] charString;
   }

   charString = NULL;
}

// End ~text_string
//-----------------------------------------------------------------------------



//-----------------------------------------------------------------------------
/*
Function Name:        operator =
Member of:            text_string
Input Parameters:     textString - The object the characters will be copied
                         from.
Output Parameters:    None.
Return Value:         Returns a reference to *this.
Comments:             This function copies characters from a text_string
                      object into the current text_string object. It calls
                      the private member function Copy() to perform the
                      copy.
*/

text_string &text_string::operator = (const text_string &textString)
{
   assert(&textString != this);

   if (charString!=NULL)
   {
      delete [] charString;
   }

   Allocate(textString.Length());
   Copy(textString);
   return (*this);
}

// End operator =
//-----------------------------------------------------------------------------



//-----------------------------------------------------------------------------
/*
Function Name:        operator =
Member of:            text_string
Input Parameters:     charArray - The array from which the characters will be
                         copied.
Output Parameters:    None.
Return Value:         Returns a reference to *this.
Comments:             This function copies characters from a character array
                      into the current text_string object. It calls the private
                      member function Copy() to perform the copy.
*/

text_string &text_string::operator = (const char * const charArray)
```

```
{
   if (charString!=NULL)
   {
      delete [] charString;
   }

   Allocate(strlen(charArray));
   Copy(charArray);
   return (*this);
}

// End operator =
//-----------------------------------------------------------------------------



//-----------------------------------------------------------------------------
/*
Function Name:       operator +
Member of:           text_string
Input Parameters:    textString - The object containing characters to
                        concatenate onto the end of the current object.
Output Parameters:   None.
Return Value:        Returns the concatenated text_string object.
Comments:            This function concatenates the string in the textString
                     parameter onto the end of the current text_string. This
                     function does not change the textString object or the
                     current object.
*/

text_string text_string::operator + (const text_string &textString)
{
   text_string tempString;
   int i,j;
   int leftStringLength,rightStringLength;

   leftStringLength = Length();
   rightStringLength = textString.Length();

   tempString.Allocate(leftStringLength+rightStringLength);
   tempString.Copy(charString);

   for (i=tempString.Length(),j=0;
        (i<leftStringLength+rightStringLength) && (textString.charString[j]);
        i++,j++)
   {
      tempString.charString[i]=textString.charString[j];
   }
   charString[i] = '\0';

   return (tempString);
}

// End operator +
//-----------------------------------------------------------------------------



//-----------------------------------------------------------------------------
/*
Function Name:       operator +
```

```
Member of:            text_string
Input Parameters:     charArray - The array containing characters to
                         concatenate onto the end of the current object.
Output Parameters:    None.
Return Value:         Returns the concatenated text_string object.
Comments:             This function concatenates the string in the array
                      charArray onto the end of the current text_string. This
                      function does not change the character array or the
                      current object.
*/


text_string text_string::operator + (const char * const charArray)
{
   return (*this+text_string(charArray));
}

// End operator +
//-----------------------------------------------------------------------------




//-----------------------------------------------------------------------------
/*
Function Name:        operator +=
Member of:            text_string
Input Parameters:     textString - A text_string object containing characters
                         to append onto the end of the current object.
Output Parameters:    None.
Return Value:         Returns a reference to *this.
Comments:             This function appends characters onto the end of a
                      text_string object. It uses the text_string::operator +()
                      function to do most of its work. This function modifies
                      the current object (*this).
*/

text_string &text_string::operator += (const text_string &textString)
{
   assert(&textString != this);
   *this = *this + textString;
   return (*this);
}

// End operator +=
//-----------------------------------------------------------------------------




//-----------------------------------------------------------------------------
/*
Function Name:        operator +=
Member of:            text_string
Input Parameters:     charArray - An array of characters that this function
                         will append onto the end of the current object.
Output Parameters:    None.
Return Value:         Returns a reference to *this.
Comments:             This function appends characters onto the end of a
                      text_string object. It uses the text_string::operator +()
                      function to do most of its work. This function modifies
                      the current object (*this).
```

```
*/

text_string &text_string::operator += (const char * const charArray)
{
   *this = *this + charArray;
   return (*this);
}

// End operator +=
//-----------------------------------------------------------------------



//-----------------------------------------------------------------------
/*
Function Name:       operator +=
Member of:           text_string
Input Parameters:    oneChar - A character that this function will append
                        onto the end of the current object.
Output Parameters:   None.
Return Value:        Returns a reference to *this.
Comments:            This function appends a single character onto the end
                     of a text_string object. This function modifies
                     the current object (*this).
*/

text_string &text_string::operator += (const char oneChar)
{
   int length = Length();

   char *tempString = charString;   // Save the current chars.
   Allocate(length);   // Allocate a new array of characters.
   Copy(tempString);   // Copy the chars into the new array.

   // Append the new character.
   tempString[length]=oneChar;
   tempString[length+1]='\0';

   // Delete the old array.
   delete tempString;

   return (*this);
}

// End operator +=
//-----------------------------------------------------------------------



//-----------------------------------------------------------------------
/*
Function Name:       operator []
Member of:           text_string
Input Parameters:    index - The index number of the character to set.
                        Numbering starts with zero.
Output Parameters:   None.
Return Value:        If the index is in range, this function returns a
                     reference to the requested character.
Comments:            The intent of this function is to enable developers to
                     get and set individual characters in a text_string
                     object.
```

```
                        It provides bounds checking on the index value. If the
                        developer tries to access a character that is out of
                        bounds, this function uses the assert() macro to abort
                        the program.
*/

char &text_string::operator [](const int index)
{
   assert((index >= 0) && (index<Length()));
   return charString[index];
}

// End operator []
//-----------------------------------------------------------------------------



//-----------------------------------------------------------------------------
/*
Function Name:          operator >>
Member of:              None. Friend of text_string.
Input Parameters:       inputStream - The stream from which the input will be
                           read.
Output Parameters:      destinationString - The string that will contain the
                        input when this function completes.
Return Value:           Returns a reference to the input stream.
Comments:               This friend function overloads the extraction operator
                        for the text_string class.
*/

istream &operator >> (istream &inputStream,
                      text_string &destinationString)
{
   char tempString[MAX_INPUT_STRING_LENGTH];

   // Read the string into a temp variable.
   inputStream >> tempString;

   // If the object's char array is not empty...
   if (destinationString.charString)
   {
      // Delete it.
      delete destinationString.charString;
   }

   // Allocate space for the input string.
   destinationString.Allocate(strlen(tempString));

   // Copy the input string into the object's char array.
   destinationString.Copy(tempString);

   return (inputStream);
}

// End operator >>
//-----------------------------------------------------------------------------
```

```
//-----------------------------------------------------------------------------
/*
Function Name:        operator <<
Member of:            None. Friend of text_string.
Input Parameters:     sourceString - The string from which characters will be
                         read.
Output Parameters:    outputStream - The stream to which output will be
                         written.
Return Value:         A reference to the output stream.
Comments:             This function overloads the insertion operator for the
                      text_string class.
*/

ostream &operator << (ostream &outputStream,
                      const text_string &sourceString)
{
   if (sourceString.Length() > 0)
   {
      outputStream << sourceString.charString;
   }

   return (outputStream);
}
// End operator <<
//-----------------------------------------------------------------------------




//-----------------------------------------------------------------------------
/*
Function Name:        CppString
Member of:            text_string
Input Parameters:     None.
Output Parameters:    None.
Return Value:         Returns a constant reference to the character array that
                      this text_string object contains.
Comments:             See Return Value section.
*/

const char *text_string::CppString(void)
{
   return (charString);
}

// End CppString
//-----------------------------------------------------------------------------




//-----------------------------------------------------------------------------
/*
Function Name:        Length
Member of:            text_string
Input Parameters:     None.
Output Parameters:    None.
```

```
Return Value:        Returns the length of the string. This is the same as the
                     number of printable characters (excluding the null
                     character).
Comments:            See Return Value section.
*/

int text_string::Length(void)
{
   int length=0;

   if (charString)
   {
      for (length=0;charString[length];length++)
      {
         // Empty loop body. The stuff in the () does the counting.
      }
   }

   return (length);
}

// End Length
//-----------------------------------------------------------------------------




//-----------------------------------------------------------------------------
/*
Function Name:       Allocate
Member of:           text_string
Input Parameters:    totalChars - An integer number of printable characters to
                        allocate space for.
Output Parameters:   None.
Return Value:        None.
Comments:            To accommodate the null character at the end of a string,
                     this function allocates totalChars+1. It also initializes
                     the memory it allocates to null characters.
*/

void text_string::Allocate(const int totalChars)
{
   if (totalChars>0)
   {
      charString = new char [totalChars+1];
      for (int i=0;i<totalChars+1;i++)
      {
         charString[i]='\0';
      }
   }
   else
   {
      charString = NULL;
   }
}

// End Allocate
//-----------------------------------------------------------------------------
```

```
//-----------------------------------------------------------------------
/*
Function Name:       Copy
Member of:           text_string
Input Parameters:    sourceString - The string from which the characters will
                        be copied.
Output Parameters:   None.
Return Value:        Returns a reference to the current object (*this).
Comments:            This private member function copies characters from a
                     text_string object into the current object.
*/

text_string &text_string::Copy(const text_string &sourceString)
{
   if (sourceString.charString)
   {
      int i;

      for (i=0;sourceString.charString[i];i++)
      {
         charString[i] = sourceString.charString[i];
      }
      charString[i] = '\0';
   }
   else
   {
      if (charString)
      {
         delete [] charString;
      }

      charString=NULL;
   }

   return (*this);
}
// End Copy
//-----------------------------------------------------------------------



//-----------------------------------------------------------------------
/*
Function Name:       Copy
Member of:           text_string
Input Parameters:    charArray - The character array from which the characters
                        will be copied.
Output Parameters:   None.
Return Value:        Returns a reference to the current object (*this).
Comments:            This private member function copies characters from a
                     character array into the current object.
*/

text_string &text_string::Copy(const char * const charArray)
{
   int i;
```

```
    if (charArray)
    {
        for (i=0;charArray[i];i++)
        {
            charString[i] = charArray[i];
        }
        charString[i] = '\0';
    }
    else
    {
        if (charString)
        {
            delete [] charString;
        }

        charString=NULL;
    }

    return (*this);
}

// End Copy
//---------------------------------------------------------------------------

// End TString.cpp
//---------------------------------------------------------------------------
```

The copy constructor and default assignment operator in Example 25.3 illustrate the patterns often followed by copy constructors and default assignment operators for classes using dynamic allocation. A copy constructor should allocate memory in the destination object for a copy of the source object's data. It should then copy the data from the source object to the destination object. A default assignment operator should check for assignment to self. If the pointer in the destination object points to dynamically allocated memory, the default assignment operator should delete it. The assignment operator function should then allocate memory for the data in the destination object and copy the data from the source object.

Sometimes it is not good to let programmers copy objects. Let's suppose, for example, that we're creating a generic set of user interface classes that will run on any operating system that supports a graphical user interface. In this type of a program, the statements

```
window window1, window2;
window1.Title("This is a window");
window2=window1;
```

could cause problems. Windowing classes are generally very complex. It usually does not make sense to assign one window object to another.

If you want to prevent such assignments, you must restrict access to the default assignment operator and the copy constructor. Restricting access to them is as easy as making them private. Example 25.4 demonstrates this technique.

EXAMPLE 25.4 Preventing Calls to the Copy Constructor and Default Assignment Operators

```
class window
{
public:
    // Public member functions go here.

private:
    window(window &sourceWindow);
    window &operator = (window &sourceWindow);
```

```
    // Other private functions go here.

private:
    // Private data goes here.
};
```

This example declares the copy constructor and the default assignment operator to be private. Because it finds the prototypes for these functions, the C++ compiler will not automatically generate them. However, nothing forces you to put the bodies of these functions into your programs. Making these functions private and leaving out the definitions of the function bodies causes the compiler to generate an error if it finds calls to them. This prevents the object from being copied.

Type Casting

By design, C++ enables programmers to change the type of virtually any piece of data by type casting. There are two methods your programs can use for type casting. The first is to use the type cast operator, which we've seen in previous chapters. The second is to use constructors.

Type Casting Using `operator` *`type`* `()`

Any object you create can be cast to any other valid C++ data type using a type cast operator function. A type cast operator function is a member function that takes the form

```
operator type();
```

where *type* represents the name of the type to which you are casting. For example, any object you create can provide a type cast operator function that will cast the object into an integer. This function would have the prototype

```
operator int();
```

The type cast operator function takes no parameters. It does have an implied parameter, which is the object on which it is invoked. A type cast operator function should not have a return type. That's because the return type is the name of the function. Example 25.5 defines a simple class with a type cast operator function. Example 25.6 shows how to call the type cast operator function defined in Example 25.5.

EXAMPLE 25.5 A Class with a Type Cast Operator Function

```
class my_object
{
public:
    my_object(int data=0);
    // Other public member functions go here.

    operator int();    // The type cast operator function.

private:
    int privateIntData;
};
```

EXAMPLE 25.6 Calling the Type Cast Operator Function

```
int main()
{
    my_object = 10;
    int anInt;
```

```
    anInt = (int)my_object;

    return (0);
}
```

The C++ code fragment in Example 25.7 shows a version of the `text_string` class that uses a type cast operator function to change the `text_string` object to a C++ character pointer. It also demonstrates the implementation of the `operator char *()` function.

EXAMPLE 25.7 Type Casting

```
class text_string
{
// Public member functions.
public:
   // Other public member functions.

   operator char *(void);

// Private member data.
private:
   char *charString;
};

text_string::operator char *()
{
   return (charString);
}
```

The `operator char *()` function returns the address contained in the private data member `charString`. Previous chapters illustrated the potential problems with type cast operator functions that return pointers. In addition, adding a type cast operator to your class enables the C++ compiler to perform silent type conversions without your being aware of it. The Troubleshooting Guide at the end of this chapter discusses this potential problem in greater detail.

Type Casting Using Constructors

Your program can also use constructors to convert the type of a piece of data. In Example 25.8, the program defines a color class. It uses constructors to change integers into colors.

EXAMPLE 25.8 Converting Data Types with Constructors

```
#include <iostream.h>


#define   BLACK 0
#define   RED 1
#define   BLUE 2
#define   GREEN 3
#define   MAGENTA 4
#define   YELLOW 5
#define   CYAN 6
#define   DARK_RED 7
#define   DARK_BLUE 8
#define   DARK_GREEN 9
#define   PURPLE 10
#define   BROWN 11
#define   DARK_CYAN 12
#define   ORANGE 13
```

```
#define   PINK 14
#define   WHITE 15

class color
{
public:
   color(int currentColor = BLACK);

   operator int();

private:
   int colorNumber;
};



color::color(int currentColor)
{
   colorNumber = currentColor;
}


color::operator int()
{
   return (colorNumber);
}



int main()
{
   color theColor = DARK_RED;

   int theColorValue = (int)theColor;
   cout << theColorValue << endl;

   color anotherColor = 12;
   theColorValue = (int)anotherColor;
   cout << theColorValue << endl;

   return (0);
}
```

The color object in Example 25.8 contains an integer color value. Its constructor has the effect of converting integers into colors. We could also provide constructors to convert long integers, short integers, or even strings into colors. When you're designing your objects, you can allow any type conversions you want.

The program in Example 25.8 also demonstrates converting colors to integers using a type cast operator.

Troubleshooting Guide

After reading this section, you should be able to:

- Determine where in your program to put inline functions.
- Fix recursive calls to the copy constructor.
- Be aware of the dangers of silent type casts.

Where Do Inline Functions Go?

Inline functions are a great asset in a C++ program. Although they tend to make a program larger, they also make it faster. As you move from one job to another, you'll find a variety of opinions about where to put the definitions of inline functions.

Some C++ programmers are of the opinion that the bodies of inline functions should go with their prototypes in the class definition. Hands On 25.1 demonstrated this technique. The advantage of this approach is that it makes the inline function code easy to find. The primary disadvantage is that it makes the class definition harder to read. It also typically makes the header file very long.

Conversely, since C++ enables us to define the bodies of inline functions after the class definition, other C++ programmers prefer to put them there. This gets the inline function code out of the class definition, leaving only function prototypes and member data. However, since the code for inline functions is contained in the header file, it still tends to be very long. Many C++ programmers don't consider this a serious disadvantage. Most of the time, that's true. In very complex programs, however, header files can contain thousands of class, constant, macro, and inline function definitions. Dealing with an extremely long header file can be tedious and confusing.

Developers of large, complex programs sometimes tend to favor putting inline function code in a special file, which they give an INL extension. In this style of programming, every object has three files associated with it. The definition of the class itself goes in a header file. The header file also contains all of the constants, macros, and other definitions needed to use the class. The CPP file contains all of the member functions that you do not define as inline. The INL file contains all of the code for the inline functions. Near the end of the header file, you insert an `#include` directive to include the INL file. The preprocessor reads everything in the INL file into the header file. It then reads the header file into the CPP file. When the preprocessor passes the results to the compiler, it can't tell the difference.

This method provides a nice, uniform way of organizing programs. The downside of it is that some debuggers will not recognize INL files. They will not save debugging information for functions that come from INL files. This makes it harder to debug inline functions.

Another disadvantage to some developers is that they do not like having `#include` directives in two places in a header file. Usually, `#include` statements go at the beginning of a header file. Some programmers think that using `#include` directives at the end of a header file to include an INL file is confusing. They tend to prefer creating a second header file that includes everything else.

For example, suppose I am writing a class called `text_string`. I could put the class definition in *TStr.h* and the code for the inline functions in *TStr.inl*. I could then create a header file called *TString.h*. Programs using the `text_string` object would include *TString.h*. This file would contain nothing but two `#include` directives. One would include *TStr.h;* the other would include *TStr.inl*. That way, *TString.h* could have all of its `#include` directives in one place.

The disadvantage of this method is that it creates another file to manage. If there are lots of objects in the program, it creates lots of extra files.

Most of the new compilers contain a setting that enables you to tell the compiler to decide which functions should be treated as inline. If your compiler has this switch, the entire question of where inline functions go completely disappears. You simply set the option to let the compiler decide. Never define any member functions as inline. Put all of your member functions in the CPP file. The compiler will scan all member functions and turn any of them that it can into inline functions.

This is the easiest solution for programmers. It's always great when we can get our tools to relieve us of these types of chores. However, if your compiler does not support this option, you'll need to use one of the other methods.

Recursive Calls to the Copy Constructor

It's a good idea to take a second look at copy constructors before we move on. Copy constructors have one mistake associated with them that nearly everyone makes at one time or another.

A class's copy constructor must take one parameter that is a reference to the source object. The parameter *must* be passed by reference. It may not be passed by value or by address (with a pointer).

It is possible to define a copy constructor with a pass by value parameter. Example 25.9 shows a copy constructor with a pass by value parameter.

EXAMPLE 25.9 A Copy Constructor with a Pass By Value Parameter

```
my_object::my_object(my_object sourceObject)
{
 data = sourceObject.data;
}
```

Programs call copy constructors whenever they pass an object to a function by value. For instance, a function with the prototype

```
void DoSomething(my_object myObject);
```

will cause the program to call the copy constructor every time it encounters a statement like this:

```
DoSomething(thisObject);
```

When `DoSomething()` starts, the program allocates space for the parameter `myObject`. It calls the copy constructor to copy the contents of `thisObject` into `myObject`.

If the copy constructor uses a parameter that is passed by value, the program will automatically call the copy constructor to copy the parameter value. This will, in turn, cause the program to call the copy constructor to copy the parameter value, which will cause the program to call the . . . well, you get the idea. The call chain will not end until the program suffers a stack overflow. This may bring down the entire computer, depending on which operating system you're using.

If the copy constructor uses a reference parameter, as it should, it will not have this problem. Whenever the program calls the copy constructor, it passes the copy constructor a reference to the source object. Because it does not receive a copy of the source object's value, it does not need to call itself.

If you find that an object's copy constructor recursively calls itself until the program crashes, it means you've accidentally left the & off of the parameter declaration. To keep the copy constructor from continually calling itself, insert the ampersand. Example 25.10 demonstrates the correct way to define the copy constructor we saw in Example 25.9.

EXAMPLE 25.10 A Correct Version of the Copy Constructor

```
my_object::my_object(my_object &sourceObject)
{
   data = sourceObject.data;
}
```

The Dangers of Silent Type Casts

In an effort to be helpful, the C++ compiler will sometimes generate type conversions without telling you. Many times, this is an *extremely* useful feature. However, it can cause unintended side effects.

Example 25.11 illustrates this problem by defining a `vector` class with an `operator float()` function. This enables vectors to be converted to floating point numbers.

EXAMPLE 25.11 An Implicit Type Conversion

```
#include <iostream.h>


class vector
{
```

```
public:
   vector(void);
   vector(float vectorDirection,float vectorMagnitude);

   void Direction(float vectorDirection);
   float Direction(void);

   void Magnitude(float vectorMagnitude);
   float Magnitude(void);

   operator float();

private:
   float direction;
   float magnitude;
};



inline vector::vector(void)
{
   direction = magnitude = 0.0;
}


inline vector::vector(float vectorDirection,float vectorMagnitude)
{
   direction = vectorDirection;
   magnitude = vectorMagnitude;
}


inline void vector::Direction(float vectorDirection)
{
   direction = vectorDirection;
}


inline float vector::Direction(void)
{
   return (direction);
}


inline void vector::Magnitude(float vectorMagnitude)
{
   magnitude = vectorMagnitude;
}


inline float vector::Magnitude(void)
{
   return (magnitude);
}


inline vector::operator float()
```

```
{
   return (magnitude);
}



int main()
{
   vector aVector(1.23,4.56);

   cout << aVector;

   return(0);
}
```

If you look at the class definition, you'll see that it doesn't define an insertion operator. However, this program will compile and run just fine. When the C++ compiler compiles this program, it sees that there is no insertion operator function for the `vector` class. The compiler tries to find a set of conversions that makes the call to the insertion operator function in `main()` succeed. The rules for this conversion are complex, but suffice it to say that the compiler detects the `operator float()` function. It uses the `operator float()` function to convert a `vector` to a `float`. The `operator <<()` function for `float`s is part of the C++ Standard Library, so the compiler uses it.

While this behavior is probably not a devastating mistake, it's still not correct. When a program outputs a `vector` object to a stream, it should print both the direction and magnitude of the `vector` to be complete. The program in Example 25.11 only prints the magnitude of the `vector`. This example shows that silent, or implicit, type conversions can cause many unexpected or incorrect side effects.

You can prevent implicit type casts like this by not providing a type cast operator function. Instead, provide another function that does the same thing but doesn't have a "magic" name. For example, we could rename the `operator float()` function in Example 25.11 to something like

```
float ToFloat();
```

Because this is not an `operator` *`type`*`()` function, the C++ compiler will not see `ToFloat()` as an acceptable way to convert a `vector` to a `float`. When you want to convert a `vector` to a `float`, you would need to call the `ToFloat()` function. The conversion would not happen automatically.

Recall that another way to perform type conversions is to use constructors. The C++ compiler will use constructors to perform type conversions whenever it can. In most cases, you can't just leave off constructors as you can with `operator` *`type`*`()` functions. However, you can prevent implicit type conversions using the C++ keyword `explicit`. Whenever a constructor is labeled `explicit`, the C++ compiler will not use the constructor to do implicit type conversions. Example 25.12 shows a class that uses the keyword `explicit`.

EXAMPLE 25.12 A Class with an `explicit` Constructor

```
class my_object
{
public:
   explicit my_object(int dataValue);

   // Other public functions go here.

private:
   int data;
   // Other private data goes here.
};
```

Summary

C++ enables programmers to define inline functions. Inline functions have many of the benefits of macros, but few of the drawbacks.

All classes that perform dynamic allocation should implement an assignment operator and a copy constructor function. Both should take a parameter that is a reference to the source object.

Type casting can be performed using constructors or the `operator type()` function. Allowing type casting can have unintended side effects. In most programming situations, it is advisable to control type casting by making all type casts explicit.

Review Questions

1. What is the difference between an inline function and a macro?
2. What are the advantages of inline functions? What are their disadvantages?
3. What is a copy constructor? For what is it used?
4. Why is it necessary for classes using dynamic allocation to provide a default assignment operator and a copy constructor?
5. How do you limit access to assignment operators and copy constructors?
6. How do you implement a type cast operator function? What potential problems do type cast operator functions cause?
7. What techniques can you use to prevent implicit type conversions with type cast operators?
8. How do you perform type casts with constructors?
9. What is an explicit constructor? Why might you need them in C++?
10. Why do assignment operators need to check for assignment to self?

Exercises

1. Explain where you think inline functions should go in your program. Tell why.
2. Write a program (other than the examples provided in this chapter) that demonstrates a problem that can occur with implicit type conversions. Explain how you would solve this problem.
3. Write a program that defines an object called `bird`. Make the `bird` class usable as a base class. Derive two classes from `bird`. Call the first `flightless_bird` and the second `flying_bird`. Make both of these classes usable as base classes. Use inheritance to provide all classes derived from `bird` with a function called `Noise()`. When the `Noise()` function is called for any particular type of `bird`, it should print a unique string to the screen that represents the noise the `bird` makes. The string should be dynamically allocated. When the `bird` object (or the object derived from `bird`) goes out of scope, it should delete the string containing the `bird`'s noise. The noise string should always be set in the `bird`'s constructor. In addition, the `flightless_bird` class, and all classes derived from it, should have two overloaded functions called `RunningSpeed()`. Use these to get and set the running speed of the `flightless_bird`. The `flying_bird` class, and all classes derived from it, should have a pair of functions called `MaxFlightAltitude()` that get and set the maximum altitude a bird can reach when flying. Make as many of these functions as you can inline functions. If any could not be made inline functions, explain why. Write a program demonstrating that your classes work. Make sure that you have implemented virtual member functions, virtual destructors, assignment operators, and copy constructors where they are needed.
4. Use the classes you created for Exercise 3. Derive a class called `penguin` from `flightless_bird`. When the program creates a `penguin`, the `penguin`'s constructor should set its noise to "Squawk". Modify the classes you wrote to enable every type of `bird` to contain a string that holds the `bird`'s name. Implement `Name()` functions for getting and setting the `bird`'s name. Make sure that you have

implemented virtual member functions, virtual destructors, assignment operators, and copy constructors where they are needed. Write a program that declares two `penguin` variables, `aPenguin` and `anotherPenguin`. Give `aPenguin` the name "Waddles." Assign appropriate values to the other private data members in `aPenguin`. Print the values in the member data of `aPenguin`. Assign the values in `aPenguin` to `anotherPenguin`. Print the values in the member data of `anotherPenguin`.

5. Use the program you created for Exercise 4. Derive the classes `eagle`, `sparrow`, and `robin` from the `flying_bird` class. Give each of them an appropriate noise string in their constructors. Derive the `ostrich` and `moa` classes from the `flightless_bird` class. Make up noise strings for these birds. You'll have to guess the noise of a moa—they're extinct (there are no moa). Write a program demonstrating that these classes work properly.
6. Use the program you created for Exercise 5. Create a class called `flock`. The `flock` class should contain a dynamically allocated array of pointers to `bird` objects. It should provide an appropriate set of member functions for using the `flock` class. Write a program that declares a list of ten `birds` of any type in a `flock`. Call the `flock` variable `aFlock`. Assign each type of `bird` the appropriate values it needs and store the `bird` in the `flock`. The `flock` object should assume ownership of each `bird` object it contains. Print all of the values in each `bird`'s member data. Declare a second variable of type `flock`. Call the second `flock` variable `anotherFlock`. Assign `aFlock` to `anotherFlock`. Change some of the values in the `birds` in `anotherFlock`. Print `aFlock` and `anotherFlock`. If any of the values in `aFlock` changed, you have not implemented your copy constructor correctly.
7. Modify the program you created for Exercise 6. Change the `bird`, `flying_bird`, and `flightless_bird` classes so that only derived classes can create them. That is, make all of their constructors `protected`. Explain why you might or might not want to use this technique in an actual program.
8. Explain the advantages and disadvantages of making assignment operators and copy constructors `private`. Give an example (other than the one in this chapter) of when this might be useful.
9. Use the program given in Hands On 22.5 (see Chapter 22). Wherever possible, make the functions in this program inline. Explain which ones could not be made inline and why.
10. Use the program you wrote for Exercise 9. Explain why the `text_string` class has a copy constructor and assignment operators. Could you leave them off this class? Why or why not? Also tell whether the `text_buffer` class needs an assignment operator and copy constructor. Give the reasons for your answer. Should the copy constructor and assignment operator prototypes be `private`? Why or why not?

Chapter Glossary

Inline Functions Functions whose code is substituted into the program's source code by the compiler. Program execution does not jump to the definition of the inline function's code.

26 Other Programmer-Defined Types

Objectives

After reading this chapter, you should be able to:

- Use structures to create new types in your programs.
- Use unions to make variable data types.
- Use enumerated types to specify groups of related constants.
- Use the `typedef` keyword to create an alias for a type.

Preview

The centerpiece of the C++ programming language is the class. It provides us with the ability to define our own types and how those types behave. In addition to classes, C++ also provides other methods of defining types. In this chapter, we'll look at what those methods are. We'll also discuss some of their most common uses.

Structures

C++ classes are based on a C language element called *structures*. C structures can contain member data, but no member functions. Since C++ is backward-compatible with C, C++ supports structures. It also extends them. C++ structures can contain both member data and member functions, just like classes. Actually, the only difference between a C++ class and a C++ structure is that the default for all class members is `private`, while the default for all structure members is `public`. Example 26.1 demonstrates how to declare structures.

EXAMPLE 26.1 Using Structures and Classes

```
#include <iostream.h>

class my_class
{
   // Inline member functions.
   my_class(int dataValue=0)
   {
   data = dataValue;
   }

   void SetData(int dataValue)
   {
      data = dataValue;
```

```
    }

    int GetData(void)
    {
        return (data);
    }

    // Member data
    int data;
};


struct my_structure
{
    // Inline member functions.
    my_structure(int dataValue=0)
    {
        data = dataValue;
    }

    void SetData(int dataValue)
    {
        data = dataValue;
    }

    int GetData(void)
    {
        return (data);
    }

    // Member data
    int data;
};



int main()
{
    my_class yourClass;
    my_structure yourStruct;

    yourClass.SetData(10);

    yourStruct.SetData(yourClass.GetData+20);

    cout << yourClass.GetData();
    cout << yourStruct.GetData();

    yourStruct.data = 40;
    cout << yourStruct.data;

    return(0);
}
```

Example 26.1 uses a structure and a class. You define structures in exactly the same manner that you would define a class. The only difference is the use of the keyword `struct`.

The keywords public and private have been omitted from the class and structure definitions in Example 26.1. If you compile this program, your compiler will complain that the member functions in the class my_class are not accessible. Since the default scope for class members is private, we can't even access the class's constructor.

The member functions of objects of type my_structure are accessible to any function in the program. Because the default scope for structure members is public, even the member data is directly accessible.

Example 26.2 contains another version of the program in Example 26.1. This time, the keywords public and private have been added where you would expect them.

EXAMPLE 26.2 A Class and a Structure with Public Functions and Private Data

```
#include <iostream.h>

class my_class
{
public:
   my_class(int dataValue=0)
   {
   data = dataValue;
   }

   void SetData(int dataValue)
   {
      data = dataValue;
   }

   int GetData(void)
   {
      return (data);
   }

private:
   int data;
};


struct my_structure
{
public:
   my_structure(int dataValue=0)
   {
      data = dataValue;
   }

   void SetData(int dataValue)
   {
      data = dataValue;
   }

   int GetData(void)
   {
      return (data);
   }

private:
   int data;
};
```

```
int main()
{
   my_class yourClass;
   my_structure yourStruct;

   yourClass.SetData(10);

   yourStruct.SetData(yourClass.GetData+20);

   cout << yourClass.GetData();
   cout << yourStruct.GetData();

   yourStruct.data = 40;        // This no longer works!
   cout << yourStruct.data;     // This no longer works!

   return(0);
}
```

The keywords `public` and `private` define the scope of the members of the structure and class in this example. They override the defaults, so the structure and the class behave in essentially the same manner. The member functions of both are `public`. The member data of both are `private`. Statements that access the member functions of the class now work properly. However, the statements in Example 26.2 that directly access the member data of the structure will no longer compile.

In practice, there is little difference in the use of structures and classes. Most C++ programmers tend to prefer classes and seldom use structures. They primarily use structures as a tool for backward-compatibility with C programs.

Unions

A union is a C++ language element that enables you to define variable types. Unions encapsulate multiple data types into the same memory space. You define a union similar to the way you would define a class or structure.

C does not allow member functions in structures or unions. It does not support classes at all.

Because unions were used commonly in C programs, they typically contain member data, not member functions. Unions may have member functions. However, none of them can be virtual. A union cannot have a base class or be used as a base class. They cannot have static member data.

Like classes and structures, unions can have several member data items. However, unlike classes and structures, the member data in unions all share the same memory space. The C++ compiler allocates memory for the largest member in the union. You can access that memory using any of the union members. No matter which member you use, you are accessing the same memory location.

TIP: The C++ compiler allocates enough memory only for the largest member of a union. All union members share that memory.

By default, all union members are `public`. You may use the keywords `public` and `private` inside unions just as you can with structures and classes. You can't use `protected` because unions do not support inheritance.

Hands On 26.1 demonstrates how unions work.

Hands On 26.1

Objective

Write a program that defines a class called number. The class should enable you to convert short, int, or long values to number objects. It should also let you convert number objects to short, int, or long values.

Experiment

Type the following program into your IDE or text editor. Compile, link, and run it.

```
#include <iostream.h>


union number
{
public:
   number(long dataValue = 0)
   {
      longData=dataValue;
   }

   number &operator =(short dataValue)
   {
      shortData = dataValue;
      return (*this);
   }

   number &operator =(int dataValue)
   {
      intData = dataValue;
      return (*this);
   }

   number &operator =(long dataValue)
   {
      longData = dataValue;
      return (*this);
   }

   operator short()
   {
      return(shortData);
   }

   operator int()
   {
      return(intData);
   }

   operator long()
   {
      return(longData);
   }

private:
   short shortData;
   int intData;
   long longData;
};



int main()
{
   number aNumber;
```

```
    short aShort = 10;
    int anInt = 1000;
    long aLong = 100000L;

    aNumber = aShort;
    cout << (short)aNumber << endl;

    aNumber = anInt;
    cout << (int)aNumber << endl;

    aNumber = aLong;
    cout << (long)aNumber << endl;

    number shortNumber = 10, intNumber = 100;
    cout << (short)shortNumber << endl;
    cout << (int)intNumber << endl;

     return(0);
}
```

Results

```
10
1000
100000
10
100
```

Analysis

The union in Hands On 26.1 has three private data members; `shortData`, `intData`, and `longData`. When this program declares variables of type `number`, it will allocate enough memory for one long integer. All three of the data members will share that same space.

Let's suppose this program runs on a computer that has a 16-bit short integer, a 32-bit integer, and a 64-bit long integer. When the program declares the variable `aNumber`, it will allocate 64 bits (enough to hold the largest data member). If you access the memory of the variable `aNumber` using the `shortData` member, you will access only the first 16 bits of the variable's memory. If you access the data using the `intData` member, you'll be accessing 32 bits of `aNumber`'s memory. Using the `longData` member enables you to access all 64 bits that the program allocates for `aNumber`.

The program begins by declaring a variable of type `number`, a `short`, an `int`, and a `long`. The declaration of `aNumber` will call the `number` constructor. The statement

```
aNumber = aShort;
```

invokes the `operator =()` function that takes a short integer as its parameter. This stores the value 10 into `shortData`. The program then outputs the contents of `aNumber` to the `cout` stream as a `short`. The

```
(short)aNumber
```

portion of the statement

```
cout << (short)aNumber << endl;
```

calls the type cast `operator short()` function. This returns the value in the `shortData` member.

REMINDER: Be careful with type cast operator functions. See the Troubleshooting Guide in Chapter 24 for details.

It's time for a pop quiz. Suppose once again that we're using a computer with a 16-bit `short`, a 32-bit `int`, and a 64-bit `long`. If the first `operator =()` function stores a `short` into the memory allocated for `aNumber`, it is storing a value into only the first 16 bits of `aNumber`'s memory. What do the other 48 bits of memory contain?

The answer is: I don't know. Only your compiler manufacturer knows for sure. The vast majority of compilers will store zeros into the unused bits of a union's memory. However, you can't depend on that in absolutely *every* case because some don't. Check your compiler manufacturer's documentation. Another way to find out is to try it. If we put the statement

Of the few compilers that don't fill the uninitialized bits with zeros, some copy the highest-order bit assigned and others simply let it be garbage. Either way, this behavior is rare.

```
cout << (long)aNumber << endl;
```

right after

```
cout << (short)aNumber << endl;
```

in this program, it will show the contents of the entire 64 bits of memory allocated to `aNumber`. Only rarely will the output be anything other than 10.

After the program outputs the contents of the variable `aNumber` to the `cout` stream as a `short`, it uses the statement

```
aNumber = anInt;
```

to assign the value 1000 to `aNumber`. When it compiles this program, the C++ compiler detects that `anInt` is an integer, so it inserts a call to the `operator =()` function that takes an `int` as its parameter. This assigns the value 1000 into `intData`. The program uses the statement

```
cout << (int)aNumber << endl;
```

to output the contents of `aNumber` to the screen as an integer.

TRAP: Not all compilers support the use of an uppercase L at the end of a large number. The majority do.

The program also assigns the value in `aLong` into `aNumber`. The variable `aLong` contains 100,000. Notice that there is an uppercase L at the end of the 100000 in the initialization of `aLong`. This tells the compiler to treat 100000 as a `long`. By default, many compilers will treat all literal numbers in programs as integers. They will warn you if they encounter numbers too big to fit in an `int`. The compiler will automatically treat a large number like 100000 as a `long`, so the program will compile. However, you get a warning. To tell the compiler that you definitely want a literal number treated as a `long`, you can put an uppercase L at the end of it.

The statements

```
number shortNumber = 10, intNumber = 100;
cout << (short)shortNumber << endl;
cout << (int)intNumber << endl;
```

demonstrate that you can assign short integers and integers into a variable of type `number`. The parameter to the `number` constructor is a `long`. However, since a `long` can hold short integers and integers, the C++ compiler will automatically convert them to long integers when it calls the number constructor.

Enumerated Types

It's not unusual to need to define lists of related constants. C++ provides a method of creating groups of constants and associating them with a type. Because this method enumerates values for a type, it is called an *enumerated type*. The values associated with the enumerated type are called *enumerants* or *enumerated values*.

You declare enumerated types with the C++ keyword `enum`. The enumerated values are actually integers in disguise. To put it technically, enumerated values are mapped onto the set of integers.

Hands On 26.2 illustrates one way to use an enumerated type.

Hands On 26.2

Objective

Write a program that uses an enumerated type to enumerate colors.

Experiment

Type the following program into your IDE or text editor. Compile, link, and run it.

```
#include <iostream.h>

enum colors
{
    BLACK,
    RED,
    GREEN,
    BLUE,
    YELLOW,
    CYAN,
    MAGENTA,
    DARK_RED,
    DARK_GREEN,
    DARK_BLUE,
    BROWN,
    DARK_CYAN,
    PURPLE,
    WHITE
};


int main()
{
    colors rainbow;

    for (rainbow=BLACK; rainbow<=WHITE; rainbow++)
    {
        cout << rainbow << endl;
    }

    rainbow = 45;

    return(0);
}
```

Results

```
0
1
2
3
4
5
6
7
8
9
```

```
10
11
12
13
```

Analysis

This program enumerates a group of related constants. The constants are colors. Using the `enum` keyword, this program creates a list of constants and associates them with the type `color`. It can declare variables of type `color` and assign color values to them. For example, it declares the `color` variable `rainbow`, which it uses in a `for` loop.

The `for` loop iterates through the list of color values. Because color values are actually integers, we can use any operator on `color` variables that we can use on integer variables. In this case, the program uses the `++` operator to increment `rainbow` each time the `for` loop iterates.

To see what values `rainbow` takes on each time through the loop, look at the Results section. The first constant in the list is assigned the value of 0. Every subsequent constant is one greater than the constant before it.

The statement

```
rainbow = 45;
```

shows that any integer can be assigned to a variable of an enumerated type. This is true even if the integer value is not one of the enumerated values. Sort of. Your compiler will at least give you a warning about this. It will tell you that the program is trying to assign an integer value to an enumerated type. With some compilers, this is an error. Most of the compilers that flag this with a warning will allow you to upgrade that warning to an error.

TIP: You may need to modify your compiler settings so that it will generate an error when your program treats enumerated types as integers. This is usually a good change to make.

Enumerated types are primarily used for documenting programs. They can help you make your programs much clearer to read. If I wrote the loop in Hands On 26.2 like this:

```
for (int i=0; i<=13; i++)
{
    cout << i << endl;
}
```

It would not be at all clear what the loop is for. Using the type name `color` and the enumerated color values makes it clear that the `for` loop iterates through a list of colors.

Enumerated types are also a more convenient way of defining lists of constants. Many programs define their error codes as enumerated types. Example 26.3 demonstrates this technique.

EXAMPLE 26.3 To Err Is Human

```
enum error_code
{
    NO_ERROR,
    NOT_ENOUGH_MEMORY,
    INVALID_NUMERIC_VALUE,
    INPUT_STRING_TOO_LONG,
    EMPTY_INPUT_STRING,
    VALUE_OUT_OF_RANGE,
    INVALID_INPUT_DATA,
    FILE_READ_ERROR,
    FILE_WRITE_ERROR,
    CANT_FIND_FILE,
    INVALID_DIRECTORY_NAME,
```

```
        INVALID_FILE_NAME,
        NO_FILE_READ_PERMISSION,
        NO_FILE_WRITE_PERMISSION
    };
```

In professional programs, these lists of error codes can get *very* long. I have seen programs with literally thousands of enumerated error codes. It would be a real chore to maintain a list of error codes if they all were declared as constant integers.

Declaring error codes as enumerated values makes the compiler assign them values. You can switch them around, add new ones, or delete values from the list without having to renumber anything yourself.

You can also assign specific integer values to enumerants. Example 26.4 demonstrates this.

EXAMPLE 26.4 Assigning an Integer Value to Enumerants

```
    enum error_code
    {
        NO_ERROR,
        NOT_ENOUGH_MEMORY,
        INVALID_NUMERIC_VALUE,
        INPUT_STRING_TOO_LONG,
        EMPTY_INPUT_STRING = 10,
        VALUE_OUT_OF_RANGE,
        INVALID_INPUT_DATA,
        FILE_READ_ERROR,
        FILE_WRITE_ERROR,
        CANT_FIND_FILE,
        INVALID_DIRECTORY_NAME = 100,
        INVALID_FILE_NAME,
        NO_FILE_READ_PERMISSION,
        NO_FILE_WRITE_PERMISSION
    };
```

As in Example 26.3, the constant `NO_ERROR` is assigned the value 0. The next three constants are assigned the values 1, 2, and 3 successively. The constant `EMPTY_INPUT_STRING` is assigned the value 10. After that, the values increase by one. So `VALUE_OUT_OF_RANGE` gets 11, `INVALID_INPUT_DATA` gets 12, and so on. `INVALID_DIRECTORY_NAME` is assigned the value 100. From there, the values increase by one.

Enumerated types can also be declared inside classes. This is a very nice feature of the C++ language. It enables us to associate constants with a class. The program in Hands On 26.3 defines a class with an enumerated type in it.

Hands On 26.3

Objective

Write a program that demonstrates the use of enumerated types in classes.

Experiment

Type the following program into your IDE or text editor. Compile, link, and run it.

```
#include <iostream.h>


class my_object
{
// Public types.
```

```
public:
   enum object_value
   {
      FIRST_VALUE,
      SECOND_VALUE,
      THIRD_VALUE
   };

// Public functions.
public:
   my_object(my_object::object_value dataValue = my_object::FIRST_VALUE)
   {
      data = dataValue;
   }

   void Data(my_object::object_value dataValue)
   {
      data = dataValue;
   }

   my_object::object_value Data(void)
   {
      return (data);
   }

   void DoSomething(void);

private:
   object_value data;
};



void my_object::DoSomething(void)
{
   for (object_value i=FIRST_VALUE; i<= THIRD_VALUE; i++)
   {
      cout << i << endl;
   }
}



int main()
{
   my_object myObject;

   myObject.Data(my_object::THIRD_VALUE);
   cout << myObject.Data() << endl;

   my_object::object_value objectValue = my_object::SECOND_VALUE;

   myObject.Data(objectValue);
   cout << myObject.Data() << endl;

   myObject.DoSomething();

   return (0);
}
```

Results

```
2
1
0
1
2
```

Analysis

An enumerated type is defined in the `my_object` class in this program. It contains three values and is defined in the `public` section of the class. You'll undoubtedly notice that I put the keyword `public` in the class twice. This is not really necessary. The first occurrence of the word `public` tells the compiler to make everything public until it encounters the words `private` or `protected`. However, many C++ programmers like to make separate sections for each type of language element in the interface, so they'll have a public section for enumerated types, another for public functions, a protected section for protected enumerated types, a protected section for protected functions, a private section for private enumerated types, a private section for private functions, and a private section for member data. When class definitions get very large, this is a good way of helping you find things.

The enumerated type `object_value` can be seen by the entire `my_object` class. Because it is public, it can also be seen outside the class. However, outside the class, the scope resolution operator must be used to access the enumerated type and the enumerated values. If you look at `main()`, it contains statements such as

```
my_object::THIRD_VALUE
```

and

```
my_object::object_value objectValue
```

Since the value `THIRD_VALUE` is defined inside an enumerated type in the `my_object` class, everything outside the class must use the scope resolution operator to tell the compiler that the enumerated type and the enumerated values are inside the `my_object` class.

This rule also applies to the definitions of member functions in the public class interface. For example, the `my_object` constructor takes a parameter that is of type `object_value`. The parameter is part of the definition of the public interface. As a result, we must use the scope resolution operator on both the type and the default value for the parameter.

This rule does not apply to the private parts of the class definition. Notice that there is no scope resolution operator on the declaration of the class's private member data. Also, the scope resolution operator is not required inside the function `DoSomething()`. The inside of a member function is private to the class. In the private parts of the class, the C++ compiler will automatically search the class definition for the enumerated type name and the enumerated values.

The `main()` function demonstrates that you can declare variables of type `my_object` and `object_value`. As stated above, `main()` is not a member of `my_object`. So it must use the scope resolution operator to access the type `object_value`. If it uses the scope resolution operator, `main()` can and does access the enumerated values.

You have already used enumerated types in the course of reading this book. Back in Chapter 20, Hands On 20.1 demonstrated the use of the `ios` formatting flags. The `ios` formatting flags, such as `ios::oct` and `ios::hex`, are enumerated values in the `ios` class.

Typedefs

In C++ programming literature, typedef also said to be a way to create an "alias" for a type name.

Type definitions are a way to rename a type. You can rename any type to another name, regardless of whether it is a built-in type or a type that you create. Example 26.5 shows a few type definitions.

EXAMPLE 26.5 Some Type Definitions

```
typedef int integer;
typedef float real;
typedef my_class your_class;
typedef int * int_pointer;
```

The type definitions in this example each rename an existing type to a new name. The first renames `int` to `integer`. The second renames `float` to `real`. After these type definitions are processed, you can use both type names in your program. You can declare variables of type `real` or `float`. Both are valid type names after the compiler processes the `typedef`.

You can rename classes, structures, unions, or enumerated types. The statement

```
typedef my_class your_class;
```

renames the class `my_class` to `your_class`. Again, both type names are valid after the type definition. You can declare variables of type `my_class` or `your_class`.

You can even use pointers in type definitions. The example shows how you can rename the type `int *` to `int_pointer`. Any valid C++ type works in a type definition—even types created with type definitions.

When you use type definitions with classes, structures, and unions, you can give names to anonymous types. An anonymous type is a type that doesn't have a name. However, the type definition gives it a name.

Example 26.6 illustrates a structure that creates an anonymous type. It is anonymous because there is no type name after the keyword `struct`. Everything from the keyword `struct` to the closing curly bracket (}) defines the type. The `typedef` statement renames that type from nothing to `my_struct`.

EXAMPLE 26.6 Renaming an Anonymous Type

```
typedef struct
{
   int intData;
   double doubleData;
} my_struct;
```

This style of programming was common in C, but you don't see it too much in C++ programs. However, the C++ language supports it.

Troubleshooting Guide

After reading this section, you should be able to:

- Recognize and avoid problems stemming from creating duplicate enumerated values.
- Use type definitions to avoid portability problems.

Duplicate Enumerated Values

It's possible to create two or more enumerated values in an enumerated type that have exactly the same value. Example 26.7 shows how this problem occurs.

EXAMPLE 26.7 Duplicate Enumerated Values

```
enum my_values
{
   VALUE1 = 1,
```

```
    VALUE2 = -1,
    VALUE3,    // =0
    VALUE4     // =1
};
```

The enumerated value VALUE1 in this example is assigned the value 1. VALUE2 receives the value –1. The other enumerated values in the enumerated type are not explicitly assigned a value by a programmer. The C++ compiler will give VALUE3 a value of one more than the value of VALUE2. So VALUE3 gets 0, as the comment indicates. The C++ compiler increases the value of VALUE3 by one and assigns it to VALUE4, which is 1. That gives VALUE4 the same value as VALUE1. Example 26.8 contains a fragment of a C++ program. The program fragment tests the value of a variable to see whether it is equal to VALUE4. Because VALUE1 and VALUE4 are equal, the test will evaluate to true. Usually, this is an error.

EXAMPLE 26.8 A Logical Error

```
my_values aValue = VALUE1;

if (aValue == VALUE4)
{
 // Do some processing
}
```

The way to avoid this problem is to make sure that you never define the same value twice in an enumerated type. With *very* rare exceptions, each enumerated value should be unique.

Using typedef for Portability

When we're creating programs, it's easy to assume that the purpose of the software we're writing will always be the same. In practice, that's seldom true. Developer assumptions often come back to haunt maintenance programmers. The Year 2000 bug is a perfect example of an incorrect programmer assumption.

In Example 26.9, we see the definition of a very useful class for a graphics program. For the simple task it accomplishes, it's well designed. The interface is minimal but complete. However, it contains a potentially serious error. Can you tell what it is?

EXAMPLE 26.9 A Seemingly Well-Designed Class

```
class rgb_color
{
public:
    rgb_color(void);
    rgb_color(int redValue,int greenValue,int blueValue);

    void Red(int redValue);
    int Red(void);

    void Green(int greenValue);
    int Green(void);

    void Blue(int blueValue);
    int Blue(void);

private:
    int red, green, blue;
};
```

Any programmer writing a class like this one makes one basic assumption that is probably not true. The assumption is that the program will never be ported to a another type of computer or another operating system.

The rgb_color class is intended for use in a graphics-oriented program. It defines an object that stores red, green, and blue color levels. The color values are defined as integers. On an operating system with a 16-bit integer, there are 65,536 color values. However, half of those are negative. Most hardware can't deal with negative color values. So a programmer who writes a class like this is probably assuming that the values will never be negative, which means that there are really 32,768 possible color values each for red, green, and blue. This may be exactly what the programmer wants, given the computer and operating system for which he/she is developing the program.

Now let's suppose the company that produces this program decides to port it to many other computers and operating systems. On some of these systems, the number of possible colors is only 256 each for red, green, and blue. On other systems, there are over 4 million possible colors.

Do you see the porting problem here? On some systems, every occurrence of the word `int` must be changed to `short`. On others, it needs to be `unsigned`, `long`, or `unsigned long`. One or more maintenance programmers will need to search through the entire program looking for integers that must be changed to another type.

Example 26.10 illustrates an easy way to avoid this entire problem. It uses a `typedef` to create a type called `color_value`. When the program is ported, the developer doing the port needs only to change the `int` in the `typedef` statement to `short` (or `long`, or `unsigned`, or whatever else is appropriate) and then recompile. The job will be done.

EXAMPLE 26.10 A More Portable `rgb_color` Class

```
typedef int color_value;

class rgb_color
{
public:
   rgb_color(void);
   rgb_color(color_value redValue,
             color_value greenValue,
             color_value blueValue);
   void Red(color_value redValue);
   color_value Red(void);

   void Green(color_value greenValue);
   color_value Green(void);

   void Blue(color_value blueValue);
   color_value Blue(void);

private:
   color_value red, green, blue;
};
```

Summary

In addition to classes, C++ provides structures, unions, enumerated types, and type definitions. You can use all of these to create types for your programs.

Structures are just like classes, with one exception. By default, everything in a class is private. In a structure, everything is public by default.

Unions are similar to structures and classes. However, unlike structures and classes, all of the data members of unions share the same space. When a program declares a union variable, it allocates only enough space for the largest data member. All of the union's data members share that same memory space.

Enumerated types give us a way to create a type and associate constants with it. Many compilers map the enumerated values onto the set of integers. However, some compilers give you the option of not allowing the program to treat the enumerants as integers.

You can define enumerated types in a class. If you do, all nonmember functions must use the scope resolution operator to tell the compiler that the enumerated type and its values are in the class. The same is true of the class's public interface.

Type definitions give you a way to rename types. This helps document your program. It can also increase your program's portability.

Review Questions

1. What is the difference between a structure and a class?
2. What are the differences between unions and classes?
3. What is an enumerated type?
4. What are some of the advantages of using enumerated types? What are some of the disadvantages?
5. Why would having duplicate enumerated values be a potential problem in a program?
6. What does a type definition do?
7. What is an anonymous type? How are they used in conjunction with `typedef` statements?
8. How can type definitions be used to increase the portability of a program?
9. How can programmer assumptions cause problems later in a program's life cycle?
10. What are some of the techniques you've learned in this book to decrease potential maintenance problems in your software?

Exercises

1. Write a program that uses a union called `type_change`. The union should have two data members. The first should be an integer and the second should be a floating point number. In your program, declare a `type_change` variable and store the value 123.456 into it as a floating point number. Retrieve the value from the variable as an integer and print it. Explain the results.
2. Write a program that uses a union called `int_to_char`. The union should have an integer and a character data member. Declare a variable of type `int_to_char`. Store the values 7, 10, and 65 into the variable as integers. Retrieve them as characters and print each character.
3. Create an enumerated type called `logical`. The `logical` type should have the constants `TRUE` and `FALSE` associated with it. The value of `TRUE` should be 1. The constant `FALSE` should equal zero. Write a program that demonstrates your enumerated type. Do not use `#define` statements in this program.
4. Suppose you are writing a multiplayer network game. Create an enumerated type called `network_message`. Imagine that the game uses this enumerated type to send event messages over the network. Associate ten constants that you make up with the `network_message` type. These should indicate player events such as `PLAYER_MOVED_LEFT`, `PLAYER_MOVED_RIGHT`, and so forth. Also include a constant at the beginning called `NETWORK_MESSAGE_FIRST`, and another at the end of the list called `NETWORK_MESSAGE_LAST`, which indicates the lowest and highest message values. Write a program that prompts the user for an integer between the highest and lowest message values. If the user inputs a value outside that range, your program should output an error message.
5. Use the program in Hands On 22.5 (in Chapter 22) for this exercise. Rewrite the `text_buffer` class so that it contains an enumerated type called `buffer_error`. Create a list of error constants that can occur in a `text_buffer` object and associate it with the `buffer_error` type. Rewrite the text editor program to make use of these error constants.
6. Explain why you chose the error messages you did for the `string_error` enumerated type in Exercise 5.
7. Use the program you wrote for Exercise 5. Rewrite the `text_string` class so that it contains an enumerated type called `string_error`. Create a list of errors that can

occur in a `text_string` object and associate it with the `string_error` type. Rewrite the program to make use of these error constants.

8. Explain why you chose the error messages you did for the `string_error` enumerated type in Exercise 7.
9. Use one type definition to design a portable class called `point_3d`. The `point_3d` class should have data members that contain *X, Y,* and *Z* integer values of a point in 3-D space. Make sure your class has the appropriate member functions. Write a program to demonstrate that your `point_3d` class works.
10. Use the `point_3d` class you designed for Exercise 9. Change the class so that it stores the *X, Y,* and *Z* values as floating point numbers instead of integers. Recompile your program and demonstrate that it works. You should need to change only one statement in your program.

27 Designing the Text Editor

Objectives

After reading this chapter, you should be able to:

- List the objectives for writing a program.
- Make a program specification.
- Design the functionality of a program.
- Design the objects in a program.
- Use the bull's-eye approach to make a project plan.

Preview

This chapter is the beginning of where the "rubber meets the road," so to speak. Throughout the course of this book, I've attempted to present a balanced approach between C++ language proficiency, software design skills, and practical programming skills. In this chapter, we attempt to pull everything together to design a working text editor.

The Purpose of the Program

We write software for definite reasons. If we can't state those reasons in one paragraph or less of written text, we probably should not write the software. This applies to any software project you will ever do.

Here is our statement of purpose:

> The program we will write for this chapter is a text editor. It is first and foremost a teaching tool. It will demonstrate how to design and develop an object oriented program in C++.

This statement tells us exactly what we are creating and why. Because this program is primarily a teaching tool, we will have a certain set of priorities while developing it. These are:

1. *The software must teach as many of the techniques presented in this book as possible.* Because of this need, the design of the software will probably not be as consistent with itself as a real, professional program. You'll see that I sometimes design and implement the same type of task different ways just to demonstrate multiple methods.
2. *The source code must be easy to understand.* As you look through the code presented in this chapter, you may see ways that the program could be made more efficient. In some cases, I've deliberately sacrificed efficiency for clarity. There are things you'll be able to do to make the program take less memory and run faster. However, they will make the program less readable to students who are new to C++.

3. *The software must work reasonably well.* In some cases, the error checking and error handling are not done as well as they would be in professional software. This program must be clear; error checking and error handling statements tend to make a program's logic less clear. Therefore, I've omitted some of it. There is enough error checking and error handling to demonstrate the techniques, but not enough for this to be a professional program. Also, I've deliberately left some errors in the program for you to find and debug in the exercises at the end of the remaining chapters.
4. *The program should be as close to a real text editor in appearance and function as can reasonably be expected.* Let's face it, neither you nor I can implement a top-notch, professional programmer's text editor with all the bells and whistles in a one-semester class. However, the goal of writing this program is to create an experience that is as close to real job experience as possible.
5. *The software must be extensible and portable.* C++ is available on a variety of hardware platforms using a variety of operating systems. This book must be usable to all of them. Therefore, so must the software. However, there are constraints on both the size of this book and the time available to produce it. As a result, only the MS DOS version of the text editor will be demonstrated here. I'll demonstrate how to build the text editor in such a way that you should be able to create a version for *any* operating system on *any* computer.

The Program Specification

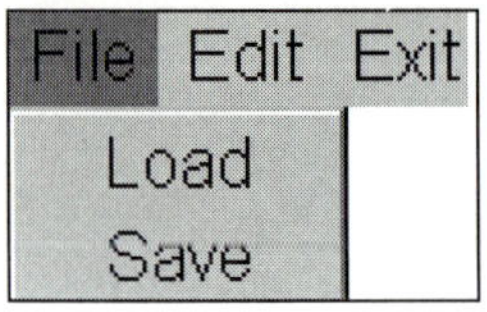

FIGURE 27.1 One View of the Menu System for the Text Editor

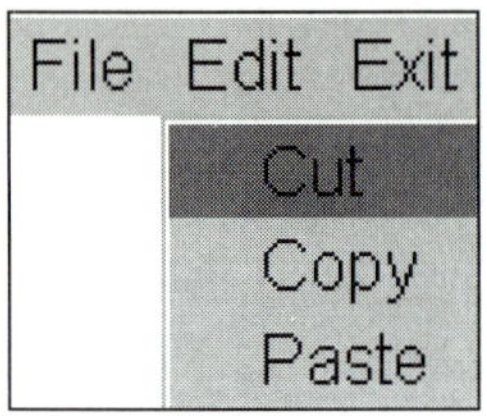

FIGURE 27.2 More of the Menu System for the Text Editor

Program specifications are a list of everything the program does. That's often harder to arrive at than it sounds. We typically write our programs for users other than ourselves. In fact, most programs are used by people who are not programmers. Since the vast majority of users are not familiar with software development, they often have difficulty stating what they want the software to do. Few users can specify all of the features of a program in the terms that programmers use.

I've learned by experience that one helpful way to design the program in a way that the users will understand is to design the user interface first. Most of what the software does is done in response to a user command. When the user types something on the keyboard, uses the mouse, or selects a menu item, the software must respond. Therefore, designing the user interface first shows the user most of what the program does.

Figures 27.1 and 27.2 show a design of the user interface for the text editor. The program will be menu-driven. That is, the user will enter most commands by selecting menu items. However, there will also be commands that are entered from the keyboard. Table 27.1 specifies the keyboard commands.

Unlike many programs you see on the market today, I've put the Exit menu item in the main menu, not in the File menu. If you think about it, that's sensible. Exiting the program

TABLE 27.1 Text Editor Keyboard Commands

Keyboard Command	Action
^c	Activate the menu system.
^a	Move cursor left.
^s	Move cursor right.
^w	Move cursor up.
^z	Move cursor down.
^u	Page up.
^d	Page down.
^e	Scroll up one line.
^x	Scroll down one line.
^t	Move to the top of the text file.
^b	Move to the bottom of the text file.
Enter	Command Mode: Select a menu item. Edit Mode: New line of text.
Esc	Cancel the current menu.

There are very few "rights" and "wrongs" when it comes to user interface design. The right style is the style that your users like. The wrong one is the one they hate. In general, though, you should try to follow accepted practice, or have a very good reason for not doing so.

isn't an action that you perform on a file, so it shouldn't go in the File menu. I know most software designers wouldn't agree. It's just an alternative point of view.

However, the real reason I did that was to demonstrate the classes that do menus. They can work with or without submenus. Any item in any menu can have a submenu. However, they don't have to have one.

The keyboard commands are all characters from the ASCII set. While they aren't as nice to use as, say, the arrow keys, they make the text editor easily portable to any type of computer and operating system. There are ways of using the arrow keys, function keys, and the Page Up and Page Down keys. However, their use is different on each type of computer.

Good object oriented design enables us to create one or more classes that hide the hardware dependencies of input and output devices. We will be using this technique to hide the hardware-specific attributes of the display. We could do the same for the keyboard. However, there's only so much that we can cover in one book, so we'll take the easy way out and use the characters shown in Table 27.1.

By looking at menus and command characters in the user interface, we can tell that the user must be able to use the program to:

1. Load a text file.
2. Save a text file.
3. Delete a line of text.
4. Copy a line of text.
5. Paste a line of text.
6. Exit the program.
7. Activate the menu system (command mode).
8. Highlight the menu item that is currently selected.
9. Move the cursor up, down, left, and right. When the user is in command mode, the cursor should only move left or right in horizontal menus. The cursor should only move up or down in vertical menus. In edit mode, the user should be able to move in all four directions. However, the cursor should never go beyond the end of the line of text.
10. Select a menu item.
11. Cancel a menu.
12. Enter text into the current text file.
13. Overwrite existing text in the text file.
14. Delete characters in the text file.
15. Scroll the text up one screenful at a time. The user should not be able to scroll beyond the beginning of the buffer.
16. Scroll the text down one screenful at a time. The user should not be able to scroll beyond the end of the buffer.
17. Scroll the text up one line at a time. The user should not be able to scroll beyond the beginning of the buffer.
18. Scroll the text down one line at a time. The user should not be able to scroll beyond the end of the buffer.

There are actually many types of program specifications. Common names for them are *functional specification, internal specification,* and *external specification.* The types of specifications you use depend on the software design methodology your company uses. The specification presented here is a generic approach to program specifications.

This is the specification for the text editor. Not all of these items will be implemented in this chapter. Some of them are left for you to do in the exercises.

Top-Down Design

The program specification in the previous section describes most of the functionality of the text editor. The top-down design shows it graphically.

We start the top-down design with the most generic statement of what the program does. Figure 27.3 shows the first level of the top-down design.

Next, we break the program down into some of its specific tasks. The text editor, like most programs, will need to perform some initializations when it starts up. While the user doesn't want to quit, the editor will get user input, execute the user's commands, and enter the user's text into the text buffer. When the user wants to quit, the program will perform any necessary cleanup and exit. See Figure 27.4.

FIGURE 27.3 The First Level of the Top-Down Design

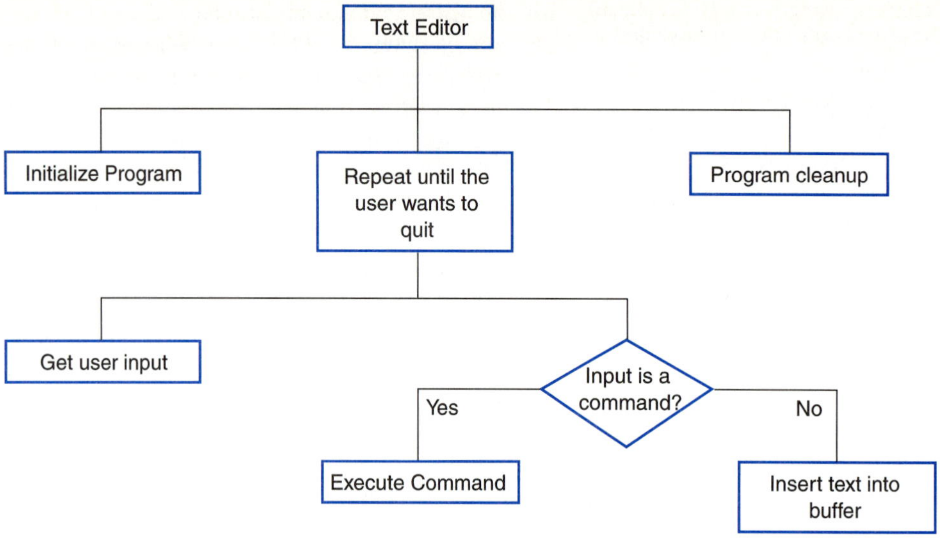

FIGURE 27.4 A More-Detailed Top-Down Design

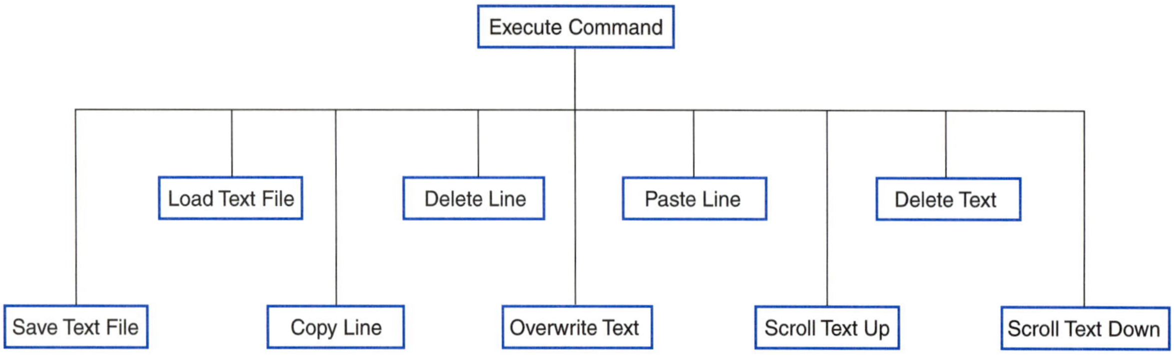

FIGURE 27.5 The Details of Execute Command

While it's easy to say, "The program will execute the user's command," there's quite a bit involved in making that happen. Therefore, we need another diagram that shows more of the details of executing user commands.

Figure 27.5 shows the commands to which the text editor will respond. Of course, these commands were taken from the specification we saw earlier. Each box on this diagram represents a function. Each function is a response to a particular command.

Notice that the Scroll Text Up and Scroll Text Down functions don't specify how much to scroll. That information is part of the command. In other words, we'll write a function that will scroll text up by any number of lines. We'll use that function to scroll the text up a line at a time. We'll also use it to scroll the text up a screenful at a time. The Scroll Text Down function will work in a similar manner.

Obviously, there is more detail to this program than is shown in the figure. However, this is enough for our purposes.

Designing the Program's Objects

Our next step is to design the objects that will do the work of the program. First, we'll need an edit area in which to work. Let's say that our text editor will use a portion of the screen as the edit area. Above the edit area, we'll leave a few lines for the program's main menu.

We'll need a way to communicate certain information to user. Specifically, we'll need to ask the user for a file name when we're saving or loading a file. Also, we'll need a way to output error messages to the user. Normally, programs accomplish this with dialog boxes. However, because we need to keep the scale of this project small, we'll create a status area below the edit area.

Since the menu system, the edit area, and the status area are all part of the same working environment, we'll create an object to contain all three of them.

So now we have four of the objects that we'll need:

1. The menus.
2. The edit buffer.
3. A status area.
4. A "desktop" object to contain the other three.

The C++ I/O streams are oriented toward line input and output. We won't be able to use them in the GUI-style, full-screen interface we're creating for our text editor. We'll need to create something to take their place. Also, we'll need classes we can use to hide the hardware dependencies of the input and output devices. So that adds two more items to our list of objects:

5. An input device object.
6. An object to represent the display.

If we look at each of these items in our object list, we'll see that some of them require additional objects. A menu contains menu items. Some of the menu items have submenus, others don't. A text buffer contains text strings.

When we get input from the user, the user will be entering both text and commands. Our input system will need to be able to get either kind of input and package it in a way the program will understand. One way to do this is to encapsulate it in a user input object.

So now we need to add these items to our object list:

7. Menu items.
8. Text strings.
9. User input objects.

Table 27.2 shows the entire list of objects we'll create for our text editor. Let's look at each of these objects and define their functionality.

Menus and Menu Items

Our menu object will represent horizontal and vertical menus. Most programs these days use a horizontal main menu. The rest of the menus are vertical. They appear when the user selects an item from the main menu or from one of the submenus. Because a menu may be either horizontal or vertical, the menu object must keep track of what type it is. This should be a private data item. The group of menu items should also be kept as private data. The menu object will need to keep track of how many menu items it contains. It will also need to store its current position on the screen. In order to display the menu properly, the program will need to know the height and width of each menu. These items should also go in the private data area.

TABLE 27.2 The Text Editor's Object List

Object	Purpose
Menu	Displays horizontal and vertical menus.
Text buffer	Contains text strings. Enables the program to edit the strings.
Status bar	Displays error messages. Enables the program to get file names for saving and loading files.
Desktop	Contains the text buffer, menu system, and status bar.
Input device	Encapsulates the keyboard.
Display	Encapsulates the display.
Menu item	An item in a menu object.
Text string	A string of characters in the text buffer.
User input	A generic format that enables the user to input commands and text.

Example 27.1 shows a pseudocode description of the menu object so far.

EXAMPLE 27.1 A First Stab at the Menu Object

```
class menu
{
private data
   The menu type (either horizontal or vertical)
   The collection of one or more menu items.
   The total number of menu items.
   The position of the menu on the screen.
   The height and width of the menu.
}
```

Naturally, the menu will have public member functions. It will need a constructor. It should probably use dynamic allocation for its list of menu items. All objects that use dynamic memory allocation should have a destructor.

In addition, we must be able to set the position of the menu. We'll keep track of the menu's position by setting the row and column of its upper left corner.

When we implement the menu object, we can have it calculate its own width and height based on the number and length of the items it contains. Therefore, we won't need public member functions to get and set the height and width.

The menu object will need to provide a function that enables the program to add items to the menu. When the program performs its initialization, it will build each menu item by item.

Lastly, the menu object will need to provide a function that actually executes the menu. If we put all of these public member functions into the description of the menu object, we get the pseudocode shown in Example 27.2.

EXAMPLE 27.2 An Improved Menu Object

```
class menu
{
public functions
   A constructor.
   A destructor.

A function to set the position of the menu's upper left corner on the screen.
   A function to get the row of the menu's upper left corner.
   A function to get the column of the menu's upper left corner.
   A function to add items to the menu.
   A function that executes the menu.

private data
   The menu type (either horizontal or vertical).
   The collection of one or more menu items.
   The total number of menu items.
   The position of the menu on the screen.
   The height and width of the menu.
}
```

A menu contains a collection of menu items. Each menu item needs a character string to display in the menu. When the user selects an item, the menu might have a submenu. If it does, the submenu needs to be executed.

Every menu item also needs a unique identifier. When a user selects a menu item, the menu system will send the text editor identifier of the item the user selected.

The program will need functions to set and get the menu item string, the item identifier, and the submenu. We'll implement the submenu using a pointer to a menu. Because the menu item object contains a pointer to dynamically allocated memory, the object should have a copy constructor, an assignment operator, and a destructor.

Example 27.3 shows a pseudocode description of the menu item object.

EXAMPLE 27.3 The Menu Item Object

```
class menu_item
{
public functions
   A constructor.
   A copy constructor.
   A destructor.

   A function to set the menu item's text string.
   A function to get the menu item's text string.

   A function to set the item's identifier.
   A function to get the item's identifier.

   A function to set the submenu.
   A function to get the submenu.

private data
   The item's text string.
   The unique identifier.
   The pointer to the submenu.
}
```

Text String Objects

We've been using various types of text string objects throughout this book. At this point, we need to decide on a design for this version of the text editor.

Because I want to demonstrate dynamic allocation as much as possible in this book, I'll rather arbitrarily decide that the text string object will use dynamic allocation. It will use lazy allocation. The text string object will not allocate memory for characters until the program tries to store characters in the object. That way, the program will use only as much memory for characters as it needs to.

We know that the object will need a constructor. Because it uses dynamic allocation, it must have a copy constructor and a destructor. It should also have an assignment operator.

When creating the text string object, we'll want to be able to initialize it to a character string. Therefore, we'll need a constructor that takes a pointer to characters as its parameter. This also implies that we'll need an assignment operator that has a character pointer parameter.

Our text string object should enable us to concatenate strings. We will need to append text string objects onto each other. In addition, we should be able to append C++ character strings onto a text string object. We'll definitely need the ability to append a single character onto the end of a text string.

C++ strings are character arrays. If they are created with pointers and dynamic allocation, they can still be treated like arrays. Most C++ programmers will be happier with any kind of string objects you create if you provide them with a subscript operator (`[]`) so they can treat your object the way they do C++ strings. Therefore, we'll add an `operator[]()` function to our text string object.

In most of the implementations of the text string objects we've created for this book, we've overloaded the insertion and extraction operators. We won't be using stream input and output for reading from the keyboard and writing to the display. The text editor will use the `ios::getline()` function to load a file into a text buffer. So we really don't need to overload the extraction operator for text strings. However, you may want to use the insertion operator to write strings to text files when you save a buffer. Therefore, the text string class will provide an overloaded insertion operator. For the sake of completeness, we'll overload the extraction operator even though we won't be using it.

The text editor will need to convert text string objects to C++ strings from time to time. Our implementation will provide a function to do that. Our program will also need a function to find the length of a text string.

Example 27.4 contains a pseudocode description of the text string object.

EXAMPLE 27.4 The Text String Object

```
class text_string
{
public functions
   A default (no-arg) constructor.
   A constructor that takes a character pointer parameter.
   A copy constructor.
   A destructor.

   An assignment operator that takes a text string parameter.
   An assignment operator that takes a character pointer parameter.

   A function for concatenating a text string to a text string.
   A function for concatenating a character array to a text string.

   A function that appends a text string to a text string.
   A function that appends a character string to a text string.
   A function that appends a single character to a text string.

   A subscript operator function.

   An insertion operator function.
   An extraction operator function.

   A function that converts the text string to a character string.

   A function that returns the length of the string.


private data
   A character pointer.
}
```

The Text Buffer Object

For the text editor, the text buffer object must contain at least one text buffer. This chapter will use a text buffer object that contains a statically allocated array of text strings. You will add dynamic allocation to the text buffer object in the exercises at the end of the chapter.

The user will primarily use a text buffer to display and edit text. The text buffer object will contain some private data members that will aid in those uses. For example, it will keep track of the first line of text that the buffer is currently displaying. It will also contain the row and column number of the insertion point.

The insertion point is the spot in the text buffer where the next text character the user types will be inserted. This is not the same as the cursor you see on the screen.

It might be helpful to think of the screen and the text buffer as two different spaces (almost like two different universes). The cursor is in screen space. In fact, we're restricting it to only a portion of the screen. The cursor on the screen must stay within the boundaries of the screen's edit area.

The insertion point is in text buffer space. It can move anywhere in the text buffer. Let's say that the current cursor position is row number 10. It's very common for the insertion point to be on a completely different row. For instance, it can be on row 55. If the user scrolls the screen up 20 lines, the cursor will most likely stay on row 10 of the display. However, the insertion point must move to line 35 of the text buffer.

Keeping the cursor and the insertion point synchronized is one of the hardest tasks you'll deal with when you're writing the text editor.

In addition to containing the array of text strings, the first line displayed, and the insertion point location, the text editor must know whether the text strings have been modified by the user. In programmer jargon, it must keep track of whether the buffer is dirty. If the buffer has been modified since it was saved, it's dirty and needs to be saved again. If the buffer is dirty, the program should ask whether the user wants to save before it exits.

The text buffer is one of the more complex objects in this program. It will need a uniform method of handling errors. One option is to make all of the text buffer member functions return error codes. Another is to have the text buffer object contain an error status variable. Whenever the program needs to check the error status, it can call a member function to get the value of the error status data member.

So the next logical question is, which method do you use and why?

Having member functions return error codes is good to do when there are many instances of an object in the program. For example, the text editor uses a lot of text string objects. If we were to make the text string object contain an error status variable, each text string in the text buffer would have an error status variable. We would end up using a large amount of memory. Having member functions return error codes saves that memory.

However, having member functions return error codes also causes complications of its own. You may find that the place where you need to test for and handle an error is not in the function where it occurred. Suppose the function `DoSomething()` is currently executing. `DoSomething()` was called by `ThatFunction()`. `DoSomething()` calls a function named `this_object::Evaluate()`. Also suppose that an error needs to be handled in `ThatFunction()`. If an error occurs in `this_object::Evaluate()`, that error code will have to be passed through `DoSomething()` to `ThatFunction()`. This situation can make it difficult to pass back other types of errors that can also occur in `DoSomething()`. If `this_object` contains an error status data member, `ThatFunction()` can call a member function that reports the error status of the object. This leaves `DoSomething()` to return error codes that deal with its own errors.

The long and short of it is that if there are many occurrences of an object in a program, it probably shouldn't contain an error status data member. If there are only a few, then having an error status data member can be a real advantage.

In our text editor, there is only one text buffer. (You'll add additional text buffers in one of the exercises.) So keeping an error status data member in the text buffer object is efficient and flexible.

What about the text buffer's member functions?

It will need a constructor. It will need a function that will retrieve the row number of the first line that is displayed. We'll need functions to get and set the row and column values of the insertion point. We'll also need a function to insert characters at the insertion point. We'll need a function that reports the number of lines of the buffer that contain text.

Since the text buffer has a collection of text string objects, we'll need a function to access them. One common way is to provide a subscript operator function, `operator[]()`. Portions of the object oriented design community dislike subscript operator functions. In C++, you typically return a reference when you implement a subscript operator function. Returning a reference or a pointer can enable a programmer to modify the contents of an object without calling the object's member functions.

For this implementation, we'll provide access to the text strings in the text buffer with a subscript operator function. The primary reason for this is simplicity. It makes the text editor code simpler and more readable. However, in a professional program, you may want to consider another approach.

The text buffer must also provide member functions that scroll the buffer up and down. It will have functions for loading and saving files. It will need a function that reports whether or not the text buffer is dirty. It will also have a function to report the error status, and another to clear it.

Example 27.5 gives a pseudocode description of the text buffer object.

EXAMPLE 27.5 The Text Buffer Object

```
class text_buffer
{
public functions
   A default (no-arg) constructor.
   A function that inserts a character at the insertion point.
   A function that reports the first line of the buffer that is currently displayed.
   A function that reports the total number of lines with text on them.
   A subscript operator function.
   A function to scroll the buffer up.
   A function to scroll the buffer down.
   A function that scrolls the buffer to a particular line.
   A function that sets the insertion point row.
   A function that gets the insertion point row.
   A function that sets the insertion point column.
   A function that gets the insertion point column.
   A function that loads a text file into the buffer.
   A function that saves the buffer to a text file.
   A function that reports whether the buffer is dirty.
   A function that reports the buffer's current error status.
   A function that clears the buffer's current error status.

private data
   The collection of text strings.
   The first row of text displayed.
   The number of lines containing text.
   The insertion point row.
   The insertion point column.
   The "dirty" status.
   The error status.
}
```

The Status Bar Object

The status bar takes the place of dialog boxes in the text editor. It will occupy an area across the bottom of the screen. It a sense, it will be like a miniature screen with a cursor of its own. However, unlike the cursor in the edit area, the status bar cursor will not be visible.

The status bar is a simple object. It will have an origin, which is its upper left corner. The status bar object will also contain the bar's height and width. It must keep track of the row and column values of its insertion point.

The bar will require member functions to get and set the row and column numbers of the origin. It must have member functions to get and set the height and width. It will need functions to print a single character or a text string at the insertion point. Also, it must be able to get input at the insertion point. Finally, it must provide a function to clear the portion of the screen that the status bar uses.

The pseudocode description of the status bar object is given in Example 27.6.

EXAMPLE 27.6 The Status Bar Object

```
class status_bar
{
public functions
   A default (no-arg) constructor.
   A function to set the origin (upper left corner) of the status bar.
   A function to get the row of the origin.
   A function to get the column of the origin.
   A function to set the height of the status bar.
   A function to get the height of the status bar.
   A function to set the width of the status bar.
   A function to get the width of the status bar.
```

```
      A function to print a text string at the current insertion point.
      A function to print a character at the current insertion point.
      A function that gets user input at the current insertion point.
      A function that clears the portion of the screen used by the status bar.
   private data
      The row and column numbers of the insertion point.
      The height and width of the status bar.
      The row and column numbers of the origin.
   }
```

The Display Object

The display object will hide the hardware dependencies of the user's video subsystem. It will provide a standard interface to the computer's screen. Computer monitors are controlled by a video adaptor. The adaptor keeps track of the current state of the display. As a result, our display object will not need to keep much information about the display's state. Whenever the text editor calls a display object function to ask about the current state of the monitor, the display object will query the adaptor for the information.

Programmers call this type of class a **wrapper class.** We can put wrappers on any hardware device. We can also put wrappers on other software. Either way, the wrapper class doesn't provide its own functionality. If the class is a wrapper for hardware, the class interfaces to the hardware and the hardware provides the class's functionality.

That's exactly what our display class will do. It will have functions to print text to the screen. However, those functions will simply pass the text to the hardware and let the video hardware print the text on the screen. The functionality of printing is provided by the video subsystem. We just use the wrapper to give the video subsystem an object oriented interface for the rest of our program.

Using wrappers is a common technique in professional programs. Very often, C++ developers need to use code libraries written in C. In such situations, it is extremely common to create a class to wrap the C library.

We would also have to rewrite the input device class for the new hardware or operating system. The input device class will be presented shortly.

By providing a wrapper for the video subsystem, we enable our text editor to be easily ported to another operating system or other computer hardware. To do the port, we would just rewrite the display class for the new hardware or operating system. None of the other classes in this program that we've discussed so far would change. None of them are dependent on the hardware or operating system that the text editor runs on. So with some advance planning, the text editor can be made to run on virtually any computer with a minimal porting effort.

There are other ways to make a display object global that don't involve global variables. It's a good idea to try and think of as many approaches that don't require global variables as you can. You may find that you really don't need any globals after all.

Making the Display Object Global Earlier in this book, I made a very strenuous effort to discourage you from using global variables. While I don't want to undermine that effort, the display class provides an example of when it may be worthwhile to use a global variable.

In this case, the display object should be available anywhere in the program. After all, the `cout` stream is available to an entire program. In fact, `cout` *is* a global variable. In this implementation, we'll make the display object a global variable, just like `cout`.

The Characteristics of a Display Object A display object has a cursor. Some types of displays can be set to different modes. This version of the text editor will work in MS DOS compatible PCs. On MS DOS compatible PCs, there are several possible video modes. In fact, there are several possible text modes.

Our program will run in one of the most common text modes. However, when the program starts, the user's screen may be in a graphics mode. It may be in a different text mode than the text editor uses. Therefore, the display object will save the current video mode when the program starts. It will set the user's display into the video we want to use. When the program ends, the display object will set the user's monitor back to the user's original video mode. When you do this kind of thing for users, they consider your program well-mannered.

When the text editor displays a menu on the screen, it will need to save whatever text is in the spot where the menu will be displayed. After it removes the menu, it will put the saved text back onto the screen. This is a very hardware-dependent screen operation. Since we're wrapping the hardware dependencies of the video subsystem in the display object class, we'll have the display object class save and restore blocks of text on the screen. So the display object will need to keep a list of the text blocks it's saving.

The Display Object's Member Functions The basic purpose of a computer display (at least while we're using the text editor) is to display text. Our program will sometimes need to display text at the current cursor location. At other times, it will need to display text anywhere on the screen. Our display object should provide the program with the ability to do both of these tasks.

The program will also need to clear the screen. At times, it must clear just a portion of the screen. The display object will need to have function to do both.

Of course, the text editor will need functions to move the cursor up, down, left, and right. It must have the ability to set the cursor's row and column separately. It will have to query for the current row and column.

In addition, the editor program should be able to ask the display object what the number of the first row is. The row number can be different for different types of displays. Some displays and display modes have row numbers that begin with zero. On others, the first row is row 1. Similarly, the text editor will need to be able to ask the display object the number of the last row, the first column, and the last column.

Most text editors use a monospaced font. That is, every letter has the same width and height. However, the width and height of the monospaced font vary on different types of displays. To make our program more portable, we will give our display object member functions that report the height and width of a character.

In text mode, each spot on the screen is a character position. If our text editor were ported to a graphics mode, each location on the screen would be a pixel. In text mode, the length of a string is just the number of characters it contains. In graphics mode, the length of a string is the number of characters it contains multiplied by the number of pixels per character. Again, for the sake of portability, we'll provide the display object with a function that returns the length of a string when it is displayed on the screen.

As was previously mentioned, the display object will keep a list of the blocks of text it saves. The object must provide functions to save and restore blocks of text.

The last member function the display object will require is a function to query the display's error status.

Example 27.7 shows a pseudocode description of the display object.

EXAMPLE 27.7 Pseudocode for the Display Object

```
class display
{
public functions
   A default constructor.
   A destructor.

   A function to clear the entire screen.
   A function that clears a specified portion of the screen.
   A function to print a character at the current cursor location.
   A function to print a string at the current cursor location.
   A function that prints a character at a specified location on the screen
      (not at the current cursor location).
   A function that prints a string at a specified location on the screen
      (not at the current cursor location).
   A function to move the cursor up a specified number of lines.
   A function that moves the cursor down a specified number of lines.
   A function that moves the cursor left a specified number of character columns.
   A function that moves the cursor right a specified number of character columns.

   A function to set the cursor's row.
   A function to get the cursor's row.
   A function which sets the cursor's column.
```

```
   A function which gets the cursor's column.

   A function that returns the width of a character in the current display mode.

   A function that returns the width of a character in the current display mode.
   A function that returns the height of a character in the current display mode.
   A function that returns the height of a string in the current display mode.
   A function that returns the width of a string in the current display mode.

   A function which returns the row number (either 0 or 1) of the first row of
      the display in the current mode.
   A function which returns the row number of the last row of the display in
      the current mode.

   A function which returns the column number (either 0 or 1) of the first
      column of the display in the current mode.
   A function which returns the column number of the last column of the
      display in the current mode.


   A function that saves the contents of a rectangular area of the display.
   A function that restores the contents of a rectangular area of the display.

   A function that returns the error status of the display.

private data
   The display's error status.
   A collection of data saved from the screen.

   MS DOS: The user's original display mode.
}
```

The Input Device Object

Like the display object, the input device object will hide many hardware dependencies. It will mimic the behavior of the `iostream` class in that it will declare a global variable to represent the keyboard.

For the sake of brevity, the input device class will limit itself to only taking input that is in the ASCII set. However, if you have the proper hardware documentation, you can easily extend it to recognize keystrokes that are not in the ASCII set (such as Page Up, Page Down, and the arrow keys).

The input device class will get characters from the keyboard. It will not require any member data. The only public functions it needs are a constructor and a function that gets input.

When it gets input, the input device class will convert some keystrokes to constants. In Table 27.1, we defined the commands we'd use to move the cursor up, down, left, and right. The input device class will convert these four keystrokes to constants defined in the program. These constants are often called **tokens.** It will also define tokens for the Enter and Escape keys on the keyboard.

Example 27.8 gives the pseudocode description of the input device class.

EXAMPLE 27.8 A Description of the Input Device Class

```
class input_device
{
public constants
   Constants defining the keystrokes for the Enter key and the Escape key.
   Constant tokens that identify the keystrokes for moving the cursor up,
      down, left, and right.
```

```
public functions
    A constructor.
    A function to get user input.
}
```

The Desktop Object

The desktop object could also contain the display and input device object, depending on your point of view. This would make global variables unnecessary in this program. However, it would not be following the style of `cin` and `cout`.

The desktop object binds together most of the other objects. It contains a text buffer (which contains text strings), a status bar, and a menu system.

The desktop object must get input from the input device. Recall that the input device doesn't recognize commands. It just gets characters. The exceptions to this are the Enter and Escape keys, and keystroke commands that move the cursor up, down, left, and right. The desktop object will need to recognize all other command keystrokes that it uses.

It's logical to ask why the input device converts some keystrokes to commands and why the desktop object must convert all the others. The answer is that the input device objects recognize only the most fundamental keystroke commands. All others are specific to the application. The input device class interprets only commands common to all (or nearly all) programs. In this way, the input device object becomes usable in a wide variety of programs.

Some readers might decide that this design isn't correct. They may move commands such as Page Up and Page Down from the desktop object into the input device class. This is a reasonable and logical decision to make. Other readers, for equally reasonable and logical reasons, may decide that having the input device object recognize other command keystrokes is not a good idea.

The point here is that it primarily depends on your point of view. Much of software design does. If you can justify your design in terms of your project's goals, program speed and efficiency, and program maintainability, then your design is justified. You should move forward with implementing it.

In our text editor, the Enter key is used both as an end-of-line marker and to select menu items. So it means different things depending on the context.

The input device passes most characters through to the program without changing them in any way. The few keystrokes that it does convert to tokens are not specific to the application. For example, the Enter key may mean different things in different applications. It can even mean different things in the same application.

Because the input device gets input that is not specific to the application, we say that it gets **raw input.** The desktop class converts the raw input to **cooked input.** That is, it converts the raw input into commands or tokens that the program recognizes and uses internally.

Cooked input can either be a command or a character to be inserted in the text buffer. The desktop object will examine all raw input. If the raw input is a command, it will cook the input by packaging it into an object and marking it as a command. If it is text, it will package the character into an object and mark it as text to go into the text buffer.

This tells us that our object list is not complete. We need a cooked input object. It must have a private data member to store characters and commands. It also requires a **discriminator** to tell the difference between the two. Simply put, a discriminator tells what kind of thing an object is. In this case, the discriminator tells the program that the cooked input object is either a command or a text character.

The cooked input object will need functions to get the character or command it contains. It also must have a function that gets the value of the discriminator. It will not need any functions to set these values.

As you become more experienced with C++, you'll easily see how the cooked input object can be modified to be generic enough to be used with most applications.

Recall that the cooked input class is specifically for use with the desktop class. As such, it is *highly* specific to the desktop object. The desktop object will set all of the values in a cooked input object. All other objects in the program will strictly be reading those values. They will not write any data into the cooked input class. So we'll make the desktop object a friend of the cooked input class.

Many object oriented designers do not like the use of the `friend` keyword. It tends to undermine the object oriented structure of C++ software. Giving an object direct access to another class's private data members is generally not a good idea.

However, if the class you are creating is very dependent on its `friend` class, then having them be friends may be appropriate. Use your best judgment. Generally speaking, though, you should minimize the use of the `friend` keyword.

You may wonder if we could implement the cooked input class without making the desktop object its friend. The answer is yes. However, it would be complicated to give only the desktop object the ability to write to a cooked input object. We want this because no other object in the system should be cooking input.

So the question becomes, which do you dislike more, the use of the keyword `friend` or complicated code? In this case, I've chosen to make the code simple and use the keyword `friend`.

Example 27.9 contains the pseudocode description of the cooked input object.

EXAMPLE 27.9 The Cooked Input Object

```
class cooked_input
{
public constants
   An enumerated type called user_input_data_type that tells whether the user
      input is a command or a character.
   Enumerated constants for the user_input_data_type.

public functions
   A constructor.
   A function to get the discriminant value.
   A function to get the command.
   A function to get the character.

private data
   A declaration indicating that the desktop class is a friend.
   A discriminant of user_input_data_type.
   A variable that will contain the character or command.
}
```

Now that we have the cooked input class, we can design the desktop object.

The desktop object will need an enumerated type that defines the commands for the text editor. Of course, the desktop will contain a text buffer. The contents of the text buffer will be displayed in an area of the screen called the *edit area*. The desktop object must keep track of where the edit area is on the screen.

Also, the desktop object is going to have a status bar and a menu system. To make the text editor more extensible, we'll dynamically allocate the menus. So the desktop object will contain a pointer to the main menu.

In addition, the desktop object will need a data member to hold its current error status.

For its public member functions, the desktop object must have a constructor and a destructor. The destructor is necessary because the desktop object will contain a pointer to menus.

Additionally, the desktop object requires functions that give the program access to the status bar and menus. It must have a function to set the text area in which the buffer contents will be displayed. The desktop class also needs a function that activates the menu system when the user enters the proper keystroke command.

The desktop object needs to provide the program with functions to manipulate the text buffer. Specifically, it will need functions to display the buffer's text, put a character into the buffer, load the buffer from a file, save the buffer to a file, and scroll the buffer. The program will need to be able to test to see whether the buffer is dirty or not. It must be able to check the number of lines that contain text. It will need to move the cursor and check the buffer's error status. When the user presses the Enter key, the program must be able to perform a line feed (newline).

Example 27.10 shows the pseudocode description of the desktop class.

EXAMPLE 27.10 The Desktop Object

```
class desktop
{
public constants
```

```
   An enumerated type called commands. It contains a list of constants defining all
      commands the text editor recognizes.

public functions
   A default constructor.
   A destructor.

   A function providing access to the status bar.

   A function to set the main menu pointer.
   A function to get the main menu pointer.

   A function that sets the boundaries of the screen area used to display text.

   A function that activates the main menu.

   A function to display one screenful of text from the text buffer.
   A function that inserts a character into the text buffer at the current
      insertion point location.
   A function to load a text file into the text buffer.
   A function to save the text buffer to a file.
   A function that tells whether the text buffer is dirty or not.
   A function which scrolls the text buffer up by a specified number of lines.
   A function which scrolls the text buffer down by a specified number of lines.
   A function that scrolls the text buffer to a particular line of text.
   A function that returns the number of lines containing text.
   A function that returns the text buffer error status.
   A function to clear the text buffer error status.

   A function that moves the cursor up a specified number of lines.
   A function that moves the cursor down a specified number of lines.
   A function to move the cursor left a specified number of character columns.
   A function to move the cursor right a specified number of character columns.
   A function to do a line feed in the text buffer.

   A function to cook user input.

   A function which returns the error status of the desktop object.
   A function which clears the desktop object error status.

private data
   The text buffer.
   The dimensions of the text display area.
   The status bar.
   A pointer to the main menu.
   The desktop object error status.
}
```

A Project Plan for the Text Editor

At this point, we have a pretty good overview of the code we'll be writing. In a real job situation, a developer would next develop a project schedule.

To develop a realistic schedule, you must determine which objects you need to implement first. Then you can estimate how long it will take to write and debug the objects. You use the bull's-eye approach we discussed earlier.

For the text editor, you may first decide to write a simple `main()` function, the text string object, and the text buffer object. Your `main()` function would only recognize user keyboard commands. This would enable you write a program that implements text strings and the text buffer. The text buffer would load a file, save a file, and scroll it. You could also work on cursor movement within the text buffer.

This approach gives you much of the core functionality of the text editor. It doesn't require you to implement the display object, the input device object, the desktop object, the menu system, or the status bar. Each of these objects would be added one by one in successive versions of the text editor. Your project plan would show the completion date of the core system. It would also show the dates you would complete each object and have it integrated into the text editor.

This is an important point. When you write a schedule, you must allow time for integrating the object into the software. It's very rare that a component will go into a program without any hitches.

Actually, software testing is an art in itself. Many software testers have backgrounds in development. Software testing provides an alternative career path for those with development skills.

Table 27.3 illustrates a possible project schedule for the text editor.

After this development is finished, you'll need to allow time for testing the software as a complete system. This can take days, weeks, or months.

The approach shown in the schedule in Table 27.3 is not the only one you can use. You may decide that it's most important to get the desktop and menu object up and running first. That way, you can plug each additional object into a working environment. With this approach, you'd first write and debug a bare-bones desktop object. Next, you'd create the menu system. Table 27.4 demonstrates a development schedule for this approach.

Which schedule you use depends on the priorities of your project.

When you're creating a schedule, write out your first estimate of the time it will take you to develop your program code. Look it over to ensure it's correct. Then double it. Create a completely new schedule that shows twice the amount of time for writing, debugging, and integrating your software. Turn that in to your manager. Chances are, she'll double it again.

I'm quite serious about using this technique. Schedules must take into account weekends, holidays, sick time, family concerns, and so on. Your initial time estimate will almost never be correct. That's OK. Most managers are experienced enough to know that. So are

TABLE 27.3 A Schedule for Implementing the Text Editor

Component(s)	Start Date	Code Completion Date	Start Debugging and Integration	Complete Debugging and Integration
Core: Text string, text buffer, simple version of `main()`	Feb. 1	Feb. 28	March 1	March 14
Desktop	March 15	April 2	April 2	April 8
Menu, menu item	April 9	April 29	April 30	May 8
Status bar	May 9	May 18	May 19	May 24

TABLE 27.4 An Alternate Schedule for Developing the Text Editor

Component(s)	Start Date	Code Completion Date	Start Debugging and Integration	Complete Debugging and Integration
Desktop	Feb. 1	Feb. 15	Feb. 16	Feb. 24
Menu, menu item	Feb. 25	March 20	March 21	March 28
Text string	March 29	April 7	April 8	April 15
Text buffer	April 16	May 2	May 3	May 10
Status bar	May 11	May 19	May 20	May 24

Most software design methodologies require you to produce more design diagrams than we have produced using the generic methods shown in this chapter. They'll also require you to provide some sort of textual explanation (like pseudocode) of the processes in your program.

most programmers. If you want realistic time estimates that accurately reflect when you'll complete the software, double your first time estimate.

Pseudocoding the Text Editor

When you begin writing a program, it's often good to pseudocode it first. The process of pseudocoding a program forces you to think about the design of each object and function before you actually write it.

One technique for pseudocoding is to create a function as if you were really going to write it. Instead of writing C++ statements in the body of the function, write comments. Example 27.11 shows pseudocode for the text editor's `main()` function.

EXAMPLE 27.11 Pseudocode for the `main()` Function

```
int main(int argc,char *argv[])
{
   int returnStatus = NO_ERROR;

   // Clear the screen.
   // If the user entered too many arguments on the command line...
      // Beep the speaker.
      // Output an error message.
   // Else there were not too many arguments on the command line...
      // Create the desktop.
      // If the desktop was created successfully...
         // Initialize the status bar.
         // Allocate memory for the main menu.
         // If the main menu was allocated...
            // Set the location of the menu on the screen.
            // Build the menu system.
            // If the menu system was built...
               // Attach the menus to the work area.
               // Set the text display area.
         // Else the menu system could not be built...
            // Output an error message.
            // Set an error code for the return status.
         // Else the main menu could not be allocated...
            // Output an error message.
            // Set an error code for the return status.
      // Else the desktop could not be created...
         // Output an error message.
         // Set an error code for the return status.

      // If the user specified a file to load...
           // Convert the file name to a text_string object.
           // Load the file.
           // If the file could not be loaded...
              // Output an error message.
              // This is not a fatal error. Clear it and go on.

      // While there is no error and the user doesn't want to quit...
         // Get input from the user.
         // Cook the user input.
         // If there was an error...
            // Beep the speaker.
            // This is not a fatal error, just clear it and go on.
         // Else if the input is a command...
```

```
            // Execute the command.
               // If the user pressed the Enter key...
                  // Move the cursor to the beginning of the next line.
               // If the user pressed PageUp...
                  // Scroll up one screenful.
               // If the user pressed PageDown...
                  // Scroll down one screenful.
               // If the user wants to scroll up one line...
                  // Scroll up one line.
               // If the user wants to scroll down one line...
                  // Scroll down one line.
               // If the user wants to jump to the top of the buffer...
                  // Jump to the top of the text buffer.
               // If the user wants to jump to the bottom of the buffer...
                  // Jump to the bottom of the text buffer.
               // If the user wants to move the cursor up one line...
                  // Move the cursor up.
               // If the user wants to move the cursor down one line...
                  // Move the cursor down.
               // If the user wants to move the cursor left one column...
                  // Move the cursor left.
               // If the user wants to move the cursor right one column...
                  // Move the cursor right.
               // If the user wants to load a file...
                  // Load a text file into the buffer.
                  // Display the new contents of the buffer.
               // If the user wants to save a file...
                  // Save the buffer contents.
                  // Redisplay the text buffer.
               // If the user wants to copy the current line of text...
                  // Copy the text string.
               // If the user wants to cut the current line of text...
                  // Cut the text string from the buffer.
                  // Redisplay the contents of the buffer.
               /* If the user wants to paste a text string that was
               cut or copied... */
                  // Insert the text string into the buffer.
                  // Redisplay the contents of the buffer.
               // If the user wants to exit the program...
                  // If the buffer is dirty...
                     /* Ask the user if she/he wants to save
                     before exiting. */
                     // If the user wants to save the buffer...
                        // Save it.
                        done = true;
               // If the command was not recognized...
                  // Beep the speaker.
                  // Clear the error.
        // Else if the user input is text...
           // Put the text in the buffer.
    // Return the error status.
}
```

Designing software is an iterative process. Often, many of the implementation details are not clear on the first design pass. Writing a pseudocode version of each object and function before we implement it helps us focus on the details we may have missed.

On a professional design project, we would go back and update the design after writing the pseudocode. By the time we wrote the actual program code, most of the details would be ironed out.

Pseudocoding also helps developers document their programs. If you look at the `main()` function in Example 27.11, you'll see that all you have to do now is insert the appropriate C++ statements after each comment.

Troubleshooting Guide

After reading this section, you should be able to:

- Avoid potential problems in stating the purpose of a program.
- Avoid selecting objects that do not belong in the program.
- Do iterative design to find details you've previously omitted.

What's the Purpose?

As you go through your career, you'll find that users sometimes cannot clearly state the purpose of the software they want. Typically, this is because they have not studied the need that the software is intended to fit. They hired you to do it instead. What they want you to do is study the situation and suggest one or more solutions.

The problem comes when users don't tell you that this is what you're being hired to do. They make a general statement like, "We need to computerize our business." Naturally, they hire you because you're the local computer expert. They tell you, "We need a computer system." After a brief pause, they usually add, "But we need one that doesn't cost too much."

The company's need here is real. Management genuinely needs to computerize parts of the business. However, they can't specify which parts unless they have carefully studied how they operate.

You know you're in this situation when the people paying you to write the program can't clearly state what it's for in one paragraph or less. When they use broad, general terms to describe what the program should do, they don't know what they really want.

Another problem occurs when management tells you, "We want you to computerize what Jane does." Your logical response is "What does Jane do?" If the reply is something like, "She coordinates customer relations information," then you're in trouble. There are many situations in which a person's job can't be done by a computer. Management recognizes that Jane performs valuable functions. She may have been doing her job for many years. Someone suggests that it would be good to capture her knowledge in software before Jane retires. This may or may not work.

You may find that you can get a computer to do some of what Jane does by putting a Web page on the company's Internet server. You can write a C++ program that interfaces with the Web page and collects information from customers. The program can then route the information where it needs to go. However, the essence of doing many jobs well lies in the judgment and experience of the person doing it. A computer will never learn every customer's face and inquire about a spouse's operation or a child's baseball game.

Although this may sound like it has nothing to do with software design, in fact it does. To be successful, you must be able to clearly see what the software should do and what it should not do. You must be willing and able to propose both software and nonsoftware solutions. In the example presented here, the solution might be to create a customer database and have Jane type in her extensive knowledge of each customer. It might also require suggesting to management that Jane pick and train the person who's going to replace her when she retires. The problem requires both a software and a nonsoftware solution.

Whenever the statement of purpose for the software is vague or involves the names of specific people, be careful. Tell management that you must study the problem for a while before you can begin to design the system. Suggest a schedule that will allow you to identify the company's software needs and report back. When you present your report, suggest alternatives. Describe what each alternative will cost and what the company will get for its money.

To be a software designer, you must work at developing all of these skills. The primary task of a software designer is communication. You must be able to communicate with management, users, and technology workers.

When you present your proposal and management selects one of the alternatives you've given them, you should have a short, clear statement of purpose for your program. Only then can you move forward with the project.

Watch Out for Improper Objects

When you're designing C++ classes, be wary of objects that have only verbs in their names. For example, you should avoid objects with names such as calculate, print, or manage. An object's name is ideally a noun. It should not be "print", but rather "report_printer". Or better yet, "report_generator". Your program should not contain an object called "manage_windows". It should be a "window_manager".

If you can't state the name of an object as a noun, it probably shouldn't be an object. It should be a function. Software objects represent something. They act as models of *things*. An object's member functions—not the object itself—should perform actions.

Objects with verbs for names will almost always make your system more complex and less object oriented. They indicate an need to redesign the software.

Play It Again, Sam

Designing software is an iterative process. You will always need to go back and redesign parts of the system when you implement it. Therefore, you must plan for change. Design your software so that it can be easily modified and extended, because it probably will be before you release version 1.0.

Having said that, you still need to try do as much design as you can the first time around. You should try to anticipate everything you'll need to implement in the software. For instance, several items have been purposely omitted from the design of the text editor. In the exercises at the end of this chapter, you'll describe what you think they are. However, I'll give you a hint. Most of the objects in the text editor will either need to return an error code or set an internal error status variable. Did you see any error codes defined in the design? They must be there for the design to be complete.

One way to gain an insight into details that you might have missed in the initial design is to write the pseudocode for each object and function. This will show you the majority of the details that are missing from your design. It also enables you to redesign before you start writing any actual code. This lowers the cost of redesigning the software.

Summary

When writing software, developers need to begin by stating what the software is for. If you can write a short, clear statement of why you are writing the program and what need it will fill, you will have a much better chance of being able to write the program.

Before you start writing the program, you need to create a program specification. The specification should list everything the program does. This can often be accomplished by designing the user interface.

You must also be able to describe the functionality of the program. Top-down design methods enable you to do this graphically.

After the program's functionality is defined, you can design the objects that will provide the functionality. As you design them, you will find that pseudocoding them helps you clarify the object's implementation details.

In almost every professional situation, you will need to make a schedule for your project (or your part of it). Use the bull's-eye approach to implement manageable portions of the program. This focuses your attention on the particular parts you are implementing. It enables you to get parts of the program written and debugged before you go on to the rest.

Remember that design is an iterative process. You'll most probably need to redesign parts of your software. If you pseudocode the functions for each of your objects, you'll often find many details that you missed in the first design pass.

Review Questions

1. What problems can occur while writing the objectives of a program? What are some ways you can solve these problems?
2. Why is a program specification necessary? How would it affect the project if you just didn't write one?
3. What does it mean to design the functionality of a program? How does this help you implement it?
4. How does top-down design help you design the functionality of a program?
5. How do you go about picking objects for a program?
6. What are some problems that can occur when you're designing objects for a program?
7. Why is a project schedule necessary? How does it help you as a developer?
8. What is the bull's-eye approach to software development? Why is it useful?
9. What would happen if you wrote the software for the entire program you were working on, then did testing, integrating, and debugging?
10. Why is design an iterative process? What prevents you from just doing it once?

Exercises

1. Give five examples of poor purpose statements for programs. Explain why they are poor examples.
2. Give five examples of good program purpose statements. Explain why they are good examples.
3. Explain why designing a program's user interface helps create the program specification. Tell why designing the user interface may not be enough to provide a complete program specification. Give at least three examples.
4. Your boss asks you to write a program that mimics a pocket calculator. Design the user interface. Use that design to generate a program specification.
5. Explain the process of top-down design. Give an example.
6. Your boss asks you to write a program that mimics a pocket calculator. Do a top-down design of the calculator program's functionality.
7. Explain why you must design a program's objects. Give an example of how to do it.
8. Your boss asks you to write a program that mimics a pocket calculator. Design the program's objects.
9. Describe how to make a project schedule. Explain the benefits of doing so. Give an example schedule.
10. Your boss asks you to write a program that mimics a pocket calculator. Make a schedule for this project. Tell which objects you would implement first and why.

Chapter Glossary

Cooked Input Input that is specific to an application. Typically, some part of the program converts raw input to tokens or commands that the program uses internally.

Discriminator A data member that tells what kind of data an object contains. Objects that contain more than one type of data use discriminators to mark the type of the data the object currently contains.

Raw Input Input whose meaning is not specific to any particular application. The input is just passed through from the input device to the program.

Token An identifier. Tokens in programs are often defined as constants to represent strings or characters in an efficient way.

Wrapper Class A class that only provides an interface into hardware or other software. The hardware or other software provides the class's underlying functionality. The wrapper just provides an object oriented interface.

28 Developing the Text Editor: TEdit.cpp, Desktop.h, and Desktop.cpp

Objectives

After reading this chapter, you should be able to:

- Implement the text editor source files *TEdit.cpp, Desktop.h,* and *Desktop.cpp*.
- Integrate and debug the objects and functions in these files.
- Name and explain other implementation alternatives.

Preview

In this chapter, we'll begin implementing the software for the text editor. Over the course of the next few chapters, I'll present the basic text editor program. Look it over carefully. You'll be debugging and enhancing it in the exercises at the end of the next few chapters.

Since this program is so long, the source files are provided for you on the CD that comes with this book. In the root directory of the CD, you will find a directory named *Examples*. The *Examples* directory contains a directory named *TEdit*. The files for this chapter are in the *TEdit* directory. To build the basic text editor system, compile and link all of the files together.

A Quick Look at the Finished Program

As you can see from Figures 28.1 and 28.2, the executable version of the text editor enables you to load a text file and edit it. You can also type text into an empty text buffer. Saving the buffer to a file is not implemented. You'll do that in an exercise. In addition, the Cut, Copy, and Paste items in the Edit menu are not implemented. These are also left as exercises.

An important thing to notice is that the text editor may display some odd-looking symbols when you load a text file. For instance, Figure 28.1 displays a line of text that reads

```
ENTER = 13,
```

Notice that there are two small circles before the E in the word Enter. This is not a program bug. The MS DOS version of this program (which is what we developed here) uses a PC's BIOS to do full-screen input and output rather than the C++ stream classes. When you send characters with an ASCII value of 31 or less to the screen using a PC's BIOS, it will try to print the character rather than interpret it. In this case, the text file contained tab characters. When the tabs were printed to the screen, the BIOS did not perform tabs. It simply printed the character. The result is the symbol you see in these two figures.

When you start the text editor, it displays a blank screen. You can begin typing text directly into the empty buffer. The program uses all of the command keys defined in Table 27.1.

FIGURE 28.1 **The Text Editor**

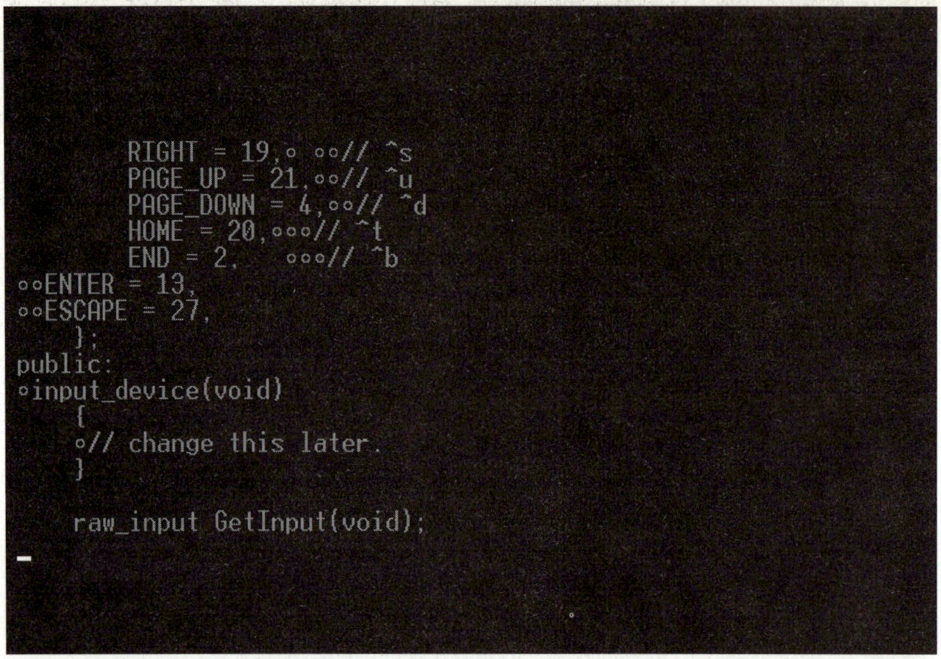

FIGURE 28.2 **The Text Editor's Menu System**

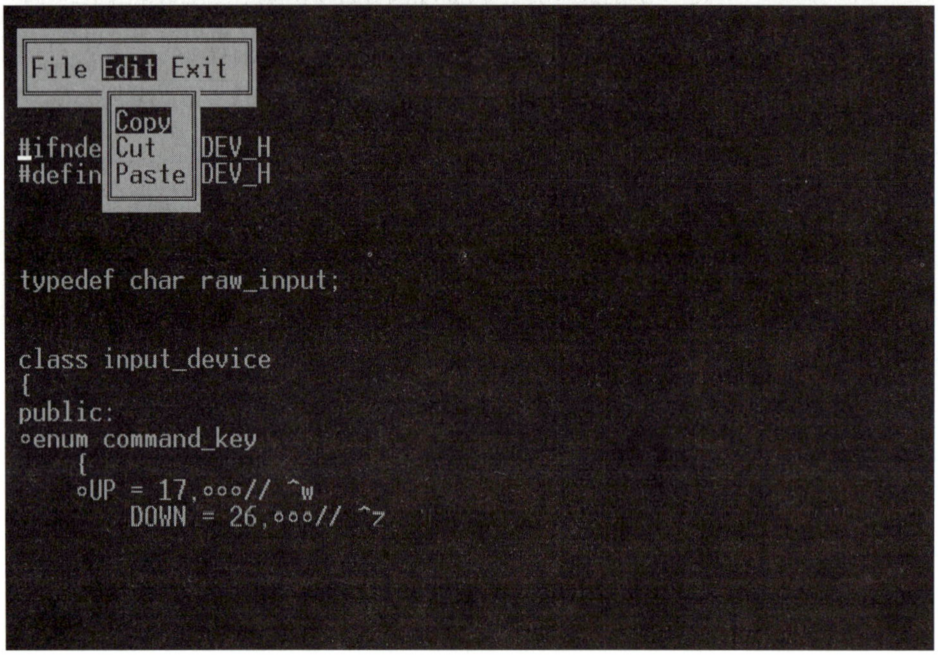

To activate the main menu, press ^c. When you do, the main menu is displayed on the screen. You can use the ^a and ^s keys to move the menu's cursor right and left in a horizontal menu. In vertical menus, you can use the ^w and ^z keys to move the menu cursor up and down. Pressing the Enter key selects an item in the current menu. Pressing the Escape key cancels the current menu.

Writing TEdit.cpp

The file *TEdit.cpp* contains the highest-level functions in the program. The contents of this file essentially state in source code what the program does. Looking through *TEdit.cpp* gives us an overview of the implementation of the text editor.

Listing 28.1 shows contents of the file *TEdit.cpp*.

LISTING 28.1 TEdit.cpp

```
//-------------------------------------------------------------------------------
/*
File Name:  TEdit.cpp
Comments:   This is the primary file in the text editor. It contains the
            main(). It also has functions to set up the status bar and the
            menu system. In addition, it contains functions to do most of the
            work of saving and loading text files.
*/
//-------------------------------------------------------------------------------



//-------------------------------------------------------------------------------
// Include Files

#define EXTERN

#include "Menu.h"
#include "MenuItem.h"
#include "StatBar.h"
#include "TString.h"
#include "TBuffer.h"
#include "InputDev.h"
#include "Display.h"
#include "Desktop.h"
#include <assert.h>

// End Include Files
//-------------------------------------------------------------------------------



//-------------------------------------------------------------------------------
// Constants

const menu_item_id MIID_FILE_LOAD = MIID_FIRST;
const menu_item_id MIID_FILE_SAVE = MIID_FIRST+1;
const menu_item_id MIID_FILE_MENU = MIID_FIRST+2;
const menu_item_id MIID_EDIT_COPY = MIID_FIRST+3;
const menu_item_id MIID_EDIT_CUT = MIID_FIRST+4;
const menu_item_id MIID_EDIT_PASTE = MIID_FIRST+5;
const menu_item_id MIID_EDIT_MENU = MIID_FIRST+6;
const menu_item_id MIID_EXIT_ITEM = MIID_FIRST+7;

const char *MIS_FILE_LOAD = "Load";
const char *MIS_FILE_SAVE = "Save";
const char *MIS_FILE_MENU = "File";
const char *MIS_EDIT_COPY = "Copy";
const char *MIS_EDIT_CUT = "Cut";
const char *MIS_EDIT_PASTE = "Paste";
const char *MIS_EDIT_MENU = "Edit";
const char *MIS_EXIT_ITEM = "Exit";

const int MAX_COMMAND_LINE_ARGUMENTS = 2;
const char BEEP_CHARACTER = (char)7;
```

```
const char *CANT_LOAD_FILE_MESSAGE = "Can't load file";
const char *CANT_SAVE_FILE_MESSAGE = "Can't save file";

const int WORK_AREA_HEIGHT = 15;

const int MAIN_MENU_UP_LEFT_ROW = 1;
const int MAIN_MENU_UP_LEFT_COL = 1;

const STATUS_BAR_UP_LEFT_ROW = 20;
const STATUS_BAR_UP_LEFT_COL = 1;
const STATUS_BAR_HEIGHT = 4;
const STATUS_BAR_WIDTH = 80;

const unsigned TEXT_AREA_FIRST_ROW = 5;
const unsigned TEXT_AREA_LAST_ROW = 20;
const unsigned TEXT_AREA_FIRST_COL = 1;
const unsigned TEXT_AREA_LAST_COL = TEXT_AREA_FIRST_COL+TEXT_BUFFER_WIDTH;

const char *FILE_LOAD_PROMPT_STRING = "Enter the name of the file to load: ";
const char *FILE_SAVE_PROMPT_STRING = "Enter the name of the file to save: ";

// End Constants
//-----------------------------------------------------------------------------



//-----------------------------------------------------------------------------
// Enumerated Types

enum program_error
{
   NO_ERROR = 0,
   CANT_CREATE_MENUS = -1,
   CANT_ALLOCATE_MENU = -2,
   CANT_CREATE_DESKTOP = -3,
   INVALID_COMMAND = -4,
   CANT_ADD_MENU_ITEM = -5,
   CANT_ALLOCATE_STRING = -6
};
// End Enumerated Types
//-----------------------------------------------------------------------------



//-----------------------------------------------------------------------------
// Prototypes

static int MakeMenus(menu *mainMenu);
static void MakeStatusBar(desktop &workArea);
static void LoadFile(desktop &workArea);
static void SaveFile(desktop &workArea);

// End Prototypes
//-----------------------------------------------------------------------------



int main(int argc,char *argv[])
{
```

```
int returnStatus = NO_ERROR;

// Clear the screen.
theScreen.Clear();

// If the user entered too many arguments on the command line...
if (argc > MAX_COMMAND_LINE_ARGUMENTS)
{
   // Beep the speaker.
   cout << BEEP_CHARACTER;

   // Output an error message.
   cout << "Error: Too many command-line arguments." << endl;
   cout << "Usage:" << endl << "tedit <filename>" << endl;
   cout << "where <filename> is the name of the file you ";
   cout << "want to load." << endl;
   cout << "The file name is optional. It may be omitted." << endl;
}
// Else there were not too many arguments on the command line...
else
{
   desktop workArea;

   // If the desktop was created successfully...
   if (workArea.ErrorStatus() == desktop::NO_ERROR)
   {
      // Initialize the status bar.
      MakeStatusBar(workArea);

      // Allocate memory for the main menu.
      menu *mainMenu;
      mainMenu = new menu;

      // If the main menu was allocated...
      if (mainMenu)
      {
         // Set the location of the menu on the screen.
         mainMenu->UpLeftRow(MAIN_MENU_UP_LEFT_ROW);
         mainMenu->UpLeftCol(MAIN_MENU_UP_LEFT_COL);
         returnStatus = MakeMenus(mainMenu);

         // If the menu system was built...
         if (returnStatus == NO_ERROR)
         {
            // Attach the menus to the work area.
            workArea.Menu(mainMenu);
            workArea.SetTextArea(TEXT_AREA_FIRST_COL,
                                 TEXT_AREA_FIRST_ROW,
                                 TEXT_AREA_LAST_COL,
                                 TEXT_AREA_LAST_ROW);
          }
          // Else the menu system could not be built...
          else
          {
             // Output an error message.
             returnStatus = CANT_CREATE_MENUS;
          }
      }
      // Else the main menu could not be allocated...
```

```
        else
        {
            // Output an error message.
            returnStatus = CANT_ALLOCATE_MENU;
        }
    }
    // Else the desktop could not be created...
    else
    {
        // Output an error message.
        returnStatus = CANT_CREATE_DESKTOP;
    }

    text_string outputMessage;

    // If the user specified a file to load...
    if ((returnStatus == NO_ERROR) && (argc > 1))
    {
        // Convert the file name to a text_string object.
        text_string fileName(argv[1]);

        // Load the file.
        workArea.LoadTextBuffer(fileName);

        // If the file could not be loaded...
        if (workArea.TextBufferErrorStatus() != text_buffer::NO_ERROR)
        {
            // Output an error message.
            outputMessage = CANT_LOAD_FILE_MESSAGE;
            workArea.StatusBar().Print(outputMessage);
            workArea.StatusBar().Print(BEEP_CHARACTER);

            // This is not a fatal error. Clear it and go on.
            workArea.ClearTextBufferError();
        }
    }

    bool done=false;
    raw_input rawUserInput;
    cooked_input cookedUserInput;

    // While there is no error and the user doesn't want to quit...
    while ((!done) && (returnStatus == NO_ERROR))
    {
        // Get input from the user.
        rawUserInput = inputDevice.GetInput();
        cookedUserInput = workArea.CookInput(rawUserInput);

        // If there is an error...
        if (workArea.ErrorStatus() != desktop::NO_ERROR)
        {
            // Beep the speaker.
            cout << BEEP_CHARACTER;

            // This is not a fatal error, just clear it and go on.
            workArea.ClearError();
        }
```

```
// Else if the input is a command...
else if (cookedUserInput.InputType() == cooked_input::COMMAND)
{
   // Execute the command.
   switch (cookedUserInput.Command())
   {
      // If the user pressed the Enter key...
      case desktop::ENTER_KEY:
         // Move the cursor to the beginning of the next line.
         workArea.LineFeed();
      break;

      // If the user pressed PageUp...
      case desktop::PAGE_UP:
         // Scroll up one screenful.
         workArea.ScrollTextBufferUp(WORK_AREA_HEIGHT-1);
      break;

      // If the user pressed PageDown...
      case desktop::PAGE_DOWN:
         // Scroll down one screenful.
         workArea.ScrollTextBufferDown(WORK_AREA_HEIGHT-1);
      break;

      // If the user wants to scroll up one line...
      case desktop::SCROLL_UP:
         // Scroll up one line.
         workArea.ScrollTextBufferUp(1);
      break;

      // If the user wants to scroll down one line...
      case desktop::SCROLL_DOWN:
         // Scroll down one line.
         workArea.ScrollTextBufferDown(1);
      break;

      // If the user wants to jump to the top of the buffer...
      case desktop::TO_BUFFER_TOP:
         // Jump to the top of the text buffer.
         workArea.ScrollTextBufferTo(0);
      break;

      // If the user wants to jump to the bottom of the buffer...
      case desktop::TO_BUFFER_END:
         // Jump to the bottom of the text buffer.
         workArea.ScrollTextBufferTo(
            workArea.TextBufferLinesUsed()-1);
      break;

      // If the user wants to move the cursor up one line...
      case desktop::MOVE_UP:
         // Move the cursor up.
         workArea.CursorUp(1);
      break;

      // If the user wants to move the cursor down one line...
      case desktop::MOVE_DOWN:
```

```
      // Move the cursor down.
      workArea.CursorDown(1);
   break;

   // If the user wants to move the cursor left one column...
   case desktop::MOVE_LEFT:
      // Move the cursor left.
      workArea.CursorLeft(1);
   break;

   // If the user wants to move the cursor right one column...
   case desktop::MOVE_RIGHT:
      // Move the cursor right.
      workArea.CursorRight(1);
   break;

   // If the user wants to load a file...
   case MIID_FILE_LOAD:
      // Load a text file into the buffer.
      LoadFile(workArea);
      // Display the new contents of the buffer.
      workArea.DisplayTextBuffer();
   break;

   // If the user wants to save a file...
   case MIID_FILE_SAVE:
      // Save the buffer contents.
      SaveFile(workArea);
      // Redisplay the text buffer.
      workArea.DisplayTextBuffer();
   break;

   // If the user wants to copy the current line of text...
   case MIID_EDIT_COPY:
      // Copy the text string.
   break;

   // If the user wants to cut the current line of text...
   case MIID_EDIT_CUT:
      // Cut the text string from the buffer.
      // Redisplay the contents of the buffer.
   break;

   /* If the user wants to paste a text string that was
   cut or copied... */
   case MIID_EDIT_PASTE:
      // Insert the text string into the buffer.
      // Redisplay the contents of the buffer.
   break;

   // If the user wants to exit the program...
   case MIID_EXIT_ITEM:
      // If the buffer is dirty...
      if (workArea.IsTextBufferDirty())
      {
         /* Ask the user if she/he wants to save
         before exiting. */
```

```
                    // If the user wants to save the buffer...
                       // Save it.
                    }

                    done = true;
              break;

              case MENU_CANCELED:
                 // Do nothing
              break;

              case MENU_FAILED:
                 cout << BEEP_CHARACTER;
                 done = true;
              break;

              default:
                 cout << BEEP_CHARACTER;
                 workArea.ClearError();
              break;
           }
         }
         // Else if it is text...
         else if (cookedUserInput.InputType()==cooked_input::CHARACTER)
         {
            // Put the text in the buffer.
            workArea.PutCharacterIntoTextBuffer(
               cookedUserInput.Character());
         }
      }
   }

   // Return the error status.
   return (returnStatus);
}



//------------------------------------------------------------------------------
/*
Function Name:        MakeMenus
Input Parameters:     mainMenu - Memory space for the main menu.
Output Parameters:    mainMenu - The completed main menu with all submenus
                          attached.
Return Value:         This function returns NO_ERROR if it is successful.
                      Otherwise, it returns an error code defined in the
                      program_error enumerated type.
Comments:             The MakeMenus() function builds the menu system for the
                      text editor. Memory must be allocated for the main menu
                      before this function is called. MakeMenus() allocates
                      memory for all of the other menus and menu items.
*/

static int MakeMenus(menu *mainMenu)
{
   int returnStatus = NO_ERROR;
   menu_item tempItem;
```

```
text_string tempString;
menu *tempMenu;

assert(mainMenu!=NULL);

// The main menu is horizontal.
mainMenu->MenuStyle(menu::HORIZONTAL_MENU_STYLE);

// Allocate the File menu.
tempMenu = new menu;

// If the File menu could be allocated.
if (tempMenu)
{
   // Set the menu's text string.
   tempString = MIS_FILE_LOAD;
}
// Else there was not enough memory...
else
{
   // Set the error status.
   returnStatus = CANT_ALLOCATE_MENU;
}

// If the string was created...
if ((returnStatus == NO_ERROR) && (tempString.Length() > 0))
{
   // Create the File | Load item.
   tempItem.Text(tempString);
   tempItem.ID(MIID_FILE_LOAD);
   tempItem.Menu(NULL);

   // Add it to the File menu.
   if (tempMenu->AddItem(tempItem) != menu::NO_ERROR)
   {
      returnStatus = CANT_ADD_MENU_ITEM;
   }
}
// Else memory for the item's string couldn't be allocated...
else
{
   // Set the error status.
   returnStatus = CANT_ALLOCATE_STRING;
}
// If there's no error so far...
if (returnStatus == NO_ERROR)
{
   // Create the text_string object that holds the name of the item.
   tempString = MIS_FILE_SAVE;

   // If the string was created...
   if (tempString.Length() > 0)
   {
      // Create the File | Save item.
      tempItem.Text(tempString);
      tempItem.ID(MIID_FILE_SAVE);
      tempItem.Menu(NULL);
```

```
         // Add it to the File menu.
         // If the item couldn't be added...
         if (tempMenu->AddItem(tempItem) != menu::NO_ERROR)
         {
            returnStatus = CANT_ADD_MENU_ITEM;
         }
         // Else the item was added...
         else
         {
            /* Create the text_string object that holds the name of
            the item.*/
            tempString = MIS_FILE_MENU;

            // If the item's string couldn't be created...
            if (tempString.Length() == 0)
            {
               // Set the error status.
               returnStatus = CANT_ALLOCATE_STRING;
            }
         }
      }
      // Else the string could not be created...
      else
      {
         returnStatus = CANT_ALLOCATE_STRING;
      }
   }

   // If there's no error so far...
   if (returnStatus == NO_ERROR)
   {
      // Add the File menu to the main menu.
      tempItem.Text(tempString);
      tempItem.ID(MIID_FILE_MENU);
      tempItem.Menu(tempMenu);

      // If the menu item couldn't be added...
      if (mainMenu->AddItem(tempItem) != menu::NO_ERROR)
      {
         // Set the error status.
         returnStatus = CANT_ADD_MENU_ITEM;
      }
   }

   // If everything's ok...
   if (returnStatus == NO_ERROR)
   {
      // Allocate the Edit menu.
      tempMenu = new menu;

      // If the menu was allocated...
      if (tempMenu)
      {
         // Create the item's string.
         tempString = MIS_EDIT_COPY;
      }
      // Else the menu couldn't be allocated...
```

```
      else
      {
         // Set the error status.
         returnStatus = CANT_ALLOCATE_MENU;
      }

      // If the string was created...
      if ((returnStatus == NO_ERROR) && (tempString.Length() > 0))
      {
         // Create the Edit | Copy item.
         tempItem.Text(tempString);
         tempItem.ID(MIID_EDIT_COPY);
         tempItem.Menu(NULL);

         // Add the item to the Edit menu.
         if (tempMenu->AddItem(tempItem) != menu::NO_ERROR)
         {
            returnStatus = CANT_ADD_MENU_ITEM;
         }
      }
      // Else the string could not be created...
      else
      {
         returnStatus = CANT_ALLOCATE_STRING;
      }
   }

   // If there's no error so far...
   if (returnStatus == NO_ERROR)
   {
      // Create the item's string.
      tempString = MIS_EDIT_CUT;

      // If the string was allocated...
      if (tempString.Length() > 0)
      {
         // Create the Edit | Cut item.
         tempItem.Text(tempString);
         tempItem.ID(MIID_EDIT_CUT);
         tempItem.Menu(NULL);

         // Add the item to the Edit menu.
         if (tempMenu->AddItem(tempItem) != menu::NO_ERROR)
         {
            returnStatus = CANT_ADD_MENU_ITEM;
         }
      }
      // Else the string could not be created...
      else
      {
         returnStatus = CANT_ALLOCATE_STRING;
      }

   }

   // If there's no error so far...
   if (returnStatus == NO_ERROR)
   {
```

```
      // Create the item's string.
      tempString = MIS_EDIT_PASTE;

      // If the string could be allocated...
      if (tempString.Length() > 0)
      {
         // Create the Edit | Paste item.
         tempItem.Text(tempString);
         tempItem.ID(MIID_EDIT_PASTE);
         tempItem.Menu(NULL);

         // Add the item to the Edit menu.
         // If the item was not added...
         if (tempMenu->AddItem(tempItem) != menu::NO_ERROR)
         {
            returnStatus = CANT_ADD_MENU_ITEM;
         }
         // Else the item was added to the menu...
         else
         {
            // Create the new item's string.
            tempString = MIS_EDIT_MENU;

            // If the item's string wasn't allocated...
            if (tempString.Length() == 0)
            {
               // Set the error status.
               returnStatus = CANT_ALLOCATE_STRING;
            }
         }
      }
      // Else the string could not be created...
      else
      {
         returnStatus = CANT_ALLOCATE_STRING;
      }
   }

   // If there's no error so far...
   if (returnStatus == NO_ERROR)
   {
      // Add the Edit menu to the main menu.
      tempItem.Text(tempString);
      tempItem.ID(MIID_EDIT_MENU);
      tempItem.Menu(tempMenu);

      // If the item can't be added...
      if (mainMenu->AddItem(tempItem) != menu::NO_ERROR)
      {
         // Set the error status.
         returnStatus = CANT_ADD_MENU_ITEM;
      }
   }

   // If there's no error so far...
   if (returnStatus==NO_ERROR)
   {
      // Create the string for the next item.
```

```
      tempString = MIS_EXIT_ITEM;

      // If the string was allocated...
      if (tempString.Length() > 0)
      {
         // Create the Exit item.
         tempItem.Text(tempString);
         tempItem.ID(MIID_EXIT_ITEM);
         tempItem.Menu(NULL);

         // Add it to the main menu.
         if (mainMenu->AddItem(tempItem) != menu::NO_ERROR)
         {
            returnStatus = CANT_ADD_MENU_ITEM;
         }
      }
      // Else the item's string wasn't allocated...
      else
      {
         // Set the error status.
         returnStatus = CANT_ALLOCATE_STRING;
      }
   }

   // Return the error status.
   return (returnStatus);
}

// End MakeMenus
//-----------------------------------------------------------------------------




//-----------------------------------------------------------------------------
/*
Function Name:       MakeStatusBar
Input Parameters:    workArea - A reference to the desktop object. Memory
                        for workArea must be allocated before this
                        function is called. It can be allocated statically
                        or dynamically.
Output Parameters:   workArea - The desktop object with the status bar
                        initialized.
Return Value:        None.
Comments:            This function initializes the desktop's status bar.
*/

static void MakeStatusBar(desktop &workArea)
{
   // Set the upper left corner.
   workArea.StatusBar().Origin(STATUS_BAR_UP_LEFT_ROW,
                               STATUS_BAR_UP_LEFT_COL);

   // Set the height.
   workArea.StatusBar().Height(STATUS_BAR_HEIGHT);

   // Set the width.
   workArea.StatusBar().Width(STATUS_BAR_WIDTH);
}
```

```
// End MakeStatusBar
//-----------------------------------------------------------------------




//-----------------------------------------------------------------------
/*
Function Name:      LoadFile
Input Parameters:   workArea - A reference to the desktop object. Memory
                       for workArea must be allocated and initialized
                       before this function is called. It can
                       be allocated statically or dynamically.
Output Parameters:  workArea - The desktop object with the file loaded into
                       the text buffer.
Return Value:       None.
Comments:           The LoadFile() function does most of the work
                    associated with loading a file. Specifically, it
                    prompts the user for a file name and loads the file
                    if it can. If it can't, it beeps the speaker and
                    prints an error message in the status bar.
*/

static void LoadFile(desktop &workArea)
{
   text_string fileName;
   text_string outputMessage;

   // Clear the status bar.
   workArea.StatusBar().Clear();

   // Prompt the user for a file name.
   outputMessage = FILE_LOAD_PROMPT_STRING;
   workArea.StatusBar().Print(outputMessage);
   workArea.StatusBar().GetInput(fileName);

   // Clear the status bar.
   workArea.StatusBar().Clear();

   // If the user typed in a file name.
   if (fileName.Length() > 0)
   {
      // Load the file.
      workArea.LoadTextBuffer(fileName);
   }

   // If there was an error loading the file...
   if (workArea.TextBufferErrorStatus() != text_buffer::NO_ERROR)
   {
      // Output an error message.
      outputMessage = CANT_LOAD_FILE_MESSAGE;
      workArea.StatusBar().Print(outputMessage);
      workArea.StatusBar().Print(BEEP_CHARACTER);

      // This is not a fatal error. Clear it and go on.
      workArea.ClearTextBufferError();
   }
}
```

```
// End LoadFile
//----------------------------------------------------------------------------



//----------------------------------------------------------------------------
/*
Function Name:       SaveFile
Input Parameters:    workArea - A reference to the desktop object. Memory
                        for workArea must be allocated and initialized
                        before this function is called. It can
                        be allocated statically or dynamically.
Output Parameters:   workArea - The desktop object with the text buffer
                     saved to a file.
Return Value:        None.
Comments:            The SaveFile() function does most of the work
                     associated with saving a file. Specifically, it
                     prompts the user for a file name and saves the file
                     if it can. If it can't, it beeps the speaker and
                     prints an error message in the status bar.
*/

static void SaveFile(desktop &workArea)
{
   text_string outputMessage;
   text_string fileName;

   // Clear the status bar.
   workArea.StatusBar().Clear();

   // Prompt the user for a file name.
   outputMessage = FILE_SAVE_PROMPT_STRING;
   workArea.StatusBar().Print(outputMessage);
   workArea.StatusBar().GetInput(fileName);

   // Clear the status bar.
   workArea.StatusBar().Clear();

   // If the user typed in a file name...
   if (fileName.Length() > 0)
   {
      // Save the buffer to a file.
      workArea.SaveTextBuffer(fileName);
   }

   // If there was an error...
   if (workArea.TextBufferErrorStatus() != text_buffer::NO_ERROR)
   {
      // Output an error message.
      outputMessage = CANT_SAVE_FILE_MESSAGE;
      workArea.StatusBar().Print(outputMessage);
      workArea.StatusBar().Print(BEEP_CHARACTER);

      // This is not a fatal error. Clear it and go on.
      workArea.ClearTextBufferError();
   }
}
```

```
// End SaveFile
//-----------------------------------------------------------------------


// End TEdit.cpp
//-----------------------------------------------------------------------
```

Let's begin our examination of this program by looking at the file *TEdit.cpp*. The file begins by including the header files that it needs. It then defines groups of constants.

The first group of constants defines unique menu item identification numbers. They are all defined in terms of `MIID_FIRST`, which is defined in *Menu.h*. The constant `MIID_FIRST` is the first number that can be used as a menu item identifier. Providing `MIID_FIRST` enables *Menu.h* to define other menu item IDs that it needs (`MENU_CANCELED`, `MENU_FAILED`, and `NO_ITEM_SELECTED`). A programmer using the `menu` object can define as many menu item identifiers as she wants. None of them will conflict with the IDs defined in *Menu.h* if the constants that the programmer defines are greater than or equal to `MIID_FIRST`.

The other constants defined at the beginning of *TEdit.cpp* are the text strings for menu items, user prompts, and error messages. There are also constants for positioning the menu, edit area, and status bar on the screen. In addition, there are a few constants needed for other miscellaneous tasks in the program.

The file *TEdit.cpp* defines an enumerated type called `program_error`, which contains a list of errors that can occur in the program. It also declares the prototypes for several functions used in this program. These are high-level functions that are not members of any class. The `main()` function calls them. Since they should not be called by any function in any other file, they are declared `static`. Recall that static functions can't be seen by functions outside the file in which they're declared.

Next is the `main()` function. The first thing that `main()` does is clear the screen. It determines the number of parameters the user typed in on the command line. If there are too many, it prints an error message and exits. If there are not too many, it declares a variable of type `desktop`, called `workArea`. The program will use this variable as its work space. When the program declares `workArea`, it must check to ensure that the `desktop` object was created without any errors. If an error does occur, the program will set the error status and exit. It returns error status value to the operating system. Because the return value of `main()` is not zero, the operating system considers this an abnormal termination. It will print an error message on the user's screen.

If the `desktop` constructor successfully creates the `desktop` object, `main()` calls the `MakeStatusBar()` function. `MakeStatusBar()` performs application-specific initialization on the status bar.

The `main()` function's next task is to allocate memory for the main menu. If the memory can't be allocated, the error status is set and the application exits. Because of a nonzero return status, the operating system prints a message telling the user that the program terminated abnormally. If the program was able to allocate memory for the main menu, it sets the location of the main menu on the screen and calls `MakeMenus()` to build the menu system.

The `MakeMenus()` function returns an error status, which `main()` checks. If `MakeMenus()` failed to create and initialize the menu system, the program exits and returns an error status code. Again, the operating system tells the user that the program terminated abnormally.

You may wonder why `main()` doesn't print out an error message explaining what happened. Just printing out an error code and telling the user that the program terminated abnormally isn't very helpful to most users. The reason for using this method is that when a computer is out of memory, it may not reliably print error messages to the screen. Most of the time, it will. However, I've run into instances on some popular operating systems where the program will lock up if it prints an error message when it runs out of memory. If it just returns an error code, it will exit the program and free the memory the program was using. This provides it with enough memory to print the error status code and the abnormal termination message. While circumstances like this are rare, you must be aware that they do occur.

If the MakeMenus() function was able to allocate and initialize the menu system, the main ( ) function attaches the main menu (and, consequently, all the submenus) to the desktop.

Assuming that the program completes all of these tasks successfully, it next checks argc to see if the user specified a file name on the command line. If it did, main() tries to load the file. Not being able to load a file is not a fatal error. The user may have just typed the file name incorrectly. If, for some reason, the program can't load the file, it prints a message, clears the error, and continues.

Next, the main() function enters a while loop. The loop continues while there is no error and the user doesn't want to quit. Inside the loop, main() uses the input_device object to get input from the user. It uses the desktop object to cook the input into a form it understands. If the input is a command, it uses a switch statement to react to the command. When the user types in a character rather than a command, the program puts it into the text buffer.

As stated previously, the MakeMenus() function builds the menu system. It calls the assert() function to ensure that memory is allocated for the main menu before MakeMenus() gets called. Recall that we use assert() to enforce assumptions and test for programmer errors. If we want to handle run time errors such as the user typing incorrect input or running out of memory, we should use branching statements like if or switch.

The MakeMenus() function creates the menu system by allocating memory for each of the main menu's submenus. For every submenu, it initializes each item in the submenu. It then adds each item to the submenu. It continues with the next item in the submenu until the submenu is complete. When finished with a menu, MakeMenus() adds the completed submenu to the main menu.

Each menu object, menu_item object, and text_string object must be dynamically allocated. If there are any allocation errors while MakeMenus() is building the menu system, it sets an error status. The error status is returned to main(), which returns it to the operating system.

The file *TEdit.cpp* also contains the function MakeStatusBar(). This short function initializes the status_bar object to values that are correct for this application.

The next function, LoadFile(), uses the status bar to prompt the user for a file name. It attempts to load the file name using the string that the user enters. If it is not successful, it prints an error message in the status bar. Otherwise, it loads the file into the text buffer.

The SaveFile() function, which is the last function in *TEdit.cpp,* follows the same essential flow of logic as LoadFile(). The primary difference is that it writes text from the buffer to the file rather than reading it from the file to the buffer.

Writing Desktop.h

Of all of the objects in the text editor, the desktop object is the highest level. It contains the most important objects in the system. The functions in *TEdit.cpp* primarily use the desktop object to do the high-level tasks that they perform.

To understand the implementation of the desktop object, we need to examine its class definition. Listing 28.2 shows the definition of the desktop class.

LISTING 28.2 Desktop.h

```
//------------------------------------------------------------------------
/*
File Name:  Desktop.h
Comments:   This file contains the definition of the desktop class. It also
            defines the cooked_input class, which it utilizes to convert raw
            user input to a form it can easily use.
*/
//------------------------------------------------------------------------
```

```
#ifndef DESKTOP_H
#define DESKTOP_H

//---------------------------------------------------------------------------
// Include Files

#include "Menu.h"
#include "MenuItem.h"
#include "StatBar.h"
#include "TString.h"
#include "TBuffer.h"
#include "InputDev.h"
#include "Display.h"

// End Include Files
//---------------------------------------------------------------------------



//---------------------------------------------------------------------------
// Class Definitions

class cooked_input
{
// Public types.
public:
   enum user_input_data_type
   {
      UNKNOWN,
      COMMAND,
      CHARACTER
   };

// Public functions.
public:
   cooked_input(void);

   cooked_input::user_input_data_type InputType(void) const;

   int Command(void) const;
   char Character(void) const;

// Private types.
private:
   union user_input_data
   {
      int command;
      char character;
   };

// Private data.
private:
   friend class desktop;   // Indicate that the desktop class is a friend.

   user_input_data inputData;
   user_input_data_type dataTypeDiscriminant;
};
```

```
class desktop
{
// Public types.
public:
   enum desktop_error
   {
      NO_ERROR,
      INVALID_INPUT
   };

   enum commands
   {
      MOVE_UP = input_device::UP,
      MOVE_DOWN = input_device::DOWN,
      MOVE_LEFT = input_device::LEFT,
      MOVE_RIGHT = input_device::RIGHT,
      ENTER_KEY = input_device::ENTER,
      ESCAPE_KEY = input_device::ESCAPE,
      PAGE_UP = 21,              // ^u
      PAGE_DOWN = 4,             // ^d
      SCROLL_UP = 5,             // ^e
      SCROLL_DOWN = 24,          // ^x
      TO_BUFFER_TOP = 20,        // ^t
      TO_BUFFER_END = 2,         // ^b
      ACTIVATE_MENU = 3          // ^c
   };

// Public functions.
public:
   desktop(void);
   ~desktop();

   // Possible aliasing problems with this function.
   status_bar &StatusBar(void);

   void Menu(menu *desktopMenu);
   const menu *Menu(void) const;

   void SetTextArea(display_coordinate left, display_coordinate top,
                    display_coordinate right, display_coordinate bottom);

   menu_item_id ActivateMainMenu(void);

   // Text buffer access functions.
   void DisplayTextBuffer(void);
   void PutCharacterIntoTextBuffer(char newCharacter);
   void LoadTextBuffer(const text_string &fileName);
   void SaveTextBuffer(const text_string &fileName);
   bool IsTextBufferDirty(void);
   unsigned ScrollTextBufferUp(const unsigned linesToScroll);
   unsigned ScrollTextBufferDown(const unsigned linesToScroll);
   unsigned ScrollTextBufferTo(const unsigned newTopLine);
   unsigned TextBufferLinesUsed(void);
   text_buffer::text_buffer_error TextBufferErrorStatus(void);
   void ClearTextBufferError(void);

   void CursorUp(unsigned linesToMove);
   void CursorDown(unsigned linesToMove);
```

```
    void CursorLeft(unsigned charactersToMove);
    void CursorRight(unsigned charactersToMove);
    void LineFeed(void);

    cooked_input CookInput(raw_input rawInput);

    desktop_error ErrorStatus(void) const;
    void ClearError(void);

// Private functions.
private:
    void AdjustCursorColumn(void);
    void AdjustCursorAndInsertionPointRows(void);

// Private data.
private:
    text_buffer editBuffer;
    display_coordinate editAreaLeft,editAreaTop;
    display_coordinate editAreaRight,editAreaBottom;
    status_bar messageBar;
    menu *mainMenu;
    desktop_error errorStatus;
};

// End Class Definitions
//-----------------------------------------------------------------------

#endif

// End Desktop.h
//-----------------------------------------------------------------------
```

The file *Desktop.h* closely reflects the pseudocode design of the `cooked_input` and `desktop` classes. After including some header files, it defines the class `cooked_input`. The `cooked_input` class creates the `user_input_data_type` enumerated type. It also defines three constants: `UNKNOWN`, `COMMAND`, and `CHARACTER`. The `cooked_input` class will use these constants to differentiate the various types of user input.

As we saw in Chapter 27, the `cooked_input` class has no public functions to set its member data. It has public functions for constructing a `cooked_input` object and for getting information out of it. The private data members are set by the `desktop::CookInput()` function. The `cooked_input` class declares the `desktop` class as its friend so `desktop::CookInput()` can have access to a `cooked_input` object's private data members. Because `desktop` and `cooked_input` are friends, they are very dependent on each other. Technically, we say that they have high modular cohesion.

The `cooked_input` class defines a union, called `user_input_data`, that it uses to store the user's input. Because it uses a union, the input can be stored as a command or as text. When the program declares a `cooked_input` object, space is allocated for the largest member of the union, which is the `int`. The program accesses the same memory whether it accesses the data as a character or as a command. Both of the union's data members share the same space.

If we look at the `desktop` class, we see that it is also implemented very much like the design in Chapter 27. Notice, however, that it contains an enumeration for the error codes that the desktop object will use. This did not appear in the original design. This is why design is an iterative process. It is precisely this type of detail that pseudocoding (and more advanced design techniques that are beyond the scope of this book) will help us find.

As specified in the design, the `desktop` class defines an enumeration of all of the commands that it recognizes. It may seem unusual that the `desktop` class redefines some of the constants defined in the `input_device` class. The reason it does is because the commands defined in input_device mean different things in different contexts. In edit mode, the command input_device::UP moves the display's hardware cursor and the text buffer's insertion point up. However, in command mode the menu object receives the input_device::UP command. It tells the menu object to move the menu's highlight bar up. These two operations are conceptually related. They both move a cursor (or something cursor-like) up. However, they are not exactly the same operation. The difference is the context. In the context of the desktop object, the input_device::UP command means move the hardware cursor and insertion point up. In the context of the menu object, the input_device::UP command means move the menu highlight bar up. It's important to understand that these are different commands because they call different functions.

The public member functions and the private data members of the desktop object all follow the design presented in Chapter 27.

Writing Desktop.cpp

The file *Desktop.cpp* contains the member functions for both the cooked_input and the desktop classes. Listing 28.3 displays the contents of *Desktop.cpp*.

LISTING 28.3 Desktop.cpp

```
//-----------------------------------------------------------------------
/*
File Name:  Desktop.cpp
Comments:   This file contains the implementation of the desktop and
            cooked_input classes.
*/
//-----------------------------------------------------------------------



//-----------------------------------------------------------------------
// Include Files

#include "display.h"
#include "desktop.h"
#include "assert.h"

// End Include Files
//-----------------------------------------------------------------------



//-----------------------------------------------------------------------
// Constants

const char *TEXT_BUFFER_FULL_MESSAGE =
   "The text buffer is full. You can't enter any more text.";

// End Constants
//-----------------------------------------------------------------------


//-----------------------------------------------------------------------
// cooked_input member functions

//-----------------------------------------------------------------------
/*
```

```
Function Name:       cooked_input
Member of:           cooked_input
Input Parameters:    None.
Output Parameters:   None.
Return Value:        Constructed object.
Comments:            This function initializes a cooked_input obect.
*/

cooked_input::cooked_input(void)
{
   dataTypeDiscriminant = UNKNOWN;
   inputData.command = 0;
}

// End cooked_input
//-----------------------------------------------------------------------------



//-----------------------------------------------------------------------------
/*
Function Name:       InputType
Member of:           cooked_input
Input Parameters:    None.
Output Parameters:   None.
Return Value:        One of the following values from the
                     cooked_input::user_input_data_type enumeration:
                     UNKNOWN     Unidentified user input.
                     COMMAND     The input is a command.
                     CHARACTER   The input is a text character.
Comments:            This function retrieves the value of the discriminant in
                     a cooked_input object. It is used to distinguish user
                     commands from text input.
*/

cooked_input::user_input_data_type cooked_input::InputType(void) const
{
   return (dataTypeDiscriminant);
}

// End InputType
//-----------------------------------------------------------------------------



//-----------------------------------------------------------------------------
/*
Function Name:       Command
Member of:           cooked_input
Input Parameters:    None.
Output Parameters:   None.
Return Value:        An integer command identifier from the desktop::command
                     enumerated type.
Comments:            This function returns the cooked user input as a command.
                     Note that the cooked_input class uses a union to store
                     user input. The user input can be accessed as a command
                     or as a character. To tell which it really is, a program
                     using this object must check the discriminant.
*/
```

```
int cooked_input::Command(void) const
{
   return (inputData.command);
}

// End Command
//-----------------------------------------------------------------------------




//-----------------------------------------------------------------------------
/*
Function Name:        Character
Member of:            cooked_input
Input Parameters:     None.
Output Parameters:    None.
Return Value:         The character contained in the cooked_input object.
Comments:             This function returns the cooked user input as a
                      character. Note that the cooked_input class uses a union
                      to store user input. The user input can be accessed as a
                      command or as a character. To tell which it really is, a
                      program using this object must check the discriminant.
*/

char cooked_input::Character(void) const
{
   return (inputData.character);
}

// End Character
//-----------------------------------------------------------------------------

// end cooked_input member functions
//-----------------------------------------------------------------------------




//-----------------------------------------------------------------------------
// desktop member functions

//-----------------------------------------------------------------------------
/*
Function Name:        desktop
Member of:            desktop
Input Parameters:     None.
Output Parameters:    None.
Return Value:         A constructed desktop object.
Comments:             This is the default constructor for the desktop class.
*/

desktop::desktop(void)
{
   editAreaLeft = editAreaTop = editAreaRight = editAreaBottom = 0;
   mainMenu = NULL;
   errorStatus = NO_ERROR;
}

// End desktop
//-----------------------------------------------------------------------------
```

```
//-----------------------------------------------------------------------------
/*
Function Name:        ~desktop
Member of:            desktop
Input Parameters:     None.
Output Parameters:    None.
Return Value:         None.
Comments:             The destructor for the desktop class. Its primary purpose
                      is to delete the mainMenu if the desktop has one.
*/

desktop::~desktop()
{
   if (mainMenu!=NULL)
   {
      delete mainMenu;
      mainMenu != NULL;   // Not really necessary.
   }
}

// End ~desktop
//-----------------------------------------------------------------------------



//-----------------------------------------------------------------------------
/*
Function Name:        StatusBar
Member of:            desktop
Input Parameters:     None.
Output Parameters:    None.
Return Value:         Returns a reference to the status_bar object.
Comments:             This function enables programs to get a reference
                      to the desktop's status bar object. Note that there are
                      possible problems caused by providing this function in
                      the desktop class. This implementation was used to
                      demonstrate some of those problems.
*/

status_bar &desktop::StatusBar(void)
{
   return (messageBar);
}

// End StatusBar
//-----------------------------------------------------------------------------



//-----------------------------------------------------------------------------
/*
Function Name:        Menu
Member of:            desktop
Input Parameters:     desktopMenu - A pointer to the main menu.
Output Parameters:    None.
Return Value:         None.
Comments:             Use this function to set the desktop object's main menu.
                      Once you do, the desktop object takes over ownership of
                      the menu pointed to by the parameter desktopMenu. When
```

```
                    the desktop object is deleted, it will automatically
                    delete its main menu and all submenus.
*/

void desktop::Menu(menu *desktopMenu)
{
   assert(mainMenu != desktopMenu);
   assert(desktopMenu != NULL);

   if (mainMenu != NULL)
   {
      delete mainMenu;
   }

   mainMenu = desktopMenu;
}

// End Menu
//-----------------------------------------------------------------------------



//-----------------------------------------------------------------------------
/*
Function Name:      Menu
Member of:          desktop
Input Parameters:   None.
Output Parameters:  None.
Return Value:       A constant pointer to the desktop's main menu.
Comments:           Use this function to get a pointer to the desktop's main
                    menu.
*/

const menu *desktop::Menu(void) const
{
   return (mainMenu);
}

// End Menu
//-----------------------------------------------------------------------------



//-----------------------------------------------------------------------------
/*
Function Name:      SetTextArea
Member of:          desktop
Input Parameters:   left - The column number of the left edge of text display
                       area on the screen.
                    top - The row number of the top edge of text display
                       area on the screen.
                    right - The column number of the right edge of text
                       display area on the screen.
                    bottom - The column number of the bottom edge of text
                       display area on the screen.
Output Parameters:  None.
Return Value:       None.
```

```
Comments:             This function sets the text display area on the screen.
                      The contents of the text buffer are displayed in the
                      text display area.
*/

void desktop::SetTextArea(display_coordinate left, display_coordinate top,
                          display_coordinate right, display_coordinate bottom)
{
   editAreaLeft = left;
   editAreaTop = top;
   editAreaRight = right;
   editAreaBottom = bottom;
   theScreen.CursorRow(editAreaTop);
   theScreen.CursorCol(editAreaLeft);
   editBuffer.InsertionPointRow(editBuffer.TopLine());
   editBuffer.InsertionPointCol(0);
}

// End SetTextArea
//---------------------------------------------------------------------------



//---------------------------------------------------------------------------
/*
Function Name:        DisplayTextBuffer
Member of:            desktop
Input Parameters:     None.
Output Parameters:    None.
Return Value:         None.
Comments:             The DisplayTextBuffer function displays text from the
                      text buffer on the screen. The first line it displays is
                      the buffer's current top line. It then displays as many
                      rows of text as will fit in the text display area.
*/

void desktop::DisplayTextBuffer(void)
{
   display_coordinate row;
   int currentLine;
   display_coordinate cursorRow,cursorCol;

   // Clear the text display area.
   theScreen.Clear(editAreaLeft,editAreaTop,editAreaRight,editAreaBottom);

   // Save the current cursor location.
   cursorRow = theScreen.CursorRow();
   cursorCol = theScreen.CursorCol();

   // Move the cursor to the beginning of the text area.
   theScreen.CursorRow(editAreaTop);
   theScreen.CursorCol(editAreaLeft);

   // For each row that's visible...
   for (row = editAreaTop,currentLine=editBuffer.TopLine();
       (row < editAreaBottom) && (currentLine < editBuffer.LinesUsed());
        row++,currentLine++)
```

```
   {
      // Move the cursor to the beginning of the row.
      theScreen.CursorRow(row);
      theScreen.CursorCol(editAreaLeft);

      // Print the line of text.
      theScreen.Print(editBuffer[currentLine]);
   }

   // Put the cursor back.
   theScreen.CursorRow(cursorRow);
   theScreen.CursorCol(cursorCol);
}

// End DisplayTextBuffer
//-----------------------------------------------------------------------------



//-----------------------------------------------------------------------------
/*
Function Name:        PutCharacterIntoTextBuffer
Member of:            desktop
Input Parameters:     newCharacter - The character to insert into the text
                         buffer.
Output Parameters:    None.
Return Value:         None.
Comments:             This function inserts a character into the text buffer
                      at the current insertion point. If there is already
                      a character there, it will be overwritten.
*/

void desktop::PutCharacterIntoTextBuffer(char newCharacter)
{
   if (theScreen.CursorCol() < editAreaRight)
   {
      editBuffer.PutCharacter(newCharacter);
   }
   else
   {
      theScreen.CursorCol(editAreaRight-1);
   }
}

// End PutCharacterIntoTextBuffer
//-----------------------------------------------------------------------------



//-----------------------------------------------------------------------------
/*
Function Name:        LoadTextBuffer
Member of:            desktop
Input Parameters:     fileName - A reference to the name of the text file to
                         be loaded into the text buffer.
Output Parameters:    None.
Return Value:         None.
Comments:             This function loads a text file into the text buffer.
*/
```

```
void desktop::LoadTextBuffer(const text_string &fileName)
{
   editBuffer.Load(fileName);
}

// End LoadTextBuffer
//-----------------------------------------------------------------------------



//-----------------------------------------------------------------------------
/*
Function Name:       SaveTextBuffer
Member of:           desktop
Input Parameters:    fileName - A reference to the name of the text file
                        into which the text buffer will be saved.
Output Parameters:   None.
Return Value:        None.
Comments:            This function saves the text buffer into a text file.
*/

void desktop::SaveTextBuffer(const text_string &fileName)
{
   editBuffer.Save(fileName);
}

// End SaveTextBuffer
//-----------------------------------------------------------------------------



//-----------------------------------------------------------------------------
/*
Function Name:       IsTextBufferDirty
Member of:           desktop
Input Parameters:    None.
Output Parameters:   None.
Return Value:        This function returns true if the text buffer is dirty,
                     or false if not.
Comments:            The Return Value section says it all.
*/

bool desktop::IsTextBufferDirty(void)
{
   return (editBuffer.IsDirty());
}

// End IsTextBufferDirty
//-----------------------------------------------------------------------------



//-----------------------------------------------------------------------------
/*
Function Name:       ScrollTextBufferUp
Member of:           desktop
Input Parameters:    linesToScroll - An integer number of lines to scroll.
Output Parameters:   None.
```

```
Return Value:        This function returns the number of lines that it
                     actually scrolls.
Comments:            The ScrollTextBufferUp function scrolls the top line
                     of the text buffer up toward the beginning of the buffer.
                     It is possible that the buffer cannot be scrolled as far
                     as requested. For example, attempting to scroll the
                     buffer up one page of text when the current top line is
                     the first line of the buffer will result in the buffer
                     not being scrolled at all.
*/

unsigned desktop::ScrollTextBufferUp(const unsigned linesToScroll)
{
   unsigned linesScrolled = editBuffer.ScrollUp(linesToScroll);
   DisplayTextBuffer();
   AdjustCursorColumn();
   AdjustCursorAndInsertionPointRows();
   return (linesScrolled);
}

// End ScrollTextBufferUp
//-----------------------------------------------------------------------------



//-----------------------------------------------------------------------------
/*
Function Name:       ScrollTextBufferDown
Member of:           desktop
Input Parameters:    linesToScroll - An integer number of lines to scroll.
Output Parameters:   None.
Return Value:        This function returns the number of lines that it
                     actually scrolls.
Comments:            The ScrollTextBufferDown function scrolls the top line
                     of the text buffer down toward the end of the buffer.
                     It is possible that the buffer cannot be scrolled as far
                     as requested. For example, attempting to scroll the
                     buffer down one page of text when the current top line is
                     the last line of the buffer will result in the buffer
                     not being scrolled at all.
*/

unsigned desktop::ScrollTextBufferDown(const unsigned linesToScroll)
{
   unsigned linesScrolled = editBuffer.ScrollDown(linesToScroll);
   DisplayTextBuffer();
   AdjustCursorColumn();
   AdjustCursorAndInsertionPointRows();
   return (linesScrolled);
}

// End ScrollTextBufferDown
//-----------------------------------------------------------------------------



//-----------------------------------------------------------------------------
/*
Function Name:       ScrollTextBufferTo
```

```
Member of:            desktop
Input Parameters:     newTopLine - The new top line of the buffer.
Output Parameters:    None.
Return Value:         This function returns the number of lines that it
                      actually scrolls.
Comments:             The ScrollTextBufferTo function scrolls the top line
                      of the text buffer to the specified line. It is possible
                      that the buffer cannot be scrolled as far
                      as requested. For example, attempting to scroll the
                      buffer to its first line when the current top line already
                      is the first line will result in the buffer not being
                      scrolled at all.
*/

unsigned desktop::ScrollTextBufferTo(const unsigned newTopLine)
{
   unsigned linesScrolled = editBuffer.ScrollTo(newTopLine);

   editBuffer.InsertionPointRow(editBuffer.TopLine());
   editBuffer.InsertionPointCol(0);

   DisplayTextBuffer();

   theScreen.CursorRow(editAreaTop);
   theScreen.CursorCol(editAreaLeft);

   return (linesScrolled);
}

// End ScrollTextBufferDown
//-----------------------------------------------------------------------



//-----------------------------------------------------------------------
/*
Function Name:        TextBufferLinesUsed
Member of:            desktop
Input Parameters:     None.
Output Parameters:    None.
Return Value:         This function returns the number of lines with text on
                      them.
Comments:             The TextBufferLinesUsed function returns the number of
                      lines of text currently in use in the text buffer. This
                      includes lines with nothing on them but a line feed.
*/

unsigned desktop::TextBufferLinesUsed(void)
{
   return (editBuffer.LinesUsed());
}

// End TextBufferLinesUsed
//-----------------------------------------------------------------------



//-----------------------------------------------------------------------
/*
```

```
Function Name:       TextBufferErrorStatus
Member of:           desktop
Input Parameters:    None.
Output Parameters:   None.
Return Value:        This function returns the text buffer's current error
                     status.
Comments:            See the Return Value section.
*/

text_buffer::text_buffer_error desktop::TextBufferErrorStatus(void)
{
   return (editBuffer.ErrorStatus());
}

// End TextBufferErrorStatus
//-----------------------------------------------------------------------------



//-----------------------------------------------------------------------------
/*
Function Name:       ClearTextBufferError
Member of:           desktop
Input Parameters:    None.
Output Parameters:   None.
Return Value:        None.
Comments:            This function clears the text buffer error status. Use
                     it when non-fatal errors occur and you just want to
                     ignore them and continue the program.
*/

void desktop::ClearTextBufferError(void)
{
   editBuffer.ClearError();
}

// End ClearTextBufferError
//-----------------------------------------------------------------------------



//-----------------------------------------------------------------------------
/*
Function Name:       ActivateMainMenu
Member of:           desktop
Input Parameters:    None.
Output Parameters:   None.
Return Value:        This function returns the unique identifier
                     of the menu item that the user selected. If the user
                     cancelled the menu, it returns MENU_CANCELED.
Comments:            Use this function to execute the desktop's main menu.
*/

menu_item_id desktop::ActivateMainMenu(void)
{
   return (mainMenu->Execute());
}
```

```
// End ActivateMainMenu
//-----------------------------------------------------------------------------




//-----------------------------------------------------------------------------
/*
Function Name:       CursorUp
Member of:           desktop
Input Parameters:    linesToMove - The number of lines to move the cursor
                        upward.
Output Parameters:   None.
Return Value:        None.
Comments:            This function moves the cursor up by the specified number
                     of lines. It moves the insertion point in sync with the
                     cursor. If the cursor encounters the top of the text area
                     before it has moved the specified number of lines, it
                     scrolls the text buffer up.
*/

void desktop::CursorUp(unsigned linesToMove)
{
   assert(linesToMove > 0);

   int newInsertionPointRow = editBuffer.InsertionPointRow()-linesToMove;
   unsigned newInsertionPointColumn = editBuffer.InsertionPointCol();
   int newHardwareCursorRow = theScreen.CursorRow()-linesToMove;
   unsigned newHardwareCursorColumn = theScreen.CursorCol();

   // This keeps the text from scrolling off the screen.
   if (newInsertionPointRow >= 0)
   {
      // If the hardware cursor will move out of the text area...
      if (newHardwareCursorRow < editAreaTop)
      {
         ScrollTextBufferUp(linesToMove);
         newHardwareCursorRow = editAreaTop;
      }

      editBuffer.InsertionPointRow(newInsertionPointRow);
      theScreen.CursorRow(newHardwareCursorRow);
      AdjustCursorColumn();
   }
}

// End CursorUp
//-----------------------------------------------------------------------------




//-----------------------------------------------------------------------------
/*
Function Name:       CursorDown
Member of:           desktop
Input Parameters:    linesToMove - The number of lines to move the cursor
                        downward.
```

```
Output Parameters:   None.
Return Value:        None.
Comments:            This function moves the cursor down by the specified
                     number of lines. It moves the insertion point in sync
                     with the cursor. If the cursor encounters the bottom of
                     the text area before it has moved the specified number
                     of lines, it scrolls the text buffer down.
*/

void desktop::CursorDown(unsigned linesToMove)
{
   assert(linesToMove > 0);

   unsigned newInsertionPointRow = editBuffer.InsertionPointRow()+linesToMove;
   unsigned newInsertionPointColumn = editBuffer.InsertionPointCol();
   unsigned newHardwareCursorRow = theScreen.CursorRow()+linesToMove;
   unsigned newHardwareCursorColumn = theScreen.CursorCol();

   // This keeps the text from scrolling off the screen.
   if ((newInsertionPointRow < editBuffer.LinesUsed()) &&
       (newInsertionPointRow < TEXT_BUFFER_LENGTH-1))
   {
      // If the hardware cursor will move out of the text area...
      if (newHardwareCursorRow > editAreaBottom)
      {
         ScrollTextBufferDown(linesToMove);

         // Move the cursor to the last row of the text area.
         newHardwareCursorRow = editAreaBottom;
      }

      editBuffer.InsertionPointRow(newInsertionPointRow);
      theScreen.CursorRow(newHardwareCursorRow);
      AdjustCursorColumn();
   }
}

// End CursorDown
//-----------------------------------------------------------------------------



//-----------------------------------------------------------------------------
/*
Function Name:       CursorLeft
Member of:           desktop
Input Parameters:    charactersToMove - The number of character columns to
                        move to the left.
Output Parameters:   None.
Return Value:        None.
Comments:            This function moves the cursor to the left by the
                     specified number of characters. It also moves the
                     insertion point the same distance. It will not let
                     the cursor move out of the text area. Neither will it
                     let the insertion point move before the beginning of
                     the string.
*/
```

```
void desktop::CursorLeft(unsigned charactersToMove)
{
   assert(charactersToMove > 0);

   unsigned currentCol = theScreen.CursorCol();

   /* If the hardware cursor won't move out of the text area and the
   insertion point won't move before the beginning of the string... */
   int newCol = (int)currentCol-(int)charactersToMove;
   if (newCol > editAreaLeft)
   {
      // Move the hardware cursor left.
      theScreen.CursorLeft(charactersToMove);
   }
   // Else the hardware cursor will move out of the text area...
   else
   {
      theScreen.CursorCol(editAreaLeft);
   }

   /* The text buffer will not move the insertion point before the beginning
   of the row. */
   editBuffer.InsertionPointCol(currentCol-charactersToMove);
}

// End CursorLeft
//-----------------------------------------------------------------------------



//-----------------------------------------------------------------------------
/*
Function Name:       CursorRight
Member of:           desktop
Input Parameters:    charactersToMove - The number of character columns to
                        move to the right.
Output Parameters:   None.
Return Value:        None.
Comments:            This function moves the cursor to the right by the
                     specified number of characters. It also moves the
                     insertion point the same distance. It will not let
                     the cursor move out of the text area. Neither will it
                     let the insertion point move after the end of the
                     string.
*/
void desktop::CursorRight(unsigned charactersToMove)
{
   assert(charactersToMove > 0);

   unsigned currentCol = theScreen.CursorCol();

   int newCol = currentCol+charactersToMove;
   int length = editBuffer[editBuffer.InsertionPointRow()].Length();

   // If the hardware cursor won't move out of the text area...
   if (newCol < editAreaRight)
   {
```

```
      /* If the text buffer insertion point won't move beyond the
      end of the string...*/
      if (newCol-editAreaLeft < length)
      {
         // Move the hardware cursor right.
         theScreen.CursorRight(charactersToMove);

         editBuffer.InsertionPointCol(newCol);
      }
      // Else it will move beyond the end of the string...
      else
      {
         theScreen.CursorCol(editAreaLeft+length);
      }
   }
   // Else the hardware cursor will move out of the text area
   else
   {
      theScreen.CursorCol(editAreaRight);
   }
}

// End CursorRight
//-----------------------------------------------------------------------------



//-----------------------------------------------------------------------------
/*
Function Name:       LineFeed
Member of:           desktop
Input Parameters:    None.
Output Parameters:   None.
Return Value:        None.
Comments:            Call this function when the user presses the Enter key
                     on the keyboard. It terminates the line of text, and
                     moves the cursor and the insertion point to the beginning
                     of the next line.
*/

void desktop::LineFeed(void)
{
   /* If the insertion point row is less than the max
   lines in the buffer... */
   if (editBuffer.InsertionPointRow() < TEXT_BUFFER_LENGTH-1)
   {
      int currentRow = theScreen.CursorRow();

      // If the cursor is on the last line of the text area...
      if (currentRow == editAreaBottom)
      {
         // Scroll one line toward the end of the buffer.
         ScrollTextBufferDown(1);
      }
      // Else the cursor isn't on the last line of the text area...
      else
      {
```

```
            // Move the cursor to the next line.
            theScreen.CursorRow(currentRow+1);
        }

        // Move the cursor to the beginning of the line.
        theScreen.CursorCol(editAreaLeft);

        /* Move the insertion point in the text buffer to the beginning
        of the next line. */
        editBuffer.InsertionPointRow(editBuffer.InsertionPointRow()+1);
        editBuffer.InsertionPointCol(0);

        // If the new row is not last line of the buffer that contains text...
        if (editBuffer.InsertionPointRow() < editBuffer.LinesUsed()-1)
        {
            /* Move all rows in the buffer down one. This creates a
            blank line. New text can be typed on the blank line. */
            for (int i=editBuffer.LinesUsed()-1;
                 i>=editBuffer.InsertionPointRow();
                 i++)
            {
                editBuffer[i+1] = editBuffer[i];
            }
        }
        /* Else the new row is the last line of the buffer that contains text.
        New text can be typed on this line. */
    }
    // Else the buffer can't take any more rows of text...
    else
    {
        text_string errorMessage = TEXT_BUFFER_FULL_MESSAGE;
        messageBar.Print(errorMessage);

        // This is not a fatal error. Clear it and go on.
        editBuffer.ClearError();
    }
}

// End LineFeed
//-----------------------------------------------------------------------------



//-----------------------------------------------------------------------------
/*
Function Name:       CookInput
Member of:           desktop
Input Parameters:    rawInput - User's input as it was received.
Output Parameters:   None.
Return Value:        This function returns the cooked input.
Comments:            The CookInput function converts the user's raw input
                     into an object. The object can be queried as to
                     whether the user's input was a command or a character
                     to go into the text buffer.
*/

cooked_input desktop::CookInput(raw_input rawInput)
```

```
{
    cooked_input cookedUserInput;

    switch (rawInput)
    {
        // If the input is a command character...
        case MOVE_UP:
        case MOVE_DOWN:
        case MOVE_LEFT:
        case MOVE_RIGHT:
        case ENTER_KEY:
        case ESCAPE_KEY:
        case PAGE_UP:
        case PAGE_DOWN:
        case SCROLL_UP:
        case SCROLL_DOWN:
        case TO_BUFFER_TOP:
        case TO_BUFFER_END:

            // Store the command.
            cookedUserInput.inputData.command = rawInput;

            // Mark it as a command.
            cookedUserInput.dataTypeDiscriminant = cooked_input::COMMAND;
        break;

        // Else if the user activated the menu...
        case ACTIVATE_MENU:
        {
            // Execute the main menu.
            menu_item_id menuSelection = mainMenu->Execute();

            // Store the command.
            cookedUserInput.inputData.command = (int)menuSelection;

            // Mark it as a command.
            cookedUserInput.dataTypeDiscriminant = cooked_input::COMMAND;
        }
        break;

        // Else if it is not a command...
        default:
            // If the input is an invalid character...
            if ((rawInput<' ') || (rawInput>'~'))
            {
                // Set an error condition.
                errorStatus = INVALID_INPUT;
            }
            // Else this is text...
            else
            {
                // Store the character.
                cookedUserInput.inputData.character = rawInput;

                // Mark it as a character.
                cookedUserInput.dataTypeDiscriminant = cooked_input::CHARACTER;
            }
        break;
    }
```

```
   return (cookedUserInput);
}

// End CookInput
//---------------------------------------------------------------------------



//---------------------------------------------------------------------------
/*
Function Name:       ErrorStatus
Member of:           desktop
Input Parameters:    None.
Output Parameters:   None.
Return Value:        This function returns the current error status of the
                     desktop object.
Comments:            See the Return Value section.
*/

desktop::desktop_error desktop::ErrorStatus(void) const
{
   return (errorStatus);
}

// End ErrorStatus
//---------------------------------------------------------------------------



//---------------------------------------------------------------------------
/*
Function Name:       ClearError
Member of:           desktop
Input Parameters:    None.
Output Parameters:   None.
Return Value:        None.
Comments:            This function clears the desktop object's error status.
*/

void desktop::ClearError(void)
{
   errorStatus = NO_ERROR;
}

// End ClearError
//---------------------------------------------------------------------------



//---------------------------------------------------------------------------
/*
Function Name:       AdjustCursorColumn
Member of:           desktop
Input Parameters:    None.
Output Parameters:   None.
Return Value:        None.
Comments:            This function synchronizes the cursor column and the
                     insertion point column.
*/
```

```
void desktop::AdjustCursorColumn(void)
{
   unsigned newInsertionPointColumn = editBuffer.InsertionPointCol();
   unsigned newHardwareCursorColumn = theScreen.CursorCol();

   // Prevent the cursor from moving beyond the end of the string.
   int length = editBuffer[editBuffer.InsertionPointRow()].Length();
   if (newInsertionPointColumn >= length)
   {
      newInsertionPointColumn = length;
      newHardwareCursorColumn = editAreaLeft+length;
   }

   // Move the hardware cursor.
   theScreen.CursorCol(newHardwareCursorColumn);

   // Move the insertion point.
   editBuffer.InsertionPointCol(newInsertionPointColumn);
}
// End AdjustCursorColumn
//-----------------------------------------------------------------------



//-----------------------------------------------------------------------
/*
Function Name:       AdjustCursorAndInsertionPointRows
Member of:           desktop
Input Parameters:    None.
Output Parameters:   None.
Return Value:        None.
Comments:            This function synchronizes the cursor row and the
                     insertion point row.
*/

void desktop::AdjustCursorAndInsertionPointRows(void)
{
   int hardwareCursorRow =
      theScreen.CursorRow() * theScreen.CharacterHeight();

   int insertionPointRow =
      (hardwareCursorRow - (editAreaTop*theScreen.CharacterHeight())) +
      editBuffer.TopLine();

   /* If the insertion point is beyond the end of the portion of the buffer
   currently in use... */
   if (insertionPointRow >= editBuffer.LinesUsed())
   {
      insertionPointRow = editBuffer.LinesUsed() - 1;

      /* hardware cursor row = (# of lines displayed) * height of a row +
      the location of the first row of text. */
      hardwareCursorRow =
         (editBuffer.LinesUsed() - editBuffer.TopLine()) *
         theScreen.CharacterHeight() + editAreaTop;
   }
```

```
    assert((insertionPointRow >= 0) &&
           (insertionPointRow < editBuffer.LinesUsed()));
    assert((hardwareCursorRow >= editAreaTop) &&
           (hardwareCursorRow<=editAreaBottom));

    editBuffer.InsertionPointRow(insertionPointRow);
    theScreen.CursorRow(hardwareCursorRow);
}

// End AdjustCursorAndInsertionPointRows
//---------------------------------------------------------------------




// end desktop member functions
//---------------------------------------------------------------------



// end Desktop.cpp
//---------------------------------------------------------------------
```

Like most of the files in a C++ program, *Desktop.cpp* begins by including the header files that it requires. Next, it declares a constant string that it uses as a error message. It then presents the `cooked_input` member functions.

After the `cooked_input` member functions, *Desktop.cpp* contains the `desktop` object member functions. The `desktop` object requires both a constructor and a destructor. Notice that not all of a `desktop` object's private data members need to be initialized. If an object contains a data member that is also a class, the data member's constructor is called automatically when the object is created. For example, the `desktop` object contains the `text_buffer` and `status_bar` object. When a `desktop` object is created, the constructors for the `text_buffer` and `status_bar` classes are automatically called. The constructors will set these two private data members into a known state.

The other data members in the `desktop` class are not objects. We must initialize them in the `desktop` constructor. Before the program uses a `desktop` object, we should ensure that every data member in the `desktop` class is initialized to a known state.

In addition to everything else it does, the `desktop` class is a container class. Specifically, it contains a list of menus. When the program assigns a main menu to the `desktop` object, the `desktop` assumes ownership of the menu. Because a `desktop` assumes ownership of a `menu` object (and all of its submenus), it must delete the `menu` object in its destructor. That's exactly what the destructor for the `desktop` class does.

The `desktop` class provides a function called `StatusBar()` that returns a reference to the private data member `messageBar`. Although this is very handy in some cases, the Troubleshooting Guide for this chapter will demonstrate why it's not a good idea.

In addition, the `desktop` class provides functions to set and get the main menu pointer. It has a function to set the boundaries of the text edit area on the screen. It also contains a group of functions to provide access to the functionality of the `desktop`'s `text_buffer` object. Let's take a careful look at each of these.

The `desktop::DisplayTextBuffer()` function clears and saves the current cursor location. As it displays text on the screen, it will move the cursor. The user will not be happy if we do not put the cursor back where it was. `desktop::DisplayTextBuffer()` saves the cursor location, uses the cursor for its own purposes, and puts the cursor back where the user left it.

After saving the current cursor location, the `desktop::DisplayTextBuffer()` function moves the cursor to the beginning of the text display area. It utilizes a `for` loop to iterate through all of the text buffer rows to be displayed on the screen. On each pass through the loop, it prints the contents of the current row of the text buffer. After the text is printed, the `desktop::DisplayTextBuffer()` function puts the cursor back where the user left it and exits.

The desktop::PutCharacterIntoTextBuffer() function is very straightforward. If the cursor is within the boundaries of the text edit area, desktop::PutCharacterInto-TextBuffer() will attempt to insert the character into the text buffer at the insertion point location. If the cursor has moved outside the text edit area, the desktop::PutCharacterIntoTextBuffer() function sets it to the right edge of the edit area.

The desktop::LoadTextBuffer(), desktop::SaveTextBuffer(), and desktop::Is- TextBufferDirty() functions simply call the appropriate functions in the text_buffer class. They provide no real functionality of their own. On the other hand, the desktop::ScrollTextBufferUp() function does provide additional functionality. Specifically, it uses the text_buffer::ScrollUp() function to scroll the buffer, displays text from the buffer on the screen, and calls some private member functions to keep the insertion point and cursor synchronized.

The desktop::ScrollTextBufferDown() function follows this same pattern. The only difference is that it scrolls down instead of up.

The logic of desktop::ScrollTextBufferTo() is simpler than the logic of the other two scrolling functions in this class. When the program scrolls to a specific line of the text buffer, it does not preserve the location of the insertion point and cursor. The assumption here is that if you're scrolling to a particular line of the buffer, you want to start typing text onto that line. Under that assumption, the desktop::ScrollTextBufferTo() function scrolls the current top line of the buffer to the line the program requested. It sets the insertion point to the beginning of the line and displays a screenful of text. Before it returns, desktop::ScrollTextBufferTo() sets the cursor position to the first row and column of the text edit area on the screen.

The desktop::TextBufferLinesUsed(), desktop::TextBufferErrorStatus(), and desktop::ClearTextBufferError() functions are wrappers for the appropriate text_buffer member functions. The desktop::ActivateMainMenu function executes the desktop object's main menu.

The names of the desktop::CursorUp(), desktop::CursorDown(), desktop::CursorLeft(), and desktop::CursorRight() functions are not entirely accurate. They move both the hardware cursor and the text buffer's insertion point. They all contain logic to prevent the hardware cursor from moving out of the text edit area. Additionally, desktop::CursorLeft() must keep the cursor and the insertion point from moving before the beginning of the current row in the text buffer. desktop::Cursor-Right() contains logic to keep the cursor and insertion point from moving beyond the end of the current line of text.

When the user is editing text and presses the Enter key, the program calls the desktop::LineFeed() function. LineFeed() terminates the current line of input and moves the cursor to the beginning of the next line. It will not insert more lines into the buffer than the buffer can hold. If the cursor is on the last line of the text edit area when the user presses the Enter key, LineFeed() scrolls the text up a line. The cursor remains on the last line of the text area so that the user can begin typing text there. If the cursor is not on the last line of the text edit area, both the cursor and the insertion point are moved down a line. The LineFeed() function also will shift rows of text downward to open up a blank line.

The desktop class uses the CookInput() function to interpret all user input. It consists primarily of a large switch statement. The case labels for all of the keyboard commands are grouped together with no break statements between them. You can see that this is definitely a handy technique. Recall, however, that some designers recommend against it.

If the user presses any keyboard command except ^c, the command is stored in a cooked_input object, marked as a command, and returned to the program. If the user presses ^c, the CookInput() function activates the menu system. When the user makes a selection, CookInput() packages that into a cooked_input object, marks it as a command, and passes it back to the program.

If the input is a character to be inserted into the buffer, CookInput() stores it in a cooked_input object as a character rather than a command. It marks the input as a character and returns it to the program.

For handling its error status data member, the desktop object provides the desktop::ErrorStatus() and desktop::ClearError() functions. The functions desktop::AdjustCursorColumn() and desktop::AdjustCursorAndInsertionPoint-

Rows() keep the hardware cursor and the text buffer's insertion point synchronized. These two functions also keep them within the bounds imposed by the screen and the text buffer.

Troubleshooting Guide

After reading this section, you should be able to:

- Understand the pitfalls of non-const returning references or pointers to private objects.
- Keep functions to a reasonable length.

Returning References and Pointers to Private Data

The desktop class contains a menu, a text_buffer, and a status_bar object. It provides access to each of them in a different way. When the text editor program needs to access the functionality of the menu, it calls the Menu() function to get a pointer to the main menu. Once it has the pointer, it can call any of the public member functions of the menu class.

Similarly, the desktop class provides a StatusBar() function that returns a reference to the desktop object's status bar. The text editor program can use the reference to call any status_bar public member function.

On the other hand, only member functions of the desktop class have direct access to the text_buffer object. The desktop class does not return a pointer or a reference to the text_buffer object it contains.

The question is, which of these three methods is best and why?

The short answer is that you should always be careful of returning pointers or references to private objects.

Let's use the private data member editBuffer as an example. Suppose the desktop class provided the function in Example 28.1.

EXAMPLE 28.1 Providing Access to Private Data

```
text_buffer &desktop::TextBuffer(void)
{
    return (editBuffer);
}
```

Now suppose that the cursor is on line 10 of the user's screen. Imagine that the text editor makes the following call

```
workArea.TextBuffer().InsertionPointRow(0);
```

The insertion point in the text buffer is moved by this call. But what about the cursor on the screen? The user is typing on line 0 of the text buffer and line 10 on the screen. That's almost certainly an error.

By providing access to its private data, the desktop class would enable the text editor program to bypass its member functions. The program would not need to call any of the scrolling or cursor movement functions in the desktop class to move the insertion point. It could manipulate the insertion point directly.

When objects return references to their private data, programs can change the state of the private data without using the object's member functions. This essentially defeats the idea of encapsulation.

The desktop::StatusBar() function returns a reference to the private status_bar object. This doesn't cause the text editor to fail because changing the state of the status_bar object doesn't affect the rest of the desktop object. It also works because I was very careful to make it work when I wrote the program. In large, professional programs, you can't assume that other programmers will use your objects the way you would. You must enforce all of your assumptions. If you assume that the programmer will never put the status_bar object into a state that crashes the desktop object, enforce that assumption. In this case, we would do that by controlling access to the status_bar object. We must force the programmer to use the desktop member functions to change the state of the status_bar.

It is possible to avoid many of these problems by returning a const reference. That would change the StatusBar() function to

```
const status_bar &desktop::StatusBar(void)
{
 return (messageBar);
}
```

Returning a const reference to private data is definitely better. It prevents the program from changing the state of the private data. However, in the text editor, the program *must* be able to change the state of the status_bar to get input and print output. Therefore, the desktop class can't return a const reference. The only safe thing to do is follow the pattern that we used for the text_buffer.

Returning a const pointer, as desktop::Menu() does, isn't much better. In the text editor, we get away with it because we don't change the internal state of the menu object when we execute the menu system. Once the menus are built, they don't change. Therefore, we can call menu member functions through a const pointer with no problems. Also, calling the menu object's member functions doesn't change the state of anything else in the desktop object. It's a relatively safe object to use in this way.

These examples in the desktop class demonstrate that an object *can* work even though it returns pointers or references to its private data. However, the programmer using your object must be extremely careful. Also, the pointer or reference can only provide access to data that doesn't affect the rest of the object. These are very special and restrictive conditions. Most of the time, returning pointers and references to private data is a shortcut to problems.

Keeping It Short and Sweet

Do you notice anything about the main() function? What I notice most is that it's very long—275 lines long, to be exact. As a general rule of thumb, functions should be only about one printed page in length. You'll always encounter one or two functions in your program that are much longer than that. Sometimes, it just doesn't make sense to shorten them. However, that's not the case with this main() function.

If we look at main() we can see that it falls into some natural blocks of code. The primary tasks it does are:

1. It checks to see that the correct arguments were sent on the command line.
2. It performs program initialization.
3. If the user specified a file to load on the command line, it loads the file.
4. It enters a loop to get user input and react to it.

It seems to me that at least two or three of these tasks could be put into separate functions that main() calls. For example, we could write a function with the prototype

```
int InitializeDesktop(desktop &theDesktop);
```

This function would return an error status, or zero if no error occurred. It would contain all of the code from main() that initializes the desktop object.

We could also easily create a function, called RunProgram(), to contain the loop main() uses to get the user's input and react to it. The main() function would call RunProgram().

By creating these two functions, we could chop more than 200 lines of code out of main(). That would make it much easier to read and understand.

Once you've written them, it's a good idea to look over your programs for functions you can shorten. Of course, breaking your program up into smaller pieces in this fashion causes an increase in the number of functions. Each time you call a function, it increases program overhead. However, in the text editor, adding these two functions does not affect the performance of the program. The main() function would only call InitializeDesktop() and RunProgram() once. Adding just two more function calls to the text editor would not affect its performance at all.

Summary

This chapter gives one possible implementation of the files *TEdit.cpp, Desktop.h,* and *Desktop.cpp.* These files demonstrate some possible approaches to the problem of implementing the text editor. They also present some possible variations. For example, *Desktop.h* and *Desktop.cpp* show what happens when objects make references and pointers to private data available through public member functions.

Several improvements can be made to the implementation of these files. You'll find some of them in the Review Questions and Exercises for this chapter.

Review Questions

1. The three files presented in this chapter all define their constants in a group near the beginning of each file. Do you agree with this implementation? Why or why not? Which of the constants defined in these files could be moved closer to where they are used?
2. In the `desktop` class the private data member `mainMenu` is declared as a pointer, unlike `editBuffer` and `messageBar`. What advantages do you think this gives? What disadvantages do you see in it?
3. Could you use inheritance in the `desktop` class? For example, would it be advisable to change the definition of the `desktop` class to the one shown below? Why or why not?

```
class desktop : public status_bar, public text_editor, public menu
{
// Public types.
public:
   // The definitions of the public types go here.

// Public functions.
public:
   // The prototypes of the public functions go here.

// Private functions.
private:
   // The prototypes of the private functions go here.

// Private data.
private:
   display_coordinate editAreaLeft,editAreaTop;
   display_coordinate editAreaRight,editAreaBottom;
   desktop_error errorStatus;
};
```

   Note that the definitions of the public types and the prototypes for the member functions were omitted from this class definition to save space.

4. Is it reasonable to think that other programmers might want to use a variation of the `desktop` class in their programs? How would you use inheritance to make the `desktop` class into a generic `desktop` class that could be used for any program? Write a class called `generic_desktop` and use it as a base for a class called `text_editor_desktop`. Which data members and member functions did you move from `desktop` into `generic_desktop`? Why? Which did you put into `text_editor_desktop`? Why?
5. If you were implementing the text editor program, would you shorten the `main()` function as suggested in the Troubleshooting Guide? Why or why not? Do you think your answer meets with good design guidelines? Is it practical to shorten functions in this way, or does it create too much overhead?

6. Do you think that the `desktop` object's text display area should be made into an object? What private data would the object have? What member functions would it have? What are the possible advantages of doing this? What are the possible disadvantages? Do you think it is worth the effort? Why or why not?
7. Look at the `desktop::SetTextArea()` function. To what range of values should the parameters be limited? Insert calls to the `assert()` function to enforce these programmer assumptions.
8. Can you find programmer assumptions in functions besides `desktop::SetTextArea()`? List the functions with assumptions. What `assert()` statements would you add to these functions to fix them?
9. The `text_editor` uses the `input_device` class to get raw input from the user. It then uses the `desktop::CookInput()` function to convert the input to a form specific to the text editor program. What advantages does this approach have? What disadvantages does it have? Would you use this approach if you were implementing the text editor? Why or why not?
10. The `cooked_input` class contains a private data type called `user_input_data`. It is a union. Could it be changed to a class or a structure? If you were implementing `user_input_data`, would you use a union, class, or structure? Why?

Exercises

1. The file and function introductory comments in the source code of the text editor are rather minimal. Most companies will require a modification history in the comments at the beginning of every file and function in a program. Explain what other information you think should go into the comments and why.
2. There is an implementation error in the `cooked_input` class. If the user types in a command, the `desktop::CookInput()` function correctly stores it as a command and sets the discriminant so that the program can tell a command was entered. However, the program can still call the `cooked_input::Character()` function to retrieve the data in the `cooked_input` object. The reverse is also true. If the user types text, the program can retrieve it as a command. Change the member functions of the `cooked_input` class so that they will not let the program retrieve commands as text or text as commands. Explain your implementation. Also tell why you chose the implementation that you did.
3. The keyword `const` was not used in the prototypes of many of the functions in the text editor. Rewrite the files presented in this chapter. Make as many `const` functions, parameters, and return types as you can. Explain which functions cannot be made `const` and why. Explain which parameters cannot be made `const` and why. Explain which return types cannot be made `const` and why.
4. It would not be sensible to have more than one `desktop` object in a program. However, the `desktop` object does not stop a programmer from declaring more than one variable of type `desktop`. Modify the constructor of the `desktop` object so that it will not allow more than one `desktop` to be created. *Hint:* Try using a `static` data member or a `static` local variable.
5. As discussed in this chapter, the `desktop` object should not return a reference to its `status_bar` object. Modify the `desktop` class so that it does not do this. Add the `desktop` member functions the text editor program needs to access the functionality of the `status_bar` without having direct access to the `status_bar` data member.
6. As discussed in this chapter, it is not a good idea for the `desktop` object to return a pointer to the main menu. Rewrite the `desktop` class so that it does not do this. Add the `desktop` member functions the text editor program needs to access the functionality of the `menu` without having direct access to the `menu` data member.
7. Some of the member functions of the `cooked_input` and desktop classes are simple enough to be `inline` functions. Change as many functions in these two classes to `inline` functions. Put the `inline` functions in an *.INL* file or the *Desktop.h* file. Explain why you chose to put the inline functions where you did.

8. The `desktop::DisplayTextBuffer()` function is written with the assumption that `editAreaLeft` is less than `editAreaRight`. It also assumes that `editAreaTop` is less than `editAreaBottom`. Rewrite this function so that it enforces these assumptions. Do whatever you reasonably can to make sure that a programmer can't use the `desktop::DisplayTextBuffer()` if the edit area is not properly initialized. Look for other programmer assumptions in functions in the file *Desktop.cpp*. Modify the functions so that they enforce these programmer assumptions.
9. Rewrite *TEdit.cpp* so that it declares and uses the functions `InitializeDesktop()` and `RunProgram()` as discussed in the Troubleshooting Guide.
10. The `MakeMenus()` function in *TEdit.cpp* is rather long. Explain why you think it may or may not be a good idea to shorten it by moving some of its code to functions called by `MakeMenus()`.

29 Developing the Text Editor: InputDev.h, InputDev.cpp, Display.h, and Display.cpp

Objectives

After reading this chapter, you should be able to:

- Implement the text editor source files *InputDev.h, InputDev.cpp, Display.h,* and *Display.cpp*.
- Integrate and debug the objects and functions in these files.
- Name and explain other implementation alternatives.

Preview

Chapter 28 presented the text editor files *TEdit.cpp, Desktop.h,* and *Desktop.cpp.* These files give an overview of how the text editor program works. This chapter implements *InputDev.h, InputDev.cpp, Display.h,* and *Display.cpp.* These four files encapsulate the portions of the program that are dependent on the hardware and operating system. If you port the text editor program to another computer or operating system, you need only change these four files. No other files in the program need to be altered.

Recall that you'll find the source files for the text editor on the CD that comes with this book. The root directory of the CD contains a directory named *Examples*. In the *Examples* directory is a directory named *TEdit*. The files for this chapter are in the *TEdit* directory.

Writing InputDev.h

InputDev.h contains the definition of the `input_device` class. The purpose of the `input_device` class is to encapsulate the keyboard in a portable way. It can also be extended to encapsulate other input devices.

Hiding hardware dependencies in this way is often a valuable technique to companies that employ us. It makes our programs highly portable. You may justifiably wonder why companies producing software don't just use the `cin` stream. It's implemented identically on all computers.

Although stream input with `cin` is portable, it often does not serve us well in programs intended for graphical user interfaces. Streams do not recognize input from keys on the keyboard such as Page Up and Page Down. They can't be used to check the status of keys such as the Ctrl and Alt keys. Input streams don't recognize function keys. They may or may not be buffered.

Streams such as `cin` perform line-oriented input. Line-oriented input means you must type in a line of data, then press the Enter key. Most programs today use screen-oriented input. In screen-oriented input, the user can enter information anywhere on the screen. Programs that use the mouse *must* have screen-oriented input so that the user can click the mouse anywhere on the screen.

For these reasons, many developers write their own input classes. If it's written properly, an input class can be implemented on virtually any computer and operating system. It can have the same interface of public member functions on all systems. That's the goal of the `input_device` class.

Listing 29.1 contains the source code for *InputDev.h.*

LISTING 29.1 InputDev.h

```
//-------------------------------------------------------------------------
/*
File Name:    InputDev.h
Comments:     This file contains the definitions required for the input_device
              class. The input_device class hides the operating system and
              hardware dependencies of getting input. It currently supports
              only the keyboard. However, it can be extended to support nearly
              any user input device.

              This file contains a global variable definition. In the same way
              that iostream.h defines the global streams cin and cout, this file
              defines the global variable inputDevice.

              Note that, in order for the memory for the variable inputDevice
              to be allocated, one (and only one) of the CPP files in your
              program must contain the following statements:
              #define EXTERN
              #include "InputDev.h"

              Any CPP or header file may include this file. However, only one
              CPP file should define the constant EXTERN before it includes
              this file.
*/
//-------------------------------------------------------------------------


#ifndef INPUTDEV_H
#define INPUTDEV_H



//-------------------------------------------------------------------------
// Types

typedef char raw_input;

// End Types
//-------------------------------------------------------------------------



//—-----------------------------------------------------------------------
// Class Definitions

class input_device
{
// Public enumerations.
public:
```

```
   enum key_id
   {
      ENTER = 13,
      ESCAPE = 27,
      UP = 23,            // ^w,
      DOWN = 26,          // ^z
      LEFT = 1,           // ^a
      RIGHT = 19,         // ^s
   };

   enum echo_mode
   {
      NO_ECHO,
      ECHO
   };

// Public member functions.
public:
   input_device(void);

   raw_input GetInput(echo_mode echoInput = input_device::ECHO);
};

// End Class Definitions
//-----------------------------------------------------------------------------



//-----------------------------------------------------------------------------
// input_device class inline member functions

inline input_device::input_device(void)
{
   // Nothing to do in this implementation.
}

// End input_device class inline member functions
//-----------------------------------------------------------------------------



//-----------------------------------------------------------------------------
// Global variable definition

#ifndef EXTERN
#define EXTERN extern
#endif

EXTERN input_device inputDevice;

#endif

// End Global variable definition
//-----------------------------------------------------------------------------


// End InputDev.h
//-----------------------------------------------------------------------------
```

The file *InputDev.h* begins by utilizing a `typedef` statement to define a type called `raw_input`. In this implementation, the `raw_input` type is just a character. However, if we were to extend the `input_device` class, we would likely want to use integers for raw input. Using integers for raw input enables us to define constants for keys that are not in the ASCII set.

Every type of computer provides programmers with ways of getting a unique identifier for each key on the keyboard. If the key represents a character in the ASCII set, the `input_device` class can convert the unique identifier to an ASCII character. ASCII characters can be stored in integers. Therefore, using integers for the `raw_input` type would enable us to store characters in `raw_input` variables.

If the user presses a key that is not in the ASCII character set, the `input_device` class can convert its unique identifier to an integer constant defined in *InputDev.h*. For example, we could define the constant `F1_KEY` in the `key_id` enumerated type. Applications could then use the `input_device` class to see if the user pressed the F1 key.

Recall that programmers often use `typedef` statements to define new names for the built-in types. If the developers think the type might need to change, they will use this technique to make the change easier to perform.

The file *InputDev.h* also defines the `input_device` class. It contains two public enumerations. The first defines constants for keys that nearly any application will need. The second enables a program to control whether or not the `input_device` class echoes user input to the screen. This was not in our original design in Chapter 27. It demonstrates the need for careful, iterative design.

The `input_device` class has only two member functions, and no member data. Its two functions are a constructor and the `GetInput()` function.

The `input_device` constructor is defined as an `inline` function. Currently, it doesn't do anything because the `input_device` class has no private data members.

The `GetInput()` function performs the work for the `input_device` class. It uses a default parameter of type `echo_mode`. By default, `GetInput()` will print the user's input to the screen. At times, the text editor overrides this behavior by passing in the enumerated value `NO_ECHO`.

Near the end of *InputDev.h,* the file declares a global variable using the preprocessor trick we saw in earlier chapters. This method requires that we put the statement

```
#define EXTERN
```

at the beginning of *TEdit.cpp* to allocate memory for the global variable `inputDevice`.

Writing InputDev.cpp.

The implementation of the `input_device` class is contained in *InputDev.cpp*. It is shown in Listing 29.2.

LISTING 29.2 InputDev.cpp

```
//-----------------------------------------------------------------
/*
File Name:    InputDev.cpp
Comments:     This file contains the implementation of the input_device class.
              It currently supports MS DOS-compatible PCs, but can be extended
              to support most hardware and operating system combinations.
*/
//-----------------------------------------------------------------



//-----------------------------------------------------------------
// Include Files

#include "InputDev.h"
```

```
#include "Platform.h"
#include "Display.h"
#ifdef PLATFORM_MS_DOS
#include <dos.h>
#endif

// End Include Files
//----------------------------------------------------------------------------



//----------------------------------------------------------------------------
// Constants

#ifdef PLATFORM_MS_DOS
const unsigned OS_SERVICES = 0x021;
const unsigned UNFILTERED_CHARACTER_INPUT = 0x07;
#endif

// End Constants
//----------------------------------------------------------------------------



//----------------------------------------------------------------------------
// input_device class member functions



//----------------------------------------------------------------------------
/*
Function Name:       GetInput
Member of:           input_device
Input Parameters:    echoInput - An optional parameter. If set to NO_ECHO, it
                        will not echo the input it gets to the display. If
                        set to ECHO, it will echo the input to the display.
                        The default is ECHO.
Output Parameters:   None.
Return Value:        Returns the input it retrieves.
Comments:            This function gets input from a keyboard. It uses the
                     PC Basic Input/Output System (BIOS) interrupts to do its
                     work. The interrupts are generated using the int86()
                     function, which is part of the C/C++ Standard Library
                     for most MS DOS-compatible compilers.
                     Once called, the GetInput() function waits until the user
                     enters input on the keyboard. It then returns that input
                     to the program that called the function.
*/

raw_input input_device::GetInput(echo_mode echoInput)
{
   raw_input userInput;

   #ifdef PLATFORM_MS_DOS
   REGS registers;

   // Select character input.
   registers.h.ah = UNFILTERED_CHARACTER_INPUT;
```

```
    // Get character input.
    int86(OS_SERVICES,&registers,&registers);
    userInput = registers.h.al;

    /* If the user's input is a printable character and it should be
    echoed to the screen... */
    if (((char)userInput >= ' ') && ((char)userInput <= '~') &&
        (echoInput == ECHO))
    {
        // Print the character on the screen.
        theScreen.Print((char)userInput);
    }

    #endif
    return (userInput);
}

// End GetInput
//-----------------------------------------------------------------------



// End input_device class member functions
//-----------------------------------------------------------------------



// End InputDev.cpp
//-----------------------------------------------------------------------
```

This implementation of the `input_device` class is specific to MS DOS–compatible computers. All of the platform-specific code is contained in `#ifdef` statements. The constant `PLATFORM_MS_DOS` is defined in the file *Platform.h*. If `PLATFORM_MS_DOS` is defined, then the code in the `#ifdef` statements in this file will be compiled. If it is not defined, the preprocessor will remove everything in the `#ifdef` statements.

If we wanted to port this program to other platforms, we would need to add `#elif defined()` statements to the program. Other possible constants include `PLATFORM_LINUX` for the Linux operating system and `PLATFORM_MAC` for the Apple Macintosh.

The `GetInput()` function uses services provided by MS DOS to get input from the user. If the user types a character that can be printed on the screen (some can't), and the program told `GetInput()` to echo the user's input, `GetInput()` prints the input on the screen at the current cursor location. It then returns the user's input.

You don't necessarily have to understand the internal details of how this function works. It is extremely dependent on IBM-compatible hardware and the MS DOS operating system. All you really need to understand is the public interface. To retrieve input from the user, you call the `GetInput()` function. If you want the user's input echoed on the screen, you either pass nothing in the parameter list or you pass the value `input_device::ECHO`. If you don't want the user's input echoed, you pass `input_device::NO_ECHO`.

Writing Display.h

As with the keyboard, the text editor program defines an object to encapsulate the video display. Nothing defined in the `display` object's public interface is dependent on any particular hardware or operating system. The `display` object provides the text editor with a portable way of printing to any location on the screen. Listing 29.3 contains the source code for *Display.h*.

LISTING 29.3 Display.h

```
//---------------------------------------------------------------------------
/*
File Name:  Display.h
Comments:   This file contains the class definition of the display object.
            The display object is used to hide the hardware specifics of
            the computer's display. It gives a generic way to do full screen
            text manipulation.
*/
//---------------------------------------------------------------------------

#ifndef DISPLAY_H
#define DISPLAY_H

//---------------------------------------------------------------------------
// Include Files

#include "TString.h"
#include "Platform.h"

// End Include Files
//---------------------------------------------------------------------------


//---------------------------------------------------------------------------
// Constants

const int MAX_STACK_SIZE = 20;

// End Constants
//---------------------------------------------------------------------------



//---------------------------------------------------------------------------
// Types

typedef int display_coordinate;

// End Types
//---------------------------------------------------------------------------


//---------------------------------------------------------------------------
// Class Definitions

class display
{
// Public types.
public:
   enum display_error
   {
      NO_ERROR,
      CANT_SAVE_BACKGROUND
   };

   enum display_style
   {
```

```
      NO_STYLE,
      BOLD,
      UNDERLINED,
      INVERSE
   };

// Public member functions.
public:
   display(void);
   ~display(void);

   void Clear(void);
   void Clear(int left,int top,int right,int bottom);

   void Print(const char characterToPrint,
              const display::display_style characterStyle = NO_STYLE);
   void Print(text_string &stringToPrint,
              const display::display_style characterStyle = NO_STYLE);

   void PrintAt(const display_coordinate row,
                const display_coordinate col,
                const char characterToPrint,
                const display::display_style characterStyle = NO_STYLE);
   void PrintAt(const display_coordinate row,
                const display_coordinate col,
                text_string &stringToPrint,
                const display::display_style characterStyle = NO_STYLE);

   void CursorUp(unsigned linesToMove);
   void CursorDown(unsigned linesToMove);
   void CursorLeft(unsigned charactersToMove);
   void CursorRight(unsigned charactersToMove);

   void CursorRow(unsigned newRow);
   unsigned CursorRow(void) const;

   void CursorCol(unsigned newCol);
   unsigned CursorCol(void) const;

   display_coordinate CharacterWidth(void) const;
   display_coordinate CharacterHeight(void) const;
   display_coordinate StringHeight(const text_string &aString) const;
   display_coordinate StringWidth(const text_string &aString) const;

   display_coordinate FirstRow(void) const;
   display_coordinate LastRow(void) const;
   display_coordinate FirstCol(void) const;
   display_coordinate LastCol(void) const;

   void SaveArea(display_coordinate left,
                 display_coordinate top,
                 display_coordinate right,
                 display_coordinate bottom);

   void RestoreArea(const display_coordinate left,
                    const display_coordinate top,
                    const display_coordinate right,
                    const display_coordinate bottom);
```

```
   display::display_error ErrorStatus(void) const;

// Private types.
private:
   class buffer_pointer_stack
   {
   public:
      buffer_pointer_stack();
      void Push(unsigned *bufferPointer);
      unsigned *Pop(void);

      int Top(void);

   private:
      unsigned *stack[MAX_STACK_SIZE];
      int top;
   };

// Private data.
private:
   display_error errorStatus;
   buffer_pointer_stack bufferStack;

   #ifdef PLATFORM_MS_DOS
   unsigned displayMode;
   #endif
};

// End Class Definitions
//-----------------------------------------------------------------------


//-----------------------------------------------------------------------
// Global variable definition

#ifndef EXTERN
#define EXTERN extern
#endif

EXTERN display theScreen;

// End Global variable definition
//-----------------------------------------------------------------------
#endif

// End Display.h
//-----------------------------------------------------------------------
```

This file begins by including the file *TString.h* and *Platform.h*. *Platform.h* contains a constant that the preprocessor uses to conditionally compile parts of the `display` object. *TString.h* defines the `text_string` object. If you look at the `display` class member functions, you'll see that we've given the `display` object the ability to print `text_string` objects. Doing this reduces the reusability of the `display` object. Every program in which we use the `display` object must also contain the `text_string` object. Technically, we say that these modules have high cohesion. They're stuck together. We must have one to use the other.

For this program, and many other programs, that's not a serious problem. However, it is likely that there are programs in which it is not appropriate to use the `text_string` object. The current implementation of the display object forces us to either rewrite it or forget about using it. In the exercises at the end of this chapter, you'll look at an alternative implementation that will lessen these problems.

There is also high cohesion between the display object and any other program module that uses it. The file *Display.h* defines a global variable called theScreen at the end. Recall from Chapter 28 that the file *Desktop.cpp* contains references to the global variable theScreen, which means that *Display.h* must be used in any program that uses the desktop object.

Both the input_device and display objects encapsulate hardware. Neither stores much in the way of private data. It is unlikely that making the input_device and display variables global will somehow result in them getting into an invalid state (however, it could happen!). Therefore, they both avoid most of the pitfalls of global variables. Even so, you can see that the high cohesion global variables cause can potentially result in problems. Cohesion tends to cut down the reusability of objects.

After *Display.h* includes the header files it needs, it defines a constant and a type that it needs. The display object uses the type, called display_coordinate, to specify *x* and *y* coordinates on the screen. In this implementation, display_coordinate is just another name for integers. However, it is likely that this type may need to change when the display object is implemented on other platforms. Many implementations will require that the display_coordinate type be unsigned integers instead of integers.

The file then defines the display object. The display class contains a section for public types. Neither of these enumerated types were defined in the design in Chapter 27. The need for them quickly became apparent when I was pseudocoding and coding the display object. I purposely gave only my original design in Chapter 27 to demonstrate the need for iteration when designing. As we examine the implementations of the objects in this program, it becomes increasingly plain that I left many details out of my original design. You will do the same as you design programs. Take the time to redesign and pseudocode your programs so that you pick up these sorts of details before you write code.

The display object defines a number of member functions. About half of them are for the purpose of providing portability. The others enable programs to print output or control the screen.

The text editor program must save the contents of rectangular sections of the screen whenever it displays a menu. It does this so that it can store the stuff on the screen that the menu covers up. When the program erases a menu, it needs to restore the contents of the screen. Saving rectangular sections of the screen is an operation that is very dependent on the hardware and operating system the computer uses. To make this operation more portable, the display object keeps an internal list of rectangular sections it saves. Any other object can tell the display to save a section of the screen. The display object will deal with all of the hardware and operating system dependencies when it saves the screen section. No other object needs to worry about it.

To save the background areas, the display object uses a **data structure** called a **stack.** A data structure is an organized collection of data. A stack is a common data structure in C++ programming. It operates very simply. You push items onto the stack and pop them off. The last one you pushed on is the first one that will pop off. The display object defines the stack as a private type. The buffer_pointer_stack object has its own member functions and private data. The member functions appear in *Display.cpp.*

Writing Display.cpp

The file *Display.cpp* contains the implementation of the display and buffer_pointer_stack classes. It is shown in Listing 29.4.

LISTING 29.4 Display.cpp

```
//-----------------------------------------------------------------------
/*
File Name:  Display.cpp
Comments:   This file contains the implementation of the display and
            the buffer_pointer_stack classes.
```

```
*/
//-------------------------------------------------------------------------------




//-------------------------------------------------------------------------------
// Include Files

#include "Display.h"
#include <assert.h>

#ifdef PLATFORM_MS_DOS
#include <dos.h>

// End Include Files
//-------------------------------------------------------------------------------


//-------------------------------------------------------------------------------
// Constants

const unsigned VIDEO_BIOS_SERVICES = 0x10;
const unsigned SET_VIDEO_MODE = 0x00;
const unsigned GET_VIDEO_MODE = 0x0F;
const unsigned TEXT_80x25_VIDEO_MODE = 0x07;
const unsigned SET_CURSOR_TYPE = 0x01;
const unsigned WRITE_CURSOR_POSITION = 0x02;
const unsigned READ_CURSOR_POSITION = 0x03;
const unsigned WRITE_CHARACTER_AND_ATTRIBUTE = 0x09;
const unsigned READ_CHARACTER_AND_ATTRIBUTE = 0x08;

const int CURSOR_STARTING_LINE = 11;
const int CURSOR_ENDING_LINE = 12;

const int TEXT_MODE_MAX_ROWS = 25;
const int TEXT_MODE_MAX_COLS = 80;
const int TEXT_MODE_FIRST_ROW = 1;
const int TEXT_MODE_LAST_ROW = TEXT_MODE_MAX_ROWS;
const int TEXT_MODE_FIRST_COL = 1;
const int TEXT_MODE_LAST_COL = TEXT_MODE_MAX_COLS;
const int TEXT_MODE_CHARACTER_WIDTH = 1;
const int TEXT_MODE_CHARACTER_HEIGHT = 1;
const int TEXT_MODE_STRING_HEIGHT = 1;

// Two bytes: 1 for the char and 1 for the attribute.
const int TEXT_MODE_BYTES_PER_CHAR = 2;

const unsigned ATTRIBUTE_NORMAL = 0x07;
const unsigned ATTRIBUTE_BOLD = 0x08;
const unsigned ATTRIBUTE_UNDERLINE = 0x01;
const unsigned ATTRIBUTE_INVERSE = 0x70;

// End Constants
//-------------------------------------------------------------------------------


//-------------------------------------------------------------------------------
// Macros
```

```
#define BuildAttribute(attrib)                                         \
            (attrib == display::NO_STYLE) ? ATTRIBUTE_NORMAL:          \
            (attrib == display::BOLD) ? ATTRIBUTE_BOLD:                \
            (attrib == display::UNDERLINED) ? ATTRIBUTE_UNDERLINE:     \
            (attrib == display::INVERSE) ? ATTRIBUTE_INVERSE:          \
            0

// End Macros
//---------------------------------------------------------------------




//---------------------------------------------------------------------
/*
Function Name:          GetVideoMode
Input Parameters:       None.
Output Parameters:      None.
Return Value:           This function returns the current video mode.
Comments:               The GetVideoMode function is for use only on MS DOS
                        compatible PCs. It gets the video mode that the user's
                        screen is currently set to.
*/

static unsigned GetVideoMode(void)
{
   REGS registers;

   registers.h.ah = GET_VIDEO_MODE;

   int86(VIDEO_BIOS_SERVICES,&registers,&registers);

   return ((unsigned)registers.h.al);
}

// End GetVideoMode
//---------------------------------------------------------------------




//---------------------------------------------------------------------
/*
Function Name:          SetVideoMode
Input Parameters:       videoMode - The display mode that the user's screen will
                           be set to.
Output Parameters:      None.
Return Value:           None.
Comments:               The SetVideoMode function is for use only on MS DOS
                        compatible PCs. It sets the user's screen to the
                        specified video mode. If the user's screen doesn't
                        support the specified mode, this function does nothing.
*/

static void SetVideoMode(unsigned videoMode)
{
   REGS registers;

   registers.h.ah = SET_VIDEO_MODE;
```

```
   registers.h.al = videoMode;

   int86(VIDEO_BIOS_SERVICES,&registers,&registers);
}

// End SetVideoMode
//-----------------------------------------------------------------------------




//-----------------------------------------------------------------------------
/*
Function Name:          GetCursorPosition
Input Parameters:       None.
Output Parameters:      row - The cursor's current row number on the screen.
                        col - The cursor's current column number on the screen.
Return Value:           None.
Comments:               This function retrieves the cursor's current row and
                        column numbers on the screen. It can only be used on MS
                        DOS compatible computers.
*/
inline void GetCursorPosition(int *row,int *col)
{
   REGS registers;

   registers.h.ah = READ_CURSOR_POSITION;
   registers.h.bh = 0;   // Memory page zero.

   int86(VIDEO_BIOS_SERVICES,&registers,&registers);
   *row = registers.h.dh;
   *col = registers.h.dl;
}

// End GetCursorPosition
//-----------------------------------------------------------------------------




//-----------------------------------------------------------------------------
/*
Function Name:          SetCursorPosition
Input Parameters:       row - The new row number that the cursor will be set to
                        on the screen.
                        col - The new column number that the cursor will be set
                        to on the screen.
Output Parameters:      None.
Return Value:           None.
Comments:               This function sets the cursor's current row and column
                        numbers on the screen. It can only be used on MS DOS
                        compatible computers.
*/


inline void SetCursorPosition(const int row,const int col)
{
   assert(row<=TEXT_MODE_MAX_ROWS);
   assert(col<=TEXT_MODE_MAX_COLS);
```

```
   REGS registers;

   registers.h.ah = WRITE_CURSOR_POSITION;
   registers.h.bh = 0;   // Memory page zero.
   registers.h.dh = row;
   registers.h.dl = col;
   int86(VIDEO_BIOS_SERVICES,&registers,&registers);
}

// End SetCursorPosition
//-----------------------------------------------------------------------



//-----------------------------------------------------------------------
/*
Function Name:        WriteCharacterAndAttribute
Input Parameters:     character - The character to write to the screen.
                      attribute - The attribute that the character will be
                         displayed with.
Output Parameters:    None.
Return Value:         None.
Comments:             This function writes a character to the display on
                      an MS DOS compatible computer. Every character must
                      have an attribute. MS DOS supports the attributes
                      specified by the constants ATTRIBUTE_NORMAL,
                      ATTRIBUTE_BOLD, ATTRIBUTE_UNDERLINE, and
                      ATTRIBUTE_INVERSE.
*/

inline void WriteCharacterAndAttribute(char character,unsigned attribute)
{
   REGS registers;

   registers.h.ah = WRITE_CHARACTER_AND_ATTRIBUTE;
   registers.h.al = character;
   registers.h.bh = 0;   // Memory page zero.
   registers.h.bl = attribute;
   registers.x.cx = 1;
   int86(VIDEO_BIOS_SERVICES,&registers,&registers);
}

// End WriteCharacterAndAttribute
//-----------------------------------------------------------------------



//-----------------------------------------------------------------------
/*
Function Name:        ReadCharacterAndAttribute
Input Parameters:     None.
Output Parameters:    character - A pointer to a character variable. This will
                         contain the character read from the screen.
                      attribute - A pointer to an unsigned integer variable.
                         This will contain the attribute of the character read
                         from the screen.
Return Value:         None.
```

```
Comments:            This function reads a character and its associated
                     attribute from the screen of an MS DOS compatible
                     computer.
*/

inline void ReadCharacterAndAttribute(char *character,unsigned *attribute)
{
   REGS registers;

   registers.h.ah = READ_CHARACTER_AND_ATTRIBUTE;
   registers.h.bh = 0;   // Memory page zero.

   int86(VIDEO_BIOS_SERVICES,&registers,&registers);
   *character = registers.h.al;
   *attribute = registers.h.ah;
}

// End ReadCharacterAndAttribute
//-----------------------------------------------------------------------------



//-----------------------------------------------------------------------------
/*
Function Name:       CursorOn
Input Parameters:    None
Output Parameters:   None.
Return Value:        None.
Comments:            This function can only be used on an MS DOS compatible
                     computer. It makes the hardware cursor visible on the
                     screen.
*/

void CursorOn(void)
{
   REGS registers;

   registers.h.ah = SET_CURSOR_TYPE;
   registers.h.ch = CURSOR_STARTING_LINE;
   registers.h.cl = CURSOR_ENDING_LINE;
   int86(VIDEO_BIOS_SERVICES,&registers,&registers);
}

// End CursorOn
//-----------------------------------------------------------------------------



//-----------------------------------------------------------------------------
/*
Function Name:       CursorOff
Input Parameters:    None
Output Parameters:   None.
Return Value:        None.
Comments:            This function can only be used on an MS DOS compatible
                     computer. It turns the hardware cursor off so that it is
                     not displayed on the screen. This may not work with some
```

```
                    computers, depending on how compatible they are. However,
                    it will work fine with the majority of PCs.
*/

void CursorOff()
{
   REGS registers;

   registers.h.ah = SET_CURSOR_TYPE;
   registers.h.ch = CURSOR_ENDING_LINE;
   registers.h.cl = CURSOR_STARTING_LINE;
   int86(VIDEO_BIOS_SERVICES,&registers,&registers);
}

// End CursorOff
//-----------------------------------------------------------------------------

#endif


//-----------------------------------------------------------------------------
/*
Function Name:      display
Member of:          display
Input Parameters:   None.
Output Parameters:  None.
Return Value:       Constructed display object.
Comments:           This is the default constructor for the display class.
                    On MS DOS compatible computers, it saves the current
                    display mode. The destructor restores the display mode
                    when the program exits.
*/

display::display(void)
{
   #ifdef PLATFORM_MS_DOS
   displayMode = GetVideoMode();
   SetVideoMode(TEXT_80x25_VIDEO_MODE);
   CursorOn();
   #endif

   errorStatus = NO_ERROR;
}

// End display
//-----------------------------------------------------------------------------



//-----------------------------------------------------------------------------
/*
Function Name:      ~display
Member of:          display
Input Parameters:   None.
Output Parameters:  None.
Return Value:       None.
Comments:           This is the destructor for the display class. The MS DOS
                    implementation of this function restores the user's
```

```
                      screen to whatever display mode it was in when the
                      program started.
*/

display::~display(void)
{
   #ifdef PLATFORM_MS_DOS
   SetVideoMode(displayMode);
   #endif
}

// End ~display
//-----------------------------------------------------------------------------



//-----------------------------------------------------------------------------
/*
Function Name:        Clear
Member of:            display
Input Parameters:     None.
Output Parameters:    None.
Return Value:         None.
Comments:             This function clears the user's entire screen.
*/

void display::Clear(void)
{
   Clear(TEXT_MODE_FIRST_COL,TEXT_MODE_FIRST_ROW,
         TEXT_MODE_LAST_COL,TEXT_MODE_LAST_ROW);
}

// End Clear
//-----------------------------------------------------------------------------




//-----------------------------------------------------------------------------
/*
Function Name:        Clear
Member of:            display
Input Parameters:     left - The column number of the left edge of the screen
                         area to be cleared.
                      top - The row number of the top edge of the screen
                         area to be cleared.
                      right - The column number of the right edge of the screen
                         area to be cleared.
                      bottom - The column number of the bottom edge of the
                         screen area to be cleared.
Output Parameters:    None.
Return Value:         None.
Comments:             This function clears the portion of the screen specified
                      by the input parameters.
*/

void display::Clear(int left,int top,int right,int bottom)
{
```

```
    display_coordinate row,col;

    GetCursorPosition(&row,&col);

    #ifdef PLATFORM_MS_DOS

    // For each row...
    for (int i=top;(i<TEXT_MODE_MAX_ROWS) && (i<=bottom);i++)
    {
        // For each column...
        for (int j=left;(j<TEXT_MODE_MAX_COLS) && (j<=right);j++)
        {
            SetCursorPosition(i,j);
            WriteCharacterAndAttribute('\0',ATTRIBUTE_NORMAL);
        }
    }

    #endif

    SetCursorPosition(row,col);
}

// End Clear
//---------------------------------------------------------------------------



//---------------------------------------------------------------------------
/*
Function Name:        Print
Member of:            display
Input Parameters:     characterToPrint - The character that will be printed on
                         the screen.
                      characterStyle - The display style of the character. This
                         parameter can be set to any value from the
                         display::display_style enumerated type.
Output Parameters:    None.
Return Value:         None.
Comments:             This version of the overloaded Print function prints a
                      character to the screen at the current cursor location.
                      It uses the print attribute specified by the
                      parameter characterStyle.
*/

void display::Print(const char characterToPrint,
                    const display::display_style characterStyle)
{
    #ifdef PLATFORM_MS_DOS
    int cursorRow,cursorCol;

    // Convert the character style to an MS DOS character attribute.
    unsigned attribute = BuildAttribute(characterStyle);

    // Print the character with its attribute.
    WriteCharacterAndAttribute(characterToPrint,attribute);

    // Get the current cursor position.
    GetCursorPosition(&cursorRow,&cursorCol);
```

```
    // Increment it.
    cursorCol++;

    // If the cursor will move out of the text area...
    if (cursorCol>TEXT_MODE_MAX_COLS)
    {
        // Move it to the beginning of the next row.
        cursorRow++;
        cursorCol = TEXT_MODE_FIRST_COL;
    }

    // If the cursor will move past the last row of the text area...
    if (cursorRow>TEXT_MODE_MAX_ROWS)
    {
        // Set it to the last row.
        cursorRow=TEXT_MODE_MAX_ROWS;
    }

    SetCursorPosition(cursorRow,cursorCol);
    #endif
}

// End Print
//-----------------------------------------------------------------------------




//-----------------------------------------------------------------------------
/*
Function Name:      Print
Member of:          display
Input Parameters:   stringToPrint - A reference to the string that will be
                       printed on the screen.
                    characterStyle - The display style of the characters in
                       the string. This parameter can be set to any value
                       from the display::display_style enumerated type.
Output Parameters:  None.
Return Value:       None.
Comments:           This version of the overloaded Print function prints an
                    entire string to the screen using the specified
                    character attribute.
*/

void display::Print(text_string &stringToPrint,
                    const display::display_style characterStyle)
{
    for (int i=0;i<stringToPrint.Length();i++)
    {
        Print(stringToPrint[i],characterStyle);
    }
}

// End Print
//-----------------------------------------------------------------------------




//-----------------------------------------------------------------------------
```

```
/*
Function Name:       PrintAt
Member of:           display
Input Parameters:    row - The row number where the character will be printed.
                     col - The column number where the character will be
                        printed.
                     characterToPrint - The character to be printed on the
                        screen.
                     characterStyle - The display style of the character. This
                        parameter can be set to any value from the
                        display::display_style enumerated type.
Output Parameters:   None.
Return Value:        None.
Comments:            This function prints a character to the screen at the
                     location specified by row and col. The character is
                     printed using the attribute contained in characterStyle.
*/

void display::PrintAt(const display_coordinate row,
                      const display_coordinate col,
                      const char characterToPrint,
                      const display::display_style characterStyle)
{
   #ifdef PLATFORM_MS_DOS
   // Save the current cursor location.
   int cursorRow,cursorCol;
   GetCursorPosition(&cursorRow,&cursorCol);

   // Make the cursor invisible.
   CursorOff();

   // Move the invisible cursor to the print location.
   SetCursorPosition(row,col);

   // Print the character.
   Print(characterToPrint,characterStyle);

   // Move the cursor back.
   SetCursorPosition(cursorRow,cursorCol);

   // Turn it back on.
   CursorOn();

   #endif
}



//---------------------------------------------------------------------------
/*
Function Name:       PrintAt
Member of:           display
Input Parameters:    row - The row number where the character will be printed.
                     col - The column number where the character will be
                        printed.
                     stringToPrint - The string to be printed on the screen.
                     characterStyle - The display style of the character
                        string. This parameter can be set to any value from
                        the display::display_style enumerated type.
```

```
Output Parameters:   None.
Return Value:        None.
Comments:            This function prints a string to the screen at the
                     location specified by row and col. The string is
                     printed using the attribute contained in characterStyle.
*/

void display::PrintAt(const display_coordinate row,
                      const display_coordinate col,
                      text_string &stringToPrint,
                      const display::display_style characterStyle)
{
   for (int i=0;i<stringToPrint.Length();i++)
   {
      PrintAt(row,col+i,stringToPrint[i],characterStyle);
   }
}

// End PrintAt
//-----------------------------------------------------------------------------




//-----------------------------------------------------------------------------
/*
Function Name:       CursorUp
Member of:           display
Input Parameters:    linesToMove - The number of rows to move upward from the
                        current position.
Output Parameters:   None.
Return Value:        None.
Comments:            This function moves the hardware cursor up by the
                     specified number of rows. It will not let the cursor
                     move out of the text area.
*/

void display::CursorUp(unsigned linesToMove)
{
   int row,col;
   GetCursorPosition(&row,&col);
   row-=linesToMove;
   if (row>=TEXT_MODE_FIRST_ROW)
   {
      SetCursorPosition(row,col);
   }
}

// End CursorUp
//-----------------------------------------------------------------------------




//-----------------------------------------------------------------------------
/*
Function Name:       CursorDown
Member of:           display
Input Parameters:    linesToMove - The number of rows to move downward from
                        the current position.
Output Parameters:   None.
```

```
Return Value:         None.
Comments:             This function moves the hardware cursor down by the
                      specified number of rows. It will not let the cursor move
                      out of the text area.
*/

void display::CursorDown(unsigned linesToMove)
{
   int row,col;
   GetCursorPosition(&row,&col);
   row+=linesToMove;
   if (row<=TEXT_MODE_LAST_ROW)
   {
      SetCursorPosition(row,col);
   }
}

// End CursorDown
//-----------------------------------------------------------------------------



//-----------------------------------------------------------------------------
/*
Function Name:        CursorLeft
Member of:            display
Input Parameters:     charactersToMove - The number of character columns the
                         cursor will be moved to the left.
Output Parameters:    None.
Return Value:         None.
Comments:             This function moves the hardware cursor left by the
                      specified number of character columns. It will not let
                      the cursor move out of the text area.
*/

void display::CursorLeft(unsigned charactersToMove)
{
   int row,col;
   GetCursorPosition(&row,&col);
   col-=charactersToMove;
   if (col>=TEXT_MODE_FIRST_COL)
   {
      SetCursorPosition(row,col);
   }
}

// End CursorLeft
//-----------------------------------------------------------------------------



//-----------------------------------------------------------------------------
/*
Function Name:        CursorRight
Member of:            display
Input Parameters:     charactersToMove - The number of character columns the
                         cursor will be moved to the right.
Output Parameters:    None.
Return Value:         None.
```

```
Comments:              This function moves the hardware cursor right by the
                       specified number of character columns. It will not let the
                       cursor move out of the text area.
*/

void display::CursorRight(unsigned charactersToMove)
{
   int row,col;
   GetCursorPosition(&row,&col);
   col+=charactersToMove;
   if (col<=TEXT_MODE_LAST_COL)
   {
      SetCursorPosition(row,col);
   }
}

// End CursorRight
//-----------------------------------------------------------------------------



//-----------------------------------------------------------------------------
/*
Function Name:         CursorRow
Member of:             display
Input Parameters:      newRow - The row number that the cursor will be moved to.
Output Parameters:     None
Return Value:          None.
Comments:              The CursorRow function moves the cursor to the specified
                       row.
*/

void display::CursorRow(unsigned newRow)
{
   int row,col;
   GetCursorPosition(&row,&col);
   SetCursorPosition(newRow,col);
}

// End CursorRow
//-----------------------------------------------------------------------------



//-----------------------------------------------------------------------------
/*
Function Name:         CursorRow
Member of:             display
Input Parameters:      None.
Output Parameters:     None.
Return Value:          This function returns the hardware cursor's current row
                       number.
Comments:              See Return Value section.
*/

unsigned display::CursorRow(void) const
{
   int row,col;
   GetCursorPosition(&row,&col);
```

```
   return (row);
}

// End CursorRow
//---------------------------------------------------------------------------




//---------------------------------------------------------------------------
/*
Function Name:        CursorCol
Member of:            display
Input Parameters:     newRow - The column number that the cursor will be moved
                         to.
Output Parameters:    None
Return Value:         None.
Comments:             The CursorCol function moves the cursor to the specified
                      column.
*/

void display::CursorCol(unsigned newCol)
{
   int row,col;
   GetCursorPosition(&row,&col);
   SetCursorPosition(row,newCol);
}

// End CursorCol
//---------------------------------------------------------------------------




//---------------------------------------------------------------------------
/*
Function Name:        CursorCol
Member of:            display
Input Parameters:     None.
Output Parameters:    None.
Return Value:         This function returns the hardware cursor's current
                      column number.
Comments:             See Return Value section.
*/

unsigned display::CursorCol(void) const
{
   int row,col;
   GetCursorPosition(&row,&col);
   return (col);
}

// End CursorCol
//---------------------------------------------------------------------------




//---------------------------------------------------------------------------
/*
Function Name:        CharacterWidth
```

```
Member of:           display
Input Parameters:    None.
Output Parameters:   None.
Return Value:        This function returns the width of a character in the
                     current display mode.
Comments:            See the Return Value section.
*/

display_coordinate display::CharacterWidth(void) const
{
   return (TEXT_MODE_CHARACTER_WIDTH);
}

// End CharacterWidth
//-----------------------------------------------------------------------------



//-----------------------------------------------------------------------------
/*
Function Name:       CharacterHeight
Member of:           display
Input Parameters:    None.
Output Parameters:   None.
Return Value:        This function returns the height of a character in the
                     current display mode.
Comments:            See the Return Value section.
*/

display_coordinate display::CharacterHeight(void) const
{
   return (TEXT_MODE_CHARACTER_HEIGHT);
}

// End CharacterHeight
//-----------------------------------------------------------------------------



#pragma argused

//-----------------------------------------------------------------------------
/*
Function Name:       StringHeight
Member of:           display
Input Parameters:    None.
Output Parameters:   None.
Return Value:        This function returns the width of a string in the
                     current display mode.
Comments:            See the Return Value section. Note that the value this
                     function returns should be the same as the value
                     returned by the display::CharacterHeight() function.
                     It is provided primarily for completeness.
*/

display_coordinate display::StringHeight(const text_string &aString) const
{
   return (TEXT_MODE_STRING_HEIGHT);
```

```
}

// End StringHeight
//---------------------------------------------------------------------


//---------------------------------------------------------------------
/*
Function Name:       StringWidth
Member of:           display
Input Parameters:    aString - A reference to the string whose width will be
                        returned.
Output Parameters:   None.
Return Value:        This function returns the width of a string in the
                     current display mode.
Comments:            See the Return Value section.
*/

display_coordinate display::StringWidth(const text_string &aString) const
{
   #ifdef PLATFORM_MS_DOS
   return (aString.Length());
   #endif
}

// End StringWidth
//---------------------------------------------------------------------


//---------------------------------------------------------------------
/*
Function Name:       FirstRow
Member of:           display
Input Parameters:    None.
Output Parameters:   None.
Return Value:        This function returns the number of the first row of the
                     display in the current video mode.
Comments:            In some display modes, the first row number is zero. In
                     others, it's one. The FirstRow function returns the
                     number of the first row for the current video mode.
*/

display_coordinate display::FirstRow(void) const
{
   return (TEXT_MODE_FIRST_ROW);
}

// End FirstRow
//---------------------------------------------------------------------


//---------------------------------------------------------------------
/*
Function Name:       LastRow
Member of:           display
```

```
Input Parameters:    None.
Output Parameters:   None.
Return Value:        This function returns the number of the last row of the
                     display in the current video mode.
Comments:            The row number of the last row on the display varies
                     with the display mode. The LastRow function returns the
                     number of the last row for the current video mode.
*/

display_coordinate display::LastRow(void) const
{
   return (TEXT_MODE_LAST_ROW);
}

// End LastRow
//-----------------------------------------------------------------------------



//-----------------------------------------------------------------------------
/*
Function Name:       FirstCol
Member of:           display
Input Parameters:    None.
Output Parameters:   None.
Return Value:        This function returns the number of the first column of
                     the display in the current video mode.
Comments:            In some display modes, the first column number is zero.
                     In others, it's one. The FirstCol function returns the
                     number of the first column for the current video mode.
*/

display_coordinate display::FirstCol(void) const
{
   return (TEXT_MODE_FIRST_COL);
}

// End FirstCol
//-----------------------------------------------------------------------------



//-----------------------------------------------------------------------------
/*
Function Name:       LastCol
Member of:           display
Input Parameters:    None.
Output Parameters:   None.
Return Value:        This function returns the number of the last column of
                     the display in the current video mode.
Comments:            The column number of the last column on the display
                     varies with the display mode. The LastCol function
                     returns the number of the last column for the current
                     video mode.
*/

display_coordinate display::LastCol(void) const
{
   return (TEXT_MODE_LAST_COL);
```

```
}

// End LastCol
//-----------------------------------------------------------------------------



//-----------------------------------------------------------------------------
/*
Function Name:       SaveArea
Member of:           display
Input Parameters:    left - The column number of the left edge of the screen
                        area to be saved.
                     top - The row number of the top edge of the screen
                        area to be saved.
                     right - The column number of the right edge of the screen
                        area to be saved.
                     bottom - The row number of the bottom edge of the screen
                        area to be saved.
Output Parameters:   None.
Return Value:        None.
Comments:            This function saves the contents of a rectangular area
                     of the screen. It puts a pointer to the saved area onto
                     a list of saved areas associated with the display object.
*/

void display::SaveArea(display_coordinate left,
                       display_coordinate top,
                       display_coordinate right,
                       display_coordinate bottom)
{
   // Allocate enough memory to hold the contents of the background.
   unsigned totalRows = bottom-top;
   unsigned totalCols = right-left;
   unsigned totalBytes = totalRows * totalCols * TEXT_MODE_BYTES_PER_CHAR;

   unsigned *buffer = new unsigned [totalBytes];

   // If the memory could be allocated...
   if (buffer != NULL)
   {
      char character;
      unsigned attribute;

      // Make the cursor invisible.
      int cursorRow,cursorCol;
      GetCursorPosition(&cursorRow,&cursorCol);
      CursorOff();

      // Save the contents of the screen at the specified location.
      for (int i=0,index=0;i<totalRows;i++)
      {
         for (int j=0;
              j<totalCols;
              j++,index += TEXT_MODE_BYTES_PER_CHAR)
         {
            SetCursorPosition(top+i,left+j);
```

```
Input Parameters:    None.
Output Parameters:   None.
Return Value:        A constructed buffer_pointer_stack object.
Comments:            This is the default constructor for the
                     buffer_pointer_stack class. This object is used
                     internally by the display object.
*/

display::buffer_pointer_stack::buffer_pointer_stack()
{
   top = 0;
   for (int i=0;i<MAX_STACK_SIZE;i++)
   {
      stack[i] = NULL;
   }
}

// End buffer_pointer_stack
//-----------------------------------------------------------------------------



//-----------------------------------------------------------------------------
/*
Function Name:       ~buffer_pointer_stack
Member of:           buffer_pointer_stack
Input Parameters:    None.
Output Parameters:   None.
Return Value:        None.
Comments:            This is the destructor for the buffer_pointer_stack
                     class. If there are any saved areas left on the stack,
                     they are deleted.
*/

display::buffer_pointer_stack::~buffer_pointer_stack()
{
   for (int i=0;i<top;i++)
   {
      delete stack[i];
   }
}

// End buffer_pointer_stack
//-----------------------------------------------------------------------------



//-----------------------------------------------------------------------------
/*
Function Name:       Push
Member of:           buffer_pointer_stack
Input Parameters:    bufferPointer - A pointer to the rectangular screen area
                        to be saved.
Output Parameters:   None.
Return Value:        None.
Comments:            This function saves a pointer to a rectangular screen
                     area on the stack.
*/
```

```
void display::buffer_pointer_stack::Push(unsigned *bufferPointer)
{
   // If the stack is not full...
   if (top < MAX_STACK_SIZE)
   {
      // Get the pointer on the top of the stack.
      stack[top++]=bufferPointer;
   }
}

// End Push
//----------------------------------------------------------------------------



//----------------------------------------------------------------------------
/*
Function Name:       Pop
Member of:           buffer_pointer_stack
Input Parameters:    None.
Output Parameters:   None.
Return Value:        This function returns a pointer to a rectangular screen
                     area.
Comments:            See the Return Value section.
*/

unsigned *display::buffer_pointer_stack::Pop(void)
{
   unsigned *buffer;

   // If the stack is not empty...
   if (top>0)
   {
      // Get the pointer on the top of the stack.
      buffer = stack[--top];
      stack[top] = NULL;
   }
   // Else the stack is empty...
   else
   {
      buffer = NULL;
   }

   return (buffer);
}

// End Pop
//----------------------------------------------------------------------------



//----------------------------------------------------------------------------
/*
Function Name:       Top
Member of:           buffer_pointer_stack
Input Parameters:    None.
Output Parameters:   None.
```

```
Return Value:         This function returns the index number of the top item
                      on the stack.
Comments:             See the Return Value section.
*/

int display::buffer_pointer_stack::Top(void)
{
   return (top);
}


// End Top
//-----------------------------------------------------------------------------


// End Display.cpp
//-----------------------------------------------------------------------------
```

The file *Display.cpp* begins by including the header files it uses. One of these, *dos.h,* is specific to MS DOS. Therefore, *Display.cpp* uses an `#ifdef` directive to conditionally include it. In addition, *Display.cpp* defines a number of constants, a macro, and some functions that are specific to MS DOS. These are also conditionally compiled.

The constructor for the `display` object contains code statements that are specific to MS DOS. These statements save the user's current video mode. They then set the video mode to a commonly used text mode and turn the cursor on. The destructor uses the video mode that the constructor saved. It restores the user's screen to whatever video mode it was in prior to launching the text editor.

Display.cpp defines two `Clear()` functions for the `display` class. The first takes no parameters. It clears the entire screen. The second clears a portion of the screen. It takes four parameters, which define the top, bottom, left, and right edges of the area to be cleared.

The `display` class also provides two overloaded `Print()` functions. The first prints a single character in a specified style. The styles in which the functions print are contained in the `display_style` enumerated type. The `Print()` function converts the generic styles defined in the `display_style` enumerated type into print styles that are specific to MS DOS. The MS DOS–specific print styles are called *attributes*. `Print()` writes the character, with its attribute, out to the screen. It then advances the hardware cursor. If the cursor will move off of the screen, the `Print()` function moves it to the beginning of the next line. If not, it simply moves the cursor one column to the right. When it has calculated the appropriate position for the cursor, the `Print()` function sets the cursor's position.

The second version of `display::Print()` prints a string to the screen. It uses a loop to call the first version of `Print()` and print each character in the string.

Display.cpp defines two overloaded functions for the display class called `PrintAt()`. These two functions print output at a specific location on the screen. The first `PrintAt()` function prints a single character. The second prints a string. When a program calls either one of the two `PrintAt()` functions, it can specify where on the screen the output should be printed.

The `display` class provides the cursor movement functions `CursorUp()`, `CursorDown()`, `CursorLeft()`, and `CursorRight()`. In addition, it enables programs to set and get the hardware cursor's row and column position with the overloaded functions `CursorRow()` and `CursorCol()`.

The file *Display.cpp* defines some functions that programs use to increase their portability. These are `CharacterWidth()`, `CharacterHeight()`, `StringHeight()`, `StringWidth()`, `FirstRow()`, `LastRow()`, `FirstCol()`, and `LastCol()`. The `display` class provides these functions so that the program has a way of asking about the physical characteristics of the screen. The current version of the text editor is implemented for MS DOS text mode. In this mode, screen locations are measured in character positions. The upper left corner of the display is numbered row 1, column 1. If we wanted to port this program to MS Windows, locations on the screen would be specified by pixel positions, not character positions. In MS DOS text mode, there are 80 characters across and 25 rows of text. Under Windows, there might be 640 pixels across the screen and 460 rows of pixels. The user may have his screen set to 800 pixels across and 600 rows of pixels. Or he may be using another screen resolution that Windows supports. Under Windows, we don't know the dimensions of the screen in advance. The same may be true under other operating systems.

The point is, we want to provide our program with a way of positioning and sizing its output that is independent of the screen resolution. This makes the program portable to other hardware and operating systems. To accomplish this, the `display` class provides functions the program can use to query the current characteristics of the screen.

As mentioned previously, the `display` class provides functions to save and restore rectangular areas of the screen. The text editor uses these functions to save areas where it displays menus. To make saving and restoring easier, the `display` class keeps a private list of screen areas it saves. Recall that this list is a stack.

Two primary operations can be performed on a stack: push and pop. To push data onto the stack means that the program is saving data. When a program pops data off the stack, it retrieves and removes the data from the stack.

In this program, the stack is implemented as an object with an array of pointers. The pointers on the stack contain the address of a block of memory. The block of memory holds the contents of the rectangular area that was saved from the screen. The array of pointers contains the number of elements specified by the constant `MAX_STACK_SIZE`. In this implementation, `MAX_STACK_SIZE` is set to 20. This limits the number of rectangular screen areas that can be saved at any one time to 20. In the exercises at the end of this chapter, you'll rewrite the `buffer_pointer_stack` class so that it uses dynamic allocation.

The `buffer_pointer_stack` class provides a constructor, a destructor, a `Push()` function, a `Pop()` function, and a `Top()` function. The constructor initializes every pointer in the stack array to `NULL`. If there are any rectangular areas left on the stack when the program exits, the `buffer_pointer_stack` destructor deletes them. The `Push()` function puts a pointer to a rectangular area onto the stack. The `Pop()` function retrieves it. The `Top()` function returns the index number of the top of the stack. The top of the stack is where the next item will be placed. The `display` class can use the `Top()` function and the `MAX_STACK_SIZE` constant to test to see whether the stack is full.

Troubleshooting Guide

After reading this section, you should be able to:

- Appropriately control the scope of functions.
- Recognize and implement design alternatives for the display class.

The Scope of Functions

If you look at some of the functions in *Display.cpp*, you may notice that they're defined differently. The functions `GetVideoMode()` and `SetVideoMode()` are declared static. They cannot be accessed by functions defined outside *Display.cpp*. The functions `GetCursorPosition()`, `SetCursorPosition()`, `WriteCharacterAndAttribute()`, and `ReadCharacterAndAttribute()` are inline functions. Inline functions are available only in the file in which they're defined. If we wanted them available in files besides *Display.cpp*, we would need to move them to *Display.h* or create a file called *Display.inl*.

Both the static and inline functions in *Display.cpp* are visible only to functions in *Display.cpp*. Which is better to use for functions whose scope we want to restrict to a particular *CPP* file, static or inline functions?

As you might expect, the answer is, it depends. Both static and inline functions are invisible outside the *CPP* file in which they're defined. Static functions are true functions. When the program calls a static function, it jumps to the function's code. The compiler substitutes the code of an inline function into the executable file wherever the program calls the inline function. An inline function results in faster, but bigger programs. Static functions result in smaller, but slightly slower programs. The trade-off is speed versus size.

The text editor calls the static functions `GetVideoMode()` and `SetVideoMode()` when the program is starting up and shutting down. It calls the inline functions `GetCursorPosition()`, `SetCursorPosition()`, `WriteCharacterAndAttribute()`, and `ReadCharacterAndAttribute()` repeatedly throughout the program. To balance speed and size, the helper functions in this file that aren't called much are made static. The helper functions in this file that are called a lot are inline. That's generally the style that experienced C++ programmers follow.

Notice also that the functions `CursorOn()` and `CursorOff()` are neither static nor inline. This makes them potentially visible throughout the entire program. Is that really what we want? Well, that depends on the program. It is reasonable that we might want programs to be able to turn the cursor on and off. If that's the case, then `CursorOn()` and `CursorOff()` should be members of the `display` class. Their prototypes should appear in the public section of the `display` class. If that's not the case, then these functions should either be made inline or static.

So why are these functions defined the way they are in this implementation?

It was a mistake. I left it in to show how the design process really works. When I first designed the `display` class, the `CursorOn()` and `CursorOff()` functions were public members of the `display` class. I later decided to remove them from the class and make them invisible outside *Display.cpp*. While revising my design, I removed them from the class but didn't decide at that time whether they should be inline or static. I wanted to wait until I designed the class more completely to see how much they were called. The problem with doing that is that I never did go back and finish revising my design. I forgot to make the decision as to whether these two functions should be inline or static.

As a result, I implemented the functions according to my design, which was wrong. I followed my design exactly and didn't make these functions inline or static. An error like this is easy to make. I should have revised my design so that the scope of these two functions was strictly controlled. It would have been easy to go back and make them visible outside of *Display.cpp* if I later found it necessary. By putting off the decision and not revising the design, I opened a way for errors to creep into my program.

You will make mistakes similar to this. We all do. If we're aware of the types of mistakes we make, we can often spot them before they get into program code.

Redesigning the `display` Object

The `buffer_pointer_stack` object in the `display` class keeps a list of pointers to buffers that contain rectangular areas saved from the screen. The rectangular areas hold characters and their attributes. The list in the `buffer_pointer_stack` class is a stack. The last pointer pushed onto the stack is the first one that will be popped off.

This implementation works well for the text editor's menu system. However, it's possible that we may not want to use this last-in-first-out style of data storage. For example, if we implement dialog boxes in the editor, the program will need to save a rectangular area where it will display the dialog box. It may also need to leave the menus active. If so, then it's very possible that the program will need to restore a screen area other than the last one saved. This presents us with a problem.

There are two solutions we could use. We could use a different kind of rectangle list in the `display` object. If we did, it would enable us to save and restore screen rectangles in any order. Another possible solution is to not have the list be internal to the `display` class. We can define a type in *Display.h* called `screen_data`, like this:

```
typedef unsigned screen_data;
```

Using this implementation, we can change the prototypes of `SaveArea()` and `RestoreArea()` in the display class definition to the following:

```
screen_data *SaveArea(display_coordinate left,
                      display_coordinate top,
                      display_coordinate right,
                      display_coordinate bottom);
```

```
void RestoreArea(screen_data *screenBuffer,
                 const display_coordinate left,
                 const display_coordinate top,
                 const display_coordinate right,
                 const display_coordinate bottom);
```

This implementation has SaveArea() allocate memory for the rectangular area it saves. It returns a pointer to that memory to the text editor program. This makes the text editor responsible for keeping its own list of screen areas. However, the text editor doesn't have to "know" how the screen areas are implemented. The screen_data type can be different for every type of computer and every operating system.

The advantage of this implementation is that it provides the programmer with quite a bit of flexibility. One of the disadvantages is that it does not prevent the program from restoring a rectangular area to the wrong location on the screen. Another problem with this implementation is that it doesn't prevent a program from directly manipulating the contents of a rectangular screen area it saved. The contents of the rectangular screen areas are dependent on the hardware and operating system. We want the program to be portable.

We can fix these problems by making the screen_data an object. Example 29.1 demonstrates a possible implementation of the screen_data object.

EXAMPLE 29.1 The screen_data Object

```
class screen_data
{
public:
   screen_data(void);
   ~screen_data();

private:
   friend class display;
private:
   unsigned *screenBuffer;
   display_coordinate left, right, top, bottom.
};
```

Example 29.1 shows that the screen_data object stores the data saved from the screen. It also stores the location from which it saved the data. This implementation prevents a program from manipulating the screen buffer data directly. It also makes sure the data gets restored to its original location.

Notice that the only two public member functions of the screen_data class are its constructor and destructor. The display class is a friend of the screen_data class. These two classes have high cohesion. A program must use both of them to use either of them.

In this implementation, the display::SaveArea() function would set the private data members of a screen_data object. The display::RestoreArea() function would use the screen_data object's private member data to restore the screen area.

Implementing the display class in this way enables programmers to have the flexibility they want without introducing too much potential for errors.

Summary

The input_device and display objects encapsulate the input and output hardware. They make the text editor program more portable. Together, these two classes also give the program full-screen editing capabilities.

The input_device class declares a global variable called inputDevice. The display class declares a global variable named theScreen. The global variables increase convenience when writing the text editor. However, they also increase the cohesion in the code. It becomes less modular. If you use global variables you must be aware of these trade-offs.

Review Questions

1. What are the advantages of using the global variables defined in *InputDev.h* and *Display.h*? What are the disadvantages?
2. What are the advantages of encapsulating the hardware with C++ classes? What are the disadvantages?
3. Why do programmers often find it necessary to write their own input and output classes when `istream` and `ostream` are provided by the C++ Standard Library?
4. How do you use conditional compilation to make portable software?
5. What functions in the `display` class make it more portable? How do they accomplish that?
6. Why does *Display.h* define the type `display_coordinate`? What are the advantages of using this type? Are there any disadvantages?
7. Is it better to define the `buffer_pointer_stack` as a private type inside the `display` class, or as a public type with its own *H* and *CPP* files? What are your reasons for your answer?
8. Why does *InputDev.h* define the `raw_input` type? Wouldn't it be better just to use characters? Why or why not?
9. Are there differences between the implementations of the `input_device` and `display` classes? Why do you think that is? What would you do to remedy problems such as this when you are designing software?
10. Which is better to use for functions that you don't want seen outside of a *CPP* file: inline functions or static functions? Why?

Exercises

1. The keyword `const` was not used in the prototypes of many of the functions in the text editor. Rewrite the files presented in this chapter. Make as many `const` functions, parameters, and return types as you can. Explain which functions cannot be made `const` and why. Explain which parameters cannot be made `const` and why. Explain which return types cannot be made `const` and why.
2. The `display` class requires the use of the `text_string` class. This means that there is high cohesion between these two modules. One way to lower the cohesion is to change all of the references to `text_string` objects to use the type `char *`. Explain the advantages and disadvantages of this approach.
3. The files *InputDev.h* and *Display.h* declare global variables. One possible way to eliminate these global variables is to create private members of the `desktop` object that are of type `input_device` and `display`. Explain the advantages and disadvantages of this approach.
4. Explain the advantages and disadvantages of implementing the background rectangle buffer using the `screen_data` object described in the Troubleshooting Guide. Implement a version of the text editor that uses the `screen_data` object.
5. In the current implementations of the `input_device` and the `display` classes, there is nothing to stop a programmer from declaring more than one `input_device` and `display` object in a program. Rewrite these two objects so that there can be only one `input_device` object and one `display` object in each program.
6. Rewrite the `buffer_pointer_stack` class to use a dynamically allocated array of pointers. When the stack gets full, have the class double the size of the pointer array. Explain the advantages and disadvantages of this approach.
7. Decide whether the `CursorOn()` and `CursorOff()` functions should be inline, static, or members of the display class. Explain the reasons you chose the implementation you did. Rewrite the text editor to use the implementation you chose.
8. The version of the `display::Clear()` function that has this prototype:

   ```
   void display::Clear(int left,int top,int right,int bottom);
   ```

   is written with the assumption that the parameters `top`, `bottom`, `left`, and `right` are all greater than or equal to zero. Rewrite this function so that it enforces these assumptions.

9. Find functions in the file *Display.cpp* besides `display::Clear()` that have programmer assumptions built into them. Rewrite those functions so that they enforce the assumptions. *Hint:* Focus on the allowable values of input parameters to functions.
10. Most of the member functions in the `display` class have the `void` return type. Some of these functions can and should return an error status value. Explain which functions should return an error status. List the error status values each function should return.

Chapter Glossary

Data Structure An organized collection of data.

Stack A data structure commonly used in computer programming. The last data item pushed onto the stack is always the first one that will be popped off.

30 Developing the Text Editor: TBuffer.h, TBuffer.cpp, TString.h, and TString.cpp

Objectives

After reading this chapter, you should be able to:

- Implement the text editor source files *TBuffer.h, TBuffer.cpp, TString.h,* and *TString.cpp.*
- Integrate and debug the objects and functions in these files.
- Name and explain other implementation alternatives.

Preview

The `text_buffer` and `text_string` objects implement the text editor's lower-level string handing. This chapter presents the files *TBuffer.h, TBuffer.cpp, TString.h,* and *TString.cpp.*

Writing TBuffer.h

The `text_buffer` contains a collection of `text_string` objects. It provides functions for inserting characters into the buffer, moving the insertion point, and scrolling the buffer. It also has functions for loading a text file into the buffer, saving the buffer to a text file, and getting the buffer status. Listing 30.1 displays the source code for *TBuffer.h.*

LISTING 30.1 TBuffer.h

```
//-----------------------------------------------------------------------
/*
File Name:   TBuffer.h
Comments:    This file contains the definition of the text_buffer class. It
             also defines the constants needed to use the text_buffer class.
*/
//-----------------------------------------------------------------------


#if !defined (TBUFFER_H)
#define TBUFFER_H


//-----------------------------------------------------------------------
// Include Files

#include "TString.h"
```

```
// End Include Files
//---------------------------------------------------------------------------



//---------------------------------------------------------------------------
// Constants

const int TEXT_BUFFER_LENGTH = 100;
const int TEXT_BUFFER_WIDTH = 75;

// End Constants
//---------------------------------------------------------------------------



//---------------------------------------------------------------------------
// Class Definitions

class text_buffer
{
// Public types.
public:
   enum text_buffer_error
   {
      NO_ERROR = 0,
      CANT_LOAD_FILE = -1,
      CANT_SAVE_FILE = -2,
      CANT_ADD_CHAR_TO_BUFFER = -3
   };

// Public functions.
public:
   text_buffer(void);

   void PutCharacter(char newCharacter);
   unsigned TopLine(void);
   int LinesUsed(void);

   text_string &operator [](int index);

   unsigned ScrollUp(const unsigned linesToScroll);
   unsigned ScrollDown(const unsigned linesToScroll);
   unsigned ScrollTo(const unsigned newTopLine);

   unsigned InsertionPointRow(const unsigned destinationRow);
   unsigned InsertionPointRow(void);
   unsigned InsertionPointCol(const unsigned destinationCol);
   unsigned InsertionPointCol(void);

   void Load(const text_string &fileName);
   void Save(const text_string &fileName);

   bool IsDirty(void);

   text_buffer::text_buffer_error ErrorStatus(void);
   void ClearError(void);

// Private data.
```

```
private:
   text_string textBuffer[TEXT_BUFFER_LENGTH];
   unsigned topLine;
   unsigned linesUsed;
   unsigned insertionPointRow, insertionPointCol;
   bool dirty;
   text_buffer_error errorStatus;
};

// End Class Definitions
//-------------------------------------------------------------------------

#endif

// End TBuffer.h
//-------------------------------------------------------------------------
```

The array in the `text_buffer` contains `text_string` objects. Therefore, *TBuffer.h* includes the file *TString.h*. It next defines a pair of constants. These constants define the size of the array of text strings.

Like most of the objects in this program, the `text_buffer` class definition contains a public enumerated type that defines a list of error identifiers. As with many of the other classes in this program, the error status constants were not thought out in the design (see Chapter 27). During the design process, it is wise to try to anticipate as many error conditions an object may have as you possibly can. This will help decrease the likelihood of design errors.

Writing TBuffer.cpp

The implementation of the `text_buffer` class is in *TBuffer.cpp,* which is shown in Listing 30.2.

LISTING 30.2 TBuffer.cpp

```
//-------------------------------------------------------------------------
/*
File Name:   TBuffer.cpp
Comments:    This file contains the implementation of the member functions for
             the text_buffer class.
*/
//-------------------------------------------------------------------------



//-------------------------------------------------------------------------
// Include Files

#include <fstream.h>
#include "TString.h"
#include "TBuffer.h"
#include <assert.h>

// End Include Files
//-------------------------------------------------------------------------



//-------------------------------------------------------------------------
/*
```

```
Function Name:        text_buffer
Member of:            text_buffer
Input Parameters:     None.
Output Parameters:    None.
Return Value:         Initialized text_buffer object.
Comments:             This function is the default constructor for the
                      text_buffer class.
*/

text_buffer::text_buffer(void)
{
   topLine=0;
   linesUsed=0;
   insertionPointRow = 0;
   insertionPointCol = 0;
   dirty = false;
   errorStatus = NO_ERROR;
}

// End text_buffer
//---------------------------------------------------------------------------




//---------------------------------------------------------------------------
/*
Function Name:        PutCharacter
Member of:            text_buffer
Input Parameters:     newCharacter - The character to insert into the text
                         buffer.
Output Parameters:    None.
Return Value:         None.
Comments:             This function inserts a character into the text buffer
                      at the current insertion point. If a character is
                      already there, it will be overwritten. This function
                      asserts that the insertion point is not beyond the end
                      of the current line of text. Characters can be inserted
                      anywhere within the current line. They can also be
                      appended to the end of the line.
*/

void text_buffer::PutCharacter(char newCharacter)
{
   int length = textBuffer[insertionPointRow].Length();

   assert(insertionPointCol <= length);
   assert(newCharacter != '\0');

   // If the line is shorter than the maximum allowed length...
   if (insertionPointCol < TEXT_BUFFER_WIDTH)
   {
      // If we're inserting a character somewhere inside the string...
      if (insertionPointCol < length)
      {
         // Type over the existing character
         textBuffer[insertionPointRow][insertionPointCol++] = newCharacter;

      }
```

```
        // Else we're appending it to the end of the string...
        else
         {
            // Put it on the end (The += function adjusts the length).
            textBuffer[insertionPointRow] += newCharacter;

            // Set the insertion point column to the new length of the string.
            insertionPointCol = textBuffer[insertionPointRow].Length();

        }

        // If the insertion point is beyond the the last line in use...
        if (insertionPointRow >= linesUsed)
        {
            // Set the number of lines used.
            linesUsed = insertionPointRow + 1;
        }

        // A character was added. Mark the buffer as dirty.
        dirty=true;
    }
    // Ignore the character if it's not added.
}

// End PutCharacter
//-----------------------------------------------------------------------------



//-----------------------------------------------------------------------------
/*
Function Name:       TopLine
Member of:           text_buffer
Input Parameters:    None.
Output Parameters:   None.
Return Value:        This function returns the top line of the buffer.
Comments:            See the Return Value section.
*/

unsigned text_buffer::TopLine(void)
{
    return (topLine);
}

// End TopLine
//-----------------------------------------------------------------------------



//-----------------------------------------------------------------------------
/*
Function Name:       LinesUsed
Member of:           text_buffer
Input Parameters:    None.
Output Parameters:   None.
Return Value:        Returns the number of lines of text currently in use in
                     the buffer.
Comments:            See the Return Value section.
*/
```

```
int text_buffer::LinesUsed(void)
{
   return (linesUsed);
}

// End LinesUsed
//-------------------------------------------------------------------------------



//-------------------------------------------------------------------------------
/*
Function Name:       operator []
Member of:           text_buffer
Input Parameters:    index - The index number of the line being accessed.
Output Parameters:   None.
Return Value:        This function returns a reference to a text string in
                     the text buffer.
Comments:            The operator [] function makes a text_buffer object
                     look and act very much like an array. Note, however,
                     that any function that returns a reference to an
                     object inside it can suffer from aliasing problems.

                     In particular, this function enables a programmer
                     using this object to write text into the buffer
                     without using the text_buffer::PutCharacter function.
                     If that happens, the buffer will not be marked as
                     dirty, and the private data member linesUsed may not
                     contain the correct value.
*/

text_string &text_buffer::operator [](int index)
{
   assert((index>=0) && (index<linesUsed));
   return (textBuffer[index]);
}

// End operator []
//-------------------------------------------------------------------------------



//-------------------------------------------------------------------------------
/*
Function Name:       ScrollUp
Member of:           text_buffer
Input Parameters:    linesToScroll - Integer number of lines to scroll toward
                         the beginning of the text buffer.
Output Parameters:   None.
Return Value:        Returns the number of lines actually scrolled.
Comments:            This function moves the current top line of the buffer
                     that is displayed on the screen toward the beginning of
                     the buffer. It prevents the top line from being moved
                     before the beginning of the buffer.

                     If, for instance, the current top line is 5, and the
                     input parameter specifies that the function should
                     scroll the buffer up 20 lines, it will only scroll 5
                     lines to the beginning of the buffer. The return value
```

```
                    reports the number of lines the function actually
                    scrolls.
*/

unsigned text_buffer::ScrollUp(const unsigned linesToScroll)
{
   assert(linesToScroll > 0);

   unsigned linesScrolled;

   // If the top line is less than the number of lines to scroll...
   if (topLine <= linesToScroll)
   {
      /* The first screenful of the buffer is currently displayed.
      Display the buffer from the beginning. */
      linesScrolled = topLine;
      topLine=0;
   }
   // Else scroll the screen toward the beginning of the buffer.
   else
   {
      topLine -= linesToScroll;
      linesScrolled = linesToScroll;
   }
   return (linesScrolled);
}

// End ScrollUp
//----------------------------------------------------------------------------



//----------------------------------------------------------------------------
/*
Function Name:       ScrollDown
Member of:           text_buffer
Input Parameters:    linesToScroll - The number of lines to scroll down.
Output Parameters:   None.
Return Value:        Returns the number of lines actually scrolled.
Comments:            This function moves the current top line of the buffer
                     that is displayed on the screen toward the end of
                     the buffer. It prevents the top line from being moved
                     after the end of the buffer.

                     Suppose, for instance, that the buffer is 100 lines of
                     text in length. If the current top line is 95, and the
                     input parameter specifies that the function should
                     scroll the buffer down 20 lines, it will only scroll 5
                     lines toward the end of the buffer. The return value
                     reports the number of lines the function actually
                     scrolls.
*/

unsigned text_buffer::ScrollDown(const unsigned linesToScroll)
{
   assert(linesToScroll > 0);

   unsigned linesScrolled;
   unsigned newTopLine = topLine+linesToScroll;
```

```
    // If the last few lines of the buffer are currently displayed...
    if ((newTopLine >= linesUsed-linesToScroll) ||
        (newTopLine >= TEXT_BUFFER_LENGTH-linesToScroll))
    {
        // Set the top line to display the last few lines of the buffer.
        topLine = linesUsed-linesToScroll;
        linesScrolled = newTopLine-topLine;
    }
    // Else the end of the buffer is not currently displayed...
    else
    {
        // Scroll down the requested number of lines.
        topLine = newTopLine;
        linesScrolled = linesToScroll;
    }
    return (linesScrolled);
}

// End ScrollDown
//-----------------------------------------------------------------------------



//-----------------------------------------------------------------------------
/*
Function Name:      ScrollTo
Member of:          text_buffer
Input Parameters:   newTopLine - The line that the buffer will be scrolled to.
Output Parameters:  None.
Return Value:       Returns the number of lines actually scrolled.
Comments:           This function moves the current top line of the buffer
                    that is displayed on the screen toward the end of
                    the buffer. It prevents the top line from being moved
                    after the end of the buffer.
*/

unsigned text_buffer::ScrollTo(const unsigned newTopLine)
{
    unsigned linesToScroll=0;
    unsigned tempTopLine = newTopLine;

    if (newTopLine>=linesUsed)
    {
        tempTopLine = linesUsed-1;
    }

    if (tempTopLine < topLine)
    {
        linesToScroll = topLine-tempTopLine;
    }
    else if (tempTopLine > topLine)
    {
        linesToScroll = newTopLine - topLine;
    }

    topLine = tempTopLine;
    return (linesToScroll);
}
```

```
// End ScrollTo
//-----------------------------------------------------------------------------



//-----------------------------------------------------------------------------
/*
Function Name:       Load
Member of:           text_buffer
Input Parameters:    fileName - Name of the file to load.
Output Parameters:   None.
Return Value:        If the file is loaded successfully, this function
                     returns NO_BUFFER_ERROR. If not, it returns
                     CANT_LOAD_FILE.
Comments:            This function loads the specified file into the
                     text buffer. Any file error will generate a
                     CANT_LOAD_FILE error. A text_buffer object for a
                     professional application would need to provide more
                     specific feedback to the function that calls this
                     routine.
*/

void text_buffer::Load(const text_string &fileName)
{
   // If the file name string is not empty...
   if (fileName.Length() > 0)
   {
      char tempString[MAX_INPUT_STRING_LENGTH];

      // Open the file.
      ifstream inputStream(fileName.CppString());

      // If the file could be opened...
      if (inputStream)
      {
         // Read in each line of text.
         unsigned i;
         bool done = false;
         for (i=0;
              (i<TEXT_BUFFER_LENGTH) && (!done);
              i++)
         {
            /* If the line of text in the file is longer than
            MAX_TEXT_STRING_LENGTH, it is truncated. */
            inputStream.getline(tempString,MAX_INPUT_STRING_LENGTH,'\n');

            // If this is not the end of the file...
            if (!inputStream.eof())
            {
               // Put the string into the buffer.
               textBuffer[i] = tempString;
            }
            // Else we're at the end of the file...
            else
            {
               done=true;
            }
         }
```

```
            // Set the number of lines used...
            linesUsed = i;
         }
         // Else the file could not be opened...
         else
         {
            errorStatus = CANT_LOAD_FILE;
         }
      }
      // Else the file name string was empty...
      else
      {
         errorStatus = CANT_LOAD_FILE;
      }
   }

   // End Load
   //--------------------------------------------------------------------------



   //--------------------------------------------------------------------------
   /*
   Function Name:       Save
   Member of:           text_buffer
   Input Parameters:    fileName - The name of the file to save.
   Output Parameters:   None.
   Return Value:        This function returns NO_BUFFER_ERROR if it successfully
                        saves the specified file. If there is any kind of file
                        error, it returns CANT_SAVE_FILE.
   Comments:            This function saves the text buffer into the
                        specified file. Any file error will generate a
                        CANT_SAVE_FILE error. A text_buffer object for a
                        professional application would need to provide more
                        specific feedback to the function that calls this
                        routine.
   */

   void text_buffer::Save(const text_string &fileName)
   {
      // If the file name string is not empty...
      {
         // Open the file.
         // If the file could be opened...
         {
            // Write each line of the buffer to the file.
            // Mark the buffer as not dirty.
         }
         // Else the file could not be opened...
         {
         }
      }
      // Else the file name string is empty...
      {
      }
   }

   // End Save
```

```
//-----------------------------------------------------------------------------



//-----------------------------------------------------------------------------
/*
Function Name:       InsertionPointRow
Member of:           text_buffer
Input Parameters:    destinationRow - The row to which the insertion point
                        will be moved.
Output Parameters:   None.
Return Value:        This function returns the actual insertion point row.
Comments:            The InsertionPointRow function sets the row number
                     of the insertion point in the text buffer. Row numbering
                     begins with zero.

                     The insertion point is not set to the requested row if
                     the requested row is beyond the end of the buffer.
*/

unsigned text_buffer::InsertionPointRow(const unsigned destinationRow)
{
   if (destinationRow<TEXT_BUFFER_LENGTH)
   {
      insertionPointRow = destinationRow;

      if (destinationRow >= linesUsed)
      {
         linesUsed = destinationRow+1;
      }
   }

   return (insertionPointRow);
}
// End InsertionPointRow
//-----------------------------------------------------------------------------



//-----------------------------------------------------------------------------
/*
Function Name:       InsertionPointRow
Member of:           text_buffer
Input Parameters:    None.
Output Parameters:   None.
Return Value:        This function returns the current insertion point row.
Comments:            See the Return Value section.
*/

unsigned text_buffer::InsertionPointRow(void)
{
   return (insertionPointRow);
}

// End InsertionPointRow
//-----------------------------------------------------------------------------
```

```
//-----------------------------------------------------------------------------
/*
Function Name:       InsertionPointCol
Member of:           text_buffer
Input Parameters:    None.
Output Parameters:   None.
Return Value:        This function returns the insertion point column.
Comments:            Column numbering begins with zero.
*/

unsigned text_buffer::InsertionPointCol(void)
{
   return (insertionPointCol);
}

// End InsertionPointCol
//-----------------------------------------------------------------------------



//-----------------------------------------------------------------------------
/*
Function Name:       InsertionPointCol
Member of:           text_buffer
Input Parameters:    destinationCol - The column to which the insertion point
                        will be moved.
Output Parameters:   None.
Return Value:        This function returns the actual insertion point column.
Comments:            The InsertionPointCol function sets the column number
                     of the insertion point in the text buffer. Column
                     numbering begins with zero.

                     The insertion point is not set to the requested row if
                     the requested column is beyond the width of the buffer.
*/

unsigned text_buffer::InsertionPointCol(const unsigned destinationCol)
{
   if (destinationCol<TEXT_BUFFER_WIDTH)
   {
      insertionPointCol = destinationCol;
   }
   else
   {
      insertionPointCol = TEXT_BUFFER_WIDTH -1;
   }

   return (insertionPointCol);
}

// End InsertionPointCol
//-----------------------------------------------------------------------------



//-----------------------------------------------------------------------------
/*
```

```
Function Name:       IsDirty
Member of:           text_buffer
Input Parameters:    None.
Output Parameters:   None.
Return Value:        This function returns true if the buffer has been
                     modified since it was last saved. Otherwise, it returns
                     false.
Comments:            See the Return Value section.
*/

bool text_buffer::IsDirty(void)
{
   return (dirty);
}

// End IsDirty
//---------------------------------------------------------------------------



//---------------------------------------------------------------------------
/*
Function Name:       ErrorStatus
Member of:           text_buffer
Input Parameters:    None.
Output Parameters:   None.
Return Value:        This function returns the text buffer's current error
                     status.
Comments:            See the Return Value section.
*/

text_buffer::text_buffer_error text_buffer::ErrorStatus(void)
{
   return (errorStatus);
}

// End ErrorStatus
//---------------------------------------------------------------------------



//---------------------------------------------------------------------------
/*
Function Name:       ClearError
Member of:           text_buffer
Input Parameters:    None.
Output Parameters:   None.
Return Value:        None.
Comments:            The ClearError function clears the text buffer's error
                     status. This is useful if a non-fatal error occurs. Your
                     program can just print an error message, clear the error
                     status, and go on.
*/

void text_buffer::ClearError(void)
{
   errorStatus = NO_ERROR;
}
```

```
// End ClearError
//-----------------------------------------------------------------------

// End TBuffer.cpp
//-----------------------------------------------------------------------
```

Like most files in this program, *TBuffer.cpp* begins by including the header files it requires. The text_buffer object reads from and writes to text files. For this reason, it includes the C++ Standard Library file *fstream.h*.

As all constructors should, the text_buffer constructor initializes a text_buffer object into a known state. Since the text_buffer class does not currently use dynamic allocation, it doesn't need a destructor. If we modified the class to dynamically allocate memory for the text_string objects it contains, we would need to add a destructor.

The text_buffer::PutCharacter() function provides the text editor program with the ability to insert a character into the text_buffer at the current insertion point location. The PutCharacter() function inserts the character within the bounds of the array of text_string objects. It adjusts the state of the text_buffer as necessary. For example, if it inserts a character into the text_buffer, it marks the text_buffer as dirty. Saving the text_buffer to a file makes it clean.

The text_buffer class provides the TopLine() and LinesUsed() functions. Programs use them to query the state of the text_buffer.

The next function in the text_buffer class, operator [](), is potentially rather dangerous. It's discussed in the Troubleshooting Guide near the end of this chapter.

The ScrollUp(), ScrollDown(), and ScrollTo() functions control the private data member topLine. ScrollUp() moves it toward the beginning of the file. ScrollDown() moves it toward the end. ScrollTo() sets topLine to the line number specified in the parameter newTopLine. Together, these three functions ensure that topLine stays within the bounds of the private array textBuffer.

If it can open the file, the Load() function opens the text file specified by the parameter fileName. If, for some reason, the Load() function can't open the file, it sets an error status variable. If it does open the file, it reads text from the file using the istream::getline() function from the C++ Standard Library.

Notice that the Load() function throws away excess text. If the file contains too many characters on a line, the Load() function throws away the extra characters on that line. If there are more lines in the file than the text_buffer can contain, Load() doesn't read them into the buffer. In a professional program, users would not appreciate this behavior. Using dynamic memory allocation, you can alter the text_buffer object to accept lines of text of any length. You can also enhance it to allocate a larger array of text_string objects. In fact, you can use dynamic allocation to enable the array to grow to the limits of memory.

Although the text_buffer class contains the prototype for the Save() function, it is not fully implemented. It generally follows the same logic as the Load() function. The primary difference is the direction the text is moving. You will implement this function in one of the exercises at the end of this chapter.

The overloaded InsertionPointRow() and InsertionPointCol() functions enable the program to control the position of the insertion point. They also ensure that the insertion point is always at a valid location inside the text buffer.

The functions IsDirty(), ErrorStatus(), and ClearError() are all quite straightforward. They provide the text editor with the ability to query the status of a text_buffer object.

Writing TString.h

TString.h presents the class definition of the text_string object. This object is fundamental to our design of the text editor. Many of the other objects in this program depend on it. Listing 30.3 shows the code for *TString.h*.

LISTING 30.3 TString.h

```
//-----------------------------------------------------------------------------
/*
File Name:  TString.h
Comments:   This file contains the constants and class definition needed to
            use the text_string class.
*/
//-----------------------------------------------------------------------------


#if !defined(TSTRING_H)
#define TSTRING_H

//-----------------------------------------------------------------------------
// Include Files

#include <iostream.h>

// End Include Files
//-----------------------------------------------------------------------------


//-----------------------------------------------------------------------------
// Constants

const int MAX_INPUT_STRING_LENGTH = 256;

// End Constants
//-----------------------------------------------------------------------------



//-----------------------------------------------------------------------------
// Class Definitions

class text_string
{
// Public member functions.
public:
   text_string(void);
   text_string(const char * const charArray);
   text_string(const text_string &sourceString);
   ~text_string();

   text_string &operator = (const text_string &textString);
   text_string &operator = (const char * const charArray);

   text_string operator + (const text_string &textString);
   text_string operator + (const char * const charArray);

   text_string &operator += (const text_string &textString);
   text_string &operator += (const char * const charArray);
   text_string &operator += (const char oneChar);

   char &operator [](const int index);

   friend istream &operator >> (istream &inputStream,
                                text_string &destinationString);
```

```
    friend ostream &operator << (ostream &outputStream,
                                 const text_string &sourceString);

    const char *CppString(void) const;

    int Length(void) const;

// Private member functions.
private:
    void Allocate(const int totalChars);
    text_string &Copy(const text_string &sourceString);
    text_string &Copy(const char * const charArray);

// Private member data.
private:
    char *charString;
};

// End Class Definitions
//-----------------------------------------------------------------------

#endif

// End TString.h
//-----------------------------------------------------------------------
```

Because the `text_string` class uses the constant `NULL`, *TString.h* includes the C++ Standard Library file *iostream.h*.

In addition, *TString.h* defines a constant that specified the maximum length of an input string. This is done to simplify the `text_buffer::Load()` function. This is a design error. Unfortunately, it's all too common for programmers to define constants in header files to make a class more usable with another class.

The reason this is a design flaw is that the `text_string` class should stand by itself. It is one of the primary building blocks of the text editor. As such, it shouldn't "know" about other classes in the program. Other classes may "know" how to use a `text_string`. However, the `text_string` class should be completely independent of all other classes for maximum reusability. The definition of the constant `MAX_INPUT_STRING_LENGTH` should be in *TBuffer.h,* not *TString.h.* It is the `text_buffer` object, not the `text_string` object, that declares input string variables (see the `text_buffer::Load()` function). Therefore, it should be *TBuffer.h* that declares this constant.

The `text_string` class dynamically allocates the array it uses to store characters. So in addition to its default no-argument constructor, the `text_string` class defines a copy constructor, an assignment operator, and a destructor. It also defines a constructor that enables programs to initialize a `text_string` object to an array of characters.

If you look at the `text_string` class definition, you'll see that a `text_string` can be used in programs together with character arrays and character pointers. Operations such as + and += accept both `text_string` objects and character arrays. Any `text_string` object can be converted to a character array by using the member function `CppString()`.

Like the `text_buffer` class, the `text_string` class provides an `operator []()` function. The advantages and disadvantages of this are discussed in the Troubleshooting Guide at the end of the chapter.

Writing TString.cpp

As you undoubtedly expect, the implementation of the `text_string` class is in *TString.cpp*. The source code is given in Listing 30.4.

LISTING 30.4 TString.cpp

```
//-----------------------------------------------------------------------------
/*
File Name:   TString.cpp
Comments:    This file contains the implementation of the text_string class.
*/
//-----------------------------------------------------------------------------




//-----------------------------------------------------------------------------
// Include Files

#include "TString.h"
#include "string.h"
#include <assert.h>

// End Include Files
//-----------------------------------------------------------------------------




//-----------------------------------------------------------------------------
/*
Function Name:      text_string
Member of:          text_string
Input Parameters:   None.
Output Parameters:  None.
Return Value:       Constructed text_string object.
Comments:           No-arg constructor. Sets the object to a known state.
*/

text_string::text_string(void)
{
   charString = NULL;
}

// End text_string
//-----------------------------------------------------------------------------




//-----------------------------------------------------------------------------
/*
Function Name:      text_string
Member of:          text_string
Input Parameters:   charArray - A pointer to characters. These chars are
                       copied into the object.
Output Parameters:  None.
Return Value:       Constructed text_string object.
Comments:           One-arg constructor. Allocates the memory for the
                    character string. It then calls the private member
                    function Copy() to copy the characters from charArray
                    into the private member data array charString.
*/
```

```
text_string::text_string(const char * const charArray)
{
   // Allocate the memory for the characters.
   Allocate(strlen(charArray));
   Copy(charArray);
}
// End text_string
//-----------------------------------------------------------------------------




//-----------------------------------------------------------------------------
/*
Function Name:       text_string
Member of:           text_string
Input Parameters:    sourceString - A text_string that will be copied into
                        the object.
Output Parameters:   None.
Return Value:        Constructed text_string object.
Comments:            Copy constructor.
*/

text_string::text_string(const text_string &sourceString)
{
   Allocate(sourceString.Length());
   Copy(sourceString);
}

// End text_string
//-----------------------------------------------------------------------------




//-----------------------------------------------------------------------------
/*
Function Name:       text_string
Member of:           ~text_string
Input Parameters:    None.
Output Parameters:   None.
Return Value:        None.
Comments:            Deletes the character array in this object. Sets the
                     private data member charString to NULL just to be safe.
*/

text_string::~text_string()
{
   if (charString)
   {
      delete [] charString;
   }

   charString = NULL;
}

// End ~text_string
//-----------------------------------------------------------------------------
```

```
//---------------------------------------------------------------------------
/*
Function Name:        operator =
Member of:            text_string
Input Parameters:     textString - The object the characters will be copied
                         from.
Output Parameters:    None.
Return Value:         Returns a reference to *this.
Comments:             This function copies characters from a text_string
                      object into the current text_string object. It calls
                      the private member function Copy() to perform the
                      copy.
*/

text_string &text_string::operator = (const text_string &textString)
{
   assert(&textString != this);

   if (charString!=NULL)
   {
      delete [] charString;
   }

   Allocate(textString.Length());
   Copy(textString);
   return (*this);
}

// End operator =
//---------------------------------------------------------------------------



//---------------------------------------------------------------------------
/*
Function Name:        operator =
Member of:            text_string
Input Parameters:     charArray - The array from which the characters will be
                         copied.
Output Parameters:    None.
Return Value:         Returns a reference to *this.
Comments:             This function copies characters from a character array
                      into the current text_string object. It calls the private
                      member function Copy() to perform the copy.
*/

text_string &text_string::operator = (const char * const charArray)
{
   if (charString!=NULL)
   {
      delete [] charString;
   }

   Allocate(strlen(charArray));
   Copy(charArray);
   return (*this);
}
```

```
// End operator =
//-----------------------------------------------------------------------------



//-----------------------------------------------------------------------------
/*
Function Name:      operator +
Member of:          text_string
Input Parameters:   textString - The object containing characters to
                       concatenate onto the end of the current object.
Output Parameters:  None.
Return Value:       Returns the concatenated text_string object.
Comments:           This function concatenates the string in the textString
                    parameter onto the end of the current text_string. This
                    function does not change the textString object or the
                    current object.
*/

text_string text_string::operator + (const text_string &textString)
{
   text_string tempString;
   int i,j;
   int leftStringLength,rightStringLength;

   leftStringLength = Length();
   rightStringLength = textString.Length();

   // Allocate the destination string.
   tempString.Allocate(leftStringLength+rightStringLength);

   // Copy the source string to the destination string.
   tempString.Copy(charString);

   // Copy any additional characters to the destination string.
   for (i=tempString.Length(),j=0;
        (i<leftStringLength+rightStringLength) && (textString.charString[j]);
        i++,j++)
   {
      tempString.charString[i]=textString.charString[j];
   }

   // Put a null character on the end of the destination string.
   charString[i] = '\0';

   return (tempString);
}

// End operator +
//-----------------------------------------------------------------------------



//-----------------------------------------------------------------------------
/*
Function Name:      operator +
Member of:          text_string
```

```
Input Parameters:    charArray - The array containing characters to
                        concatenate onto the end of the current object.
Output Parameters:   None.
Return Value:        Returns the concatenated text_string object.
Comments:            This function concatenates the string in the array
                     charArray onto the end of the current text_string. This
                     function does not change the character array or the
                     current object.
*/

text_string text_string::operator + (const char * const charArray)
{
   return (*this+text_string(charArray));
}

// End operator +
//--------------------------------------------------------------------------



//--------------------------------------------------------------------------
/*
Function Name:       operator +=
Member of:           text_string
Input Parameters:    textString - A text_string object containing characters
                        to append onto the end of the current object.
Output Parameters:   None.
Return Value:        Returns a reference to *this.
Comments:            This function appends characters onto the end of a
                     text_string object. It uses the text_string::operator +()
                     function to do most of its work. This function modifies
                     the current object (*this).
*/

text_string &text_string::operator += (const text_string &textString)
{
   assert(&textString != this);

   *this = *this + textString;
   return (*this);
}

// End operator +=
//--------------------------------------------------------------------------



//--------------------------------------------------------------------------
/*
Function Name:       operator +=
Member of:           text_string
Input Parameters:    charArray - An array of characters that this function
                        will append onto the end of the current object.
Output Parameters:   None.
Return Value:        Returns a reference to *this.
Comments:            This function appends characters onto the end of a
                     text_string object. It uses the text_string::operator +()
```

```
                     function to do most of its work. This function modifies
                     the current object (*this).
*/

text_string &text_string::operator += (const char * const charArray)
{
   *this = *this + charArray;
   return (*this);
}

// End operator +=
//-----------------------------------------------------------------------------




//-----------------------------------------------------------------------------
/*
Function Name:      operator +=
Member of:          text_string
Input Parameters:   oneChar - An character that this function will append
                       onto the end of the current object.
Output Parameters:  None.
Return Value:       Returns a reference to *this.
Comments:           This function appends a single character onto the end
                    of a text_string object. This function modifies
                    the current object (*this).
*/

text_string &text_string::operator += (const char oneChar)
{
   int length = Length()+1;

   char *tempString = charString;   // Save the current chars.
   Allocate(length);                // Allocate a new array of characters.

   //If we're not appending to an empty string...
   if (length>1)
   {
      Copy(tempString);             // Copy the chars into the new array.
   }

   // Append the new character.
   charString[length-1]=oneChar;
   charString[length]='\0';

   // Delete the old array.
   if (tempString != NULL)
   {
      delete tempString;
   }

   return (*this);
}

// End operator +=
//-----------------------------------------------------------------------------
```

```
//-----------------------------------------------------------------------------
/*
Function Name:       operator []
Member of:           text_string
Input Parameters:    index - The index number of the character to set.
                        Numbering starts with zero.
Output Parameters:   None.
Return Value:        If the index is in range, this function returns a
                     reference to the requested character.
Comments:            The intent of this function is to enable developers to
                     get and set individual characters in a text_string
                     object. It provides bounds checking on the index value.
                     If the developer tries to access a character that is out
                     of bounds, this function uses the assert() macro to
                     abort the program.
*/

char &text_string::operator [](const int index)
{
   assert((index >= 0) && (index<Length()));
   return charString[index];
}

// End operator []
//-----------------------------------------------------------------------------



//-----------------------------------------------------------------------------
/*
Function Name:       CppString
Member of:           text_string
Input Parameters:    None.
Output Parameters:   None.
Return Value:        Returns a constant reference to the character array that
                     this text_string object contains.
Comments:            See Return Value section.
*/

const char *text_string::CppString(void) const
{
   return (charString);
}

// End CppString
//-----------------------------------------------------------------------------



//-----------------------------------------------------------------------------
/*
Function Name:       Length
Member of:           text_string
Input Parameters:    None.
Output Parameters:   None.
Return Value:        Returns the length of the string. This is the same as the
```

```
                        number of printable characters (excluding the null
                        character).
Comments:               See Return Value section.
*/

int text_string::Length(void) const
{
   int length=0;

   // If the string is not empty...
   if (charString)
   {
      // Count the number of characters in the string.
      for (length=0;charString[length];length++)
      {
         // Empty loop body. The stuff in the () does the counting.
      }
   }

   return (length);
}

// End Length
//-----------------------------------------------------------------------------



//-----------------------------------------------------------------------------
/*
Function Name:          Allocate
Member of:              text_string
Input Parameters:       totalChars - An integer number of printable characters to
                           allocate space for.
Output Parameters:      None.
Return Value:           None.
Comments:               To accommodate the null character at the end of a string,
                        this function allocates totalChars+1. It also initializes
                        the memory it allocates to null characters.
*/

void text_string::Allocate(const int totalChars)
{
   // If the string is not empty...
   if (totalChars>0)
   {
      // Allocate the new string.
      charString = new char [totalChars+1];

      // If the new string was allocated...
      if (charString)
      {
         // Initialize it to null characters.
         for (int i=0;i<totalChars+1;i++)
         {
            charString[i]='\0';
         }
      }
      // Else the new string was not allocated...
      else
```

```
        {
           charString=NULL;
        }
     }
     // Else the string is empty...
     else
     {
        charString = NULL;
     }
}

// End Allocate
//----------------------------------------------------------------------------



//----------------------------------------------------------------------------
/*
Function Name:       Copy
Member of:           text_string
Input Parameters:    sourceString - The string from which the characters will
                        be copied.
Output Parameters:   None.
Return Value:        Returns a reference to the current object (*this).
Comments:            This private member function copies characters from a
                     text_string object into the current object. This function
                     is written with the assumption that the memory for the
                     destination string has been allocated before Copy is
                     called.
*/

text_string &text_string::Copy(const text_string &sourceString)
{
   // If the source string is not empty...
   if (sourceString.charString)
   {
      int i;

      // Copy characters from the source to the destination string.
      for (i=0;sourceString.charString[i];i++)
      {
         charString[i] = sourceString.charString[i];
      }
      charString[i] = '\0';
   }
   // Else the source string is empty...
   else
   {
      // If the destination string is not empty...
      if (charString)
      {
         // Delete it.
         delete [] charString;
      }

      charString=NULL;
   }

   return (*this);
}
```

```
// End Copy
//-----------------------------------------------------------------------



//-----------------------------------------------------------------------
/*
Function Name:       Copy
Member of:           text_string
Input Parameters:    charArray - The character array from which the characters
                         will be copied.
Output Parameters:   None.
Return Value:        Returns a reference to the current object (*this).
Comments:            This private member function copies characters from a
                     character array into the current object.
*/

text_string &text_string::Copy(const char * const charArray)
{
   int i;

   // If the source string is not empty...
   if (charArray)
   {
      // Copy characters from the source to the destination.
      for (i=0;charArray[i];i++)
      {
         charString[i] = charArray[i];
      }
      charString[i] = '\0';
   }
   // Else the source string is empty...
   else
   {
      // If the destination string is not empty...
      if (charString)
      {
         // Delete it.
         delete [] charString;
      }

      charString=NULL;
   }

   return (*this);
}

// End Copy
//-----------------------------------------------------------------------

// End TString.cpp
//-----------------------------------------------------------------------
```

After *TString.cpp* includes the header files it requires, it provides a constructor for the `text_string` class. The constructor initializes the private data member `charString` to `NULL`.

In addition, the `text_string` class furnishes the text editor program with a constructor that takes a character array as a parameter. It enables us to declare a `text_string` object and initialize it to a C++ character string. The `text_string` class also has a copy constructor and a destructor. These are both necessary for classes that do dynamic allocation.

TString.cpp also defines two `operator =()` functions. Programs use the first one to assign `text_string` objects to `text_string` objects. They use the second `operator =()` function to assign character arrays to `text_string` objects. When a `text_string` object or a character array is assigned to a `text_string`, both of the `operator =()` functions allocate memory and make a copy of the source string. Note that the first `operator =()` function checks for assignment to self.

Since users often want to concatenate one string onto the end of the other, the `text_string` class supplies the text editor program with two `operator +()` functions. The first concatenates two `text_string` objects. The second concatenates a character array onto the end of a `text_string` object. Neither of these functions change its arguments. The `operator +()` functions return the resulting string. The string can then be assigned to a `text_string` object with the `text_string::operator =()` function.

The `text_string` class provides three functions for appending to a `text_string`. The first appends a `text_string` onto a `text_string`. The second appends a character array onto the end of a `text_string`. The third appends a single character to a `text_string`. All three of these functions change the destination `text_string` object.

The `text_string::operator []()` function returns a reference to a character in the `text_string` object. As was mentioned previously, this can cause problems. It is discussed in the Troubleshooting Guide for this chapter.

The `CppString()` function enables the text editor program to explicitly convert a `text_string` to a character pointer. It does so without providing the potential problems that adding an `operator char *()` function could create.

To provide the functionality of the C Standard Library function `strlen()`, the `text_string` class has a function called `Length()`. It simply counts the number of printable characters in the string and returns the count.

The `text_string` class needs three private member functions. One is called `Allocate()`. The other two are a pair of overloaded `Copy()` functions. `Allocate()` dynamically allocates memory to which the private data member `charString` can point. The first `Copy()` function copies characters from a `text_string` object to a `text_string` object. The second version of the `Copy()` function copies a character array to a `text_string` object. Both of these functions are written with the assumption that `charString` points at memory that was allocated before `Copy()` is called. This is a safe assumption, since only members of `text_string` call `Copy()`.

Troubleshooting Guide

After reading this section, you should be able to:

- Recognize potential problems with providing an `operator []()` function in a class.
- Create and execute the basic tests needed to find major errors in the text editor.

Potential Problems with the `operator []()` Function

Both the `text_buffer` and the `text_string` class provide an `operator []()` function. This is extremely handy for accessing characters in the text buffer. Example 30.1 illustrates why.

EXAMPLE 30.1 Using the [ ] Operators

```
text_buffer aBuffer;
aBuffer[0][0] = 'a';
```

The `operator []()` function of the `text_buffer` class enables us to get direct access to any `text_string` object. The `operator []()` function in the `text_string` class allows us to get direct access to any character in a `text_string` object. The two statements in Example 30.1 show that we can combine these to give the `text_buffer` object the appearance of a two-dimensional array. The statement

```
aBuffer[0]
```

evaluates to a `text_string` object. It provides us with a reference to the first `text_string` in the buffer. The statement

```
aBuffer[0][0]
```

gets the first `text_string` and uses that `text_string` object to call the `text_string::operator []()` function. The `text_string::operator []()` returns a reference to the first character in the `text_string`.

Nearly any object, or combination of objects, can be made to look like a two-dimensional array. All we need to do is provide the appropriate `operator []()` function in the class or classes.

So what could possibly be wrong with this? It's quick, convenient, and it makes the `text_buffer` look like a built-in data type. Isn't that what we want in our programs?

If you look again at Example 30.1, you'll see that any function having access to a `text_buffer` object can store a character anywhere in the buffer. However, doing so bypasses the insertion point. To give users a coherent experience when they're using the text editor, the program must synchronize the insertion point and the cursor. In our current implementation of the `text_buffer` class, it's possible to insert characters anywhere in the buffer. Any desktop member function could potentially insert characters without updating the cursor or the insertion point. It could happen accidentally. A maintenance programmer could also do it on purpose, not realizing the potential side effects.

Example 30.2 demonstrates another pitfall of returning references to private data. The program fragment uses the `operator []()` functions of the `text_buffer` and `text_string` classes to get access to an individual character in the text buffer. It sets a pointer to that character. This code fragment uses the pointer to create another name, or alias, for the data. Once it does, the program can use the pointer to change the contents of the buffer without calling any more member functions. This defeats the purpose of using an object oriented language.

EXAMPLE 30.2 Creating an Alias

```
char *aPointer;
text_buffer theBuffer;
aPointer = &theBuffer[1][2];
*aPointer = 'C';
```

Previous chapters mentioned that it is always a potential problem for member functions to return references or pointers to private data. Now we can see why. Giving programs direct access to private data can result in an object getting into an invalid state. In this case, the program could insert a line of text into the text buffer after the line specified by the `linesUsed` data member. The `linesUsed` member would contain invalid data. That would probably cause a program malfunction.

If you look over the code for the `desktop` class in Chapter 28, you'll see that having the `operator []()` function in the `desktop` class makes the code simpler and clearer. The same is true the `text_buffer` class. The `PutCharacter()` function is simpler and more readable because the `text_string` class provides an `operator []()` function. However, you must decide whether the advantages of having `operator []()` functions are worth the potential for problems. In this implementation of the text editor, I've been extremely careful to use the `operator []()` functions in a way that will benefit the program. On a large project, all the other programmers might be just as careful. Or they might not.

Testing the Text Editor

The core functionality of the text editor is provided by the `text_buffer` and `text_string` classes. Any major errors the program has will most likely be found in these two classes. Therefore, the Troubleshooting Guide and Exercises in this chapter focus more on debugging than in other chapters.

When you're developing a program, it's up to you to test it as much as you can. It's much faster (and cheaper) to find your errors yourself rather than leave them for a tester to find. You'll also be more likely to develop a good reputation with your co-workers if your code is largely bug-free when they see it.

How do you go about testing the `text_buffer` and `text_string` classes? There are multiple approaches. Most developers just go ahead and build the text editor and test it together with the rest of the program. That's not the best method.

Professional software testers will test code three to four times more thoroughly than a professional developer. They test the code under as many conditions as they can. Typically, a tester will work from the program's design. All of the tests will be created to ensure that the code follows the design.

To do this, most testers develop small programs that test one object at a time. Developers hate doing that. Their attitude is, "Why write code I'll just have to throw away?" Having been both a professional developer and a professional tester, I've seen this situation from both points of view.

Code that you write for tests is never wasted. You will almost always use it again. As you test each object, you'll find errors. After you've fixed the bugs, you'll need to run the tests again to ensure that the bugs truly are fixed. This is called *regression testing*. Any code you wrote for the original tests will be used again for the regression tests.

When you write a program to test an object, it should test every member function. You must test it in ways that simulate normal operation. You must also test it in ways that simulate operation under extreme conditions.

For example, one feature of the `text_string` class is that it allocates any length of string. To test that feature, we should write a program that declares a `text_string` and stores characters to it. The program should enter a loop and keep appending characters to the string until the computer runs out of memory. In this way, we can verify that the `text_string` really does grow to the limits of memory. We can also validate that the `text_string` class can gracefully handle the problem of running out of memory. Gracefully handing a problem does not include crashing the program.

Other tests on the `text_string` object might involve assigning huge strings to one another, concatenating huge strings together, and assigning a huge string to an empty string. We would also need to test to see what happens when you concatenate two empty strings together. Our test program should check to see that an empty string can be assigned to an empty string, a huge string can be assigned to an empty string, and an empty string can be assigned to a huge string. (Note that this list of possible tests on the `text_string` object is by no means exhaustive.)

Each object in a program should be tested individually. Afterward, integration testing can begin. In the text editor, the `test_string` object should be tested by itself. The `text_buffer` object can then be built and tested together with the `text_string`. Once these two objects are integrated, the `text_buffer` can be put into the `desktop` object. They can then all be tested together.

All of this sounds like a lot of work. It is. Most of it will be done by people who exclusively test software for a living. However, it will benefit you to take some time to do a fair portion of the tester's job before you show anyone your code. If you add this time into the development schedule when you make it, testing won't be a problem. Unfortunately, most of us don't even think of allowing time for testing when we first get into professional programming situations. Hard experience teaches us that we can schedule it in from the beginning, or we can make up the time with 14- or 16-hour work days later on. Either way, we *will* put in the time.

Summary

The `text_buffer` and `text_string` objects provide the core functionality of the text editor. If they are well-written and well-tested, much of the text editor program will work properly.

Review Questions

1. To lower cohesion in the program, would it be advisable to make the `text_buffer` use C++ character arrays rather than `text_string` objects so that it doesn't need to include *TString.h?* Why or why not?
2. Is it really necessary that the `text_string` class work together with character arrays? Shouldn't we just require the programmer using the `text_string` class to never use character arrays? Why or why not?

3. Is the design of the text_string class complete? What other member functions could be added to the text_string class? *Hint:* The C Standard Library that comes with your compiler contains a number of functions for string handling. Look through your compiler's documentation and see what these do. Which of them should be included in the member functions of text_string? If you think your list of member functions is complete, do you also think it's minimal? Why or why not?
4. Is the design of the text_buffer class both minimal and complete? Why or why not? What other member functions could be included in this class? Do you think they *should* be included? Why or why not?
5. If we modify the text_buffer class to dynamically allocate its list of strings, we must add a destructor to deallocate the list. What other functions would we need to add? Why?
6. Should we as designers of the text_buffer class allow other programmers to assign or copy text_buffer objects? Why or why not? What can we do to prevent it?
7. The two overloaded text_string::Copy() functions are written with the assumption that memory for charString was allocated before Copy() was called. Can you use calls to assert() to enforce that assumption? Where would you insert the calls to assert()?
8. Do you think the text_buffer and text_string objects should have operator []() functions? Why or why not?
9. What tests do you think need to be performed on the text_string object to ensure that it works properly?
10. What tests do you think need to be performed on the text_buffer object to ensure that it works properly?

Exercises

1. It is possible that someone might want to use the text_string class from the text editor as a base class. Explain what changes must be made to it to make it usable as a base class and why.
2. The keyword const was not used in the prototypes of many of the functions in the text editor. Rewrite the files presented in this chapter. Make as many const functions, parameters, and return types as you can. Explain which function cannot be made const and why. Explain which parameters cannot be made const and why. Explain which return types cannot be made const and why.
3. The Save item in the File menu of the text editor is not fully implemented. Write the rest of the code needed to save the text buffer to a file.
4. The Cut, Copy, and Paste items in the Edit menu of the text editor are not implemented. Write the code necessary for these menu items to work.
5. The text_buffer class uses a statically allocated array of text_string objects. Enhance the text_buffer class to use a dynamically allocated array of text_string objects. If the text_buffer object's array gets full, it should dynamically increase the size of the array.
6. There is a bug in the text editor. To see this bug, load a text file into the editor that is at least 60 lines long. Move to the last line of text and press Enter. Type some characters, but don't press Enter. Now use ^w to scroll up until the last line of text scrolls off the screen. Use ^z to move down to the end of the buffer. Notice that the last line of text is not displayed. Fix this bug.
7. The text editor contains a major program error. To see this bug, type in a line of text that is at least 20 characters long. Use ^a to move to the middle of the line you just typed. Press Enter. Explain what happened. Explain what you expected to happen. Fix the bug.
8. The text editor contains a bug. When you run it from a command-line prompt, it will not load a file as it's supposed to. Fix this bug.
9. There are additional bugs in the text editor. Find as many as you can. Explain how you produced each bug so that anyone else can reproduce it.
10. Add a new item to the text editor's Edit menu called Delete. The Delete item should remove the current line of text from the text buffer. However, unlike the Cut command, it should not save the line of text for pasting.

31 Developing the Text Editor: Menu.h, Menu.cpp, MenuItem.h, MenuItem.cpp, StatBar.h, StatBar.cpp, and Platform.h

Objectives

After reading this chapter you should be able to:

- Implement the text editor source files *Menu.h, Menu.cpp, MenuItem.h, MenuItem.cpp, StatBar.h, StatBar.cpp,* and *Platform.h.*
- Integrate and debug the objects and functions in these files.

Preview

This chapter presents the final group of files needed for the text editor. These files implement the menu system and the status bar. *Platform.h* defines portability constants.

Writing Menu.h

The text editor's menu system is flexible and powerful. Yet it has a simple programming interface. Programmers using the `menu` object can get and set its origin, which is its upper left corner. They can get and set the menu's style, add items to the menu, and execute it. These are the only operations needed for this menu system.

The class definition of the `menu` object is found in *Menu.h,* which appears in Listing 31.1.

LISTING 31.1 Menu.h

```
//-----------------------------------------------------------------------------
/*
File Name:     Menu.h
Comments:      This file contains the definition of the menu class. It also
               defines constants and types needed to use menus.
*/
//-----------------------------------------------------------------------------


#ifndef MENU_H
#define MENU_H

//-----------------------------------------------------------------------------
// Include Files

#include "MenuItem.h"
```

```
#include "Display.h"
#include "InputDev.h"

// End Include Files
//-----------------------------------------------------------------------------



//-----------------------------------------------------------------------------
// Constants

const menu_item_id MENU_CANCELED = -1;
const menu_item_id MENU_FAILED = -2;
const menu_item_id NO_ITEM_SELECTED = -3;

// End Constants
//-----------------------------------------------------------------------------



//-----------------------------------------------------------------------------
// Class Definitions
class menu
{
// Public types.
public:
   enum menu_display_style
   {
      VERTICAL_MENU_STYLE,
      HORIZONTAL_MENU_STYLE
   };

   enum menu_error
   {
      NO_ERROR = 0,
      CANT_ALLOCATE_MENU = -1
   };

// Public functions.
public:
   menu(void);
   ~menu();

   void UpLeftRow(display_coordinate row);
   display_coordinate UpLeftRow(void);

   void UpLeftCol(display_coordinate col);
   display_coordinate UpLeftCol(void);

   void MenuStyle(menu::menu_display_style style);
   menu::menu_display_style MenuStyle(void);

   menu::menu_error AddItem(menu_item &newItem);

   menu_item_id Execute(void) const;

// Private functions.
private:
```

```
    void AdjustVerticalMenuSize(void);
    void AdjustHorizontalMenuSize(void);
    menu_item_id ExecuteVerticalMenu(void) const;
    menu_item_id ExecuteHorizontalMenu(void) const;
    void HighlightVerticalMenuItem(int highlightedItem) const;
    void HighlightHorizontalMenuItem(int highlightedItem) const;
    void UnhighlightVerticalMenuItem(int highlightedItem) const;
    void UnhighlightHorizontalMenuItem(int highlightedItem) const;

// Private data.
private:
    menu_item *allItems;
    int totalItems;
    display_coordinate upLeftX, upLeftY;
    display_coordinate height,width;
    menu_display_style menuStyle;
};

// End Class Definitions
//-----------------------------------------------------------------------------

#endif

// End Menu.h
//-----------------------------------------------------------------------------
```

Any menu contains menu items, so the objects for the text editor's menu system are modeled that way. The `menu` class has a dynamically allocated list of `menu_item` objects. Because *Menu.h* needs access to the definition of `menu_item` objects, it includes *MenuItem.h*.

Every program's menus must display the menu on the screen. A menu must also get the user's selection. The text editor's menus are no different. For this reason, *Menu.h* also includes *Display.h* and *InputDev.h*.

When the text editor executes a menu, the `menu` object `Execute()` function displays the `menu` and waits for the user to select a `menu_item`. It returns the unique identifier of the item the user chose. However, the user can also cancel the `menu`. If this occurs, the `Execute()` function must notify the text editor. It must also return an error status constant if it can't display the `menu`.

To accommodate these needs, *Menu.h* defines three constants of type `menu_item_id`. The first, `MENU_CANCELED`, is returned by the `Execute()` function when the user presses the Escape key to cancel the menu. The `Execute()` function returns the constant `MENU_FAILED` if it can't display the menu. *Menu.h* also defines the constant `NO_ITEM_SELECTED` to indicate that the user hasn't chosen a menu item yet.

Menu.h then defines the `menu` class. The `menu` object definition begins with a section for public enumerated types. A menu can be either horizontal or vertical. The main menu of most programs is horizontal. The rest of the menus are usually vertical. The `menu` class also contains an enumeration of its error codes.

Since the `menu` class keeps a dynamically allocated list of `menu_item` objects, the `menu` class must have a destructor. When a `menu` is deleted, it will delete all of the `menu_item` objects in its list.

The `menu` class contains almost as many private member functions as public member functions. This is because it does a lot of work behind the scenes. When a `menu` executes, it determines whether the `menu` is horizontal or vertical. There are two different functions for executing the two different `menu` styles. Menus in this menu system size themselves. They calculate their size based on the width of the items they contain. The `menu` class contains private functions to aid in those calculations. Menus also highlight and unhighlight their items as needed. The `menu` class definition contains private functions to help with these tasks.

Writing Menu.cpp

The implementation of the menu class is more complex than the class definition indicates. Listing 31.2 gives the source code for *Menu.cpp*.

LISTING 31.2 Menu.cpp

```
//---------------------------------------------------------------------------
/*
File Name:    Menu.cpp
Comments:     This file contains the implementation of the menu class.
*/
//---------------------------------------------------------------------------



//---------------------------------------------------------------------------
// Include Files

#include "Platform.h"
#include "Menu.h"
#include "assert.h"

// End Include Files
//---------------------------------------------------------------------------

#ifdef PLATFORM_MS_DOS

//---------------------------------------------------------------------------
// Constants

static const display_coordinate MENU_BORDER_WIDTH = 1;
static const display_coordinate MENU_BORDER_HEIGHT = 1;

static const display_coordinate HORIZONTAL_MENU_ITEM_SEPARATOR_WIDTH = 1;
static const char HORIZONTAL_MENU_SEPARATOR_CHARACTER = ' ';

static const char UPPER_LEFT_MENU_CORNER_CHARACTER = (char)201;
static const char HORIZONTAL_BORDER_CHARACTER = (char)205;
static const char UPPER_RIGHT_MENU_CORNER_CHARACTER = (char)187;
static const char VERTICAL_BORDER_CHARACTER = (char)186;
static const char LOWER_LEFT_MENU_CORNER_CHARACTER = (char)200;
static const char LOWER_RIGHT_MENU_CORNER_CHARACTER = (char)188;

#endif

static const display::display_style MENU_BACKGROUND_STYLE = display::INVERSE;
static const display::display_style MENU_CURSOR_BACKGROUND_STYLE  =
   display::NO_STYLE;

// End Constants
//---------------------------------------------------------------------------



//---------------------------------------------------------------------------
/*
Function Name:       menu
Member of:           menu
```

```
Input Parameters:    None.
Output Parameters:   None.
Return Value:        Constructed menu object.
Comments:            This is the default constructor for the menu class.
*/

menu::menu(void)
{
   allItems = NULL;
   totalItems = 0;
   upLeftY = -1;
   upLeftX = -1;
   height = 0;
   width = 0;
   menuStyle = VERTICAL_MENU_STYLE;
}

// End menu
//-----------------------------------------------------------------------------



//-----------------------------------------------------------------------------
/*
Function Name:       ~menu
Member of:           menu
Input Parameters:    None.
Output Parameters:   None.
Return Value:        None.
Comments:            This is the destructor for the menu class. If there are
                     any items in the menu, they are deleted.
*/

menu::~menu()
{
   if (totalItems > 0)
   {
      assert(allItems != NULL);
      delete [] allItems;
   }
}

// End ~menu
//-----------------------------------------------------------------------------



//-----------------------------------------------------------------------------
/*
Function Name:       UpLeftRow
Member of:           menu
Input Parameters:    row - The new row number of the upper left corner of the
                        menu.
Output Parameters:   None.
Return Value:        None.
Comments:            This function sets the row number of the upper left
                     corner of the menu.
*/
```

```
void menu::UpLeftRow(display_coordinate row)
{
   assert((row >= theScreen.FirstRow()) &&
          (row+height <= theScreen.LastRow()));
   upLeftY = row;
}

// End UpLeftRow
//-----------------------------------------------------------------------



//-----------------------------------------------------------------------
/*
Function Name:       UpLeftRow
Member of:           menu
Input Parameters:    None.
Output Parameters:   None.
Return Value:        This function gets the row number of the upper left
                     corner of the menu.
Comments:            See the Return Value section.
*/

display_coordinate menu::UpLeftRow(void)
{
   return (upLeftY);
}

// End UpLeftRow
//-----------------------------------------------------------------------



//-----------------------------------------------------------------------
/*
Function Name:       UpLeftCol
Member of:           menu
Input Parameters:    col - The new column number of the upper left corner
                        of the menu.
Output Parameters:   None.
Return Value:        None.
Comments:            This function sets the column number of the upper left
                     corner of the menu.
*/

void menu::UpLeftCol(display_coordinate col)
{
   assert((col >= theScreen.FirstCol()) &&
          (col+width <= theScreen.LastCol()));
   upLeftX = col;
}

// End UpLeftCol
//-----------------------------------------------------------------------



//-----------------------------------------------------------------------
/*
```

```
Function Name:       UpLeftCol
Member of:           menu
Input Parameters:    None.
Output Parameters:   None.
Return Value:        This function gets the column number of the upper left
                     corner of the menu.
Comments:            See the Return Value section.
*/

display_coordinate menu::UpLeftCol(void)
{
   return (upLeftX);
}

// End UpLeftCol
//-----------------------------------------------------------------------------



//-----------------------------------------------------------------------------
/*
Function Name:       MenuStyle
Member of:           menu
Input Parameters:    style - A member of the menu::menu_display_style
                        enumerated type.
Output Parameters:   None.
Return Value:        None.
Comments:            This function sets the menu's style. Available styles
                     are listed in the menu::menu_display_style enumerated
                     type.
*/

void menu::MenuStyle(menu::menu_display_style style)
{
   assert((style == VERTICAL_MENU_STYLE) ||
          (style == HORIZONTAL_MENU_STYLE));
   menuStyle = style;
}

// End MenuStyle
//-----------------------------------------------------------------------------



//-----------------------------------------------------------------------------
/*
Function Name:       MenuStyle
Member of:           menu
Input Parameters:    None.
Output Parameters:   None.
Return Value:        This function gets the menu's style.
Comments:            See the Return Value section.
*/

menu::menu_display_style menu::MenuStyle(void)
{
   return (menuStyle);
}
```

```
// End MenuStyle
//---------------------------------------------------------------------------



//---------------------------------------------------------------------------
/*
Function Name:        AddItem
Member of:            menu
Input Parameters:     newItem - A reference to the item to be added to the
                         menu.
Output Parameters:    None.
Return Value:         Returns error status values from the menu::menu_error
                      enumerated type.
Comments:             This function adds a menu_item object to a menu. It
                      allocates memory for the new item, and copies the data
                      from the newItem parameter into the item it allocates.
                      When it does, it takes over ownership of the data in
                      newItem. So if newItem contains a submenu, the allocated
                      item takes ownership of it. When newItem is deleted,
                      it won't delete the submenu. The submenu will be
                      deleted when the allocated item is deleted.

                      This function allocates space in the current menu for
                      the new item. It adjusts the size and position of the
                      menu, and any submenus in the menu item.
*/

menu::menu_error menu::AddItem(menu_item &newItem)
{
   menu_error errorStatus = NO_ERROR;

   // Calculate the new size of the array.
   int newLength = totalItems + 1;

   // Allocate the new array.
   menu_item *tempArray = new menu_item [newLength];

   // If the array was allocated...
   if (tempArray)
   {
      // Copy the contents of the current array into the new array.
      int i;
      for (i=0;i<totalItems;i++)
      {
         tempArray[i] = allItems[i];
      }

      // Add the new item to the new array.
      tempArray[i] = newItem;

      // Delete the current array.
      if (allItems)
      {
         delete [] allItems;
      }
```

```
        // Set the new array as the current array.
        allItems = tempArray;
        totalItems = newLength;

        // If the new item has a submenu...
        if (allItems[i].Menu()!=NULL)
        {
            display_coordinate x,y;

            // Set the position of the submenu.

            // If the current menu is horizontal...
            if (menuStyle == HORIZONTAL_MENU_STYLE)
            {
                // Calculate the location of the submenu.
                x=upLeftX+MENU_BORDER_WIDTH;
                y=upLeftY+MENU_BORDER_HEIGHT+theScreen.CharacterHeight();

                for (int i=0;i<totalItems-1;i++)
                {
                    x+=theScreen.StringWidth(allItems[i].Text());
                    x+=HORIZONTAL_MENU_ITEM_SEPARATOR_WIDTH;
                }
            }
            // Else it must be vertical...
            else
            {
                // Calculate the location of the submenu.
                x=upLeftX+MENU_BORDER_WIDTH;
                y=upLeftY+MENU_BORDER_HEIGHT;
                y += totalItems * theScreen.CharacterHeight();
            }
            allItems[i].Menu()->upLeftX = x;
            allItems[i].Menu()->upLeftY = y;
        }

        // Adjust the size of the menu to accommodate the new item.
        if (menuStyle==VERTICAL_MENU_STYLE)
        {
            AdjustVerticalMenuSize();
        }
        else
        {
            AdjustHorizontalMenuSize();
        }
    }
    // Else the array could not be allocated...
    else
    {
        errorStatus = CANT_ALLOCATE_MENU;
    }

    return (errorStatus);
}

// End AddItem
//-----------------------------------------------------------------------------
```

```
//-----------------------------------------------------------------------------
/*
Function Name:       Execute
Member of:           menu
Input Parameters:    None.
Output Parameters:   None.
Return Value:        This function returns the identifier of the menu item
                     that the user selected. If the user cancels the menu,
                     this function returns MENU_CANCELED. If there is not
                     enough memory to execute the menu, this function
                     returns MENU_FAILED.
Comments:            This function determines whether the menu is horizontal
                     or vertical and calls the appropriate private member
                     function to execute the menu.
*/

menu_item_id menu::Execute(void) const
{
   menu_item_id selectedMenuItem;
   // If this is a vertical menu...
   if (menuStyle == VERTICAL_MENU_STYLE)
   {
      selectedMenuItem = ExecuteVerticalMenu();
   }
   // Else this is a horizontal menu...
   else
   {
      selectedMenuItem = ExecuteHorizontalMenu();
   }

   return (selectedMenuItem);
}

// End Execute
//-----------------------------------------------------------------------------



//-----------------------------------------------------------------------------
/*
Function Name:       ExecuteVerticalMenu
Member of:           menu
Input Parameters:    None.
Output Parameters:   None.
Return Value:        This function returns the identifier of the menu item
                     that the user selected. If the user cancels the menu,
                     this function returns MENU_CANCELED. If there is not
                     enough memory to execute the menu, this function
                     returns MENU_FAILED.
Comments:            This function executes a vertical menu by displaying it
                     on the screen and waiting for user input. If the user
                     selects an item with a submenu, it executes the submenu.
*/

menu_item_id menu::ExecuteVerticalMenu(void) const
{
   menu_item_id selectedMenuItem = MENU_FAILED;
   int i;
   display_coordinate lowRightX,lowRightY;
```

```
display_coordinate x;
display_coordinate y;
// Assumes monospaced character font.
display_coordinate characterWidth = theScreen.CharacterWidth();
display_coordinate characterHeight = theScreen.CharacterHeight();



// Save the background where the menu will appear on the screen.
lowRightX = upLeftX+width+(2*MENU_BORDER_WIDTH);
lowRightY = upLeftY+height+(2*MENU_BORDER_HEIGHT);
theScreen.SaveArea(upLeftX,upLeftY,lowRightX,lowRightY);

// If the background was saved...
if (theScreen.ErrorStatus() == display::NO_ERROR)
{
   // Display the menu.

   // Print the upper left corner.
   x = upLeftX;
   y = upLeftY;
   theScreen.PrintAt(y,x,UPPER_LEFT_MENU_CORNER_CHARACTER,
                     MENU_BACKGROUND_STYLE);

   // Print the top border.
   x+=MENU_BORDER_WIDTH;
   for (i=0;i<width;i++)
   {
      theScreen.PrintAt(y,x++,HORIZONTAL_BORDER_CHARACTER,
                        MENU_BACKGROUND_STYLE);
   }

   // Print the upper right corner.
   theScreen.PrintAt(y,x,UPPER_RIGHT_MENU_CORNER_CHARACTER,
                     MENU_BACKGROUND_STYLE);

   // For each item in the menu...
   x = upLeftX;
   y = upLeftY + MENU_BORDER_HEIGHT;
   for (i=0;i<totalItems;i++)
   {
      // Print the left border.
      theScreen.PrintAt(y,x,VERTICAL_BORDER_CHARACTER,
                        MENU_BACKGROUND_STYLE);

      // Print the item text.
      x+=MENU_BORDER_WIDTH;
        theScreen.PrintAt(y,x,allItems[i].Text(),MENU_BACKGROUND_STYLE);

      /* If the item doesn't cover the width of the menu,
      fill in the background. */
      for (x+=theScreen.StringWidth(allItems[i].Text());
           x<lowRightX-1;
           x+=characterWidth)
      {
         theScreen.PrintAt(y,x,' ',MENU_BACKGROUND_STYLE);
      }

      // Print the right border.
```

```
   theScreen.PrintAt(y,x,VERTICAL_BORDER_CHARACTER,
                     MENU_BACKGROUND_STYLE);
   y+=characterHeight;
   x=upLeftX;
}

// Print the lower left corner.
theScreen.PrintAt(y,x,LOWER_LEFT_MENU_CORNER_CHARACTER,
                  MENU_BACKGROUND_STYLE);

// Print the bottom border.
x+=characterWidth;
for (i=0;i<width;i++)

   theScreen.PrintAt(y,x,HORIZONTAL_BORDER_CHARACTER,
                     MENU_BACKGROUND_STYLE);
   x+=characterWidth;
}

// Print the lower right corner.
theScreen.PrintAt(y,x,LOWER_RIGHT_MENU_CORNER_CHARACTER,
                  MENU_BACKGROUND_STYLE);

// Display the menu cursor.
int highlightedItem = 0;
HighlightVerticalMenuItem(highlightedItem);

raw_input userKeyPress;

/* While a menu item is not selected and the user hasn't
canceled the menu... */
selectedMenuItem = NO_ITEM_SELECTED;
while ((selectedMenuItem == NO_ITEM_SELECTED) &&
       (selectedMenuItem != MENU_CANCELED))
{
   // Get input from the user.
   userKeyPress = inputDevice.GetInput(input_device::NO_ECHO);

   switch (userKeyPress)
   {
      // If the user pressed up...
      case input_device::UP:
         // If the menu cursor is not at the top of the menu...
         if (highlightedItem > 0)
         {
            UnhighlightVerticalMenuItem(highlightedItem);

            // Move the menu cursor up one.
            highlightedItem--;
            HighlightVerticalMenuItem(highlightedItem);
         }
      break;

      // Else if the user pressed down...
      case input_device::DOWN:
         // If the menu cursor is not at the bottom of the menu...
         if (highlightedItem < totalItems-1)
         {
            UnhighlightVerticalMenuItem(highlightedItem);
```

```
                    // Move the menu cursor down one.
                    highlightedItem++;
                    HighlightVerticalMenuItem(highlightedItem);
                }
            break;

            // Else if the user pressed Enter...
            case input_device::ENTER:
                // Select the current item.
                selectedMenuItem = allItems[highlightedItem].ID();

                // If the user selected an item and it's a submenu...
                if ((selectedMenuItem != MENU_CANCELED) &&
                    (allItems[highlightedItem].Menu()!=NULL))
                {
                    // Execute the submenu.
                    selectedMenuItem =
                        allItems[highlightedItem].Menu()->Execute();

                    if (selectedMenuItem == MENU_CANCELED)
                    {
                        selectedMenuItem = NO_ITEM_SELECTED;
                    }
                }

            break;

            // Else if the user pressed Esc...
            case input_device::ESCAPE:
                // Cancel this menu.
                selectedMenuItem = MENU_CANCELED;
            break;
        }

    }

    // Restore the background image.
    theScreen.RestoreArea(upLeftX,upLeftY,lowRightX,lowRightY);
  }
  // Else the background could not be saved...
  else
  {
    selectedMenuItem = MENU_FAILED;
  }

  return (selectedMenuItem);
}

// End ExecuteVerticalMenu
//------------------------------------------------------------------------




//------------------------------------------------------------------------
/*
Function Name:        ExecuteHorizontalMenu
Member of:            menu
Input Parameters:     None.
Output Parameters:    None.
```

```
Return Value:        This function returns the identifier of the menu item
                     that the user selected. If the user cancels the menu,
                     this function returns MENU_CANCELED.
Comments:            This function executes a horizontal menu by displaying it
                     on the screen and waiting for user input. If the user
                     selects an item with a submenu, it executes the submenu.
*/

menu_item_id menu::ExecuteHorizontalMenu(void) const
{
   menu_item_id selectedMenuItem;
   int i;
   display_coordinate lowRightX,lowRightY;
   display_coordinate x;
   display_coordinate y;
   // Assumes monospaced character font.
   display_coordinate characterWidth = theScreen.CharacterWidth();
   display_coordinate characterHeight = theScreen.CharacterHeight();

   // Save the background where the menu will appear on the screen.
   lowRightX = upLeftX+width+(2*MENU_BORDER_WIDTH);
   lowRightY = upLeftY+height+(2*MENU_BORDER_HEIGHT);
   theScreen.SaveArea(upLeftX,upLeftY,lowRightX,lowRightY);

   // If the background could be saved...
   if (theScreen.ErrorStatus() == display::NO_ERROR)
   {

      // Draw the horizontal menu.

      // Print the upper left corner.
      x = upLeftX;
      y = upLeftY;
      theScreen.PrintAt(y,x,UPPER_LEFT_MENU_CORNER_CHARACTER,
                        MENU_BACKGROUND_STYLE);

      // Print the top border.
      x+=characterWidth;
      for (i=0;i<width;i++)
      {
         theScreen.PrintAt(y,x++,HORIZONTAL_BORDER_CHARACTER,
                           MENU_BACKGROUND_STYLE);
      }

      // Print the upper right corner.
      theScreen.PrintAt(y,x,UPPER_RIGHT_MENU_CORNER_CHARACTER,
                        MENU_BACKGROUND_STYLE);
      // Print the left border.
      x = upLeftX;
      y = upLeftY + characterHeight;
      theScreen.PrintAt(y,x,VERTICAL_BORDER_CHARACTER,
                        MENU_BACKGROUND_STYLE);

      // For each item in the menu...
      x = upLeftX + HORIZONTAL_MENU_ITEM_SEPERATOR_WIDTH;
      for (i=0;i<totalItems;i++)
      {
         // Print the item text.
```

```
      theScreen.PrintAt(y,x,allItems[i].Text(),
                        MENU_BACKGROUND_STYLE);

      x += theScreen.StringWidth(allItems[i].Text());

      // Print the item separator.
      theScreen.PrintAt(y,x,HORIZONTAL_MENU_SEPARATOR_CHARACTER,
                        MENU_BACKGROUND_STYLE);
      x += HORIZONTAL_MENU_ITEM_SEPARATOR_WIDTH;
   }

   theScreen.PrintAt(y,x,VERTICAL_BORDER_CHARACTER,
                     MENU_BACKGROUND_STYLE);

   x = upLeftX;
   y = upLeftY + (2*characterHeight);

   // Print the lower left corner.
   theScreen.PrintAt(y,x,LOWER_LEFT_MENU_CORNER_CHARACTER,
                     MENU_BACKGROUND_STYLE);

   // Print the bottom border.
   x+=characterWidth;
   for (i=0;i<width;i++)
   {
      theScreen.PrintAt(y,x,HORIZONTAL_BORDER_CHARACTER,
                        MENU_BACKGROUND_STYLE);

      x+=characterWidth;
   }

   // Print the lower right corner.
   theScreen.PrintAt(y,x,LOWER_RIGHT_MENU_CORNER_CHARACTER,
                     MENU_BACKGROUND_STYLE);
   // Display the menu cursor.
   int highlightedItem = 0;
   HighlightHorizontalMenuItem(highlightedItem);

   raw_input userKeyPress;

   /* While a menu item is not selected and the user hasn't
   canceled the menu... */
   selectedMenuItem = NO_ITEM_SELECTED;
   while ((selectedMenuItem == NO_ITEM_SELECTED) &&
          (selectedMenuItem != MENU_CANCELED))
   {
      // Get user input.
      userKeyPress = inputDevice.GetInput(input_device::NO_ECHO);

      switch (userKeyPress)
      {
         // If the user pressed left...
         case input_device::LEFT:
            // If the menu cursor is not at the left of the menu...
            if (highlightedItem != 0)
            {
               UnhighlightHorizontalMenuItem(highlightedItem);
```

```
                // Move the menu cursor left one.
                highlightedItem--;
                HighlightHorizontalMenuItem(highlightedItem);
            }
        break;

        // Else if the user pressed right...
        case input_device::RIGHT:
            // If the menu cursor is not at the right of the menu...
            if (highlightedItem < totalItems-1)
            {
                UnhighlightHorizontalMenuItem(highlightedItem);

                // Move the menu cursor right one.
                highlightedItem++;
                HighlightHorizontalMenuItem(highlightedItem);
            }
        break;

        // Else if the user pressed Enter...
        case  input_device::ENTER:
            // Select the current item.
            selectedMenuItem = allItems[highlightedItem].ID();

             // If the user selected an item and it's a submenu...
             if ((selectedMenuItem != MENU_CANCELED) &&
                 (allItems[highlightedItem].Menu()!=NULL))
             {
                // Execute the submenu.
                selectedMenuItem =
                   allItems[highlightedItem].Menu()->Execute();

                if (selectedMenuItem == MENU_CANCELED)
                {
                   selectedMenuItem = NO_ITEM_SELECTED;
                }
            }
        break;

        // Else if the user pressed Esc...
        case  input_device::ESCAPE:
            // Cancel this menu.
            selectedMenuItem = MENU_CANCELED;
        break;

      }
   }

   // Restore the background image.
   theScreen.RestoreArea(upLeftX,upLeftY,lowRightX,lowRightY);
}
// Else the background could not be saved...
else
{
   selectedMenuItem = MENU_FAILED;
}

return (selectedMenuItem);
```

```
}

// End ExecuteHorizontalMenu
//---------------------------------------------------------------------------



//---------------------------------------------------------------------------
/*
Function Name:       AdjustVerticalMenuSize
Member of:           menu
Input Parameters:    None.
Output Parameters:   None.
Return Value:        None.
Comments:            This function adjusts the width and height of a vertical
                     menu. If the newest item in the menu is too wide to
                     fit, it widens the menu. It also increases the height
                     of the menu so the new item will fit.

                     Note that this function does not check to see if the
                     menu exceeds the boundaries of the screen.
*/

void menu::AdjustVerticalMenuSize(void)
{
   // Find the width and height of the new item.
   display_coordinate itemWidth =
   theScreen.StringWidth(allItems[totalItems-1].Text());
   display_coordinate itemHeight =
      theScreen.StringHeight(allItems[totalItems-1].Text());

   // If the width of the item is greater than the width of the menu...
   if (itemWidth > width)
   {
      // Adjust the width of the menu.
      width = itemWidth;
   }

   // Adjust the height of the menu.
   height += itemHeight;

}

// End AdjustVerticalMenuSize
//---------------------------------------------------------------------------



//---------------------------------------------------------------------------
/*
Function Name:       AdjustHorizontalMenuSize
Member of:           menu
Input Parameters:    None.
Output Parameters:   None.
Return Value:        None.
Comments:            This function adjusts the width and height of a
                     horizontal menu so that the newest item will fit.

                     Note that this function does not check to see if the
```

```
                    menu exceeds the boundaries of the screen.
*/

void menu::AdjustHorizontalMenuSize(void)
{
   // Find the width and height of the new item.
   display_coordinate itemWidth =
      theScreen.StringWidth(allItems[totalItems-1].Text());
   display_coordinate itemHeight =
      theScreen.StringHeight(allItems[totalItems-1].Text());

   // Adjust the width of the menu.
   width += itemWidth + HORIZONTAL_MENU_ITEM_SEPARATOR_WIDTH;

   // Adjust the height of the menu.
   if (height == 0)
   {
      height = itemHeight;
   }
}

// End AdjustHorizontalMenuSize
//---------------------------------------------------------------------------



//---------------------------------------------------------------------------
/*
Function Name:      HighlightVerticalMenuItem
Member of:          menu
Input Parameters:   highlightedItem - The integer index number of the item
                       to be highlighted. Index numbering begins with zero.
Output Parameters:  None.
Return Value:       None.
Comments:           This function highlights an item in a vertical menu when
                    it is displayed.
*/

void menu::HighlightVerticalMenuItem(int highlightedItem) const
{
   display_coordinate x,y;


   x=upLeftX+MENU_BORDER_WIDTH;
   y=upLeftY+MENU_BORDER_HEIGHT;
   y += highlightedItem * theScreen.CharacterHeight();
   theScreen.PrintAt(y,x,allItems[highlightedItem].Text(),
                  MENU_CURSOR_BACKGROUND_STYLE);
}

// End HighlightVerticalMenuItem
//---------------------------------------------------------------------------



//---------------------------------------------------------------------------
/*
Function Name:      HighlightHorizontalMenuItem
Member of:          menu
```

```
Input Parameters:    highlightedItem - The integer index number of the item
                        to be highlighted. Index numbering begins with zero.
Output Parameters:   None.
Return Value:        None.
Comments:            This function highlights an item in a horizontal menu
                     when it is displayed.
*/

void menu::HighlightHorizontalMenuItem(int highlightedItem) const
{
   display_coordinate x,y;


   x=upLeftX+MENU_BORDER_WIDTH;
   y=upLeftY+MENU_BORDER_HEIGHT;

   for (int i=0;i<highlightedItem;i++)
   {
      x+=theScreen.StringWidth(allItems[i].Text());
      x+=HORIZONTAL_MENU_ITEM_SEPARATOR_WIDTH;
   }
   theScreen.PrintAt(y,x,allItems[highlightedItem].Text(),
                     MENU_CURSOR_BACKGROUND_STYLE);
}

// End HighlightHorizontalMenuItem
//------------------------------------------------------------------------------



//------------------------------------------------------------------------------
/*
Function Name:       UnhighlightVerticalMenuItem
Member of:           menu
Input Parameters:    highlightedItem - The integer index number of the item
                        to be unhighlighted. Index numbering begins with zero.
Output Parameters:   None.
Return Value:        None.
Comments:            This function restores an item in a vertical menu to its
                     normal appearance by removing the menu cursor bar.
*/

void menu::UnhighlightVerticalMenuItem(int highlightedItem) const
{
   display_coordinate x,y;

   x=upLeftX+MENU_BORDER_WIDTH;
   y=upLeftY+MENU_BORDER_HEIGHT;
   y += highlightedItem * theScreen.CharacterHeight();
   theScreen.PrintAt(y,x,allItems[highlightedItem].Text(),
                     MENU_BACKGROUND_STYLE);
}

// End UnhighlightVerticalMenuItem
//------------------------------------------------------------------------------



//------------------------------------------------------------------------------
```

```
/*
Function Name:       UnhighlightHorizontalMenuItem
Member of:           menu
Input Parameters:    highlightedItem - The integer index number of the item
                        to be unhighlighted. Index numbering begins with zero.
Output Parameters:   None.
Return Value:        None.
Comments:            This function restores an item in a horizontal menu to
                     its normal appearance by removing the menu cursor bar.
*/

void menu::UnhighlightHorizontalMenuItem(int highlightedItem) const
{
   display_coordinate x,y;


   x=upLeftX+MENU_BORDER_WIDTH;
   y=upLeftY+MENU_BORDER_HEIGHT;

   for (int i=0;i<highlightedItem;i++)
   {
      x+=theScreen.StringWidth(allItems[i].Text());
      x+=HORIZONTAL_MENU_ITEM_SEPARATOR_WIDTH;
   }
   theScreen.PrintAt(y,x,allItems[highlightedItem].Text(),
                     MENU_BACKGROUND_STYLE);
}


// End UnhighlightVerticalMenuItem
//-----------------------------------------------------------------------


// End Menu.cpp
//-----------------------------------------------------------------------
```

Menu.cpp begins by including the header files it requires and defining some constants it uses. The `menu` constructor initializes the private data members to a known state. Its destructor deletes the list of `menu_item` objects. The overloaded `UpLeftRow()` and `UpLeftCol()` functions enable the text editor to get and set the position of the `menu` object on the screen. A pair of overloaded `MenuStyle()` functions enables it to get and set the style of a menu. This implementation supports two menu styles, horizontal and vertical.

The `AddItem()` function is one of the workhorses of the `menu` class. When it adds an item, it allocates memory and copies the contents of the `menu_item` passed in through the `newItem` parameter. The `menu_item` may contain submenus. If it does, the `menu` object that invoked `AddItem()` assumes ownership of the submenu. When the program deletes the `menu` object, its destructor deletes the list of `menu_item` objects. When a menu deletes a `menu_item` with a submenu, the `menu_item` destructor deletes the submenu. If the submenu contains items with submenus, they are deleted as well. This design enables us to delete all of the menus and submenus in the program by simply deleting the program's main menu.

Each time the program adds a `menu_item` to a `menu`, the `AddItem()` function allocates more memory for the list. If the item being added to the `menu` has a submenu, the `AddItem()` function sets the position of the submenu. It also increases the size of the `menu` if the item is too big to fit. It determines this by calculating the size of the string in the `menu_item`. The `AddItem()` function returns an error status if it was unable to allocate and build the `menu`.

Whenever a program needs to display a menu and get the user's input, it calls the `Execute()` function. `Execute()` determines whether the menu is horizontal or vertical. If it is vertical, it calls the private member function `ExecuteVerticalMenu()`. If it is horizontal, it calls the private member function `ExecuteHorizontalMenu()`. These two functions perform the actual work in executing a menu.

Both `ExecuteVerticalMenu()` and `ExecuteHorizontalMenu()` follow the same general logic. They save the contents of the screen where the `menu` will be displayed. After the background is saved, they each print the `menu` on the screen and enter a `while` loop. Inside the loop, they each get input from the user and react to it. `ExecuteVerticalMenu()` allows the user to move the cursor up and down. `ExecuteHorizontalMenu()` lets the user move the cursor left and right. They both enable the user to press Enter to select an item or Escape to cancel the menu. All other input is ignored. If the user selects an item that has a submenu, the submenu is executed.

The loop finishes when a `menu_item` with no submenu is selected. It will also terminate when the user cancels the `menu`. After the loop finishes, the `ExecuteVerticalMenu()` and `ExecuteHorizontalMenu()` functions restore the background where the `menu` appeared. They then return the user's selection or the value `MENU_CANCELED`.

The private member functions `AdjustVerticalMenuSize()` and `AdjustHorizontal-MenuSize()` help the `AddItem()` function set the height and width of `menu` objects. The private functions `HighlightVerticalMenuItem()`, `HighlightHorizontalMenuItem()`, `UnhighlightVerticalMenuItem()`, and `UnhighlightHorizontalMenuItem()` are called by `ExecuteVerticalMenu()` and `ExecuteHorizontalMenu()` to control the menu selection bar.

Writing MenuItem.h

In any menu system, a menu contains items. Each item must have a string associated with it that the menu can display. It can also have a submenu. Professional user interface classes also enable programmers to attach dialog boxes to menu items. For simplicity, our text editor does not support dialog boxes. However, they would be fairly straightforward to add.

The definition of the `menu_item` class is in *MenuItem.h*. The source code for *MenuItem.h* appears in Listing 31.3.

LISTING 31.3 MenuItem.h

```
//---------------------------------------------------------------------------
/*
File Name:   MenuItem.h
Comments:    This file contains the definition of the menu_item class. It also
             defines some types and constants used with the menu_item class.
*/
//---------------------------------------------------------------------------


#ifndef MENUITEM_H
#define MENUITEM_H

//---------------------------------------------------------------------------
// Include Files

#include "TString.h"

// End Include Files
//---------------------------------------------------------------------------

//---------------------------------------------------------------------------
// Forward references
```

```
class menu;

// End Forward references
//---------------------------------------------------------------------------



//---------------------------------------------------------------------------
// Types

typedef int menu_item_id;

// End Types
//---------------------------------------------------------------------------



//---------------------------------------------------------------------------
// Constants

const menu_item_id MIID_UNKNOWN = -1;
const menu_item_id MIID_FIRST = 1000;

// End Constants
//---------------------------------------------------------------------------


//---------------------------------------------------------------------------
// Class Definitions

class menu_item
{
// Public functions.
public:
   menu_item(void);
   menu_item(menu_item &sourceItem);
   ~menu_item();

   menu_item &operator =(menu_item &sourceItem);

   void Text(text_string &itemText);
   text_string &Text(void);

   void ID(menu_item_id idNumber);
   menu_item_id ID(void);

   void Menu(menu *itemSubmenu);
   menu *Menu(void);

// Private data.
private:
   text_string itemString;
   menu_item_id itemID;
   menu *subMenu;
   bool ownsSubMenu;
};
```

```
// End Class Definitions
//-----------------------------------------------------------------------

#endif
// End MenuItem.h
//-----------------------------------------------------------------------
```

MenuItem.h uses some techniques that make it unusual in this program. First, it declares a **forward reference.** A forward reference is a reference to a type before it is declared. The forward reference in *MenuItem.h* is the statement

```
class menu;
```

The reason that this is a forward reference is that menu is not defined at this point in *MenuItem.h.* Using a forward reference enables us to use the menu type even if it is not yet defined.

You may wonder why we don't just include the file *Menu.h* at the beginning of *MenuItem.h.* The answer can be found by looking at the beginning of *Menu.h.* If you do, you'll see the statement

```
#include "MenuItem.h"
```

The file *MenuItem.h* can't include *Menu.h* if *Menu.h* includes *MenuItem.h.*

Recall that an object of type menu can contain menu_item objects. A menu_item can also contain a menu. Forward references resolve this "chicken and egg" situation. When the compiler processes *MenuItem.h,* the only thing it needs to "know" about the menu object is that menu_item has a private data member that is a pointer to a menu. The forward reference in *MenuItem.h* tells the compiler that the menu type is defined somewhere in the program. It's a way of saying, "Don't worry about the menu type now. Just let me use it. I'll give the definition for it elsewhere." The compiler will accept that and process the file. Since forward references are somewhat unusual, some compilers give a warning to let you know that you did something out of the ordinary. In this case, you can safely ignore that warning.

MenuItem.h defines the menu_item_id type. In this case, the menu_item identifiers are integers. My experience with porting programs tells me that this type would likely change if the program needed to be enhanced. That's why I used the typedef to define the menu_item_id type rather than just use integers.

This program uses the convention of having all menu_item identifiers start with the characters MIID_, which stands for *menu item identifier.* When the program creates a menu_item, its constructor must initialize it to a known state. *MenuItem.h* defines the constant MIID_UNKNOWN for this purpose. It also defines the constant MIID_FIRST. To see why, take a look at main() in *TEdit.cpp* (see Chapter 28). You'll see that the switch statement that processes user input contains cases for character commands and menu commands. When we define the unique identifiers for the menu items, we must be sure they don't conflict with the character commands a user can type in. For this reason, I've provided the constant MIID_FIRST. I've given MIID_FIRST a value that no character command can have. All menu_item identifiers must be greater than or equal to MIID_FIRST. A quick look back at *TEdit.cpp* will show that all of the menu_item identifiers are indeed defined in terms of MIID_FIRST.

Next, *MenuItem.h* defines the menu_item class. Since the menu_item class contains a pointer to a dynamically allocated menu, it must have a destructor. It also provides a copy constructor and an assignment operator. The other public member functions are used for getting and setting the item's text, ID, and menu pointer.

Writing MenuItem.cpp

Listing 31.4 displays the source code for the menu_item member functions.

LISTING 31.4 MenuItem.cpp

```
//---------------------------------------------------------------------------
/*
File Name:  MenuItem.cpp
Comments:   This file contains the implementation of the menu_item class.
*/
//---------------------------------------------------------------------------



//---------------------------------------------------------------------------
// Include Files

#include "TString.h"
#include "menuitem.h"
#include "assert.h"

// End Include Files
//---------------------------------------------------------------------------



//---------------------------------------------------------------------------
/*
Function Name:       menu_item
Member of:           menu_item
Input Parameters:    None.
Output Parameters:   None.
Return Value:        Constructed menu_item object.
Comments:            This function initializes a menu_item object.
*/

menu_item::menu_item(void)
{
   itemID = MIID_UNKNOWN;
   subMenu = NULL;
   ownsSubMenu=true;
}

// End menu_item
//---------------------------------------------------------------------------



//---------------------------------------------------------------------------
/*
Function Name:       menu_item
Member of:           menu_item
Input Parameters:    sourceItem - The menu_item object to be copied.
Output Parameters:   None.
Return Value:        Constructed menu_item object.
Comments:            This is the copy constructor for the menu_item class.
*/

menu_item::menu_item(menu_item &sourceItem)
{
```

```
   *this = sourceItem;
}

// End menu_item
//-----------------------------------------------------------------------------



//-----------------------------------------------------------------------------
/*
Function Name:          ~menu_item
Member of:              menu_item
Input Parameters:       None.
Output Parameters:      None.
Return Value:           None.
Comments:               This is the destructor for the menu_item class. If the
                        current menu item contains a submenu and it owns the
                        submenu, it will delete the submenu.
*/

menu_item::~menu_item()
{
   // If the items contains a submenu and it owns the submenu...
   if ((subMenu != NULL) && (ownsSubMenu == true))
   {
      // Delete the submenu.
      delete (subMenu);
   }
}

// End ~menu_item
//-----------------------------------------------------------------------------



//-----------------------------------------------------------------------------
/*
Function Name:          operator =
Member of:              menu_item
Input Parameters:       sourceItem - The menu item that will be copied.
Output Parameters:      None.
Return Value:           Returns a copied menu_item object.
Comments:               This function copies one menu_item object to another.
                        When the copy is done, the destination object assumes
                        ownership of the submenu (if there is one).
*/

menu_item &menu_item::operator =(menu_item &sourceItem)
{
   itemString = sourceItem.itemString;
   itemID = sourceItem.itemID;
   subMenu = sourceItem.subMenu;
   ownsSubMenu=true;
   sourceItem.ownsSubMenu=false;
   return (*this);
}
```

```
// End operator =
//-----------------------------------------------------------------------------


//-----------------------------------------------------------------------------
/*
Function Name:       Text
Member of:           menu_item
Input Parameters:    itemText - The item's new text string.
Output Parameters:   None.
Return Value:        None.
Comments:            Use the Text function to set the text string that will
                     be displayed for this item in the menu.
*/

void menu_item::Text(text_string &itemText)
{
   itemString = itemText;
}

// End Text
//-----------------------------------------------------------------------------



//-----------------------------------------------------------------------------
/*
Function Name:       Text
Member of:           menu_item
Input Parameters:    None.
Output Parameters:   None.
Return Value:        This function returns the menu item's text string.
Comments:            See the Return Value section.
*/

text_string &menu_item::Text(void)
{
   return (itemString);
}

// End Text
//-----------------------------------------------------------------------------



//-----------------------------------------------------------------------------
/*
Function Name:       ID
Member of:           menu_item
Input Parameters:    idNumber - A constant that uniquely identifies this
                        menu item.
Output Parameters:   None.
Return Value:        None.
Comments:            Use this function to set the menu_item object's
                     identifier.
*/

void menu_item::ID(menu_item_id idNumber)
```

```
{
   itemID = idNumber;
}

// End ID
//-------------------------------------------------------------------------



//-------------------------------------------------------------------------
/*
Function Name:         ID
Member of:             menu_item
Input Parameters:      None.
Output Parameters:     None.
Return Value:          This function returns the menu_item object's unique
                       identifier.
Comments:              See the Return Value section.
*/

menu_item_id menu_item::ID(void)
{
   return (itemID);
}

// End ID
//-------------------------------------------------------------------------



//-------------------------------------------------------------------------
/*
Function Name:         Menu
Member of:             menu_item
Input Parameters:      itemSubmenu - A pointer to the item's submenu.
Output Parameters:     None.
Return Value:          None.
Comments:              Use this function to set an item's submenu. If the item
                       already has a submenu that it owns, the old submenu is
                       deleted and replaced by the new submenu. When your
                       program uses the Menu() function to set an item's
                       submenu, the item assumes ownership of the submenu.
*/

void menu_item::Menu(menu *itemSubmenu)
{
   /* If the parameter is not null, assert that the item's current
   submenu and the new submenu do not point at the same submenu. */
   assert((itemSubmenu!=NULL) ? subMenu != itemSubmenu:true);

   // If the item has a submenu and it owns the submenu...
   if ((subMenu != NULL) && (ownsSubMenu==true))
   {
      delete (subMenu);
   }

   subMenu = itemSubmenu;
   ownsSubMenu=true;
}
```

```
// End Menu
//--------------------------------------------------------------------


//--------------------------------------------------------------------
/*
Function Name:      Menu
Member of:          menu_item
Input Parameters:   None.
Output Parameters:  None.
Return Value:       A pointer to the item's submenu.
Comments:           See the Return Value section.
*/

menu *menu_item::Menu(void)
{
   return (subMenu);
}

// End MenuItem.cpp
//--------------------------------------------------------------------
```

The menu_item class uses two constructors. The first is a default (no-arg) constructor that sets the object to a known state. The second is a copy constructor. The copy constructor calls the `operator =()` function to copy the contents of the source item.

Like all classes that use dynamic allocation, the menu_item provides a destructor. The destructor checks to see if the menu_item has a submenu that it owns. If it does, the destructor deletes it.

You may wonder when a menu_item owns its submenu and when it does not. The answer lies in the default constructor, the `operator =()` function, and the overloaded `Menu()` function. By default, a menu_item owns its submenu. When a program uses the `Menu()` function to set a menu_item object's submenu, the menu_item assumes ownership of the submenu. Ownership is lost in the `operator =()` function. Whenever a program contains a statement like this:

```
thisMenuItem = thatMenuItem;
```

the `operator =()` function assigns ownership of the submenu to the menu_item on the left of the equal sign. If the object on the right of the equal sign is deleted, it will not delete the submenu because it doesn't own it. The submenu will not be deleted until the menu_item that owns it is deleted.

The rest of the menu_item member functions are straightforward, and should require no explanation.

Writing StatBar.h

The status bar acts much like a miniature display. The text editor prints messages in it. The status bar is also used to get user input such as the name of a file to load or save. Listing 31.5 presents the source code for *StatBar.h*.

LISTING 31.5 StatBar.h

```
//--------------------------------------------------------------------
/*
File Name:  StatBar.h
Comments:   This file contains the definition of the status_bar object.
*/
```

```
//-------------------------------------------------------------------


#ifndef STATBAR_H
#define STATBAR_H


//-------------------------------------------------------------------
// Include Files

#include "TString.h"
#include "Display.h"

// End Include Files
//-------------------------------------------------------------------



//-------------------------------------------------------------------
// Class Definitions

class status_bar
{
// Public functions.
public:
   status_bar(void);

   void Origin(display_coordinate row,display_coordinate col);
   display_coordinate OriginRow(void);
   display_coordinate OriginCol(void);

   void Height(display_coordinate statusBarHeight);
   display_coordinate Height(void);

   void Width(display_coordinate statusBarWidth);
   display_coordinate Width(void);

   status_bar &Print(text_string &outputString);
   status_bar &Print(const char outputChar);
   void GetInput(text_string &inputString);

   void Clear(void);

// Private data.
private:
   display_coordinate originX,originY;
   display_coordinate height,width;
   display_coordinate insertionPointX,insertionPointY;
};

// End Class Definitions
//-------------------------------------------------------------------

#endif

// End StatBar.h
//-------------------------------------------------------------------
```

The file *StatBar.h* defines the `status_bar` class. The public member functions of the `status_bar` class enable the text editor to get and set its attributes. They also allow the program to print strings and get user input.

Like the `text_buffer`, the `status_bar` has an insertion point. However, the `status_bar` does not store text in a buffer and enable the program to scroll it. When the insertion point reaches the end of the last line of the `status_bar`, any further attempts to print to the `status_bar` cause it to be cleared. This simplifies the code for the `status_bar`.

Writing StatBar.cpp

Listing 31.6 shows the source code for the `status_bar` class.

LISTING 31.6 StatBar.cpp

```
//-----------------------------------------------------------------
/*
File Name:   StatBar.cpp
Comments:    This file contains the implementation of the status_bar class.
*/
//-----------------------------------------------------------------



//-----------------------------------------------------------------
// Include Files

#include "InputDev.h"
#include "Display.h"
#include "StatBar.h"
#include <assert.h>

// End Include Files
//-----------------------------------------------------------------


//-----------------------------------------------------------------
// Constants

const int ORIGIN_START_X = 0;
const int ORIGIN_START_Y = 0;
const int INSERTION_POINT_START_POSITION_X = ORIGIN_START_X+1;
const int INSERTION_POINT_START_POSITION_Y = ORIGIN_START_Y+1;

// End Constants
//-----------------------------------------------------------------


//-----------------------------------------------------------------
/*
Function Name:       status_bar
Member of:           status_bar
Input Parameters:    None.
Output Parameters:   None.
Return Value:        Returns a constructed status_bar object.
Comments:            This is the default constructor for the status_bar
                     class.
*/
```

```
status_bar::status_bar(void)
{
    originX=ORIGIN_START_X;
    originY=ORIGIN_START_Y;
    height=0;
    width=0;
    insertionPointX = INSERTION_POINT_START_POSITION_X;
    insertionPointY = INSERTION_POINT_START_POSITION_Y;
}

// End status_bar
//------------------------------------------------------------------------



//------------------------------------------------------------------------
/*
Function Name:       Origin
Member of:           status_bar
Input Parameters:    row - The row number of the upper left corner of the
                        status_bar object on the screen.
                     col - The column number of the upper left corner of the
                        status_bar object on the screen.
Output Parameters:   None.
Return Value:        None.
Comments:            Use this function to set the location of the upper left
                     corner of the status bar on the screen.
*/

void status_bar::Origin(display_coordinate row,display_coordinate col)
{
   originX=col;
   originY=row;
}

// End Origin
//------------------------------------------------------------------------



//------------------------------------------------------------------------
/*
Function Name:       OriginRow
Member of:           status_bar
Input Parameters:    None.
Output Parameters:   None.
Return Value:        Returns the row number of the upper left corner of the
                     status_bar object on the screen.
Comments:            See the Return Value section.
*/

display_coordinate status_bar::OriginRow(void)
{
   return (originY);
}

// End OriginRow
//------------------------------------------------------------------------
```

```
//-----------------------------------------------------------------------------
/*
Function Name:      OriginCol
Member of:          status_bar
Input Parameters:   None.
Output Parameters:  None.
Return Value:       Returns the column number of the upper left corner of
                    the status_bar object on the screen.
Comments:           See the Return Value section.
*/

display_coordinate status_bar::OriginCol(void)
{
   return (originX);
}

// End OriginCol
//-----------------------------------------------------------------------------



//-----------------------------------------------------------------------------
/*
Function Name:      Height
Member of:          status_bar
Input Parameters:   statusBarHeight - The height of the status_bar object.
Output Parameters:  None.
Return Value:       None.
Comments:           This function sets the height of a status_bar object.
*/

void status_bar::Height(display_coordinate statusBarHeight)
{
   height = statusBarHeight;
}

// End Height
//-----------------------------------------------------------------------------



//-----------------------------------------------------------------------------
/*
Function Name:      Height
Member of:          status_bar
Input Parameters:   None.
Output Parameters:  None.
Return Value:       Returns the height of the status_bar object.
Comments:           See the Return Value section.
*/

display_coordinate status_bar::Height(void)
{
   return (height);
}

// End Height
//-----------------------------------------------------------------------------
```

```
//-----------------------------------------------------------------------------
/*
Function Name:       Width
Member of:           status_bar
Input Parameters:    statusBarWidth - The width of the status_bar object.
Output Parameters:   None.
Return Value:        None.
Comments:            This function sets the width of a status_bar object.
*/

void status_bar::Width(display_coordinate statusBarWidth)
{
   width = statusBarWidth;
}

// End Width
//-----------------------------------------------------------------------------



//-----------------------------------------------------------------------------
/*
Function Name:       Width
Member of:           status_bar
Input Parameters:    None.
Output Parameters:   None.
Return Value:        Returns the width of the status_bar object.
Comments:            See the Return Value section.
*/

display_coordinate status_bar::Width(void)
{
   return (width);
}

// End Width
//-----------------------------------------------------------------------------



//-----------------------------------------------------------------------------
/*
Function Name:       Print
Member of:           status_bar
Input Parameters:    outputString - A string that will be printed in the
                        status bar.
Output Parameters:   None.
Return Value:        Returns a reference to a status_bar object.
Comments:            This function prints a string in the status bar on the
                     screen. It is intended to operate similar to, but not
                     exactly the same as, C++ streams.

                     This Print() function keeps the string it prints from
                     going outside the boundaries of the status bar. If
                     there are too many lines of text output in the status
                     bar, this function clears the bar and begins printing
                     again at the upper left corner.
*/
```

```
status_bar &status_bar::Print(text_string &outputString)
{
   assert(originX>=0);
   assert(originY>=0);

   static bool insertionPointInitialized = false;

   // If the status bar's insertion point has not been initialized...
   if (!insertionPointInitialized)
   {
      // Set it to the upper left corner.
      insertionPointX = originX+1;
      insertionPointY = originY+1;
      insertionPointInitialized = true;
   }

   int stringWidth = theScreen.StringWidth(outputString);
   int stringHeight = theScreen.StringHeight(outputString);

   // If the string fits entirely within the status box...
   if ((originX+stringWidth < originX+width) &&
       (originY+stringHeight < originY+height))
   {
      // Print the string.
      theScreen.PrintAt(insertionPointY,insertionPointX,outputString);

      // Find the new insertion point.
      insertionPointX += outputString.Length()*theScreen.CharacterWidth();

      // If the insertion point has moved past the right edge...
      if (insertionPointX >= originX+width)
      {
         // Move it to the beginning of the next line.
         insertionPointX = INSERTION_POINT_START_POSITION_X;
         insertionPointY++;
      }
   }
   // Else if the string goes past the right edge of the status box...
   else if (insertionPointX >= originX+width)
   {
      // Print each character that fits.
      for (int i=0;
           (i<outputString.Length()) && (insertionPointX<originX+width);
           i++)
      {
         theScreen.PrintAt(insertionPointY,insertionPointX,outputString[i]);
         insertionPointX += theScreen.CharacterWidth();
      }

      // Set the insertion point to the beginning of the next line.
      insertionPointX = INSERTION_POINT_START_POSITION_X;
      insertionPointY++;
   }

   // If the insertion point has moved down too many rows...
   if (insertionPointY >= originY+height)
   {
      // Clear the status box.
```

```
        Clear();

        // Set the insertion point back to the upper left corner.
        insertionPointX = INSERTION_POINT_START_POSITION_X;
        insertionPointY = INSERTION_POINT_START_POSITION_Y;
    }

    return (*this);
}

// End Print
//-----------------------------------------------------------------------------



//-----------------------------------------------------------------------------
/*
Function Name:       Print
Member of:           status_bar
Input Parameters:    outputChar - A character that will be printed in the
                        status bar.
Output Parameters:   None.
Return Value:        Returns a reference to a status_bar object.
Comments:            This function prints a character in the status bar on
                     the screen. It is intended to operate similar to, but
                     not exactly the same as, C++ streams.

                     This Print() function keeps the character it prints
                     from going outside the boundaries of the status bar. If
                     there are too many lines of text output in the status
                     bar, this function clears the bar and begins printing
                     again at the upper left corner.
*/
status_bar &status_bar::Print(const char outputChar)
{
    text_string tempString;
    tempString+=outputChar;
    return (Print(outputChar));
}

// End Print
//-----------------------------------------------------------------------------



//-----------------------------------------------------------------------------
/*
Function Name:       GetInput
Member of:           status_bar
Input Parameters:    None.
Output Parameters:   inputString - The string where the user input will be
                        stored.
Return Value:        None.
Comments:            This function gets input in the status bar from the
                     user. Since the input string is a text_string object,
                     it will automatically allocate enough memory for the
                     user's input.
*/
```

```
void status_bar::GetInput(text_string &inputString)
{
   assert(originX>=0);
   assert(originY>=0);

   raw_input userInput = ' ';
   text_string tempInputString;

   for (bool done = false; !done; )
   {
      raw_input userInput = inputDevice.GetInput(input_device::NO_ECHO);

      if (userInput != input_device::ENTER)
      {
         tempInputString+=(char)userInput;

         theScreen.PrintAt(insertionPointY,insertionPointX,(char)userInput);
         insertionPointX+=theScreen.CharacterWidth();

         // If the insertion point has moved past the right edge...
         if (insertionPointX >= originX+width)
         {
            // Move it to the beginning of the next line.
            insertionPointX = INSERTION_POINT_START_POSITION_X;
            insertionPointY++;
         }

         // If the insertion point has moved down too many rows...
         if (insertionPointY >= originY+height)
         {
            // Clear the status box.
            Clear();

            // Set the insertion point back to the upper left corner.
            insertionPointX = INSERTION_POINT_START_POSITION_X;
            insertionPointY = INSERTION_POINT_START_POSITION_Y;
         }
      }
      else
      {
         done = true;
      }
   }
   inputString = tempInputString;
}
// End GetInput
//-----------------------------------------------------------------------------



//-----------------------------------------------------------------------------
/*
Function Name:       Clear
Member of:           status_bar
Input Parameters:    None.
Output Parameters:   None.
Return Value:        None.
```

```
Comments:            This function clears the status bar.
*/

void status_bar::Clear(void)
{
   theScreen.Clear(originX,originY,originX+width,originY+height);
}

// End Clear
//-----------------------------------------------------------------------

// End StatBar.cpp
//-----------------------------------------------------------------------
```

Since the `status_bar` object interacts with the user, `status_bar` includes both *InputDev.h* and *Display.h*. It then defines some constants that it requires to set the `status_bar` in a known state. The constructor uses these constants.

The `status_bar` does not do dynamic allocation, so it doesn't need a destructor. It provides functions to set and get the origin of the `status_bar`. The origin is its upper left corner. It also provides functions for getting and setting its height and width. Programs can use the two overloaded `Print()` functions to print `text_string` object or single characters to the screen.

Also, *StatBar.cpp* contains the source code for the `status_bar::GetInput()` function. Unlike the `input_device::GetInput()` function, the `status_bar::GetInput()` function does not have a parameter for controlling the echo of the user's input. `status_bar::GetInput()` always echoes whatever the user types into the program.

The `status_bar::Clear()` function uses the `display::Clear()` function to clear the portion of the screen devoted to the `status_bar`.

Writing Platform.h

Certain files in the text editor are platform-specific. They must be modified if the program is ported to another operating system or computer. All platform-specific files include the file *Platform.h,* which is shown in Listing 31.7. The only thing that *Platform.h* contains is the definition of a constant that specifies which platform the text editor is being compiled for.

LISTING 31.7 Platform.h

```
//-----------------------------------------------------------------------
/*
File Name:  Platform.h
Comments:   This file contains preprocessor definitions that control which
            type of computer and operating system this program is being
            compiled for.
*/
//-----------------------------------------------------------------------

#ifndef PLATFORM_H
#define PLATFORM_H

#define PLATFORM_MS_DOS

// The following platforms are not implemented in this version.

// To compile this program for Linux, uncomment the next line.
// #define PLATFORM_LINUX
```

```
// To compile this program for the Macintosh, uncomment the next line.
// #define PLATFORM_MAC

#endif

// End Platform.h
//-----------------------------------------------------------------------
```

Summary

The menu and menu_item classes provide the text editor with a fully functional menu system. The status_bar class defines a simple object that substitutes for dialog boxes and other user interface items. The text editor uses the file *Platform.h* to define its target platform.

Review Questions

1. Do you think that object oriented programming techniques have helped in implementing the text editor? Why or why not?
2. Should the menu object allow programs to assign menus to other menus? In other words, should it allow such statements as

   ```
   menu thisMenu, thatMenu;
   // Code to store items in thisMenu goes here.
   thatMenu = thisMenu;
   ```

   If you think the menu object should allow such statements, what modifications to the menu class need to be made to the class? If you think such statements should not be allowed, how will you change the definition of the menu class to prevent them?
3. The comments in the source code for the menu_item class do not document the assumption that all menu_item identifiers must be greater than or equal to MIID_FIRST. Where should that documentation go? Are there other places where it should appear as well?
4. Why do menu_item identifiers begin with 1000?
5. Why does a menu_item need to contain information about whether or not it owns a submenu? What would happen if it did not contain this information?
6. Should the status_bar class allow a program to declare more than one status_bar? Why or why not? What modifications would you need to make to the status_bar class to prevent a program from declaring more than one status_bar?
7. How do the constant definitions in *Platform.h* make the text editor more portable?
8. What is a forward reference? Why does the file *MenuItem.h* declare a forward reference?
9. What limitations does the status_bar class place on the length of output strings? Where should these limitations be documented?
10. Are there any limitations on the length of an input string the status_bar can read? Are these limitations documented? Where does such documentation belong?

Exercises

1. The keyword const was not used in the prototypes of many of the functions in the text editor. Rewrite the files presented in this chapter. Make as many const functions, parameters, and return types as you can. Explain which functions cannot be made const and why. Explain which parameters cannot be made const and why. Explain which return types cannot be made const and why.
2. Many enhancements could be made to the text editor. The edit area does not have a visible border. Neither does the status box. The menu object, however, draws a border

around each menu. Using the menu object as a guide, enhance the text editor so that it draws a border around the text edit area and around the status box. Name at least five other enhancements you could add to this program.

3. The menu class defines and uses some MS DOS–specific constants. It needs these to draw borders for menus. If you were to port the text editor to MS Windows or the Apple Macintosh, you would use graphics functions to draw these lines rather than print them character-by-character. All code in *Menu.cpp* that draws menus would need to change, depending on which operating system you were using. Mark the code that would change with conditional compilation directives.
4. The menu::AddItem() function is not very efficient in the way it allocates space. For example, it could allocate the menu_item list to a default size of ten items. If the list gets full, it could allocate space for another five items. Explain the advantages and disadvantages of this approach.
5. One of the menu_item::ID() functions enables programmers to set a menu_item object's unique identifier. The menu_item class is written with the assumption that all menu_item identifiers are greater than or equal to MIID_FIRST. However, the ID() function does not enforce this assumption. Modify the ID() function to force programmers to pass in an identifier value greater than or equal to MIID_FIRST.
6. Look closely at the copy constructor for the menu_item class. It calls the operator =() function to copy the contents of the source item into the newly constructed menu_item. The operator =() function transfers ownership of the submenu to the destination object. This means that if you defined a menu_item parameter for a function and pass it by value, ownership of the submenu will be transferred to the parameter inside the function. After the function terminates, the parameter will be deleted. When it is, it will delete the submenu. Modify the menu_item copy constructor so that it does not suffer from this problem.
7. Create a third version of the overloaded status_bar::Print() function that prints character arrays to the status_bar.
8. The status_bar::Print() and status_bar::GetInput() functions are written with the assumption that the height and width of the status_bar are greater than zero. However, they do not enforce this assumption. Rewrite all three functions to enforce this assumption.
9. The status_bar does not display a cursor when the user is prompted for input. This can be a little disconcerting to users. Write a version of the status_bar class that displays a cursor for the user when the GetInput() function is executed.
10. Write a brief discussion of your opinion of the text editor presented in this book. Describe the strengths and weaknesses of the design. Describe the strengths and weaknesses of the implementation. Tell why the design and implementation does or does not meet the design goals.

Chapter Glossary

Forward Reference A reference to a type before it is declared.

Appendix Installing and Using Metrowerks CodeWarrior

The CD-ROM that comes with this book contains a copy of Metrowerks CodeWarrior Lite, a full-featured C and C++ development environment. CodeWarrior Lite is a special trial version of Metrowerks CodeWarrior. It has all of the tools that come with CodeWarrior. However, it cannot create new C++ files or projects. Therefore, all of the empty C++ files are provided on the CD. The CD also contains all of the project files you will need for this book.

The CD contains versions of CodeWarrior Lite for Microsoft Windows and the Apple Macintosh. The installation procedure for the Windows version is presented in this appendix.

Installing CodeWarrior Lite for Windows

Before you install CodeWarrior Lite, check the amount of space available on your hard drive. You will need about 100 MB of free space.

To install CodeWarrior Lite:

1. Insert the CD that accompanies this book into your CD-ROM drive.
2. From the Windows 95/98 Start menu, select Run. The Run dialog box will appear.
3. In the Run dialog box, type

   ```
   <d>:\CW_Lite_Tools
   ```

   where <d> represents the drive letter of your CD-ROM drive. Select OK.
4. The Setup program for CodeWarrior Lite Tools will execute. Follow the instructions presented by the Setup program.
5. When the Setup program completes, choose the Close button in the Finished dialog box.
6. From the Windows 95/98 Start menu, select Run.
7. In the Run dialog box, type

   ```
   <d>:\CW_Lite_C
   ```

   where <d> represents the drive letter of your CD-ROM drive. Select OK.
8. When the Setup program completes, choose the Close button in the Finished dialog box.

Copying the Example Files

Before you use the example files provided on the CD, you'll need to copy them to your hard drive. To copy the files:

1. From the Windows Start menu, select Programs.
2. From the Programs menu, choose Windows Explorer.

3. When Windows Explorer opens, it will display a list of disk drives installed in your computer. Select your CD-ROM drive.
4. In the root directory of the CD, you will see a directory named *Examples*. Drag that directory from the CD to the hard drive where you want the example files to reside.

Once you have completed this procedure, Windows Explorer will copy the files to your hard drive.

Running CodeWarrior Lite

To run CodeWarrior Lite:

1. Select Programs from the Windows 95/98 Start menu.
2. Choose CodeWarrior Lite for Windows.
3. In the menu that appears, select CodeWarrior Lite.

CodeWarrior Lite will begin operation.

Developing Programs with CodeWarrior Lite

You can use CodeWarrior Lite to write the Hands On programs and the programs from the exercises at the end of each chapter. You must first copy the *Examples* directory from the CD to your hard drive. If you have done that, use the following procedure to write a program.

To write a program with CodeWarrior Lite:

1. Run CodeWarrior Lite.
2. From the File menu, choose Open.
3. Use the Look In pull-down list to select the hard drive the *Examples* directory is on.
4. Select the *Examples* directory. When you do, the Open dialog box will display all of the subdirectories of *Examples*.
5. Choose the directory for the chapter in which you're working.
6. All of the project files have the extension *.mcp*. Select the project file for the program you want to write.

You can now open the blank *.cpp* and *.h* files for each program.

Index

The letter *n* denotes information in the margin.